SHORT STORIES
for Students

Advisors

Jayne M. Burton is a teacher of English, a member of the Delta Kappa Gamma International Society for Key Women Educators, and currently a master's degree candidate in the Interdisciplinary Study of Curriculum and Instruction and English at Angelo State University.

Tom Shilts is the youth librarian at the Okemos branch of Capital Area District Library in Okemos, Michigan. He holds an MSLS degree from Clarion University of Pennsylvania and an MA in U.S. History from the University of North Dakota.

Amy Spade Silverman has taught at independent schools in California, Texas, Michigan, and New York. She holds a bachelor of arts degree from the University of Michigan and a master of fine arts degree from the University of Houston. She is a member of the National Council of Teachers of English and Teachers and Writers. She is an exam reader for Advanced Placement Literature and Composition. She is also a poet, published in *North American Review*, *Nimrod*, and *Michigan Quarterly Review*, among others.

SHORT STORIES
for Students

**Presenting Analysis, Context, and Criticism
on Commonly Studied Short Stories**

VOLUME 41

Matthew Derda, Project Editor

Foreword by Thomas E. Barden

GALE
CENGAGE Learning

Farmington Hills, Mich • San Francisco • New York • Waterville, Maine
Meriden, Conn • Mason, Ohio • Chicago

Short Stories for Students, Volume 41

Project Editor: Matthew Derda

Rights Acquisition and Management: Lynn Vagg

Composition: Evi Abou-El-Seoud

Manufacturing: Rhonda A. Dover

Imaging: John Watkins

Product Design: Pamela A. E. Galbreath, Jennifer Wahi

Digital Content Production: Edna Shy

Product Manager: Meggin Condino

For product information and technology assistance, contact us at
Gale Customer Support, 1-800-877-4253.
For permission to use material from this text or product,
submit all requests online at **www.cengage.com/permissions.**
Further permissions questions can be emailed to
permissionrequest@cengage.com

Gale
27500 Drake Rd.
Farmington Hills, MI, 48331-3535

ISBN-13: 978-1-5730-2317-7
ISSN 1092-7735

This title is also available as an e-book.
ISBN-13: 978-1-5730-2325-2
Contact your Gale, a part of Cengage Learning sales representative for ordering information.

Printed in Mexico
1 2 3 4 5 6 7 19 18 17 16 15

Table of Contents

Why Study Literature At All?

Short Stories for Students is designed to provide readers with information and discussion about a wide range of important contemporary and historical works of short fiction, and it does that job very well. However, I want to use this guest foreword to address a question that it does *not* take up. It is a fundamental question that is often ignored in high school and college English classes as well as research texts, and one that causes frustration among students at all levels, namely why study literature at all? Isn't it enough to read a story, enjoy it, and go about one's business? My answer (to be expected from a literary professional, I suppose) is no. It is not enough. It is a start; but it is not enough. Here's why.

First, literature is the only part of the educational curriculum that deals directly with the actual world of lived experience. The philosopher Edmund Husserl used the apt German term *die Lebenswelt*, "the living world," to denote this realm. All the other content areas of the modern American educational system avoid the subjective, present reality of everyday life. Science (both the natural and the social varieties) objectifies, the fine arts create and/ or perform, history reconstructs. Only literary study persists in posing those questions we all asked before our schooling taught us to give up on them. Only literature gives credibility to personal perceptions, feelings, dreams, and the "stream of consciousness" that is our inner voice. Literature wonders about infinity,

wonders why God permits evil, wonders what will happen to us after we die. Literature admits that we get our hearts broken, that people sometimes cheat and get away with it, that the world is a strange and probably incomprehensible place. Literature, in other words, takes on all the big and small issues of what it means to be human. So my first answer is that of the humanist we should read literature and study it and take it seriously because it enriches us as human beings. We develop our moral imagination, our capacity to sympathize with other people, and our ability to understand our existence through the experience of fiction.

My second answer is more practical. By studying literature we can learn how to explore and analyze texts. Fiction may be about *die Lebenswelt*, but it is a construct of words put together in a certain order by an artist using the medium of language. By examining and studying those constructions, we can learn about language as a medium. We can become more sophisticated about word associations and connotations, about the manipulation of symbols, and about style and atmosphere. We can grasp how ambiguous language is and how important context and texture is to meaning. In our first encounter with a work of literature, of course, we are not supposed to catch all of these things. We are spellbound, just as the writer wanted us to be. It is as serious students of the writer's art that we begin to see how the tricks are done.

Seeing the tricks, which is another way of saying "developing analytical and close reading skills," is important above and beyond its intrinsic literary educational value. These skills transfer to other fields and enhance critical thinking of any kind. Understanding how language is used to construct texts is powerful knowledge. It makes engineers better problem solvers, lawyers better advocates and courtroom practitioners, politicians better rhetoricians, marketing and advertising agents better sellers, and citizens more aware consumers as well as better participants in democracy. This last point is especially important, because rhetorical skill works both ways when we learn how language is manipulated in the making of texts the result is that we become less susceptible when language is used to manipulate us.

My third reason is related to the second. When we begin to see literature as created artifacts of language, we become more sensitive to good writing in general. We get a stronger sense of the importance of individual words, even the sounds of words and word combinations. We begin to understand Mark Twain's delicious proverb "The difference between the right word and the almost right word is the difference between lightning and a lightning bug." Getting beyond the "enjoyment only" stage of literature gets us closer to becoming makers of word art ourselves. I am not saying that studying fiction will turn every student into a Faulkner or a Shakespeare. But it will make us more adaptable and effective writers, even if our art form ends up being the office memo or the corporate annual report.

Studying short stories, then, can help students become better readers, better writers, and even better human beings. But I want to close with a warning. If your study and exploration of the craft, history, context, symbolism, or anything else about a story starts to rob it of the magic you felt when you first read it, it is time to stop. Take a break, study another subject, shoot some hoops, or go for a run. Love of reading is too important to be ruined by school. The early twentieth century writer Willa Cather, in her novel *My Antonia*, has her narrator Jack Burden tell a story that he and Antonia heard from two old Russian immigrants when they were teenagers. These immigrants, Pavel and Peter, told about an incident from their youth back in Russia that the narrator could recall in vivid detail thirty years later. It was a harrowing story of a wedding party starting home in sleds and being chased by starving wolves. Hundreds of wolves attacked the group's sleds one by one as they sped across the snow trying to reach their village. In a horrible revelation, the old Russians revealed that the groom eventually threw his own bride to the wolves to save himself. There was even a hint that one of the old immigrants might have been the groom mentioned in the story. Cather has her narrator conclude with his feelings about the story. "We did not tell Pavel's secret to anyone, but guarded it jealously as if the wolves of the Ukraine had gathered that night long ago, and the wedding party had been sacrificed, just to give us a painful and peculiar pleasure." That feeling, that painful and peculiar pleasure, is the most important thing about literature. Study and research should enhance that feeling and never be allowed to overwhelm it.

Thomas E. Barden
Professor of English and Director of
Graduate English Studies,
The University of Toledo

Introduction

Purpose of the Book

The purpose of *Short Stories for Students* (*SSfS*) is to provide readers with a guide to understanding, enjoying, and studying short stories by giving them easy access to information about the work. Part of Gale's "For Students" Literature line, *SSfS* is specifically designed to meet the curricular needs of high school and undergraduate college students and their teachers, as well as the interests of general readers and researchers considering specific short fiction. While each volume contains entries on "classic" stories frequently studied in classrooms, there are also entries containing hard-to-find information on contemporary stories, including works by multicultural, international, and women writers.

The information covered in each entry includes an introduction to the story and the story's author; a plot summary, to help readers unravel and understand the events in the work; descriptions of important characters, including explanation of a given character's role in the narrative as well as discussion about that character's relationship to other characters in the story; analysis of important themes in the story; and an explanation of important literary techniques and movements as they are demonstrated in the work.

In addition to this material, which helps the readers analyze the story itself, students are also provided with important information on the literary and historical background informing each work. This includes a historical context essay, a box comparing the time or place the story was written to modern Western culture, a critical overview essay, and excerpts from critical essays on the story or author. A unique feature of *SSfS* is a specially commissioned critical essay on each story, targeted toward the student reader.

To further help today's student in studying and enjoying each story, information on audiobooks and other media adaptations is provided (if available), as well as reading suggestions for works of fiction and nonfiction on similar themes and topics. Classroom aids include ideas for research papers and lists of critical and reference sources that provide additional material on the work.

Selection Criteria

The titles for each volume of *SSfS* were selected by surveying numerous sources on teaching literature and analyzing course curricula for various school districts. Some of the sources surveyed include: literature anthologies, *Reading Lists for College-Bound Students: The Books Most Recommended by America's Top Colleges*; *Teaching the Short Story: A Guide to Using Stories from around the World*, by the National Council of Teachers of English (NCTE); and "A Study of High School Literature Anthologies," conducted by Arthur Applebee at the Center for the Learning and Teaching of Literature and sponsored by the National Endowment for the Arts and the Office of Educational Research and Improvement.

Input was also solicited from our advisory board, as well as educators from various areas. From these discussions, it was determined that each volume should have a mix of "classic" stories (those works commonly taught in literature classes) and contemporary stories for which information is often hard to find. Because of the interest in expanding the canon of literature, an emphasis was also placed on including works by international, multicultural, and women authors. Our advisory board members—educational professionals—helped pare down the list for each volume. Works not selected for the present volume were noted as possibilities for future volumes. As always, the editor welcomes suggestions for titles to be included in future volumes.

How Each Entry Is Organized

Each entry, or chapter, in *SSfS* focuses on one story. Each entry heading lists the title of the story, the author's name, and the date of the story's publication. The following elements are contained in each entry:

Introduction: a brief overview of the story which provides information about its first appearance, its literary standing, any controversies surrounding the work, and major conflicts or themes within the work.

Author Biography: this section includes basic facts about the author's life, and focuses on events and times in the author's life that may have inspired the story in question.

Plot Summary: a description of the events in the story. Lengthy summaries are broken down with subheads.

Characters: an alphabetical listing of the characters who appear in the story. Each character name is followed by a brief to an extensive description of the character's role in the story, as well as discussion of the character's actions, relationships, and possible motivation.

Characters are listed alphabetically by last name. If a character is unnamed—for instance, the narrator in "The Eatonville Anthology"— the character is listed as "The Narrator" and alphabetized as "Narrator." If a character's first name is the only one given, the name will appear alphabetically by that name.

Themes: a thorough overview of how the topics, themes, and issues are addressed within the story. Each theme discussed appears in a separate subhead.

Style: this section addresses important style elements of the story, such as setting, point of view, and narration; important literary devices used, such as imagery, foreshadowing, symbolism; and, if applicable, genres to which the work might have belonged, such as Gothicism or Romanticism. Literary terms are explained within the entry, but can also be found in the Glossary.

Historical Context: this section outlines the social, political, and cultural climate in which the author lived and the work was created. This section may include descriptions of related historical events, pertinent aspects of daily life in the culture, and the artistic and literary sensibilities of the time in which the work was written. If the story is historical in nature, information regarding the time in which the story is set is also included. Long sections are broken down with helpful subheads.

Critical Overview: this section provides background on the critical reputation of the author and the story, including bannings or any other public controversies surrounding the work. For older works, this section may include a history of how the story was first received and how perceptions of it may have changed over the years; for more recent works, direct quotes from early reviews may also be included.

Criticism: an essay commissioned by *SSfS* which specifically deals with the story and is written specifically for the student audience, as well as excerpts from previously published criticism on the work (if available).

Sources: an alphabetical list of critical material used in compiling the entry, with bibliographical information.

Further Reading: an alphabetical list of other critical sources which may prove useful for the student. Includes full bibliographical information and a brief annotation.

Suggested Search Terms: a list of search terms and phrases to jumpstart students' further information seeking. Terms include not just titles and author names but also terms and topics related to the historical and literary context of the works.

In addition, each entry contains the following highlighted sections, set apart from the main text as sidebars:

Media Adaptations: if available, a list of audio-books and important film and television adaptations of the story, including source information. The list also includes stage adaptations, musical adaptations, etc.

Topics for Further Study: a list of potential study questions or research topics dealing with the story. This section includes questions related to other disciplines the student may be studying, such as American history, world history, science, math, government, business, geography, economics, psychology, etc.

Compare and Contrast: an "at-a-glance" comparison of the cultural and historical differences between the author's time and culture and late twentieth century or early twenty-first century Western culture. This box includes pertinent parallels between the major scientific, political, and cultural movements of the time or place the story was written, the time or place the story was set (if a historical work), and modern Western culture. Works written after 1990 may not have this box.

What Do I Read Next?: a list of works that might give a reader points of entry into a classic work (e.g., YA or multicultural titles) and/ or complement the featured story or serve as a contrast to it. This includes works by the same author and others, works from various genres, YA works, and works from various cultures and eras.

Other Features

SSfS includes "Why Study Literature At All?," a foreword by Thomas E. Barden, Professor of English and Director of Graduate English Studies at the University of Toledo. This essay provides a number of very fundamental reasons for studying literature and, therefore, reasons why a book such as *SSfS*, designed to facilitate the study of literature, is useful.

A Cumulative Author/Title Index lists the authors and titles covered in each volume of the *SSfS* series.

A Cumulative Nationality/Ethnicity Index breaks down the authors and titles covered in each volume of the *SSfS* series by nationality and ethnicity.

A Subject/Theme Index, specific to each volume, provides easy reference for users who may be studying a particular subject or theme rather than a single work. Significant subjects from events to broad themes are included.

Each entry may include illustrations, including photo of the author, stills from film adaptations (if available), maps, and/or photos of key historical events.

Citing Short Stories for Students

When writing papers, students who quote directly from any volume of *SSfS* may use the following general forms to document their source. These examples are based on MLA style; teachers may request that students adhere to a different style, thus, the following examples may be adapted as needed.

When citing text from *SSfS* that is not attributed to a particular author (for example, the Themes, Style, Historical Context sections, etc.), the following format may be used:

> "How I Met My Husband." *Short Stories for Students.* Ed. Sara Constantakis. Vol. 36. Detroit: Gale, Cengage Learning, 2013. 73–95. Print.

When quoting the specially commissioned essay from *SSfS* (usually the first essay under the Criticism subhead), the following format may be used:

> Dominic, Catherine. Critical Essay on "How I Met My Husband." *Short Stories for Students.* Ed. Sara Constantakis. Vol. 36. Detroit: Gale, Cengage Learning, 2013. 84–87. Print.

When quoting a journal or newspaper essay that is reprinted in a volume of *SSfS*, the following form may be used:

> Ditsky, John. "The Figure in the Linoleum: The Fictions of Alice Munro." *Hollins Critic* 22.3 (1985): 1–10. Rpt. in *Short Stories for Students.* Vol. 36. Ed. Sara Constantakis. Detroit: Gale, Cengage Learning, 2013. 92–94. Print.

When quoting material from a book that is reprinted in a volume of *SSfS*, the following form may be used:

> Cooke, John. "Alice Munro." *The Influence of Painting on Five Canadian Writers.* Lewiston, NY: Edwin Mellen Press, 1996. 69–85. Rpt. in

Short Stories for Students. Vol. 36. Ed. Sara Constantakis. Detroit: Gale, Cengage Learning, 2013. 89–92. Print.

We Welcome Your Suggestions

The editorial staff of *Short Stories for Students* welcomes your comments and ideas. Readers who wish to suggest short stories to appear in future volumes, or who have other suggestions, are cordially invited to contact the editor. You may contact the editor via E-mail at: **ForStudents Editors@cengage.com.** Or write to the editor at:

Editor, *Short Stories for Students*
Gale
27500 Drake Road
Farmington Hills, MI 48331-3535

Literary Chronology

1832: Louisa May Alcott is born on November 29 in Germantown, Pennsylvania.

1854: Oscar Wilde is born on October 16 in Dublin, Ireland.

1862: Edith Wharton is born on January 24 in New York, New York.

1869: Louisa May Alcott' "Back Windows" is published in *Merry's Museum*.

1875: Jacques Futrelle is born on April 9 in Pike County, Georgia.

1885: Ring Lardner is born on March 6 in Niles, Michigan.

1888: Louisa May Alcott dies of a stroke on March 6 in Boston, Massachusetts.

1888: Oscar Wilde's "The Nightingale and the Rose" is published in *The Happy Prince and Other Tales*.

1900: Oscar Wilde dies of cerebral meningitis on November 30 in Paris, France.

1902: Beryl Markham is born on October 22 in Ashwell, England.

1905: Jacques Futrelle's "The Problem of Cell 13" is published in *Boston American*.

1910: Edith Wharton's "Afterward" is published in *Century Magazine*.

1912: Jacques Futrelle dies in the *Titanic* disaster on April 15.

1916: Roald Dahl is born on September 13 in Cardiff, Wales.

1918: Muriel Spark is born on February 1 in Edinburgh, Scotland.

1921: Edith Wharton is awarded the Pulitzer Prize for Fiction for *The Age of Innocence*.

1925: Flannery O'Connor is born on March 25 in Savannah, Georgia.

1925: Ring Lardner's "Haircut" is published in *Liberty Magazine*.

1926: John Knowles is born on September 16 in Fairmont, West Virginia.

1929: Charles Beaumont is born on January 2 in Chicago, Illinois.

1933: Ring Lardner dies of a heart attack on September 25 in East Hampton, New York.

1937: Edith Wharton dies of a stroke on August 11 in St.-Brice-sous-Forêt, France.

1945: Beryl Markham's "Brothers Are the Same" is published in *Collier's Weekly*.

1948: Roald Dahl's "Man from the South" is published in *Collier's*.

1952: Charles Beaumont's "The Beautiful People" is published in *IF* magazine.

1952: Naomi Shihab Nye is born on March 12 in St. Louis, Missouri.

1961: Muriel Spark's "Bang-Bang You're Dead" is published in *Voices at Play*.

1963: Yann Martel is born on June 25 in Salamanca, Spain.

1964: Flannery O'Connor dies of complications from lupus on August 3 in Milledgeville, Georgia.

1965: Flannery O'Connor's "Parker's Back" is published in *Everything that Rises Must Converge*.

1967: Charles Beaumont dies of Alzheimer's disease on February 21 in Woodland Hills, California.

1968: John Knowles's "A Turn with the Sun" is published in *Phineas*.

1973: Julie Orringer is born on June 12 in Miami, Florida.

1986: Beryl Markham dies of complications from a broken leg on August 4 in Nairobi, Kenya.

1990: Roald Dahl dies from myelodysplastic syndrome on November 23 in Oxfordshire, England.

1993: Naomi Shihab Nye's "Hamadi" is published in *America Street: A Multicultural Anthology of Stories*.

1993: Yann Martel's "The Facts Behind the Helsinki Roccamatios" is published in *The Facts Behind the Helsinki Roccamatios: Short Fiction*.

2001: John Knowles dies after a short illness on November 29 in Ft. Lauderdale, Florida.

2003: Julie Orringer's "The Isabel Fish" is published in *How to Breathe Underwater*.

2006: Muriel Spark dies of cancer on April 13 in Florence, Italy.

Acknowledgements

The editors wish to thank the copyright holders of the excerpted criticism included in this volume and the permissions managers of many book and magazine publishing companies for assisting us in securing reproduction rights. We are also grateful to the staffs of the Detroit Public Library, the Library of Congress, the University of Detroit Mercy Library, Wayne State University Purdy/Kresge Library Complex, and the University of Michigan Libraries for making their resources available to us. Following is a list of the copyright holders who have granted us permission to reproduce material in this volume of SSfS. Every effort has been made to trace copyright, but if omissions have been made, please let us know.

COPYRIGHTED EXCERPTS IN SSfS, VOLUME 41, WERE REPRODUCED FROM THE FOLLOWING SOURCES:

All Things Considered, March 30, 2009. Copyright © 2009 by National Public Radio. Reproduced by permission of the publisher.—*Aviation History*, v. 20.1, September, 2009. Copyright © 2009 by *Aviation History*. Reproduced by permission of the publisher.—Beer, Janet. From *Kate Chopin, Edith Wharton and Charlotte Perkins Gilman: Studies in Short Fiction*. Macmillan Press, 1997. Copyright © Macmillan Press, 1997. Reproduced by permission of the publisher.—*Belfast Telegraph*, December 29, 2012. Copyright © 2009 by *Belfast Telegraph*. Reproduced by permission of the publisher.—*Booklist*, 100.1, September 1, 2003; 101.5, November 1, 2004; 108.8, December 15, 2011. Copyright © 2003, 2004, 2011 by *Booklist*. Reproduced by permission of the publisher.—*Bookman*, 25, June 1907; 27, June 1908. Public Domain.—Doyle, Christine. From *Louisa May Alcott : Transatlantic Translations*. University of Tennessee Press, 2000. Copyright © University of Tennessee Press, 2000. Reproduced by permission of the publisher.—Dyman, Jenni. From *Lurking Feminism: The Great Stories of Edith Wharton*. Peter Lang, 1996. Copyright © Peter Lang, 1996. Reproduced by permission of the publisher.—Friedrich, Otto. From *Ring Lardner*. University of Minnesota Press, 1965. Copyright © University of Minnesota Press, 1965. Reproduced by permission of the publisher.—*Guardian*, June 22, 2010; July 23, 2010. Copyright © 2010 by *Guardian*. Reproduced by permission of the publisher.—Horan, Patrick M. From *The Importance of Being Paradoxical: Maternal Presence in the Works of Oscar Wilde*. Fairleigh Dickinson University Press, 1997. Copyright © Fairleigh Dickinson University Press, 1997. Reproduced by permission of the publisher.—*Horn Book*, 87.6, November-December 2011. Copyright © 2011 by *Horn Book*. Reproduced by permission of the publisher.—*Kirkus Reviews*, 71.15, August 1, 2003; 72.20, October 15, 2004. Copyright © 2003, 2004 by *Kirkus Reviews*. Reproduced by permission of the publisher.—*Kliatt*, 39.4, July 2005. Copyright © 2005 by *Kliatt*. Reproduced by permission of the publisher.—*Library Journal*, 129.18, November 1, 2004. Copyright © 2004 by *Library Journal*. Reproduced by permission of the publisher.—Martel, Yann. From *This is My Best: Great Writers Share Their Favorite Work*. Edited by Retha Powers and Kathy Kiernan. Chronicle Books, 2004. Copyright © Chronicle Books, 2004. Reproduced by permission of the publisher.—McDowell, Margaret B. From *Edith Wharton*. Edited by Joseph M. Flora. Twayne Publishers, 1991. Copyright © 1991, Cengage Learning. Reproduced by permission of Gale, a part of Cengage Learning.—*Nation*, 84.2185, May 16, 1907. Public Domain.—Orvell, Miles. From *Flannery O'Connor: An Introduction*. University Press of Mississippi, 1991. Copyright © University Press of Mississippi, 1991. Reproduced by permission of the publisher.—*Pif Magazine*, August 1, 1999. Copyright © 1999 by *Pif Magazine*. Reproduced by permission of the publisher.—*Publishers Weekly*, 244.30, July 28, 1997; 246.39, September 27, 1999; 248.46, November 12, 2001; 250.34, August 25, 2003; 251.44, November 1, 2004; 252.47, November 28, 2005. Copyright © 1997, 1999, 2001, 2003, 2004, 2005 by *Publishers Weekly*. Reproduced by permission of the publisher. —Ruddick, Nicholas. From *Approaches to Teaching the Works of Oscar Wilde*. Edited by Philip E. Smith. Modern Language Association of America, 2008. Copyright © Modern Language Association of America, 2008. Reproduced by permission of the publisher.—*School Library Journal*, 51.10, October 2005. Copyright © 2005 by *School Library Journal*. Reproduced by permission of the publisher.—Smith, Gail K.

From *American Women Short Story Writers: A Collection of Critical Essays*. Edited by Julie Brown. Garland Publishers, 1995. Copyright © Garland Publishers, 1995. Reproduced by permission of the publisher.—*Spectator*, 287.9037, October 20, 2001; 296.9192, October 9, 2004. Copyright © 2001, 2004 by *Spectator*. Reproduced by permission of the publisher.—Sproxton, Judy. From *The Women of Murial Spark*. St. Martinapos;s Press, 1992. Copyright © St. Martin's Press, 1992. Reproduced by permission of the publisher.—*Studies in Short Fiction*, I.2, Winter 1964. Copyright © 1964 by *Studies in Short Fiction*. Reproduced by permission of the publisher.—*Voice of Youth Advocates*, 34.4, October 2011. Copyright © 2011 by *Voice of Youth Advocates*. Reproduced by permission of the publisher.—*Weekend All Things Considered*, October 18, 2003. Copyright © 2003 by National Public Radio. Reproduced by permission of the publisher.—*Weird Fiction Review*, October 23, 2012. Copyright © 2012 by *Weird Fiction Review*. Reproduced by permission of the publisher.—West, Mark I. From *Roald Dahl*. Twayne Publishers, 1992. Copyright © 1992, Cengage Learning. Reproduced by permission of Gale, a part of Cengage Learning.—White, Barbara A. From *Edith Wharton: A Study of the Short Fiction*. Twayne Publishers, 1991. Copyright © 1991, Cengage Learning. Reproduced by permission of Gale, a part of Cengage Learning.—Worthington, Heather. From *Roald Dahl*. Edited by Ann Alston and Catherine Butler. Palgrave MacMillan, 2012. Copyright © Palgrave MacMillan, 2012. Reproduced by permission of the publisher.

Contributors

Susan K. Andersen: Andersen is a writer and teacher with a PhD in English literature. Entry on "The Nightingale and the Rose." Original essay on "The Nightingale and the Rose."

Bryan Aubrey: Aubrey holds a PhD in English. Entry on "Hamadi." Original essay on "Hamadi."

Rita M. Brown: Brown is an English professor. Entry on "Parker's Back." Original essay on "Parker's Back."

Catherine Dominic: Dominic is a novelist and a freelance writer and editor. Entries on "The Facts behind the Helsinki Roccamatios" and "Haircut." Original essays on "The Facts behind the Helsinki Roccamatios" and "Haircut."

Klay Dyer: Dyer is a freelance editor and writer specializing in topics relating to literature, popular culture, and emerging technologies. Entry on "Man from the South." Original essay on "Man from the South."

Kristen Sarlin Greenberg: Greenberg is a freelance writer and editor with a background in literature and philosophy. Entry on "The Problem of Cell 13." Original essay on "The Problem of Cell 13."

Michael Allen Holmes: Holmes is a writer with existential interests. Entries on "Bang-Bang You're Dead" and "Brothers Are the Same." Original essays on "Bang-Bang You're Dead" and "Brothers Are the Same."

David Kelly: Kelly is an instructor of creative writing and literature. Entry on "The Beautiful People." Original essay on "The Beautiful People."

Michael J. O'Neal: O'Neal holds a PhD in English. Entry on "Afterward." Original essay on "Afterward."

April Paris: Paris is a freelance writer with a background in creating educational materials. Entry on "Back Windows." Original essay on "Back Windows."

Laura B. Pryor: Pryor has a master's degree in English literature and almost thirty years of experience as a professional writer. Entry on "The Isabel Fish." Original essay on "The Isabel Fish."

Bradley A. Skeen: Skeen is a classicist. Entry on "A Turn with the Sun." Original essay on "A Turn with the Sun."

Afterward

EDITH WHARTON
1910

"Afterward," a short story by Pulitzer Prize–winning American author Edith Wharton, was first published in the January 1910 edition of *Century*. It then appeared in Wharton's 1910 short-story collection *Tales of Men and Ghosts*.

As a ghost story, "Afterward" uses to full effect many of the conventions of gothic literature: supernatural subject matter; the uncanny, in the Freudian sense of something being familiar and alien at the same time; a dilapidated setting, usually a house with secret passages or rooms; images of darkness and shadows; repressed secrets; and such motifs as punishment and retribution, despair, terror, and the lingering impact of past events on the present. Wharton used these conventions to explore broader subjects that can be found in most of her fiction: marriage, social class, and the role and position of women.

"Afterward" is available in *The Collected Stories of Edith Wharton* (1998), selected by Anita Brookner, and in Wharton's *Collected Stories, 1891–1910*, edited by Maureen Howard for the Library of America in 2001. The story is also available online at the East of the Web website at http://www.eastoftheweb.com/short-stories/UBooks/Afte.shtml.

AUTHOR BIOGRAPHY

Edith Newbold Jones was born on January 24, 1862, in New York City into an "Old New

Wharton wrote "Afterward" in 1910.
(© *Classic Image* | *Alamy*)

married, but the engagement was broken off because she was too intellectual for her husband-to-be—at least according to the gossip columns. In 1883, she met Edward Wharton, whom she would marry in 1885.

Throughout the late 1880s, Wharton read voraciously and continued to write poetry. In 1891, *Scribner's* published "Mrs. Manstey's View," her first published short story. The Whartons purchased a home in Newport, Rhode Island, in 1893. Wharton decorated the house with the help of well-known interior designer Ogden Codman Jr. Later, in 1897, she and Codman would publish a well-received book, *The Decoration of Houses*. Meanwhile, she continued her extensive travels, primarily in Italy; in the late 1890s, the purpose of much of this travel was to find a climate that would help cure her recurring respiratory illnesses.

In 1902, the Whartons moved into The Mount, a home they had built in western Massachusetts (and that today operates as a Wharton museum). That same year, she published her first novel, *The Valley of Decision*. Her next published work was *The House of Mirth* (1905), a novel that remained on the best-seller list until 1906 and established her as both a critical and a popular success. By the end of the year, some 140,000 copies were in print. In 1907, the Whartons settled in France, where Edith lived for most of the rest of her life, only rarely visiting the United States. She began a love affair with London *Times* journalist William Morton Fullerton in 1908, and in 1913, she was divorced from Edward Wharton, who for years had been growing mentally unstable.

In 1910, Wharton began writing what is one of her most widely known works, the novella *Ethan Frome*, though its sales at the time were disappointing. That year, she also published "Afterward" in *Century*. In 1913, her novel *The Custom of the Country* was published, selling nearly 60,000 copies. After World War I broke out, she returned to Paris from further travels to establish American Hostels for Refugees, a relief agency for the many Belgian refugees who flooded Paris after the battles of the Marne and Ypres. During the war, she worked as a war correspondent for *Scribner's*, writing articles based on her visits to military hospitals at the fronts at Argonne, Ypres, and Verdun. Overall, she worked tirelessly for the French war effort, raising funds for refugees, for women displaced

York" family with impeccable social credentials. Her father was George Frederic Jones, whose income derived from Manhattan landholdings; her mother was Lucretia Rhinelander Jones. Because of a depression in the post–Civil War real-estate market, the family lived overseas during much of Edith's early life, first in Rome, then in Paris, and later in Bad Wildbad, Germany. After the family returned to their home on West 23rd Street in New York City, she was tutored at home. Her mother refused to allow her to read contemporary fiction, so she immersed herself in the classics and the study of modern languages.

In the mid-1870s, the young Edith wrote her first known work of fiction, a novella titled *Fast and Loose*, as well as a collection of poetry, *Verses*, which her mother paid to have privately printed. Worried that their daughter's intellectual and artistic pursuits would render her unfit for marriage, her parents arranged her social debut in 1879, a year earlier than they normally would have. In 1882, she was engaged to be by the war, and for charities such as the Children of Flanders Rescue Committee. She was named Chevalier de l'Ordre National de la Legion d'Honneur by the French government in 1916 for her war work. This work included the chairmanship of the Franco-American General Committee, which oversaw various relief projects.

In 1920, Wharton published what is arguably her major novel, *The Age of Innocence*. The following year, she was awarded the Pulitzer Prize for the novel. She was the first woman to win the prize. During the 1920s, she continued to write travel articles, short stories, and poems, all while traveling throughout Europe. She was a prominent member of the Anglo-American literary set, forging close relationships with such figures as Henry James, Hamlin Garland, Joseph Conrad, Aldous Huxley, and others, along with such French authors as André Maurois and André Gide. She maintained a close relationship with American novelist Sinclair Lewis even after the Pulitzer advisory board overturned the selection committee's decision to award the 1921 prize to Lewis for *Main Street*.

Wharton's health began to decline in 1929, but she nonetheless published *Hudson River Bracketed* that year. In 1932, she published its sequel, *The Gods Arrive* (a novel rejected for serial publication by several magazines because it features an unmarried couple who live together), and in 1934, she published an autobiography, *A Backward Glance*. In 1933, she began work on her last novel, *The Buccaneers*, which was published posthumously in 1938. Also published posthumously was the short-story collection *Ghosts* (1937), reprinting several of her previously published ghost stories.

In 1935, Wharton suffered a stroke, from which she largely recovered. However, on June 1, 1937, she suffered a heart attack, and her symptoms suggested that she also had another stroke. She suffered a further stroke on August 7 and died on August 11 at her home in St.-Brice-sous-Forêt, France.

PLOT SUMMARY

I

"Afterward" is divided into five numbered parts. Part I begins with Mary Boyne in her new home in England awaiting her husband,

MEDIA ADAPTATIONS

- A dramatization of "Afterward" is available on a DVD titled *Shades of Darkness: Six Mysterious Tales of the Paranormal*. The DVD was released by Koch Studios in 1986. The production was originally broadcast on television in 1983 as part of the *Shades of Darkness* series by Granada Television of England.

- An audio version of "Afterward" is available online at the LibriVox website (https://librivox.org/afterward-by-edith-wharton). The story is read by Charlie Blakemore. Running time is about one hour and seventeen minutes.

- LibriVox also has an audio version of all of the stories in *Tales of Men and Ghosts*, including "Afterward," at https://librivox.org/tales-of-men-and-ghosts-by-edith-wharton/. The reader is Nicholas Clifford, and the running time of "Afterward" is about an hour and ten minutes.

- A radio adaptation of "Afterward" was first broadcast by BBC4 Radio in England on October 30, 2009, as part of the network's *The Female Ghost* series.

- An audio dramatization of "Afterward," written and performed for national radio broadcast, is available on the Scribbling Women website at http://www.scribblingwomen.org/ewafterwardfeature.htm. The story was dramatized by Donna DiNovelli.

Edward ("Ned"), in the library. In the December dusk, she broods over the events of the past six months leading up to the present. She recalls the conversation they had with a cousin, Alida Stair, in June, when she and Ned were looking for a country house to purchase in southern England. Alida, who had herself purchased such a house, suggested a home named Lyng in Dorsetshire. Mary and Ned found the house attractive because it had the charm of being old, isolated, and in disrepair, with no modern conveniences. They jokingly indicated to Alida, however, that they wanted the house only if it had a ghost. Alida indicated that there was a ghost but that Mary and Ned would never know it, for according to legend, the inhabitants of Lyng never know they have encountered any ghost until long afterward.

The narration indicates that Mary and Ned lived in the American Midwest for a number of years until Ned, an engineer with the Blue Star Mine, reaped a sudden windfall that would enable him and Mary to settle into a life of more harmonious pursuits: Mary wanted to garden and paint, and Ned hoped to write a book. Mary goes on to recall that after they moved into Lyng, her husband became withdrawn and worried. She remembers a day in October when she came across a hidden stairwell that led to a coign (a projecting corner of a building) on the roof. After she and Ned climbed the stairs to take in the view, a stranger appeared below, causing Ned to grow anxious and run after him. Mary gave the incident little thought because numerous tradesmen came and went each day to work on the house. When she asked Ned about the stranger, he replied that he thought the man was Peters, one of the workmen, and that he dashed away to have a word with him about work on the property. Now, however, she recalls more vividly the incident and her husband's anxiety.

II

That December day in the library, Mary observes a person coming up the walk to the house. She initially believes it to be the ghost, but it turns out to be Ned. She is determined to discover what is troubling Ned, and she asks him whether he has seen the ghost yet; he replies that he has not. She then sees a change in his bearing while he opens the mail, for it seems as though he has been suddenly relieved of the cares harassing him. Mary, too, is relieved until she opens her own mail to find a newspaper clipping about a lawsuit filed by a man named Elwell against Ned in connection with the Blue Star Mine. When Mary questions Ned about the matter, he dismisses her concerns by replying that the suit has been withdrawn and wondering why Mary would suddenly take any interest in his business affairs.

III

Mary wakes up early the following day, refreshed at the alteration in Ned. She concludes that she does not have to be concerned about his business affairs because she trusts him. As she is awaiting a workman in her garden, a stranger appears and asks for her husband. She sends the man to the library to find Ned, not giving the matter much thought until later that day, when she learns from Trimmle, the parlor maid, that Ned left with the stranger. When Ned fails to return, Mary grows increasingly troubled. Looking in the library for clues to his absence, she finds a note that reads: "My dear Parvis, I have just received your letter announcing Elwell's death, and while I suppose there is now no further risk of trouble, it might be safer—."

IV

Mary remembers the extensive search by the authorities for Ned over the last two weeks. She continued to search for clues to his disappearance, and again she examined the note, which in fact was a letter that Ned had just begun writing to Parvis when he left with the stranger. She managed to get in touch with Parvis, a lawyer in Wisconsin, but he cabled back to her saying that he had no direct concern in the lawsuit. Mary has gradually come to accept her situation, concluding that no one will ever discover what happened to Ned. She thinks that the house itself was an accomplice in her husband's disappearance.

V

Parvis is in England on business, so he has decided to pay his respects to Mary. He arrives at Lyng, and during their conversation he explains the events surrounding the Blue Star Mine. She learns that her husband had acted dishonorably, for the business deal that had enriched her and Ned had in fact been an underhanded speculation that ruined Elwell's life. In despair, after his lawyers advised him that he would be unable to make a case against Ned in court, Elwell shot himself. Parvis goes on to explain that Elwell's widow, burdened with responsibilities, has appealed publicly for aid, causing the affair surrounding the Blue Star Mine to return to the news. Parvis shows Mary a newspaper clipping with a picture of Elwell, whom Mary now recognizes as the man who appeared at Lyng and led Ned away—in fact Elwell's ghost. The ghost first appeared on October 20, the day Elwell shot himself; this was the occasion when Ned and Mary saw a stranger from their rooftop vantage point. Elwell, however, was not dead, so he was unable to reach Ned. He lingered for two months before dying, and just after his death, his ghost again appeared at Lyng, exacting retribution by spiriting Ned away. Mary now understands that what Alida had told them was true: she did not know that the ghost had appeared until afterward.

CHARACTERS

Agnes
Agnes, one of the Boynes' servants, never directly appears but is referred to by Trimmle.

Edward "Ned" Boyne
Before the story begins, Ned was an engineer for the Blue Star Mine. He took part in a business arrangement that earned him a large windfall, but his enrichment came at the expense of Robert Elwell, who was left ruined. Ned and Mary moved to an isolated country house in England, and it becomes apparent in retrospect that Ned was trying to escape the consequences of his actions. He is dismissive of Mary's concerns about a newspaper clipping she receives in the mail about a lawsuit Elwell filed against him. In the end, Ned disappears, and later, after Mary investigates and contacts a lawyer in Wisconsin, she understands that the stranger she had seen on the property that day was in fact Elwell's ghost seeking retribution, and that it was he who spirited Ned away.

Mary Boyne
Mary Boyne is the protagonist of "Afterward," and the story is told from her perspective. She and her husband, Ned, have been married for a number of years. They lived in the American Midwest (apparently Wisconsin), but after Ned reaped large but ill-gotten profits on a speculative business deal, the couple decided to move to England and live at Lyng, a remote country house in Dorsetshire. Mary becomes increasingly disturbed, for her husband seems troubled and withdrawn. Later in the story, after he disappears, Mary investigates the disappearance.

Ultimately, she learns that Ned's profits came at the expense of Robert Elwell, whose ghost appeared and took Ned away. The story, then, is in large part an examination of the role of women at the time. Mary is depicted as somewhat naïve and innocent, and she is kept in a kind of "gilded cage," entirely dependent on her husband, who turns out to be unworthy of her trust. The story traces her shocked enlightenment as she gradually comes to understand the circumstances of her life.

Mrs. Dockett
Mrs. Dockett, the head servant in the Boyne household, does not appear directly but is referred to by Trimmle.

Robert Elwell
Robert Elwell was an American business associate of Ned Boyne. Ned took advantage of Elwell through a highly speculative investment that enriched the Boynes but ruined Elwell. Elwell, in despair, shoots himself, but he lingers for two months before he dying. It is Elwell's ghost that appears at Lyng, first when Mary and Ned are up on the roof taking in the view, and then later, at the time of Ned's disappearance. The first occurrence takes place when Elwell shoots himself, the second just after he actually dies. The essence of the story is that Elwell's ghost appears at Lyng to exact retribution for Ned's duplicity.

Parvis
Parvis is a lawyer from Waukesha, Wisconsin, whose name appears on a letter Ned Boyne was writing at the time of his disappearance. Mary contacts him, but he replies that his involvement in the lawsuit involving Elwell was tangential. Later, when he is in England on other business, he appears at Mary's home in Dorsetshire and reveals to her the essence of the mystery surrounding Ned's business dealings as well as his disappearance.

Peters
Peters is one of the tradesmen working on the Boyne house. Peters is mentioned only by name and never appears.

Alida Stair
Alida Stair, identified as a friend, acts as an adviser to the Boynes when they are making

plans to purchase a country house and move to England. It is she who suggests Lyng in Dorsetshire as a property that will meet their expectations, including their hope that the house be haunted by a ghost. She wryly points out to the couple that they will know about the ghost only long after they encounter it.

Trimmle

Trimmle is the Boynes' parlor maid. Trimmle maintains something of an air of superiority and expresses mild impatience with what she regards as obtuseness on the part of Mary.

THEMES

Revenge

The principal theme of "Afterward" is the inescapability of retribution. As the story unfolds, the reader learns that Ned, Mary's husband, reaped a large windfall in a business deal involving the Blue Star Mine. Although the details are not specified, it becomes clear that Ned acted dishonorably in his business dealings with Robert Elwell, bringing the latter to ruin. Although he tries to escape the consequences of his actions, in part by moving to a remote corner of England, he grows increasingly troubled and anxious, suggesting that he feels guilt about his actions—or at least that he is worried about legal consequences. He is relieved when he learns that Elwell's lawsuit against him has been abandoned, but it soon becomes apparent that Elwell will exact another form of retribution. After he shoots himself in despair, he tries to reach Ned, but he is unable to do so because he is not yet dead; nevertheless, his spirit appears at Lyng, to Ned's consternation. Two months later Elwell dies. Now he is able to appear at Lyng in spectral form and carry out his purpose. Mary directs him to the library, where Ned is working. Later, she discovers that the stranger has disappeared with her husband. Only after the arrival of the lawyer Parvis from Wisconsin does the reader, along with Mary, fully understand that the stranger who arrived at Lyng was Elwell's ghost, bent on exacting retribution for Ned's actions.

Sex Roles

A theme that runs throughout Wharton's fiction is the role and position of women and the author's perception that women at the time were too often kept in a "gilded cage," meaning that they were kept in comfortable, even affluent, circumstances by their husbands (or other men, such as fathers and brothers) but were denied full participation in the affairs of adult life. In this regard, Mary Boyne resembles many of Wharton's female characters. She is something of an innocent appendage to Ned and his professional life, an ornament, not a partner. This is made especially apparent after Mary learns of the lawsuit and her husband dismisses her concerns:

> His wife felt a sting of compunction. Theoretically, she deprecated the American wife's detachment from her husband's professional interests, but in practice she had always found it difficult to fix her attention on Boyne's report of the transactions in which his varied interests involved him. Besides, she had felt during their years of exile, that, in a community where the amenities of living could be obtained only at the cost of efforts as arduous as her husband's professional labours, such brief leisure as he and she could command should be used as an escape from immediate preoccupations, a flight to the life they always dreamed of living.

This passage suggests that Mary feels guilty about her lack of participation in her husband's business affairs, as in theory she opposes the view, held by many American women, that they have no role to play in their husbands' professional interests. She acknowledges, however, that she simply finds it difficult to maintain interest in those affairs. Further, she recognizes that her husband has to devote considerable time and effort to his business dealings, so rather than involving herself in his affairs, she chooses to avoid mention of them during his brief periods of leisure.

Mary goes on to reflect:

> Once or twice, now that this new life had actually drawn its magic circle about them, she had asked herself if she had done right, but hitherto such conjectures had been no more than the retrospective excursions of an active fancy. Now, for the first time, it startled her a little to find how little she knew of the material foundation on which her happiness was built.

It was likely Wharton's view that most women at the time knew little about "the material

TOPICS FOR FURTHER STUDY

- Stephanie Carroll's *A White Room* (2013) is a modern gothic tale set in the late nineteenth century. The protagonist is Emeline Evans, who dreams of becoming a nurse but has to save her family from poverty by marrying John Dorr, an attorney, after her father dies. Dorr moves her to a gothic house in a remote town, where she appears to begin to go mad. Read the novel, then write a report comparing its themes to those of Wharton's "Afterward."

- Investigate the history of the spiritualist movement in the late nineteenth and early twentieth centuries. What did spiritualists believe? Who were the major figures in the movement? What hoaxes were perpetrated? To what extent did the interest in spiritualism make the reading public more receptive to ghost stories? Present your findings in an oral report for your classmates.

- Select one of Wharton's ghost stories other than "Afterward." Possibilities include "Pomegranate Seed," "The Eyes," "All Souls," "The Looking Glass," and "The Triumph of Night." Convert the story into a dramatic script and, with the help of a willing companion, perform your play for your classmates.

- *The Secret Keepers* (2012), by Chinese Canadian author Paul Yee, is a young-adult novel set in San Francisco's Chinatown in the early twentieth century. It tells the story of a boy, Jackson Leong, who lost his brother in the 1906 San Francisco earthquake. Jackson has to deal with the ghost of his brother, as well as the ghost of a young woman. Read the novel, and then prepare a written report about how both the novel and "Afterward" make use of the theme of hidden secrets.

- Investigate English country houses similar to the one that forms the setting of "Afterward." Locate descriptions and images of these kinds of properties on the Internet and, using a tool such as Jing.com or Flickr, share your findings with your classmates.

- Investigate the history of gothic literature in British and American literature. What is gothic literature, and why is the word *gothic* used to refer to it? What is the relationship between gothic and the ghost story? Who were prominent writers of gothic literature? What are the conventions of gothic literature? Present the results of your research in a chart, which you can share with your classmates on a social networking site.

- During Wharton's lifetime, the "woman question" was a topic of discussion, and Wharton was very much concerned about the roles and positions of women. Locate the article titled "The Woman Question Again," by Francis Parkman, published originally in the *North American Review* in January 1880 and available online (http://digital.library.cornell.edu/cgi/t/text/page-viewer-idx?c=nora;cc=nora;rgn=full%20text;idno=nora0130-1;didno=nora0130-1;view=image;seq=28;node=nora0130-1%3A1;page=root;size=s;frm=frameset). Imagine and script a debate between Wharton at age eighteen and the author of the article on the issues he addresses. With a willing classmate, perform your debate for the class.

foundation" on which their lives were built. In both of these ruminative passages, Wharton conveys a sense of isolation, of being encircled and cut off. The circle may be a "magic circle," one that enables Mary and her husband to achieve "the life they always dreamed of living," but that life, for Mary at least, is built on ignorance and a lack of full participation in the affairs of adult life.

The Boynes look for a country home where they can spend quiet evenings by the fire.
(© blindfire / Shutterstock.com)

STYLE

Gothic Stories and Ghost Stories

Ghost stories such as "Afterward" can be thought of as a subcategory of gothic literature, an early romantic form of literature that emerged in the eighteenth century and grew increasingly popular in the nineteenth. Gothic literature is generally characterized by a murky atmosphere of gloom and horror, with events taking place in a setting of decay and desolation. The ghost story seizes on these characteristics of gothic literature and uses them in often predictable ways.

"Afterward" provides a good example of the genre. The story consists of a nested story in which past events are framed by present ones, suggesting that the reader is entering the frame of mind of a character actively engaging her memory, in this case Mary Boyne. The tale also relies on contrasts between light and dark, suggesting differing degrees of illumination, awareness, and understanding. The setting for gothic stories is often a mysterious house, usually with

some kind of secret passage (such as the stairs that Mary discovers), which functions as a symbol by encouraging the merger of conscious and subconscious thought. Characters often climb to heights to attain a revealing perspective, as Mary does when she ascends the stairs and first sees Elwell's apparition.

Such stories often feature an intellectual man who tries to seclude his wife and himself from the human community, just as Ned Boyne, the engineer/scientist, tries to seclude himself and his wife in the English countryside. Additionally, such stories often feature a childlike woman who accepts her seclusion but then achieves a terrifying awareness; for example, Mary gradually learns that her husband acted dishonorably. Finally, and perhaps most importantly, the gothic ghost story exposes the limitations of the rational, suggested by this story's spectral library and the disappearance of Ned.

Symbolism

Symbolism is evident in "Afterward." The ghost of Robert Elwell hunts Ned Boyne down and spirits him away in a symbolic act of retribution for his dishonesty. A more specific symbol in "Afterward" is the library. The library at Lyng is dark and shadowy, and its shadows suggest Ned's concealment of his shady business dealings. Additionally, the darkness of the library suggests Mary's ignorance—but it allows for her eventual illumination. The library is the story's emotional center, the site of accumulated but suppressed knowledge, retribution for secret transgressions, and Mary's belated education.

Setting

In connection with the conventions of gothic literature, setting plays an important role. A ghost story is likely to be most effective in a setting that is in some measure eerie, otherworldly, and perhaps dilapidated. Secret passages, hidden rooms, and the like are commonplace. In "Afterward," the Boynes deliberately seek out an obscure setting, a home lacking in modern conveniences and needing repairs—in modern terms, a "fixerupper." As the story unfolds, it becomes apparent that the house is hiding other secrets. As Mary becomes increasingly troubled by her husband's anxiety, she reflects:

> The thought that there *was* a secret somewhere between them struck her with a sudden rap of wonder, and she looked about her down the long room.
>   "Can it be the house?" she mused.
>   The room itself might have been full of secrets. They seemed to be piling themselves up, as evening fell, like the layers and layers of velvet shadow dropping from the low ceiling, the rows of books, the smoke-blurred sculpture of the hearth.

Later, Mary has this thought:

> It was the house itself, of course, that possessed the ghost-seeing faculty, that communed visually but secretly with its own past; if one could only get into close enough communion with the house, one might surprise its secret, and acquire the ghost-sight on one's own account.

Passages such as this underscore the themes of the novel by impressing on the reader the notion of hidden secrets, of a "lurking mystery," that will eventually be revealed.

Imagery

A dominant set of images in "Afterward" comprises those concerning darkness, gloom, obscurity, and shadows on the one hand and light, illumination, and brightness on the other. The images of darkness not only contribute to the ghostly atmosphere of the story but also signify the notion of secrets, of hidden knowledge that will eventually be revealed; similarly, images of light come to signify the enlightenment and illumination that Mary experiences as she gradually comes to understand that her husband is not the man she thought he was. A passage at the beginning of part II is representative of Wharton's use of images of darkness and light.

> Weary with her thoughts, she moved to the window. The library was now quite dark, and she was surprised to see how much faint light the outer world still held.
>   As she peered out into it across the court, a figure shaped itself far down the perspective of bare limes: it looked a mere blot of deeper grey in the greyness.

After Ned arrives, as Mary sits in the shadowy library, the parlour maid enters with a lamp and a tray with letters. The light "struck up into Boyne's face as he bent above the tray she presented." The maid leaves after finishing her "errand of illumination." Ned speaks to Mary, "the light bringing out the sharp stamp of worry between his brows as he turned over the letters." After Ned offers reassurance to Mary, the maid brings in a second lamp: "With the dispersal of shadows...Mary Boyne felt herself less oppressed by that sense of something mutely imminent which had darkened her afternoon."

Such passages pervade "Afterward." At the start of part III, for example, Mary's "recovery of her sense of security" seems to be

> in the air when she woke in her low-ceiled, dusky room; it went with her down-stairs to the breakfast-table, flashed out at her from the fire....It was as clear, thank heaven, as the bright outer light that surprised her almost with a touch of summer when she issued from the house.

HISTORICAL CONTEXT

Social Changes in the Early Twentieth Century

In the preface to her 1937 collection *Ghosts*, Wharton maintained, "Deep within us as the ghost instinct lurks, I seem to see it being

COMPARE & CONTRAST

- **1910:** Although spiritualism and the belief that one can commune with the ghosts of the dead are beginning to wane in popularity, spiritualism still maintains a large following.

  Today: Spiritualism in numerous forms is practiced by many proponents of the New Age movement.

- **1910:** Despite a growing women's suffrage movement, women are still denied the right to vote in the United States, and most women remain largely dependent on husbands or other men for support.

  Today: Women enjoy a full range of legal rights, and through the first decade of the twenty-first century, 57 percent of college students, and of college graduates, are women, demonstrating the ability of women to be self-supporting.

- **1910:** In the first decade of the new century, the psychoanalytic movement led by Sigmund Freud is growing in popularity, leading authors in new directions in the exploration of character and motivation.

  Today: Freudian psychoanalysis, while having undergone revisions, continues to be practiced. The American Psychological Association's Division 39 is devoted to psychoanalysis.

---

gradually atrophied by those two world-wide enemies of the imagination, the wireless and the cinema." That Wharton would make such a remark comes as little surprise, for Wharton's life straddled the later nineteenth and early twentieth centuries. She was born during the Civil War into an older, pretechnological age, the age of the horse and buggy, the oil lamp, and the stage. She came of age, however, as new technological wonders—electricity, the radio, motion pictures, the automobile, air travel—were coming into existence.

This era was marked by momentous changes not only in technology but also in social and political affairs. During the first years of the new century, for example, new schools of painters, composers, and writers were beginning to question traditional ways of practicing their arts. New definitions of what was meant by "modern" were evolving, and new understandings of the human mind, developed by such thinkers as Sigmund Freud and the American psychologist William James, offered artists new ways of conceiving of character and personality in their works. That Wharton straddled this emergence of modernity

is evident in her writing. On the one hand, she retained her interest in the more traditional novel of manners, as represented by such titles as *The House of Mirth* and *The Age of Innocence.* Yet at the same time she remained fascinated by the uncanny, the eerie, and the inexplicable, and she exercised this fascination in ghost stories.

The twentieth century can be said to have begun with the death of England's Queen Victoria in 1901. With her death, a long era of tradition died as well, to be replaced by the brief, optimistic Edwardian era, named after her son, King Edward VII—an optimism that would be shattered by World War I. During much of this period, Wharton lived in Europe, which enjoyed comfort and wealth, at least among the higher social classes, and which reveled in the possibilities for material and social progress and amelioration of the human condition. Although much of her work during this period could hardly be regarded as cheerily optimistic, she nevertheless set her work in a familiar social landscape, one that would have been immediately recognizable to her readers.

Mary sees a mysterious man walking down the avenue of trees, coming toward the house, but only much later does she realize this is the ghost.
(© Vitaly Ilyasov / Shutterstock.com)

In "Afterward," for example, Edward Boyne makes his fortune in American trade and then moves to England to enjoy his windfall. There, he plans to assume the role of the English country squire, stroll through his gardens, write a book, and enjoy the company of his pliant wife. These are common motifs in the Anglo-American literature of the time. Yet his gains are ill-gotten, or at least of dubious legitimacy, suggesting Wharton's critique of Edwardian wealth and comfort within a still-rigid social class structure. Wharton, in other words, used familiar social and economic settings to embed her interest in the "uncanny" and the alien therein.

Throughout her work, Wharton presents new, more modern views of women, taking on the problems of gender that were growing more pressing in the new century. Again, she was peculiarly well positioned to do so, having been raised in a stifling social environment that offered women limited opportunities, but being surrounded in her middle years with new views concerning the roles of women. Demands for the right to vote were intensifying. Margaret Sanger's advocacy of birth control seemed to open new possibilities for women by freeing them from childbirth, if desired, and household drudgery. The public was growing more aware of the economic predicament of women who had to make do without the protection of men. Women could envision greater possibilities for social, political, artistic, and biological freedom—yet they continued to meet with resistance from a male power structure. They remained trapped, just as Mary Boyne in "Afterward" is trapped in a marriage in which she is an ornament. Her husband does not regard her as a full participant in life, as seen in his dismissal of her concern about his business affairs; she has little ability to exercise personal choice. Mary, however, is a product of her social class, and the prison of social class was a persistent theme in Wharton's fiction. Later writers would attack the male power structure more vigorously, yet Wharton, herself a member of society's upper-crust, tradition-bound social structure, struck early blows against it.

CRITICAL OVERVIEW

Tales of Men and Ghosts, in which "Afterward" is included, met with mixed reactions when the collection was published in 1910. A reviewer for the London *Independent* judges the stories to be of "strangely unequal merit" and concludes with the somewhat enigmatic judgment, "There is a cramping of influence discernible in these pages." The reviewer for *Nation* finds the stories "ingenious and readable" but goes on to write that "their ingenuity is altogether too patent: they are too clearly trumped up out of the author's fancy." The reviewer further comments on what he regards as the magazine-fiction style of the stories:

> Not the least puzzling thing about this collection is its uncertainty of style. Two of the stories, "Afterward" and "The Letters," are (rather ineffectively) in her earlier manner—that Anglo-Gallic manner, with its nuances, its compunctions, its hiatuses.... Their style is rather that alert and commonplace style of the magazine fiction of the day as turned out by an army of skillful practitioners.

A reviewer for *Athenaeum* is more positive, commenting that

> the most genuine attempt at a material ghost appears in "Afterward," where the man whom Boyne has wronged, and who has attempted to commit suicide, comes after his death to fetch him. Here the skill of the writer is shown chiefly in the manner in which Boyne's wife sees the ghost through her husband's eyes, and gradually understands the situation.

The reviewer for *Bookman* remarks that "her ghosts are not very terrible creatures" but goes on to comment, "It is in . . . studies of human nature that Miss Wharton excels. Her volume is three parts brilliant and always readable."

Modern scholars take a number of approaches to Wharton's ghost stories in general and "Afterward" in particular. Margaret B. McDowell, in "Edith Wharton's Ghost Tales Reconsidered," comments on the thematic role of Wharton's ghosts, noting that their presence

> is less important than the cause of that appearance and the shocked response of a character to the supernatural phenomenon. . . . The interest in the story centers on the living and the human individual, on the relationships among the characters, and the exploration of the situation in which they find themselves.

Other critics take a more psychological approach to the ghost stories. In *Edith Wharton: A Study of the Short Fiction*, Barbara A. White remarks that "the ghost stories of Wharton's middle period bear a close relation to other stories of the time about reason versus intuition." Referencing a character in one of the collection's other stories, "The Long Run," White comments: "Possibly Wharton shares Merrick's belief that reason and intuition cannot be balanced; she has her character conclude that one cannot serve two masters, 'theory and instinct.' . . . Similarly, Mary Boyne does not see the ghost until 'afterward,' or too late." In the same vein, Gloria C. Erlich, in "The Female Conscience in Edith Wharton's Shorter Fiction"—in which she calls "Afterward" "one of Wharton's best ghost stories"—hints at a Freudian interpretation of the story, writing that it depicts the "bewildered consciousness of a woman singularly ignorant of the realities of life." Erlich goes on to write:

> Mary Boyne had been so protected from the sordid ways of the world that she was unaware of her husband's business activities and the lawsuit concerning them. . . . Viewed in this light, the ghost that appears "afterward," or belatedly,

can be seen as the return of what Mary had repressed, some knowledge deemed unsuitable for young ladies. Here . . . economic ignorance can serve as a metaphor for sexual ignorance.

Numerous modern scholars explore feminist interpretations of Wharton's ghost stories. Kathy Fedorko, in *Gender and the Gothic in the Fiction of Edith Wharton*, comments: "As in earlier Gothic stories, Mary Boyne and her husband Ned are distinctly gendered, the passive and nurturing nonintellectual female and the emotionally distant and controlling male intellectual." Fedorko goes on to point out that

> unlike earlier heroines, however, Mary probes her way into awareness, even though such understanding is threatening and terrifying. . . . [Readers] observe her learning to read the subconscious and uncanny in her experience, putting pieces together that bring her new understanding, albeit at great cost.

For Allan Gardner Smith, in "Edith Wharton and the Ghost Story,"

> The ghostly ectoplasm is a coalescence of her husband's guilt, a veridical haunting to dramatize the suppressions of business mores, kept from the wife but surfacing in conditions of "continuity and silence." The ghost itself dramatizes, in its indeterminateness, the difficulty she experiences in bringing this material to consciousness.

Similarly, Candace Waid, in *Edith Wharton's Letters from the Underworld: Fictions of Women and Writing*, examines the ghost stories in terms of the efforts of women writers at the time to find a voice:

> Wharton's ghost stories reveal her efforts to imagine a voice for the woman writer, to place the woman writer in relation to the unwritten (and in some sense unspeakable) story of women's silence. Through the medium of the ghost story, Wharton peers into (what she calls in the story "Afterwards" [*sic*]) the "deep dim reservoir of life" and the "back-waters of existence" that "breed, in their sluggish depths, strange acuities of emotion."

CRITICISM

Michael J. O'Neal

O'Neal holds a PhD in English. In the following essay, he examines point of view in Wharton's "Afterward."

In constructing a work of fiction, one of the first and most important decisions an author

> THE READER ACCOMPANIES MARY ON HER
> JOURNEY OF DISCOVERY. THE READER ACQUIRES
> HINTS AND SUGGESTIONS OF A MYSTERY TO BE
> SOLVED BUT REMAINS IGNORANT OF THE NATURE OF
> THAT MYSTERY UNTIL THE STORY'S DENOUEMENT,
> JUST AS MARY DOES."

has to make concerns the selection of a point of view, a decision that asks and answers two questions: Who is going to narrate the story, and from whose perspective will the story be narrated? A common point of view is first person, a grammatical term that refers to the use of "I" and "me" on the part of the narrator. In a first-person narrative, such as Mark Twain's *Huckleberry Finn* or J. D. Salinger's *The Catcher in the Rye*, a character in the story narrates the events from his or her perspective. Usually, that character is the narrative's main character, the protagonist, but in some cases, the first-person narrator can be a minor character who observes and comments on the actions of others.

The other major point of view is third person—again a grammatical term, this time referring to the use of "he/him," "she/her," and "they/them." With this narrative point of view, the story is told from the outside by a voice that may or may not represent the views of the author. Third-person narratives come in two broad types. A third-person omniscient narrator can move freely in time and space and, in particular, can enter into the thoughts, feelings, and motivations of all the characters. The narrator is conceived as godlike—that is, as "omniscient," or "all knowing." The other type is generally referred to as third-person limited, meaning that while the narrative is told in the third person—Mary Boyne, for example, is referred to as "she" and "her"; she does not tell the story herself—the point of view is limited to the perspective of a single character.

The history of fiction during the nineteenth century and into the twentieth reflects in part an evolution during which the omniscient point

of view was supplanted by the limited point of view. This evolution was the handiwork in large part of Edith Wharton's friend, fellow author, and mentor Henry James, who was an avid proponent of the view that a work of fiction should create a center of consciousness whose thoughts, perceptions, and attitudes form the subject of the work. The notion, then, is that the subject of a work of fiction is not X but rather a central mind's perception of or attitude toward X.

This brings us to "Afterward." The story is about Mary Boyne. The story could have been told by Mary in the first person, for after all, the story chronicles events that took place in her life. However, this point of view would not have worked for Wharton's purposes, for what the story is really about is the evolution of Mary's awareness of the implications of the events taking place around her. Only by adopting the third-person limited point of view can Wharton effectively re-create the *gradual* unfolding of Mary's understanding. Indeed, the very title of the story, "Afterward," emphasizes the notion that Mary was able to understand the events of the story only later, with the passage of time. In this sense, the use of the "nested story" is important. The story is often told from the perspective of sometime later, of "afterward," toggling back and forth between earlier events as they unfolded in the past and Mary's present understanding of those events.

That the story is replete with portents and auguries is made apparent early on in part I, and Mary's sensitivity to those portents suggests that her education will ultimately be achieved. For years, she had stifled her feelings in the "soul-deadening ugliness of a Middle Western town" in the United States. Shortly after moving into Lyng, Mary reflects on the "special charm" of the manse, "the charm of having been for centuries a deep dim reservoir of life." She thinks of the house's isolation, but the narrator reflects on her behalf that "these backwaters of existence sometimes breed, in their sluggish depths, strange acuities of emotion, and Mary Boyne had felt from the first the mysterious stir of intenser memories." The narration continues: "The feeling had never been stronger than on this particular afternoon when, waiting in the library for the lamps to come, she rose from her seat and stood among the shadows of the hearth."

WHAT DO I READ NEXT?

- *The Ghost Stories of Edith Wharton* (1997) collects eleven of Wharton's best ghost stories, including "Pomegranate Seed," "The Eyes," "All Souls," "The Looking Glass," and "The Triumph of Night."

- Wharton's Pulitzer Prize–winning novel, *The Age of Innocence* (1999), was selected by the Modern Library as one of the hundred best novels of all time. It tells the story of Newland Archer, engaged to the seemingly ideal May Welland but drawn into the dangerous and exotic world of May's cousin, the Countess Olenska.

- One of Wharton's literary mentors and friends was Henry James, the author of ten ghost stories, collected in *Ghost Stories of Henry James* (2008). Among them is his famous novella, the disturbing psychological story *The Turn of the Screw* (1898).

- In 1899, African American author Charles W. Chesnutt published *The Conjure Woman*, seven tales dealing with racial issues in the American South after the Civil War. The stories, narrated for a white northern couple by Uncle Julius McAdoo, are derived from African American folktales and include numerous supernatural occurrences built around the voodoo conjuring tradition.

- Roald Dahl sifted through over seven hundred ghost stories to select the fourteen included in *Roald Dahl's Book of Ghost Stories* (1984), a volume for young adults. Included are tales by such storytellers as E. F. Benson, Sheridan Le Fanu, Rosemary Timperley, and Wharton.

- Alex Owen's *The Darkened Room: Women, Power and Spiritualism in Late Victorian England* (2004) is a historical study about the role of women in the spiritualist movement in England during the late nineteenth century.

- Sir Arthur Conan Doyle is best known for his highly logical character Sherlock Holmes, yet Doyle also wrote numerous books about spiritualism, the most famous of which is *The History of Spiritualism* (2003), first published in 1926.

- Michael Ford's *The Poisoned House* (2011) is a good old-fashioned ghost story by a modern author. It tells the story of a fifteen-year-old servant girl in 1850s London. She works in an elegant house, Greave Hall, but the house contains deadly secrets, and an otherworldly presence is making itself known. The book is recommended for both adults and young adults.

Soon Mary reflects on the frame of mind of her husband, who suddenly seems perplexed, restless, and anxious; of course, Mary will only "afterward" learn the source of this anxiety. She thinks: "The thought that there *was* a secret somewhere between them struck her with a sudden rap of wonder.... 'Can it be the house?' she mused." The house, with its gothic atmosphere of shadows and darkness, as well as its history in breeding "strange acuities of emotion," is conspiring in Mary's emotional education. She understands that the library might be full of

secrets, but what she does not yet understand is that the most salient secret is the one her husband harbors. At this point, she exists in the "shadows of the hearth."

That Mary gains in understanding is made apparent in such passages as this one, still in part I:

> Now, as she stood on the hearth, the subject of their earlier curiosity revived in her with a new sense of its meaning—a sense gradually acquired through daily contact with the scene of the lurking mystery.

It must be remembered that in order for the story to work effectively as a piece of fiction, the nature of the "lurking mystery" has to be withheld from the reader. Otherwise, the "punch line" of the story would be apparent from the very beginning, rendering the story pointless. Accordingly, the reader accompanies Mary on her journey of discovery. The reader acquires hints and suggestions of a mystery to be solved but remains ignorant of the nature of that mystery until the story's denouement, just as Mary does.

This process continues throughout the remainder of the story. Mary discovers the panel that opens onto a flight of stairs that lead to a coign, or vantage point on a flat ledge on the roof. She notices the anxiety and perplexity on her husband's face when a figure appears on the avenue of lime trees below. Ned descends in pursuit of the figure, and when his wife later questions him about his reaction to the stranger, he dismisses her concerns and distracts her by proposing a walk up the nearby Meldon Steep. The narration then returns to the present: "Yet now, as she reviewed the scene, she felt her husband's explanation of it to have been invalidated by the look of anxiety on his face."

Much of the story's imagery reinforces this narrative perspective. For example, in part II, Mary is sitting in the library with her husband as dusk falls and the maid brings a second lamp:

> With the dispersal of shadows, and the repetition of the daily domestic office, Mary Boyne felt herself less oppressed by that sense of something mutely imminent which had darkened her afternoon.

Indeed, much of the story involves images of light penetrating the darkness, of Mary achieving illumination as she comes to understand her husband's falsity. In part III, after the appearance of the stranger whom she directs to Ned in the library, she has this reaction:

> Then of a sudden she was seized by a vague dread of the unknown. She had closed the door behind her on entering, and as she stood alone in the long silent room, her dread seemed to take shape and sound, to be there breathing and lurking among the shadows. Her short-sighted eyes strained through them, half-discerning an actual presence, something aloof, that watched and knew.

Ned receives news in the mail that seems to relieve his worry. (© *Blinka / Shutterstock.com*)

Mary is in fact short-sighted, but with much straining she will finally be able to penetrate the shadows.

Thus, "Afterward" is a story about seeing, about penetrating the gloom and the shadows. It is about a conventional woman who lives her life as an accessory to her husband and his activities. Ned made a fortune, however ignominiously, in the rough-and-tumble world of business, while Mary is given to such stereotypically feminine pursuits as gardening and painting. To her chagrin, she remains in ignorance of the nature and consequences of her husband's business dealings, and that ignorance persists when the inevitable retribution overtakes Ned in the form of the ghost of Robert Elwell. She investigates her husband's disappearance, but it is only after the lawyer Parvis explains the circumstances of Elwell's suicide that the full realization of the significance of past events hits her:

> She nodded at Parvis with the look of triumph of a child who has worked out a difficult puzzle. But suddenly she lifted her hands with a desperate gesture, pressing them to her temples.

Mary realizes that in her ignorance, she became the midwife of Elwell's retribution by sending him to Ned in the library. And she now fully understands the enigmatic words of Alida Stair: that she would not know of the presence of the ghost until long afterward.

Source: Michael J. O'Neal, Critical Essay on "Afterward," in *Short Stories for Students*, Gale, Cengage Learning, 2015.

Janet Beer

In the following excerpt, Beer discusses some of the difficulties women faced in getting their works published in the 1890s as well as the role of the short story in Wharton's development as a writer.

... All three writers felt the constraints of what was deemed acceptable by the magazine editors and sought to find ways and means to accommodate the strictures of the censoring eye of those in charge at the journals and publishing houses whilst remaining in control of their own discursive practice. But, in being dismissive of any writing which did not aim at the achievement of the radical reform of the existing social order through the power of polemic, whether in the form of fiction or sociology, Charlotte Perkins Gilman did not, at any point, accede to either the censorship of the magazine editor or the imposition of a subject, for to have done so would have invalidated her work entirely. She was briefly the editor of a radical magazine, the *Impress*, in 1894 in San Francisco, for which she wrote reviews, articles, poetry and editorials, but the magazine failed after a short period and until she established *The Forerunner* in 1909 she did not publish any more fiction, concentrating instead on writing works of social theory: *Women and Economics* was published in 1898, *Concerning Children* in 1900, *The Home: Its Work and Influence* in 1903 and *Human Work* in 1904.

Despite the apparent unanimity of the editorial establishment as regards appropriate themes and subjects for the magazine audience, all three writers knew that there were differences between editors and exploited these in so far as they could by submitting and resubmitting stories to different journals.

... Whilst the short story served an important role in the continuing artistic development of all these writers, Edith Wharton might easily be assumed to be the least focused upon it as a

> **WHARTON REGARDED THE SHORT STORY AS THE MOST ACCESSIBLE OF LITERARY MODES AND THE ONE IN WHICH SHE FELT MOST COMPETENT AND ASSURED."**

form since she worked in so many different genres and was a prolific novelist. However, as I shall discuss in the context of the novellas, her experimentations in short fiction were excellent preparation for the business of the construction of longer works although this does not mean that her short stories are, in some way, to be construed as inferior to her novels. Barbara White, in her *Edith Wharton: A Study of the Short Fiction*, comments on the immediate proficiency of Wharton as a writer of short stories: 'her early stories cannot really be considered apprentice work. As a writer Wharton sprang full-grown, as it were, from the head of Zeus.' There is no sense in which Wharton's short stories are to be considered as anything other than texts in which she was able to do different things than in her novels and also, and more importantly, in and around the writing of short stories she found a medium in which to theorise her craft. Wharton regarded the short story as the most accessible of literary modes and the one in which she felt most competent and assured; in her oft-quoted letter to Robert Grant, written in response to his comments on her novel, *The Fruit of the Tree*, published in 1907, she says: 'As soon as I look at a subject from the novel-angle I see it in its relation to a larger whole, in all its remotest connotations; & I can't help trying to take them in, at the cost of the smaller realism that I arrive at, I think, better in my short stories. This is the reason why I have always obscurely felt that I didn't know how to write a novel. I feel it more clearly after each attempt, because it is in such sharp contrast to the sense of authority with which I take hold of a short story.' That 'sense of authority' is given expression not only in her stories but in her writing about the short story genre, particularly in her 1925 book, *The Writing of Fiction* where she talks with confidence about the responsibilities of the writer in the construction of the tale: 'One of the chief obligations, in a short story, is to give the reader an immediate sense of security. Every phrase should be a sign-post, and never (unless intentionally) a misleading one: the reader must feel that he can trust to their guidance.' The importance of paying attention to detail, to the 'smaller realism,' is the consistent theme of Wharton's writing about the short story but her dominating concern is always with the establishment of an intimate relationship between writer and reader. In her Preface to *Ghosts*, the collection published in 1937, she says 'But when I first began to read, and then to write ghost stories, I was conscious of a common medium between myself and my readers, of their meeting me halfway among the primeval shadows, and filling in the gaps in my narrative with sensations and divinations akin to my own.' It is also in this Preface that she makes the statement: 'for reading should be a creative act as well as writing,' and in the composition of her short stories and novellas Wharton was as much pre-occupied with the achievement of a consonance of form and content, which would ensure that her readers were given the opportunity to be active in the construction of meaning and effect, as she was with the mechanisms of the plot.

There is always a distinct morality on offer in Wharton's fiction and, whilst taking it as given that all three women wrote because they wanted to write, felt the imperative to create, to leave their mark on the world of letters, they had distinctive positions as to their purposes as writers.

...At the beginning of her writing career Wharton relied upon the advice of Edward L. Burlingame and William Brownell of *Scribner's* as well as her close friend, Walter Berry, who provided a good deal of support by both suggesting revisions and assisting with matters of organisation and style. As Wharton says in tribute to Berry in her autobiography, *A Backward Glance*: 'The instinct to write had always been there; it was he who drew it forth, shaped it and set it free. From my first volume of short stories to *Twilight Sleep*, the novel I published just before his death, nothing in my work escaped him, no detail was too trifling to be examined and discussed, gently ridiculed or quietly praised.' Notwithstanding the elegiac nature of her tribute to Berry in the context of

an autobiography which has a generally ameliorative tone, the advice Wharton received from both editors and friends was an enabling principle in her development as an artist; she sought the company of artists and men and women of letters, the literary world was her chosen milieu and the practice of her art was intimately bound up with her social life and the people with whom she chose to associate. Wharton's background and income gave her access to the kind of international culture of letters unavailable to Chopin, primarily for reasons of money and location. Whilst Kate Chopin's personal and professional network was therefore naturally more restricted than Wharton's, she did actively avoid participation in the kind of 'literary set' which St Louis had to offer. Chopin was always vigilant in defending herself against any charges of literary preciousness; both in her public and private writings she established a persona for herself which pretended to humility whilst actually ironising the pretensions of those people who belonged to the kind of improvement 'Clubs' which were proliferating in the 1890s. An essay Chopin wrote for the *Century* magazine, entitled 'In the Confidence of a Story-Writer,' published in 1899 without the author's name, makes plain her disdain for any intellectual or artistic affectation: 'I hurried to enroll myself among the thinkers and dispensers of knowledge, and propounders of questions. And very much out of place did I feel in these intellectual gatherings. I escaped by some pretext, and regained my corner, where no "questions" and no fine language can reach me.'

So, whilst Edith Wharton can be said to have taken up a position of almost total immersion in the business, the practice and the social life of what she called the 'Land of Letters,' Chopin engaged only selectively with the literary establishment....

Source: Janet Beer, Introduction to *Kate Chopin, Edith Wharton and Charlotte Perkins Gilman: Studies in Short Fiction*, Macmillan Press, 1997, pp. 4, 6–10.

Jenni Dyman

In the following excerpt, Dyman points out that in "Afterward" Mary acts childlike in many ways.

...In keeping with the social code and her husband's desires, Mary Boyne has developed habits of submissiveness, repression, and absence of direct communication in her daily life. For instance, when Ned Boyne begins to look worried, she conjectures that he may be ill or may have seen the Lyng ghost, but rather than ask about his anxiety, she is "tongue-tied in his presence as though it were she who had a secret to keep from him." The first time Elway appears and Ned Boyne panics, Mary acts as though she believes her husband's fabricated explanation for suddenly dashing off without a word, but she really feels "her husband's explanation . . . to have been invalidated by the look of anxiety on his face" and later his "look of relief" when the stranger vanishes. When Boyne receives the letter about Elway's suicide, she sees he is worried at first. When Boyne's "lines of tension had vanished," she remains silent and does not ask about what has troubled him.

Mary's need for preservation of the status quo is so strong that she conveniently ignores or forgets any information that might alter her life. When she receives a letter with a newspaper clipping about Elway, she finds she knows nothing about "the squabble over interests in the Blue Star." Boyne says he told her earlier about it. "I must have forgotten," she says. "Vainly she strained back among memories." She does not press for details when Boyne reminds her, "It's all rather technical and complicated. I thought that kind of thing bored you." Although "it startled her a little to find how little she knew of the material foundation on which her happiness was built," she does not question at all the appearance of the business-like stranger whom she directs to Boyne. When Boyne does not appear for lunch, she questions the servants about him, at first not even remembering the visit of the stranger. When Parvis, the lawyer, arrives, Mary Boyne admits, "I know nothing." He is "surprised at her continued ignorance. . . . Was it possible that she really knew as little as she said?" It is only when Parvis raises the curtain on the sordid affair: Boyne's cheating Elway out of a share of the mine, Elway's attempted suicide and eventual death, the impoverished condition of Elway's family, that her "confused perceptions, and imperfectly initiated vision" allow her to finally see "something dishonorable" about her husband's actions. Looking at a news photo of Elway, at last she realizes that Elway is the ghost of Lyng and the dis-embodiment of the "dreadful moral secret that haunted her." She hears "the faint boom of half-forgotten words," "You won't know till afterward. . . . You won't know till long, long afterward."

Mary's repressive tendency, however, is not airtight; nagging questions sometimes surface. She "could not say that any one of these questions had occurred to her [earlier], yet, from the promptness with which they now marshalled themselves at her summons, she had a sense that they must all along have been there, waiting their hour." There is really nothing wrong with Mary's memory. When Boyne disappears, she has an "unwonted exactness of visual memory" that his papers "lay precisely as they had lain." Under stress, she is capable of "leaping back to an image . . . lost under layers of subsequent impressions." She has within her recesses and resources that she does not explore or tap, similar to Lily Bart in *The House of Mirth*. Lily was "always scrupulous about keeping up appearances to herself. Her personal fastidiousness had a moral equivalent, and when she made a tour of inspection in her own mind there were certain closed doors she did not open" (Benstock ed.). Society's role of "lady" requires women to deny the uncomfortable material realities around them.

One door that Mary Boyne, in her childish dependency, never opens on her own is the door to an understanding of American business and her husband's part in it. "Theoretically, she deprecated the American wife's detachment from her husband's professional interests, but in practice she had always found it difficult to fix her attention on Boyne's report of the transactions in which his varied interests involved him." She had always preferred during their leisure "escape from immediate preoccupations, a flight to the life they always dreamed of living." Mary rationalizes her lack of interest and attention to business and the financial foundation of her life. "If she had indeed been careless of her husband's affairs, it was . . . because her faith in him instinctively justified such carelessness." When Ned assures her that everything is "all right" with the Blue Star Mine, she thinks that "his right to her faith had now affirmed itself in the very face of menace and suspicion."

Wharton uses telling imagery to describe Mary's dependent, immature existence. Like a child, she is soothed and comforted by Boyne. She seats herself on the sofa beside him. He clasps her hand. As she experiences a "flood of . . . dissolving doubts," he tells her things were "never righter" and holds her close. Mary is soothed by the father authority figure who knows all, tells little, and promises her safety. Several times Wharton compares Mary to a child. Mary has the conviction that "[The house's] secrets were all beneficent, kept, as they said to children, 'for one's good'...." Mary is also compared to "a savage on whom the meaningless processes of civilization make but the faintest impression." And she is described as an object acted upon, "part of the routine, a spoke of the wheel, revolving with its motion; she felt almost like the furniture of the room in which she sat, an insensate object to be dusted and pushed about with the chairs and tables." In her repressive and dependent state, she is ignorant of the actual world that sustains her. When Parvis finally breaks through her shell and tells her that her husband's business dealings were questionable ("I don't say it wasn't straight, and yet I don't say it was straight. It was business"), her first impulse is to do what she has always done, deny disturbing reality. Parvis gives her a sensational news clipping about her husband, and "she felt it would be impossible to read what was said of him, and closed her eyes with the sharpness of pain." Finally then, she can deny no longer. She understands the information that threatens not only her physical world and her husband's reputation, but also the entire internal construct by which she has lived her life: "She nodded at Parvis with the look of triumph of a child who has worked out a difficult puzzle...."

Source: Jenni Dyman, "'Afterward' and 'The Eyes,'" in *Lurking Feminism: The Ghost Stories of Edith Wharton*, Peter Lang, 1996, pp. 42–44.

Barbara A. White

In the following excerpt, White examines the significance of how some of Wharton's characters can see ghosts and some cannot.

...The ghosts in Wharton's middle stories are basically protective. They either challenge the villain directly or try to warn the observer or protagonist of impending danger. In "The Triumph of Night," an underrated story, the ghost warns the reflector, George Faxon, that his new friend's uncle plans to kill his nephew for his money. As the smiling uncle gets his young nephew to sign his will, a ghostly double appears to George; the ghost regards the nephew with "eyes of deadly menace" (2: 336) and tries to keep George from witnessing the will. Even in "The Eyes" the young Culwin might have been saved by the apparition had he been able to

interpret it. Despite ghostly intervention, however, the victims always seem to perish. Culwin becomes a vampire, and Mrs. Brympton and the rich nephew die, having been weakened in health by the villains. The wife in "Kerfol" is tried for murder and goes mad. In all cases the power of the "father" surpasses that of the ghost: Culwin's wealth and position allow him to act as he pleases; similarly, the evil uncle is a powerful businessman who can easily neutralize George, and lady's maids are no match for Mr. Brympton.

Wharton presents the situation most elegantly in "Kerfol," where she reveals the extent of the patriarchs' power and the nature of their mentality. At her trial the wife, Anne de Cornault, tells the judges the following story. Her father had married her as a young woman to Yves de Cornault, the sixty-year-old lord of Kerfol. Her husband forbade her to leave home but brought her a little dog for company when he was away on his frequent trips. After Anne had some innocent meetings with a young neighbor and gave him her necklace, she found the dog on her pillow strangled with the necklace. Each subsequent dog she was given would appear on her pillow strangled to death. One night when about to escape to the neighbor she discovered her husband dead with dog bites all over him. The judges have Anne shut up in the keep of Kerfol. Of course, they do not believe that canine ghosts killed Yves de Cornault, nor are they impressed by the story of the strangled dogs: "What did it prove? That Yves de Cornault disliked dogs, and that his wife, to gratify her own fancy, persistently ignored this dislike" (2: 296).

The narrator of the story can conjure up the ghost dogs of Kerfol three hundred years later because of his sensitivity to the "long accumulation of history" (2: 283) connected with the place. He opens himself to "be penetrated by the weight of its silence"; instead of trying to "see more" and "know more," he seeks to "feel more: feel all the place had to communicate" (2: 283). The possession of this unusual facility, called by Mary Boyne of "Afterward" (1910) the "ghost-seeing faculty," might have allowed some of the victims just discussed to work with the ghosts in challenging the power of the patriarchs. Mary Boyne unfortunately lacks the ghost-seeing faculty. When she and her husband move into an English country house, she romantically thinks she wants to see a ghost. But she is the kind of person who feels at home only in the "bright outer light" (2: 162). Mary seeks "the dispersal of shadows" and needs constant reassurance that everything is "all right" (2: 159–60). So when the ghost comes to reveal her husband's business dishonesty and demand restitution, she does not want to know the truth and fails to heed the ghost. Ghosts are ignored at one's peril, and the second time it appears it takes Mary's husband. Perhaps if the young Andrew Culwin had been less of a rationalist, if he had not "belonged to the stout Positivist tradition" and possessed a "light, spacious and orderly mind" (1: 115–16), he could have heeded the first admonition of the eyes.

The ghost stories of Wharton's middle period bear a close relation to other stories of the time about reason versus intuition. There is a dialogue between the two, a "strange duel" (2: 317), in a marriage/divorce story called "The Long Run" (1912). The married Paulina Trant tries to convince Halston Merrick to run away with her because their love should not be concealed and denied (Paulina has the same name as the angel at the grave, Paulina Anson). Merrick responds with rational arguments against an impulsive act. He thinks she lacks "logic and understanding" and invites her to the "dissecting table." She claims that his logical demonstration is "a dead body, like all the instances and examples and hypothetical cases that ever were!" (2: 319). Although Merrick eventually wins the argument and the two separate, in the long run they lead miserably impoverished lives and realize they made a mistake. Possibly Wharton shares Merrick's belief that reason and intuition cannot be balanced; she has her character conclude that one cannot serve two masters, "theory and instinct. The gray tree and the green. You've got to choose which fruit you'll try; and you don't know till afterward which of the two has the dead core" (2: 306). (Similarly, Mary Boyne does not see the ghost until "afterward," or too late.)

. . . As in the ghost stories, the trick would be to gain the ghost-seeing faculty but not be overwhelmed by the ghosts, and Wharton cannot envision this happening. The seers occupy the same position as incest victims with limited recall, who are described as struggling between "needing to know and being afraid to see." Wharton can only imagine the characters being destroyed by their insight. When Mary Boyne finally realizes "long afterward" that she saw the ghost, she feels her insides crumble, "like inward falling ruins," through which she cannot communicate (2: 176). George Faxon misses saving his friend from the evil uncle because he flees from the ghost in terror, thereby assuring "the triumph of night" in the story's title. Several months later, as he tries to recuperate from his "nervous collapse," he imagines blood on his hands; if he had not run away, "he might have broken the spell of iniquity, the powers of darkness might not have prevailed" (2: 344). . . .

Source: Barbara A. White, "Young Gentleman Narrators, Ghosts, and Married Couples in the Middle Stories," in *Edith Wharton: A Study of the Short Fiction,* Twayne Publishers, 1991, pp. 69–73.

Margaret B. McDowell
In the following excerpt, McDowell explains how Wharton uses supernatural events to highlight problems in interpersonal relationships.

. . . In roughly thirty of her stories, as well as in several of her novels and novellas, Wharton examined the role and status of women, the implications of marriage as seen through the eyes of a woman, the relationship between mother and child, and the rapidly changing views about divorce and about liaisons outside of marriage. Though she explored these subjects insistently, she approached the issues from varying angles and arrived at contradictory conclusions. If any consistent pattern of conviction emerges from the stories, which cover almost fifty years, it is that each woman must decide for herself what is best in her own situation. When Wharton began writing, divorce in many parts of America spelled disgrace not only to the divorcee but to her relatives; yet divorce was commonplace only a few years later. Views on love affairs outside marriage changed much more slowly. In any event, it is remarkable that in the 1890s and even at the turn of the century a woman from Wharton's conservative milieu could examine so vigorously and so searchingly issues related to divorce and to love, legal or illicit. Certainly no American author before 1930 produced such penetrating studies of women who, instead of marrying, decide to risk social ostracism by contracting temporary alliances based on mutual trust and sexual desire.

In other stories from this early period, Wharton deplores the fact that women in 1900 knew little about the lives their husbands led.

> IN SEVERAL OF WHARTON'S GHOST STORIES, A CHARACTER IS LURED OR FORCED AWAY TO A LAND OF THE DEAD—IF NOT ACTUALLY TO DEATH— THROUGH THE INFLUENCE OF THE GHOST OF A PERSON FROM THE PAST."

While she saw such sheltered existence as stultifying, she nevertheless recognized that when women did gain worldly understanding, they had no power to change whatever they found amiss. Only painful disillusionment and resigned acceptance result from enlightenment, as in "The Lamp of Psyche" (1895), when a woman learns that her husband had avoided military service by questionable means, and in "The Letters" (1910), when a woman discovers unopened all the love letters she had written her husband before their marriage. In both stories, ironic endings suggest that the husbands never even notice that the adoration of their wives has turned to patient forbearance.

Wharton's humorous approach to divorce in "The Other Two" (1904) was remarkable for its time. Despite its light tone, it raised questions about the benefits and dangers of the growing incidence of divorce and remarriage as these are reflected from the point of view of Alice's third husband, Waythorn. At the close of the story, he takes the third cup of tea—after the other two men are served—and does so with a laugh. But the reader is aware of his ambivalence toward his new marriage, toward his wife who accommodates easily to all three men, and toward himself as a man who feels himself superior to the other two and possibly to Alice and may be embarrassed about such feelings. Perhaps the sense of possession, intimacy, and privacy cannot be attained in a marriage to a partner who has shared her love and life too completely with others.

Wharton suggests varying answers to the question of the degree of choice that remains to a woman after marriage in three of her astringent tales: "Fullness of Life" (1891), "The Reckoning" (1904), and "The Quicksand" (1904). In "Souls Belated" (1899) she implies that marriage may be an artificial formality and a mere extraneous convention when love invests a liaison outside of marriage, but that compromise with conventions may undergird love more satisfactorily than the troublesome seeking of freedom from conventions. She was still wrestling with such problems almost three decades later in *The Children* and *The Gods Arrive*, indicating that the personal, psychological, and sexual problems confronting women at the turn of the century were not to be resolved in her lifetime. Later excellent stories centering on these themes, which R. W. B. Lewis designates "The Marriage Question," include "Autres Temps," "The Day of the Funeral," "Joy in the House," "Diagnosis," "Roman Fever," and "Pomegranate Seed." Wharton's final story, "All Souls," presents a woman who has had a satisfying marriage that has left her with the confidence to live alone and the wish to do so in the home that she and her husband enjoyed. Nevertheless, she finds herself vulnerable to fear and less able to cope independently without her husband than she had expected. "Roman Fever," "Pomegranate Seed," and "All Souls" hold special significance in Wharton's work because they are sure evidence that she retained the ability to write good fiction to the end of her life.

... Wharton used a wide variety of psychic phenomena in her stories of terror, including the evocation of ghosts, the uncertainty of memory, the occurrence of the demonic or the uncanny, the mystery of spirit-possession, and the distortions of time and nature as one finds them in a dream. Through these means, she provided unusual angles of penetration and a new perspective from which to view the strange or unfamiliar in human experience as it impinges on the mundane. She used psychic phenomena symbolically, and saw no need to document exactly the supernatural occurrence, preferring to hover between the worlds of the natural and the supernatural. Ambiguity characterizes the situations and tone of her best stories, particularly their endings. Consequently, the effect lingers as the reader ponders the tale long after it has been told.

In her later stories, Wharton establishes such ambiguities even more effectively, as in "Pomegranate Seed" and "All Souls." In "Pomegranate Seed" she introduces the ordinary routines of home life and marriage to establish a substratum for the action. When Kenneth Ashby marries Charlotte, he is careful, for one thing, to remove his dead wife's picture to the children's playroom. Over several months, however, the mysterious appearance in the mail at nine separate times of a gray envelope addressed in pale ink destroys the harmony of Kenneth's present marriage. Each time a letter appears, he becomes disturbed, leaves the room, and refuses to discuss it or to let his wife, Charlotte, read it. Charlotte decides that a beautiful home is not enough for them and that travel might reestablish harmony between herself and her husband. The morning Kenneth agrees to book passage for their journey, he disappears. Rushing to her mother-in-law for reassurance, Charlotte is lost in despair after the older woman recognizes the handwriting on the envelopes as that of Kenneth's domineering dead wife, Elsie. So shocked is she by the sight that she cannot even speak the name but communicates the identity of the writer to Charlotte simply by gazing fixedly at the wall where Elsie's picture had formerly hung. The material nature of the letters and the recognized penmanship validate the power of an actual ghost in this tale, although Charlotte's jealousy and lack of trust and Kenneth's inability to talk about his problems would adequately account for his leaving home.

In Wharton's late ghost stories the emphasis generally shifts to problems of relationships that are illuminated by some suggestion of a supernatural or extraordinary psychic experience. The difficult situations faced by characters in these stories can seldom be completely changed or the problems resolved, but the confrontation of the strange occurrence not only brings fear but forces an exploration of common human experience. Death and aging are recognized as inevitable, but Wharton explores other issues such as the need for spiritual sensitivity; the longing for independence; the crucial concern for others, or the lack of it; the misuse of power by the strong over the powerless; the juxtaposition of gossip, superstition, or custom with accurate historical information; the breakdown of communication, particularly among family members; and the temptation to live in a serene past rather than to face a disturbing present. Perhaps the most common theme running through Wharton's late ghost stories is her warning not to forfeit the sanctity of the soul through worship of the past, through nostalgia for a vanished society, or through grief for those who have died. Wharton recognized the

temptation to look toward the past and to relinquish too easily the rewards that life may still offer. Stories developing this central theme include "After Holbein," "Kerfol," "Mr. Jones," "Pomegranate Seed," "The Looking Glass," and "All Souls."

In several of Wharton's ghost stories, a character is lured or forced away to a land of the dead—if not actually to death—through the influence of the ghost of a person from the past. In "Mr. Jones," a housekeeper exists in a state of nervous submission and finally dies because she has succumbed to the power of an already dead tyrant whose purpose had always been to imprison and dominate her, whereas a woman who challenges his mythic power by reading historical documents survives. In "Bewitched," Saul Rutledge is lured into a torpid, deathlike state, at first through fixation on a dead girl and the compelling memories of a lost love to which he tenaciously clings. In "Pomegranate Seed," Kenneth Ashby is lured away from his ongoing life with his new wife and children (and supposedly to death) because he hears in letters from his dead wife—letters illegible to others—the voice upon whose strength he had too completely depended. In "After Holbein," the senile Evelina Jasper and Anson Warley dance toward their own deaths in their ritual reversion to an already vanished aristocratic New York society.

Our understanding of Edith Wharton as a mature artist and as an older human being is enlarged by study of her late ghost stories, particularly when we consider them in relation to her autobiography, her finished and unfinished novels, and her other late stories. Her dedication of *Ghosts* (published just after her death) to Walter de la Mare leaves unanswerable questions. We can discover no record of his knowing Wharton, nor of his response to the dedication. We cannot be sure of the reasons for her attraction to his work—particularly his "ghostly" fiction—nor can we be sure of his influence upon her own stories. Nevertheless, it is clear that she saw in him a kindred soul and that the relationships between the stories of the supernatural and terror by these two authors enrich the reading of all of Wharton's late work.

In their ambiguous suggestion of the supernatural in the context of the natural, both Wharton and de la Mare create the eerie through an emphasis upon silence, suffocation, emptiness, or solitude. Wharton comes closest to de la Mare's dreamy, hypnotic style in "A Bottle of Perrier" as she presents Medford's state of mind in his five days at the desert compound, where he languidly accepts inactivity, isolation, and intense heat until an uneasy restlessness imperceptibly grows into an overwhelming fear.

In their stories both Wharton and de la Mare impressively relate silence to fear, although occasionally silence symbolizes peace. Characters are struck dumb after seeing an apparition; ghosts are often unable to make a sound; people fear that ghosts may be listening to them in the silence enveloping them; and silence may even become palpable—something one can touch or that weighs one down or smothers a victim. The two writers intensify the effects of silence by the use of natural conditions, such as fog, snow, soft wind, intense heat, or paralyzing cold. Both authors dramatically communicate the sense of a silence so absolute and unending that some of their stories suggest an atmosphere of total emptiness, impenetrable solitude, and exposure of the infinite— in fact, the presence of death in life. . . .

Source: Margaret B. McDowell, "Novellas and Short Stories," in *Edith Wharton*, edited by Joseph M. Flora, Twayne Publishers, 1991, pp. 82–83, 87–89.

SOURCES

Anderson, Nick, "The Gender Factor in College Admissions: Do Men or Women Have an Edge?," in *Washington Post*, March 26, 2014, http://www.washingtonpost.com/local/education/the-gender-factor-in-college-admissions/2014/03/26/4996e988-b4e6-11e3-8020-b2d790b3c9e1_story.html (accessed July 10, 2014).

"Chronology," in *Collected Stories, 1891–1910*, by Edith Wharton, edited by Maureen Howard, Library of America, 2001, pp. 901–19.

"A Controversial Pulitzer Prize Brings Edith Wharton and Sinclair Lewis Together," in *Reader's Almanac: The Official Blog of the Library of America*, June 28, 2011, http://blog.loa.org/2011/06/controversial-pulitzer-prize-brings.html (accessed July 14, 2014).

"Current Fiction: *Tales of Men and Ghosts*," in *Edith Wharton: The Contemporary Reviews*, edited by James W. Tuttleton, Kristin O. Lauer, and Margaret P. Murray, Cambridge University Press, 1992, p. 175; originally published in *Nation*, November 24, 1910, p. 496.

"An Edith Wharton Chronology," Edith Wharton Society, Washington State University website, http://public.wsu.edu/~campbelld/wharton/wchron.htm (accessed July 5, 2014).

Erlich, Gloria C., "The Female Conscience in Edith Wharton's Shorter Fiction: Domestic Angel or Inner Demon," in *The Cambridge Companion to Edith Wharton*, edited by Millicent Bell, Cambridge University Press, 1995, p. 104.

Fedorko, Kathy, *Gender and the Gothic in the Fiction of Edith Wharton*, University of Alabama Press, 1995, p. 54.

"History of the Spiritualist Movement," Church of the Living Spirit website, http://www.churchofthelivingspirit.com/index.php?option=com_content&view=article&id=22:historyspiritualistmovement&catid=31:general&Itemid=59 (accessed July 8, 2014).

Marklein, Mary Beth, "College Gender Gap Remains Stable: 57% Women," in *USA Today*, January 26, 2010, http://usatoday30.usatoday.com/news/education/2010-01-26-genderequity26_ST_N.htm (accessed July 10, 2014).

McDowell, Margaret B., "Edith Wharton's Ghost Tales Reconsidered," in *Edith Wharton: New Critical Essays*, edited by Alfred Bendixen and Annette Zilversmit, Garland Publishing, 1992, pp. 298–99.

"Psychoanalysis: Division 39," American Psychological Association website, http://apadivisions.org/division-39/ (accessed July 14, 2014).

Review of *Tales of Men and Ghosts*, in *Edith Wharton: The Contemporary Reviews*, edited by James W. Tuttleton, Kristin O. Lauer, and Margaret P. Murray, Cambridge University Press, 1992, p. 176; originally published in *Athenaeum*, December 3, 1910, p. 700.

Review of *Tales of Men and Ghosts*, in *Edith Wharton: The Contemporary Reviews*, edited by James W. Tuttleton, Kristin O. Lauer, and Margaret P. Murray, Cambridge University Press, 1992, p. 176; originally published in *Bookman*, Spring 1911, p. 14.

Review of *Tales of Men and Ghosts*, in *Edith Wharton: The Contemporary Reviews*, edited by James W. Tuttleton, Kristin O. Lauer, and Margaret P. Murray, Cambridge University Press, 1992, p. 175; originally published in *Independent* (London, England), November 17, 1910, p. 1089.

Robinson, B. A., "New Age Spirituality," Ontario Consultants on Religious Tolerance website, 2011, http://www.religioustolerance.org/newage.htm (accessed July 10, 2014).

Smith, Allan Gardner, "Edith Wharton and the Ghost Story," in *Edith Wharton*, edited by Harold Bloom, Bloom's Modern Critical Views, Chelsea House Publishers, 1986, p. 94.

Waid, Candace, *Edith Wharton's Letters from the Underworld: Fictions of Women and Writing*, University of North Carolina Press, 1991, p. 177.

Wharton, Edith, "Afterward," in *Collected Stories, 1891–1910*, edited by Maureen Howard, Library of America, 2001, pp. 830–60.

———, Preface to *Ghosts*, in *Edith Wharton: A Study of the Short Fiction*, edited by Barbara A. White, Twayne

Publishers, 1991, p. 140; originally published in *Ghosts*, Appleton-Century, 1937, p. ix.

"Wharton, Edith," in *Merriam-Webster's Encyclopedia of Literature*, Merriam-Webster, 1995, p. 1195.

White, Barbara A., *Edith Wharton: A Study of the Short Fiction*, Twayne Publishers, 1991, pp. 70–71.

Yeazell, Ruth Bernard, "Self-Made Man," Review of *Edith Wharton*, by Hermione Lee, in *Edith Wharton in the News*, April 1, 2007, http://edithwharton.blogspot.com/2007/04/ruth-bernard-yeazell-on-hermione-lees.html (accessed July 7, 2014).

FURTHER READING

Dalby, Richard, ed., *The Mammoth Book of Victorian and Edwardian Ghost Stories*, Carroll & Graf, 1995.
This volume is part of a series of "mammoth" volumes of ghost stories. It contains ghost stories by such major nineteenth- and early twentieth-century writers as Charles Dickens, Sheridan Le Fanu, Henry James, Bram Stoker, and Ambrose Bierce, as well as such lesser-known figures as Rhoda Broughton, Amelia B. Edwards, and Lettice Galbraith. Other volumes in the series include *The Mammoth Book of Ghost Stories*, *The Mammoth Book of Haunted House Stories*, and *The Mammoth Book of 20th-Century Ghost Stories*.

Lewis, R. W. B., *Edith Wharton: A Biography*, Harper & Row, 1975.
This is the definitive critical biography of Wharton. It details the relationship between her work and her life, evaluates her accomplishments, and argues that she was a writer of first importance in American letters.

Lewis, R. W. B., and Nancy Lewis, eds., *The Letters of Edith Wharton*, Scribner's, 1989.
About four thousand of Wharton's letters survive. This collection, edited by a husband-and-wife team, includes just under four hundred of those letters. The letters peel away Wharton's aloof public image to reveal her evolving relationships with such major figures as Henry James, Kenneth Clark, and Bernard Berenson and her love affair with journalist William Morton Fullerton.

Wegener, Frederick, *Edith Wharton: The Uncollected Critical Writings*, Princeton University Press, 2014.
This volume gathers Wharton's many pieces of literary criticism, including reviews, essays, literary eulogies, and forewords and introductions both to her own work and to that of others. Among the entries are examinations of novels, of lyric and dramatic verse, and of the work of other critics of art, architecture, and literature.

Wright, Sarah Bird, *Edith Wharton A to Z: The Essential Guide to the Life and Work*, Facts on File, 1998.
This volume, as the title suggests, is an encyclopedic reference work to Wharton. It includes brief articles on her writings, her personal associations and other biographical details, and literary, historical, and aesthetic terms used in connection with her work. Of particular value are the appendices, including lists of media adaptations of her works, a chronology of her writings and publications, the author's genealogy and family tree, a time line, and a bibliography.

SUGGESTED SEARCH TERMS

Edith Wharton

Edith Wharton AND Afterward

Edith Wharton AND Tales of Men and Ghosts

ghost stories

gothic literature

The Mount AND Lenox, Massachusetts

Old New York AND Wharton

psychoanalysis

Sigmund Freud

spiritualism

woman question

Back Windows

LOUISA MAY ALCOTT
1869

"Back Windows," by Louis May Alcott, was first published in 1869 in the girls' periodical *Merry's Museum*. It was later included in the first volume of *Aunt Jo's Scrap-Bag*, which was released in 1872. This popular short story is didactic, created to teach moral lessons to the children reading it. Alcott uses domestic realism as she explores the themes of family, duty, and self-reliance. The story is told in the first person by an anonymous narrator who simply identifies herself as an old woman watching her neighbors through their back windows. The story blends humor and sadness to bring to life the characters in the different domestic scenes the narrator creates as she shows her readers the path to harmony and the domestic ideal. The volume of *Aunt Jo's Scrap-Bag* containing "Back Windows" is available in a 2013 edition.

AUTHOR BIOGRAPHY

Alcott was born on November 29, 1832, in Germantown, Pennsylvania. She shared her birthday with her father, Amos Bronson Alcott, who was a teacher at the time of her birth. According to Marjorie Worthington in *Miss Alcott of Concord*, he lost his teaching job for attempting to integrate his class. The second of four daughters, Louisa was homeschooled and profoundly influenced by her father's transcendental philosophy.

American novelist Louisa May Alcott (© Lebrecht Music and Arts Photo Library / Alamy)

The Alcott family associated with prominent transcendentalists, including Ralph Waldo Emerson and Henry David Thoreau.

Bronson Alcott's passion for his philosophy resulted in the family's brief stay at Fruitlands in Harvard, Massachusetts, in 1843. Fruitlands was his experiment in communal living, which failed in a matter of months. After Fruitlands, the family moved to Concord, Massachusetts. Abigail Alcott, Louisa's mother, worked to support the family because Bronson's work with transcendentalism did little to bring the family money.

As a child, Alcott was active and independent. She grew to follow her mother's hardworking example and started working at age fifteen to help support her family. She took on different jobs, including sewing, teaching, and domestic work. She published her first poem, "Sunshine," at the age of eighteen under the name Flora Fairfield. She also wrote a number of gothic thrillers under the name A. M. Barnard.

Alcott volunteered to work as a nurse during the Civil War and left home in 1862. She contracted typhoid fever while away and was treated with mercury, which is believed to have caused health problems throughout her life. Alcott wrote a fictional account of her life as a war nurse called *Hospital Sketches* in 1863. Her first published novel, *Moods*, followed a year later. *Moods* sold well, but *Hospital Sketches* enhanced her reputation as an author.

Alcott was working as an editor for the children's magazine *Merry's Museum* when she was encouraged to write a book for girls. She completed her first children's novel, *Little Women*, in a matter of months, and it was published in 1868. Loosely based on Alcott's own family, *Little Women* was a commercial and critical success that defined her career. Many of Alcott's subsequent stories, such as "Back Windows" in 1869, continued the themes of home and family. Alcott continued writing about the fictional March family in later works, including *Good Wives*, which completed *Little Women*, the two being combined into a single volume in 1880. Her other volumes include *Little Men, Jo's Boys and How They Turned Out*, and *Aunt Jo's Scrap-Bag*.

Alcott was socially active throughout her life. She was a proponent of abolition, women's rights, animal rights, and temperance. She also wrote, toured, and championed her causes. Toward the end of her life, Alcott cared for her father after he had a stroke. She also raised her sister May's daughter after May died of complications of childbirth in 1879. The girl was named Louisa May but called Lulu. Alcott died on March 6, 1888. Her death is commonly attributed to mercury poisoning, but the exact cause is not known.

PLOT SUMMARY

"Back Windows" is a short story written in the first person. The narrator, an inquisitive old lady, describes what she observes when she

MEDIA ADAPTATIONS

- The recording *Aunt Jo's Scrap-Bag* is an audiobook of Alcott's short-story collection read by different performers. It was released by LibriVox in 2010. "Back Windows" lasts a total of nine minutes and fifty-nine seconds.

looks out of her back windows and into the back windows of her neighbors, claiming that she cannot help but see them. She focuses on the children in her area and reveals that she knows them well even though she has never met them and does not know their names. She also acknowledges that she has her own opinion of each one, based on her observations. She begins her narrative by describing the babies in her view. There are three of them.

The first baby is the aristocratic baby. This baby has the most comfortable life among the neighbors. The parents dote on the baby, and the grandmother amuses the baby with a beautiful toy. The aristocratic baby has an attractively furnished room and beautiful clothes with ribbons on them. The sex of the baby is not known because all infants wore the same type of clothing in the nineteenth century. The narrator sums up her description by saying that the baby has an easy life.

The next baby described is the happy-go-lucky baby, and he is the narrator's favorite. This baby is older than the aristocratic baby. He is a toddler, capable of walking on his own. The boy is always happy, and the narrator compares the yellow nightgown that he wears with his sunny disposition. Although he is still a baby, he takes care of himself. He helps the maid make the beds and wanders downstairs where the women are working in the kitchen. The narrator expresses concern that he might fall down the stairs on his own. He also goes outside alone and plays in his little garden, where he has planted various objects, including one of his red shoes.

The last baby is the forlorn baby, and the narrator is very sorry for him. A cruel nurse tends to him, but no one comforts him. The narrator believes that this baby is gaining the courage to fight back, but she also hints that he may not live much longer under such harsh conditions. After describing the babies, the narrator moves on to the children she can see.

The first child the narrator introduces is Henry, the only child in the story identified by name. He is a ten-year-old boy who keeps chickens. The birds are continually escaping, and he is continually chasing after them. The narrator hopes that they will be eaten for Thanksgiving so that Henry will not have to chase them. She is certain that he will only be able to stop chasing after his chickens when they are eaten.

The next boy scares his mother by acting as though he is in a circus every week. His behavior causes the narrator to conclude that he has seen Leotard. This statement references Jules Léotard, a French acrobat who performed on the trapeze in the late nineteenth century. She admires the energy and resolve that the boy displays in his pursuits.

The domestic boy is described as both well behaved and virtuous, and he has the narrator's respect. He cares for his three younger sisters, curling their hair in the morning. The girls love him very much and wait for him to come home every day.

There is also a naughty boy, and the narrator finds him amusing. He constantly fights with the cook. The narrator witnesses him sneaking in when the cook steps out of the house to dance around on her clean floors in muddy shoes. The narrator believes, however, that the cook could cause the boy's behavior to change if she were to handle him in a better way. After muddying the floors, the boy is annoyed about being punished and sent on an errand. The narrator has seen the boy's father whip him, but the punishments do not seem to bother the child for long. He finds another form of amusement soon after he is whipped. Although she knows that she should disapprove of his behavior, the narrator finds the naughty boy to be the most fascinating of her neighbors.

After describing the neighboring boys, the narrator moves on to the girls. The three sisters of the domestic boy enjoy playing with their dolls, which are the same sizes as the girls are. There is also a little girl who acts as though she prefers to be dirty and unkempt, refusing to cooperate with the adults who try to make her tidy. The narrator realizes, however, that the girl prefers being dressed up and pretty to being clean after observing the child's reaction when she is dressed for special occasions. Another little girl is mean to her cat, hits her sister, and disobeys her mother. She stands in stark contrast to the housewifely girl, who is always sweet, helps with the baby, washes dishes, and goes to school early. The narrator calls her a neighbor worth having.

The narrator ends her accounts of the children and mentions the adults. She comments that they are hardly worth mentioning because they are much like the children. One man is lazy and alcoholic, and another man is short-tempered, swearing at gates. There are also a fatherly gentleman and a cheery old man who reminds the narrator of the happy-go-lucky baby.

The narrator comments that some of the women take on the role of wife and mother well, whereas others do not. She explains that she never sees the forlorn baby's mother comfort him, and she believes the woman will regret her behavior if the baby dies. She comments that the mother of the naughty boy could change him for the better if she would talk to him. The narrator is convinced that this course of action would be much more effective than hitting him. She also mentions the fine lady who cares more about her bonnets and panniers, that is, hats and dresses, than she does about looking after her children. The narrator concludes that she does not want anything to do with the fine lady.

The narrator ends the description of her neighbors because she knows that people would object to her sharing what she has witnessed. She completes her story by wondering whether spirits observe humans and how they would view humans' behavior when they think no one is watching. She wonders how the spirits would record and reward different actions. She believes that watchful spirits would be more accurate and more charitable than she is.

CHARACTERS

Aristocratic Baby

The aristocratic baby has an easy life with comfortable surroundings and doting parents.

Cheery Old Man
The cheery old man lives in an attic and has a flower in his window. He reminds the narrator of the happy-go-lucky baby.

Circus Boy
About once a week this boy frightens his mother with circus-like acrobatics.

Cross Man
The man swears when his shed door will not shut.

Cross Nurse
The forlorn baby's nurse is largely responsible for his unhappiness.

Dandified Man
This man is lazy, is obsessed with fashion, and drinks alcohol.

Dirty-Faced Girl
This girl ordinarily does not allow anyone to make her neat and clean, but the narrator knows that although she enjoys being dressed up, she is not clean.

Domestic Boy
This boy takes care of his three sisters and curls their hair in the morning.

Domestic Boy's Sisters
The three girls greet their brother every day when he comes home.

Fatherly Man
This father spends time with his children.

Fine Lady
This mother spends more time managing her wardrobe than she does taking care of her children.

Forlorn Baby
A cruel nurse is responsible for the forlorn baby, and his mother never comforts him.

Forlorn Baby's Mama
The mother never comforts her unhappy son, and the narrator believes she will regret the neglect if he dies.

Girl Who Torments Her Kitty
This girl irritates her cat, slaps her sister, and runs away.

Happy-Go-Lucky Baby
This toddler takes care of himself and finds his own amusement. He is always content and cheerful on his own.

Henry
The only character named in the story, Henry raises chickens. They escape often, and he has to catch them.

Housewifely Girl
The narrator admires this little girl, who helps take care of the baby, washes dishes, and goes to school with a cheerful attitude.

Narrator
The identity of the narrator is never revealed, but she describes herself as an old lady. She looks out of her back windows and into the back windows of her neighbors and observes their behavior without their knowledge.

Naughty Boy
The most interesting child to the narrator is the naughty boy. He is constantly in trouble, and the narrator recounts how he fools the cook and tracks dirt on the clean floors.

Naughty Boy's Mother
The narrator does not describe the naughty boy's mother, but she is certain that this mother could help her son change by speaking gently to him.

THEMES

Family
Family is a central theme in "Back Windows." Alcott associates devotion to family with goodness and morality in this story. The narrator considers the boy who cares for his younger sisters virtuous, and his actions create harmony in the family unit. In return for his care, his sisters are always happy to see him. They "run to meet him, sure of being welcomed as sisters like to be met by their big brothers whom they love."

In addition to pictures of domestic tranquility, Alcott examines unhappy families. The

TOPICS FOR FURTHER STUDY

- Read *The Road to Yesterday*, by L. M. Montgomery, a Canadian author of children's classics in the early twentieth century. Choose one short story from the collection to consider alongside "Back Windows." Then write your own short story incorporating at least one character from each story. Be creative with your story, and illustrate it by hand or using computer graphics.

- Research women's suffrage in the United States. Create a website that provides an overview of the history and includes different activists and their individual contributions. Be sure to include a link for Alcott.

- Read the book *Becoming Naomi León* (2004), by Pam Muñoz Ryan, winner of the Tomás Rivera Book Award. This is the story of Naomi's fight to keep her family together when her absentee mother returns and tries to take Naomi and her brother. Choose a partner; one of you create a blog for Naomi and the other a blog for the narrator of "Back Windows." Write entries about family for your characters, and respond to each other's posts.

- Research the American family in the nineteenth century. Create a multimedia presentation that outlines the changes in family and society throughout the century. Be sure to include changes in laws, philosophy, and gender roles.

- Investigate transcendentalism and its influence on American society. Consider the following question in your research: What does transcendentalism teach, and how did it become a cultural movement? Write a research paper on the topic, and present your information in class. Enhance your presentation using slides or other presentation tools.

naughty boy, for example, is redeemable according to the narrator. She finds him interesting to watch. She is convinced that the boy could change for the better if his family, specifically his mother, were to treat him differently and speak "to him as only mothers can speak." A mother's love, the narrator is convinced, would be more effective than the whippings that the boy already receives. Ultimately, Alcott places a great deal of responsibility on mothers. The forlorn baby's mother is absent when the miserable child needs her, and the narrator is concerned that the child will die without her care. She also believes that the young mother will regret her behavior when it is too late.

Duty

Many of the characters whom the narrator describes in "Back Windows" have family duties to perform. Some live up to their obligations, but others do not. The theme of duty affects both children and adults. The domestic boy, for example, performs his duty toward his sisters, and he is rewarded with love and harmony. The naughty boy is disobedient and intentionally causes trouble, forsaking his duty to his family.

Like the domestic boy, the housewifely girl performs her duty to her family. She cheerfully helps around the house, goes to school, and assists with taking care of the baby. Another little girl is an example of someone who does not fulfill her familial duties. She is abusive to her cat and sister, and she constantly disobeys her mother. The lives of the children who fulfill their duties are described in much happier terms than are the lives of the disobedient children. For example, the naughty boy is occasionally whipped.

When the narrator moves on to the adults, she notes that they are just like the children. There is a fatherly man who cares for his family and performs his duty. There is also a fine lady who ignores her children so that she can spend her time trimming bonnets. Failing in her domestic duty as a wife and mother, the woman becomes someone the narrator "wouldn't be introduced to on any account."

Self-Reliance

Alcott inserts the theme of self-reliance into the narrator's story. An example of this self-reliance is the happy-go-lucky baby. He is a toddler who creates his own joy. Constantly alone and overlooked, he manages to find his own amusement. This separates him from the other

The narrator watches the activities of her neighbors from her back window.

(© Anna Bogush / Shutterstock.com)

happy baby, the aristocratic baby, who is constantly being amused by family members with pretty toys. The toddler has learned to develop the self-reliance that the aristocratic baby may lack in the future. He is responsible for his own happiness and manages to find it in any circumstance. As the narrator says, he is content to "find endless wonders and delights."

Even at his early age, the happy-go-lucky baby is learning to become a dutiful child and adult. He helps make the beds, and he creates his own garden, even though nothing that he plants has a chance to grow. The narrator never sees anyone with the child, which indicates that he has taken the tasks upon himself. He does not rely on others to tell him what he should do; he relies on his innate understanding of the world. This self-reliance creates a sense of serenity in the boy that the narrator sees in his smile. It is the same smile that she finds in the cheery old man.

STYLE

Realism

The descriptions that the narrator provides in "Back Windows" are examples of realism, specifically domestic realism. Laura Dabundo, in *The Encyclopedia of Romantic Literature*, describes domestic realism as fiction that "concerns issues of home and family, courtship and marriage."

In this story, Alcott focuses on the topics of home and family. She displays family scenes that would be realistic to people from different walks of life. Babies are neglected or doted on, children are naughty or moral, and parents perform their duties or shun them. There is nothing idealized or magical about the families. The image of a grandmother in a wealthy family hovering over an infant with toys is just as believable as the image of a toddler underfoot in a kitchen full of women at work.

Point of View

Alcott uses a first-person, or personal, point of view in "Back Windows." M. H. Abrams, in *A Glossary of Literary Terms*, defines the first-person point of view as one that "limits the matter of the narrative to what the first person narrator knows, experiences, or finds out by talking to other characters." The narrator does not speak with the other characters, but she makes inferences about them that are based on her observations. For example, she infers that the happy-go-lucky baby would not mind falling down the stairs very much because he is always so cheerful.

Didactic

"Back Windows" is an example of a didactic story, according to Abrams, because the author intends to teach a moral lesson. She provides an outline for both good and bad behavior, encouraging readers to perform their duty both as children and as adults. For example, the domestic boy is both "good" and "virtuous," and the housewifely girl is "a neighbour worth having." Alcott also heavily examines the role that mothers play in the happiness of children because it was an important lesson in the nineteenth century for her target audience, young girls.

COMPARE & CONTRAST

- **1860s:** The women's rights movement fights for the equality of women, including the rights to vote, inherit property, and have legal custody of children. Small economic and familial changes are made at the state level, but the right to vote is not granted.

  Today: Women gained the right to vote with the ratification of the Nineteenth Amendment in 1920. The debate on the roles of women in society continues; there are, however, legal protections against discrimination.

- **1860s:** The cult of domesticity is widely accepted in American society. Women are expected to remain home with their families after they marry and become mothers; many independent women, like Alcott, choose to stay single.

  Today: It is socially acceptable for women to work outside the home after having children. Many households rely on the income generated by wives and mothers.

- **1860s:** Children spend more time with their mothers as men work and women remain home. The burden of raising children falls mainly to the women in the family.

  Today: Although many women choose to stay home with their children, a growing number of men are choosing to be stay-at-home fathers. The role of primary caregiver to children is no longer determined by gender.

HISTORICAL CONTEXT

Family Life in the 1860s

There was an evolution of the American family in the mid- to late nineteenth century. As people moved to cities, women and children no longer needed to work as they had on family farms. As Tiffany K. Wayne explains in *Women's Roles in Nineteenth-Century America*, "Middle class families began to focus more on children as individuals." This transition in society resulted in children's spending more time at home and in school. Children also fell solely under the domain of their mothers, and the cult of domesticity developed. Wayne goes on to state, "Women's roles in the household, including mothering, became rationalized and professionalized just as men's work away from home had become."

Having the ideal family was a goal for many Americans when "Back Windows" was first published in 1869. Women were seen as guardians of the family; they needed to ensure harmony and happiness. Alcott demonstrated this ideal family dynamic in her work. For example, she states that the naughty boy's mother should "put her arms around him sometimes" to tame his wild ways. Although the fixed concept of women as leaders of the house and home may seem to conflict with feminist views, it is important to note that Alcott was an active suffragist who advocated for the women's vote.

In the mid-nineteenth century, even feminist activists rarely questioned the role of married women as homemakers and mothers. Many women who valued their independence, such as Alcott and the activist Abby Kelly, hesitated to marry. Françoise Basch discusses this concept in an article for *History Workshop*, providing the example of Kelly, who was reluctant to marry because "public opinion, she feared, would impose on her the wife's traditional role."

Women's Rights

The issue of women's rights developed out of the abolition movement. As an entry in Digital History notes, "A public debate over the proper role of women in the antislavery movement,

The narrator cannot help but be amused at the antics of the naughty boy, particularly when he tracks mud all over the kitchen to aggravate the cook. (© iravgustin | Shutterstock.com)

especially their right to lecture to audiences composed of both sexes, led to the first organized movement for women's rights." The first convention took place in July 1848, at Seneca Falls, New York. Organized by Lucretia Mott and Elizabeth Cady Stanton, the convention resulted in the Declaration of Grievances, a document outlining fifteen changes necessary for women's equality. There was a delay in the fight for equality, however, as many suffragists put their efforts on hold in favor of the fight for abolition before the Civil War. There were, nonetheless, minor advancements in state laws. Some states recognized joint custody and made it easier for women to divorce their husbands.

After the Thirteenth Amendment abolished slavery in 1865, there was a greater push for women's suffrage. As James Kirby Martin and his coauthors point out in *A Concise History of America and Its People*, "the National Woman Suffrage Association (NWSA) in 1878 succeeded in getting a constitutional amendment introduced into the Senate." Although the amendment would not be passed until 1919, the movement saw greater success in state legislatures. Certain states allowed women to vote on educational issues. For example, as Madeleine B. Stern states in *Louisa May Alcott*, on May 29, 1880, Alcott "attended Concord's town meeting, where for the first time, women could cast their vote for the school committee."

CRITICAL OVERVIEW

Alcott wrote steadily from the time she was sixteen even before achieving major commercial or critical success. She wrote under pen names such as Flora Fairfield and A. M. Barnard. Barnard was the name she used for publishing her gothic thrillers. These short stories were created to entertain, and although they were popular, they did not receive much critical acclaim at the time. Modern scholars, however, have shown great interest in them. As Stefan Dziemianowicz writes in the foreword to *A Whisper in the Dark*, "any embarrassment she felt toward them is wholly unjustified. The literary quality that distinguished these stories from others of their kind is still evident today."

Alcott's autobiographical account of being a war nurse, *Hospital Sketches*, was published in 1863 and was praised by critics. For instance, the review in the *Boston Evening Transcript* calls the stories in the book "productions of uncommon merit." Alcott's first novel, *Moods*, was published in 1864, and the criticism was divided. Madeleine B. Stern paraphrases Henry James's review for *North American*, stating that he called her "ignorant of human nature" while praising her ability to write "a novel above the average."

Although Alcott developed a reputation as an author with her earlier works, it was *Little Women* that changed her life and career. Written at the suggestion of her editor, the book was predominantly praised by critics and adored by girls after its 1868 publication. The *Boston Post Supplement* points out that books for boys typically dominated the holidays, but "here is one equal to the best of theirs." The popularity of *Little Women* led Alcott to write other children's books, many of them including the characters from *Little Women*. Published in 1872, *Aunt Jo's Scrap-Bag*, which includes "Back Windows," is such a book. The *Literary World Review*, as quoted in *Louisa May Alcott: The Contemporary Reviews*, calls the collection "simple, natural, full of unaffected feeling, and luminous with that property, almost peculiar to Miss Alcott's compositions, of brightness."

Although scholarly interest in Alcott's work began to fade in the mid-twentieth century, her literature continued to be popular into the early twenty-first century. Several of her works were adapted for film. As Stern explains in "Louisa M. Alcott: An Appraisal," "Her appeal will continue as long as domesticity and adolescence remain experiences of human life."

CRITICISM

April Paris

Paris is a freelance writer with a background in creating educational materials. In the following essay, she examines the moral lessons Alcott teaches in "Back Windows."

"Back Windows" is a moral tale that Alcott wrote for teaching her young, female audience valuable life lessons. Although her intention is to teach, Alcott does more than point out and praise virtue. She understands that educating children requires creativity and entertainment. Madeleine B. Stern notes this concept in "Louisa M. Alcott: An Appraisal" when she quotes "Helping Along." In that piece, Alcott states that "young people like stories better than sermons" and adds that children she knew had "great skill in finding the moral if there was any." By presenting an amusing and compassionate view of the different children in her story, including the naughty ones, Alcott shows readers the value of self-restraint and the path toward the domestic ideal.

In the various domestic scenes of "Back Windows," the narrator describes everything from ideal tranquility to reprehensible abuse. The negative stories are about selfishly following personal passions without regard for others, and the positive ones are about choosing self-restraint. This path toward domesticity is common in Alcott's other works, as Karen Halttunen explains in "The Domestic Drama of Louisa May Alcott." Halttunen cites an episode from *Little Women* as an example: "When Jo's

friend Laurie tempts her to run away with him to visit her sick father in wartime Washington, she replies that her duty lies at home." In "Louisa M. Alcott," Stern calls Alcott's moral tales propaganda stories and states that they "were devoted to more general lessons in work and industry, cleanliness and pluck, cheerfulness and love." Throughout "Back Windows," these lessons are demonstrated by the characters who are able to exercise self-restraint.

The domestic ideal is shown in both babies and children. The happy-go-lucky baby with his self-reliance and cheerful nature demonstrates that happiness is found within. The domestic boy and housewifely girl are ideal children who care for their siblings. The narrator briefly mentions a cheerful old man and a fatherly man, but she spends little time describing the adults in her neighborhood. These images of virtue are examples to follow, but the author knows that she must do more to encourage wayward children to make moral choices in life. For example, she spends much more time examining the naughty boy than she does the virtuous children. This indicates the narrator understands that naughty children, not virtuous ones, are in greater need of her lesson. The narrator also seems to identify with the naughty boy and his endless trouble.

The narrator's partiality to mischievous children is clear from her amusing description of the naughty boy. She recounts his escapades with humor. For example, she says "that sly dog whipped up one of the low windows, scrambled in, and danced a hornpipe all over the kitchen, while the fat cook scolded and fumbled for her key." She hints that the child is not cruel or evil; he simply lacks judgment and self-control. She

WHAT DO I READ NEXT?

- *Little Women* (1868) is the book that launched Alcott's career. It is a fictional account of her family. The book has been reprinted throughout the years, including in a 2014 edition.

- Edited by Lawrence Buell, *The American Transcendentalists: Essential Writings* is a collection of work by transcendental writers along with responses to the movement. Published in 2006, the book is a valuable resource for anyone wishing to better understand transcendentalism.

- Published in 2011, *Under the Mesquite* is a young-adult novel by Guadalupe Garcia McCall that tells the story of Lupita, a girl in high school who struggles to care for her family as her mother fights cancer. Like "Back Windows," the story is deeply rooted in themes of family and love.

- *United States History: Beginning to 1877* (2009), by William Francis Deverell and Deborah Gray White, is a social studies book that provides an overview of American history and how the nation transformed over the years.

- Lucy Maude Montgomery's *Emily of the New Moon* is a fictional story of an orphaned girl with dreams of being a writer. Montgomery was a Canadian author in the early twentieth century who, like Alcott, used her home for inspiration. Originally published in 1923, the book was reprinted in 2008.

- *Louisa May Alcott*, by Amy Ruth, is written for young readers. Published in 1999, the biography provides valuable information for readers of all ages who are interested in learning more about Alcott and her family.

- *Family Life in 19th-Century America*, by James M. Volo and Dorothy Denneen Volo, is a nonfiction book that examines the changes that affected families during Alcott's lifetime. Published in 2007, the book provides insight into the daily lives of American families.

ends her account of the boy by explaining, "I . . . am afraid I find this little black sheep the most interesting of the flock." The narrator in fact creates a kinship with this character by her own actions. When the reader stops to consider the situation, it is clear that the narrator is breaking social customs by spying on her neighbors through their back windows.

As she abruptly ends her descriptions of her neighbors, the narrator admits that recounting her observations of them is not socially acceptable. She says, "But as some might think it was unjustifiable curiosity on my part to see these things, and an actionable offence to speak of them, I won't mention them." Here she acknowledges giving in to her curiosity, which reverses her claim at the beginning of the story that she cannot help but see into her neighbors' homes. If this old lady is still misbehaving, it is safe to assume that she was not the housewifely girl in her youth. By admitting her own ill-advised actions, the narrator makes herself an authority on misguided behavior. When she says, "I know there is a true boy's heart, warm and tender, somewhere under that jacket that gets dusted so often," she speaks from both observation and personal experience. She knows that the self-destructive nature of passionate self-expression can be conquered in favor of domestic restraint, as Halttunen points out.

The narrator enjoys the happy-go-lucky baby as much as the naughty boy and places them prominently in her story. She favors the happy-go-lucky baby because of his cheerful disposition. Unlike the aristocratic baby, the happy-go-lucky baby does not have doting adults and nice toys to amuse him. He finds his own amusements and makes his own happiness. There are clues to his character and what type of adult the boy may become. For example, "Sometimes he is up in the chambers with the girl, while she makes the beds, and he helps." In his activities, the helpful toddler shows both cheerfulness and industry. The cheerful old man is a foreshadowing of the toddler's future. The old man has the same smile as the baby, and he grows a flower, which reflects the baby's ill-fated attempts to plant his garden. If he remains cheerful and industrious, the baby has the opportunity to live a happy life.

Some of the adults the narrator mentions represent possible futures for the children in the story, if their lives remain unaltered. As she explains, adults "go on very much as the children do." For example, the fatherly man is the possible future of the domestic boy, who is developing parenting skills by taking care of his younger sisters. The cross man is the possible foreshadowing of both the forlorn baby and the naughty boy, who are treated harshly and do not receive the love that they need. The man swearing at the gate in frustration recalls the scene of the naughty boy glowering fiercely and muttering about his "confounded errand."

The aristocratic baby is at risk of a completely different fate. Although the infant has a beautiful and comfortable start to life, the child needs to learn industry to become virtuous. If the baby lives too comfortably and never becomes industrious, the fate of the lazy, dandified man awaits. The dandy cares far too much for fashion, and his laziness is compounded by alcoholism, making him a dire warning to the readers of the story.

The girls in "Back Windows" play at house, and some of them are successful in their duties, whereas others are not. The cruel little girl who abuses her cat and hits her sister is clearly lacking in domestic ability. Her cruel and selfish behavior differs from that of the naughty boy. His actions are misguided, but they are not violent or mean. If this girl does not learn to exercise self-restraint, she may become like the mother of the forlorn baby or the naughty boy. Selfishness and lack of love create the worst parents, and poor parenting does not teach children well.

Given that "Back Windows" was written for the female audience of *Merry's Museum*, Alcott's focus on the importance of motherhood in domesticity is understandable. The narrator states that mothers have a special ability to guide their children. She states that the naughty boy's mother would change him if she "spoke to him as only mothers can speak." Motherly love is better at guiding and rehabilitating wayward children than are traditional methods of punishment, such as scolding and whipping. In making this statement, the narrator places the power of domestic stability in the hands of mothers, a lesson that would have been relevant to her young readers in 1869.

By showing the naughty boy as someone who is capable of being rehabilitated by a mother's love and a gentle hand, the narrator provides hope that his future is not sealed because

of his mischievous nature. She offers encouragement rather than condemnation to the boy, and this encouragement is extended to other naughty children who may read the story. Although the narrator emphasizes the importance of proper parenting skills, she does not give naughty children the excuse to blame others for their shortcomings. If the happy-go-lucky baby is capable of industry and self-reliance, then older children should have a greater understanding of how they ought to behave.

By the end of the story, the narrator encourages children to exercise self-restraint at all times by invoking other familiar stories and lessons. She reminds readers that unseen spirits are watching them, observing their "trouble, vanities, and sins." When she questions whether the spirits keep records and hand out rewards, she reminds her audience of common spiritual lessons in American culture. As Stern points out, much of early children's literature was limited to religious literature such as *Missionary Stories* and *The Holy Land*. Incorporating spirits into "Back Windows" makes perfect sense. The threat of unseen spirits watching and judging them at all times becomes very real when the narrator reveals what she can see simply by looking out her windows. Even with her warning, the narrator offers hope as she looks to the charity of the spirits. Here she implies that naughty children who take the path to virtue will not be judged harshly for their past mistakes.

Source: April Paris, Critical Essay on "Back Windows," in *Short Stories for Students*, Gale, Cengage Learning, 2015.

Christine Doyle
In the following excerpt, Doyle discusses Alcott's view on the differences between "talent" and "genius."

. . . However, the American "cultural space" in which Louisa May Alcott forged her career as a writer adds another layer of complexity to the issue of professionalism. The rise of the American periodical press, beginning in the 1840s, and the particulars of its early growth helped to shape the writing career Alcott was trying to shape for herself. The 125 or so American magazines that existed in 1825 burgeoned to 600 by 1850. Periodicals expanded their subscription bases at astounding rates; during the 1850s, several journals had over 100,000 subscribers (Baym, *Novels*). The *New York Ledger*, founded in 1855, had 180,000 subscribers by 1857, and its numbers

The narrator watches little girls have tea parties and "play mother." (© *Maryna Kulchytska / Shutterstock.com*)

doubled soon after (Brodhead). Further, while the various periodicals represented a wide range of reading tastes, from the lowbrow story-papers to the middle-class domestic fiction to the high art of magazines like the *Atlantic Monthly*, the fact that the periodicals came into existence at more or less the same time meant that, in the beginning, "writers were not in any necessary way aligned with one or another of these distinct cultures but faced an array of literary possibilities, and had several publics and several models of authorship equally available to them" (Brodhead). The lines dividing "high" literary art from "low" became more sharply drawn by about 1870, nearly the exact chronological midpoint of Alcott's career, but during the first half of her career, it was a fairly simple enterprise for a writer to participate at all the different levels; in fact, Brodhead uses Alcott as his prime example of a writer who did exactly that, publishing in the *Atlantic Monthly* at the same time she was producing sensation stories for *Frank Leslie's Illustrated Newspaper*. Her insightful understanding of the conventions of various genres and the ability to shape her talents to fit them carried

her successfully through the mid-1860s. Brodhead suggests that the success of *Little Women* in 1868–69 was another stroke of fortuitous timing, coming at a time when the *Atlantic* was courting Henry James but not Louisa May Alcott. Cut off from high art, excelling at her own brand of domestic fiction—a genre whose conventions she "stretched" by her secularism, her humor, and her use of vernacular language, among other things—enabled her to be a recognized successful author and to stay afloat financially without having to continue to participate in the "sensation" genre, now becoming more clearly lower class (Brodhead).

Brodhead's cultural reasoning goes a long way toward explaining Alcott's choice of post-1870 genre, but he defines it almost completely in terms of the American marketplace, then adds the personal element that this also allowed Alcott to fulfill her need for self-sacrifice, to "set aside personal pleasures [i.e., writing artistic but possibly ones not well-received critically or rewarding financially] for socially useful work," a moral virtue inculcated in her from childhood. This, however, seems much less important than the

> **EVIDENCE SUGGESTS THAT ALCOTT MAY
> HAVE BEEN MORE AMBIVALENT, OR
> PERHAPS RELUCTANT TO 'SETTLE' FOR FAME
> AND FORTUNE AND ABANDON 'GENIUS' THAN SHE
> WOULD LIKE TO HAVE BELIEVED."**

way Alcott made the increasing tension between "artist" and "professional writer," an American cultural struggle, also an intensely personal one, or as she frequently defined it, her own struggle with the issues of "talent" and "genius."

Frequently in both her private and public writings, Alcott discusses the difference between the two terms, claiming the first for herself; but not the second. For example, in a letter to her publisher James Redpath, she wrote, "people mustn't talk about genius, for I drove that idea away years ago. . . . The inspiration of necessity is all I've had" (rpt. in Stern, "Self-Criticism"). Questions of genius often come under consideration in Alcott's work. For example, in *Little Women*, when Laurie asks Amy why she has abandoned her dream of becoming the next Raphael, she replies, "Because talent isn't genius, and no amount of energy can make it so," Laurie himself uses this criterion when he gives up his own dreams of becoming a famous musician. It may, finally, have been the criterion she herself used when she wrote, "I can't be a C.B., but I may do a little something yet." Despite these frequent disclaimers, evidence suggests that Alcott may have been more ambivalent, or perhaps reluctant to "settle" for fame and fortune and abandon "genius" than she would like to have believed.

For example, there are indications that she may have looked upon at least her adult novels with even more artistic yearnings during the post-1870 portion of her career. For one thing, she did something with these novels that she did seldom in her writing career—she worked on them over long periods of time and revised them. Alcott struggled with *Work* for over a decade before finally publishing it in 1872. She received back the copyright from *Moods*, which had originally been published in 1864, and

rewrote it for publication in 1882, changing major portions, including the ending.

Upon sending *A Modern Mephistopheles* to her publisher in 1877, she commented, "Enjoyed doing it, being tired of providing moral pap for the young." The entry continues, "Long to write a novel, but cannot get time enough" (*Journals* 204; January, February 1877). Here Alcott makes new distinctions in her work, not only between her children's books and her novels, but also between the novel-length work she had just written for Roberts Brothers and something else she had in mind as a "novel," possibly something more artistic. Considering the entry as a whole suggests that she was doing more than complaining about being "trapped" in the world of children's fiction, which is how the quote is frequently read; she may also have been grappling with the larger question of artistic ambition.

In any case, Alcott's claim that she had no time is arguable, for by this point in her life, the security of her financial status (for four years, she had been recording investments made, as well as income, in her ledgers) should have allowed her to retreat at least temporarily from the demands of her family and her public. The book she "Enjoyed doing" for Roberts Brothers provides another insight into her inability to retreat long enough to write that novel. Early in the book, the young heroine Gladys defuses the boast of the Faust character Felix that his next book will surpass the first by so much "that this first attempt will be forgotten," when she warns him:

> You will never do better; for this came from your heart, without a thought of what the world would say. Hereafter all you write may be more perfect in form but less true in spirit, because you will have the fear of the world and the loss of fame before your eyes. (*AMM* 24–25)

Possibly by this point in her career, when she might finally have been able to take the time to nurture a more artistic novel, the specter of not being able to produce a novel greater than *Little Women*, a true work of genius, intimidated her as much as the *Atlantic*'s rejections. Her journals suggest that the question of genius was never settled in her own mind, for she was at work on a never-finished book she called "Genius" in the last years of her life (*Journals* 238; February 1883). The *Modern Mephistopheles* tale, in fact, is based on a story she had published anonymously in 1866 entitled "The Freak of a Genius." At the same time that her own development as a writer and the cultural climate around her might have been encouraging her to reconsider her own position as an artist, then, it is possible that by 1877 she feared that *Little Women,* her most acclaimed work but a children's novel, was only a freak of her genius, a work in which things came together as they never would again, certainly never for an adult work, however much time she might take. She may have been anxious lest the world that lionized her as a professional writer might not be so kind if she claimed to be an artist; it might say of her that her talent was not genius....

Source: Christine Doyle, "Transatlantic Ties: The 'Dear Girls' of Haworth and Concord," in *Louisa May Alcott & Charlotte Brontë: Transatlantic Translations,* University of Tennessee Press, 2000, pp. 18–21.

Gail K. Smith

In the following excerpt, Smith examines how Alcott creatively uses the "confidence woman" in some of her short stories.

On June 22, 1862, a budding young author from Concord, Massachusetts, wrote these lines to her friend Alf Whitman. From 1862 to 1868, she would pen numerous "blood & thunder tales," with thrilling titles like "Pauline's Passion and Punishment" or "The Mysterious Key and What It Opened." Printed in sensational illustrated weeklies like *Frank Leslie's Illustrated Newspaper* and *The Flag of Our Union,* they brought much-needed cash to the writer and thrills, spills, and chills to thousands of readers. But virtually no one knew that the author, "A.M. Barnard," was none other than "The Children's Friend," the author of *Flower Fables* and—in 1868–1869—*Little Women.* "A.M. Barnard" was Louisa May Alcott.

At the suggestion of Alcott collector Carroll Atwood Wilson, Leona Rostenberg, an antiquarian bookseller, set out in the early 1940s to find Alcott's pseudonymous and anonymous "blood and thunder" stories. While Ednah D. Cheney had mentioned the stories in passing in her 1889 biography of Alcott, both the titles and Alcott's pseudonym were as yet unknown. No manuscripts existed, and it was uncertain where Alcott had published the stories. Rostenberg, along with business partner Madeleine B. Stern, found at the Houghton Library several letters between Alcott and James R. Elliott of Elliott, Thomes, and Talbott, publishers of *The Flag of Our Union.* Here were the titles and locations of several Alcott thrillers, in addition to the revelation that Alcott was writing as "A.M. Barnard."

> THE VICTIMS ARE IN SOME WAY WILLING PARTICIPANTS IN THE DECEPTION THEY UNDERGO, AND THE STORIES PROCEED WITH THE USUAL PERIODS OF THE SETUP, THE SUCCESSFUL DECEPTION, AND THE FINAL DISCOVERY."

Comparing cryptic references in Alcott's journals to the crumbling pages of "A.M. Barnard" in the cheap weeklies yielded story after story by Alcott. Rostenberg announced her discovery in the *Papers of the Bibliographical Society of America* in 1943, and after years of continued sleuthing she and Stern published three landmark collections under Stern's editorship: *Behind a Mask: The Unknown Thrillers of Louisa May Alcott* (1975), *Plots and Counterplots: More Unknown Thrillers of Louisa May Alcott* (1976), and *A Double Life: Newly Discovered Thrillers of Louisa May Alcott* (1988). The American public discovered, to their amazement, that like Jo March in *Little Women,* Alcott began her career as a writer of lurid stories she was reluctant to own as hers.

Initially the reception of these stories has focused on the hitherto-unknown "side" of Alcott herself. Critics have mainly assumed that these tales reveal the "real" Alcott, who later retires behind a mask of domesticity to write the *Little Women* series. Accompanying this interpretation of Alcott's life are parallel readings of her sensational heroines as angry women who must screen their passion with the mask of conventional womanhood. Studies by Ann Douglas, Judith Fetterley, and Martha Saxton, along with Madeleine Stern's introductions to all three thriller collections, draw on the mask image to explain how Alcott—amateur actress and pseudonymous writer as she was—expressed her real self both "behind the mask" of "A.M. Barnard" and through her actress/trickster characters. But while there is a good deal of evidence from letters and journal entries that Alcott found release in writing her "blood and thunder" tales, the image of the mask, which recurs in these stories and in the criticism about them, is more complex in Alcott's hands than a simple distinction between reality and assumed identity. Examining Alcott's play with masks, acting, and deception reveals that these stories consciously manipulate fictional conventions about identity, character, and the task of the author.

A number of the rediscovered "blood and thunder" stories feature a female protagonist who uses trickery and theatrical ability to hoodwink her audience, usually male. The stories, in fact, are more than "obliquely feminist" (Stern, Introduction, *Behind a Mask* xxviii). Alcott, an outspoken supporter of women's rights and the first woman to vote in a Concord (Massachusetts) election, might be expected to depart from the typical gender roles of the Gothic cliffhanger or the sensational romance—the sinister male mastermind, for instance, or the melting, virtuous heroine. Nowhere is Alcott's skillful reworking of gender and identity more apparent than in her stories of women who gain the trust and devotion of their willing victims in order to outwit them and gain what they desire. Stories like "V.V., Or, Plots and Counterplots," *Behind a Mask, Or, A Woman's Power*, and "Pauline's Passion and Punishment" revise the male tradition of the confidence story. In fact, Alcott writes story after story featuring what we might call a "confidence woman." To understand the significance of that act, we must first examine the tradition of the confidence man in American fiction.

The term "confidence man" was apparently coined to describe an American criminal, William Thompson, arrested in 1849 for playing on the gullibility of strangers whom he asked to leave their watches with him (Lindberg). As John G. Blair and Gary Lindberg point out, the figure of the confidence man is related to but distinct from both the mythic trickster figure (Odysseus, Hermes, or Esu the Signifying Monkey, for example) and the picaro (Blair; Gates). The confidence man, unlike the nearly universal trickster figure, "inhabits a modern, highly differentiated, literate society" (Lindberg); unlike the picaro, the confidence man "has usually lost his sense of the ludicrous. Game-playing . . . is the source of his being. Hence such figures commonly evoke a moral seriousness rare among picaresque rogues" (Blair). And, as Blair notes, the confidence man owes his success to the willing complicity of his victims.

From early American works onward, the confidence man has played his part. Preceding the American confidence story were the orally influenced tales of the early nineteenth century, now known as "Southwestern humor," which gave the related genres of the trickster tale and the picaresque an especially crude, violent, aggressive, and intensely masculine—often misogynistic—flavor. Johnson Jones Hopper's gambler character, Simon Suggs, sets the theme for the nascent confidence-man tradition with his maxim, "It is good to be shifty in a new country." Subsequent writers would represent again and again the shifty character that America seemed to breed. Edgar Allan Poe's slippery confidence men and his own authorial deceptions owe much to the precursor genre of the Southwestern trickster tale or picaresque. Herman Melville's *The Confidence-Man: His Masquerade* (1857) pulls a joke on the reader attempting to identify the confidence man's avatars, and satirizes both his characters and the America they represent.

Studies by Gary Lindberg, John G. Blair, and Victor Myers Hoar, Jr., have considered the confidence man in American and European literature, commenting on its moral qualities and its appropriateness to America. These critics, however, have based their conclusions on a literary canon made up solely of men who created male confidence artists. It has long been assumed that the confidence artist in American literature is necessarily masculine because the confidence man was a stock figure in the supposedly "man's world" of the frontier (Cohen and Dillingham). There were, however, actual "confidence women" succeeding at matrimonial swindles in young America (Nash), as well as women writers who explored the confidence theme and created female tricksters in their fiction. And the female trickster figure was hardly new; writers could draw on a long tradition of the *femme fatale* (often called a witch or sorceress)—Circe, Jezebel, Morgan le Fay—and the female spinner of plots—Athena, Penelope, Scheherezade.

Concerns with female deceivers were common in American politics and literature up to Alcott's time. In early America, the Puritans exhibited a particular fear of women who were "shifty characters" in their extremely "new country." Anne Hutchinson was accused of sorcery and banished from the Bay Colony when her lay prayer meetings were perceived as a challenge to the primacy of the male clergy. Cotton Mather executed many women deemed witches; often, they were midwives or others who in some way crossed traditional gender boundaries (in the case of the midwives, women were infiltrating the male world of medicine). The figure of the confidence artist became prevalent in the literature of Jacksonian America, along with concerns about unheard-of social mobility and the rule of the formerly disenfranchised. Several American women writers from the 1830s onward were rethinking both the supposed masculinity of confidence games and the male condemnation of female tricksters. Caroline Kirkland's *A New Home, Who'll Follow* (1839) satirized the gullibility of male pioneers whose greed and delusions of grandeur make them susceptible to the land speculator's confidence schemes. The fugitive slave in Harriet Jacobs's autobiographical novel, *Incidents in the Life of a Slave Girl* (1860), described her clever machinations from her attic hiding place, where she arranges to have letters from herself posted from faraway cities to her old master, so he will never suspect she is living within sight of his house. Far from being a "sorceress," Jacobs is a highly moral trickster who manages to hoodwink her depraved master in order to save herself and her family.

By the time of Alcott's productive years, as Susan P. Casteras has noted, images of "female sages and sorceresses" were particularly prevalent in British Victorian art. Casteras speculates that these images express the anxieties of male artists—especially the Pre-Raphaelites—toward the "New Woman" of intellect and achievement, who was gaining political, social, and legal power. Across the Atlantic, Louisa May Alcott was delving into the same concerns through the vehicle of the confidence woman and the confidence story.

It is interesting to note that literary confidence games seem to fit best in the tale or short story. Lindberg points out that "the confidence man belongs in an episodic plot because he possesses no ground of continuity on the basis of which to perpetuate 'himself.'...A story centered around a con man must share his impermanence." Even *The Confidence-Man*, sometimes called a novel, is organized in discrete encounters. The short, self-contained narrative, with a setup, a period of deception, and a discovery (on the part of the characters, or the reader, or both), is the norm in a confidence story. In fact, the short story is admirably suited to the subject. In a "con,"

in literature as in life, timing is all-important. The quickness—or at least the sudden turns—needed for a "trick" to be successful before it is found out dictates the length of the event and hence the length of the narrative.

Alcott's confidence women clearly partake of elements of the confidence-man tradition, as well as the tales of a mythical female trickster or *femme fatale*. The victims are in some way willing participants in the deception they undergo, and the stories proceed with the usual periods of the setup, the successful deception, and the final discovery. Yet unlike Poe, Alcott does not always wish to leave us with a clear picture of what is real and what is false. The "discovery," for instance, is in some stories rather ambiguous. In addition, unlike Poe and Melville, Alcott is highly conscious of traditional gender roles in this genre. Her confidence women cross gender boundaries, acting in traditionally masculine ways and forcing men into "feminized" roles of subservience, ignorance, passivity, and powerlessness. In exploring the machinations of a confidence woman, Alcott complexifies both the conventions of gender roles and the conventions of the confidence story.

As in other confidence stories, timing is of the utmost importance in Alcott's stories. In fact, Alcott's confidence women frequently comment on their careful attention to timing as they weave their plots and cast their scenes—as do Alcott's narrators. Using the language of the dramatic director and the author, they encourage the reader to consider the ways in which the stories they enact reflect the form they take. Alcott's confidence women consciously manipulate their victims' access to knowledge, their emotions, their gendered perceptions, and their assumptions about gender in others; in doing so these heroines "write" the confidence tale we read. At the same time, Alcott herself, we realize, shapes her story to manipulate our access to knowledge, our emotions, and our assumptions about gender—and, finally, our assumptions about the relation between author and reader.

...Alcott's greatest contribution to the short story is her regendering of the confidence story. Alcott's confidence woman bends both gender and form while she manipulates conventions of character and identity. With the creation of the confidence woman, Alcott takes her place as one of the innovators of the American short story. Her experimentation with "blood & thunder" accomplished, perhaps, more than she knew.

Source: Gail K. Smith, "Who Was That Masked Woman? Gender and Form in Louisa May Alcott's Confidence Stories," in *American Women Short Story Writers: A Collection of Critical Essays*, edited by Julie Brown, Garland Publishers, 1995, pp. 45–50, 57.

SOURCES

Abrams, M. H., "Didactic Literature" and "Point of View," in *A Glossary of Literary Terms*, 7th ed., Cornell University Press, 1999, pp. 65, 233.

Alcott, Louisa May, "Back Windows," in *Aunt Jo's Scrap-Bag*, CreateSpace Independent Publishing Platform, 2013, pp. 93–97.

Basch, Françoise, "Women's Rights and the Wrongs of Marriage in Mid-Nineteenth-Century America," in *History Workshop*, Vol. 22, No. 1, Fall 1986, pp. 18–40.

Dabundo, Lauren, "Domestic Realism," in *The Encyclopedia of Romantic Literature*, Vol. 1, *A–G*, edited by Frederick Burwick, John Wiley & Sons, 2012, p. 371.

Dziemianowicz, Stefan, ed., Foreword to *A Whisper in the Dark: Twelve Thrilling Tales*, by Louisa May Alcott, Barnes & Noble Books, 1996, p. viii.

Halttunen, Karen, "The Domestic Drama of Louisa May Alcott," in *Feminist Studies*, Vol. 10, No. 2, Summer 1984, pp. 233–54.

"Literary Notices," in *Boston Post Supplement*, No. 81, October 3, 1868.

"Louisa May Alcott," History.net, http://www.history net.com/louisa-may-alcott (accessed September 8, 2014).

Martin, James Kirby, Randy Roberts, Steven Mintz, Linda O. McMurry, James H. Jones, and Sam W. Haynes, *A Concise History of America and Its People*, HarperCollins, 1995, p. 506.

Review of *Aunt Jo's Scrap-Bag*, in *Louisa May Alcott: The Contemporary Reviews*, edited by Beverly Lyon Clark, Cambridge University Press, 2004, p. 163; originally published in *Literary World*, December 1, 1871.

Review of *Hospital Sketches*, in *Louisa May Alcott: The Contemporary Reviews*, edited by Beverly Lyon Clark, Cambridge University Press, 2004, p. 9; originally published in *Boston Evening Transcript*, June 4, 1863.

Stern, Madeleine B., *Louisa May Alcott*, University of Oklahoma Press, 1950, pp. 146, 289, 349.

———, "Louisa M. Alcott: An Appraisal," in *New England Quarterly*, Vol. 22, No. 4, December 1949, pp. 475–98.

Wayne, Tiffany K., *Women's Roles in Nineteenth-Century America*, Greenwood Press, 2007, p. 3.

"Women's Rights," Digital History, http://www.digital history.uh.edu/disp_textbook.cfm?smtID=2&psid=3539 (accessed September 8, 2014).

Worthington, Marjorie, *Miss Alcott of Concord: A Biography*, Doubleday, 1958, p. 18.

FURTHER READING

Alcott, Louisa May, *Behind a Mask: The Unknown Thrillers of Louisa May Alcott*, edited by Madeleine B. Stern, William Morrow Paperbacks, 1997.

This book is a collection of some of Alcott's blood and thunder stories, as she called them. These stories show her versatility as a writer.

Barney, William L., ed., *A Companion to 19th-Century America*, Wiley-Blackwell, 2006.

This collection of essays from different scholars examines the many changes that occurred in the century. The book is a valuable resource for anyone interested in understanding the history and culture that shaped Alcott and her work.

Bender, Thomas, *Toward an Urban Vision: Ideas and Institutions in Nineteenth-Century America*, University Press of Kentucky, 1975.

Bender examines the correlations between cities and industry. He also explores how urban and industrial developments brought changes to American society and culture.

Eiselein, Gregory, and Anne K. Phillips, eds., *The Louisa May Alcott Encyclopedia*, Greenwood Press, 2001.

This nonfiction text provides valuable information about the entire Alcott family. The history and culture of the time are also examined.

Emerson, Ralph Waldo, *Nature*, Penguin Classics, 2003.

Emerson was a friend of the Alcott family and a leading transcendentalist. *Nature* is considered the book that spearheaded the transcendentalist movement.

Faulkner, Carol, *Lucretia Mott's Heresy: Abolition and Women's Rights in Nineteenth-Century America*, University of Pennsylvania Press, 2013.

This biography of one of the leaders of the movement for women's rights provides valuable insight into women and society in the nineteenth century. Faulkner also examines the different ways women viewed the goal of the movement.

Gura, Philip F., *American Transcendentalism: A History*, Hill and Wang, 2007.

Gura explores the history of transcendentalism and its influence on the United States. The text provides invaluable information on the prominent figures of the movement and how it developed over the years.

SUGGESTED SEARCH TERMS

Louisa May Alcott

Louisa May Alcott AND Back Windows

Louisa May Alcott AND biography

Louisa May Alcott AND feminism

Louisa May Alcott AND suffrage

transcendentalism

Louisa May Alcott AND criticism

1860s AND United States

nineteenth century AND American family

Bang-Bang You're Dead

MURIEL SPARK

1961

With a title suggestive of gangster drama or a crime thriller, Muriel Spark's story "Bang-Bang You're Dead" actually draws its phrasing from a childhood game played by the protagonist, Sybil—though it also involves life-or-death intrigue later in Sybil's life. Spark was a Scottish writer who began as a poet but eventually devoted her time to fiction, writing some twenty novels, as well as over forty short stories. One of the most significant events of her life was her conversion to Roman Catholicism in her mid-thirties. Some of her stories bear comparison to those of renowned American author Flannery O'Connor, who also had a religious perspective that manifested itself not in romanticized tales of salvation but in witty, perceptive, sometimes dark, often comical looks at the foibles of ordinary humans and the violence that their weaknesses somehow lead to.

Another significant event in Spark's life was her stay in Britain's African colony of Southern Rhodesia—modern-day Zimbabwe—a stay that lasted through most of World War II. Several of her stories are set in Rhodesia or Africa generally. "Bang-Bang You're Dead" partly takes place in an unnamed colony just off the Zambezi River, which divided Northern and Southern Rhodesia. In the story's present, Sybil and a few acquaintances are watching films from that time in her life, perhaps in London or thereabouts, nearly twenty years later. The tale of what happened and why, back

Scottish novelist Muriel Spark
(© Pictorial Press / Alamy)

then in the colony, is a curious one indeed. First published in 1961 in the collection *Voices at Play*, "Bang-Bang You're Dead" has appeared in several later Spark volumes, including *Collected Stories I* (1967), *Bang-Bang You're Dead and Other Stories* (1982), and *Open to the Public: New and Collected Stories* (1998).

AUTHOR BIOGRAPHY

Muriel Sarah Camberg was born on February 1, 1918, in Edinburgh, Scotland, to a Jewish father and an English mother. The otherness of her parents contributed to an underlying sense of not quite belonging to the society around her. Spark is said, by the *New Criterion* editors who eulogized her, to have been "intensely literary from the dawn of reason."

Spark herself, quoted by Ruth Whittaker in *The Faith and Fiction of Muriel Spark*, reported that "it came down as family legend that I could write before I could talk."

She attended James Gillespie's Girls' School, a Presbyterian institution, and wrote a great deal of verse from the age of nine onward. In her words, cited by Dorothea Walker in *Muriel Spark*, she was "the school's Poet and Dreamer." Spark also kept a diary, and, as if preparing herself for intimate involvement with her own fiction, she developed the habit of writing herself love letters from imaginary boyfriends, which she would leave around the house for her first audience, her mother, to find. At age fourteen Spark was crowned "Queen of Poetry" by film actress Esther Ralston on behalf of the Heather Club, for writing the best poem commemorating the death of Sir Walter Scott.

Spark left Scotland in 1937 to join and marry S. O. Spark in Southern Rhodesia, and she soon gave birth to a son, Robin. Spark and her husband divorced the following year, but she nonetheless stayed in Africa as World War II got underway. She lamented the lack of the sort of culture she had enjoyed back in Great Britain and longed to return to the books and ideas to be found there. She returned in 1944, when wartime circumstances finally permitted her to gain passage on a merchant steamer. She gained work with the British Foreign Office at Woburn Abbey in England, writing anti-Nazi propaganda; one of her most notable efforts was a story about the Führer having his pants burned off in a bombing. After the war, she researched and wrote for a jewelry trade magazine, *Argentor*, and then became secretary of the Poetry Society and later editor of its *Poetry Review*. She helped attract young poets by insisting they be paid for their work. She started her own magazine, *Forum*, in 1949, but only two issues were published.

In 1951, Spark's first story, "The Seraph and the Zambesi," won the London *Observer*'s short-story contest, and she issued her first volume of poems in 1952. She was baptized as an Anglican in 1953, attending the same church as T. S. Eliot, but then converted to Catholicism, which she felt better accorded with her innate worldview, in 1954. Around this time, being fairly impoverished, she suffered from nervous strain, and with the encouragement of several generous patrons—one of whom was English writer Graham Greene—she sought psychological assistance. Taking interest in the theories of Carl Jung, she recovered her sense of well-being, and from there her vocation as a writer took off.

Her first novel, *The Comforters* (1957), was a success, to be followed by well-known works such as *Memento Mori* (1959) and *The Prime of Miss Jean Brodie* (1961). "Bang-Bang You're Dead" first appeared in the collection *Voices at Play* in 1961. Moving to New York in 1962, Spark published a number of stories in the *New Yorker*, which provided her with an office. She left for Italy in 1966 and would remain there for the rest of her life, writing prolifically. Spark was made a dame of the British Empire in 1993, and in 1997, she won the prestigious David Cohen British Literature Prize for lifetime achievement. Spark died at the age of eighty-eight in Florence, Italy, on April 13, 2006, on the eve of Good Friday.

PLOT SUMMARY

The opening lines of "Bang-Bang You're Dead" invoke the image of Rupert Brooke—an English poet who died in World War I—in describing the faces of Englishmen in Africa. Scenes from a trip taken by the protagonist, Sybil Greeves, to "the Colony" are being shown to a group of people in a darkened room by the hosts for the evening, Ted, who is a distant cousin of Sybil's, and his wife, Ella. Sybil has not seen the eighteen-year-old films before. The viewers admire the vivid colors and people. Another young woman in the film is mistaken for Sybil, who quickly corrects the impression.

In 1923, young Sybil's mother points out a girl who looks just like her, in both clothing and countenance, on the street. They see her other times, and when Sybil begins school, she learns that the girl, Désirée Coleman, is a year older. Adults mistake them for each other, though children do not. When Sybil is nine—and the girls are now only mistaken for each other in poor late-afternoon light—Désirée's family moves to the square where Sybil lives, as do the Dobell boys, Hugh and Jon. When they all play, the somewhat daft Désirée always prematurely shoots Sybil dead, against the established rules, spoiling the game for Sybil. She tries to muster the resolve to insist on staying alive, but

MEDIA ADAPTATIONS

- "Bang-Bang You're Dead" can be found on the audio version of Spark's volume *The Complete Short Stories*, released by Canongate Books in 2011. The readings by Juliet Stevenson, Richard E. Grant, and Emilia Fox cover a running time of seventeen hours and twenty-four minutes.

Désirée's screeching always wins out. Eventually, Sybil decides to read instead of playing with the other children.

As the host puts the third film on the reel, Sybil remarks that her companions, including her look-alike, were about to go out on a hunt; she was only posing with a gun "for effect." Sybil relates that the look-alike and her husband, as well as a fair-haired fellow, all died, having been mixed up in "shooting affairs." The film rolls.

As Sybil and her husband, Donald Greeves, prepare to leave for two years in Africa, their relatives warn them not to die from a lion attack or a shooting affair—a recent fixture in news from the colonies, attributed to various aspects of colonial life, including the shortage of white women. A year and a half into their marriage, Donald dies after a lioness mauls him. His archaeologist friends encourage Sybil to stay on anyway, and she does—until World War II leaves her stranded in the Colony (while they all went home in time). She takes a job teaching at a girls' private school.

On film, the colonial party rides up the Zambezi River, in south-central Africa; in the dark room, Sybil explains that she was asking a canoeing native about the hippos. The projector misfires, and Ted and another young man fix it while they all chat. An elderly woman learns that Sybil is somewhat famous.

Sybil finds the colors in Africa overwhelming. She rents a house with Ariadne Lewis. Over a couple of years, Sybil has three affairs despite not being terribly interested in such things; they end when she inevitably comes down with tropical flu and writes the man off. She dismisses the supposition that she might be a lesbian; she simply finds physical intimacy boring. Ariadne reports having met a look-alike of Sybil's who even knows her. Désirée comes over for tea, and the two women reunite warmly. When Sybil's school goes on break and Ariadne meets up with her husband in Cairo, Sybil begins visiting the remote home of Désirée and her husband, Barry Weston. Barry and Désirée insist that she keep visiting, and Sybil realizes they are using her to prop up their union through excessive displays of affection in front of her. She repeatedly submits to the unpleasant experience. They posit that she must need romance in her life. Barry reads his poems after dinner, and Sybil obliges him with dishonest and increasingly paltry compliments. In the mornings, Barry and Désirée fight. Désirée suggests that Sybil is infatuated with Barry, which Sybil denies by calling him "an all-round third-rater." Désirée heatedly defends her husband's honor.

In the dark room, the viewers admire the Westons' estate. The third reel finishes. The fair-haired man in the film is identified as David Carter, the manager of Barry's passion-fruit plantation. Sybil reports that the Africans never gave her trouble; only the white people did.

Although the Westons' quarrels are purportedly driven by jealousy—Désirée's over Sybil and Barry's over David—Sybil realizes that while Barry has a mind to abandon his juicing operation to focus on his poetry, Désirée finds him inadequate if he is not actively increasing their wealth. Beyond boredom, Sybil starts hating them. Barry reports that David also writes poetry, which apparently interests Sybil, and the Westons encourage a match. Hearing David's poetry, Sybil mildly criticizes it, which angers him. Later, however, she warms to it, and they begin an affair, unbeknownst to the Westons. David believes Barry will soon cede the business to him. Sybil comes down with the flu, and when David arrives to propose marriage, she denies him. When he tries to insist, she insults his poetry. Later, Désirée reports that David has become an alcoholic and has been put on a month's leave. Sybil again visits the Westons, only to learn that David has already returned.

As the hostess, Ella, admires the Westons' awning, Ted observes that Carter looks miserable.

The young man wonders if this was a "*typical*" colonial afternoon. Sybil responds ambiguously.

With the camera out, the Westons overlay their life with theatricality—happy children, well-dressed servants, a frisky dog, dancing, and clapping. Arriving from across the lake, David moors his boat and walks solemnly up the lawn, stopping to stare at Sybil for a spell; at length, Barry calls for the cook-boy to pause the filming. The Westons wonder when Sybil will finally have an affair. With the camera put away and the sun setting, everyone changes, and Sybil sits outside the dining room while Désirée busies herself inside. Désirée gasps, a gun is fired, and Désirée crumples; with another gunshot, David collapses. In his dying moment, he observes Sybil, his intended victim, still alive.

Weeks later, Barry puzzles over David's murder of Désirée. He tells Sybil there was no real hint of romance between them. He says he will now enlist because the world needs a good poet-soldier. Sybil obliquely reveals her true opinion of his poetry, saying he will "make a better soldier . . . than a poet." He imagines she is simply "upset." He sends her the films from Cairo a month before being killed in action.

The viewers think about the films they have watched. The elderly woman laments the people's deaths; the host and hostess want to enjoy the colors and vegetation again. Sybil agrees to their showing the last reel one more time, as for her, watching is—in a phrase echoing a remark of the hostess's at the story's beginning—"an interesting experience."

CHARACTERS

David Carter
David Carter manages Barry's passion-fruit plantation. The "cool and fair" Carter seems apt cause for jealousy on Barry's part, but Carter has designs only on Barry's business, not on his wife. Sybil overlooks the mediocrity of David's poems to allow herself an affair with him, but he loses his grip when she rejects him. Sybil recognizes danger in the look in his eyes, but he accidentally kills the wrong woman.

Hugh and Jon Dobell
The Dobell boys have a natural placidity or acceptance of others' faults that allows them

to tolerate Désirée's petulance without effort. They try to side with Sybil when Désirée plays unfairly, but they are no match for Désirée's inflexible will. To Sybil's dismay, the boys cannot conceive of playing their favored game of bandits and riders with just three people.

Elderly Lady

One of the guests at Ted and Ella's, the elderly lady asks fundamental questions from time to time.

Ella

The hostess, named Ella, constantly admires the colors in the Africa films. Her recognition of Sybil's fame is a source of arrogance for her. Generally speaking, the hostess seems to have only a superficial appreciation for life.

Donald Greeves

An archaeologist who is content to coast through his obligatory time in the field before returning to intellectual stasis in academia, Donald proves unable to hold Sybil's romantic interest. He dies from his wounds after a lioness mauls him.

Sybil Greeves

Sybil is the story's protagonist. She proves indifferent to romantic relations and to socializing with people who bore her, which is most everyone. As such, she castigates herself by allowing the Westons to torment her with their nauseating romantic displays, with the torment stemming not from jealousy, as the Westons would expect and even want, but, as usual, from boredom. Early in life Sybil recognizes herself as exceptionally intelligent, which contributes to an isolation she is generally content with (aside from the games of bandits and riders), seeing as how mundane friendships hold little interest for her. She struggles with her tendency toward isolation while in Africa, where, ironically—one would think finding time alone would be easy in an African colony—it becomes impossible because of the white people's insistence on sticking together there, especially the men to the women, as well as the Westons to Sybil. She only manages to win back her solitude when the Westons and her last lover all meet early deaths. Although Sybil plays no conscious role in bringing about their tragic ends, her actions greatly affect, even outright determine, some of the behavior of the

others. Nearly twenty years after those colonial days, she seems satisfied with her lot in life.

Sybil Greeves's Mother

What little is said by Sybil's mother suggests that Sybil was raised under somewhat oppressive encouragement to be the classic "good girl"—though Sybil's precocious awareness of this oppression perhaps lessened its impact. Sybil's mother is glad when Sybil stops playing rowdy games with the Dobells and Désirée.

Ariadne Lewis

Sybil's housemate during the war, Ariadne has a husband who is off fighting. According to Sybil, Ariadne is one of human society's "conventional nitwits."

The Natives

Reflecting less the author's values than the era in which she was writing, as well as her focus elsewhere in this particular story, the native Africans are virtual nonentities. They are never described individually and rarely depicted in action, aside from when the Westons' servants are made to clap while their employers dance and when the cook-boy plays cinematographer. Just one is even named, Elijah ("black Elijah," he is called, as if his race is a necessary prefix). In the self-centered lives of these colonials, the Africans are little more than background music.

Ted

The showing of the films apparently comes about because Ted, a distant cousin of Sybil's by marriage, has a projector. While his wife as hostess focuses on keeping conversation and drinks flowing, he as host manages the technical side of things, offering appropriate husbandly comments from time to time.

Barry Weston

Late in the story, the reader learns that Barry is "over-weight, square and dark," and "his face had lines, as of anxiety or stomach trouble." Barry has two young daughters from a previous marriage, and he and Désirée have a baby. He is a successful businessman but dreams of being a poet, as encouraged both by hearty sales of his *Home Thoughts* in the Colony and by Sybil's praise; yet he receives no indication that he could ever be successful back in England. Unfortunately for him, he has married a woman who has no interest in being allied with a potential starving artist, leading to their frequent quarrels. Regardless, he loves Désirée and is devastated by her death; his saving grace, he affirms, is his poetry. Contributing to the war effort partly out of grief, partly out of the vain dream that he could be the next Rupert Brooke, Barry is killed.

Désirée Weston (née Coleman)
A veritable doppelganger for Sybil in their youth, Désirée grows to resemble Sybil less, perhaps as a reflection of her mental mediocrity in comparison to Sybil's profound intelligence. Coincidentally, the two women meet up in the African colony, where their lives again become intertwined. Désirée and Barry make Sybil a foil to their overdramatized—and ingenuine—wedded bliss, and they constantly encourage her to remedy her lonesomeness. Ironically, Sybil's bowing to their encouragement ultimately leads to both Désirée's and Barry's deaths.

Young Man
The young man viewing the films with Sybil and the others seems to be the only one who sees past the surface layer of the occasion. Sybil responds enigmatically to his insightful inquiries.

THEMES

Memory
The framework for "Bang-Bang You're Dead" is a trip down memory lane: Sybil is being shown films of her life in colonial Africa, from around 1941 or 1942. This would make the story set around 1960. The host and hostess and their two other guests are intrigued by the films and ask questions that, one might think, would prod Sybil toward deeper recollections and perhaps a few good stories, especially considering the absence of any soundtrack. It is possible that, in unnarrated stretches of time, Sybil does tell the viewers more about what is going on, just as the reader learns through the narration itself what happened back then. However, the brief interludes of conversation, during which Sybil is concisely witty and ambiguous rather than waxing eloquent, suggest that she is quite content to say as little about these memories as possible. Indeed, despite hints that Sybil herself

is the story's narrator, practically nothing is said about what emotional effects these memories have on her. It is almost as if the story itself has been written, by Sybil, to counter her silence before those fawning viewers with a fuller, if yet reserved, revelation of the truth before the anonymous reader.

Doubles
Thus primed by the narrator's selective attention to consider as carefully as possible the events being depicted, the reader likely takes note of the fair proliferation of doubles in the story. In various ways, the doubles, beyond their striking similarities, bring out each other's or others' characteristics through contrast. In addition to the obvious pairing of Désirée and Sybil, there are the two indistinguishable Dobell boys, who may or may not be twins and are the perfect complementary playmates for the two girls: while the girls touch on the two extremes of intellect versus ego, the boys seem to together follow a middle path, absorbing Désirée's negative energy without needing to express any of their own, trying to resolve conflicts but not compromising their own peace of mind to do so.

Barry and David serve similarly complementary functions in relation to the doubled women later in life. Both are poets and passion-fruit men—their business is mining *passion*. However, while Barry's passion is foremost for his poetry, David's is more for the juicing business. Neither seems to have much of a grip on his passion for the opposite sex, in part because of their preconceptions of the roles of men and women. It is as if Barry expects Désirée to remain loyal to him even if he can no longer support her, while David's notions lead him to tell Sybil, once they have had an affair, "It's your duty to marry me."

Sex Roles
Spark wrote "Bang-Bang You're Dead" around 1960, at the dawning of significant, if gradual, changes in the societal and domestic roles of women and men. However, the colonial African scenes are set prior to and during the Second World War, around 1940. While that war itself brought about significant, if temporary, changes to gender roles, with many women in Britain, America, and elsewhere entering the workforce, these changes were not necessarily felt in colonial

TOPICS FOR FURTHER STUDY

- Read two more among Spark's five other African short stories—"The Seraph and the Zambesi," "The Pawnbroker's Wife," "The Portobello Road," "The Go-Away Bird," and "The Curtain Blown by the Breeze." Then write an essay in which you offer individual evaluations of those two stories and then discuss what they and "Bang-Bang You're Dead" have in common, the extent to which the African setting seems to have affected or determined their contents, and what the reader might surmise about Spark's stay in Africa based on these stories.

- Just as the names of Charles Dickens's characters are often boldly significant, the names of the characters in "Bang-Bang You're Dead" resonate with meaning. Write an essay in which you conjecture on the significance behind the names of that story's characters and explain how they contribute to an overall understanding of the story. Be sure to make reference to *sibyls*, as well as the story of Sibylla in chapter XIV of Ovid's *Metamorphoses*.

- Write a short story in which you emulate "Bang-Bang You're Dead" by using as a framework the showing of home movies to

a protagonist, whose reactions to them in the company of others reveal more or less how the protagonist feels about that time in his or her life.

- Read *The Ear, the Eye, and the Arm* (1994), a Newbery Honor work of speculative fiction by Nancy Farmer. The story is set in Zimbabwe in the year 2174, following three children on a harrowing adventure. Like Spark, Farmer lived in Africa for several years, near Zimbabwe and the Zambezi River, and married her husband and bore a son there. After reading Farmer's novel, write an essay about its positive and negative qualities, and discuss the extent to which Farmer's familiarity with Africa legitimizes the content of her fiction set there.

- Read Chapter Four of Spark's *Curriculum Vitae: Autobiography* (1992), which covers her stay in Africa. Distill what you learn into a multimedia presentation to give before your class, using photographs and a soundtrack—employing more than just music—to help set the scene for your exploration of this period of Spark's life and its significance to her future life and work.

---

situations. Indeed, although Sybil and Désirée were free to join hunts and carry guns, for example, the reader gets the impression that the respective gender roles were somewhat dated in the colonies.

As Eleanor Byrne relates in "Muriel Spark Shot in Africa," emigration to the colonies was encouraged by the British government in an antifeminist context: women were to ignore the liberation movement back in England so as to marry and support their adventuresome men from within the colonial home. Dialed especially far back was the consciousness of the colonial Englishmen, all the way back to a

primitive state, owing not to their proximity to the natives but to their own possessiveness, lust, anxiety, and anger. The shortage of white women—there was one for every three white men—heightened the treatment of women as sexual objects. This does not seem to bother Ariadne, for one, who is content to let men fawn over her even while maintaining her integrity and forgoing any affairs in her husband's absence (she may be a "nitwit," but at least she is a decent one).

Sybil copes less well with the pressure to oblige the white men with intimate attention. She tries to play the role of captivated female, willing herself to feel enough attraction to engage in a few affairs, but to do so she must completely suppress her intellectual inclinations and pay attention only to voice and appearance. It takes a good bit of brain-deadening alcohol for her to accomplish this, or perhaps "the hangovers were frightful" only metaphorically. Either way, she gains nothing from these interactions, and eventually she realizes that she must come to terms with her own conception of her identity as a woman.

Dishonesty

Engaging in affairs that she cares nothing about is just one way that Sybil is dishonest with herself and others—one which seems (at first) to be relatively harmless, allowing a few men the pleasure they primarily seek but ending things when the time is right. More pervasive is the dishonest veneer she adopts whenever she joins the Westons. She visits them although she really does not want to. She sits through their public displays of affection despite her distaste for them, instead of, say, pointedly rising and walking around whenever they start up, or even simply saying something. She eventually allows the couple to go on believing that she and Barry could be a dangerous combination if left alone, and she feeds Barry's poetic ego rather than offer her true opinions about his verse.

Sybil does struggle with this dishonesty, and one sees the seed of this struggle in her childhood troubles with Désirée. Back then, her problem in bandits and riders stemmed from her compulsion to do what was most socially acceptable (doubtless as conditioned by her mother), which left her to die prematurely in every game in accordance with her having been shot, bowing to Désirée's own bending of the rules. Rather than stir up trouble, Sybil follows the rules of the game about dying and dies.

In the Colony with the Westons, Sybil likewise follows the rules of conduct as implicitly laid out by her friends, namely, to endure their displays of affection and help coddle their self-images. This all amounts to quite an effort for Sybil; it seems that every moment she is with the Westons, she is being dishonest. Once the pattern has been set, there seems to be no way out for Sybil, unless she is willing to compromise her reputation by spoiling the friendship entirely. Perhaps aptly, it takes one last dishonest endeavor to get Sybil out of her trouble: even after she realizes that she is honestly disinterested in having affairs, she has one last affair with David Carter—as if to spite the Westons by secretly doing what they have suggested but have doubted is possible. (Barry has told her, "You haven't a chance.")

It is after this relationship goes sour, for once deeply distressing the man in question, that Sybil's interpersonal troubles are neatly (from her perspective) resolved: David's anguish accidentally leads to Désirée's and David's deaths and later to Barry's death. Just before Barry enlists, Sybil has her revelation that thenceforth she must not be dishonest, even in casual friendships. Whether she holds to this resolution while socializing with Ted and Ella, for example, is a bit of an open question.

Intelligence

Sybil's relational difficulties all tie back to her profound intelligence. It seems to have been Désirée's jealousy of Sybil's intellect that led her to target Sybil so unrelentingly in the games of bandits and riders when they were children. In Africa, Sybil's intellectual expectations for a romantic partner lead to the waning of her interest in Donald, and her high standards for conversation are hardly met by the likes of Ariadne and Désirée, whose interests rarely rise above run-of-the-mill romantic gossip. With a less exacting mind, Sybil might have been able to genuinely appreciate the poetry of Barry and David.

Beyond all the trouble Sybil's intellect gives her, the story ultimately supports its premier role in Sybil's life: once she has resolved her perception of herself as a woman, once she has dissociated from her double and thus freed herself from the dichotomy that the two of them represented, and once she has cemented the importance of honesty in her life, she is able to go on and become, as the story has it, famous. The nature of her fame goes unstated, but given that she is the sort of famous person known only to a select few, it is not unreasonable to conceive of her as a gifted writer, just like Spark, an admirable model of not just feminine but human intelligence.

According to Spark, "Bang Bang You're Dead" was inspired by an event that happened to her during her time in Rhodesia (modern-day Zimbabwe). (© Jez Bennett | Shutterstock.com)

STYLE

Realism

The style of Spark's fiction is a point of much interest. Many of her stories verge on magic realism or perhaps fantasy, with the likes of ghosts and angels appearing as narrators or characters. Even when her stories are technically realistic, unique characters and confluences of events often create a fantastic feel. In this respect, she has been compared to Charles Dickens. The poet W. H. Auden once observed that while Dickens was often seen as a "fantastic creator of over-life-size characters," he was "much more of a 'realist' than he is generally taken for," as there really are such over-life-size characters in the world. The *New Criterion* editors, who quote Auden in their obituary of Spark, observe, "It is the same with Muriel Spark."

"Bang-Bang You're Dead" is an excellent example of a story in which, as Anne Herrmann formulates in a review, "the literary techniques Spark employs are both realistic ... and surrealistic."

In terms of realism, the events of the story all take place within the bounds of real possibility. In terms of surrealism, there is the fact of the unnerving similarity in the appearances of Sybil and Désirée, who quite coincidentally meet up in colonial Africa and then get mixed up in a shooting affair that leaves one of them dead; this course of events is improbable enough to push the bounds of realism.

The fascinating thing is that the story is very much derived from Spark's real experiences: there was, in fact, a person who bore such a striking similarity to her—named Nita McEwan—and they did, in fact, coincidentally meet up in Southern Rhodesia, and McEwan was, in fact, killed by her husband in a shooting affair. Thus do the facts demonstrate that reality itself can lend life a surrealistic feel. Spark once objected, in an interview with Sara Frankel, that her writing is "certainly not realistic," but she qualified this by adding: "Realism has come to mean something rather stark, anyway it's a category of literature that doesn't really mean the 'real.'" Even if "Bang-Bang You're Dead" would not be marked as a work of ordinary realism, it stands on a realistic foundation.

Postmodernism

Another label that is not ordinarily applied to Spark but which may be fitting in the case of this story is *postmodernism*. The story comes in the early phase of the postmodern era, often dated to the end of World War II, though hard-and-fast postmodernist works tend to feature more deliberate narrative self-consciousness, ambiguity, and structural complexity. The structure of "Bang-Bang You're Dead" is certainly complex, with the alternation between the present and an incrementally progressing past, but this is not beyond the reach of modernism.

What characterizes the story as more postmodern, however, is the interplay between Sybil's conception of her self in the present and her self in the scenes from her past. Only in the postmodern era has technology allowed people to relive their experiences in forms such as home movies. Sybil's past recalibrations of her identity have been intriguing enough: in childhood, her identity was effectively thrown into doubt by the appearance of her physical double, whose dullness of wit became the all-too-apparent foil to Sybil's intelligence. Sybil was very good at casually playing with her friends, as seen with the Dobells, but the frustrations wrought by the egotistic Désirée push Sybil to bury herself in books instead. Her sense of self is put under a microscope by her relocation to Africa, where she realizes, through her inability to adhere to conventional male-female dynamics, that she simply is not a conventional person. Finally, her sense of identity is resolved when the deaths of her double and the other agents of dishonesty and doubt (David and Barry) allow her to settle into the self-conception that feels right to her.

Postmodernism comes into play when Sybil watches scenes from the Colony in the company of people who seem to be little more than strangers. On the one hand, the reader might expect the scenes to provoke much self-reflection on Sybil's part. On the other hand, Sybil knows that those scenes were staged for the camera and therefore falsified; it is not true reality they are all witnessing. Thus might Sybil's reflections on that past be foregone conclusions: she solidified her identity at the close of

these events, that identity has served her well, and the films do not, or do not appear to, lead her to reassess either her identity or her role in the events of that era. This creates a rift between Sybil and the reader, who, like the young man in attendance at the showing, is given cause to assess those events differently from how Sybil has assessed them. This rift is the postmodern disruption that leaves room for markedly different readings of Sybil's character.

HISTORICAL CONTEXT

Colonial Southern Rhodesia

Southern Rhodesia, now called Zimbabwe, would prove one of the most problematic of the British African colonies in terms of the eventual transition to independence. Its colonial beginnings were much like those of its neighbors, Northern Rhodesia (now Zambia) and Nyasaland (now Malawi). In the 1830s, just before armed white settlers began infiltrating the region from South Africa, the Ndebele people pushed northward in order to escape those settlers and their military pressures. In 1889, Cecil Rhodes's British South Africa Company was directed by the British government to establish colonial rule there, and Lobengula, king of the Ndebele, was brought down through both deception and force by 1893. The Ndebele and Shona people surprised the British by allying to stage what has been called the Great Rebellion or First Chimurenga War in 1896–1897, but the British, with their overwhelming firepower and brutal, even torturous, tactics, won the day.

Over half a century would pass before another armed uprising would occur. In the meantime, the white settlers proceeded to claim as much as half of the land in what was now called Southern Rhodesia, pushing the Africans onto reservations and instituting a system that mirrored South African apartheid. Native Africans lived in separate areas and were prohibited from voting, gaining political office, or achieving officer status in the ranks of the army or police.

Therefore Spark arrived in Southern Rhodesia in 1937 into a colonial situation that was relatively stable, despite occasional labor protests and political agitation. The 55,000 white people, alongside the 1.5 million

COMPARE
&
CONTRAST

- **1940s:** The black population in Southern Rhodesia is approximately 1.5 million, while whites number some 55,000.

  1960s: At the time of the illicit declaration of independence in 1965, there are some 5 million black Africans living alongside some 270,000 whites in what is now called the Republic of Rhodesia.

  Today: By 2010, only some 40,000 white people remain alongside the more than 12 million black Africans in the modern Republic of Zimbabwe.

- **1940s:** World War II touches on the continent of Africa with battles occurring in North and East Africa. Many Africans volunteer to fight or are even forcibly conscripted by their colonial governments, and altogether, some 1.36 million Africans from some thirty countries serve in the war.

  1960s: The decade opens with seventeen African nations gaining their independence in 1960, mostly in peaceful manners, and sixteen more follow suit within the decade. Following the illegitimate white-minority declaration of Rhodesian independence in 1965, black African nationalists begin waging guerrilla war to reclaim their homeland.

  Today: Having been the third-to-last African nation to gain independence, in 1980, Zimbabwe endured civil strife between competing factions that led to government massacres in the mid-1980s. Zimbabwe's troops have contributed to wars in Congo and Mozambique, while violence has marred multiple presidential elections, all of which have been won by Robert Mugabe.

- **1940s:** British colonials in Southern Rhodesia enjoy a time of power and relative ease. Despite labor strikes and other agitations, African resistance does not currently threaten the settlers' well-being.

  1960s: After the white-minority government's unilateral declaration of independence, the strength of Rhodesian military forces is sufficient to minimize the effectiveness of guerrilla actions. The apartheid-style separation of society and a lack of environs offering decent cover (jungles, swamps) prevent nationalists from surreptitiously infiltrating or attacking settler areas.

  Today: After true independence was gained in 1980, some three-fifths of the nation's white population fled the country. In the 1990s, lingering resentment of the prolonged white-minority rule was inflamed when the British government withdrew promises to fund peasant resettlement schemes. Mugabe passes legislation from 2000 onward ousting white farmers from their lands. With essential financial sources like the World Bank and IMF cutting aid in response to the land seizures, the Zimbabwean economy collapses.

native Africans, had carved out social niches for themselves, working in the upper echelons and fraternizing exclusively with each other. Spark found this insularity both unappealing and absurd, given the beauty to be found in both the land and the people. She was also amazed that the white colonials seemed to expect to spend their lives in Rhodesia with the Africans under their thumb, where in her mind, the end of the colonial era was inevitable.

Spark's marriage quickly fell apart, and she came to fear that she, like Nita McEwan, would be a victim of a murderous/suicidal husband. She hid the revolver that her husband, affected by the broader colonial gun culture, was fond of shooting off in courtyards. A moment of clarity came when she visited Victoria Falls, one of the most magnificent watercourses in the world, and grew determined to find her way back to England, which she eventually did.

Sybil, who enjoys reading philosophy, is much more studious than her husband.
(© Lenar Musin | Shutterstock.com)

As for the colony itself, while Zambia and Malawi gained independence and the leadership of black Africans, Southern Rhodesia was declared independent by the white-minority government that was in charge in 1965, leading to international reprobation and sanctions. The Second Chimurenga War was initiated in 1966 as nationalists fought against the Rhodesian security forces, who were backed by the South African army. Through the 1970s, other independent African nations, as well as China and the Soviet Union, assisted the nationalists, and victory was achieved in 1979, with Zimbabwe proclaimed independent in 1980. The country's name was taken from the great stone ruins, second only to Egypt's pyramids on the African continent, attesting to the region's advanced ancient cultures. Unfortunately, the social situation in Zimbabwe did not greatly improve with independence, as Robert Mugabe, originally the prime minister and later the longtime president, would prove to be one of Africa's most incorrigible tyrants, rigging elections through violence, suppressing all opposition, and upending the economy through the premature reclamation of land from white farmers and other disastrous decisions. Zimbabwe remained unstable into the 2010s.

CRITICAL OVERVIEW

Critics have produced an abundance of positive commentary on Spark's writing ability and the value of her works. Regarding her short stories in particular, a *Publishers Weekly* review of Spark's *Open to the Public* declares, "By turns (and twists) comic, whimsical and sinister (but always sparklingly sharp), this latest collection... nicely reflects her marvelously varied career." Rebecca Abrams, reviewing Spark's *The Complete Short Stories*, finds that "there is not a single disappointment" in the volume, and a *Publishers Weekly* review of *All the Stories of Muriel Spark* calls the volume a "treasure trove" marked by stories "that combine elements that other writers wouldn't dare bring together." The stories' narrators are deemed "astute observers of race, class and society," and the reviewer declares that "Spark's marvelous control of ambiguities and language continues to dazzle."

"Bang-Bang You're Dead," along with a couple of her other African stories, has received close and admiring attention. Dean Flower, reviewing *Open to the Public*, notes that Sybil's story is among those of Spark's that "are richly evolved and prolonged, almost miniature novels." Derek Stanford, in his *Muriel Spark*, labels Sybil's story and two others "brilliant constructions." Abrams calls the African stories "hard-edged, harshly lit," and affirms that "each tale craftily weaves its way into something startling"; "Bang-Bang You're Dead" is her foremost example. Abdel-Moneim Aly, writing for the *Scottish Studies Review*, holds that "the African short stories represent a watershed in Spark's fiction. They are a breakthrough to the fuller form in her art." Karl Malkoff, in his *Muriel Spark*, considers "Bang-Bang You're Dead" the "most successful" of the stories in its original volume.

If there has been one consistent note of disapproval it has related to the moral feel of Spark's works. The *New Criterion* editors, for example, note that her employment of typically clever, detached narrators "grants insight but tends to discount such homely virtues as warmth, human attachment, affection. Not everyone finds this attractive." The wording here attests that this is more a sentimental objection than a literary one. Nonetheless, others have suggested likewise. Gabriele Annan, in the *Spectator*, finds that alongside "wit" and "cleverness," "heartlessness" is one of Spark's trademarks.

Nonetheless, the *New Criterion* editors affirm, "No other contemporary writer commanded Muriel Spark's combination of comic seriousness, narrative grit, and pellucid prose." Dorothea Walker, in her preface to the Twayne volume *Muriel Spark*, notes, "That Muriel Spark is a celebrated writer is attested by the abundance of critical comment as well as by her popular success." Focusing on the Scottish author's longer works, Walker notes that "Spark's talent is unique": "In intricacy of plot, wit of dialogue, and inventiveness of character, Muriel Spark remains a gifted novelist who shows in each novel an innate originality. She cannot be categorized." Vern Lindquist, in the

ONE MIGHT GO SO FAR AS TO SUGGEST THAT ALL THE MORAL WEIGHT OF THE STORY IS CONCENTRATED HERE IN TWO RELATIVELY INNOCUOUS SENTENCES."

Dictionary of Literary Biography, remarks, "Spark's status as one of the most widely read contemporary British writers stems in part from the power, wit, and elegance of her short-story collections." In his introduction to *Theorizing Muriel Spark*, Martin McQuillan states, "Muriel Spark is one of the most important novelists of the twentieth century."

CRITICISM

Michael Allen Holmes

Holmes is a writer with existential interests. In the following essay, he considers how Sybil might, perhaps even ought to, feel guilty over Désirée's death in "Bang-Bang You're Dead" but nonetheless attains peace of mind.

Some consider the moral component the most essential component of any story. If a story's morality is misaligned with higher values or perhaps lacking entirely, the story is compromised. Some commentators on Muriel Spark, noting how detached and ironic her narrators can be, have conceived that accordingly the stories are lacking in moral direction. Regarding "Bang-Bang You're Dead," for example, Velma Bourgeois Richmond, in her *Muriel Spark*, suggests a lamentable absence of compassion in Sybil in observing that "the superior intellect observes and notes, but feels little."

An absence of morality is also suggested when the deaths that prove so convenient to Sybil are fairly applauded by critics. Richmond crassly suggests that Sybil, having grown weary of Donald, is "relieved when he is killed by a lion." Dean Flower misguidedly declares that Désirée's being shot to death is "the happiest of endings." However, perceptive critics recognize that the reader may have to probe more deeply to grasp the morality in Spark's stories. Rebecca Abrams,

WHAT DO I READ NEXT?

- After getting a taste of Spark's short stories, the reader might next turn to one of her novels. Her most famous is *The Prime of Miss Jean Brodie* (1961), about a teacher at a Scottish Presbyterian school (not unlike the one Spark attended as a girl) who wields her influence over a number of girls in less-than-moral ways as they go through adolescence.

- Doris Lessing, who won the Nobel Prize in Literature in 2007, did not just visit but grew up in the colony of Southern Rhodesia, living there from the age of six until two dozen years later. Lessing's first novel, *The Grass Is Singing* (1950), is set in Southern Rhodesia and focuses on race relations. Her relevant short fiction is collected in the volume *African Stories* (1964).

- While Spark and Flannery O'Connor have different styles in many respects, Spark's African stories have earned comparison with O'Connor's largely because of the higher frequency of violence to be found in them. O'Connor's collections, with stories invariably set in her native American South, include *A Good Man Is Hard to Find* (1955)—the title story being one of her most famous—and *Everything That Rises Must Converge* (1965).

- Graham Greene, one of the most popular English writers in history, was also affected by stays in Africa, including travels in Liberia and a stint working for British intelligence in Sierra Leone during World War II. Greene's novel *The Heart of the Matter* (1948) takes place in Sierra Leone and centers on marital drama between a solitary, literary-minded white woman and her husband.

- Early in her writing career, Spark considered the English author Max Beerbohm to be an important influence, especially with regard to his subtle, concise, and witty style. One of his best-known collections is *Seven Men* (1919), which presents fictional biographies of such characters as rival novelists and a poet who deals with the devil.

- Spark and Virginia Woolf have been considered alongside each other in light of their shared use of comic elements as an aspect of a feminist worldview. Both Spark and her character Sybil are evoked by Woolf's feminist essay *A Room of One's Own* (1929).

- The young-adult novel *Out of Shadows* (2011), by Jason Wallace, who grew up in Zimbabwe, treats the nation's postindependence drama by portraying the experiences of a thirteen-year-old whose family moves to Zimbabwe and places him in an elite, desegregated boarding school, where race relations and bullying are topics of supreme interest.

for example, praises her fiction's "deceptive lightness, the way it seems almost to shrug its shoulders at the people and lives it so piercingly brings to life." Abrams duly notes that "Spark's fictional observers invariably occupy uncertain moral ground." To reach the true depths of "Bang-Bang You're Dead," a reading of the story must account for the moral perspective inhabited by Sybil beyond the mere impression of a lack of compassion.

On the surface, of course, the story does intimate that Sybil suffers from a lack of warmth toward others, in particular the others who meet their deaths in Africa in the course of a drama in which she plays no small part. The scenes from Rhodesia alone do not necessarily support such an assessment: Sybil cannot be directly blamed for any of her three companions' deaths, and the story simply does not incorporate her emotional responses to those deaths. Yet the coolness Sybil evinces when discussing those deaths with Ted, Ella, and their guests cannot be denied. When she first mentions the deaths and one of the company asks, "Don't tell me *they* were mixed up in shooting affairs," Sybil wryly responds, "They were mixed up in shooting affairs." Rather than delve into or even just hint at the details of the shootings in question or her feelings about them, she has delivered an echoing punch line that leads only to a toss-off, cul-de-sac expression of exasperation by the elderly woman: "Oh, these colonials...and their shooting affairs!" With nowhere else for the line of thought to proceed, right on cue, the host announces that the third reel shall begin, and Sybil's response has proven quite effective in deflecting from the heart of the matter.

The topic is broached again when the hostess asks regarding David Carter, "He was in a shooting affair, did you say?" Once again Sybil parries the question with a neutral comment that invites no further inquiry: "Yes, it was unfortunate." The hostess (or one of the others) nonetheless tries to lead the discussion onward, supposing that it must have been a dangerous place to live in, but Sybil's response is again ambiguous: "It was dangerous for some people. It depended." Finally, when asked about whether the native Africans caused any difficulty for her, Sybil drops the slightest hint regarding the origins of her companions' shooting affair by acknowledging that she had trouble "only with the whites." However, this remark, too, is delivered like a punch line, echoing the questioner in an unexpected way. Everyone laughs, and once again Sybil is able to avoid discussing the matter further, whether she intended as much or not.

Later, discussing the scenes filmed on the very day that the shooting occurred, Sybil makes no reference to it. The shooting proves the climax of the story, but it is broached only one more time in the present-day discussion and only in a generic sense, when the elderly lady remarks, "How tragic, those people being killed in shooting affairs." None of the other guests tries to draw out any explanation of the shooting affair that afflicted Sybil's friends, and the topic rests in peace. Finally, after all this, one cannot help thinking that perhaps Sybil has avoided discussing the affair not because she was traumatized, as the film viewers seem to

conceive, but because she feels guilty about it. She has been said to feel guilty, in fact, but only about her lack of interest in intimacy, not about the manner in which her companions died.

It is not difficult to conceive of Sybil as sharing the blame for what happened, if not deserving the blame foremost, despite the fact that she never pulled a trigger. On the one hand, Désirée and Barry placed inordinate pressure on Sybil to visit their home; veritably, they insisted, and there was little she could do but relent. Still, she was never obligated to play along with all of their silly romantic performances, serving as the validating audience. It might have been difficult for her to avoid those performances without removing herself from the friendship entirely, and this might have had consequences in the larger but limited white social circle of which they were all a part. Being dishonest was a choice that she made, however—a choice she validated by conceiving of the inevitable unpleasant experience as (divine) punishment for her supposed abnormality, such that her despairing anticipation of another evening at the Westons' amounts to "an offering to the gods." Deception is deception, no matter how it is justified.

Similarly, Sybil ultimately succumbs to an affair with David Carter for little reason other than that it seems the acceptable thing to do. The affair is even conceived of "as an act of virtue done against the grain" (that is, her grain), as if, because indifference to intimacy is considered wrong by her white colonial friends, to have an affair must be right and therefore virtuous. This is entirely spurious reasoning, equating the (relative) expectations of any given group of people with the (absolute) quality of virtue. Her affair with David may have "absolved her from the reproach of her sexlessness," but this reproach came not from those "gods" she was making offerings to, but from Barry and Désirée, whom she actually despises—and thus why should their reproaches have determined her behavior?

It is always difficult, of course, not to conform to peer pressure. All in all, regardless of how Sybil justified her affair with David, even if she was able to end her other affairs without incident, she must have been aware—given the proliferation of shooting incidents in the colony, not to mention that mankind has proven capable of deplorable violence in all ages and eras—that sooner or later, a man could get seriously attached to her, and her dishonesty over the affair could lead to complicated, even dangerous emotions on the man's part.

Once she has spurned David, Sybil recognizes that he represents a threat. When he first suggests marriage, the narration describes how "he clung to her with violent, large hands." He "looked at her somewhat wildly" and "clung to her" again. And "to get rid of him," she ingenuinely suggests she will think about it. In this case, one can hardly blame her for doing what is necessary to end the scene—but this is only proof that she already recognizes that he is dangerous. When he responds to her ensuing letter by forcing his way into her house, she is duly "alarmed." Luckily for her, a bold figurative slap to his poetic face disposes of him this time, and she is surely relieved to hear that he has been put on a month's leave from Barry's passion-fruit business. In turn, she must be more alarmed than ever when she arrives at the Westons to hear that David has already returned.

This is the point, one might argue, when Sybil's dishonesty itself becomes dangerous, even culpable for what transpires next. Sybil might have immediately related to Désirée all the details of the surreptitious affair, precisely to make clear that in Sybil's presence, David might be dangerous. Instead, she says nothing and treats David's presence as casually as possible. As he walks up the lawn she says, "Oh hallo, David," and at Désirée's suggestion that she is low in spirits, she affirms, "Oh, I'm quite happy." She is out of David's earshot (she is not rubbing anything in), but nonetheless her remark completely obscures the notion that there might be any cause for legitimate alarm. No other chance to apprise her hosts of the potential danger will come: in his very next appearance, before he happens upon Sybil, David accidentally shoots Désirée instead and then commits suicide. It is David who has murdered Désirée and himself, but for the modern reader—in an era when US government posters, in light of potential terrorism especially, implore, "If you see something, say something"—it must be acknowledged that Sybil should, to some extent, feel guilty about Désirée's death, and perhaps also David's.

Sybil cannot entirely exculpate herself from Barry's death, either. When the two of them are processing the murder-suicide, she makes every effort to prevent him from figuring out just why it was that David shot Désirée. She suggests that it all happened simply because David "was mad," that is, crazy. She also cites the notion that, as Barry has been suggesting, David "was keen on Désirée," even though she knows full well this is a red herring. When Barry stumbles upon the realization that, in certain light, Désirée and Sybil look strikingly similar, in her mind she deliberately schemes, "I must say something... to blot this notion from his mind. I must make this occasion unmemorable, distasteful to him." Indeed, she is aiming not merely to cut short the discussion for the time being but to lead Barry to suppress the entire conversation from his conscious mind, which she accomplishes by finally and profoundly insulting what has become the defining aspect of his life: his poetry.

Sybil presumably goes to these impressive lengths to deceive Barry because if he realizes the truth, he will, without doubt, verbally formulate the notion that his wife's death is partly, if not mostly, Sybil's fault—and thus will she have to confront this unpleasant truth head on, face to face with another reasoning human being, rather than simply shrugging it off. Regardless of her reasoning, Sybil's actions invite further blame in light of the consequences: if Barry had known the truth and could have used it to erase the embarrassing public notion that his wife and David had been having an affair, he might not have felt compelled to escape the only society he knew by risking and ultimately sacrificing his life in the ongoing world war.

The matter of Sybil's complacence with her companions' deaths is compounded when the reader comes to realize that Sybil, it seems, must be seen as not just the protagonist but also the author of the story, writing about herself in the third person. There are only a couple of narratorial remarks that indicate this is the case. Early in the story, when the period after Donald's death by lioness is being described, it is mentioned that Sybil "cultivated a few friends for diversion," after which the narrator drops the valuative comment, "Charming friends need not possess minds." Such a comment is not outside the bounds of what any disinterested narrator might be entitled to say in the course of a story; but in the ensuing scene, the narrator for the first time, and quite strikingly, introduces herself in the first person. Sybil has just been told, "you haven't changed much since you were a girl," and while the Sybil in the story merely remarks, "Thank you, Ella," the narrator adds, "I haven't changed at all so far as I still think charming friends need not possess minds."

The reader, if already decided on the notion that the narrator is not one of the story's characters, might impulsively imagine that this comment, too, could be delivered by a disinterested persona. But examined closely, the pattern of the exchange must be regarded as revealing that Sybil is, in fact, the narrator; otherwise, the narrator herself would be practicing such bold deception—given the way the line both responds to the comment to Sybil and echoes the earlier narrative phrasing—that nothing in the story could be trusted, and the story would be worthless. Also, elsewhere in the story the notion of indifference to friends' mental capacity is formulated for Sybil when she is said to learn "to listen without boredom"—that is, to listen to mindless, or insufficiently mindful, chatter from friends and be charmed nevertheless. There is one last hint that Sybil must be the narrator, when the narrator remarks in the final scene, after Sybil has revealed how differently she feels from when she was in Africa, "One learns to accept oneself." Again, this is not necessarily outside the bounds of what a disinterested narrator might say; but after the earlier breach of first-person narration, the reader easily takes this line, in which the narrator directly formulates in a prescriptive way, as if based on experience, what Sybil herself has gone through, as confirmation that Sybil and the narrator are one.

Thus, if Sybil is actually narrating the story, the silences with regard to her role in and feelings about the infamous shooting affair are all the more striking. Not merely in the dialogue of the story, which is confined to what Sybil has chosen to say to other people, but in every moment of the narration, Sybil has had the opportunity to explain her feelings about, and perhaps remorse over, what occurred and thus absolve herself of whatever guilt she might feel. Yet she declines this opportunity. Or so it seems.

One first reads the story, of course, not knowing just how the shooting affair will come about, such that many significant lines of narration can only be taken at face value. Only on a second reading can their full import be recognized. (While the narrator is now understood to be Sybil, it is useful to still refer to "the narrator" to distinguish the Sybil who is writing from the Sybil in the story.) When Sybil first takes up residence with Ariadne Lewis, for example, the narrator reveals, "It was another ten years before she had learnt those arts of leading a double life and listening to people ambiguously, which enabled her to mix without losing identity, and to listen without boredom."

These lines describe not just Sybil's future personal improvement but also her past fault, if fault it might be called: she was, in Africa, unable "to mix without losing identity"—she literally could not be in the presence of others without her identity being, to some extent, absorbed into theirs. Such is the case with many adolescents, when susceptibility to peer pressure is almost a biological imperative, and Sybil would have been only nineteen or twenty, perhaps fresh out of secondary school, upon arriving in Africa. Thus, where the mixing culture is one of heightened male-female interactions, Sybil feels such a powerful compulsion to conform to this culture that when she realizes that she is sexually interested in "neither men nor women," she "felt a lonely emotion near to guilt." This is the effective guilt of not conforming, an emotion that naturally arises when one fails to live up to the moral standards of one's community; the problem is that it may also arise when one fails to live up to immoral standards, if one does not have the philosophical background to recognize the community's standards as such.

The guilt produced in such circumstances is arguably an illegitimate guilt, but Sybil cannot know this about her own guilt, entrenched as she is in this insular white colonial community. Feeling guilt, she naturally acts to assuage that guilt. In particular, "The act of visiting the Westons alleviated her sense of guilt." She went "not because her discomfort was necessary to their well-being, but because it was somehow necessary to her own." Thus, instead of being viewed as a young woman who is conducting herself dishonestly in social relations, Sybil must be recognized as one who is following the compass of her conscience without being able to realize that this compass, as magnetized by the unintellectual and often immoral people around her, is leading her astray.

Later the notion of guilt surfaces again, when Sybil reflects on her encouragement of Barry's poetry, in spite of her poor opinion of it: "Even the guilt of condoning Désirée's 'marvellous . . . wonderful' was less than the guilt of her isolated mind." Thus does the narrator make clear that the guilt Sybil feels about her indifference to the company of such people as the Westons outweighs the guilt of her dishonesty about Barry's poetry. In applauding that poetry, she is quite consciously choosing the lesser of two evils.

Little more is said to address Sybil's feelings and potential culpability about the shooting affair as it actually occurred. There is still room, then, for the reader to believe that Sybil *should* feel guilty about it, even if her previous, related guilt was unjustified. Yet this is surely a grayer moral area than has been acknowledged. The Westons constantly insisted that she act in accord with their desires, visiting at their whim, playing the role of "the other woman" without actually doing anything illicit, and finally she reached a point where she simply went along with everything. Indeed, she continued to simply go along with everything right up to the point where David shot Désirée and then himself. In hindsight, one can argue that she should have acted differently, but at any and all points she could have underestimated the danger that David represented, and of course there were Barry and Désirée explicitly directing her to "cheer up in front of the camera"—and with them, even when the material camera was off, a metaphysical camera was always rolling.

Still, the reader may wonder, has Sybil thought through the notion that she might be guilty to some extent? There is something very definite about the way she finally reveals her true opinion of Barry's poetry "with a sense of relief, almost absolution"—as if she is baptizing herself into the religion of truth: "There is no health, she thought, for me, outside of honesty." Surely, then, Sybil has been honest with herself about her role in the affair. However, the reader must still wonder, how does she *feel* about it. To answer this, all the reader has left are the questions asked by the reader's surrogate within the story, the young man, who alone asks the probing sorts of questions that the inquisitive reader must want to: "'You didn't care for the bright colours?' said the young man, leaning forward eagerly." In

response, she merely "smiled at him." Later, the young man asks in seeming amazement, "Was this a *typical* afternoon in the Colony?" And Sybil's answer is cryptic: "It was and it wasn't."

The young man's crowning question comes when, after the four reels have all been viewed, and the fact of the shooting affair has settled in his mind, he comes up with a doozy of a comment: "'A hundred feet of one's past life!' said the young man. 'If they were mine, I'm sure I should be shattered. I should be calling "Lights! Lights!" like Hamlet's uncle.'" This is quite a bold reference to the famous play-within-the-play of Shakespeare's *Hamlet*. Therein, at Hamlet's bidding, the royal players enact scenes that mimic Hamlet's uncle murdering Hamlet's father and wedding his mother—leading the uncle, King Claudius, to cry out "Give me some light:—away!" after which all the audience members exclaim, "Lights, lights, lights!"

If Sybil, like Spark, is a British writer, this reference could not have escaped her; and it is as if the young man has specifically veiled his intended question to Sybil—do you feel the weight of the guilt of a murder on your shoulders as you watch these films?—so that she might respond without necessarily verbalizing a response for all to understand. The young man and Sybil have established a bit of a rapport, as evidenced by her first smiling, then coyly responding to his questions, and now that rapport comes to fruition. One might go so far as to suggest that all the moral weight of the story is concentrated here in two relatively innocuous sentences: "Sybil smiled at him. He looked back, suddenly solemn and shrewd." In this moment, it seems, Sybil has responded to the question of whether she feels guilty over what happened with a resounding *no*. Being, now, an irreproachably honest person, she has without doubt thought the matter through. The young man, without understanding the full extent of Sybil's experiences and the wisdom she has attained, can only sit back in solemn wonder over what might have happened back with that notorious shooting affair, while the reader, knowing more, may shrewdly accept that Sybil's clear conscience has been honestly earned.

Source: Michael Allen Holmes, Critical Essay on "Bang-Bang You're Dead," in *Short Stories for Students*, Gale, Cengage Learning, 2015.

Desirée is shot because she is mistaken for Sybil. (© *Naypong / Shutterstock.com*)

Gabriele Annan

In the following review, Annan especially commends Spark's handling of religion in her short stories.

'Inheritance, faith, suppressed passion; irony, simplicity, black comedy: these are Muriel Spark's trademarks.' Andrew Motion wrote that in a review of Spark's last novel, *Aiding and Abetting* (about Lord Lucan), and it's quoted on the dust jacket of *The Complete Short Stories*. One might add wit and cleverness to the trademarks; and heartlessness. As for Spark's simplicity, that is a bit suspect. Few of the characters, few of the happenings in this hefty new volume are what at first they seem; and that's one of the points her fiction makes.

There are 41 stories: not a book to be read at a sitting; but not a book to have by one's bedside either: many of the stories are too spooky for the insomniac small hours. There are lots of ghosts. Quite often they tell the story

in the first person. In 'The Portobello Road,' the narrator is surprised by the behaviour of an old friend when she greets him across the market stalls. 'He looked very ill, although when I had said "Hallo, George" I had spoken friendly enough.' The next paragraph begins, 'I must explain that I departed this life five years ago.' Very casual: being a ghost is just as run-of-the-mill as being a civil servant. And then you read on and discover that the reason she's dead is that George murdered her.

The neatest, wittiest, shortest, cleverest of the ghost stories is 'The Pearly Shadow.' The Shadow is a hallucination suffered first by a patient in a psychiatric hospital, then caught—like flu—by a nurse. The psychiatrist in charge of them is Dr. Felicity Grayling. Spark is wickedly sharp at defining people by their names: not in a rollicking, Dickensian way, but so that you know immediately where they come from, what kind of school they went to, how they will speak. (Always on the watch for snobbery, she pounces when she sees it. There's a story called 'The Snobs' and even a ghost who is 'a terrible snob.') Felicity puts the nurse on tranquillisers. The Shadow comes to her surgery to complain: if the nurse were to take an overdose, he says, it would kill him. 'You won't feel a thing,' Felicity comforts him. Not that that is quite the end of the Pearly Shadow. Something threatening is still to come for Felicity.

The stories are arranged not in chronological order, but more or less according to theme. The first batch are set in Africa and deal with *crimes passionels* among whites—shootings, mostly. They are variations on the Happy Valley murder, though set not in Kenya but in South Africa and the former Rhodesia, where Spark lived during her early, short, unhappy marriage. One of her characters explains that adultery is common among whites in Africa because there are three males to every female. The first African story, 'The Go-Away Bird,' is long and particularly appealing—possibly because the heroine is a typical 'girl of slender means,' poor, plucky and engaging. Girls like that are, of course, a speciality and forte of Spark's, and luckily there are quite a lot of them in this collection.

Her most famous speciality, though, is Catholicism, possibly because she is known to be a convert, and conversion is always fascinating (could it happen to me?). But religion is treated even more casually than the showier, cornier supernatural of ghosts and other strange happenings. There is no reverent hush. The monks in 'Come Along Marjorie,' for instance, make the most banal remarks imaginable as they try in vain to persuade mute Marjorie to move on from their retreat, where she has outstayed her welcome. In the end, they arrange for her to be taken to an asylum. The only words she has ever been heard to speak are 'The Lord is risen.'

> Only the very mad, I thought, can come out with the information 'The Lord is risen,' in the same factual way as one might say 'You are wanted on the telephone.'

The implication, I think, is that low-key factual is the sign of true faith.

Source: Gabriele Annan, Review of *The Complete Short Stories*, in *Spectator*, Vol. 287, No. 9037, October 20, 2001, pp. 53–54.

Publishers Weekly

In the following review, an anonymous writer praises Spark's daring elements in her short stories.

Coming just four years after the cloth edition of *Open to the Public: New and Collected Stories*, which introduced readers to 10 new Spark tales, this collection tacks on four slight additions and brings the total of Spark's stories to 41. The new entries are brief variations on familiar Spark themes: social standing is comically depicted in "The Snobs," the ownership of family history is probed through photographs in "A Hundred and Eleven Years Without a Chauffeur" and benign ghostly experiences account for the remaining two stories. Taken together, they're not a major inducement for owners of the 1997 collection to indulge again so soon. Those who know Spark mainly from her novels, however (*The Prime of Miss Jean Brodie*; *Loitering with Intent*), will be pleased to snap up this treasure trove, markedly best for the many of her earlier stories that combine elements that other writers wouldn't dare bring together. Chance encounters between strangers spiral into unexpected plots (as when a young woman meets a soldier on a train in "The House of the Famous Poet"), and Spark's narrators (including the wry, level-headed ghost of "The Portobello Road") serve as astute observers of race, class and society, particularly in the stories set in colonial South Africa. There are times when the whimsy goes screwball, and briefer pieces stemming from a word or phrase peter out, but overall Spark's marvelous control of ambiguities and language continues to dazzle.

Forecast: Following so soon on the heels of *Open to the Public*, this volume may not receive much review coverage, but as the first paperback collected edition since 1985, it should sell well, particularly to students and first-time Spark readers.

Source: Review of *All the Stories of Muriel Spark*, in *Publishers Weekly*, Vol. 248, No. 46, November 12, 2001, p. 37.

Publishers Weekly

In the following review, an anonymous writer points out Spark's skill with stories that contain both humorous and supernatural elements.

By turns (and twists) comic, whimsical and sinister (but always sparkingly sharp), this latest collection of short stories by the author of *The Prime of Miss Jean Brodie* and *Reality and Dreams* nicely reflects her marvelously varied career. Earlier stories such as "The Curtain Blown by the Breeze," "Bang-Bang You're Dead" and "The Pawnbroker's Wife" take place in the Central African region Spark coolly observed firsthand in all its colonial parochialism and overheated behavior. The best of these, a novella of ill-fated exile, "The Go-Away Bird," spans the social comedy of the colonial community and the stay-at-home English. Spark is even funnier about the English in their natural environment, as when she portrays polite mind games in "Twins" or mating habits in "A Member of the Family." This collection also shows her fascination with the ghost story, beginning with the flashback afterlife of "The Portobello Road." Spark imaginatively reworks its conventions in the living ghost of "The Leaf Sweeper," and the unquiet literary remains of "The Executor." In two of the best works here, "The House of a Famous Poet" (with its ominous "abstract funeral") and "Open to the Public" (its characters are possessed by the ghosts of ambition and literary fame), the hauntings are at once metaphorical, philosophical and unsettling. With 10 tales new to American readers, *Open to the Public* brings Spark's stories up to date with the rest of her prolific output.

Source: Review of *Open to the Public: New and Collected Stories,* in *Publishers Weekly,* Vol. 244, No. 30, July 28, 1997, pp. 54–55.

Judy Sproxton

In the following excerpt, Sproxton explains that Spark, though not precisely a feminist, gives her female characters "dignity and possession of mind."

The greatest irony in Muriel Spark's fiction is its success. Peter Owen, the publisher for whom she worked in 1958, has said that she was amazed by the warm reception accorded to her first novel, *The Comforters.* She had thought of herself as a poet and a biographer; writing fiction had never attracted her. Then, already well known in literary circles, she was commissioned by Alan Maclean of Macmillan to write a novel. She embarked on this project in the winter of 1955. The book turned out to be a revelation about her resources. The sensitivity to words and to their hidden wit which had dynamized her poetry found a new medium in the novel: the very power of words and their

hold on the mind became the major theme of this one. Her elegance of phrase, her intellectual control and capacity for stringent organization of material had already made of her a sound and efficient biographer; these talents enabled her to construct in her novel an unpredictable plot with many possibilities to exploit, many meaningful details to retain, and a forceful resolution.

. . . Spark's work has attracted a good deal of critical attention in recent years. David Lodge in *The Novelist at the Crossroads* (Routledge and Kegan Paul 1971) offers a useful discussion of the narrative stance she adopts with reference to her faith. He comments that Spark's novels are distinguished by 'a highly original and effective exploitation of the convention of authorial omniscience.' Lodge discusses at length the function of narrative presentation, showing how this inevitably depends for its coherence on assumptions about the nature of providence, or its absence. He distinguishes between the Catholic writer such as Mauriac, whose authorial structure implies a perspective such as God might well have, and the writer like Graham Greene, whose characters' responses to providence are the only indication of the writer's own apprehension of the divine. Occasionally, irony in the plot implies some deeper purpose, but this is never spelt out nor developed. Muriel Spark's use of the 'convention of authorial omniscience' is equally unpretentious: 'for most of the time,' writes Lodge, 'her satires are narrated from some human, limited point of view.'

Spark presents her characters and situation with mastery, never faltering in her control, and adding a dimension of wit and appreciation of irony which makes her prose sparkle. However, as Lodge says, she 'points to providence at work, but providence remains ultimately mysterious and incomprehensible, because the world is a fallen one and even the novelist cannot claim to understand it fully.' This elegant modesty does much to make her work at once unpredictable and yet endearing. Sometimes we marvel at events and reactions, and we feel that, instead of merely manipulating us, the writer is marvelling too. For Malcolm Bradbury (*Possibilities*—OUP, 1973) the essence of Spark's narrative is close to Waugh's detachment: 'Waugh,' he says, 'feels free to represent the contemporary world as chaos and his characters bereft of any significant moral action.' What unity there is in Spark's narrative is, he says, aesthetic; she has no sympathy for her characters, and the wholeness of coherence of her works derives from her intelligence and her sensitivity to form as a poet. Peter Kemp's study, *Muriel Spark* (Elek, 1974), asserts that Spark's artistry is not dependent merely on aesthetic economy and tautness of plot; for him there is a rigorous moral dimension implicit in all she writes. 'The fictive organization is regarded as reflecting on a small and comparatively simple scale the vaster and more complex dispositions of divinity,' he says. There is a purpose that can be glimpsed beyond the immediate moment and, without trying to define this purpose, her writing suggests that the chaos of human activity is only an illusion; ultimately there is a sense which gives proportion to all things. Kemp points out that, although there is a satisfaction to the reader in the order, pattern and resolution of her plots, there is no place for complacency. Her themes are deeply disturbing; they cast a spotlight on the moral shortcomings of people's behaviour. 'This fiction,' writes Kemp, '...is aimed at...preventing the lazy mind and torpid moral sense from lapsing into dangerous sloth...'

Critics have been, understandably, fascinated by the original and confident way in which Spark writes; it has been tempting to define the terms in which she works, and to read from her work some intimation of absolute points of reference, be they spiritual or aesthetic. However, such terms are elusive. I have found it rewarding to consider the perspectives and motivation of some of her characters individually. By rebuilding their understanding of their lives, their problems, their needs and their ability to confront challenges, it is possible to see how Spark portrays an experience of life to which the individual will contributes. I have studied her women characters exclusively. This is because little attention has been paid to Spark's presentation of women, although her achievement in constructing female character is unrivalled in the twentieth-century Catholic novel. Spark is not a feminist in the sense that she asserts specific rights for women, nor is she interested in decrying a society which might seek to repress women. However, she has, in several of her novels, depicted women in a search for a dignity and possession of mind which, in its own way, vindicates a woman's

spiritual integrity. Waugh's women are mostly mere social satellites; Greene appears unable to present the inner consciousness of a woman— the female characters in his books are shown through the eyes of men. Muriel Spark, however, conveys an insight into the minds of her women characters which enables the reader both to identify with and to appraise their behaviour. She does not intend them to stand as exemplary figures; indeed, some are clearly flawed and wilfully contrive their own malevolent relationships. Some, though, achieve their identity through their quest for self-respect, which involves an appreciation of all that they cannot understand.

Source: Judy Sproxton, Introduction to *The Women of Muriel Spark*, St. Martin's Press, 1992, pp. 9, 16–18.

SOURCES

Abrams, Rebecca, "Merciless Merriment," in *New Statesman*, Vol. 130, No. 4559, October 15, 2001, pp. 56–57.

Aly, Abdel-Moneim, "The Theme of Exile in the African Short Stories of Muriel Spark," in *Scottish Studies Review*, Vol. 2, No. 2, Fall 2001, pp. 94–104.

Annan, Gabriele, Review of *The Complete Short Stories*, in *Spectator*, Vol. 287, No. 9037, October 20, 2001, pp. 53–54.

Apostolou, Fotini E., "Deadly Desires: The Inscription of the Body as Initiation to Narrative," in *Seduction and Death in Muriel Spark's Fiction*, Greenwood Press, 2001, pp. 33–54.

Byrne, Eleanor, "Muriel Spark Shot in Africa," in *Theorizing Muriel Spark: Gender, Race, Deconstruction*, edited by Martin McQuillan, Palgrave, 2002, pp. 113–26.

Flower, Dean, Review of *Open to the Public*, in *Hudson Review*, Vol. 51, No. 1, Spring 1998, pp. 241–49.

Frankel, Sara, "An Interview with Muriel Spark," in *Partisan Review*, Vol. 54, No. 3, Summer 1987, pp. 443–57.

Gann, Lewis H., *Central Africa: The Former British States*, Prentice-Hall, 1971, pp. v–vi, 120–24, 135–41, 156–59.

Herrmann, Anne, Review of *Open to the Public*, in *America*, Vol. 178, No. 18, May 23, 1998, pp. 28–34.

"History of Zimbabwe," Embassy of Zimbabwe–Sweden website, http://www.zimembassy.se/history.html (accessed September 1, 2014).

Hubbard, Tom, "The Liberated Instant: Muriel Spark and the Short Story," in *Muriel Spark: An Odd Capacity for Vision*, edited by Alan Bold, Vision/Barnes & Noble, 1984, pp. 178–80.

Lindquist, Vern, "Muriel Spark," in *Dictionary of Literary Biography*, Vol. 139, *British Short-Fiction Writers,*

1945–1980, edited by Dean Baldwin, Gale Research, 1994, pp. 226–33.

Malkoff, Karl, *Muriel Spark*, Columbia University Press, 1968, p. 30.

McQuillan, Martin, ed., Introduction to *Theorizing Muriel Spark: Gender, Race, Deconstruction*, Palgrave, 2002, p. 1.

"Muriel Spark, RIP," in *New Criterion*, Vol. 24, No. 9, May 2006, pp. 1–2.

Plaut, Martin, "The Africans Who Fought in WWII," BBC News website, November 9, 2009, http://news.bbc.co.uk/2/hi/africa/8344170.stm (accessed September 1, 2014).

Review of *All the Stories of Muriel Spark*, in *Publishers Weekly*, Vol. 248, No. 46, November 12, 2001, p. 37.

Review of *Open to the Public*, in *Publishers Weekly*, Vol. 244, No. 30, July 28, 1997, pp. 54–55.

Richmond, Velma Bourgeois, *Muriel Spark*, Frederick Ungar Publishing, 1984, pp. 60–63.

Spark, Muriel, "Bang-Bang You're Dead," in *Collected Stories I*, Alfred A. Knopf, 1968, pp. 77–111.

Stanford, Derek, *Muriel Spark*, Centaur Press, 1963, pp. 107–19.

Stannard, Martin, *Muriel Spark: The Biography*, W. W. Norton, 2010, pp. 45–60.

"Timeline: African Independence," RFI website, February 16, 2010, http://www.english.rfi.fr/africa/20100216-timeline-african-independence (accessed September 1, 2014).

Walker, Dorothea, *Muriel Spark*, Twayne's English Authors Series No. 460, Twayne Publishers, 1988, pp. iii–v, 1–6.

Whittaker, Ruth, "Background," in *The Faith and Fiction of Muriel Spark*, Macmillan, 1982, pp. 18–36.

"Zimbabwe Profile," BBC website, http://www.bbc.com/news/world-africa-14113618 (accessed September 1, 2014).

"Zimbabwe Whites Flown Back to UK," in *Huffington Post*, July 6, 2009, http://www.huffingtonpost.com/2009/06/05/zimbabwe-whites-flown-bac_n_211858.html (accessed September 1, 2014).

FURTHER READING

Dangarembga, Tsitsi, *Nervous Conditions*, Ayebia Clarke, 2004.
> One of Zimbabwe's best-known modern writers, Dangarembga has set this novel in the 1960s, when a village girl gets the opportunity to be educated at a white-run mission school, which turns out to have advantages as well as drawbacks.

Dinesen, Isak, *Out of Africa*, Putnam, 1937.
> Celebrated in its day as a revelatory look at life for colonials in Kenya, Dinesen—the pen name of Karen Blixen—has received criticism in the modern era for her romanticization of a lifestyle that was enabled by white oppression of the native majority, an aspect of the era that she ignores. Nonetheless, the story sweeps the reader away, and the film adaptation won the Academy Award for Best Picture of 1985.

Johnson, David, *World War II and the Scramble for Labour in Colonial Zimbabwe, 1939–1948*, University of Zimbabwe Publications, 2000.
> Although Spark pays little attention to the local and regional circumstances for native Zimbabweans in "Bang-Bang You're Dead," Johnson's volume takes a close look at what native Africans experienced during that story's time period, when the British were mobilizing for World War II.

Lessing, Doris, *Under My Skin: Volume One of My Autobiography, to 1949*, HarperCollins, 1994.
> This first volume of Lessing's autobiography treats her years growing up and maturing into an adult in Southern Rhodesia. The volume ends with Lessing traveling to London with the manuscript of her first novel in tow. Like Spark, Lessing was an independent-minded woman who developed a perceptive and witty literary style.

Samkange, Stanlake, *Origins of Rhodesia*, Frederick A. Praeger, 1969.
> Inspired by elders who, attending school with him, saw fit to object to the British colonial education system's biased portrayal of British inroads into the region, Samkange determined to someday write a history conveying the truth. This is that volume, extending from the earliest knowledge of the region's history to the death of the Ndebele king Lobengula in 1894 and the christening of the territory of "Rhodesia."

SUGGESTED SEARCH TERMS

Muriel Spark AND Bang-Bang You're Dead

Muriel Spark AND African short stories

Muriel Spark AND autobiographical fiction

colonial Africa AND literature

Southern Rhodesia OR Zimbabwe AND history

Zimbabwe AND literature

Muriel Spark AND Flannery O'Connor

Muriel Spark AND Graham Greene

Muriel Spark AND Doris Lessing

The Beautiful People

CHARLES BEAUMONT
1952

"The Beautiful People" is a science-fiction story about conformity. It was first published in *If* magazine in 1952, but its insights into the human condition and the way society works are as fresh in the early twenty-first century as they were then. In this story, set in the future, everyone in the world undergoes a process called the Transformation, which turns them into ideally fleshed-out nineteen-year-olds. Surgical machines remove any flaws, altering bone structure and organs and skin, making bodies durable and beautiful.

One girl, though, sees her upcoming Transformation not as an opportunity to become beautiful but as a threat to her unique personality. Unlike everyone else, she still has books, left to her by her father, who also left her with a sense that she is beautiful as she is. Because she resists the Transformation, Mary is put under psychiatric care, loses her job, and ultimately is put before a government tribunal, where her refusal to become "beautiful" brands her as an enemy to society.

The story's author, Charles Beaumont, was one of the most prolific writers of science-fiction and fantasy stories in the 1950s and 1960s. As a skilled writer of futuristic fiction, Beaumont delivers a world that was speculative then but is more familiar to readers in 2015. Obsession with youth and the ease of cosmetic surgery are at the fore of the story, and the details, such as

In the opening scene, Mary closes her eyes rather than watch a violent meteor shower.
(© Rob van Esch / Shutterstock.com)

wall-sized televisions and windows that can be turned on or off at the push of a button, prove to be close to the values and technology of the twenty-first century.

"The Beautiful People," slightly revised from the 1952 version, was published in Beaumont's collection *Yonder* in 1958 and was reprinted in *Best of Beaumont* in 1982. The *If* version is available online from Project Gutenberg.

AUTHOR BIOGRAPHY

Beaumont was born Charles Leroy Nutt in Chicago, Illinois, on January 2, 1929. In grade school, he was teased for his name and came to hate it. He first changed it to Charles McNutt and then, after he started publishing, legally changed it to his pen name, Charles Beaumont.

When he was young, Beaumont was interested in football and baseball, not writing. At age eleven, though, he contracted spinal meningitis,

which curtailed his involvement in sports. He then became an avid reader. Beaumont hung around the editorial offices of Ziff-Davis Publishing, watching the writers churn out copy for science-fiction and fantasy magazines, including *Amazing Stories*, which would publish his first professional work years later, in 1951.

At age twelve, Beaumont was sent to Everett, Washington, where his parents thought the weather would help his meningitis. There he lived with five widowed aunts and listened night after night to their stories about how their husbands had died. He published his own amateur magazine, *Utopia*, and started drawing illustrations and cartoons for pulp magazines, placing his first cartoon in *Fantastic Adventures* in October 1943. Beaumont became involved in radio at this time, appearing on a West Coast program called *Drama Workshop*. He also wrote and directed a fifteen-minute radio program called *Hollywood Hi-Lights*.

Beaumont left high school before graduation. He served in the army for four months but left because of a bad back, receiving an honorable discharge. He used the army's education stipend—from the Servicemen's Readjustment Act of 1944, better known as the G.I. Bill—to enroll in Bliss-Hayden Acting School in California, where he was discovered in a play. Universal Studios signed him as an actor, but he never appeared in a film before his contract ran out. He worked briefly for the animation studio at MGM and sold illustrations to Fantasy Publishing, drawing cartoons and book jackets.

In 1946, at the Fowler Brothers Bookstore in Los Angeles, Beaumont struck up a conversation about cartoons with Ray Bradbury, an older, established writer of fantasy and science fiction. Bradbury would be a mentor to Beaumont for the rest of his life. Beaumont moved briefly to Mobile, Alabama, in 1948 to take a job as a clerk with the Gulf, Mobile & Ohio Railroad. There he met Helen Braun. They were soon married, and he moved back to California with her.

In 1952, Beaumont returned to Universal Studios to work in the music department copying musical scores. After being fired, he began to write full-time, which put him and his family into poverty—at a low point, his typewriter was in hock and the gas was turned off. Then, in September 1954, *Playboy* magazine accepted his novella *Black Country*. Soon *Playboy* had Beaumont on retainer for five hundred dollars per month. He started selling to major magazines such as *Esquire* and the *Saturday Evening Post*. He also had radio and television plays produced.

In 1957, Beaumont's first short-story collection, *The Hunger and Other Stories*, was published. The following year he published *Yonder: Stories of Fantasy and Science Fiction*, which includes "The Beautiful People," and in 1960 he published *Night Ride and Other Journeys*. In 1959 Rod Serling began the classic anthology television series *The Twilight Zone*. Beaumont became one of the show's principal writers, producing scripts for thirty-three of the 156 episodes.

In 1963, Beaumont became notably weak and ill. Doctors could not determine what was wrong with him at first, but the following year the diagnosis of early-onset Alzheimer's disease was made, though it was never fully confirmed. As the disease progressed and Beaumont became unable to write, friends, including the

science-fiction luminaries William F. Nolan and Jerry Sohl, ghostwrote his works for him. Beaumont died on February 21, 1967, at the age of thirty-eight.

PLOT SUMMARY

Beaumont establishes in the first paragraph that "The Beautiful People" does not take place in a world familiar to his readers. Eighteen-year-old Mary Cuberle sits watching violent war scenes that are soon identified as something called the Mayoraka Disaster, and her mother mentions that this event has worn as thin as the first landing on Mars. The television they are watching is part of a wall (technology that was just barely imaginable when this story was first published in 1952).

Mary and her mother are in the waiting room of Doctor Hortel and have been waiting for three hours. Mary's mother expresses worries about things that Mary has told her. When they go in to see the doctor, he says that he knows what is bothering Mary: that she feels bad about her body and is impatient to turn nineteen so that she can undergo the procedure that will change her looks and make her as beautiful as her mother and all the women she sees on television, in magazines, and on the streets. As he talks about the virtue of waiting for her time to come, Mary and Mrs. Cuberle try to interrupt him, but Doctor Hortel keeps explaining, in a patronizing way, how going through the procedure will change her confused attitude, if she will only be patient.

When she is able to interject, Mary tells the doctor that he is reading the situation backward. It is not that she wants to undergo the Transformation sooner but that she does not want the Transformation at all.

Doctor Hortel is astounded. He has never heard of anyone refusing the Transformation. After using a machine clipped to Mary's head to determine that she is not insane and suggesting that she may be lying about her feelings, he questions her. She tells him that she is curious about things she has read about in books. For instance, she explains—after her mother broaches the issue—that she has tried to sleep, even though nobody sleeps anymore or even remembers how to do so. Her talk about sleep and books and not wanting the Transformation

MEDIA ADAPTATIONS

- Beaumont had a long successful relationship with Rod Serling's television series *The Twilight Zone*, so it is not surprising that "The Beautiful People" would have been adapted for that show. The adaptation, called "Number Twelve Looks Just like You," ran on January 24, 1964. It is credited to Beaumont and John Tomerlin, but Tomerlin wrote the entire script because by that time Beaumont was too ill to write. The episode stars Collin Wilcox as Marilyn Cuberle, Richard Long as her uncle Rick, and Suzy Parker, a supermodel of the day, as Marilyn's mother. Because the nature of the story is that people are made to look alike, the post-Transformation actors play several roles. "Number Twelve Looks Just like You" was episode 16 in season 5 of the series and is available in *The Twilight Zone: The Definitive Collection* (2006).

makes Doctor Hortel uncomfortable. He calls off their interview abruptly and asks Mrs. Cuberle to find another psychiatrist for Mary.

The next section of the story takes place in the Cuberles' apartment, which, like all apartments in this futuristic world, is far below Earth's surface. Mary thinks about the lines from "Snow White and the Seven Dwarfs" about the mirror showing who is the fairest of them all, lines that she has read in a book. Her mother comes in and criticizes Mary for not having the windows on so that she can look at people outside and for spending too much time reading books when she could be watching taped broadcasts. She tries to convince Mary of how much better she will feel after the Transformation, but Mary is focused on a world her father described. When Mary tells her mother that her father told her she was beautiful, her mother scoffs. The father underwent *his* Transformation,

the mother explains. But Mary says that he regretted it and advised her to not make the mistake he made. Mrs. Cuberle gathers up all of the books she can find in the apartment, deciding that they are a bad influence on Mary, and takes them to the elevator to dispose of them. Mary explains that she has anticipated that very move and has hidden the best books where her mother cannot find them. The scene ends with them having "lunch": it is not a meal, like those Mary has seen described in books, but just pills to be swallowed.

In the next section, Mary is at work, designing a crane on a drafting table. Her supervisor, Mr. Willmes, approaches, looks over her work, and compliments it. He takes her into the boss's office for a private talk. He has been told by an anonymous informant (identified later in the story as Mary's mother) that Mary has refused to undergo the Transformation, and he wants to warn her about how such a decision can affect her job. Their boss, Mr. Poole, will be displeased, he says, implying that Mary's decision will reflect badly on Willmes himself. People will think of their office as if it has a mutant, a member of a lower social class, working there. She would lose out on promotions that could easily be hers after undergoing the Transformation. She would age and feel the effects of aging, which people who go through the Transformation are spared. Mary thinks over what he has said and asks Mr. Willmes to accept her resignation. He encourages her to reconsider, reminding her that she has a few months to change her mind.

The next scene takes place in the Cuberles' apartment some time later. Mrs. Cuberle arrives home from work. She is tired and worried about how they will survive financially now that Mary is out of her job. Mary points out that her mother was the one who told Mr. Willmes that Mary was not going to undergo the Transformation, so it is really Mrs. Cuberle who has caused their financial problems. Mrs. Cuberle complains that they are social outcasts now, that people will treat them as if they are mutants, and that her own job is in jeopardy.

A letter arrives for Mrs. Cuberle from a government agency identified as Dept. F, offering to give Mary a hearing about her case. Mary goes to her room to be alone. She manages to fall asleep, but sleep does not bring her peace.

The hearing resembles a public trial. A young-looking man representing the government—the senator—lays out the official position, pointing out that a panel of doctors has confirmed that there is no danger to Mary in undergoing the Transformation. All of the news media outlets throughout the galaxy, which he identifies with such futuristic names as Newstapes and Foto services, are watching to see what Mary will do, posing a potential social crisis. Too much government time is being spent, the senator says, on the question of what Mary will do.

The audience is packed with beautiful people who shout at Mary to change. The senator produces a petition signed by two thousand people who think that Mary should be forced to change. The senator signs the order to make her change.

At the Transformation Parlor, Mary, looking at the other young men and women who are about to undergo the procedure, comes to a realization about why she has been so hesitant. All along, she understands, she has had a concern about what happens to the people who transform, about where their real selves go once they become artificially beautiful people. The news media are on hand at the Transformation Parlor to cover the event, until they are asked to leave so that the machines that do the actual Transformation are able to do their job.

As the workers at the parlor set the machines to transform Mary, she keeps crying out her fear about what is going to happen to her. The workers speak soothingly to calm her fears, telling her that the Transformation will not hurt, but she is not worried about pain. She does not want to know what is going to happen, because she knows that well enough, but instead she is worried about where her identity will go and who she will be once her Transformation is complete.

As the psychiatrist Doctor Hortel explains it to her, most young people Mary's age are thrilled by the chance to undergo the Transformation. The Transformation will make them look better, smoothing out their skin and fixing any shaping of their bone structure considered imperfect. It will help them live long lives, free from the aches and pains of living. It is simply considered rational to want to have one's body altered by the Transformation, and the people Mary encounters in this story cannot understand why she would not jump at the chance.

But most people Mary's age have not had the encouragement of a parent as supportive as Mary's father was. He told her that she is beautiful as she is, and he gave her books to read. Unlike the tapes that everyone currently watches, the books provoke thought. Mary can see that going through the Transformation will not necessarily make her a better person. She does not need to have her looks altered if she believes that she is already beautiful, and by the end of the story, she begins to understand that changing her looks will inevitably change her personality. She is not sure that the new personality will be an improvement.

Mary's background and intellect make it possible for her to stand up for what she believes in even when everyone else, including her own mother, tells her that she is wrong. She is willing to try sleeping, even though neither she nor anyone she knows can say what it will do to a person. The descriptions of sleep that Mary has read in books appeal to her. She is willing to lose her job as an engineer if that is what she must do to opt out of the Transformation.

By the story's end, Mary is worn down. She wearily submits to the Transformation. She does not believe that it will make her life any better, and she suspects that it will make it worse, but she can no longer disagree with everyone in the entire universe.

CHARACTERS

Mary Cuberle

Mary is a normal-looking eighteen-year-old employed as an engineer. She is intelligent and does her job well. Over the course of the story, Mary becomes perceived as a threat to society across the world and across the galaxy because she questions the accepted standards of behavior.

Mr. Cuberle

Mary's father is dead at the time of the story and does not appear in it, but he is talked about. He was in the army, working with rockets, and died at an event referred to as the Ganymede affair. He remains a major influence on Mary, whose ideas of standing up against the government stem from things that her father taught her.

One thing that makes Mary unique is that she reads books that her father and his father left for her. From the books, she learns about self-image and about sleep. She recalls her father telling her that she is beautiful as she is, a belief that drives her to oppose her Transformation.

Mrs. Zena Cuberle

Mary's mother is the widow of a soldier who died in battle. She is frightened and confused because she does not understand her daughter's behavior. Mrs. Cuberle notes early on that Mary has been quiet and withdrawn for months. She becomes so worried about Mary that she takes her to Doctor Hortel, a psychiatrist. She knows that Mary does not want the Transformation, and she knows some of the consequences that this decision can bring on her household, but she goes to Doctor Hortel because she cannot change Mary's mind, and she hopes that he can.

After she sees how much Mary's odd behavior frightens the psychiatrist, Mrs. Cuberle makes an anonymous call to Mary's supervisor, Mr. Willmes, hoping that he can do something to change her mind. Instead, her plan backfires because Mary resigns. After that, Mrs. Cuberle is very frightened, almost manic: her daughter has been fired; the public is aware of Mary's position, and Mrs. Cuberle fears they both will be shunned as mutants; and they are in danger of slipping into poverty if public prejudices cause Mrs. Cuberle to lose her job, too.

Mrs. Cuberle angrily throws out many of the books that her dead husband left to Mary, hoping to erase the terrible danger she sees coming from the knowledge they bring. When the letter comes from Centraldome requiring Mary to submit to a hearing about whether she will undergo the Transformation, Mary is frightened, but Mrs. Cuberle is relieved. All along, she has been looking for someone who can compel the sort of behavior she wants from her child, which is something that she is unable to do.

Doctor Hortel

Doctor Hortel is a psychiatrist who represents the status quo at the beginning of the story. He describes the Transformation process in detail for Mary, which tells the reader what is at stake. He takes a dismissive, patronizing stance toward Mary and her mother, telling them that he knows what is troubling Mary. He talks over them when they both try to interrupt to tell him what the trouble really is, indicating that he thinks he knows this girl he has just met better than she knows herself.

When they finally do get to tell him that Mary is questioning the Transformation, Doctor Hortel is stumped. He has no experience with a person who does not welcome the change. He is mystified by a person who may know how to sleep. Lacking understanding, he looks for the few solutions that he can comprehend, checking Mary for insanity and suggesting that she is lying about her attitude. When neither of these turns out to be the cause of Mary's reticence about the Transformation, Doctor Hortel becomes upset, taking a few pills to calm himself. He quickly distances himself from Mary, telling her and her mother that he cannot treat her and recommending that they go somewhere else for help.

The doctor is described as a dark-haired, handsome man who looks as if he is in his middle twenties, but the way that he refers to eighteen-year-old Mary as a girl implies that he is much older than that. Having had his looks altered as has everyone else on Earth, he is much older than his looks imply.

Mr. Poole

Mr. Poole is an executive at Interplan, where Mary works. He does not appear in the story. The boss of Mr. Willmes, Mary's supervisor, Poole is mentioned as someone who may cause trouble for Mary's department if he finds out that one of the employees does not want to undergo the Transformation.

The Senator

Early in the story, Doctor Hortel believes that there is a problem with young people thinking too much about the Transformation and becoming anxious about waiting until they are nineteen. He mentions that he will suggest to someone he refers to as "the senator" that the government should start a new education program to help young people cope with the wait.

The story does not make clear whether the senator character introduced later in the story is the same person Doctor Hortel was talking about. The senator at the end of the story is in charge of deciding Mary's fate. The story makes a point of describing the senator as having a young, handsome face, even though he is clearly older. He makes the government's case before a packed hearing room. He points out how the time being spent on talking about Mary Cuberle is taking away from important intergalactic matters that should be the concern of the government. He is the one who brings up the petition, implying that the will of the people should be followed. It is his signature that sentences Mary to undergoing the forced Transformation.

Shala

Shala is Mary's friend who has undergone the Transformation. Mrs. Cuberle brings her up as a reason why Mary should welcome having the surgery. Shala is mentioned but does not appear in the story.

Mr. Willmes

Mr. Willmes is Mary's supervisor at Interplan, where she works during the first part of the story. He values Mary's work, but he is worried about negative associations that will affect his department if Mary refuses to go through with the Transformation. His superior, Mr. Poole, will be displeased. People will look down on their department as a place that employs inferior people.

Willmes tries to help Mary as much as he can. He makes the case to her about how much happier she will be after the Transformation. When Mary offers her resignation, Willmes asks whether that is what she really wants. He says that if she should ever change her mind and undergo the Transformation, her job will be available to her, but as it is, he has to let her resign.

THEMES

Coming of Age

Everyone in the society depicted in "The Beautiful People" is expected to undergo the Transformation at the same point in their lives, age nineteen. In the beginning of the story, Doctor Hortel presumes that Mary's problem is that she is impatient, wanting this procedure performed on her sooner than later. This impatience mirrors that with many of the milestones that adolescents want to reach as soon as they can, including driving, jobs, and moving out to start their own homes. The implication is that, for this society, the Transformation is considered a rite of passage into adulthood.

Ironically (from her compatriots' perspective), Mary's true rite of passage is when she develops a sense of who she is and learns to stand up against the social norms. Many coming-of-age stories follow their protagonists from childhood to adulthood, but in the vision that Beaumont presents, the world of adults is corrupt. It is something to be avoided, not embraced. Even stories that show a protagonist's coming of age as a loss of innocence show a transition into knowledge from ignorance. In "The Beautiful People," however, the traditional passage to adulthood is a passage to a narrower view of the world.

Individualism

In this story, adult figures pressure Mary to submit herself to the Transformation, becoming increasingly desperate to make sure that this one individual be willing to be like everybody else. They try to convince her with a series of logical arguments. They tell her that looking better will make her feel better about herself; that it is necessary for her job as a machine designer; that she will live longer once her body has been altered; and that she should want to be like others her age, such as her friend Shala. In the end, they go over her head to make the case that Mary is a threat to the social order of many planets if she does not behave as everyone else does.

Mary cannot help seeing the world differently than most people do. The narrator explains that she fondly remembers her father as someone who did not think the Transformation was worth having. He was someone who revered books and the complex knowledge to be gotten from them. Having become the person she is over the course of her eighteen years, Mary follows her conscience instead of following society's norms. She is not trying to change the world or to assert her legal right as an individual; she is only trying to follow the truth as she knows it. With all of the peer pressure that is directed at Mary—the entire universe wants her to change her mind—she stays true to her individual vision up to the very end of the story.

TOPICS FOR FURTHER STUDY

- Do you agree that there is a level at which plastic surgery alters a person's personality? Look online at stories from people who have had good and bad experiences with plastic surgery and quote them in an essay that explains which operations you think might intrude on an individual's sense of self.

- This story describes how plastic surgery changes bone structure and removes fat, but it does not acknowledge differences in race. Write a proposal from the perspective of someone within the Centraldome government addressing how to handle different kinds of skin. Discuss issues such as whether they would suggest bleaching or dying and whether they would be open to a few chromatic varieties in officially sanctioned beauty.

- Read Arthur Miller's classic play *The Crucible*, which is set in the seventeenth century during the trials against women accused of witchcraft in the Massachusetts Bay Colony, but is actually a reflection on the way the US government was jailing people with no evidence, backed by public fear, during the McCarthy hearings of the 1950s. (Miller's play was produced the year after "The Beautiful People" was first published.) After reading the play, rewrite the trial from Beaumont's story as a script with Mary Cuberle being accused of witchcraft. Include evidence that the prosecutors would use to support their claim.

- When he wrote this story in 1952, Beaumont was speculating—quite accurately, it turns out—about large, wall-sized television sets and television content that the viewer can choose. What do you think television will be like a hundred years from now? Speculate on whether there will be public television sets or only smaller, individual screens. Create a speculative design for the television of the future, and discuss the shows people will watch and where and how they will watch them.

- At the end of the story, Mary is forced to undergo the Transformation because a large number of people sign a petition saying that she should be forced to change. Organize a debate in your class, with one side arguing for why petitions are good for giving lawmakers guidance on their jobs and the other side arguing that petitions give too much power to small clusters of the population.

- Assemble a slide show of pictures of famous male and female models to support a presentation to your class that argues either that US society has narrow standards of beauty or that US society has a broad, open view of what is considered beautiful— or that both angles have truth to them.

- Survey people who use social media regularly to determine whether they think sites like Facebook and Twitter promote collectivist thinking or individuality. Ask the same questions of the same number of people who seldom use social media. Use the answers to describe in an essay the requirements that you think social media websites should have if their actual goal is to make a better society.

- In Lee Strauss's *Perception* series of novels for young adults, a seventeen-year-old genetically altered person (GAP), Zoe, leaves her life of luxury within a walled city where non-GAPs are kept out—treated as the mutants of Beaumont's story are—to work with a rebel among the outsiders to solve the mystery of her brother's disappearance. Love blooms. Read *Perception* (2012), the first novel in the series, and write a short story that places you in a fictional group favored by the government or in a group excluded by the government. Describe the obstacles that institutional exclusionism can put in front of people.

Mrs. Cuberle looks through magazines filled with nothing but photographs of beautiful people.
(© matka_Wariatka / Shutterstock.com)

Social Identity

Those in power in this story—Mary's supervisor, Mr. Willmes; Willmes's boss, Mr. Poole; Doctor Hortel; the senator—fear what will happen to society if one person publicly announces that the accepted standards of beauty are not absolute standards. This is not a society that believes in the benefits of multiple ideas from multiple people. It is a society that is based on the principle that any small amount of disagreement will lead to greater amounts of disagreement, threatening to bring the entire social order to a standstill.

Most social groups have characteristics that they think set them apart from other social groups. In the world "The Beautiful People" presents, though, social identity is based on something superficial and artificial. Beauty is not a characteristic that helps society expand its understanding of science, religion, or the arts. In this world, being beautiful is no achievement, because everyone is beautiful. This society puts so much value on beauty that

it can be imperiled by something as simple as a person who does not see beauty in the standard way. All it takes is someone like Mary, someone who does not remember nonstandard beauty herself but who has heard about the idea from her father and from books, to threaten collapse of the social order.

History

This story begins with televised footage of war. War stories are so much a part of this culture that Doctor Hortel, when he hears it mentioned, recalls the battle that Mary's father fought and died in. To these people, war is an important part of history that is and should be remembered: as a woman explains to Mrs. Cuberle in the doctor's waiting room, the memory of war is used to keep the young people feeling grateful for the world they have now.

This is a very narrow view of history, one that plays well on television screens but lacks depth. When Mary begins to bring up ideas that she has gotten from books—ideas that are no longer available or permissible, like sleep and food and honest self-esteem—her mother becomes frightened and angry. She throws the books out and encourages Mary to get her ideas only from videos. She insists that Mary's view of the world be formed from the images that the government has made to be acceptable. This narrow view of history makes it easy to keep all of the people on Earth and other planets believing the same ideas, whereas the wider and more realistic ideas of history, those available in books, encourage individual thought.

Courage

Mary stands up against all of society, even when it is clearly implied that her position might cause the collapse of the social order. It might seem that taking and holding such a strong position would require a tremendous amount of courage, but Beaumont makes it clear that Mary does not think of herself as courageous. She does not think that she is right. She does not even know what she thinks.

Throughout the story, Mary questions herself. She looks at herself in the mirror and is surprised that she is not disappointed by what she sees, having learned that she should be. She knows what her father told her, but that is contradicted by what her mother tells her. She likes her supervisor, so she volunteers to resign from her job when she sees that she is going to cause trouble. She is flexible about everything in her life, willing to look at the other side's argument and unable to fully formulate an argument for herself.

Even as she is not trying to force her position, Mary is adamant about her right to not hold any position. She does not know that the Transformation is wrong for her, but she feels that it probably is, and her opponents have not convinced her that it is right for her. Mary's courage is not the courage of certainty so much as the courage of probability: the things that people tell her about the Transformation make sense to her, but her skepticism about it is worth fighting for.

STYLE

Establishing a Futuristic Setting

A defining characteristic of science-fiction and fantasy stories is that they are set in worlds that have basic differences from the contemporary world with which readers are familiar. "The Beautiful People" does not announce what is unique about its setting, but it offers readers enough clues early on to put them on alert. The situation described in the first paragraph, for instance, is more violent than television of the fifties would have broadcast, showing severed limbs and a destroyed ship. By the end of that paragraph, deadly meteorites have been mentioned. Within a few lines, the television is described as being built into the wall—technology that was unavailable at the time the story was written. The scene shown on the television is described as the Mayoraka Disaster in a way that implies that the story's characters would naturally be familiar with it, just as modern television viewers would recognize footage of 9/11.

Beaumont's task is to introduce readers to the world of the work while not taking them out of the story. He does this by dropping hints and references that are not too direct but are also not too subtle for the average reader to figure out. Who, for instance, are the mutants the story refers to? Readers need only know that they are people who have not been transformed and who probably cannot be transformed, which would make them like Mary but also different from her. What is Centraldome, and, specifically, what is Dept. F? All readers need to know is that they are functions of a powerful government. Any similarity between what they do in the story and the real government that readers know is left for the reader to determine.

Writers like Beaumont are not expected to write about the real world. They do, however, have to establish the relationship between common reality and the reality that is being presented in their stories.

Scene Breaks

Although fiction writers are able to give information to readers through narration, most prefer to present their stories in a series of dramatic scenes. In "The Beautiful People," the story plays out through a series of clear, specific scenes in which the characters interact. The scene in Doctor Hortel's office is followed by Mary at home, looking in the mirror, which leads to a scene with Mrs. Cuberle confronting Mary, then Mary at her desk, Mary and Mr. Willmes in the boss's office, Mary arriving home some weeks or months later, going to her bedroom, standing before the senator's hearing, and then visiting the Transformation Parlor.

Although the location of each scene is clear, Beaumont throws readers off slightly by running some of them together. He is very clear about where the end of the scene in the doctor's office occurs: when Mrs. Cuberle leaves, there is a space break, a double-spaced gap that, like the fade to black in a film, shows that the action is over. There is no gap, though, after the scene in the boss's office: suddenly Mary is riding in an elevator, and readers must figure out that she is now at home. Then there is a discussion of what Mrs. Cuberle's coworkers think of Mary, indicating that enough time has passed for her refusal of the Transformation to become common knowledge, but nothing in the story's layout on the page helps readers understand this scene shift. The same thing happens when Mary's leaving the hearing leads to a description of the Transformation Parlor, leaving readers only a few beats behind in determining the current scene.

HISTORICAL CONTEXT

A Nervous Political Climate

In 1952, when "The Beautiful People" was first published in *If* magazine, American society was in the throes of a battle over conformity. The United States was perceived as being in the middle of a struggle against the Soviet Union, the world's other superpower, with each side poised to take control of the world in the name of ideology. Suspicions over people who held views that were different from the average views grew to levels of extremism during the Cold War.

The United States and the Soviet Union had actually worked with each other to defeat the Axis powers during World War II. Almost immediately after the end of the war in 1945, however, competition and mutual distrust began. The Americans feared that the Soviets' aim of spreading Communism across the globe, if left unchecked, would one day lead to a takeover of the United States, the only country with the military power to stop them. The Soviets feared that the Americans would wield their newly developed atomic weaponry, used against Japan during the war, to stop Soviet expansion. The late-1940s jockeying for

position culminated in a showdown between the two superpowers on the Korea Peninsula. The army of the Democratic People's Republic of Korea, a Communist country with Soviet backing, invaded South Korea in 1950. South Korea was politically aligned with the West and was quickly supported by the United States. The Korean conflict lasted three years, but the dichotomy between Communist North Korea and democratic South Korea is ongoing in the early twenty-first century. The Cold War, a term that refers to the indirect competition between the United States and the Soviet Union—the tension never actually led to direct conflict between the two superpowers—lasted until the Soviet Union disbanded in 1991.

In the United States, the political climate of the 1950s was fraught with fears that the Soviets were working to make the population more open to Communist takeover. Several politicians built careers on promising to guard the nation against the perceived Communist threat. One of them was Richard M. Nixon, who entered politics in 1945, came to national attention as a zealous Communist fighter when he joined the House Un-American Activities Committee (HUAC) in 1947, and went on to be vice president from 1953 to 1961 and president from 1969 until his resignation in 1974.

The politician most associated with America's anticommunism fever is Joseph McCarthy of Wisconsin. In 1950, McCarthy came to fame by declaring that he had proof that 205 active members of the Communist Party were working in the US State Department. A Senate subcommittee investigation found that McCarthy had no evidence to back his charges, but the popularity of McCarthy's anticommunist crusade grew. People in the entertainment industry were called before the HUAC and asked if they were or ever had been affiliated with the Communist Party (which was not illegal). If they were, or if they refused to answer, film studios refused to offer them work, blacklisting them.

After Hollywood, McCarthy focused on the government. It was only when he took on the United States military in the 1954 Army-McCarthy hearings that the country began to see McCarthy as an opportunist who was willing to accuse upstanding American patriots—and by accusing them ruin their careers—to further his own goals.

COMPARE
&
CONTRAST

- **1952:** Discrimination and lack of representation set the stage for the civil rights movement that pushes for fair treatment regardless of race, gender, ethnic origin, and physical abilities.

  Today: Laws resulting from the civil rights struggles of the 1950s and 1960s are aimed at giving people who are not born in the majority a chance to live as well as those who are.

- **1952:** The Cold War is at its most frightening period. Americans fear that a totalitarian system like the one in the Soviet Union will replace individual thought with the kind of state-sponsored idea molding that is evident in Beaumont's story.

  Today: Since the collapse of the Soviet Union in 1991, other totalitarian regimes try to control the thoughts of the citizens, but these governments are not in countries that have the power to take over the entire world.

- **1952:** Television is new, having only become widely dispersed after the end of World War II in 1945, but is already looked down on as a simplified way of storytelling that pales in comparison with books and newspapers.

  Today: The proliferation of cable television stations has made it possible for television to offer viewers extended prestige programming, such as *Breaking Bad*, *Treme*, and *Downton Abbey*. Entire networks are dedicated to in-depth news and science reporting that would not fit into the half-hour slots that the networks gave news in its infancy.

- **1952:** A woman raising her child by herself, as Mrs. Cuberle does in this story, is rare.

  According to the 1950 census, only 3.6 million households in the United States have a mother but no father. It is not surprising that Mrs. Cuberle feels she must rely on others to tell her how to raise Mary.

  Today: One-fourth of US households are led by single mothers. Social services, from student meal programs to day care to job counseling, are available to assist them. Single mothers know that they do not need men to make decisions in their homes.

- **1952:** Americans are becoming aware of the powerful influence of the advertising industry—dubbed Madison Avenue, after the street in New York City where most of the important advertising firms are centered. People are suspicious of advertisers' strategies, which often seek to create paranoid self-consciousness about natural looks in order to sell products to correct supposed flaws.

  Today: Advertising is bigger than ever, with product names appearing in places that they never appeared in before. The products being advertised may be helpful for living happy, comfortable lives, but many are, as before, trying to sow discontent in order to make unnecessary merchandise seem necessary.

- **1952:** Scientific expansion is aimed at the skies. A writer like Beaumont, speculating about what a future society will be like, naturally assumes that there will be coalitions of people living on other planets.

  Today: Speculative fiction often focuses on how societies of the future will deal with the environmental and social challenges that contemporary society has placed in their way.

The word *McCarthyism* has come to describe taking advantage of a political climate of paranoia to stir up public fears, destroying the lives of innocent people in the process. "The Beautiful People" ends with a hearing that reflects the kinds of hearings that were in the news in 1952.

Television

In "The Beautiful People," Mary is someone who can understand reality because she reads books while everyone else gets their news from television and videos. This is a common stance in literary circles in the early twenty-first century, but at the time that Beaumont was writing, television was an emerging technology.

There were various types of experimental televisions throughout the world starting in 1935, but World War II, which broke out in Europe in 1939, cut short its expansion into commercial markets. Science and technology were diverted to the war effort until the late 1940s. When the war was over, the availability of television sets and broadcasts to watch exploded. Only fifteen television stations broadcast to small, local markets in the United States in 1946, and television sets cost $375, equivalent to nearly three thousand dollars in 2014. By 1948, four television networks were broadcasting seven days a week. The number of television sets produced jumped from 975,000 in 1948 to three million the following year and continued to grow.

The development of networks of stations allowed broadcasting from coast to coast in the United States. The problem with this was that the country's width made four time zones necessary, which meant that a show originating live in Los Angeles at nine o'clock at night, for example, would have to be shown live in New York at one in the morning. Networks experimented with having actors repeat their performances, but broadcasters quickly saw the need for taping shows to offer the same performance to different time zones.

The first form of recording broadcasts was Kinescope, a method of attaching a film camera to a video monitor to capture the show with all of the cuts and camera angles that were part of the original broadcast. Kinescope images were dingy and grainy, but in most cases, they are the only records of late-1940s and early-1950s television.

Although videotape cassette recorders did not become a commercial household product until the 1970s, electromagnetic tape technology for capturing broadcast shows was available in 1951. It was developed by the production company of the popular entertainer Bing Crosby, who longed to make his own television show available for delayed broadcast in

The doctors believe that Mary might be insane because she resists the Transformation.
(© Hans Geel / Shutterstock.com)

the same way that his popular radio show was taped and repeated. When "The Beautiful People" was first published in 1952, taped television shows were possible, though uncommon. Beaumont's prescient view of a future when taped television programs would be common was as accurate as his anticipation of such twenty-first-century developments as video on demand and wall-sized screens.

CRITICAL OVERVIEW

Beaumont wrote in a wide range of styles, mostly concentrated in science fiction and fantasy. Although authors traditionally have been paid better for genre fiction, such as Beaumont's, than for literary fiction, genre fiction has not been given the critical acclaim accorded to literary fiction. Beaumont's success as a genre fiction writer is measured by his ability to sell enough works and live by the money he made as a writer in the last years of his life. He is best remembered for his long association with the television program *The Twilight Zone* (1959–1964), to which he was a frequent contributor.

In the compendium *Twentieth-Century Science-Fiction Writers*, Bill Pronzini calls Beaumont "a consummate craftsman of the popular market short story—perhaps the most accomplished writer of this type of fiction to publish in the 1950's and early 1960's." In Pronzini's analysis, Beaumont's early death, at age thirty-eight, "cut short a career which might have progressed to major stature." This view was echoed in a review in *Library Journal* by Susan L. Nickerson, who notes that his "promising career" was cut short. Reviewing the collection *Best of Beaumont* in 1982, fifteen years after the author's death, Nickerson calls him a "prolific and skillful writer" who "mingled sf [science fiction] and fantasy with bits of humor and horror." She proclaimed the book of his short stories to be a top-notch collection and recommended it to libraries, where Beaumont's works might be underrepresented.

CRITICISM

David Kelly

Kelly is an instructor of creative writing and literature. In the following essay, he looks at how the authority figures in "The Beautiful People" cannot change Mary's mind because they are too unimaginative or bound by tradition or simply too reliant on using peer pressure to get what they want.

In Beaumont's "The Beautiful People," four authority figures work, with little effect, to persuade eighteen-year-old Mary Cuberle that she will feel better about herself after undergoing face- and body-altering plastic surgery. If she agrees to this Transformation, they assure her, she will be physically sound, with a modified body that will last for decades. She will never have to worry about standing out in a crowd because she will look like everybody else. She will be beautiful. Each of the people making this case to Mary holds some degree of authority over her, but their arguments get nowhere. Mary refuses to accept the operation

DOCTOR HORTEL IS THE TRUE REPRESENTATION OF SOCIETY IN THIS STORY—WISE, WELL INTENTIONED, AND, WHEN IT COMES DOWN TO IT, USELESS."

that everyone else in the world has accepted. She holds on to her individuality until surgery is forced upon her by the government.

Mary lives with her mother. One would expect them to have the kind of closeness and intimacy that would make her mother her confidante, giving Mrs. Cuberle a powerful influence in Mary's decision making. Mrs. Cuberle is a weak woman, however. Although the story is set in the future—no precise date is mentioned, but there are references to historical events occurring in '17, so it is at least sixty years past the mid-twentieth century when it was written—the mother follows the conventional female gender role of Beaumont's time, the 1950s. When she in not successful in begging Mary to cooperate, she takes the girl to a psychiatrist and asks if he can change her attitude. When he is unsuccessful, Mrs. Cuberle informs on Mary, phoning her boss without her knowledge in the hope that he can change her. When this fails, Mrs. Cuberle wrings her hands, worrying that she and her daughter are going to fall to economic ruin once she, too, loses her job and Mary is practically tarred as one of the social underclass—the mutants.

Mary's boss at Interplan is Mr. Willmes. He seems to be compassionate, offering to help Mary keep her job and then offering to take her back if she ever changes her mind. Mr. Willmes is perhaps not such an educated man, as indicated by his speech patterns. "You got till March," he tells Mary, sounding gruffer than he probably means to while telling her that she will have to go. He calls her "kid" and says she is a "cub" and blurts out, "What the hell?" Mr. Willmes's speech pattern is more suggestive of his lower social standing than of his personality. He is in a position of authority over Mary, but being above his workers does not put Mr. Willmes high on the social ladder. He is yet vulnerable to pressures from his

WHAT DO I READ NEXT?

- Lois Lowry's 1993 novel *The Giver* has been a classic of young-adult fiction since its publication. It depicts a society like the one Beaumont describes. In *The Giver*, perfection is achieved through a policy of Sameness, and books are outlawed. *The Giver* won a Newbery Medal. *The Giver Quartet Omnibus* (2014) includes *The Giver* and its three sequels.

- Catherine Knutsson applies themes of futuristic dystopian science fiction to the traditions of Pacific Northwest Native Americans in her books. The 2012 novel *Shadows Cast by Stars*, for example, is about a future world decimated by a plague, where one gifted young girl has, like Mary Cuberle, retained the sensibilities of the old ways, which give her the power to stand up to the destruction.

- Adam Johnson won the Pulitzer Prize in Fiction for *The Orphan Master's Son* (2012), which describes a real-world totalitarian state: North Korea under Kim Jong-il. This coming-of-age story of a man involved in state-sponsored kidnappings gives a realistic view of a world that seems as if it could only be science fiction.

- Beaumont's career paralleled that of his friend Richard Matheson: they spent time together, published in the same science-fiction and fantasy magazines, and wrote frequently for *The Twilight Zone*. Matheson lived to 2013 and published frequently, but arguably his best-remembered work is the novel *I Am Legend* (1954), which has been adapted to film three times (the most recent in 2007). The plot concerns a man with a condition similar to vampirism who survives a plague that wipes out most of humanity, and the tale is considered a precursor to the trend in vampire movies and television programs in the early twenty-first century.

- Scott Westerfeld's best-selling young-adult novel *Uglies* (2005) and its sequels explore the same situation presented in "The Beautiful People": a future world where everyone undergoes an operation during adolescence (age sixteen in Westerfeld's version) to correct any physical imperfections and make them beautiful. Like Mary, one of Westerfeld's characters, Tally Youngblood, comes to question society's obsession with beauty.

- Arguably the most famous book about government control of citizens' thoughts published in modern times is George Orwell's novel *Nineteen Eighty-Four*, published in 1949. In this novel, manipulation of language and history, like the manipulation of physical characteristics in "The Beautiful People," gives the government the power to make people accept what they are told. *Nineteen Eighty-Four* is considered one of the great political novels of the twentieth century.

- Beaumont was a friend of Ray Bradbury, a writer whose work crossed over from the narrow science-fiction genre to a more broadly accepted literary audience. Bradbury's novel *Fahrenheit 451*, published in 1953, concerns a future world where, as in the world of "The Beautiful People," books are banned in the name of promoting a hollow sense of happiness, and television watching fills the emptiness of curiosity.

- One of Beaumont's most esteemed short stories is "Black Country," originally published in *Playboy* magazine in 1954—it was the first work of fiction published in that magazine—and later included in Beaumont's collection *The Hunger and Other Stories*. The story, about the romance between a white man and a black woman, is notable for the musical style of Beaumont's prose, which evokes jazz.

- Oskar Gruenwald's scholarly article "The Dystopian Imagination: The Challenge of Techno-Utopia" examines the tradition in American science fiction to imagine government control and the changes that the postindustrial age have brought, considering such issues as cybernetics and virtual reality as reflected in the ideas of Beaumont and others. The article was published in the *Journal of Interdisciplinary Studies*, Vol. 25, Nos. 1/2, in 2013.

social superiors, which is what makes him reluctantly give up a valued employee like Mary: he simply cannot afford to have her working for him, given the political trouble that a person refusing the Transformation could bring to his department.

That trouble is recognized by a man referred to as the senator, who clearly has a strong social position, given that by the end of the story he uses his authority to make Mary forcibly submit to the Transformation. Before sentencing her, though, the senator makes his case at a judicial tribunal of some sort. He points out the stress that her independence is causing other individuals, including her own mother. He brings up her mother several times and mentions the strain that even talking about Mary is putting on society. He explains that the time spent on preparing and holding the tribunal and the resources of the news media being expended on her are a burden that the world should not have to bear. He seems to be pleading for Mary to undergo the Transformation, appealing to her sense of fairness and to her sympathy for her mother as well as for everyone in the universe. This is a politician who does not want to resort to forcing someone to do what he wants her to do: he wants her to agree to the Transformation of her own free will.

After making his case that society will be harmed if one lone person does not go along with the crowd—a case that might just be a rhetorical trick to get Mary to cooperate—it turns out that the senator does see her as a threat to humanity. In part, he is right. The case that he does not make to the tribunal—because he does not dare to—is that individualism is always going to be a threat to political order. Boiled down to its simplest form, politics is about human interaction, and, more specifically, getting people to coexist peacefully in their neighborhoods and continents and, in the case of the story's futurism, throughout the galaxy. If people were to get along naturally, there would be no use for politicians.

The people of the senator's world do coexist peacefully, all having been brought, without violence, through suggestion and empathy alone, to agree to the same ideas. Erasing physical differences surely had something to do with making this possible. On some level, the Transformation is not much different from the fad for school districts to enforce dress codes, so that people cannot claim enemies or friends at a glance. On another level, getting everyone in the galaxy to agree to something—whether it is a sports team or the just way to run the economy or the way that every person should look—is in itself bound to promote political stability. But Mary's independence threatens to upset all of that.

If one accepts that the senator is working to maintain the universal harmony his people have finally established, it becomes much more difficult to see him as a villain. But he seems like a villain. The story portrays him as heartless, taking a girl's identity away from her. This question of balancing the good of one against the good of all invites readers to ask themselves about the methods that the senator uses to achieve his goal. Under what circumstances, if any, is it all right for the government to insist that someone give up his or her individuality? There is no doubt about how readers are supposed to feel about this question. The story seems like a tragedy when Mary Cuberle is led screaming toward the big machine that she does not want working on her. But just what is the right way to deal with a presumed menace to society?

As complex as the senator's position may seem, it is nothing like the position of Doctor Hortel, the psychiatrist Mary's mother takes her to. Unlike Mrs. Cuberle and Mr. Willmes, Doctor Hortel is presented in the story as an intelligent man in a position of control. His power is limited to coercing Mary to change her mind, although, unlike the senator, he does not have the ultimate authority to make her change if she does not want to.

Doctor Hortel is the true representation of society in this story—wise, well intentioned, and, when it comes down to it, useless. He is a psychiatrist in an age when psychological evaluation is done by alligator clamps and the calculations of a machine. As a girl Mary's age enters his office, his years of living in this society have left him with just one fallback position: the assumption that she is impatient to be made beautiful sooner than the law allows. When he finds out that she does not want the Transformation, and his testing device tells him that Mary is not insane, he has no way of dealing with her. His experience in a harmonious society has not prepared him for one who does not fit in with the harmony.

Worse than the narrow scope of his imagination is that Doctor Hortel ends up being frightened of the world in which he, as a professional man, should have some power. Learning that Mary is not interested in the Transformation makes him uncomfortable, but learning that she has read books about the true history of the world makes him panic. He abruptly terminates their interview and asks her to consult another psychiatrist, rushing to get her out of his office as soon as possible, as if having a person like her even near him might make him a suspect himself. Doctor Hortel not only lacks the power to make a diagnosis, the insight needed to make Mary change her mind, and the social authority to stand up to the government on his patient's behalf, but also cowers before the hint of guilt by association.

This is what makes Doctor Hortel the perfect representative, the very right person to establish what the world of "The Beautiful People" is all about. Each of the story's authority figures feels that, at some level, Mary is confused, frightened, or being rebellious for rebellion's sake. Her mother effectively turns her over to the authorities by phoning her employer; she hopes that being exposed as someone who is not willing to transform will bring Mary consequences just harsh enough to shake her into what Mrs. Cuberle considers sensibility. Her employer is willing to go along with her in her curiosity, but not far enough, and he eventually has to cut his ties with her or risk losing his shaky social standing. The senator would like Mary to change her mind on her own, but he is not smart enough to move her with a convincing argument.

Doctor Hortel should be smart enough to persuade Mary, with his impressive social position if not with the wisdom of his scientific background. He is unimaginative and fearful, though. The job that he has apparently been doing for quite some time, earning him a secure place high in the social hierarchy, turns out to be limited to telling people that things will be all right. When someone appears who is not assured by his assurances, the psychiatrist has no recourse but to shut his door on them. Which is what society does in the story. Mary is offered beauty, an ideal that like happiness and justice no one can find bad. Resisting, she becomes a threat that the most powerful authorities can answer only with force.

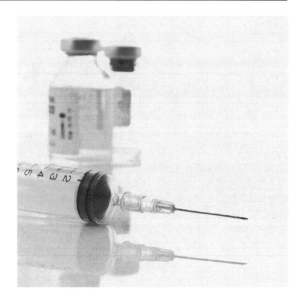

At the end of the story, a needle is pressed into Mary's flesh, suggesting that she must be sedated before they can start the procedure.
(© patpitchaya | Shutterstock.com)

Source: David Kelly, Critical Essay on "The Beautiful People," in *Short Stories for Students*, Gale, Cengage Learning, 2015.

Kat Clay

In the following essay, Clay examines Beaumont's contributions to weird fiction and regrets his early death and the lack of his work available in print.

Forget shagging backpackers and pot smoking fogies, the Abbey of St. Wulfran's is quite possibly the worst literary hostel in the world. Set in a picturesque German valley, the Abbey boasts dirty floors, straw beds and eccentric monks who refuse to answer your most basic questions. Stay for long enough and you might hear the howls of the Abbey's longest residing guest . . .

In Charles Beaumont's "The Howling Man," a Bostonian named David Ellington bicycles his way across Europe during the inter-war period. In Germany he falls ill and is taken to a monastery where a "howling man" is locked in a prison. While the monks tell him not to release the man because he is the Devil, the man cries that it is only because of his sexual transgressions that he has been imprisoned. The young man is faced with a crisis of conscience;

CHARLES BEAUMONT'S IDEAS WERE WELL
AHEAD OF HIS TIME; HIS OTHER STORIES INCLUDED
PROGRESSIVE IDEAS ON HOMOSEXUALITY, GAY
MARRIAGE AND RACISM."

does he release him or do nothing, which would surely mean the man's death?

"The Howling Man" is an effort to come to terms with the individual's role in releasing evil into the world, using weird elements to explain the rise of Hitler in Europe. Beaumont, an existential Christian, plots a thinly veiled allegory of the Christian account of creation, where sin enters the world due to the temptation of man by the devil. Ellington's desire for the knowledge of good and evil is his downfall; in doing a perceived good he brings evil into the world. It is a perfect illustration of the adage that the "road to hell is paved with good intentions."

Beaumont sets up the allegory by establishing pre-war Germany as Eden. His casual account of bicycling through Belgium and Germany draws the reader in like a travelogue. It's almost pleasant: "The Germany of that time was a land of valleys and mountains and swift dark rivers, a green and fertile land where everything grew tall and straight out of the earth."

The story is permeated by a sense of nostalgia for the pre-World War Two Germany. Beaumont begins the story by referring to "The Germany of that time," and he later writes, "I feel it's quite important to remember how completely Paradisical [sic] the land was then." Beaumont equates pre-war Germany with a fairy tale paradise; he refers to his crossing of the Belgium-German border as moving through an "invisible door, into a kingdom of winds and light." Yet post-war Germany will never return to that beauty; like Eden, the garden has been spoiled by sin.

Why did Beaumont choose historical Germany for his setting and not a futuristic world like many of his other stories? Was it to make a very clear point about his opinions on World War Two? It's difficult to speculate where

Beaumont developed his pacifist ideals. During the war years Beaumont was a bedridden teenager with spinal meningitis and he spent this time discovering science fiction. Despite having a clearly anti-war agenda in his stories, he enlisted in the army in 1947, but was discharged after three months for medical reasons. Science-fiction and war became inseparable for Beaumont. "The Beautiful People" opens with a young woman watching television in a waiting room:

> Mary sat quietly and watched the handsome man's legs blown off; watched further as the great ship began to crumple and break into small pieces in the middle of the blazing night. She fidgeted slightly as the men and the parts of the men came floating dreamily through the wreckage out into the awful silence. And when the meteorite shower came upon the men, gouging holes through everything, tearing flesh and ripping bones, Mary closed her eyes.

In "Elegy," a group of desperate spacemen seeks refuge in a galactic cemetery, only to be refused by the groundskeeper on the basis of their violence and prejudice.

> When from the moment of your departure you had wars of your own, and killed, and hurled mocking prejudice against a race of people not like you, a race who rejected and cast you out into space again!

It's not surprising then that Beaumont's twist is that the released "man" becomes Hitler.

> When the pictures of the carpenter from Braunau-am-Inn began to appear in all the papers, I grew uneasy; for I felt I'd seen this man before. When the carpenter invaded Poland, I was sure. And when the world was plunged into war and cities had their entrails blown asunder and that pleasant land I'd visited became a place of hate and death, I dreamed each night.

Hitler is the embodiment of the Devil, the serpent that tempts David Ellington to release him into the world.

"The Howling Man" is not the only weird story to attribute the Nazis' power to supernatural forces; more recent incarnations include *Raiders of the Lost Ark* and Mike Mignola's *Hellboy* comics. It would be easier to blame Hitler's actions on a supernatural, demonic power, because explanations of his behavior would then be beyond human comprehension. Sadly, Hitler was but a man, indicative of the extreme depths of human perversion, the horrors that only man is capable of.

While there are no women in the story, except for the reminiscences of the Abbot, sexual transgression becomes a metaphor for Eve. Although the original Creation story does not explicitly reference sex as a temptation, countless historical reinterpretations have associated Eve with the femme fatale and temptress archetypes.

"The Howling Man" was written for *Rogue*, and many of Beaumont's short stories were published in men's magazines such as *Playboy* and *Esquire*. His short stories often contain underlying sexual themes. Yet Beaumont seems to be advocating Christian morals in a pornographic magazine. Is Beaumont preaching? Or was he simply approaching the available markets at the time for science fiction and horror?

In "The Howling Man" the narrator dreams of *bagnios* filled with Islamic virgins (*houris*). It's not clear which definition of *bagnio* Beaumont meant; it could either be a bath-house, prison or brothel, but either way it sounds like an exotic fantasy.

It is Ellington's erotic desires that lead him to Paris and straight to the red light district of the Rue Pigalle. He only lasts a month before his health wanes and he decides that the celibate solitude of riding a bicycle across Europe is the antidote for any sexually (or otherwise) induced illnesses.

Sexual transgressions are the reason that the locked up man gives for his imprisonment:

> I was in the village, lying with my woman, when their crazy Abbot burst into the house and hit me with his heavy cross... I have sinned but who has not? With my woman, quietly, alone with my woman, my love.

It is his own experiences with sex that make Ellington empathize with the imprisoned man and not the monks. The Abbot is aware of Ellington's beliefs and elaborates on what outsiders often think of the clergy. "Monks are misfits, neurotics, sexual frustrates and aberrants. They retreat from the world because they cannot cope with the world."

Ellington remains suspicious of the Abbot, simply because a man cannot possibly be normal if he is celibate. Yet the monk's argument for containing the "Howling Man" is that their village was turned into "a resort for the sinful" after World War One, associating sexual impropriety with war. "Forsaken, fornicators paraded the streets," and "The orgies were too wild, the drunkards much too drunk." The Abbot attributes this change not to man but the very presence of the Devil. This echoes the Biblical post-sin world, where God sent a flood to destroy the corruption on Earth, indicating that this release and recapturing of the Devil goes in cycles.

In an effort to exorcise the Devil from the village, the Abbot was tempted by a woman in a passage rife with sexual innuendo:

> He said his wife was dying and begged me to give her Extreme Unction... A woman lay upon a bed, her body nude. "It is a different Extreme Unction that I have in mind," he [the Devil] whispered, laughing. "It's the only kind, dear Father, that she understands. No other will have her! Pity! Pity on the poor soul lying there in all her suffering. Give her your Sceptre!" And the woman's arms came snaking, supplicating toward me, round and sensuous and hot...

Of course, the principle of Occam's Razor applies; if caught between a man claiming he was locked up unfairly for sex outside of marriage and an Abbot claiming he's captured the Devil incarnate... it's no wonder Ellington decides to release the Devil.

Brother Christophorus represents Christ, and the story takes on the tone of a morality tale when Ellington's refusal to believe results in the Devil entering the world. Brother Christophorus, like Christ, is forgiving of Ellington's mistakes.

After Ellington realizes the consequences of his choices, Brother Christophorus says, "My son, don't blame yourself. Your weakness was *his* lever. Doubt unlocked the door."

The young man's weakness? Sympathy, induced by mutual understanding and empathy for sexual transgressions.

Michel Foucault in the *History of Sexuality* argues that sexuality, while not the most important factor in power, is the most flexible. It is "useful for the greatest number of manoeuvres and capable of serving as a point of support, as a lynchpin, for the most varied strategies." And such is the Devil's nature, to use any sort of power to strategize his escape. Sexuality is a "dense transfer point for relations of power," particularly between priests and their laity. The priest is able to resist sexual temptations, making him a morally superior person, but as David

Ellington is not a particularly religious man, the Abbot has no power over him.

Despite writing prolifically, Beaumont's books are now out of print and only a few short stories are available on e-readers. His *Twilight Zone* scripts remain in various formats; from 1960 *The Twilight Zone* won three consecutive Hugos for Best Dramatic Presentation. In these years Beaumont contributed at least 15 scripts. Although Beaumont did not write the script, "Number 12 Looks Just Like You" was based on "The Beautiful People." Sadly, Beaumont contracted either early-onset Alzheimer's disease or Pick's disease in his thirties, rapidly decreasing his mental faculties. Many of his friends ghostwrote his later credited *Twilight Zone* scripts to help him meet his commitments.

Due to his untimely death at the age of 38, Charles Beaumont does not receive the same recognition as his contemporaries Richard Matheson and Ray Bradbury. Bradbury commented that because Beaumont died before the moon landing, he wasn't able to promote himself in the way that other science fiction writers did (p19, Prosser).

Charles Beaumont's ideas were well ahead of his time; his other stories included progressive ideas on homosexuality, gay marriage and racism. His stories are often about people standing up for what they believe in, but with the consequences of their integrity being negative. While somewhat neglected as a writer, his stories are important in the timeline of weird fiction, for their progressive content and their significant role in contributing to *The Twilight Zone*.

"The Howling Man" is a warning that one man's good intentions can wreak havoc on the world. But if all we aspire is to be good without heeding the advice of others, we cannot help but release the devil.

Source: Kat Clay, "The Nature of Evil in 'The Howling Man,'" in *Weird Fiction Review*, October 23, 2012.

Publishers Weekly

In the following review, an anonymous writer describes Beaumont's stories as enjoyable, if somewhat dated.

While Beaumont may be best remembered for his contributions to *The Twilight Zone*, he also produced a considerable number of short stores that crossed a spectrum of genres, from horror and dark fantasy to more traditional noir and mystery fiction. Twelve of the 13 stories in this collection have never been published before. "Adam's Off Ox" is a folksy tall tale combining a deal-with-the-devil plot with a surprising take on the origin of Paul Bunyan and his blue ox, Babe. In "The Junemoon Spoon," the citizens of a small country town collude to take revenge on a sleazy traveling salesman. With "A Long Way from Capri," "Lachrymosa," "The Rival" and "A Friend of the Family," Beaumont uses romantic twist endings to heal his characters' wounded hearts. "Time and Again" and "The Indian Piper" are also gentle stories of healing, though without the romance. In "Moon in Gemini," a young woman's fears for her unborn baby rapidly turn to dangerous paranoia, while "Resurrection Island" will appeal to fans of pulp adventure. Although no dates are given to any of these stories, all betray their age with their old-fashioned sensibility. Fans of Beaumont's writing are sure to enjoy this collection, however.

Source: Review of *A Touch of the Creature*, in *Publishers Weekly*, Vol. 246, No. 39, September 27, 1999, p. 78.

SOURCES

Abramson, Albert, *The History of Television, 1942 to 2000*, McFarland, 2003, p. 18.

Anker, Roger, Introduction to *Charles Beaumont: Selected Stories*, Dark Harvest, 1988, pp. 11–19.

Beaumont, Charles, "The Beautiful People," in *Yonder: Stories of Fantasy and Science Fiction*, Bantam Books, 1958, pp. 134–48.

Isaacs, Jeremy, and Taylor Downing, *Cold War: An Illustrated History, 1945–1991*, Little, Brown, 1998, pp. 113–16.

"Korean War," History Channel website, 2014, http://www.history.com/topics/korean-war (accessed August 29, 2014).

Mathur, Aparna, Hao Fu, and Peter Hansen, "The Mysterious and Alarming Rise of Single Parenthood in America," in *Atlantic*, September 3, 2013, http://www.theatlantic.com/business/archive/2013/09/the-mysterious-and-alarming-rise-of-single-parenthood-in-america/279203/ (accessed August 27, 2014).

Nickerson, Susan L., Review of *Best of Beaumont*, in *Library Journal*, December 15, 1982, p. 2355.

O'Dell, Cary, "Kinescope," Museum of Broadcast Communications website, http://www.museum.tv/eotv/kinescope.htm (accessed August 29, 2014).

Phillips, Robert R., "First-Hand: Bing Crosby and the Recording Revolution," IEEE Global History Network website, 2014, http://www.ieeeghn.org/wiki/index.php/First-Hand:Bing_Crosby_and_the_Recording_Revolution (accessed August 29, 2014).

Pronzini, Bill, "Charles Beaumont," in *Twentieth-Century Science-Fiction Writers*, 2nd ed., edited by Curtis C. Smith, St. James Press, 1986, p. 44.

Wetzel, James R., "American Families: 75 Years of Change," in *Monthly Labor Review*, March 1990, p. 5, http://www.bls.gov/mlr/1990/03/art1full.pdf (accessed August 27, 2014).

FURTHER READING

Jones, Darryll, Bernice M. Murphy, and Elizabeth McCarthy, *It Came from the 1950s! Popular Culture*, Palgrave Macmillan, 2011.

In this book, the editors blend together the anxieties that made the 1950s such a fertile ground for science-fiction writers like Beaumont. Fear of nuclear devastation, fear of scientific overreach, fear of psychiatry, and social engineering are all parts of what makes "The Beautiful People" work.

McGee, Glenn, *The Perfect Baby: A Pragmatic Approach to Genetics*, Rowman & Littlefield Publishers, 1996.

In common, readable language, this book explores some of the ethical questions that are only hinted at in "The Beautiful People," the main one being, What if science *could* assure physical perfection for people? Who would it be for? Who would it be required for? The question of eugenics is often considered to be a trespass into God's terrain, but with each scientific advance, humanity comes closer.

Packard, Vance, *The Hidden Persuaders*, Ig Publishing, 2007.

Originally published in 1957, Packard's book is a milestone in explaining the techniques that advertisers around the time of this story's publication used to alter the perceptions and needs of the unsuspecting populace.

Prosser, Lee, *Running from the Hunter: The Life and Works of Charles Beaumont*, Borgo Press, 2010.

This biography of Beaumont is short—under 150 pages—but is considered thorough and accurate in its research. The book includes a bibliography and an index to aid those studying Beaumont's life and works.

Wolf, Naomi, *The Beauty Myth: How Images of Beauty Are Used against Women*, Harper Perennial, 2002.

When this book was first published in 1990, it created a firestorm of controversy. Wolf's reputation as a scholar has since grown. Women's inclusion in more and more professions is evidence that her ideas of what society expects women to look like have kept her argument relevant.

SUGGESTED SEARCH TERMS

Charles Beaumont

Charles Beaumont AND The Beautiful People

Charles Beaumont AND The Beautiful People AND psychiatry

Charles Beaumont AND The Beautiful People AND government

Charles Beaumont AND 1950s science fiction

science fiction AND self image

Charles Beaumont AND futurism

Charles Beaumont AND plastic surgery

Charles Beaumont AND The Beautiful People AND perfection

Charles Beaumont AND Yonder

Brothers Are the Same

BERYL MARKHAM

1945

"Brothers Are the Same," a story attributed to the part-rustic, part-cosmopolitan English author Beryl Markham, draws on her experience growing up in Kenya to portray the drama of a young Masai warrior's rite of initiation. By virtue of the relatively temperate climate and fertile soils of the central highlands, Kenya became a popular destination for enterprising early twentieth-century British colonials, who procured land and ran farms or other businesses. Other than former soldiers, most colonials, including Markham's father, paid the British Crown for their land, but this is not to say that it was justly obtained in the first place, and nearly all of them enjoyed the cheap domestic services of a subjugated native population. Additional Westerners made the trip to Kenya to be led by white guides on big-game hunts, with the Swahili word *safari*, meaning "journey," subsequently entering the English lexicon. A fair deal of literature came out of this pocket of the colonial world, including novels, short stories, and nonfiction by the likes of Karen Blixen, Ernest Hemingway, Elspeth Huxley, and Markham.

"Brothers Are the Same" was written in 1944, by which time was Markham was living in California with her third husband, Raoul Schumacher, who was a writer. The two are known to have collaborated on works published under Markham's name, and Schumacher is understood to have played a significant role in

Aviator Beryl Markham in 1936
(© *Everett Collection Inc.* / *Alamy*)

the production of this story. From the outset, the reader is immersed in the world of a Masai, or Maasai, youth named Temas, who is on the verge of becoming a warrior but first must face a lion—as well as his fears of failing while his rival, Medoto, looks on. The story was first published in *Collier's Weekly* on February 24, 1945, and was later collected in *The Splendid Outcast: Beryl Markham's African Stories* (1987).

AUTHOR BIOGRAPHY

Markham was born on October 26, 1902, in the village of Ashwell, Rutland, England, with the last name Clutterbuck; she was not christened Beryl until a month and a half later. She had a brother who was two years older. Her father was running a farm, and both parents enjoyed fox hunting, such that from infancy Beryl became familiar with the sounds, smells, and nearness of horses. When she was two her father, Charles Clutterbuck, set out for South Africa, looking to make his fortune as a colonial, but he was instead drawn to what was then

called British East Africa. He gained a job as a cattle manager under the famous Lord Delamere, whose estate remains a major dairy farm. Clutterbuck erected a home in Njoro, near Nakuru, northwest of Nairobi, and his family joined him in late 1905; but his social-butterfly wife, Clara, and now-sickly son, Richard, returned to England in 1906, leaving Beryl and her father behind.

Beryl's childhood was one of profound freedom from discipline or restrictions. Her father was busy establishing his own farm, so she was raised by the Africans he employed, allowing her to learn various tribes' customs and languages, especially those of the Nandi. She spent a great deal of her time hunting barefoot in the Rongai Valley, gradually learning the ways of her instructors and being permitted to wield a spear. On the Clutterbuck farm, Beryl began to help exercise and train the racehorses that her father bred on the side, as Kenya already had a burgeoning racing culture. She proved especially good with the wildest and most challenging horses. Meanwhile, indoors at night, her father read to her from the Greek classics. She was assigned governesses and tutors—many of whom did not last long, and all of whom were reluctantly tolerated—but when World War I started, she was sent to a boarding school in Nairobi. After three years, she was expelled for trying to incite a student revolt.

At age sixteen Beryl was married to a farmer twice her age, Jock Purves, and soon after, her father went bankrupt and left the country. She took up horse training as a profession and, at the age of twenty-three, trained a winner of the annual St. Leger. She soon divorced and then married a wealthy aristocrat, Mansfield Markham, with whom she would bear a son, Gervaise, and whose name she would retain for life. Captivated by developments in air travel, Markham soon took lessons and became an aviatrix, offering her services to paying clients, lost airmen needing to be found, and those with medical needs. Her daring feats included a cross-country night run to bring oxygen to an imperiled miner, with nary an electric light to be found along the way and the landing strip marked only by oil-rag torches. She also flew big-game hunters out to find their victims. Her most famous flight would be her transatlantic journey from England to North America in 1936, the first nonstop solo flight by a woman west across the Atlantic.

In 1939, after some traveling, Markham ended up in the United States, where she would join Raoul Schumacher, her eventual third husband, and live in California. By 1941, Markham was producing the book that would make her literary reputation, *West with the Night* (1942), a memoir that uses her career as an aviatrix as a framework for delving into her experiences in Kenya. In writing and editing the book, she gained assistance from her husband. According to testimony from acquaintances of Schumacher's, Markham actually did not write her memoir at all, but only outlined or recited stories that her husband turned into literature. There are similar questions about the short stories published under her name, including "Brothers Are the Same," which appeared in *Collier's Weekly* in 1945. By 1948, Markham and Schumacher were separating, and, after Markham managed to publish a story edited for her by another writer friend, Stuart Cloete, whatever else she wrote without any assistance was definitively rejected by her publisher. The following year, Markham returned to Kenya, where she would build up a revived career as a horse trainer, producing more than twenty winners of the Kenyan classics. When Kenya gained independence, she shifted her life and career to South Africa for over a dozen years, returning to Kenya in 1970. Throughout, she continued to live as freely, sometimes recklessly, as she always had. At the age of eighty-three, after breaking her leg in a fall and undergoing surgery, Markham died in Nairobi on August 4, 1986.

PLOT SUMMARY

"Brothers Are the Same" opens by describing the people of the Masai ethnic group, from the Serengeti Plain, in southern Kenya and northern Tanzania. To become full-fledged warriors, each young Masai man must pass a test by confronting a lion. During the dry season, just before dawn, sixteen-year-old Temas lies in a rock cleft waiting for the lion he and his ten companions have tracked to awaken. His companions are spread out nearby.

Temas is less nervous about the lion than about the possibility of failing his test, as Medoto, his rival for a girl's affection, is among his companions and is surely hoping for his failure. If

MEDIA ADAPTATIONS

A facsimile of the original *Collier's Weekly* publication of the story is available at http://www. unz.org/Pub/Colliers-1945feb24. The story's opening, p. 22, is found under "Brothers Are the Same," but the remainder, pp. 70–72, can be found under the later article "Anthropological Katie."

Temas falls short in his performance, his failure will follow him for the rest of his life, especially with Medoto around to report it. Temas considers his armament: a spear, a short sword in his belt, and a rawhide shield. When light strikes the thicket in the ravine, the lion will awaken.

Temas frets; all his companions have already passed their tests. He wonders if the girls will ever chant in his honor, especially Kileghen—but he gets angry after thinking of her, when he meant not to. She and Medoto sang to each other the night before. Temas remembers having been ceremonially given his spear, when Medoto had laughed and disparaged him, with Kileghen watching; for Temas the moment had been ruined.

The lion awakens and sniffs the air, picking up the scent of humans. He looks carefully out of his lair and sees Temas, who has also risen. Silence reigns as Temas awaits his comrades, who should now be leaping out to flush the lion his way. He remembers the rules of combat for facing a lion, though not all of them because he is distracted by his fear of failure. No longer believing in himself, he starts trembling.

His companions leap from their cover, shouting, and encircle the lion, with Temas standing opposite the lion, while Medoto is behind him to one side. Uncertain, conscious of Medoto's judging eyes, Temas fails to advance and draw a charge. The lion thus ignores him and prepares to leap instead at the more imposing Casaro. Temas is secretly relieved, and Casaro prepares to meet the lion's charge; but from behind Temas, a thrown pebble strikes the lion, who is infuriated and—not realizing Medoto was responsible—turns and charges at Temas.

Temas, suddenly transformed into a man, meets the charge but spears only the lion's shoulder, and his spear and shield are torn away from him. Taken down, the lion's teeth sunk into his thigh, Temas feels himself being dragged away—but after a moment he wields his sword and slices at the lion, who drops him. After a dust-clouded confrontation, Temas is the one left standing.

The comrades cheer for Temas, who smiles broadly. But he realizes that Medoto knows that had the stone not been thrown, he would have failed. Temas imagines Medoto's barbed thoughts, and as the others bear the lion off, Temas lingers and confronts Medoto, grasping his sword and insisting he will not put up with any jeering. Medoto waits, laughs, and then drops his spear and shield. He tells Temas that he, too, felt cowardly and weak during his trial, and he does not blame Temas for trembling. He threw the stone because he felt compassion for Temas.

Now only the vision of the girl lies between the two. But Medoto withdraws from his *shuka* a belt made by Kileghen, who told Medoto to give it to Temas if he proved brave, but to keep it if he failed. Medoto gives Temas the belt. But Temas, declaring that they are now brothers and that "brothers are the same," cuts the belt in half and entwines the two halves in their respective armbands. Temas declares that Kileghen, who as a woman cannot judge warriors, will have to choose between them some other way.

The two boys return home singing arm in arm. At their *manyatta*, or village encampment, everyone cheers, and Temas is brought to the *singara*, the warriors' place, with Medoto remaining by his side. Kileghen, watching, is curious about the division of her belt between the swaggering young men. She frowns, but then she smiles, as if in triumph more than wonder.

CHARACTERS

Casaro

One among the ten companions who help bring about the confrontation between Temas and the lion, Casaro is already a seasoned warrior, and thus for a moment, the lion sees fit to charge at him rather than the nearer but unintimidating Temas.

Kileghen

Though she scarcely appears in the story, Kileghen's role is crucial because of Temas and Medoto's rivalry for her affection. Temas is befuddled by the fact that she seems to vacillate between the two of them. She smiled ambiguously after Medoto made fun of Temas upon his receipt of his spear, and worse, just the night before, she and Medoto sang songs to each other, making Temas jealous. Nonetheless, curiously, Kileghen seems to favor Temas but tests Medoto, rather, by making him the bearer of her gift, giving him the chance to either honor Temas's bravery or elect to keep the belt for himself. When the two young men reappear after the lion hunt each bearing half of the belt, she is at first consternated, but then something about the circumstance leaves her smiling, as if she, or the two boys, or all of them have somehow triumphed.

The Lion

Greatly personified, the lion in this story is not just the proverbial king of the jungle but is given the character of and specifically described as a tyrant: he is said to harbor fearless disdain for all who might challenge him, including the men now gathered about his lair. The lion hesitates as neither Temas nor anyone else acts in aggression, but finally he prepares to charge Casaro—until the thrown stone irks him into a charge at Temas. The lion's impulse to carry Temas off before actually killing him proves his undoing, as it leaves Temas the chance to wield his sword.

Medoto

In Temas's mind, at least, Medoto is a sworn enemy, and their rivalry has shown itself in Medoto's occasionally caustic remarks. The other Masai in their community, including the young women, have sung songs about Medoto, who has already passed his test of warriorhood. Established as a cold-hearted villain by Temas's fears and expectations, Medoto proves otherwise when he congratulates and supports Temas rather than condemning him for nearly bowing to his fear upon confronting the lion. Medoto's throwing the rock was in fact a virtuous gesture, meant to ensure that Temas did not fail in the eyes of their comrades and community. In the end, Medoto and Temas are so close that they are like brothers.

Temas

The hero of the story, Temas is at first greatly concerned that he will prove no such thing, as lying in wait for the lion leaves his thoughts circling inexorably back to his fear of failure. Indeed, it appears that Temas is more concerned about his enemy Medoto's presence than about the lion's. When the confrontation with the lion finally comes about, Temas's fear (whatever kind it may be) gets the better of him, freezing him in place, and if not for Medoto's gesture, he would have failed through inaction, letting another man take the lion's charge in his place.

Once the lion does charge Temas, he is suddenly transformed into a warrior, fighting through his wounds and whatever pain he must be feeling to at last slay the lion. This success emboldens him to challenge Medoto about the possibility of being ridiculed, but when Medoto's own motivations prove noble, Temas is stirred to sympathetic appreciation. He divides the gift from Kileghen, declares Medoto his brother, and shares in the glory of the kill—and the glory of Kileghen's attention—with his newfound friend.

THEMES

African Culture

"Brothers Are the Same" makes a point of not just being set within an African culture, that of the Masai, but being about that culture. The opening paragraph has the ring of an ethnographic study, broadly characterizing the type of the Masai men by way of genealogical suppositions. Also appearing prominently in the story are descriptions of the characters' clothing, jewelry, and armaments, as well as their hunting behavior—such as the encirclement of the lion and the posture adopted by both Temas and Casaro upon facing the lion, down on one knee. Above all, the emotional drama that the story hinges on is specific to the Masai rite of passage of killing a lion, with the way that rite plays out for Temas being the crux of the tale. From whatever source the author derived the knowledge of Masai culture drawn on to write the story, it has been given the feel of an authentic Masai experience.

Masculinity

In any culture where physical force has come into play with regard to the culture's survival, one can expect to find manifestations and considerations of masculinity. That is, as long as it is perceived to be ideal for the boys of a culture to gain the physical prowess and confrontational attitude necessary for attacking and defending against physical threats, the culture will encourage, perhaps even demand the development of such traditionally masculine traits. In the modern era, many would rightfully argue that just because a woman possesses or gains such traits does not mean she is "masculine," but the traditional roles of the sexes are more a matter of biology than of patriarchy: on average, testosterone-fueled men have physically larger and thus stronger frames, while women, with their bodies governed more by estrogen, have evolved not to fight but to produce, feed, and care for healthy babies.

In a traditional culture such as that of the Masai, gender roles are likely to be more pronounced, as the survival of the community still depends heavily on physical prowess—if not to attack other communities, then to manage such predators as the lion—and on successful reproduction and child rearing. Thus, as the story communicates, the pivotal moment in the life of a Masai male is his test of warriorhood, his chance to prove his merit in battle by conquering a lion. For Temas, however, this test does not concern him as much as another perceived test of masculinity: the test of winning the affection of a female.

Affection

In this story, love is suggested to be an even more powerful force than the fight-or-flight instincts that kick in whenever a situation of extreme threat is encountered. As the coming fight will make perfectly clear, there is a reasonable chance that Temas could be killed in his encounter with the lion, and yet somehow—hormones, it seems, must take the blame—his mind is more occupied with the possibility that failure will result in his being rejected by the girl he holds so much affection for, Kileghen. Affection between teenagers can indeed be a stressful issue, as the excitement of flirtation can easily be mistaken for burgeoning love, by both participants and observers. Kileghen has every right to smile at and sing with whomever she chooses, but Temas (naturally) blows this out

TOPICS FOR FURTHER STUDY

- Read one of the other stories in the collection *The Splendid Outcast: Beryl Markham's African Stories*, and be sure to also read Mary S. Lovell's introduction to the story. For extra background, seek mention of the story you chose in one or more Markham biography. Write an essay in which you compare and contrast the styles of this story and "Brothers Are the Same" and the circumstances in which they were composed, concluding with a statement on whether or not the stories ring true for you.

- Research the Masai people and their culture, consulting at least two print sources, and then write a short story set in a Masai community. Post your story online, and ask your classmates to comment on how well you have reflected Masai culture. Then add your own comment discussing how successful you think your story is in this respect.

- Read *Call on the Wind* (2007), a young-adult novel by South African author David Donald that explores the affections between two youths in a small Griqua fishing village, with Isaak unsure whether to become a traveling musician or stay with Liesa and help his community survive. After reading, write an essay in which you discuss the sense of community in this novel and in "Brothers Are the Same," where the male Masai youths are expected to become warriors. Compare how successfully the communities sustain themselves as well as how much they allow for individual freedom.

- Investigate other literary representations that might be classed as those of "noble savages," and also consult at least one critical work on the so-called stereotype. Then write a personal reflection paper on what you perceive in the representation in general and in "Brothers Are the Same" in particular.

- Research the behavior, social groupings, and habitat of the African lion, and create either a poster project or a website presenting what you have learned, using text as well as photos, illustrations, charts, graphs, and other visuals to convey your acquired knowledge. Include a portion of text discussing the accuracy of the portrayal of the lion's behavior in "Brothers Are the Same."

---

of proportion in his mind, imagining that she is practically teasing him through her interaction with Medoto. This leads Temas to feel a very masculine "fury," which is to say that, incited by a rival, he has ruffled his feathers in irritation and might feel like puffing up his chest and crowing—except his low self-esteem, stemming merely from his youth (the fact that he has not passed his warriorhood test yet) and especially his uncertainty about Kileghen, leaves him doubtful of his self-worth. Thus, where the trial is meant to be one in which he proves his masculinity, he is being sabotaged not by a lack of masculinity but by his own affections: he overthinks his relation to Kileghen, and his energies are redirected away from the present and back into his uncertain adolescent mind.

Friendship
The moment after the battle with the lion in which Temas divides the belt from Kileghen shows that he has conquered the waywardness of his affections and is standing firm on the masculine ground he has just established for himself. This is somewhat unexpected, because the most "masculine" thing to do would have been to proudly claim the belt and the woman as well; but Medoto has softened Temas's heart by demonstrating brotherly affection for the initiated warrior. He possesses knowledge that

The story takes place on the Serengeti plain. (© *Gary C. Tognoni* / *Shutterstock.com*)

could ruin Temas, and he might even be able to avail himself of this knowledge to win the affections of Kileghen. However, Medoto seems to determine that, as a colloquial (and superficially sexist) modern saying suggests, companionship between brothers—whether of blood or of experience—should take priority over potential romantic partners. This formulation is often crudely applied, but the ideology behind it is borne out in the present story: with his thoughts dwelling on a woman even at the onset of potentially fatal battle with a fierce animal, Temas with his trembling hands not only nearly gets himself killed, but also puts Casaro's life in danger—though it seems the seasoned warrior would have been able to handle the lion's charge. Still, the point is that in the heat of battle, all of one's thoughts must be focused on the matter at hand, not just for one's own sake but for the sake of one's comrades in arms. In the end, with what is both an individual and a collective victory for the young Masai, Medoto and Temas are not just friends but are as good as brothers, and even Kileghen seems to appreciate that this friendship is, in its way, as valuable as a romantic relationship, if not more so. Romance allows for a community's survival into the future, but the friendship that binds the members of that community can be essential for the survival of one and all.

STYLE

Moral Dilemmas

"Brothers Are the Same" can be seen to revolve around a series of moral dilemmas. The most prominent dilemma is the one that the protagonist, Temas, faces after Medoto has presented him with the belt made by Kileghen as a gift for the bravest warrior, whoever he might be. Medoto judges Temas to be that man, and so he gallantly hands over the belt. Thus must Temas ask himself, What do I do with this belt? If he simply accepts it, he may feel he has wronged Medoto by unjustly taking full credit for proving his masculinity and killing the lion; if he turns the belt down, he will feel that his genuine accomplishment of slaying the lion will go unrecognized, and more importantly, he will lose Kileghen's hand. He resolves this dilemma by creating a third path that leads to an ending that can be satisfactory all around, for the time being, at least: the two youths share the belt, and Kileghen's judgment is deferred to another, hopefully less ambiguous day. In such two-pronged dilemmas, it is often an unexpected third solution that resolves the matter; certain choices may be presented as the only alternatives, but the open mind, thinking outside the box, may come up with a better one.

Interestingly, there are two other dilemmas behind this one, neither of which is quite as apparent simply because the protagonist is not the one who faces it; rather, they are Medoto's dilemmas. First, witnessing Temas's trial unfold, Medoto must choose whether or not to help his foe, when failing to help or perhaps even hindering Temas could lead to his winning Kileghen's affections for himself. Virtuously, Medoto helps Temas by throwing the rock. Second, after Temas slays the lion, Medoto can choose between wielding the knowledge that Temas flinched for his own designs, or hailing Temas as a true warrior. Again, he makes the virtuous choice, being truthful about his own hesitations and making Temas not a hated enemy but a brother in arms. In consequence, Temas repays the kindness.

Romanticism

Romanticism has its foundation in eighteenth-century literature giving pride of place to the authors' or characters' emotional lives, the sensibility of common people, and the beauty of nature. Markham would generally not be called a romantic writer; her admired book *West with the Night* is notable not only for a strain of existential philosophizing that is no stranger to romanticism, but also for the levelheadedness with which some fairly heart-stopping stories are told, such as the time she was attacked by a pet lion. The lion's approach is described as follows: "I cannot say that there was any menace in his eyes, because there wasn't, or that his 'frightful jowls' were drooling, because they were handsome jowls and very tidy." This, of course, is a memoir, and one who keeps an even keel in nonfiction may be nonetheless inclined to wax romantic in fiction.

"Brothers Are the Same" speaks of the Masai people, their way of life, and the thoughts and actions of the people in the story in such a way that the Masai are ennobled beyond their immediate existence through reference to distant history, the complexity of their sentiments, and the gravity of their actions. The Masai are, in a word, romanticized. There are both positive and negative aspects to such a portrayal. On the positive side, the story itself is intensified and made more dramatic by the romanticizing references, something the casual reader is likely to appreciate. The Masai are increased in stature—in a Westerner's eyes, at least—by being compared in physiognomy to the ancient Egyptians and Greeks, whose cultures have long been romanticized through combinations of adulatory history and piquant fiction; Cleopatra and Helen of Troy come to mind. In this story, a few lines in particular—like "They are the Masai," "once they were warriors and they have not forgotten that," and "legend said that no Masai had ever feared"—serve to put the tribe on a pedestal when the story has hardly begun. This admiration extends to the individual characters, who carry the connotations of their people. While the Masai broadly are romanticized in an idealizing way, the individual characters, in the first half of the story at least, are romanticized rather in dramatic ways, which is to say that their emotional aspects are enlarged and centered on, their concerns magnified, as if amounting to forces of nature. Such dramatization can indeed enhance the feel of a narrative.

Romanticizing can have negative aspects as well. For example, in Markham's story, where it is noted that Kileghen is "rightly named after the star Venus," this might seem romantic at first glance, but of course there is no reason to believe that the Masai name for Venus carries the connotations of the Western name for it. Since the name *Venus* means something only for the narrator and reader, not for the characters, it loses most of its significance. A more general problem is that characters and acts can be romanticized to such a degree that the authenticity of a story is cast into doubt, such as through improbably valiant acts or virtuous persons or noble thoughts. Romanticization of American Indians, for example, has led to skepticism, whether justified or not, whenever a "noble savage" is encountered in literature.

Only the individual reader can decide whether Markham has crossed such a line in this story, such as where Temas, having "felt the fangs tear loose the flesh of his thigh, freeing it, freeing him"—that is, having had a chunk of his leg bitten off—proceeds to make his way home on foot without having even bandaged what sounds like a gaping wound. A nitpicker might call such physical details into question, but the crux of the story is an emotional detail that may also leave the reader doubtful, namely, the complete reconciliation of two boys who had been portrayed as sworn enemies. This is believable enough, given the extraordinary circumstance that they have endured together, but it is curious how they both seem perfectly happy and at peace even while they continue to both hunger after Kileghen's affection—when they reach their *manyatta*, "both caught her glance and gave the question with their eyes." This provides for a dramatic final moment, but, given the intensity with which Temas's affection for Kileghen has been described—indirectly, his affection grips him even more than the immediate presence of a lion—it is difficult to imagine the boys' shared contentedness with their victorious friendship coexisting with their unfulfilled desire for the same young woman. That is, the friendship is inclusive, but the desire is exclusive—only one will see his desire fulfilled (presuming they both have honorable intentions), and so it is difficult to imagine them basking in that desire together nonetheless, as if actually indifferent to the outcome.

HISTORICAL CONTEXT

Kenya's White Settlers

Settlement of Kenya by white colonials began in the earliest years of the twentieth century. The British had arrived in the nineteenth century and by 1895 established the British East Africa Protectorate, with Uganda as well as Kenya falling under its control. To enable regular travel as far inland as Uganda, a railway was constructed stretching from Mombasa, on the Indian Ocean coast, to Kisumu, on the northeastern coast of Lake Victoria, at fair expense to British taxpayers—some 5.5 million pounds. To justify and perhaps recoup the costs of the project, finished in 1901, Britain aggressively encouraged white settlement. The Crown had simply claimed whatever land appeared not to be in use, ignoring the fact that the Kikuyu, for example, regularly shifted their agriculture to keep the soil healthy, meaning uninhabited land was not unclaimed. Nonetheless, the Crown rented out its newfound land to British settlers at low costs, through the Ordinance of 1902, with 160-acre allotments to be expanded if the land was developed. By April 1904, there were still only 130 settler farms—Markham's father arrived in July of that year—but a steady inflow would continue over the next decade.

At this time, Nairobi was still a minor stop on the railroad journey, on a plain where trains could stop to take on water. Nonetheless, horse racing was already an attraction, and there was even a newspaper, the *East African Standard*. In terms of mastering the land, Lord Delamere's struggles were emblematic of his fellow pioneers'. The first stretch of land he tried to graze cattle on had been dubbed by the Masai *angata natai emmin*, or "the plain of the female rhino without any milk" (cited in Elspeth Huxley's *Settlers of Kenya*); undernourished by what grew there, his imported sheep died of footrot, lung disease, intestinal worms, and other such ailments. Delamere next imported cattle, but for plowing he also brought oxen—which brought a virus, which killed many of the cattle; most of the rest were done in by diseases like red water and East Coast fever, transmitted by ticks. Delamere next tried growing an expansive crop of wheat, over some 1,200 acres, but wheat rust destroyed half and left the other half nearly worthless. Having already mortgaged his English estate several times over, Delamere persisted, employing a scientist to breed a rust-resistant strain of wheat. The colonial government eventually assumed this task, as new strains of rust constantly demanded new varieties of wheat. After years of failures, Delamere's efforts paid off. World War I slowed settlers' progress, as a majority of men volunteered to serve, but after the war, former soldiers were granted land, adding a thousand new farms.

Over the years, settler progress continued, at times haltingly, such as through an economic slump in 1921, a locust infestation from 1928 to 1931, and especially the Great Depression in the 1930s. Smaller farmers made profits through coffee, maize, and dairy works, while tea and sisal operations allowed larger companies to flourish. Additional rail lines were constructed, hospitals and schools were established for whites as well as native Africans, and Nairobi evolved into a modern city. Roads and cars eventually proliferated, and white settlers enjoyed horse racing, polo, and even golf in their spare time. White farmers' hard work and financial investments left them feeling that they had earned their pleasantly adventurous lives in Kenya. Markham, however, being raised in Kenya, came to ally herself with the native cultures to a far greater extent. As Mary S. Lovell says of Markham in introducing her short-story collection, "She became part of Africa and Africa became part of her."

The Masai

The Masai are perhaps the best known of all of East Africa's tribes, owing to the nobility of

COMPARE
&
CONTRAST

- **1940s:** In Kenya, under British rule, the Masai Mara National Reserve is formed, which nominally honors the Masai but which ultimately leads to their displacement from their few habitations on this large parcel of land—about 580 square miles—further confining them to limited territory.

  Today: Some 580 square miles of territory are slated to be taken from the Masai in the Serengeti in Tanzania for the benefit of a luxury safari company based in the United Arab Emirates, but domestic and international protests—including a global petition with more than 1.7 million signatures—help defeat the plan in 2013.

- **1940s:** Spread out among some two thousand white-owned farms, there are roughly eight thousand white agriculturists in Kenya. About 5 percent of Kenya's total land has been "alienated," or claimed by white colonials. Altogether there are some twenty-four thousand white people.

  Today: While Kenya reached a high of sixty thousand whites by the time of independence in 1963, the majority fled the country out of fear of what might have happened, with the Mau Mau rebellion of the 1950s fresh in their minds. Much of the whites' farmland ends up

back in the hands of native Kenyans, though expansive white-owned estates remain. In the twenty-first century, despite occasional violence related to terrorism or elections, the white population has climbed back up to thirty thousand.

- **1940s:** In 1941, the sensational murder of Lord Erroll, the figurehead of the "Happy Valley" set of hedonistic, drug-addled white swingers in Kenya, makes headlines. One man whose wife was having an affair with Lord Erroll is tried but acquitted for the murder, which goes unsolved.

  Today: In 2006, Tom Cholmondeley, who will inherit the title of Lord Delamere along with an estate covering about one hundred thousand acres of land, kills the second black African "trespasser" in as many years. The first was an undercover Masai game warden, and in the absence of hard evidence Cholmondeley was acquitted. The second, a stonemason, was reportedly poaching, but the impression that Cholmondeley has been killing blacks for sport helps lead to his conviction. Nonetheless, he is sentenced to only eight months' prison time and serves only five.

---

spirit evident in their picturesque stature and adherence to traditional ways. Even in the twenty-first century the Masai live much as they did centuries ago, in small, semipermanent villages used as bases for grazing livestock in the surrounding savannas. Perhaps the most significant difference is that in the past they in part secured their livelihood through cattle raids on neighboring tribes. The colonial government eventually forbade this practice, though such raids still occur in Kenya on occasion.

The thriving Masai culture was interrupted by the installation of the first rail line, as it

bisected their grazing lands and cut communities off from each other, with the British claiming all the land immediately adjacent to the railway. The Masai resisted by waging war against the whites, but, overmatched in terms of weaponry, they soon agreed to a peace treaty. A passageway between what were now the northern and southern reserves was promised, but fears of spreading cattle disease meant that this passageway never materialized. The reserves themselves, as cited in Errol Trzebinski's *The Kenya Pioneers*, were promised "so long as the Masai Race shall exist," but the British reneged on this agreement within

The brothers aspire to be Masai warriors.
(© Avatar_023 | Shutterstock.com)

a decade. Wishing to claim the rich pastureland of the northern reserve, Laikipia, against the wishes of the northern Masai, the colonial government recognized as paramount leader a southern spiritual figure who did wish to reunite the tribe, signed a treaty with him, and then undertook the removal of the northern Masai to the south. A first attempt occurred in 1911, but rains caused delays, many cattle died of disease, and many Masai died of cold; the government at last turned them back. The Masai then actually sued to remain in Laikipia, citing their original treaty, but the courts, citing the later treaty, dismissed the case. The northern Masai at last migrated south in 1912.

Aside from being contained within a strict reserve, whereas in the past their borders had fluctuated in accord with the activities of the *moran,* their warriors, the Masai now also found their cultural order disrupted. There had been a careful balance between ambitious warriors and reasonable elders, with prophets acting as mediating religious figures, but the colonial government's focus on centralized representation meant that the power of prophets increased, leaving warriors and elders alike with less influence. The colonial government intruded further by disrupting the initiation ceremony through which warriors committed to such aggressive acts as cattle raids. Elders proceeded to cooperate with the government, while the warriors resisted, continuing to conduct cattle raids despite the fines the elders were left to pay. This give-and-take would continue into the twenty-first century. The Masai yet manage to maintain traditions far more than most tribes, availing themselves of the land they have been left with to sustain their cattle while also fashioning traditional adornments not just for themselves but also for paying tourists.

CRITICAL OVERVIEW

The initial reception of the one volume Markham published during her lifetime, *West with the Night,* was highly positive; in the words of Diane Ackerman in the *New York Times,* "it was acclaimed by critics." The book nonetheless sank into the depths of cultural memory until, having been greatly praised by none other than Ernest Hemingway in a letter to his editor (Hemingway had met Markham while on a hunting safari in Kenya), the work was eventually brought to the attention of publishers and reissued in 1983. Hemingway's praise, as quoted in Mary S. Lovell's *Straight On till Morning: The Biography of Beryl Markham,* was indeed effusive:

> She has written so well, and so marvellously well, that I was simply ashamed of myself as a writer. I felt that I was simply a carpenter with words, picking up whatever was furnished on the job and nailing them together and sometimes making an OK pigpen. But this girl can write rings around all of us who consider ourselves as writers.... I wish you would get it and read it because it really is a bloody wonderful book.

Tellingly, Hemingway actually opened his letter by stating of Markham, "I knew her fairly well in Africa and never would have suspected that she could and would put pen to paper except to write in her flyer's log book." Sure enough, as the biographies published after Markham's death indicate, the degree to which she fashioned the prose of her own books remains in serious doubt. One friend, Scott O'Dell, once witnessed Markham and her third husband composing a story—the editor was waiting for it on the doorstep—with Schumacher sitting at the typewriter and Markham merely answering questions he posed. In fact, as Lovell reports, Schumacher once bared his soul, as it seemed, to O'Dell at a party when talking about his writing:

> You are my best friend and I want to make a confession. I want you to know that Beryl did not write *West with the Night*, or any of the short stories. Not one damn word of anything.

Speaking to Lovell as she was writing her biography, O'Dell confirmed, "Yes I'm sure of that. Raoul wrote them all." Given how well he knew Schumacher, it is difficult to doubt O'Dell's testimony, but Lovell does—in part because she seems to have been misinformed (perhaps by Markham herself) about a biographical fact: she suggests that Schumacher and Markham met in 1941, after the aviatrix had started writing *West with the Night*, but Trzebinski, whose biography *The Lives of Beryl Markham* came out several years later, suggests that the two actually first met as early as 1937, though they did not cohabitate until later. Markham is said to have provided Schumacher with bare facts and observations, which he turned into the memoir, despite having never been to Africa himself. He even relied upon such existing works as Elspeth Huxley's *White Man's Country* (1935) and Karen Blixen's *Out of Africa* (1937) for setting and ambience. Trzebinski goes so far as to say of Schumacher's effort, "His subtle, many-layered approach, conveying Beryl's vision of Africa, made *West with the Night* his masterpiece."

"Brothers Are the Same" appeared in *The Splendid Outcast: Beryl Markham's African Stories*, compiled by Lovell just after her biography was issued, and Lovell acknowledges the debt owed to Schumacher—to the extent that she could confirm it—in her introductions to the stories. Of this story, she states that Schumacher is understood to have devised the plot, which was embellished with details that Markham could recall—though even these had to be supplemented with information on Masai customs from the local library. In her biography, Lovell more straightforwardly acknowledges that this story, like two preceding stories, "was almost certainly also Raoul's work."

Reviewing *The Splendid Outcast* for the *New York Times*, Ackerman suggests that the collection "will delight some people and puzzle others." She classes several of the stories as "stock romantic fiction of the era." She does suggest that with the stories conveying Markham's "offbeat adventures in Africa, . . . she emerges from them as a woman of finely tuned observation, as well as courage, cunning and vulnerability." A writer for *Kirkus Reviews* was unfavorable toward the collection, stating, "The overall effect of these eight stories is to bring about an almost pitiable diminishment of the aura—at least the literary one—surrounding the famous flier, writer, and horsewoman." The reviewer says that the volume's later stories, including "Brothers Are the Same," "decline toward O. Henry-esque formula, relying increasingly on suspense and twist endings." The conclusion is that "it seems as much travesty as homage to bring the poorest of these desperate pieces back into print."

Introducing *The Splendid Outcast*, Lovell sees fit to generously affirm,

> Beryl's literary works are few, and that is our loss. But . . . she surely deserves the full, unequivocal credit for her remarkable writing ability, in addition to the acclaim that she has already received for her other achievements.

CRITICISM

Michael Allen Holmes

Holmes is a writer with existential interests. In the following essay, he argues that "Brothers Are the Same" is an artificial, or inauthentic, cultural reconstruction.

Upon reading the Beryl Markham story "Brothers Are the Same," the Western reader may very well imagine it to be a legitimate representation of Masai culture. Introducing the story in the Markham collection she edited, Mary J. Lovell contextualizes such an impression by noting that while the story "seems on first consideration to have been written out of her deep knowledge of African culture," it was in fact Raoul Schumacher, her husband at the time, who seems to have come up with the plot. Even Markham's advisory contributions are thrown into doubt when Lovell acknowledges that Schumacher needed to hit the library to determine the relevant Masai tribal customs.

WHAT DO I READ NEXT?

- The one great work published under Markham's name is *West with the Night* (1942), though her third husband, Raoul Schumacher, is understood to have played a substantial role in the shaping of the prose, perhaps having written it himself. Nonetheless, it is said to accurately depict Markham's singular life in Kenya and also conveys many fascinating philosophical observations.

- Another white author who can provide an insider's perspective on life in Kenya is Elspeth Huxley, who arrived in British East Africa in 1912, when she was five years old and Markham was ten. Huxley's family lived on a coffee farm in Thika, and her best-known work is the memoir *The Flame Trees of Thika: Memories of an African Childhood* (1959).

- Nobel Prize winner Ernest Hemingway is among the many boldfaced names whose lives intersected with Markham's. Hemingway set a variety of stories in Africa, including "The Short Happy Life of Francis Macomber," "An African Story," and "The Good Lion," all of which can be found in *The Complete Short Stories of Ernest Hemingway* (1987). He also penned the memoir *Green Hills of Africa* (1935), about a monthlong safari taken in 1933.

- Dave Eggers has proven himself one of modern literature's most versatile authors, with his novels inhabiting the perspectives of characters of various cultural backgrounds. His novel *What Is the What: The Autobiography of Valentino Achak Deng* (2006) is based on extensive interviews conducted by Eggers with the protagonist, Deng, one of Sudan's "Lost Boys," a refugee from violence who ended up in America.

- One of Markham's few friends who was, like herself, both a writer and an aviator was Antoine de Saint-Exupéry. His most famous book may be the self-illustrated *Le petit prince* (1943), or *The Little Prince*, which is superficially a children's book but features such intricate metaphorical prose about finding a place for oneself that it may ring truer for young adults. Saint-Exupéry also wrote *Terre des hommes* (1939), translated as *Wind, Sand and Stars*, a memoir detailing the time he and a navigator crashed in the Sahara Desert and barely escaped with their lives, among other aviatory experiences.

- One of the earliest works of fiction inhabiting a Masai perspective is Richard Llewellyn's *A Man in a Mirror* (1961). The novel centers on the young warrior Nterenke, who finds himself uncertainly poised between Masai tradition and encroaching Western ways of thinking.

- After Schumacher withdrew his assistance from Markham's literary efforts, the friend to whom she turned to help her polish the story "The Quitter" was South African writer Stuart Cloete. In *The Curve and the Tusk* (1952), set in Mozambique, Cloete delves into the minds of colonials as well as native Africans and even elephants in exploring the full significance of life in Africa.

- A slightly different tack to inhabiting the perspective of indigenous people is found in Conrad Richter's young-adult novel *The Light in the Forest* (1953), about a young white boy who was seized by Lenni-Lenape Indians as an infant and raised by them. When the Lenape are forced to turn him back over to his birth parents, the boy—an Indian at heart—objects and resists.

Knowing all this—or even not knowing it—the reader may experience an intuitive rejection of the premise that any "deep knowledge of African culture" is behind the story. Closer consideration of certain aspects of the story seems to justify such a rejection.

> **HOW COULD HE BE TRULY AFRAID OF FAILING IN A CONTEST WITH A LION IF HE IS NOT AFRAID OF THE LION ITSELF?"**

The unlikelihood that Markham independently wrote much of anything that was published under her name is by now well established. Friends of Markham and Schumacher's scoffed outright at the suggestion that Markham could even be called a writer. Her husband was often specifically introduced as her ghostwriter. After they had met success with both *West with the Night* and half a dozen short stories, Schumacher agreed to assist in her planned biography of Todd Sloan, a famous jockey, while jointly they would work on his own pet project, an African novel—even though, as he acknowledged, he had only been to Africa through Markham's yarns. As planned, that novel would have been published under both their names. When their marriage began to fray, however, Schumacher declared his withdrawal from any literary partnership. He is cited in Errol Trzebinski's biography *The Lives of Beryl Markham* as remarking, "You have posed as a writer for years. I am going to write my book on Africa...you can write on Todd Sloan or do any damn thing you like. But I'm not going to write another damn word for you." Trzebinski goes on to relate what happened when Markham did try to write the biography herself and submitted samples to Houghton Mifflin: "Their letter of rejection, which ultimately Raoul showed to Scott [O'Dell], was 'very curt, very short and absolutely insulting: "The person who wrote *West with the Night* did not write this."'" As a forthright declaration—indeed an accusation—from a major publisher, this seems to sum up the matter of Markham's purported authorship.

Thus, the reader almost certainly has in "Brothers Are the Same" a re-creation of Masai life written by someone, Schumacher, who had never even met a Masai. It should come as no surprise that Markham was unable to offer much assistance with regard to traditions or customs, because the culture with which she was truly familiar—and without doubt she was as intimately familiar with it as a white person could be—was that of the Nandi. In *West with the Night*, the dozen or so mentions of the Masai are mostly generalized or offhand references. (Curiously, despite the merely peripheral role played in Markham's life and memoir by the Masai, the photographs of tribesmen and women in *The Illustrated West with the Night* almost exclusively feature the Masai.) Markham's father, Charles Clutterbuck, as Trzebinski relates, regarded the Masai, whose culture praises the warriors' practice of cattle raiding, as "incorrigible thieves...as robbers, plain and simple." When Clutterbuck was managing for Lord Delamere, he once fired all of the Masai herdsmen being employed after sixty heads of cattle disappeared over the course of a week when Delamere was away. Whether Markham inherited such an attitude toward the Masai is uncertain.

One aspect of "Brothers Are the Same" that is likely to have been shaped by Markham's input is the confrontation with the lion. As it happened, at the age of ten Markham had her own run-in with a lion, from which she did not emerge unscathed. As related in *West with the Night*, once when she and her father were visiting the farm of the Elkingtons, who had captured and raised a lion cub, named Paddy, Beryl happened upon the lion out on the grounds. She walked by slowly and carefully while singing a song, but then she broke into a run, and Paddy silently chased her and, biting into her leg, took her down; fortunately the attack had been witnessed, and Jim Elkington soon came charging on, planning to beat the roaring lion—but instead getting Paddy to pursue him as he clambered up a tree. Beryl was then swept up by Bishon Singh, an Indian employee of her father's, who told Clutterbuck that his daughter "had been moderately eaten by the large lion." Paddy was later caught and spent his remaining years in a cage. Markham also had the benefit of her father's opinions about lions, which are recorded in *West with the Night*:

> "Lions are more intelligent than some men," he said, "and more courageous than most. A lion will fight for what he has and for what he needs; he is contemptuous of cowards and wary of his equals. But he is not afraid. You can always trust a lion to be exactly what he is—and never anything else."

The personification of the lion as a tyrant in "Brothers Are the Same" would appear to owe much to the conceptions propagated by Markham's father. It is possible that the personification goes a little too far. A lion would seem no more likely to "contemplate his massive paws," a somewhat Shakespearean gesture, than he would be to admire his mane while gazing into a pool of water. The reader may also have difficulty imagining that a rock the size of a grain of maize, which when thrown would perhaps hurt a lion less than the sting of a horsefly, would be enough to infuriate him and completely alter his pattern of attack. But of course, only a lion can really say how he would respond to such an insult.

The biggest problem of authenticity in the story would seem to relate to the character of the Masai. Clutterbuck's disparagement of the tribe is certainly unfair, coming as it does from a privileged white manager and landowner who was out to take advantage of the African soil and people as best he could. The Masai can hardly be blamed for taking advantage of him or his wealthy employer in return. Generally the Masai are spoken very highly of by historians and commentators on Kenya. In Markham's memoir, the Masai are said to be one of Lord Delamere's "two great loves"—East Africa at large being the other—as "he respected the spirit of the Masai, their traditions, their physical magnificence, and their knowledge of cattle." Delamere was outraged when he learned that Clutterbuck had fired his beloved Masai. In *Colonial Inscriptions: Race, Sex, and Class in Kenya*, Carolyn Martin Shaw notes that Elspeth Huxley held the Masai up as "living in harmony with nature...the best example of human integration into this environment." Shaw observes that "representations of the Maasai as noble savage" were common, leading her to indeed refer to them as "the much-praised noble Maasai."

Of particular relevance to this story is Shaw's depiction of romantic relations in Masai communities. In her words, "Maasai men were male-defined, male-identified sexual beings." She quotes a passage from Huxley that reveals more about colonial perceptions of the tribe's relational customs:

> At heart, I think, [Europeans] envied these young men's apparent freedom, their status, their physique, the spice of danger in their lives and their sexual opportunities—the warriors could take their pick of lovers among unmarried girls. In fact they had just about everything a young man could want.

Shaw quotes Huxley again as adding, "Certainly there was nothing soft or feminine about their behavior. From infancy they were trained for war." Another telling quotation can be found in *White Africans*, by fervent colonialist J. F. Lipscomb, who quotes a district officer as reporting with regard to the Masai, "They still prefer to live in the present and to let the future take care of itself."

All of these quotations bring one's mind to the key element of "Brothers Are the Same," Temas's fear of failure. To begin with, it is curious that this young Masai warrior-to-be is so worked up about a young woman in the first place. From what others have said of the Masai, the warriors were tantamount to rock stars, earning adulatory attention from young women especially. Even rock stars fall in love, of course, but angst over the attention of a single young woman is founded in the Christian tenet of monogamy, of each person being entitled to romantic partnership with just a single other person, for life. In a culture where strictly monogamous marriage is not the norm—Shaw reports that even married Masai women could feel free to take warriors as lovers—it is unlikely that a young man who has the full glory of warriorhood before him, waiting to be seized, would be so distracted by such monogamous angst.

This would seem especially true if Temas is not even afraid of the actual lion. How could he be truly afraid of failing in a contest with a lion if he is not afraid of the lion itself? The very origin of fear is the biological imperative to preserve one's life, to avoid dangerous situations or creatures that might bring death about. In Temas's case, failure in his endeavor could very well mean death; if he is afraid of failing, then he would *have* to be afraid of dying, of being killed by the lion. That life-threatening lion is there before him, a visceral presence if ever there was one, and yet even as the lion is poised within striking distance, Temas's thoughts are elsewhere: "Every eye was on him, and the strength of one pair—Medoto's—burned in his back like an unhealed scar." Anyone who has met with luck on an African safari can attest that, even from a fair distance, from within a vehicular stronghold, the sight of a lion is utterly riveting. From only yards away, on

The brothers track a lion with other young men of their tribe. (© *Maggy Meyer | Shutterstock.com*)

foot, with not a gun in sight, how could one think of anything else but the lion? Even Markham, who came face to face with Paddy on the Elkingtons' farm, could afterward report, "I remembered the rules that one remembers." If a ten-year-old white girl with no cultural investment in lion relations, other than the straightforward desire to preserve her life, can remember the rules of engagement, how could it be that the young Masai warrior Temas "remembered many of the rules, the laws that governed combat with a lion—but not enough, for stubbornly, wastefully, foolishly, his mind nagged at fear of disgrace—fear of failure."

The fear of failure may not be a Western invention, but it is certainly a notion that is exacerbated in Western culture, and the more one thinks about it, the more difficult it is to ascribe this fear to a Masai youth on the verge of warriorhood. From earlier, the narration reports, as Temas ponders the sleeping lion, "Fear of battle was a nonexistent thing—but fear of failure could be real, and was. It was real and living." After all, this seems entirely backward. Fear of battle is a real thing, fear of a real

actual thing; fear of failure is founded entirely in the imaginative conception of what might happen; it is not "real" but is entirely conceptual. A quotation about Markham seems especially apt in this context. In Lovell's biography, an old Kenyan friend of Markham's, Rose Cartwright, is quoted as saying: "She had no imagination whatsoever, it had never developed in her as a child and I think that this was why she was often brave to a foolhardy extent." These remarks relate partly to Markham's questionable status as an author of fiction, but they also relate to her inclination to live in the present, which is analogous to the natural Masai inclination to live in the present, as identified by Lipscomb's district officer. Markham was essentially raised by the Nandi, growing up within their warrior-centered culture—and not as a domesticated girl but as one of the boys, hunting in the forest and so forth. The Masai, too, have always been raised to be brave warriors, and a good part of bravery may be an unwillingness to dwell on what might go wrong, perhaps even an incapacity to *imagine* what might go wrong. But this is precisely what Temas is doing in "Brothers Are the Same," over-imagining not just *how* things might go wrong, but what the result would be if things *were* to go wrong; this is doubly removed from the reality before him. For a Masai, one of a people who "live in the present and . . . let the future take care of itself," such maladaptive removal from reality would perhaps not be possible.

In the end, in light of questions of authorship, cultural understanding, and psychological truth, it is difficult to give much credence to "Brothers Are the Same." In the references to their skin first being "the color of worn copper," then later shining "like worn gold in the sun," it is as if the Masai themselves are treasured museum pieces, or mere figures in sepia-tinted photographs, rather than actual people. Where the narrator says of Temas's killing of the lion, "It was impossible, it was mad, but it was Masai madness, and it was done," the reader cannot help realizing that this narrator is as far from truly understanding the Masai as anyone could be, with their inherent bravery and skill as warriors reduced to mere "madness." Even the title, in this light, may give offense: what Temas means in saying that "brothers are the same" is unclear, because the Masai, at least in this story, do not seem to ascribe to a theory of collective identity, whereby one person is anyhow indistinguishable from another. Also, there is no sense that this is a reference to communal sexuality, since Temas indicates that Kileghen will still be choosing between them, just in some other way. Only from the perspective of a distant, undiscerning white observer, it seems, could fellow Masai warriors be reduced to being "the same." It may have a nice noble ring to it, a universalizing sound, but for all the author's (or authors') genuine understanding of Masai culture, the title may as well be "Masai Are the Same," or perhaps even "Africans Are the Same," though Markham herself, at least, even if she did not write the story, knew better and would surely have objected to that.

Source: Michael Allen Holmes, Critical Essay on "Brothers Are the Same," in *Short Stories for Students*, Gale, Cengage Learning, 2015.

Nate Pederson

In the following review, Pederson describes Markham's memoir as "absorbing."

Beryl Markham was the first person to fly solo from England to North America from east to west, against prevailing Atlantic winds. She accomplished this remarkable feat in 1936, flying a Vega Gull dubbed *The Messenger*. Her harrowing flight, which ended with a crash landing in Nova Scotia, brought a brief flurry of international acclaim in that age of aviation firsts. Markham's record flight, however, was only one accomplishment in an unconventional life, retold beautifully in her memoir *West With the Night*, first published in 1942.

Markham was raised by her father on a remote farm in Njoro, British East Africa (present-day Kenya). After a tomboyish childhood spent roaming the Kenyan wilds, she moved upcountry to Molo, becoming a racehorse trainer. There she saw her first plane and met British pilot Tom Black, who became her flight instructor and lover.

Soon Markham earned her commercial pilot's license, the first woman in Kenya to do so, and began to freelance as a bush pilot. Much of *West With the Night* concerns itself with this period in Markham's life, detailing her flights in an Avro Avian biplane running supplies to remote outposts or scouting game for safaris.

Since airfields were essentially nonexistent in Africa at the time, Markham's flights were particularly dangerous, punctuated with white-knuckle landings in forest clearings and open fields. In fact the dangers of African flying claimed the lives of a number of aviators. Markham eloquently describes her own search for a downed pilot: "Time and distance together slip smoothly past the tips of my wings without sound, without return, as I peer downward over the night-shadowed hollows of the Rift Valley and wonder if Woody, the lost pilot, could be there, a small pinpoint of hope and of hopelessness listening to the low, unconcerned song of the Avian—flying elsewhere."

Markham's memoir shies away from personal details and straightforward chronology, instead focusing on vivid scenes gathered from a well-lived life. Rarely does one encounter such an evocative sense of a time and place as she creates. The heat and dust of Africa emanate from her prose. Anyone interested in aviation, in Africa or in simply reading an absorbing book will find much to like in its pages. Ernest Hemingway wrote of her memoir, "I wish you would get it and read it because it really is a bloody wonderful book."

Source: Nate Pederson, Review of *West with the Night*, in *Aviation History*, Vol. 20, No. 1, September 2009, p. 62.

Melissa Block and Anne Cherian

In the following radio show transcript, Cherian discusses how she was "immediately and forever enthralled" with Markham's book West with the Night.

MELISSA BLOCK, host:

You Must Read This is our series where authors talk about a book they love. Author Anne Cherian was born in India. When she took her first trip to the U.S., she was accompanied by a book about a female adventurer. It was Beryl Markham's *West With The Night*, and it conjured up a feeling of endless possibility.

ANNE CHERIAN: Ask Americans to name the pioneers of transatlantic flight, and many will come up with Charles Lindbergh and Amelia Earhart. But there were others who dared to fly that great distance. And I think the most intriguing member of those early record holders was Beryl Markham. She was a colonial child, born in Britain and raised in Africa, where she met Ernest Hemingway on safari and was rumored to have had an affair with an English prince.

She took up flying at a time when most people hadn't even seen planes, became the only professional pilot in Africa, and in 1936, accepted a challenge to fly solo across the Atlantic Ocean.

In early September, she set off from England in a tiny turquoise and silver plane filled with good luck gifts. She flew for over 21 hours, survived a crash landing on an island near Nova Scotia and went on to write her autobiography, *West With The Night*.

I read her book at age 24, while flying in a plane west from India to begin graduate studies in the United States. I was immediately and forever enthralled.

Markham was a woman who wrote about the moments that meant the most to her: hunting barefoot with the Nandi as a child, training race horses, scouting elephants in Africa, and of course, making that daring trip across the Atlantic.

Initially, what intrigued me most about *West With The Night* were the vignettes of her childhood. Growing up in India, I was used to reading stories by Western authors about landscapes and food I did not know.

But here was a young girl whose childhood I could easily imagine, for she, too, had played with servants, spoke a different language outside the house, and killed animals—wild pigs in her case, snakes in mine.

Then there was Markham's portrayal of Africa. Having read foreigners' accounts of India, like Africa, conquered and exoticized, I am quick to sense if a tale is authentic, and Markham's was exactly that.

Africa, she said, could be mystic, wild, a sweltering inferno, a photographer's paradise, a hunter's Valhalla, an escapist's utopia. But to her, it was just home.

Beryl Markham was a woman who went after what she wanted and gave it her all. Her horses won races, and she parlayed her aviation skills learned as a bush pilot into a dark flight across the Atlantic, and when she sat down to write her memoirs, she produced a dazzling book.

I still have my first copy of *West With The Night*, now frayed, the pages yellow with age, and read it for the simple beauty of its language, for the vivid description of Africa and for the amazing adventures of a woman ahead of her time.

I also reach for it whenever I worry that my youthful dream of being a writer is as foolish as reaching for the stars. Then, it is always comforting to read about a woman who sat in a small plane, suspended between earth and sky. Why? Because she wanted to and because she could.

MELISSA BLOCK, host:

Anne Cherian is the author of the novel, *A Good Indian Wife*. She recommended *West With The Night* by Beryl Markham for our series You Must Read This.

Source: Melissa Block and Anne Cherian, "Out of Africa and West with the Night," in *All Things Considered*, March 30, 2009.

Publishers Weekly

In the following review, an anonymous writer points out how the story in the picture book The Good Lion *highlights Markham's respect for nature.*

Brown (*Odd Boy Out*) brings to life a bold and enchanting girl, the young Beryl Markham.

Excerpted from *West with the Night*, the 1942 autobiography the aviator wrote about her youth in East Africa, the text relates the events of a visit she made with her father to the Elkington Farm, where Paddy, a hand-raised lion, freely roams the estate. "A tame lion is an unnatural lion," Markham's father warns her, "and whatever is unnatural is untrustworthy." Brown's sepia-tinted watercolors impart information without drawing attention to themselves. He portrays the narrator with a long brown ponytail and gray trousers. She calls the lion "harmless"; still she "remember[s] not to run," walking slowly past the giant cat when she finds him in her path. A sequence of seven suspenseful pages—one per second of elapsed time, seemingly—shows that Markham's father is right. "There was no sound or wind. Even the lion made no sound as he came swiftly behind me. What followed was my scream that was barely a whisper." During the few moments the lion actually traps her, Brown's golden spreads turn to cold shadows of purple and blue; then, as help quickly arrives, the pictures turn sunny again. "Paddy had lived and died in ways not of his choosing," Markham concludes, with unexpected compassion.

Her reverence for the majesty of Nature—even its predatory creatures—will not be lost on young readers.

Source: Review of *The Good Lion*, in *Publishers Weekly*, Vol. 252, No. 47, November 28, 2005, pp. 51–52.

Margaret Bush

In the following review, Bush is disappointed in the picture-book adaptation of an anecdote from Markham's West with the Night.

Markham included the story of her childhood encounter with a lion in her autobiographical *West with the Night* (Farrar, 1982). Brown's adaptation of it begins with a tantalizing premise that doesn't actually get much play as later events move in a slow, dreamlike sequence. "My father and I settled in East Africa in 1906. . . . And it was where, as a small girl, I was eaten by a lion." The child and her father ride out to an estate where a tamed lion roams free, and she goes off exploring. Brown's sketchy, homely watercolor views include a few animals and trees against an otherwise barren landscape of earth melding into orange sky. Beryl soon encounters the resting lion, calmly stares him down, and goes on her way, unaware that he is now following her. Help miraculously arrives from a Sikh tending horses in the deserted terrain. Brown switches color tones for the anticlimactic attack, rescue, and loss of freedom for the animal. The enlarged face of the prone child, her eyes and mouth tight shut, painted in shades of purple, is the only close-up view of her—otherwise she appears as a small, crudely sketched figure. Markham goes quickly to the message of the tale, saying that this was a good lion, who did his best at being tame, and that perhaps he shouldn't be blamed for his one mistake and caged for the rest of his long days—a simplistic summation since the lion had gone on to kill a horse, a bull, and a cow the same evening.

Source: Margaret Bush, Review of *The Good Lion*, in *School Library Journal*, Vol. 51, No. 10, October 2005, pp. 120–21.

SOURCES

Ackerman, Diane, "A High Life and a Wild One," in *New York Times*, August 23, 1987, http://www.nytimes.com/1987/08/23/books/a-high-life-and-a-wild-one.html (accessed September 5, 2014).

Ghosh, Palash, "Ex-British Army Colonel Murdered by Armed Gang: Twilight for Whites in Kenya?," in *International Business Times*, August 26, 2013, http://www.ibtimes.com/ex-british-army-colonel-murdered-armed-gang-twilight-whites-kenya-1399035 (accessed September 6, 2014).

Hughes, Lotte, "Rough Time in Paradise: Claims, Blames and Memory Making around Some Protected Areas in Kenya," in *Conservation and Society*, Vol. 5, No. 3, 2007, pp. 307–30.

Huxley, Elspeth, *Settlers of Kenya*, Greenwood Press, 1975, pp. 1–31.

Lipscomb, J. F., *White Africans*, Greenwood Press, 1974, p. 71.

Lovell, Mary S., comp., Introduction and Notes to *The Splendid Outcast: Beryl Markham's African Stories*, North Point Press, 1987, pp. ix–xv, 51–52.

———, *Straight On till Morning: The Biography of Beryl Markham*, St. Martin's Press, 1987, pp. 240–41, 261, 326.

Markham, Beryl, "Brothers Are the Same," in *The Splendid Outcast: Beryl Markham's African Stories*, compiled by Mary S. Lovell, North Point Press, 1987, pp. 52–66.

———, *The Illustrated West with the Night*, Welcome, 1994, pp. 66, 69, 72, 78.

McGreal, Chris, "A Lost World," in *Guardian* (London, England), October 25, 2006, http://www.theguardian.com/world/2006/oct/26/kenya.chrismcgreal (accessed September 6, 2014).

Pflanz, Mike, "Kenyan Aristocrat Thomas Cholmondeley Released from Prison after Five Months," in *Telegraph* (London, England), October 23, 2009, http://www.telegraph.co.uk/news/worldnews/africaandindianocean/kenya/6415490/Kenyan-aristocrat-Thomas-Cholmondeley-released-from-prison-after-five-months.html (accessed September 6, 2014).

Review of *The Splendid Outcast*, in *Kirkus Reviews*, October 21, 1987, https://www.kirkusreviews.com/book-reviews/beryl-markham-2/the-splendid-outcast-beryl-markhams-african-sto/ (accessed September 5, 2013).

Shaw, Carolyn Martin, *Colonial Inscriptions: Race, Sex, and Class in Kenya*, University of Minnesota Press, 1995, pp. 198, 200, 209, 213.

Smith, David, "Tanzania Ditches Plan to Evict Masai for Serengeti 'Wildlife Corridor,'" in *Guardian* (London, England), October 7, 2013, http://www.theguardian.com/world/2013/oct/07/tanzania-maasai-serengeti-wildlife-corridor (accessed September 6, 2014).

Trzebinski, Errol, *The Kenya Pioneers*, W. W. Norton, 1985, p. 35.

———, *The Lives of Beryl Markham: "Out of Africa"'s Hidden Free Spirit and Denys Finch Hatton's Last Great Love*, W. W. Norton, 1993, pp. 13, 35, 239, 258–59.

FURTHER READING

Bentsen, Cheryl, *Maasai Days*, Summit Books, 1989.
As a journalist, Bentsen situated herself as intimately as possible within the Masai community in order to write about their traditions, their philosophy, and their relationship to the modern world.

Dinesen, Isak, *Out of Africa*, Putnam, 1937.
Karen Blixen's memoir, published under her pen name, treats her life in Kenya through the period of time when the somewhat younger Markham was coming of age. Markham is a hidden presence in *Out of Africa*, as Denys Finch Hatton (Robert Redford to Meryl Streep's Blixen in the film version), who was the love of Blixen's later life, turned to Markham for companionship shortly before his tragic death.

Ngũgĩ wa Thiong'o, *Weep Not, Child*, Heinemann, 1964.
Ngũgĩ is the foremost literary authority on native Kenyan perspectives on the impact of British colonialism. Focusing on the experiences of his own people, the Kikuyu, his first novel, *Weep Not, Child* (originally published under the name James Ngugi), revolves around the rise of the Mau Mau insurgency, in which many Kenyans objected to British oppression and atrocities in the only practical manner left to them, through violent rebellion.

Thomson, Joseph, *Through Masai Land: A Journey of Exploration among the Snowclad Volcanic Mountains and Strange Tribes of Eastern Equatorial Africa*, Houghton Mifflin, 1883, reprint, Nabu Press, 2010.
The title makes clear that this work, perhaps the earliest treatment of Masai culture, very much comes from a condescending colonialist perspective (though it was written before British East Africa became a colony). It remains valuable in conveying both first impressions about the Masai and the biases of the British observer.

SUGGESTED SEARCH TERMS

Beryl Markham AND Brothers Are the Same

Beryl Markham AND West with the Night

Kenya AND Masai OR Maasai

Masai AND warriors AND lion

Masai AND literature

Beryl Markham AND Kenya

Beryl Markham AND aviation

Beryl Markham AND horse racing

Beryl Markham AND literature

Beryl Markham AND ghostwriter

The Facts behind the Helsinki Roccamatios

YANN MARTEL

1993

Yann Martel's story "The Facts behind the Helsinki Roccamatios" chronicles the dwindling months of a relationship between the narrator and his friend Paul, who is dying of AIDS. The narrator comes up with an idea in order to help Paul not dwell on his dying: He wants to help Paul do something constructive, distracting, and entertaining; he suggests that the two of them create a series of stories together. The narrative structure they devise is that they will take turns telling stories to each other about a fictional family. The family they concoct is an Italian family living in Helsinki, Finland, in the mid-1980s, the Roccamatio family. The first story will reflect in some way a significant event that happened in the year 1901, through an episode in the life of a Roccamatio; the second story will reflect an event from 1902; and so on. The narrator and Paul aim to continue through 1986. For each year assigned them, Paul and the narrator do a bit of historical research to determine a suitable world event, not necessarily the most significant one of that year. Martel includes snippets of the historical research—the facts behind the stories about the fictional Roccamatio family—but none of the stories are fully related to the reader. As "The Facts behind the Helsinki Roccamatios" unfolds, the narrator describes the tragic worsening of Paul's health. The reader should be aware that Martel is very detailed in his descriptions of the appalling effects of AIDS

Author Yann Martel (© David Levenson / Getty Images)

on Paul's body. "The Facts behind the Helsinki Roccamatios" was published first in the *Malahat Review* in 1990, winning Canada's Journey Prize the following year, and then in *The Facts behind the Helsinki Roccamatios* in 1993.

AUTHOR BIOGRAPHY

Born in Salamanca, Spain, on June 25, 1963, Martel is the younger of two sons of Canadian diplomat Émile Martel and Nicole Perron Martel. Having traveled extensively as a youth, Martel attended Ridgemont High School in Ottawa, Ontario, Canada, graduating in 1979. He went on to Trinity College School, in Port Hope, Ontario. After graduating, he studied at Trent University and then Concordia University. Returning to Trent in 1986, Martel received a bachelor of arts degree in philosophy in 1987.

The Facts behind the Helsinki Roccamatios was Martel's first published work; it appeared in 1993 and includes the title story. Martel then published his first novel, *Self*, in 1996. The following year, Martel traveled to India to write his next book, *Life of Pi*, which was published in 2001. He won the Man Booker Prize for the novel in 2002. The book was later adapted as a play and for film. He published a collection of short fiction, *We Ate the Children Last: Stories*, in 2004 and his third novel, *Beatrice and Virgil*, in 2010. Martel has taught at the Free University of Berlin and has served as the writer in residence at the Saskatoon Public Library.

PLOT SUMMARY

"The Facts behind the Helsinki Roccamatios" opens in 1986 in a university town in Toronto. The narrator is looking back to that time from a later date. In 1986, he was twenty-three and in his final year at Ellis University, while Paul was nineteen and entering his first year. When the narrator served as Paul's upperclassman advisor, the two became friends. At the beginning of Paul's second term, he became ill. The narrator summarizes that within nine months, Paul was dead. He then turns to detailing the course of Paul's illness, beginning with the diagnosis of AIDS, which, it was eventually determined, was contracted via a blood transfusion Paul received in Jamaica three years previously, after his family had been in a car accident.

The narrator describes the way Paul invited him to visit, and how Paul's parents reacted to the news regarding their son testing positive for HIV. His father, Jack, responded by destroying and burning the family car. The narrator relates that even though the car is not the one Jack was driving when the accident happened, and even though the accident was not Jack's fault, Jack's anger and grief were turned toward the closest vehicle at hand. Paul's mother, Mary, was in the fetal position on her bed when the narrator met her, and Jennifer, Paul's sister, was puffy-faced and distraught.

The narrator speaks of his attempts to try to continue with his studies. But watching his friend dying prevented him from focusing on school. He attempted to officially withdraw, but he missed a deadline and then, in appealing, refused to explain the source of his emotional

MEDIA ADAPTATIONS

- The collection *The Facts behind the Helsinki Roccamatios* is available as an unabridged recording published in 2004 by Audible Audio, featuring narrators Jeff Woodman, Barbara Caruso, John Randolph Jones, David LeDoux, and Johnny Stange.

distress, and consequently he simply dropped out, to fail his final year. He goes on to discuss Paul's time in the hospital. He recalls how he wanted to find something creative and intellectually meaningful that he and Paul could set their minds to while Paul was in the hospital. He thought of the way Boccaccio constructed his story cycle known as the *Decameron*. In Boccaccio's work, ten people gather at a villa outside of Florence as they attempt to isolate themselves from the plague, and in doing so, they survive. Essentially, as the narrator explains, they tell stories to one another to pass the days of their isolation.

The narrator fleshes out a similar framework, describing the way the history of the twentieth century would provide a guideline for his and Paul's work as a whole, with each episode to reflect one fact or event from each year, from 1901 through 1986. The narrator presents his idea to an unenthusiastic Paul. Despite his initial reservations, Paul soon decides he would like to participate. He is called upon to select the name of the family that will be featured in the stories as well as the contemporary location of the family. It is determined that the family members who inform the framework of the story will be of Italian heritage, but living in Helsinki. The family name, Paul decides, is Roccamatio.

The narrator does not transcribe the actual stories, which he and Paul decided to keep secret, but does include, for every year as the storytelling continues, the historical facts used as the context for each story. He states that for the first year, 1901, the historical fact associated with the story was the death of Queen Elizabeth I of England. He then mentions that the story he told was concerned with the patriarch of the Roccamatio family, Sandro, and his death. This opening story allows for the introduction of the family members gathered at the funeral. The reader is told nothing else about this story. The narrator goes on to describe the way the stories unfolded during his visits to see Paul at his home and in the hospital. They would talk about his health and current treatments, and then current events and politics, before progressing to the stories.

The remainder of Martel's story interweaves the historical events from which the narrator and Paul draw for their stories with the narrator's recounting of Paul's treatment and illness. For a while, he is mostly well but is visiting the hospital on a treatment schedule involving vitamins and medication. As his treatment wears on, Paul begins to grow demoralized, realizing how grueling his life will continue to be. The narrator comments on the way Paul's stories mirror his grim mood, his pessimism. He spends time in and out of the hospital. He relapses and returns to the hospital for some time, just after they have reached the year 1913. The narrator tries to keep his own stories upbeat, deciding to avoid discussion of World War I and focus instead on such things as women's suffrage. The two sometimes argue about the course of each other's stories.

Paul regularly receives blood transfusions because his medications make him severely anemic. He develops new complications, from infections to lesions. At one point, when they are on the year 1921 in their storytelling, Paul grows angry and frustrated. He stubbornly insists that various events that took place later in history occurred in 1921. Paul is given antidepressants. The narrator watches him grow increasingly ill, fragile, and emaciated. Frequently the narrator runs into Paul's parents, and they give him a key to their house. Paul begins to feel better for a time, and he is able to go home. His family is pleased to be able to help him. Paul thinks of beginning his college studies again through correspondence courses; he is optimistic about his chances of recovery.

After Paul spends some time with his family at their cottage, they must rush him back to the hospital in Toronto because he has severe abdominal pains. His condition worsens. He becomes increasingly depressed, and the narrator, too, is having trouble coping with what is happening to his friend. Paul's parents also become depressed, though Mary seems to find some strength through her faith. Paul develops a fungal infection in his spinal fluid. The doctors determine that he will stop taking some of his medication, as its side effects are becoming too onerous for Paul to bear.

When Paul and the narrator reach the year 1950, the narrator states that this is the last year for which Paul takes sole responsibility for his story. Paul's health begins to decline rapidly. He stops eating. He begins to talk about God, and the narrator arranges for the hospital's chaplain to come and visit Paul. Paul's vision deteriorates, quickly to the point of blindness. He tells the narrator that he will not think about making up any more stories, except for one he would like to set in the year 2001, years into the future from the standpoint of the story's setting of 1986.

Paul is allowed to go home, where he will spend his last days. Not long after, he dies. He has left the narrator a note, dictated to the live-in nurse. He has made up an event for the year 2001—the death of Queen Elizabeth II—and tells the narrator that it was the best he could do, and that the story is the narrator's to tell.

CHARACTERS

Jack Atsee

Jack is Paul's father. Jack feels a sense of guilt over Paul's illness, in addition to the natural parental grief he feels over his son's diagnosis of AIDS. The narrator explains that Jack was driving the car when they had the accident that necessitated Paul's receiving an emergency blood transfusion. The doctors surmise that Paul contracted AIDS as a result of that transfusion. The narrator further notes that the accident was not Jack's fault. Nevertheless, Jack destroys the family car, though it was not the one that was in the accident. The narrator returns to Jack and his sorrow and guilt periodically in the story. At one point, the narrator mentions that Jack, like his son, has been put on antidepressants.

Jennifer Atsee

Jennifer is Paul's sister. She does not figure prominently in the story. She is younger than Paul and is as grief-stricken as her parents at Paul's diagnosis, but she manages to remain relatively strong and optimistic longer than Mary and Jack in particular. She feels a sense of duty to remain well and healthy so that her parents will still have a child after they lose Paul.

Mary Atsee

Mary is Paul's mother. She is numb with grief when Paul is diagnosed with AIDS. The narrator makes a note of observing that at one point during Paul's illness, she seems to regain a sense of hope and appears to draw strength from her religion.

Paul Atsee

Paul is the narrator's friend. He is several years younger than the narrator and in his freshman year of college when the story opens. He becomes ill during his second semester. Paul contracted AIDS through a blood transfusion a few years prior to the beginning of the story. Although the nurse at the end of the story thinks that Paul and the narrator were romantically involved, neither man is gay. At one point Paul states that he wishes he had a girlfriend.

Paul is initially uninterested in the narrator's idea for the storytelling, but he changes his mind and selects the location and the family name. As the story progresses, Paul is initially optimistic but soon grows weary of the medicines he takes and their side effects. He weakens and begins to lose hope. The narrator helps to keep his spirits up. At times Paul argues with the narrator regarding the course the stories are taking. His condition begins to drastically worsen when he and the narrator have reached the late 1950s and early 1960s with the stories' historical frame of reference. But Paul insists on jumping ahead to a year in the future—2001—and working on the final story. He dies before he can finish it, having only formulated the "historical" fact for the year.

Narrator

The narrator, who remains unnamed throughout the story, is the protagonist. Martel's introduction to the volume of short stories that includes "The Facts behind the Helsinki

Roccamatios" indicates that the story was "inspired by the death of a friend from AIDS." Yet Martel provides little other information about the narrator, so it should not be assumed that the first-person narrator is in any way to be associated with Martel himself.

The narrator comes up with the idea of the storytelling that informs the plot; this serves as a means of helping his friend Paul cope with his disease and treatment, but it also helps them both escape the situation as much as they are able to. The narrator responds in various ways to his friend's illness. At times he is optimistic, but he also feels frustrated, angry, helpless, and hopeless. He attempts to stay upbeat for Paul, but is not always able to control his emotions, as when Paul loses his sight. He witnesses a great deal of suffering but for the most part narrates the story in an emotionally level fashion.

THEMES

Disease

In "The Facts behind the Helsinki Roccamatios," Paul is dying of AIDS. A significant portion of the narrative is dedicated to tracing the impact of the disease, not just on Paul but on his family and on the narrator. The stigma associated with AIDS is an aspect of the disease that the narrator explores. He addresses what he thinks people probably expect—that Paul is gay and had unprotected sex. When Paul first tells the narrator about his diagnosis, the narrator's reaction reveals the common fears associated with the disease. The narrator wonders if Paul had ever bled in his presence, or if he had ever drunk from Paul's glass or eaten his food. The narrator states,

> Then I thought of him. I thought of gay sex and hard drugs. But Paul wasn't gay. He had never told me so outright, but I knew him well enough and I had never detected the least ambivalence. I likewise couldn't imagine him a heroin addict. In any case, that wasn't it.

To counter these suspicions—in himself, in the reader, in people in Paul's life—the narrator explains that Paul contracted the disease when he had a blood transfusion while his family was on vacation in Jamaica.

After Paul's treatment begins, the narrator states that he does not want to discuss what AIDS does to the human body, although later he will offer some very specific details about

this. In the early weeks of Paul's treatment, the narrator focuses on what he calls "the I'm-not-going-to-die virus. It's the one that affects the most people because it attacks the living, the ones who surround and love the dying." He talks of Paul eagerly eating his peas as if it would do some good, help his body fight. He recalls how his reaction to this was that all he could think of was that it would not matter, that Paul would die anyway. Although the narrator states that this metaphoric virus affected *him*, he seems to be focusing on the way it affected Paul, the way Paul acted as if by eating his peas and shaving daily he would somehow pull through. What the narrator does not explicitly state is the way Paul's illness, the way his knowledge of Paul's imminent death, made him focus on the fact of his own vitality—Paul *was* going to die, and soon, regardless of peas and pills and shaving habits, whereas he would not, not anytime soon. The narrator depicts the arrogance of the living in the face of a loved one's imminent death.

Storytelling

The importance of storytelling is a significant element in Martel's story. The narrator comes up with the idea of storytelling as a means of doing something both productive and distracting to pass the time while Paul is effectively bedridden. He derives this idea from the way the individuals whom Boccaccio depicts in the *Decameron* escape the plague in Italy at a villa outside of Florence. That collection of stories is held together by the framework of the people's gathering; each individual tells a story to pass the time and make them all feel better. Martel's narrator states,

> What I meant was that between the two of us we had to do something constructive, something that would make something out of nothing, sense out of nonsense, something that would go beyond *talking* about life, death, God, the universe and the meaning of it all and actually *be* those things.

The stories are so private and sacred that the narrator only shares the tiniest scraps of information about the characters' lives. He does, however, reveal the historical facts that serve as the jumping-off points for the stories. In the choices he and Paul make, the reader understands the way each man is coping with Paul's illness. Sometimes the facts concern war, death, and tragedy. Other times they are optimistic—coronations, inventions, medical discoveries. Even though the narrator does not

TOPICS FOR FURTHER STUDY

- In "The Facts behind the Helsinki Roccamatios," Martel explores the death of the narrator's friend from AIDS. Research the history of the AIDS epidemic, focusing on the 1980s, during which Martel's story takes place, and create a presentation through PowerPoint or in another format to share the information you learn with your class. Incorporate statistics concerning the number of individuals affected and the number who died over the course of the decade, designing charts or graphs to convey your data.

- With a small group, read Courtney Sheinmel's 2009 young-adult novel *Positively*. In it, a thirteen-year-old girl who is HIV positive struggles with her HIV status and attempts to cope with the knowledge that she carries the virus that killed her mother. Create an online blog in which you and your group explore and discuss issues that arise in the novel. Among other topics, discuss the impact of the protagonist's diagnosis on her life. How does she cope with her challenges? What is her daily life like and how does it change once she has been diagnosed? How effectively does the author portray the character and the struggles she faces?

- In the 1996 novel *Push*, by Sapphire, the protagonist learns that she is HIV positive after her sexually abusive father dies from AIDS. Read the novel and compare it to the 2009 movie into which it was adapted, retitled *Precious*. In what ways does the film differ from the novel? Which format do you think more effectively conveys the struggles of the protagonist? Why? Which format did you prefer? Write a paper in which you compare the book and the film. Consider the ways in which characters, plot, and themes have been translated from book to film. Please note that the novel and film have explicit sexual and violent content. This assignment should be reserved for more mature students.

- Martel includes a number of historical facts in "The Facts behind the Helsinki Roccamatios." It is upon these facts that the Roccamatio stories—those created by the narrator and Paul but not related by the narrator—are based. Select one of the facts and, after conducting additional research on the fact you have selected, write your own short story inspired by that moment in history. Share your historical research and your story with your class by making it accessible online, or read it aloud.

---

offer the reader the Roccamatio stories themselves, he provides glimpses into their content, and he underscores the way the *act* of storytelling itself helped both Paul and him.

STYLE

Story-within-a-Story Structure

In "The Facts behind the Helsinki Roccamatios," Martel employs the device of embedding a story or series of stories—created by one or more characters—within his own story. In this case, Martel departs from the model slightly, varying the traditional story-within-a-story to feature the idea of the story rather than the story itself. The narrator tells the reader that he will not be relating any of the actual stories he and Paul told one another. What he does provide are the historical facts chosen for each year, facts that inspired the stories themselves. He occasionally provides hints about the fiction in mentioning a particular character, one of the Roccamatios, and maybe what happens to him or her in a story. Yet beyond these glancing hints, none of the details of the stories are

Paul is ill with AIDS, so his friend comes up with the idea of passing the time with stories.
(© Photographee.eu | Shutterstock.com)

fleshed out. Rather, the reader is provided with a paragraph or a sentence or two on the historical event selected for that year. There is sometimes a relation between this event and something going on with Paul's treatment. The narrator, seeing Paul struggling, may opt to focus on a noncontroversial event such as an invention or scientific discovery as the historical basis for his story in order to distract Paul. Often, Paul will not allow this and grows angry with the narrator, or makes his subsequent story fit his own bleak outlook.

Martel uses a similar structure in his well-known novel *The Life of Pi*. The structure embeds a larger story within a briefer one, which presents itself primarily at the beginning and end of the embedded story—hence the term "frame narrative" is often used in discussing *The Life of Pi* and similar works. In *The Life of Pi*, the adult character of Pi tells the story of what happened to him as a youth to someone interviewing him. That story of what happened to him is the main story in the novel. Essentially

the story-within-a-story and frame narrative operate in concert to produce the more complex effect of the work of fiction as a whole; the term applied to a given work depends on which part is the focus, the internal or the external story. In "The Facts behind the Helsinki Roccamatios," Martel actually embeds a number of stories, or rather the ideas of the stories and the historical facts surrounding them, within the main story of Paul's illness. As Martel here draws on the idea of serial storytelling rather than a bookend framework, leaving the external story as the focus, the term "stories-within-a-story" would perhaps be most accurate. It is the framework of Paul's illness that forms the bulk of the narrative, whereas in *The Life of Pi*, it is the embedded story, the story within the framework of the interview with the grown man, that constitutes the bulk of the narrative of his younger self.

First-Person Narration
Martel uses an unnamed first-person narrator in this short story. A first-person narrator relates the

events from his or her own perspective, referring to him- or herself as "I." In Martel's story, the narrator's tone gradually shifts. At the beginning of the story, he is matter-of-fact. The tone is conversational, but the reader understands that time has passed, that the narrator is looking back on 1986 from a later point in his life and has some emotional distance from the events. Having failed his courses that year because he was unable to withdraw in time, he simply states, "I botched my academic year." He goes on to speak about his emotions, and the toll Paul's illness and subsequent death took on him, without actually conveying those emotions.

Yet once the narrator immerses himself in narrating the time period more closely, describing conversations with Paul and his family, his tone changes. The narration becomes more intimate, more painful, and more honest, though still largely reserved. Often he pulls back to a more distant narrative stance, speaking of medical treatments and pills and Paul's physiological reaction to them, but the narrator then moves once again deeper into the events that took place during that time period, describing his own breakdowns as he watched Paul grow increasingly emaciated and weaken and lose hope. When Paul loses his vision, the narrator recounts, "for the first time ever, I can't help it and I impose my sadness onto his. I break down right in front of him. Great, cracking, uncontrollable sobs." Despite the narrator's emotional response to what has happened to his friend, there remains some distance in the way he describes the story's events. But later, he will mention touching and cleaning Paul's ear and having a whispered conversation with Paul. Here, the reader feels more intensely what both the narrator and Paul are going through. The first-person narrator, then, as he attempts to navigate his own emotional response to what has happened to his friend, allows the reader glimpses into the way he coped during that time period. His narration reflects his own emotional waves—he would pull away from the situation at times but inevitably feel the full emotional brunt of what was happening. Using a first-person narrator allows Martel to demonstrate to the reader what happens to someone who is so intimately involved in the death of a friend.

HISTORICAL CONTEXT

AIDS in the 1980s

Martel opens "The Facts behind the Helsinki Roccamatios" in 1986. The disease that became known as AIDS began to be widespread in the United States in the early 1980s. Initially, the US Centers for Disease Control and Prevention (CDC) published a statement concerning a type of pneumonia that was becoming increasingly prevalent within the homosexual male community. This strain, Pneumocystis carinii pneumonia (PCP), was often present alongside a type of cancer known as Kaposi's sarcoma. In 1982, the CDC coined the term *acquired immunodeficiency syndrome*, along with the acronym AIDS, to describe a disease that left the body vulnerable to such rare infections as PCP and cancers such as Kaposi's sarcoma. The disease became associated with gay men and intravenous drug users, and those afflicted were stigmatized by society. The increasing prevalence of AIDS and the high death rate associated with it caused it to be referred to as an epidemic by the mid-1980s.

By 1984, the CDC reported that AIDS was likely caused by a single, particular virus, which later became known as *human immunodeficiency virus*, or HIV. The US surgeon general published a report on AIDS in 1986. It advocated various prevention measures, such as the use of condoms, and encouraged parents and schools to initiate discussions with young people about how AIDS is spread. Also in 1986, clinical trials involving the use of the drug azidothymidine (AZT) to treat those infected with AIDS reported positive results, and by March of the following year, the Food and Drug Administration approved the use of AZT in treating patients with AIDS. During this time period, an activist group known as the AIDS Coalition to Unleash Power, or ACT UP, which sought to minimize the stigma associated with AIDS, advocated increased drug research for treating the disease and began staging rallies across the country. A drug trial of AZT demonstrated the way it could slow the progression of the disease in individuals who had HIV but no symptoms of the disease. More than 100,000 individuals diagnosed with AIDS had been reported to the CDC by August 1989.

Boccaccio's **Decameron**

Boccaccio was a fourteenth-century Italian writer. His most famous work, the *Decameron*,

COMPARE
&
CONTRAST

- **Mid-1980s:** AIDS has emerged in America as a deadly disease caused by a single virus that becomes known as HIV. By the end of 1986, 28,712 cases of AIDS have been reported in the United States, and 24,559 individuals have died from the disease.

  Mid-1990s: By the end of 1997, 641,086 cases of AIDS have been reported in the United States, and 390,692 individuals have died from AIDS.

  Today: Approximately 1.1 million people in the United States are currently living with HIV. Since 1981, 658,692 individuals have died from AIDS in America.

- **Mid-1980s:** Medical advancements in treatment for AIDS begin to expand once the virus that causes the disease is identified in 1984. The first report on AIDS by the surgeon general is published in 1986, making recommendations regarding the prevention of the disease. A year later, the Food and Drug Administration approves the use of AZT in the treatment of HIV-positive individuals.

  Mid-1990s: New breakthroughs in treatment are developed in 1995 and 1996. One of the new treatments is designed to suppress HIV in HIV-positive patients. The life expectancy of HIV-positive patients is increased.

  Today: New developments in HIV and AIDS research are focused on rapid testing for the presence of the virus. The impact of the Affordable Care Act on treatment for HIV/AIDS is explored in a government report focused on HIV/AIDS strategy.

- **Mid-1980s:** Novels using the frame narrative device, also known as the story-within-a-story, have been told throughout history. In 1984, the West German novel *The Neverending Story*, originally published in 1979, is released as a feature film, translating this literary device into a visual, live-action format. Another story-within-a-story novel, *The Princess Bride*, originally published in 1973, is translated to film in 1987.

  Mid-1990s: Martel's "The Facts behind the Helsinki Roccamatios" is published and employs the story-within-a-story device. The 1997 film *Titanic* employs the frame narrative structure, as the lone living survivor looks back from 1997 to the events that took place when the ship sank in 1912.

  Today: Martel uses the frame narrative technique in *Life of Pi*, published in 2001 and adapted for film in 2012.

is referenced by Martel in "The Facts behind the Helsinki Roccamatios." Boccaccio's work and especially its structure inspire the narrator in Martel's story. Mentioning how the characters in Boccaccio's story gather in a villa to escape the plague and tell each other stories to pass the time, the narrator imagines fashioning a similar work. Scholars estimate that Boccaccio composed the *Decameron* during the years 1348 through 1353. In it, ten young people, seven women and three men, flee Florence during the year of the plague there, in 1348. They escape to a villa in the countryside for two weeks. In the framework narrative, each member of the party is allowed a turn at being king or queen over the others. The current ruler dictates the way their time is spent, and is allowed the privilege of telling stories during that time. There are one hundred such stories contained within the *Decameron*. With this framework, Boccaccio narrates the events of the overarching story and then has each character tell his or her stories. Boccaccio organizes the larger story by days. The book opens with grim descriptions of the plague and the chaotic nature of the time. As the book proceeds and

The invented stories are about a family of Italian immigrants who live in Helsinki, Finland.
(© Oleksiy Mark / Shutterstock.com)

the characters divide up their time, each day has its own unique tone. Day one, for example is lively and playful. Later days are filled with stories of tragic love affairs or tales of intrigue and adventure. Some of the stories are sensual (some scholars have even described them as obscene), while others demonstrate the work's overarching spirituality and morality.

CRITICAL OVERVIEW

Martel's collection *The Facts behind the Helsinki Roccamatios* was originally published in 1993 and then reprinted in 2004, after the success of his novel *The Life of Pi*. In a review of the story collection, Christopher Priest, writing for the London *Guardian*, states, "Martel writes plain prose with surface adornments. Sometimes the extra level is sentimental, sometimes too many details appear, sometimes the author makes an implied request to the reader for confirmation of his ideas."

Of the short story for which the volume is named, Priest insists that this piece is "much less successful" than another story in the volume, "The Time I Heard the Private Donald J. Rankin String Concerto with One Discordant Violin, by the American Composer John Morton." Describing the format of "The Facts behind the Helsinki Roccamatios," including the way Paul and the narrator link a historical fact to each story, Priest notes, "They get as far as 1961, but long before then the reader is anxiously consulting the calendar, counting how many of these tedious years still lie ahead." Writing for *Entertainment Weekly*, Jennifer Reese comments that Martel's "gimmick" of the storytelling goes on "too long, but the sadness that gradually seeps through the cracks of the futile game is all the more excruciating for being so tightly repressed." She affirms that the story is "moving." In a review for the *New York Times*, Janet Maslin describes Martel's long story as a novella, one in which "Martel achieves a graceful balance." She characterizes it as "an odd hybrid: part history, part Roccamatio fiction, part poignantly evoked medical crisis." Maslin further observes the way Martel's later work is evoked in this story, commenting, "The seeds of 'Life of Pi' can be found in the engaging narrative voice, in its curious digressions, in its mixture of unexpected playfulness with the gravity of imminent death."

CRITICISM

Catherine Dominic

Dominic is a novelist and a freelance writer and editor. In the following essay, she tracks and examines the emotional distance established by the first-person narrator of "The Facts behind the Helsinki Roccamatios."

Yann Martel's long story "The Facts behind the Helsinki Roccamatios" is characterized to a marked degree by the narrator's emotional restraint. The distance he establishes between himself and his subject matter—the death of his friend—is almost astonishing. Only rarely in the text does the narrator express his grief, and even rarer still is the opportunity for the reader to *feel* the grief of the narrator. Every writer at some point, often at many points, in his or her career hears the advice "show, don't tell." And many writers argue that there are times when this is a rule that must be broken. Yet in this story about disease, dying, and grief, Martel's narrator is so reserved, so conservative in the way he doles out his true emotions to the reader, that we as readers feel almost cheated when we reach the end of the story. Usually a first-person narrator would give the reader intimate access to thoughts, emotions, and the overall interior world and psychic turmoil one would expect in the midst of such tragedy. Yet Martel's narrator serves more as a reporter. He tells us what he is feeling, he describes Paul's condition and how he reacts to it, but his comments feel clinical and observational at best.

Early in the story, the narrator offers a brief summary of Paul's early symptoms, and he recalls how he jokingly assessed Paul's condition and told him he had pneumonia. He then reveals that that is actually what Paul had. He then states, "In mid-February Paul went to Toronto to see his family doctor. Nine months later he was dead." This sort of clinical summary is typical of the way the narrator reports on Paul's illness; he summarizes in an emotionally distant fashion. Alternatively, he offers

> AS READERS, WE FOLLOW THE NARRATOR AROUND, LOOKING OVER HIS SHOULDER, SEEING WHAT HE SEES; BUT WE CAN ONLY REACT AS STRANGERS, EAVESDROPPERS INTO WHAT MUST HAVE BEEN A VERY PRIVATE, HELLISH, PAINFUL WORLD, BECAUSE THE NARRATOR ONLY RARELY DRAWS US INTIMATELY INTO HIS OWN THOUGHTS."

cold facts, as a journalist would, to describe a situation fraught with emotion. In describing the car accident that resulted in the transfusion that was the source of Paul's infection with HIV, the narrator reports the following facts (italics added for emphasis):

> *Three* years ago, when he was *sixteen*, he had gone to Jamaica on a Christmas holiday with his parents. They had had a car accident. Paul's right leg had been broken and he'd lost some blood. He had received a blood transfusion at the local hospital. *Six* witnesses of the accident had come along to volunteer blood. *Three* were of the right blood group.

The report goes on from there, noting that *one* of these *three* individuals had died *two* years afterward while undergoing treatment for pneumonia. This paragraph is data rich, full of facts, numbers, and specific details. It is also devoid of emotion.

The narrator watches how the drama of Paul's family's coming to grips with his diagnosis unfolds. He describes their reactions, the way Paul's father destroyed the family car, the way Paul's mother lies awake on her bed in the fetal position, the puffy face of Paul's sister, from all the crying, and the way they end up sleeping wherever they happen to find themselves. He notes that Paul existed in the middle of all of this, not reacting to the news himself. Meanwhile, the narrator has not conveyed in any fashion the way he himself emotionally reacted to the news; he has described only how he logically reacted, assessing whether he himself could have ever gotten infected and theorizing as to how Paul got infected. At Paul's house, the narrator simply positions himself as

WHAT DO I READ NEXT?

- Martel's first novel is a fictional autobiography. *Self* was published in 1996 and focuses on a variety of issues, including gender and identity.

- Martel's third novel, *Beatrice and Virgil*, was published in 2010. The titular characters are stuffed animals, a donkey and monkey. In this experimental work, Martel uses animals, as he did in *Life of Pi*, to explore human relationships.

- Nobel Prize–winning Canadian author Alice Munro has set the bulk of her short fiction in her home country. Her collection *Selected Stories, 1968–1994* was published in 1996.

- *When Heroes Die* is a 1994 young-adult novel by Penny Raife Durant. In it, the protagonist's uncle, who raises him after the death of his father, eventually dies from AIDS. The uncle is hospitalized for a period of time prior to his death, not unlike Paul in "The Facts behind the Helsinki Roccamatios."

- *Abyssinian Chronicles*, a novel by Moses Isegawa, was published in 2000. Isegawa's novel focuses on the life of a young man who lives through Uganda's tumultuous twentieth-century history, including the onset of the AIDS epidemic.

- *AIDS at 30: A History*, by medical historian Victoria A. Harden, was published in 2012. Harden analyzes the way American society responded to the AIDS epidemic and chronicles the advances made in the treatment and understanding of the disease from both a medical and a social perspective.

a fly on the wall to observe. He cooks and cleans. He lists other activities, and he talks about the drugs Paul took. The narrator goes on to describe the "three states" Paul's family members went through. Regarding the first state, he talks about Paul's father destroying household objects, his mother lying in bed, his sister crying, and the dog hiding and whining. In the second state, they rally around Paul and encourage each other. The third state involves them participating in normal activities and facing the day as if Paul's illness is nonexistent. These descriptions are rooted in the narrator's keen observations, but still he does not reveal his own emotional reaction to Paul's ongoing illness or to witnessing what Paul's family is enduring. As readers, we follow the narrator around, looking over his shoulder, seeing what he sees; but we can only react as strangers, eavesdroppers into what must have been a very private, hellish, painful world, because the narrator only rarely draws us intimately into his own thoughts. Though he is a first-person narrator, the story reads as if it is being told from a more distant and detached third-person point of view.

This distance is underscored by the story's emphasis on storytelling. The narrator describes the way he and Paul utilized storytelling as something constructive, creative, and distracting, but he insists on telling us almost nothing about the stories themselves. The narrator states, "Now understand that you're not going to hear the story of the Helsinki Roccamatios. Certain intimacies shouldn't be made public. They should be known to exist, that's all." Thus begins the main portion of this long short story, in which Martel interweaves the historical facts that inform the stories the narrator and Paul are telling each other with the facts about Paul's illness and prolonged dying.

What remains missing, though, is what has already been noted as absent, and will continue to be largely absent throughout the work, that is, the "certain intimacies" which the narrator refuses to share. Just as he refused to describe his "emotional distress" to the review board at college, which was reviewing his appeal for withdrawal, the narrator refuses to discuss it with his readers. He states that when the chairman of the committee "asked me in a glib little voice what exactly I meant by 'emotional distress,' I looked at him and I decided that Paul's agony wasn't an orange I was going to peel and quarter and present to him." Perhaps as readers we can accept this at face value, that this was not information the narrator felt comfortable sharing with the chairman of this committee. Yet as readers, it is not "Paul's agony" that we want to see sectioned and displayed, it is the narrator's emotional response to it. We cannot really *know* Paul; we can only know what little the narrator chooses to show us in the very limited context of his grave illness. Usually, at least, readers get to know a first-person narrator. Here, not only do we not know Paul, we also do not know the person telling us Paul's story. We glimpse what he likely feels about Paul and Paul's suffering, but we are not allowed to feel it as well. We are kept at arm's length by the narrator, and apparently we are kept there by design, as "certain intimacies shouldn't be made public."

One of the few instances where the narrator reveals his inner thoughts about the circumstances comes when Paul, apparently feeling angry and frustrated about what is happening to him, vigorously interrupts the narrator's historical facts for the year 1921 with inaccurate historical information. He interjects facts related to death and violence, until the narrator determines to set the facts straight and steer the conversation to safer territory. This further infuriates Paul, and as he becomes more agitated, the narrator thinks to himself, about himself, "*What have you done, you idiot?*" He does not reflect further on this, though. He simply attempts to soothe Paul.

A bit later in the story, after Paul improves briefly but then worsens again, he whispers to the narrator about how he wants to live, how he wants more time. The narrator confesses his thoughts to the reader, saying, "I want to speak, but the words (what words?) don't come. I want to cry, but I feel that I mustn't so I don't." He then attempts to cheer Paul by telling him about all the research that is being done all over the world to find a cure. He later berates himself for saying, "Time is on your side." The narrator's introspections are so limited, restrained. At one point he contemplates the circumstances of an old man sitting alone in the hospital. He thinks of suffering and pain, and comments to himself, "I can't face Paul yet." Here we can see the train of thought, and the narrator's feeling of being unable to face his friend, but the passage remains emotionally reserved. The narrator refuses to open up to the reader and *share* his pain, *reveal* his turmoil. Instead, he reflects, and he discusses the effects of these reflections, but he does not *feel*.

Finally, near the end of the story, the narrator says, "I feel like bursting into tears." The occasion is that Paul has decided to stop shaving. He has very few facial hairs left, while the hair on his scalp has been falling off in patches. Yet the narrator quickly transitions from this one scrap of emotion (notably he *feels* like crying but does not actually shed tears) to a discussion of the historical research Paul has been doing. We as readers are effectively distanced once again from the narrator's emotions. Shortly after, as Paul's despondency deepens, the narrator finds himself feeling numb. At the revelation that Paul has a fungus in his spinal fluid, the narrator states that he wants to forget everything, be far away from what is happening. In contrast to Paul's weakness, the narrator states that he feels "arrogant" in light of his own vitality. These small revelations of emotion build toward a slightly larger discussion of how the narrator feels when the doctors announce they are taking Paul off the primary drug used to treat HIV. The narrator states, "I sit beside his bed, trying to contain myself. My throat is tight and I feel heat in my eyes." Once again though, he moves quickly to another topic. He discusses one of the characters in the Roccamatio stories, a family member named Monika, who, in this installment, is murdered. Here, Martel pairs some of the narrator's more revelatory statements about his feelings with one of the longer descriptions about the content of a Roccamatio story. These commentaries work together to reveal the gravity and darkness surrounding Paul's dying and the narrator's response to it.

This sets up a lengthier tangent in which the narrator leaves the hospital and delights in reading the grim news headlines in which it seems as though the world is destroying itself. He is gleeful at the thought that everything, everyone, is dying. The subtext here is that if Paul has to die, so does everyone else. The narrator then observes everyday life going on around him, stating that he feels "something in me start to unwind." He notices random ads, and beautiful people and poor people. He goes to a bookstore. He seems astounded by the variety and complexity of life. The narrator comments on his ability to take pleasure from catastrophe. This section is perhaps the story's most introspective, but again, it is filled with observations that are summed up by the narrator's response of being unmoved, in a negative way, by negative events and feelings. He seems inured to human suffering.

Paul and his friend look to the Encyclopædia Britannica for facts to focus on.

(© maxim ibragimov / Shutterstock.com)

Throughout the rest of the story, the narrator's responses vary between detachment and brief, unexamined revelations of emotion. When Paul vomits blood, the narrator panics for a moment, worried that he will be infected. He describes feeling tense after running into the chaplain at the hospital, and how he runs along a path, drops to the ground, claws at the earth with his fingers, and rests his head on the cool ground. Yet he makes no attempt to analyze this panicked, erratic behavior. He does talk about feeling relief and depression when he leaves Paul, while feeling "brilliantly alive" when he is with him.

The narrator has a deeper, more thoughtfully explored burst of emotion when Paul goes blind: "For the first time ever, I can't help it and I impose my sadness onto his. I break down right in front of him. Great, cracking, uncontrollable sobs." We have seen so little emotion from the narrator at this point, that this moment is startling in its candor. It is the last moment of such emotion. The story trails off with Paul's death, and the way the narrator

learns of it, over the phone. He comments that he feels shocked by the words as they are delivered, but, again, the description of his emotional response is extremely detached. The last words of the story are Paul's, in the note that he leaves for the narrator. Martel chose to end the story here, instead of illuminating the narrator's response to the note. Once again, we are left looking over the narrator's shoulder. We read the note and watch for a response from the narrator, and see none.

As Jennifer Reese has noted in a review of the story for *Entertainment Weekly,* the little emoted sadness that does enter the story "is all the more excruciating for being so tightly repressed." Arguably, though, the moments of expressed emotion remain so repressed, so removed and so unexamined, that the story falls short of effectively exploring the prolonged death of the narrator's close friend. It leaves the reader feeling cheated and unconnected, rather like seeing a news story without the hook that draws you in. The narrator *reports* but so rarely emotes that the reader is left with an empty feeling that has more to do with never having been filled than with having something taken away.

Source: Catherine Dominic, Critical Essay on "The Facts behind the Helsinki Roccamatios," in *Short Stories for Students*, Gale, Cengage Learning, 2015.

Stephen Moss

In the following essay, Moss examines the controversy over Martel's choice to write a book about the Holocaust.

Talking about the Holocaust at nine in the morning in the elegant lounge of a trendy boutique hotel in central London is not ideal. A woman packs up and moves to the other side of the room at Yann Martel's first mention of genocide. I am conscious of the fact we may be speaking too loud. There is an additional problem that my new BlackBerry keeps ringing. I have no idea how to turn it off, and eventually have to ask the concierge to dispose of it.

Martel, the Canadian author who won the Booker prize for the outrageously successful *Life of Pi* in 2002, takes all this more or less in his stride, though he is a little put out by my incompetence and fractiousness—I rather rudely insist that the young woman who is steering him round the UK and Ireland on the publicity tour for his new novel, *Beatrice and Virgil*, absent herself from the room while we talk. I'd only finished his book the night before—reaching its dramatic denouement in the bath, if you must know—and feel at something of a disadvantage in talking about it, since he spent eight years labouring over it.

The inescapable fact about the book, Martel's long-awaited follow-up to *Life of Pi*, is that it has not been very well received. In the US the reviews were what one politely calls "mixed"; in the UK they have been uniformly hostile. The general view is that pretty well all fictional treatments of the Holocaust are doomed, and that this one—about a blocked writer who meets a taxidermist writing a play about "the horrors" who is probably a former Nazi seeking some sort of catharsis—is more doomed than most.

I have taken along a review by David Sexton, literary editor of the *London Evening Standard* and a critic with impeccable taste, who had accused Martel of being "not very bright" because of a quote in which he said the monkey and donkey which feature in the taxidermist's clunky play, large chunks of

> HE CONTRASTS THE MULTITUDE OF TREATMENTS OF THE TWO WORLD WARS OF THE 20TH CENTURY WITH THE MUCH MORE RESTRICTED FRAMEWORK WITHIN WHICH THE HOLOCAUST IS SEEN, AND QUESTIONS WHETHER THE LATTER SERVES THE VARIETY OF THE EXPERIENCES AND RESPONSES OF THOSE WHO SUFFERED AND DIED."

which appear in the novel, were appropriate representatives of Jews because they embody mental nimbleness and stubbornness respectively. Martel is keen to see the review, as he has heard about it but has yet to read it. I hand it over and lean back. All in all, I am sensing disaster here.

Apart from an "Oooh" (or maybe "Pwooh") at being accused of stupidity by Sexton, he takes it philosophically. "I think there are four kinds of reviews. There are bad bad reviews; good bad reviews; bad good reviews, and good good reviews. Good bad reviews that point out genuine flaws are useful. This is just idiotic and very personal. I'm using allegory. If he says that of me, I wonder what he feels about Art Spiegelman in *Maus*. In *Maus* the Jews are characterised as mice. But were the Jews mouselike in the Warsaw ghetto uprising? I wonder how he feels about that characterisation."

I try to move away from the specifics of this review to the general problem Martel faced with this book—that many critics recoil from the very idea of a Holocaust novel written by an author who is neither Jewish nor basing his work, as with *Schindler's Ark*, on some sanctified piece of history. Martel, who is (*pace* Sexton) very bright and enormously fluent considering the time and the fact that he has just finished having breakfast with his wife and nine-month-old son in the hotel restaurant, rejects the idea that the Holocaust is "indescribable, that is should be sacred." "It's the specialism of the artist to go where other people don't go," he says. "I don't think the Holocaust gains by having artists staying on the edges. It's always represented in the same way, in a non-fictional way, so the archetypal figures are people like Primo Levi and Elie Wiesel, or the historians. They've all done essential work, but I can't think of any other historical event that is only represented by historians and survivors. Most other historical events will be taken on by artists."

He contrasts the multitude of treatments of the two world wars of the 20th century with the much more restricted framework within which the Holocaust is seen, and questions whether the latter serves the variety of the experiences and responses of those who suffered and died. "You can't quantify human pain the way you can measure out sugar," he says. "Death comes one individual at a time."

I suggest that what the critics are trying to tell him is it's none of his business—he's not Jewish, is a different generation, is almost inevitably going to come up with a treatment which offends aesthetically. "The tragedy of the Holocaust wasn't exclusively Jewish," he says. "It was non-Jews who did it. It was an act of two groups, so it's not just for Jews to be expert on the Holocaust. In any case, we're in dialogue with history, and you no more own a historical event than people own their language. The English don't own the English language; the Jews don't own the Holocaust; the French don't own Verdun. It's good to have other perspectives. If you claim to own an event, you may suffer from group think."

Beatrice and Virgil is better than many of the critics have suggested, and certainly gripped me as I read the final third in the bath, though there is a temptation to skip the extracts from the taxidermist's tiresome, quasi-Beckettian monkey-and-donkey fable. The beginning of the book is especially compelling—a lunch at which the author, Henry, is slated for having written a book about the Holocaust deemed unpublishable by a posse of editors from the UK and North America who have assembled to tell him to do it differently, if he does it at all. Clearly, Henry is Martel and this lunch did occur, a couple of years ago, when his publishers ganged up to tell him that five years' work on his long-pondered Holocaust book had been misdirected.

The problem, as becomes clear in conversation as well as the novel, was that he had conceived of a "flip book" which could be read from both front and back. From the front,

you got the novel; from the back you got an essay on how difficult it is to represent the Holocaust. The two would presumably have met in the middle, to their mutual enlightenment. But his lunch companions were unconvinced. He sums up their feelings in *Beatrice and Virgil*: "The novel was tedious, the plot feeble, the characters unconvincing, their fate uninteresting, the point lost; the essay was flimsy, lacking in substance, poorly argued, poorly written. The idea of the flip book was an annoying distraction, besides being commercial suicide. The whole was a complete, unpublishable failure."

It sounds like quite an occasion. There's a moment in the novel when one of the editors asks where you would put the bar code on a book with, in effect, two front covers. Henry initially offers some polite suggestions; then he snaps. "I wrote my book on the Holocaust without worrying about where the fucking bar code would go." The ugly sound of art meeting commerce.

I tell him I rather liked the idea of the flip book. "So did I," he says. Did he fight for it? "I fought a lot for it, but I accepted their [his editors' and publishers'] argument that non-fiction is a very specialised product, whereas a novel is a very broad product that has great general appeal. A great novel from Colombia, *One Hundred Years of Solitude*, will be read around the world, whereas who's going to read a history of Colombia? A fraction of those people who might read *One Hundred Years of Solitude*. They said, 'Your essay will drag down the novel.'" He dropped the essay, which remains unpublished, and set about reworking the fictional element, now framed as two men (both called Henry) both trying to find a way to describe the Holocaust. The writer Henry's chance encounter with the taxidermist Henry eventually makes it possible for him to find a way through the conceptual problems posed by his publishers.

Martel strikes me as quite a tough cookie, clever and hard-edged. If he had absolutely believed in the flip-book concept, I suspect he would have got his way. After all, here was an author whose previous book, *Life of Pi*—an unlikely tale of an Indian boy drifting in a lifeboat for 277 days with only a talking Bengal tiger for company—has sold more than seven million copies around the world and is reckoned to be the most successful Booker winner of all time. It's a fair bet he could have found other publishers, but he says he respects the ones he has and in the end accepted their arguments.

Before *Life of Pi*, Martel—who had published a collection of short stories and a novel to critical acclaim and uninspiring sales—was trundling along, happy enough but earning next to nothing. *Life of Pi* catapulted him into the literary stratosphere, made him a millionaire (a film of the book due next year, to be directed by Ang Lee, will presumably add to the pot), and sent him on the road for two years doing interviews like this one in hotel lounges around the world—a purgatory he says he enjoys. The book even found him a wife, the writer Alice Kuipers, whom he met at the Cheltenham festival where he was talking about *Life of Pi* in 2003. Martel is 46, Kuipers 31, and son Theo was born last year. Martel clearly dotes on him and insists I interrupt their breakfast to meet him, even though neither of us is quite ready to make intelligible conversation.

So *Life of Pi* changed everything? "It changed everything on the outside," says Martel. "It made my life more complicated, busier. But not on the inside. The process of writing remains exactly the same—research, writing, rewriting." He seems unfazed by the sudden wealth. "I don't smoke, I don't drink, I didn't own a car until I was 39. I'm not a consumer. I hate buying clothes. I don't have a mobile. I just don't need things. I don't like things. Since boarding school days at age 16 I consciously said, 'Why am I valuing this stuff?'" His time in India in the late 1990s, when he was writing *Life of Pi*, reinforced his anti-materialism and led him to swap secularism for spirituality, to accept that there was some purpose beneath the surface anarchy, to believe that the boy and tiger being tossed about on the Pacific were going to make landfall thanks to some divine grace.

Martel and his family live on the Canadian prairies, in the town of Saskatoon, where he is loosely attached to the University of Saskatchewan. "It's a great little community in Saskatoon," he says. "I got tired of living in big cities. I lived for 10 years in Paris, I lived for 10 years in Montreal, I lived a summer in Toronto, I spent a fair bit of time in London. In all big cities the style of life is the same. Same endless array of restaurants; same big museums with the usual suspects; same anonymity, which can

be thrilling when you're young but which I found got tiresome. What I like about a small city [the population of Saskatoon is around 220,000] is it can't compete with big cities, so it can only be itself. It has a certain authenticity." He and his wife have bought a house in the town, but he says that without her prompting he probably wouldn't have bothered, preferring the life of the hermit crab that moves from borrowed shell to borrowed shell.

Martel's father was a Canadian diplomat (and award-winning poet) and his mother a translator; because of his father's job, his upbringing was peripatetic—he was born in Spain and grew up in Costa Rica, France and Mexico as well as Canada. His family spoke French but he attended English-speaking schools and has always written in English; as well as being bilingual in English and French, he is fluent in Spanish. The multilingualism and his parents' literary leanings made writing an almost inevitable calling, and he wrote his first play—which he says was very bad—at 19.

For the last three years Martel has been sending fortnightly letters and books to the Canadian prime minister Stephen Harper—an attempt to educate him in the ways of great literature. Martel was prompted to act as a literary godfather when Harper cited *The Guinness Book of Records* as his favourite book, and by his failure to recognise the importance of the arts generally. "I'm doing it to point out that literature's not just entertainment," he explains. "It is an essential tool to look at the human condition. I don't care if fellow citizens read or not; it's not up to me to say how people should live their lives. But I believe people who lead should read."

He says that, in Harper, he sensed "a man who was a narrow ideologue, in part because he hasn't read. He lacks empathy because he hasn't read literature. If literature does one thing, it makes you more empathetic by making you live other lives and feel the pain of others. Ideologues don't feel the pain of others because they haven't imaginatively got under their skins." The books Martel has sent include George Orwell's *Animal Farm*, Jane Austen's *The Watsons* and Elizabeth Smart's *By Grand Central Station I Sat Down and Wept*. He's had a few pro forma replies from the PM's office, but nothing from Harper himself, which he contrasts with the handwritten note he received from Barack Obama saying how much he and his daughter Malia had enjoyed *Life of Pi*.

Martel is already deep into his next novel, which is set in Portugal and features three chimpanzees. He is reading dozens of books about chimps and currently trying to find what kind of car would have been driven in Portugal in the 1930s. "Those kinds of questions, that kind of approach to the world, is what I find satisfying," he says. "After that, fame, money, 'Why don't you live in Bel Air?' It's like, 'Why would I want to do that?' I'm quite happy living the natural life of the writer. It is a thrilling place to be."

Source: Stephen Moss, "Yann Martel: 'Jewish People Don't Own the Holocaust,'" in *Guardian* (London, England), June 22, 2010.

Yann Martel

In the following essay, Martel explains a little about how he became a writer.

I started writing seriously when I was nineteen. I wrote a play about a young man who falls in love with a door; when a friend finds out and destroys the door, our hero commits suicide. It was as bad as it sounds. But that first effort was a capital step for me because, for the first time in my life, I wrote something for its own sake; that is, the sake of art.

Before that, writing had always been homework. Writing doesn't come easily—to anyone. Children draw without being prompted. They sing and babble without being prompted. They do all kinds of things on their own. But they don't write. Precocious children may compose sonatas, like Mozart. But you never hear parents exclaim, "Look! Junior has written a three-hundred-page novel! And he's only seven years old!" It just doesn't happen. Words are boring; they just sit there on the page. They are hard to spell. There are so many of them to learn. Some you can't even pronounce. And then you must order them into something called "sentences"—so, so difficult. Worse, there's grammar, which never gives you a break. And all this struggle for what? For something boring that just sits there on the page.

Playing cops and robbers or hide and seek is more fun. Swimming is more fun. Nearly everything is more fun. The child can't imagine anyone who would enjoy writing. Except perhaps one person: its older sibling, who is miserable and inward-looking, who is racked by doubts and covered in pimples.

Adolescence is the savior of writing, just as—to some teenagers—writing is the savior of adolescence. It is at that age that the effort involved in writing begins to bear fruit. With words, one can express oneself; and since every teenager is at one point or another misunderstood, there is much to express. Suddenly the possibilities of words begin to explode in the mind. The teenager reads and writes in search of answers.

Then, normally, in the late teen years, the angst settles, the pen is dropped and life goes on. The poems and stories one wrote as a teenager are relegated to yellowed diaries stored in boxes in attics. Normally.

But some of us don't want to drop the pen. The intoxication of words and stories goes beyond merely calming us. On the contrary. Words and stories and books fire us up. After looking in with language, we start looking out. We feel the urge to continue writing. We have more stories and poems in us. Writing becomes something serious.

Thus is born the writer. Or at least this writer. I kept writing to learn, to explore, to create, to renew.

At first what I wrote was terrible, trapped in immaturity. But by dint of practice I got better. This story is the result. "The Facts behind the Helsinki Roccamatios," and the three other stories that became my first book, are the best results of my early years as a writer. With them, the door of the imagination was flung open and I entered a room—a bejeweled world—I never wanted to leave. It was a thrill I'll never forget.

For me, the best was the first.

Source: Yann Martel, "From *Facts Behind the Helsinki Roccamatios*," in *This Is My Best: Great Writers Share Their Favorite Work*, edited by Retha Powers and Kathy Kiernan, Chronicle Books, 2004, pp. 309–10.

Barbara Hoffert

In the following review, Hoffert recommends Martel's collection, considering the stories "meditative" and "thought-provoking."

Having delivered a nail-biting narrative with *Life of Pi*, Martel chooses not to repeat himself, here offering four meditative stories that test the limits of the form. In the longest, the narrator and a friend slowly perishing of AIDS swap stories, centered on the imaginary Roccamatios of Helsinki, that reflect events of the 20th century. We don't get their stories, however, just the events that inspire them, which creates an appropriate sense of being shut out (just as the narrator can't really enter his friend's pain), though it can be a little distancing. In "Manners of Dying," variations of the same letter written by a prison warden to a woman whose son has just been executed reveal the horror of capital punishment. In the especially intriguing "The Vita Aeterna Mirror Company," an old woman reiterates memories (in a narrow column) to her newly alert grandson (whose thoughts fill the page). Startlingly, she even shows him a machine that makes mirrors out of memories. Elusive and thought-provoking, though sure to confound anyone who reads for plot, this collection is recommended for public and academic libraries.

Source: Barbara Hoffert, Review of *The Facts behind the Helsinki Roccamatios*, in *Library Journal*, Vol. 129, No. 18, November 1, 2004, p. 79.

Brad Hooper

In the following review, Hooper describes Martel's collection as "stunning."

This collection of two long and two short stories by the author of the avidly read and Booker Prize-winning novel *Life of Pi* (2002) was published a decade ago in Martel's native Canada and now is being released in the U.S. Its American appearance after all these years is due to the success of *Pi*, of course, but its postponement had nothing to do with a lack of artistry. These are stunning stories; they are drawn, like *Pi*, from the far reaches—not stretches—of the author's inventiveness. The title story is a masterpiece by any standard; the destructiveness of AIDS has rarely been rendered so universally as Martel parallels a long set of political horrors that have occurred over the twentieth century with the private ones endured over the course of a young man's fatal illness, The next story (bearing a title much too long to cite here) leaves the reader wondering what writer has understood as well as Martel the union of physical and emotional sensations that listening to beautiful music can induce. The last two stories—both much shorter—engage in elements of magic realism; in the first one, the author explores a range of personal reactions to death, and in the second, he suggests that much of what we see in ourselves is the construct of our memories. The collection is a multidimensional meditation on being and mortality and

answering to a higher spirit—cerebral exercises, no question, but the sheer luminosity of Martel's prose style opens these stories' relevance and allure to a wide audience.

Source: Brad Hooper, Review of *The Facts behind the Helsinki Roccamatios*, in *Booklist*, Vol. 101, No. 5, November 1, 2004, p. 465.

Publishers Weekly

In the following review, an anonymous writer sees the collected stories as "exemplary works of apprenticeship."

Pathos is leavened with inventiveness and humor in this collection of a novella and three short stories first published in a slightly different version in Canada in 1993, nearly 10 years before Martel's Booker-winning *Life of Pi*. The minor key is established in the title novella, a graceful, multilayered story of a young man dying of AIDS, told through the refracting lens of the history of the 20th century. Infected by a blood transmission, Paul receives the diagnosis during his freshman year of college. The narrator, Paul's student mentor, devises a plan to keep Paul engaged in life—they will invent the story of the Roccamatio family of Helsinki, which will have 100 chapters, each thematically linked to an event of the 20th century. The connection between the history, the stories and Paul's condition is subtle and always shifting, as fluid and elusive as life itself. The experience of death is delicately probed in the next two stories as well: in one, a Canadian student's life is changed when he hears the Rankin Concerto, written in honor of a Vietnam veteran; in the other, a prison warden reports to a mother on her son's last moments before he is executed. The book closes with a surreal fable in which mirrors are made from memories. These are exemplary works of apprenticeship, slight yet richly satisfying.

Source: Review of *The Facts behind the Helsinki Roccamatios*, in *Publishers Weekly*, Vol. 251, No. 44, November 1, 2004, pp. 41–42.

Kirkus Reviews

In the following review, an anonymous writer describes the collection as "a disappointment."

This mixed-bag of three stories and a novella first appeared in 1993, nine years before its Canadian author's Booker Prize winner, *Life of Pi*.

The stories are comparatively weak. "Manners of Dying" contains alternative versions of the letter a prison warden must send to the mother of a young convict over whose execution he presides. A few of the several scenarios (describing the prisoner's reaction to his imminent death) are harshly moving, but the story as a whole is distinctly gimmicky. In another, an unnamed narrator re-creates "The Time I Heard the Private Donald J. Rankin String Concerto with One Discordant Violin, by the American Composer John Morton." The chamber piece so identified memorializes the Vietnam War with awkward intensity, in "a mix of perfect beauty and cathartic error." Martel's development of the premise is disappointingly banal. "The Via Aeterna Mirror Company: Mirrors to Last till Kingdom Come" describes, in a mixture of prose and verse, its narrator's slow comprehension of his grandmother's long widowhood and stoical old age, the facts of which are "stored" in a marvelous machine that "runs on" her memories. It's a thin fantasy, filled with redundant padding, that reads like an abandoned Ray Bradbury effort. Then there's the title novella, set in 1986, about a college student's slow dying from AIDS (contracted during an emergency blood transfusion), as described by the friend who endures the ordeal with him, ceaselessly visiting and offering support, concocting an ongoing story about an imaginary Finnish family: "a story in eighty-six episodes, each echoing one event from one year of the unfolding century." As his friend's "contributions" remain hopeful and encouraging, the patient's own tales grow increasingly despairing and apocalyptic: the surrounding story's progression is precise, impressively imagined, and immensely moving.

Overall, a disappointment. "The Facts," though, represents the best reason we've been given yet to keep reading Martel.

Source: Review of *The Facts behind the Helsinki Roccamatios*, in *Kirkus Reviews*, Vol. 72, No. 20, October 15, 2004, p. 979.

Olivia Glazebrook

In the following review, Glazebrook judges the stories in the collection to be less mature than Martel's writing in his novel Life of Pi.

This collection was originally published by Faber in 1993, and was followed in 1996 by Martel's first novel, *Self*. Then Canongate bagged the prizewinning *Life of Pi* in 2002, and now, in the wake of its colossal success,

they have republished these four stories, 'slightly revised.' 'I'm happy to offer these four stories again to the reading public . . .' chuckles Martel fondly in his Author's Note, '. . . the youthful urge to overstate reined in, the occasional clumsiness in the prose I hope ironed out.'

The title story is an account of the decline and death of Paul, a young man who has contracted the HIV virus as a result of a blood transfusion in Jamaica. The narrator is a friend and fellow student of Paul's who constructs a game which he hopes will distract Paul from his illness: they will invent a family and tell its history, using an event from each year between 1901 and 1986 as a 'metaphorical guideline.' So, a saga in 86 chapters. Martel, however, is not concerned with the Roccamatio family. Instead he uses the historical events picked by Paul and the narrator to parallel the relentless advance of Paul's illness.

In 'The Time I Heard the Private Donald J. Rankin String Concerto' the narrator chances on a classical music concert in an abandoned theatre in Washington D.C. He is profoundly affected by the music, and after the concert follows its composer, John Morton, to the bank where Morton works as a janitor.

'Manners of Dying' is a collection of letters from a warden on Death Row to the mother of an executed prisoner. Each letter describes how Kevin Barlow might have lived his last moments: in one he trembles, in another he laughs; in one he is aggressive, in another incapacitated by fear; in one he is impatient to be hanged, in another he has to be dragged to the noose.

And finally, 'The Vita Aeterna Mirror Company,' a fantasy in which an old lady shows her sulky grandson how to make a mirror: by speaking memories into a machine.

In his Author's Note Martel describes what, for him, makes a story 'work': 'intellect rooted in emotion, emotion structured by intellect—in other words, a good idea that moves.' But an idea is not a plot. What is lacking in this book, although it is an interesting and at times engaging read, is story, a narrative of incidents in their sequence from which ideas and themes naturally arise. Paul's illness cannot help but be affecting: it is grim, desperate, painful. And Kevin Barlow's execution appals, just as it should. But this book contains jumbles of description, theme and emotion, rather than stories.

In 'The Vita Aeterna Mirror Company' Martel positively avoids storytelling. When the grandmother tells her memories to the mirror machine, all her bored grandson hears (and all we read) is 'blah-blah-blah-blah' over and over again. In later life the grandson regrets his inattention. 'I often,' he writes at the end of the story, 'try to imagine all the words I so stupidly ignored.' Fortunately by the time *Life of Pi* came along, Yann Martel had decided it was worth filling in the blah-blah-blah-blahs.

Source: Olivia Glazebrook, "Working with Ideas, Not Stories," in *Spectator*, Vol. 296, No. 9192, October 9, 2004, pp. 48–49.

SOURCES

Bosco, Umberto, "Giovanni Boccaccio," in *Encyclopædia Britannica*, April 25, 2013, http://www.britannica.com/EBchecked/topic/70836/Giovanni-Boccaccio (accessed September 22, 2014).

"History of HIV & AIDS in the U.S.," AVERT website, http://www.avert.org/history-hiv-aids-us.htm (accessed September 22, 2014).

"The HIV/AIDS Epidemic in the United States," Henry J. Kaiser Family Foundation website, April 7, 2014, http://kff.org/hivaids/fact-sheet/the-hivaids-epidemic-in-the-united-states/ (accessed September 22, 2014).

Martel, Yann, "The Facts behind the Helsinki Roccamatios," in *The Facts behind the Helsinki Roccamatios*, Harcourt, 2004, pp. 3–81.

Maslin, Janet, "Dark-Hued Early Works of a Booker Prize Winner," in *New York Times*, November 22, 2004, http://www.nytimes.com/2004/11/22/books/22masl.html (accessed September 22, 2014).

Priest, Chistopher, "The Song Is Ended but the Malady Lingers On," in *Guardian* (London, England), September 24, 2004, http://www.theguardian.com/books/2004/sep/25/featuresreviews.guardianreview13 (accessed September 22, 2014).

Reese, Jennifer, Review of *The Facts behind the Helsinki Roccamatios*, in *Entertainment Weekly*, December 3, 2004, http://www.ew.com/article/0,,831849,00.html (accessed September 22, 2014).

"Thirty Years of HIV/AIDS: Snapshots of an Epidemic," amfAR website, http://www.amfar.org/thirty-years-of-hiv/aids-snapshots-of-an-epidemic/ (accessed September 22, 2014).

"Yann Martel," British Council Literature, http://literature.britishcouncil.org/yann-martel (accessed September 22, 2014).

"Yann Martel," in *Canadian Encyclopedia*, http://www.thecanadianencyclopedia.ca/en/article/yann-martel/ (accessed September 22, 2014).

FURTHER READING

Gillett, James, *A Grassroots History of the HIV/AIDS Epidemic in North America*, Marquette Books, 2010.
   Gillett's work investigates the history of activism surrounding AIDS and AIDS awareness throughout the past twenty-five years.

The Journey Prize Stories 25, McClelland & Stewart, 2013.
   The Journey Prize is an award given to promising young Canadian authors. A number of stories are selected by a three-person jury and published in an anthology every year.

Martel, Yann, *What Is Stephen Harper Reading? Yann Martel's Recommended Reading for a Prime Minister and Book Lovers of All Stripes*, Vintage Canada, 2009.
   Martel began sending letters and books to the prime minister of Canada after the leader revealed he was not much of a reader. This volume collects the letters Martel used to introduce each month's selections to the prime minster. In the letters, Martel explains to the prime minister why he should be reading the volumes being sent.

Shilts, Randy, *And the Band Played On: Politics, People, and the AIDS Epidemic*, 20th Anniversary Edition, St. Martin's Griffin, 2007.
   Shilts's journalistic investigation explores the AIDS epidemic and the politics he believes contributed to the rapid spread of the disease.

SUGGESTED SEARCH TERMS

Yann Martel AND The Facts behind the Helsinki Roccamatios

Yann Martel AND AIDS

Yann Martel AND frame narrative

AIDS epidemic AND 1980s

Yann Martel AND biography

Yann Martel AND Life of Pi

HIV/AIDS treatment AND history

AIDS in fiction

Yann Martel AND Canadian short story authors

Yann Martel AND Man Booker Prize

Boccaccio AND Decameron

Yann Martel AND Boccaccio

Haircut

RING LARDNER
1925

Ring Lardner was a well-respected short-story writer who came from a background in sports writing. His short story "Haircut" is narrated by a barber, known as Whitey, who gossips with an unnamed patron—the reader. The contents of Whitey's ramblings to the patron focus on Jim Kendall, a onetime resident of the small town in which the story is set. He regales the patron with stories of Jim's practical jokes and sense of humor, which reveal Jim's cruelty and vindictiveness. In telling the patron of the events that led to Jim's death, Whitey describes Jim's delight in making fun of the mentally disabled Paul, the way his drinking affected his family, and his obsession with Julie, whom he humiliates when she does not return his advances. At the heart of the story is the tension between Whitey's casual description of Jim as a funny practical joker and the reality of Jim's baseness and cruelty. Whitey is regarded as somewhat of an unreliable narrator, and the story is regarded as a gritty exploration of the underlying brutality of a midwestern small town. "Haircut" was first published in the March 1925 issue of *Liberty* magazine. It was published the following year in *The Love Nest and Other Stories*, in the 1954 volume *Haircut and Other Stories*, which was reprinted in 1991, and in *The Best Short Stories of Ring Lardner* in 1957.

American sports columnist and short-story writer Ring Lardner, Jr. (© *Paul Dorsey | The LIFE Picture | Getty Images*)

AUTHOR BIOGRAPHY

Lardner was born in Niles, Michigan, on March 6, 1885. He was the youngest of six children in a wealthy family. His parents were Henry and Lena Lardner, a businessman and a poet, respectively. Lardner was educated at home and then at Niles High School. Despite the financial losses the family suffered following a bank failure, Lardner declined a college scholarship and instead went to Chicago, where he worked odd jobs. Then his father enrolled him in the Armour Institute of Technology, where he studied mechanical engineering. He only remained there a short time before returning to Niles to work as a postal clerk, a bookkeeper, and a meter reader.

In 1905, Lardner began working as a reporter for the *South Bend Times*. Three years later, he moved to Chicago and worked as a sports reporter for several different papers. He married Ellis Abbot in 1911. While he continued to work as a sports writer, he also began to publish epistolary fiction, writing a series of fictional letters from a baseball player to his friend. The first letters in this series, "A Busher's Letters Home," were published in 1914 in the *Saturday Evening Post*. Lardner went on to publish other works of short fiction in a variety of journals.

Lardner and his wife and four sons moved to Long Island in 1919. His literary circle of friends included F. Scott Fitzgerald. In 1925 he published the story "Haircut" in *Liberty* magazine, and it was later included in the volume *The Love Nest and Other Stories* (1926) and in other collections. His work was both popular and critically acclaimed, but his reputation and his health began to decline after 1926. He suffered from tuberculosis, a heart condition, alcoholism, and insomnia. He died of a heart attack on September 25, 1933.

PLOT SUMMARY

"Haircut" begins with the first-person narrator, a barber, who is later identified as Dick or "Whitey," describing the working-class town in which he lives and earns a living as the proprietor of a barbershop. The shop is the setting for the story. Whitey addresses the reader as if he or she is a patron of the barbershop. He begins to tell the anonymous "you" about the good times the town had before Jim Kendall was killed. He speaks of the way Jim and his friend Hod Meyers would tell stories together and keep everyone entertained and laughing.

Whitey relates how Jim and Hod teased other patrons of the shop. After explaining that Jim sold canned goods for a living and was often out of town on business, Whitey describes the way Jim would return on Saturdays and tell stories of his travels. Whitey talks about Jim losing his job, working odd jobs around town, and spending his money on gin. He mentions Jim's wife, and how she tried to collect Jim's earnings so she could feed their children before Jim spent the money on alcohol. Whitey appears amused by Jim's efforts to outsmart his wife.

In recounting an incident in which Jim promised his wife and children he would take them to the circus, Whitey states that while Jim's family waited for him to meet them to buy tickets, he was getting drunk. Doc Stair, a new young doctor in town, came along and paid for the tickets for Mrs. Kendall and the children. Whitey recounts that Doc Stair was hired as town coroner after the old coroner died.

Next Whitey talks about a young boy who fell from a tree when he was ten and hit his head. His name was Paul Dickson, and according to Whitey he was never the same after the accident. After spending some time describing the way Jim used to make fun of Paul, Whitey says that the only people in town Paul trusted were Doc Stair and a young woman named Julie Gregg. The doctor attempted to help Paul, and Whitey notes that he did seem to improve under Doc Stair's care.

Whitey then begins to talk about Julie. He describes the way, while waiting for his mother when she was seen by Doc Stair, he watched Julie walk into the office and meet the doctor for the first time. Whitey saw that Julie was

smitten from the first, but the doctor did not quite reciprocate her feelings. Whitey then describes the way Jim Kendall, though married, pursued Julie. When Julie rebuffed all of Jim's advances, he forced his way into her house; she freed herself from his grasp, locked herself in a different room in her house, and called the marshal, Joe Barnes. As Whitey tells it, Joe spoke to Jim the next day about the incident. Later, Hod Meyers teased Jim about it, and as Julie's affection for Doc Stair was well known, Hod also suggested that Doc had what Jim could not have. Whitey then describes Jim's ability to change his voice—he could sound like a woman, or any man, Whitey says.

After describing the way he had been fooled by Jim as a practical joke, Whitey relates the way Jim got his revenge after Julie spurned him. One night, when Jim knew Doc was out of town, he called Julie and said it was Doc. He told Julie he needed to see her. She agreed to go to his office. Meanwhile, Jim, who had been drinking with his friends at the pool hall, brought his friends with him to Doc's office and hid behind the stairs. Julie rang the bell outside his office. When she heard a noise, Whitey explains, she called out and asked if it was Ralph, which was Doc Stair's first name. When she realized that she had been fooled, she turned to leave, and Jim and all of his friends chased her home and mocked her the whole way.

When Doc returned, the whole town knew of the incident, but nobody told him at first. After Paul Dickson overheard Jim bragging about it at the barbershop, he informed Doc about what had happened with Julie. Whitey assumed that Doc planned to make Jim suffer for what he had done, but he did not want Julie to find out, Whitey surmises. Not long after, Jim was in Whitey's shop looking for someone to go duck hunting with. As Hod was out of town, Jim agreed to let Paul go with him. The next morning, Doc came in to Whitey's shop to ask if he had seen Paul. Whitey stated that Paul and Jim had gone hunting, but Doc explained that Paul had told him that he would never have anything to do with Jim again.

According to Whitey, Doc Stair then said that Paul had told him about the joke Jim had played on Julie, and had asked him what he thought about it. Doc Stair had told Paul that anyone who could do something like that should not be allowed to live. Whitey tried to defend Jim to the doctor, explaining Jim's actions as merely mischievous. Later that day, the doctor got a call from a man named John Scott, whose property Paul and Jim had been on while hunting. According to Whitey, Paul explained to John the way the gun had gone off accidentally when Jim had given it to him while they were hunting. Jim was dead. As Doc Stair was the coroner, he was summoned to examine the body. The death was ruled accidental. Whitey concludes his story by stating that Jim was foolish to have allowed someone so inexperienced with guns to use one.

CHARACTERS

Joe Barnes
Joe is the town's marshal. Julie phones him after Jim attacks her. He warns Jim to stay away from Julie.

Dick
See "Whitey"

Paul Dickson
Paul is described by Whitey as a simpleton who sustained a head injury as a young boy when he fell from a tree. Doc Stair worked with him to try and improve his ability to function more competently and independently, but he is still widely regarded as mentally disabled. He shoots Jim when they are hunting, and the death is ruled an accident.

Julie Gregg
Julie is a young woman who has gone away to college and returned to the small town in which the story takes place. She is different from other people in town due to her education and worldliness, Whitey notes, and she is attracted to Doc Stair, likely in part because he is an intelligent outsider who, like Julie, has experiences that extend beyond the town. Julie is the victim of one of Jim's pranks. As an object of his desire who rejected him, Julie is targeted by Jim. Seeking to humiliate her, he calls Julie, pretending to be Doc Stair. When she goes to meet him, she is taunted and chased by Jim and his friends.

Jim Kendall
Jim Kendall is the focus of the anecdotes Whitey tells the patron who is getting a haircut. He is described as a clever prankster, yet his sense of humor is often cruel and vindictive. He makes fun of the mentally challenged Paul and humiliates Julie, who expresses her disdain for him. Though he is married with children, he pursues other women, Whitey states, and Julie becomes the focus of his obsession. He is a drunk, and alcohol fuels many of his schemes. Paul shoots Jim at the end of the story. The incident is written off as a hunting accident.

Mrs. Kendall
Mrs. Kendall is Jim Kendall's wife. Whitey speaks of her desire to divorce Jim, but she has no means to support herself and care for her children without Jim, even though he spends most of what little he earns on alcohol.

Hod Meyer
Hod does not feature prominently in the story but is depicted by Whitey as a sort of sidekick to Jim. Hod goads Jim about Julie's rejection of him and points out that Doc Stair is the object of Julie's affection.

John Scott
John Scott owns the property upon which Jim Kendall and Paul Dickinson are hunting when Paul kills Jim.

Doc Stair
Doctor Ralph Stair, referred to primarily in the story as Doc Stair, is a handsome young doctor who is well regarded within the community. Julie has romantic feelings for the doctor, which the whole town has apparently noticed, if Whitey is to be believed. Doc Stair is trusted by Paul and becomes a pivotal, though apparently unwitting, figure in the tragic results of Jim's scheme. Whitey's

suggestion is that Doc Stair influenced Paul in such a way that may have led to Jim's death.

"Whitey"

Whitey, whose real name is Dick, is the barber who narrates the story. The story is essentially made up of the gossip Whitey tells a patron who comes in for a haircut. He is especially talkative and inserts some comments into his story that indicate his opinion about the events he is relating, indicating when he thought Jim was funny, or when he thought Jim got what he deserved. Whitey is somewhat of an unreliable narrator, because he expresses views of Jim that are not consistent with the actions he describes Jim as taking.

THEMES

Community

In "Haircut," Lardner attempts to realistically depict the society of a midwestern small town. Social realism is a narrative mode in which an author attempts to accurately convey the details of a particular society, including all its shortcomings, and Lardner employs elements of this mode as a means of exploring the small midwestern community in which Whitey's barbershop, the setting for "Haircut," is situated. As a gathering place for men, the barbershop is a place where men converse freely without social interaction with women. Town gossip is disseminated here, and through the exchange of information that passes between Whitey and his patrons, the town's sense of community, and the reader's view of it, coalesces.

By means of the stories Whitey tells, Lardner reveals details of the midwestern town and a profile of the community. It is populated, as Whitey's narrative indicates, largely by working-class individuals, most of whom are not well educated. There is a coarseness to the society that Lardner depicts. Jim's sense of humor is cruel, but Whitey and Jim's drinking buddies find him funny. Jim is a product of this society. He is fired from his job as a canned goods salesman, and he is an alcoholic and a womanizer. Whitey defends him, stating that Jim "was all right at heart, but just bubblin' over with mischief." Lardner depicts few characters who express a different view of Jim. Paul, who is mentally disabled, is the butt of many of Jim's jokes and does not feel the loyalty to him that Whitey does. Julie, as the object of Jim's

unwanted attention, similarly is disdainful of Jim. Doc Stair attempts to distinguish himself from the elements of the community with which he disagrees, as when he comes to the aid of Mrs. Kendall or shares his view of Jim with Whitey, but Doc is an outsider and does not represent the society that Lardner is depicting and that Whitey comments on and exemplifies. The world Lardner portrays is one that is unrefined and uneducated; it is gritty at best, and there are only passing examples of hard-working or good-hearted individuals. Lardner's focus is on a male-dominated community that gathers in the barbershop and the pool hall and elevates individuals like Jim to a prominent social position within the community.

Otherness

In the society that Lardner explores in "Haircut," those who seem to embody "otherness" are targeted as unwanted and therefore considered worthy of attack. Jim is the arbiter of a sense of justice that regards difference as an unwelcome part of the homogenous small town in which the story takes place. Jim's violent attacks against otherness are tacitly approved of by the rest of the (male) community. Three individuals stand out as "other" in the story—Doc Stair, Julie, and Paul. Although Doc is quite literally an outsider and therefore by definition "other," he is a strong, masculine figure whom Jim cannot take on directly. Nevertheless, when it becomes clear that Julie, whom Jim desires in spite of, or perhaps because of her otherness, prefers Doc Stair to him, Jim targets both of them in a prank, the doctor indirectly, and Julie directly. Julie stands out from the rest of the community due to her education and worldliness. She has left the small town and been educated in big-city colleges, only to return in order be with her ailing mother after the death of her alcoholic father. As Whitey states, this situation was difficult for Julie, because compared to the other young people in town, "well, she's too good for them." Jim's attraction to Julie is something he announces publicly, and consequently her rejection of him stings all the more. He attempts to take her by force, but she escapes and calls the marshal. Hod continues to tease and goad Jim about the way the "Doc had cut him out," or ruined his chances with Julie because she preferred the doctor to Jim. His revenge against them really has little to do with Doc. In fact, Jim waits until the doctor is out of town, then he impersonates

TOPICS FOR FURTHER STUDY

- Critics of "Haircut" repeatedly return to the story's use of an unreliable narrator. Create a small writing group. Your goal will be to write your own short story in which you employ an unreliable narrator, and to discuss this writing process. Consider the motivation your narrator will have for skewing the story. Is the narrator's unreliability intentional or unintentional? Will your narrator, like Whitey, hold a position within his or her society in which he or she is likely to be reporting on the story's events? After writing your story, post it in a blog you create. With your group members discuss the role of the unreliable narrator within one another's stories. Share your experience of using this literary device as a writer.

- Ray Bradbury's *Dandelion Wine* was published in 1957 and is often regarded as a young-adult novel. The work is set in 1928 in a midwestern town. In some ways, the young narrator, a twelve-year-old boy, may be regarded as unreliable, given his unconventional way of seeing the world. Read *Dandelion Wine* and consider Douglas's perceptions of the summer of 1928. In what ways may he be considered unreliable? Do you think Douglas's perceptions of the world around him, as colored by his belief in seemingly otherworldly or supernatural elements and events, are related to his age, or to the author's intention to create a world in which the lines between fantasy and reality are blurred? Write an analytical essay on the character of Douglas and his role as narrator.

- Gail Tsukiyama, daughter of a Chinese mother and Japanese father, explores the lives of a small group of women in rural China in 1926 in *Women of the Silk*. The novel was published in 1991. Tsukiyama studies a different kind of community from the one Lardner does, although the time frame is the same. In *Women of the Silk*, the author focuses on a community of women working in a silk factory. Protesting against brutal working conditions, the women of the village stage a labor strike. With a small group, read Tsukiyama's novel and consider the ways in which the women of the community are portrayed. How do they interact and what types of conflicts do they navigate in the way they relate to each other and in their interactions with the men of the community? Create a blog as a venue for discussing your reactions to the novel. In particular, examine the author's treatment of gender roles within the community she portrays. Consider as well the way Tsukiyama treats women and their roles within the community and the way this treatment differs from Lardner's.

- In "Haircut," Lardner writes about a small working-class community in the Midwest. As he makes references to northern Michigan in the story, and Lardner was from Michigan, the location of the fictional town is often regarded as being rural Michigan in the 1920s. Using print and online sources, research US history during the 1920s, focusing on the Midwest and on daily life in small-town America. How did economic upheavals in the US economy affect daily life? Who were the prominent political figures of the time? Who were the state politicians in Michigan during this era, and how did they interact with and have an impact on the national economy and events? Create a presentation, such as with PowerPoint or Prezi, in which you provide an overview of this time period in American and Michigan history.

---

the doctor on the phone and gets Julie to come to the doctor's office. She knocks eagerly on the door and calls out to him, using his first name, Ralph, and when she does, Jim and his inebriated friends make fun of her and chase her back home, taunting her the whole way. Her refusal to sleep

The story reads like anecdotes told by a fellow customer in a barber shop.
(© Orange Line Media / Shutterstock.com)

with him, and her preference for a better-educated, more refined individual make her, and the doctor himself in a smaller way, the target of Jim's attack on otherness.

Jim also seeks out and attacks the notion of otherness in another way. He ruthlessly taunts and humiliates Paul, who is mentally disabled following a head injury he suffered as a child. Jim sends Paul on useless errands and continuously mocks him and calls him names. Whitey states,

> You can imagine that Jim used to have all kinds of fun with Paul. He'd send him to the White Front Garage for a left-handed monkey wrench. Of course they ain't no such thing as a left-handed monkey wrench.

As Jim makes Paul the butt of so many jokes, and as community members like Whitey laugh along with Jim, or at least condone the behavior by not interfering, Paul consequently trusts no one in the community, as Whitey points out, save Julie, Doc Stair, and his own mother. After Paul learns of what Jim did to Julie, he tells Doc Stair,

who denounces Jim's actions by saying that "anybody that would do a thing like that ought not to be let live." When Jim is looking for someone to go duck hunting with, Paul volunteers, even though he had never held a gun before. Whitey supposes that Jim was planning on playing tricks on Paul, like pushing him out of the boat and into the water, and that is why he allowed him to come. Jim's view of Paul as other is so well established that Whitey knows exactly why Jim agrees to let Paul come along. Even after Paul shoots Jim—"a plain case of accidental shootin'," Whitey explains—the community, represented by the plain-speaking Whitey, still condones his behavior. Although Jim acknowledges, "it probably served Jim right, what he got," he still insists that "we miss him round here. He certainly was a card!" Essentially, Whitey maintains that Jim did the townspeople's dirty work for them—he attacked otherness by isolating and humiliating those perceived to be different, like Julie for being superior, and Paul for being inferior.

STYLE

First-Person Narration

In "Haircut," Lardner employs a first-person narrator, Whitey, who relates the events of the story. Unlike other first-person narratives in which the narrator is a participant in the action, "Haircut" is structured in such a way that Whitey, as the narrator, is merely telling the story to an anonymous patron (and the reader), rather than actively participating in the events of the story. Furthermore, Whitey has the bias of a gossiping observer. Although he does not participate in the action of the story, he is not a neutral third-person observer. In that his observations and comments clearly do not mirror the gravity of the story he is relating, he establishes himself as an unreliable narrator. Where his perceptions do not always mirror the reality of the situation he is describing, it is incumbent upon the reader to make the necessary distinctions between Whitey's interpretations and what actually happened. Whitey's unreliability is established gradually as the story progresses. He describes Jim Kendall's comical nature, and he states that the town has had good times, but nothing so good as when Jim was alive. Whitey comments, "I bet they was more laughin' done here than any town its size in America." Such an exaggeration leads the reader to believe that Jim Kendall was a man with an amazing sense of humor who kept the townspeople laughing until his death. Yet as the story progresses, the image of Jim shifts. Initially, Jim is presented as a jokester who cracks wise about Whitey's red nose and the amount of alcohol—or cologne—he must have been drinking, or who pokes fun at the large Adam's apple of another patron of Whitey's barbershop.

Later, though, Whitey describes some of Jim's other attempts at humor, such as the way Jim laughs behind his wife's back when he outsmarts her and manages to collect his earnings and spend them on gin before she can approach his employers about his wages, which she needs so she can feed their hungry children. Jim also teases and taunts the mentally disabled young man Paul, sending him on farcical errands. Whitey talks about the way Jim could change his voice to sound like anybody, and describes him as a "card" just before he relates the story of Jim's public humiliation of the woman he attempted to sexually assault. He repeats this characterization of Jim as a funny guy, a card, after Jim is "accidentally" shot by

Paul. Whitey observes, "It probably served Jim right, what he got. But still we miss him round here. He was certainly a card!" Throughout the story, Whitey describes Jim's actions in terms of pranks, jokes, and mischief making but then relates events that are cruel and heartless. The reader is forced to sift through Whitey's comments and decide what is "funny" about Jim's actions, and what may be believed about what Whitey says about Jim and his deeds.

Vernacularism

Lardner was known as a vernacular writer. *Vernacular* is a term that refers to the language or dialect spoken by people in a particular region. The vernacular that Lardner employs in his works, including "Haircut," is that of midwestern, working-class, undereducated individuals. Whitey epitomizes this style. He uses poor grammar and plenty of slang, often using words such as "ain't" in his speech. His tone is casual and friendly. Lardner even captures regional pronunciations of various words, when, for example, Whitey says "You'd of thought it was a reserved seat like they have sometimes in a *theayter*" (emphasis added). Whitey's pronunciations often leave off the last hard *g* sound in words ending in *-ing,* as when he says things such as "laughin'," "playin'," and "makin'." Whitey talks about how it was "wrote all over her face that she was gone" when he talks about the way Julie looked at and felt about Doc Stair. The effect of using this vernacular style is to situate the reader firmly in the time and place of the story. Here, the reader is treated like the patron to whom Whitey is speaking. He asks at the onset of the story if the person he is serving is a newcomer to town, and at the end of the story he asks the patron if he would like his hair combed wet or dry. The vernacular Whitey uses conveys throughout the story the essence of the gossipy murmuring of barbershop conversation.

HISTORICAL CONTEXT

Literary Movements in the 1920s

During the 1920s, fiction was influenced by several different literary modes, as traditions of the past gave way to narrative exploration and experimentation. As Robert Fulford observes in *The Triumph of Narrative: Storytelling in the Age of Mass Culture,*

COMPARE
&
CONTRAST

- **1925:** Lardner's "Haircut" employs the device of the unreliable narrator. Whitey is a first-person narrator whose reactions to and opinions of events do not accurately mirror the gravity or social import of those events.

  Today: Gillian Flynn's 2012 novel *Gone Girl*, adapted for film in 2014, employs the literary device of the unreliable narrator through the character of Nick, the husband of a woman who has disappeared.

- **1925:** Mental illness is treated in a variety of ways in America, many of which focus on the mental disability as a condition that requires affected individuals to be separated from society in some way, whether through institutionalization or sterilization. At the same time, Sigmund Freud's work in the area of psychoanalysis encourages an understanding of causality rather than simply treatment of symptoms or isolation of patients.

  Today: Mental illness awareness advocacy groups such as the National Alliance on Mental Illness fight to remove the stigma associated with mental illness and to advo-

cate for access to health care for the mentally ill. A wide range of treatment options is available for the mentally ill in twenty-first-century American society, including various types of counseling and therapy as well as medication.

- **1925:** Literary trends in the 1920s involve a mixture of traditional forms from the nineteenth century, such as realism and naturalism, with emerging modes such as modernism. Writers such as Hemingway, Fitzgerald, and Lardner merge traditional storytelling methods with modernist themes and elements.

  Today: Twenty-first-century literary trends draw on traditions of the past. Realism remains a mainstay of contemporary fiction. At the same time, there is wide experimentation and genre-blending in today's fiction. Exemplifying such experimentation is the 2014 best-selling novel *The Bone Clocks*, by David Mitchell, in which the author experiments with form, presenting six interrelated narratives with recurring protagonists and spanning the years 1984 through 2043.

---

beginning around 1900, modernism celebrated or mourned the end of all that was certain, orderly, and purposeful. In literature, modernism turned against the naturalism and realism that dominated the fiction of the nineteenth century. It taught us to look with suspicion on the idea that a straightforward narrative can tell the truth about human life.

The realism and naturalism to which Fulford refers did not disappear entirely, but coexisted alongside the new modernist modes. While realism emphasized the accurate depiction of society and daily life with few idealistic embellishments, naturalism, a closely related narrative mode, emphasized not only the depiction of reality but also the futility of humans in trying to impose their will on their

destinies. Naturalism is closely aligned with the philosophy of determinism and persisted into the 1920s. Novelists such as Theodore Dreiser, Upton Sinclair, and John Steinbeck are affiliated with naturalism. Realism continued to thrive throughout the modernist period in literature as a dominant mode, and many authors mixed realism with modernist experimentation. Modernism explored narrative techniques that broke with traditional methods of characterization and linear plotting. Some writers experimented with stream-of-consciousness narration, depicting the thoughts of their characters instead of interpreting and conveying those thoughts for the reader. Others employed episodic or nonchronological

---

Jim tries to hurt his wife by saying he will take their family to the circus, but he does not show up.
(© Brian S | Shutterstock.com)

narrative techniques. Hemingway and Fitzgerald were considered modernists who nonetheless drew heavily on traditional realist storytelling.

Treatment of the Mentally Disabled in the 1920s

In "Haircut," Lardner depicts a character who is mentally disabled after he suffered a head injury as a child. Paul is the object of Jim's derision and the butt of jokes. Though Doc Stair attempts to work with Paul to improve his cognitive function, his place within the community as a simpleton is fixed. While Paul is humiliated viciously by Jim, he lives with his mother and is allowed certain freedoms within the community, as his affliction appears to be relatively mild. Yet in the 1920s in America drastic measures were being taken to address the perceived threat those deemed mentally disabled posed to society. Many deemed "feeble-minded" were institutionalized in order to remove them from society. Often, intelligence testing was used as a method to make the determination of feeblemindedness. Sterilization was another method used to control the feared spread of mental disability, as was electroshock therapy. Some communities did implement educational programs targeted at the mentally disabled, but many of these programs lost funding not long after.

Concurrently in Europe during this time, renowned psychologist Sigmund Freud was gaining prominence within the field of mental health. He and his colleagues focused on causes of mental illness as a pivotal component of developing treatment for various mental issues. Yet Freud was highly critical of the American approach to mental illness. As Paul Roazen points out in a *Social Research* article, Freud felt that American treatment of mental illness focused on the use of the type of psychoanalysis Freud developed as a means toward a medical solution. Freud disagreed with the American method of using medical treatment, as opposed to therapy, as the first and sometimes only method of treatment for mental illness. Roazen further observes that Freud "was shocked by the tendency to commercialize and sensationalize his ideas," and that he resisted the "American tendency" to proceed quickly to the application of psychoanalysis without spending the appropriate amount of time on the study of patients. Roazen points out that to some extent Freud's fears were justified, stating, "The American inclination, even in as introspective a field as psychoanalysis, has been to emphasize behavioral changes in therapeutic treatment, rather than to retain Freud's own insistence on inner changes in personality."

CRITICAL OVERVIEW

Lardner's short story "Haircut" is often examined as an example of Lardner's vernacular style and for its use of an unreliable narrator. Robert Fulford in *The Triumph of Narrative: Storytelling in the Age of Mass Culture*, examines the narrative ambiguity of the story. Fulford maintains that as a narrator, Whitey is not deliberately obfuscating the truth: "Whitey holds back none of what he knows. He simply doesn't realize that Jim, the good old boy he's talking about, was a scoundrel."

In *Ring Lardner and the Other*, Douglas Robinson explores one of the critical debates surrounding "Haircut." Robinson explains that some critics of the story read it as a morality play in which Jim is punished for the evil he perpetrates, as if "by the hand of God, through the agency of a kind of holy fool who is exonerated by the small town's authorities." Robinson goes on to summarize and explore the work of other critics, such as Charles May, who analyzed the story in 1973. Robinson states that in the view of critics such as May, the town as a whole conspires in Jim's murder and in covering it up through their exoneration of Paul. Robinson states that in this reading, "Whitey's task as narrator is to get the reader too to conspire in the coverup."

Cynthia Miller, in *Companion to Literature: Facts on File Companion to the American Short Story*, maintains that in "Haircut," Lardner "uses small-town life to expose the weaknesses, irony, and coldhearted self-interest inherent in the social contract of relationships." Miller draws upon the earlier analysis of the story by Charles May and highlights how Lardner

implicates the reader in a number of ways. "At best," Miller insists, "readers believe, with Whitey, that 'Jim was a sucker' for handing his gun over to an inexperienced hunter, and at the worst, they believe he had it coming."

CRITICISM

Catherine Dominic

Dominic is a novelist and a freelance writer and editor. In the following essay, she argues that Lardner's unreliable narrator in "Haircut" uses storytelling as a means of maintaining the community's gender roles.

The unreliability of Lardner's narrator in "Haircut" is often the central focus of critical analysis of the work. Lardner exploits the device effectively, contrasting Whitey's casual view of Jim's actions with the inherently transgressive nature of those actions. A close reading of Whitey's unreliability as a narrator reveals the way this device informs the story's narrative and thematic structure. Essentially, Whitey is a storyteller. He appropriates information gleaned from his privileged position as the town's confidant and confessor—or at least, as the confidant and confessor to the town's male population—in order to reframe facts and reinforce gender roles. Although critics like Robert Fulford, in *The Triumph of Narrative: Storytelling in the Age of Mass Culture*, suggest that Whitey is forthcoming and honest, but simply isn't particularly astute in assessing Jim's character, Whitey arguably has some culpability of his own in that he witnesses Jim's reprehensible behavior but does nothing about it. Whitey seems invested in maintaining the status quo in town, in solidifying the notion that Jim is just a prankster. He demonstrates, through some of his comments, that he is not completely unaware that Jim's behavior is in some ways socially unacceptable. Yet Whitey participates in couching Jim's actions in such a way that they appear socially acceptable. His characterization of Jim, and of other characters in the story, including Julie and Mrs. Kendall, reinforces the town's prevailing sense of gender roles. Jim is in some ways permitted to behave in a certain way, however morally reprehensible, due to the privileged status men hold within the community. Women—represented by Julie and Mrs. Kendall—are objectified, and the actions Jim takes against them are condoned by the

WHAT DO I READ NEXT?

- Lardner's early work as a sports writer is evident in the letters he published as the work of a fictional rookie baseball player. These letters are collected in the volume *You Know Me Al*, published in 2004. The first group of letters, "A Busher's Letters Home," were among Lardner's first published works of fiction and originally appeared in 1914.

- Lardner's short fiction is collected in *Stories & Other Writings*, published in 2013 by the Library of America.

- Lensey Namioka, the Chinese-born author of *An Ocean Apart, a World Away*, explores the life of a Chinese immigrant girl who is provided with the chance to attend college in the United States in the 1920s. The young-adult novel was published in 2003.

- F. Scott Fitzgerald, a friend of Lardner's, is said to have modeled the character of Abe North in *Tender Is the Night* after Lardner. Fitzgerald's novel was published in 1934 and, like Lardner's work, also features characters whose lives are affected by alcoholism and infidelity.

- Herman Koch's *The Dinner* is a 2009 Dutch novel translated by Sam Garrett and published in English in 2012. It features an unreliable narrator and hints of mental illness.

- *New World Coming: The 1920s and the Making of Modern America*, by Nathan Miller, was published in 2004. In it, Miller examines the cultural, political, and economic forces that shaped the development of American society in the 1920s.

community. This approval is signified through male laughter and through Whitey's minimization of the impact of Jim's actions.

Lardner provides Whitey with an important role in the story. Significantly, Lardner sets the story in a locus of male communal gathering— the barbershop. As a barber, Whitey is widely exposed to the opinions of male members of the community. In some ways, he reflects their views and serves as the male spokesman for the community, filtering the opinions of the males who enter his shop into the male stance of the town. As the narrator of "Haircut," Whitey conveys what he hears, in typical barbershop gossip fashion, and colors the stories, through his own narration, with the slant approved of by the male community members.

Throughout the story, Whitey repeatedly validates Jim's actions by pointing out how funny Jim is. Notably, Whitey conveys that Jim is funny to *the whole town*, not just to him. Jim holds an exceptional place within the community. When he comes into the barbershop, whoever is sitting in the seat nearest the spittoon, where Jim always sits, vacates it for him. Whether this is because they fear him, as some critics have suggested, or because they revere him is irrelevant. Regardless of the means through which Jim has earned this deference, it is the deference that is key. He has established himself as an alpha figure, and he is unchallenged. His status is reinforced whenever he comes into the barbershop and the seat is yielded to him. The community of males within the barbershop acknowledges and validates Jim's position among them. As Whitey's discussion of Jim and his character proceeds, he reveals that Jim and his wife were not

> on very good terms. She'd of divorced him only they wasn't no chance to get alimony and she didn't have no way to take care of herself and the kids. She couldn't never understand Jim. He *was* kinda rough, but a good fella at heart.

In this paragraph, Lardner establishes Jim as a coarse or violent individual (he was "rough") and Whitey as aware of both this roughness and of Jim's wife's desire to divorce him, perhaps because of his roughness. Whitey presents these facts about Jim in such a way, though, that defers to Jim's status within the community. Jim, according to Whitey, is only "kinda rough." By rough, he may mean general coarseness of character, as Jim's womanizing and alcoholism are later referred to, or he may be referring to Jim being a physically violent person, suggested by the fact that Jim later bursts into Julie's house and physically grabs

> EVEN AFTER JIM'S DEATH, WHITEY BOTH UPHOLDS JIM'S ROLE WITHIN THE COMMUNITY AND CONFIRMS THE IMMORALITY OF JIM'S ACTIONS."

her, forcing his presence on her against her will. Yet Whitey insists that Jim is just *kinda* rough. In this way he attempts to validate Jim's acknowledged and inherent roughness as socially acceptable, at least to the male members of the community.

Jim's roughness, however it may be characterized by Whitey for the purposes of both defending Jim as socially acceptable and validating Jim's privileged position within the community, is of the type that Jim's wife and Julie find repugnant or frightening, as their own actions indicate. The first clue to Mrs. Kendall's feelings is Whitey's understanding that Mrs. Kendall wants to divorce Jim. Whitey's understanding is reflective of that of the community as a whole. Whitey states, after Hod makes a joke about how Jim's wife would not care if Jim drank wood alcohol, that "that would set everybody to laughin' because Jim and his wife wasn't on very good terms." Mrs. Kendall attempts to collect Jim's pay, so she can feed their children, before Jim gets to it, as he spends all of his money on gin. When Jim successfully gets his employers to pay him in advance, he expresses his gleefulness at having outsmarted his wife. He also punishes his wife—and children—by telling them he will take them to the circus and then not showing up to do so. Whitey conveys this story after noting that Jim felt he needed to "get even" with Mrs. Kendall for trying to get his money. By not condemning Jim's treatment of his wife, and by telling the story of Jim's humiliation of her as if it were entertaining or amusing, Whitey again validates Jim's actions and reinforces Mrs. Kendall's role in the community. Socially, as a woman, as the wife of Jim, she is the butt of jokes, the object of derision. She is a mother, reliant on an alcoholic for income, and her very real plight of trying to keep her children fed is reduced to "humorous" anecdote.

Jim further humiliates his wife when he publicly announces his desire for Julie. Whitey does not denounce Jim's actions in any way. In fact, he praises Jim. Whitey says, "Now Jim Kendall, besides bein' a jokesmith and a pretty good drinker, well, Jim was quite a lady-killer." He talks about how Jim ran "pretty wild" when he was a traveling salesman, and how he'd "had a couple little affairs of the heart right here in town." Jim's infidelity is admired alongside his alcoholism and his crude and often cruel sense of humor. Whitey concludes his summary about Jim's affairs by noting, "As I say, his wife could of divorced him, only she couldn't." Here, Whitey acknowledges that Mrs. Kendall had some cause to divorce her husband. He is aware that Jim's actions are transgressive, yet he validates them nonetheless, praising Jim's prowess as a lady-killer, even while acknowledging that the actions fall outside the boundaries of acceptable moral behavior. Whitey then describes the way Jim announces in the barbershop that he would be willing to give his house, wife, and kids to anyone who would help him "get" Julie. He reduces his family to property in this statement, yet Whitey chooses to focus on the fact that Jim is expressing how he felt about Julie. "He didn't make no bones about how he felt. Right in here, more than once, in front of the whole crowd, he said he was stuck on Julie." It is almost as if Whitey is touched by the depth of Jim's feelings for Julie, and because Jim is "stuck" on Julie, his description of his wife and children as property is understandable.

Next, Whitey relates the way Jim went to Julie's house, "and when she opened the door he forced his way in and grabbed her." Forcing and grabbing are violent actions, and clearly Jim's intentions were to follow through with further violence and possibly rape Julie. Yet Whitey, when describing this incident, refers to it as "this little affair." Like Mrs. Kendall, Julie is objectified. Mrs. Kendall is property to Jim, and Julie is an object to be used for sexual gratification. Whitey's word choice and commentary suggest that he both *knows* that Jim's actions are socially inexcusable and that he knowingly validates them anyway. His description of Jim's treatment of Mrs. Kendall and Julie authenticates Jim as a representative of maleness within this community. Whitey also reinforces Jim's notion of the female role within the community by condoning Jim's actions and Jim's view of women as *things* to *have*. Jim goes on to take revenge against Julie, publicly humiliating her and having a mob of his drunk friends chase her through the streets of town and back to her home. After Jim is killed by Paul in what is described as a hunting accident, Whitey concludes the story with the observations that Jim probably got what he deserved, but that he is missed, because he was so funny. Even after Jim's death, Whitey both upholds Jim's role within the community and confirms the immorality of Jim's actions. He at once conveys his understanding that the things Jim has done are morally unacceptable, and diminishes the wrongness of Jim's actions in order to help maintain Jim's reputation within the community, even after Jim's death.

Throughout "Haircut," Whitey, Lardner's unreliable narrator, serves as storyteller. His unreliability is often characterized as related to his inability to accurately assess the moral implications of Jim's actions. James Phelan, for example, states of Whitey in *Experiencing Fiction: Judgments, Progressions, and the Rhetorical Theory of Narrative*, "though not mean and selfish himself, he is so morally imperceptive that he does not recognize Jim's meanness and selfishness." Yet Whitey *does* perceive the wrongness of Jim's actions. He understands that Mrs. Kendall would have every reason to want to divorce a man who has been repeatedly unfaithful to her, and whose alcoholism results in her being unable to properly take care of her children. Whitey simply chooses to varnish over the moral impropriety he recognizes. His statements fairly clearly convey his understanding, but he is also certain to emphasize and praise Jim's sense of humor and his status as a "lady-killer." Similarly, Whitey observes Julie's fear of Jim, noting when he relates his story that she locked herself in another room after breaking free of Jim. He also emphasizes the force Jim used. Yet Whitey disregards these facts and writes the incident off as a small affair. Through this type of storytelling, Whitey recasts Jim's actions, de-emphasizing the transgressive nature that he also quietly acknowledges. In doing so, he highlights the privileged role Jim has within the community and the way he, Whitey, as a representative of the male community, condones behavior that objectifies women.

Source: Catherine Dominic, Critical Essay on "Haircut," in *Short Stories for Students*, Gale, Cengage Learning, 2015.

Paul shoots Jim in revenge for the attack on Julie, but Doc Stair rules it an accident.
(© FooTToo | Shutterstock.com)

Otto Friedrich

In the following excerpt, Friedrich discusses Lardner's vernacular style and his background as a sports writer.

"You could of did better if you had of went at it in a different way." This, when it first appeared in 1914, was the sound of a new voice in American fiction. It was still an age when such masters as Henry James and William Dean Howells were writing their stately periods. The masters had dealt occasionally with the uneducated proletariat, and dialect had traditionally been used as a provincial form of humor. But Ring Lardner's Jack Keefe, hero of the stories that became *You Know Me Al*, represented not only a new and realistic rhythm of speech but a new social caste, a lower class that didn't know it was lower class. Lardner's illiterates, his baseball players and salesmen and barbers and nurses, thought of themselves as clever and prospering, and so did the nation that applauded their creator.

Unlike most American writers, who have traditionally written about themselves and people like themselves, Lardner wrote about the strangers inhabiting the crass and rapacious America that he saw around him. Even when he spoke in the first person, he assumed a disguise and spoke in the prevailing language of the time. The man who came from a wealthy and cultivated family, which originally hoped he would enter the ministry, pretended that he was a yokel. The man whom Scott Fitzgerald described as "proud, shy, solemn, shrewd, polite, brave, kind, merciful, honorable," pretended that he was a bumptious extrovert. And a nation that never really recognized either Lardner's Puritan personality or his Puritan portrait of America nonetheless poured fame and wealth on the young sportswriter as one of the greatest literary folk heroes since Mark Twain. At the height of his success in the middle twenties, he was earning about fifty thousand dollars a year, and issuing folksy pronouncements on everything from disarmament to the emancipation of women. Beyond the national frontiers, Virginia Woolf took mournful pleasure in the fact that Lardner had achieved eminence by ignoring England and its literary traditions. Aside from writing "the best prose that has come our way," she said, "... it is no coincidence that the best of Mr. Lardner's stories are about games, for ... [games have] given him a clue, a centre, a meeting place for the divers activities of people whom a vast continent isolates, whom no tradition controls."

In writing about sports, Lardner had struck a hidden nerve in many Americans, at least in many men, for he described a new kind of American mythology, a mythology that more elegant writers had not observed. In the half-century before Lardner's appearance, the nation had reached and conquered its old frontiers. It had become stabilized, both economically and socially. Neither boys nor men could so easily dream of discovering gold and making millions. Since it was a fairly comfortable time, people began turning to the question that still haunts the affluent society: What shall we do with ourselves? The rich might amuse themselves in collecting bibelots or titled husbands, and the poor still struggled for survival, but the increasingly large and prosperous middle classes were more interested in the simple pursuit of leisure. And so they began to take up sports. Baseball, adapted from the English game of rounders during the forties, did not become seriously organized until 1900. Football, once largely confined to the "Big Three" of the Ivy League, exploded into a national sport shortly after the turn of the century and eventually became a hundred-million-dollar industry. Boxing was legalized in the nineties and changed from a system of barroom brawls into the snob-appeal sport it has remained since the days of Gentleman Jim Corbett. Such traditional pastimes as horse racing and such novelties as basketball all became "big time." And the boys of the period often dreamed less of making a million dollars than of being another Eddie Collins or another Red Grange. James T. Farrell, for example, wanted to become a professional baseball player long before he ever considered writing. "We American men are a nation of frustrated baseball players," he wrote. Scott Fitzgerald was prey to a similar fantasy. For twenty years, he recalled, he put himself to sleep by imagining that "Once upon a time ... they needed a quarterback at Princeton, and they had nobody and were in despair. The head coach noticed me kicking and passing on the side of the field, and he cried: 'Who is *that* man—why haven't we noticed *him* before?'"

Running and fighting have been international sports since classic times, but the major American sports have American peculiarities. The common denominator in baseball, football, basketball, and hockey is that they are highly organized, highly competitive, and that most people take part in them solely by watching them. The active pursuit of leisure does exercise a certain attraction on Americans. Some twenty-five million of them take out fishing licenses every year, according to one recent estimate, and about twenty million acquire hunting licenses, and the equipment that they take along on their domestic safaris helps to raise the business of sports to an estimated total of more than fifty billion dollars a year. Most of these activities are not sports in any sense of competition or excellence, however, but rather a matter of relaxation and self-indulgence. When it comes to the major sports events that attract the attention of millions of Americans—the World Series or the Kentucky Derby or the Rose Bowl game—the American sportsman is nothing more than a distant spectator.

Yet there is something more than entertainment in sports, some magical quality that has never quite been trapped in words. Perhaps the most perceptive effort to understand this magic was that of the Dutch historian Johan Huizinga, who presumably never got within miles of Yankee Stadium. In *Homo Ludens*, he attempted to study the whole subject of "play," not as a skill that divided men from animals but as one that men shared with their Darwinian ancestors. Play, to Huizinga, was not just baseball or football, but hopscotch and darts—and even war. He found that all play is an attempt to create order. "Into an imperfect world and into the confusion of life it brings a temporary, a limited perfection." He found that it satisfies a human need for aesthetic order. "It is invested with the noblest qualities we are capable of perceiving in things: rhythm and harmony." He found that play has no intrinsic morality but "the element of tension imparts to it a certain ethical value in so far as it means a testing of the player's prowess: his courage, tenacity, resources and last, but not least, his spiritual powers." In all its ritual, in fact, its priests in special clothing, its confinement within a consecrated area, its suspension of normal reasoning, and its insistence on arbitrary values, Huizinga found that "play" was much the same as religion—it ante-dates religion but fulfills much the same need.

Ring Lardner would naturally have scoffed at such theories. He would have insisted that he couldn't understand them. And yet this is the magic that surrounds sports. We pay hundreds of thousands of dollars to a Cassius Clay, for example, to commit assaults that would normally make us call the police. And we treat the chroniclers of such sports—the Heywood Brouns, the John Kierans, the Red Smiths, and the Ring Lardners—with a special adulation that we reserve for the magicians who know the secrets of the ultimate mystery....

Source: Otto Friedrich, "Ring Lardner," in *Ring Lardner*, University of Minnesota Press, 1965, pp. 5–8.

SOURCES

Fulford, Robert, "The Cracked Mirror of Modernity," in *The Triumph of Narrative: Storytelling in the Age of Mass Culture*, House of Anansi Press, 1999, pp. 95–122.

Hoermann, Simone, Corinne E. Zupanick, and Mark Dombeck, "The History of the Psychiatric Diagnostic System," *Metapsychology Online Reviews*, http://meta

psychology.mentalhelp.net/poc/view_doc.php?type=de&id=478 (accessed September 23, 2014).

Lardner, Ring, "Haircut," in *Haircut and Other Stories*, Collier, 1954, pp. 9–21.

Matterson, Stephen, "1890–1940s Modernism," PBS website, http://www.pbs.org/wnet/americannovel/time line/modernism.html (accessed September 23, 2014); originally published in *The Essential Glossary: American Literature*, 2003.

———, "1890–1920s Naturalism," PBS website, http://www.pbs.org/wnet/americannovel/timeline/naturalism.html (accessed September 23, 2014); originally published in *The Essential Glossary: American Literature*, 2003.

"Mental Illnesses," NAMI: National Alliance on Mental Illness website, http://www.nami.org/Template.cfm?Section=By_Illness (accessed September 23, 2014).

Miller, Cynthia J., "'Haircut,'" in *Companion to Literature: Facts on File Companion to the American Short Story*, edited by Abby H. P. Werlock, Facts on File, 2010, pp. 299–300.

"NAMI Advocacy," NAMI: National Alliance on Mental Illness—Mental Health Support, Education, and Advocacy website, http://www.nami.org/Template.cfm?section=About_Public_Policy (accessed September 23, 2014).

Noll, Stephen, "The Establishment of a National Profession: Mental Retardation, 1900–1940," in *Feeble-Minded in Our Midst: Institutions for the Mentally Retarded in the South, 1900–1940*, University of North Carolina Press, 1995, pp. 26–46.

Oriard, Michael, "Ring Lardner," in *Dictionary of Literary Biography*, Vol. 86, *American Short Story Writers, 1910–1945, First Series*, edited by Bobby Ellen Kimbel, Gale Research, 1979, pp. 172–92.

Phelan, James, Introduction to *Judgments, Progressions, and the Rhetorical Theory of Narrative*, Ohio State University Press, 2007, pp. 1–26.

Roazen, Paul, "Freud and America," in *Social Research*, Vol. 39, No. 4, Winter 1972, pp. 720–32.

Robinson, Douglas, "Lardner's Dual Audience," in *Ring Lardner and the Other*, Oxford University Press, 1992, pp. 143–80.

FURTHER READING

Botshon, Lisa, and Meredith Goldsmith, eds., *Middlebrow Moderns: Popular American Women Writers of the 1920s*, Northeastern University Press, 2003.

> Botshon and Goldsmith collect essays from critics who examine the work of the women writers of the 1920s derided as "middlebrow" by the literary elite. These authors, such as Edna Ferber, Nella Larsen, and Dorothy Canfield Fisher, nevertheless published best sellers

and won literary awards. The essays collected in this volume examine the contribution of these authors to American literature and explore issues related to gender bias.

Fitzgerald, F. Scott, *A Life in Letters: F. Scott Fitzgerald*, edited and annotated by Matthew J. Bruccoli, Scribner, 1995.
In these letters, Fitzgerald discusses matters both professional and personal. He corresponds with and about Lardner and other literary peers, about American fiction in general and his own work in particular.

Goldberg, David J., *Discontented America: The United States in the 1920s*, Johns Hopkins University Press, 1999.
Goldberg traces the major historical developments of the 1920s and examines the political and economic issues that defined the era.

Hornick, Robert N., *The Girls and Boys of Belchertown: A Social History of the Belchertown State School for the Feeble-Minded*, University of Massachusetts Press, 2012.
Hornick's study traces the history of a state school for the mentally disabled from its 1920s origins through the next several decades, documenting the various forms of treatment children received at this institution.

SUGGESTED SEARCH TERMS

Ring Lardner AND Haircut

Ring Lardner AND unreliable narrator

Ring Larder AND F. Scott Fitzgerald

Ring Lardner AND F. Scott Fitzgerald AND Abe North

Ring Lardner AND realism

Ring Lardner AND naturalism

Ring Lardner AND modernism

1920s literary movements

mental disability AND American history AND 1920s

alcoholism AND America AND 1920s

Hamadi

NAOMI SHIHAB NYE

1993

"Hamadi" is a short story by Naomi Shihab Nye. It was published in *America Street: A Multicultural Anthology of Stories* in 1993. Much of Nye's work makes use of her dual cultural background, and "Hamadi" is no exception. Set in Texas, it features a young American girl named Susan, the daughter (like Nye) of an immigrant from Palestine and an American mother, and a grandfatherly man named Saleh Hamadi, who immigrated to the United States from Lebanon when he was eighteen. Hamadi is a philosophical sort of man, given to enigmatic sayings, and Susan, a bright girl with literary tastes, finds him interesting. There is also a romantic element in the story, as Susan's friend Tracy, among others, is interested in a boy named Eddie. When Hamadi accompanies Susan's family and friends on an expedition to sing Christmas carols, the evening brings an emotional disappointment, but Hamadi is on hand with some wise words. The story is memorable not so much for its plot—not a great deal happens—but for its depiction of the outsider—the dignified, eccentric Hamadi—and of Susan, the reflective girl who is drawn to him.

AUTHOR BIOGRAPHY

Naomi Shihab Nye is a poet, essayist, and short-story writer who also writes books for children. She was born on March 12, 1952, in

Susan thinks about the Sphinx at Giza as a kind of escape. (© S-F / Shutterstock.com)

St. Louis, Missouri, to a Palestinian father and American mother. Nye's early education was in St. Louis, but during her high-school years she lived in Ramallah, Jordan; Jerusalem, Israel; and San Antonio, Texas. In 1974, she graduated from Trinity University in San Antonio with a bachelor of arts degree in English and world religions. Nye had been writing poetry since she was six years old, and she soon began to publish in that genre. *Tattooed Feet*, a chapbook containing twenty-one poems, was published in 1977, followed by *Eye-to-Eye* in 1978. Her first full-length poetry collection, *Different Ways to Pray*, was published in 1980. It was awarded the Voertman Poetry Prize from the Texas Institute of Letters. *Hugging the Jukebox* (1982) also won the Voertman Prize, as well as a Notable Book designation from the American Library Association.

Nye's poems often give expression to her Arab American identity. Subsequent poetry collections include *Yellow Glove* (1986), *Red Suitcase* (1994), *Words under the Words: Selected Poems* (1995), *Fuel* (1998), *Mint Snowball* (2001), *You and Yours* (2005), *Tender Spot: Selected Poems* (2008), and *Transfer* (2011).

Nye has also written two young-adult novels, *Habibi* (1997), which won the Jane Addams Children's Book Award in 1998, and *Going Going* (2005), and many books for children, including *Sitti's Secrets* (1994) and *Baby Radar* (2003). In 2014, she published *The Turtle of Oman*, a novel for young readers. Other prose works include *Never in a Hurry: Essays on People and Places* (1996), *I'll Ask You Three Times, Are You OK? Tales of Driving and Being Driven* (2007), and *There Is No Long Distance Now: Very Short Stories* (2011). The short story "Hamadi" appeared in *America Street: A Multicultural Anthology of Stories* in 1993.

Nye has won four Pushcart Prizes and has been a Guggenheim Fellow. In 2009, she was elected a chancellor of the Academy of American Poets. She has also been a visiting writer at the University of Hawaii in 1991, the University of Alaska, Fairbanks, in 1994, and the University of Texas at Austin in 1995 and 2001.

Nye married Michael Nye in 1978, and their son was born in 1986. As of 2014, the Nyes live in San Antonio.

PLOT SUMMARY

The story is set in an unnamed town in Texas. It begins with the thoughts of Susan, a fourteen-year-old high-school freshman, who has an American mother and a Palestinian father. She sometimes helps out in the counselors' office in school, sorting attendance cards and listening to their conversation. Many questions are on her mind about why things are done in a certain way and not in another way. She daydreams about Saleh Hamadi, a family friend, and also about her grandmother, who lived in a village north of Jerusalem. When Susan was about seven or eight years old, she and her family had lived in Jerusalem, and they would visit her grandmother on the weekend. Now, in Texas, Susan often takes long walks with her father. Some evenings, when she thinks of her grandmother, she suggests that they visit Saleh Hamadi, so they drive downtown to visit him. He lives frugally on the sixth floor of a hotel.

Hamadi, a bachelor who had immigrated to the United States from Lebanon at the age of eighteen, freely offers general advice about living, and he likes to use some Spanish words he learned when he worked in a fruit and vegetable warehouse. Sometimes he speaks Arabic, his native language. He claims to have known the famous Lebanese poet Kahlil Gibran in New York, and he loves Gibran's work, but Susan is unsure whether he ever actually met the man. On one occasion, Susan's father suggests that Hamadi should visit his relatives in Lebanon, but Hamadi is not enthusiastic about the idea. He implies cryptically that he already knows what his family members have been doing. Susan's father finds him a bit exasperating, saying that he talks in riddles.

Susan and her friend Tracy read *The Prophet*, a work by Gibran, to each other at lunch at school. Tracy talks about how she dislikes a girl called Debbie because Debbie likes a boy called Eddie, in whom Tracy has a romantic interest. Susan finds a passage in *The Prophet* where Gibran talks about what love is, and she tells Debbie she is more interested in owning Eddie than in loving him. Susan herself is not interested in having a boyfriend.

Susan is to go Christmas caroling with the English club. They will accept donations and send them to a children's hospital in Bethlehem. Susan has the idea to invite Hamadi to go as

well. Her father thinks it is not a good idea, saying that his English is old fashioned and he would not know any of the songs. But Susan insists, saying that it is tedious being with the same people all the time.

Hamadi agrees to come on the expedition, and he is excited at the prospect. Her father wonders why she is suddenly so interested in Hamadi. He wishes she would show the same interest in her own uncles. Susan thinks her uncles are conventional and boring, while she regards the interesting Hamadi as a "surrogate grandmother" who stimulates her mind.

Susan persuades both her parents to go caroling too. Hamadi makes the trip to their house by bus, and then all the carolers assemble at the school. Hamadi goes around the group introducing himself, surprising everyone with his formal manners and unfashionable clothing. Susan introduces him as one of her best friends.

They go singing from house to house. Susan is aware of the strengths and weaknesses of all the group as far as singing is concerned. Her mother knows all the words without even looking at the paper, whereas her father has more interest in looking around at people's yards than in singing. Hamadi seems to be humming more than singing, and even when he seems to pronounce a word she is not sure what language it is. One word he utters, he tells her, was in Aramaic, the language spoken by Jesus Christ.

After they have been singing for a while, moving from block to block, Eddie rushes up. He had not been expecting everyone else to assemble on time. Hamadi, whom Eddie does not know, is the only one to welcome him to the group. Eddie then goes up to Tracy and says hello, but she is less than welcoming. Nonetheless, the two of them walk on together as the carolers go on to another house. One of the carolers, Lisa, then tells Eddie that she is excited about him and Debbie (it appears they are dating) and asks why Debbie is not there. Eddie replies that she has a sore throat. Lisa talks about making reservations for dinner at a popular restaurant for after the Sweetheart Dance in February, even though that is two months in the future. Hamadi listens and congratulates her on planning ahead.

Susan watches her father staring off at the sky. She wonders whether he was thinking about refugees in camps in Palestine or about his boyhood there. She finds immigrants like her father and Hamadi interesting, and also rather sad.

Tracy is crying. Eddie has left her side and is clowning around with Cameron, another caroler. Hamadi asks Tracy why she is crying. She leans up against him and cries harder. Susan puts her arms around Tracy. Hamadi makes a wise remark about how people always endure and keep on going, even when in pain. Eventually, they turn a corner. It is a remark that Susan will remember for many years, and it will comfort her when she is sad herself.

CHARACTERS

Cameron

Cameron is one of the young carolers. He sings enthusiastically and clowns around with Eddie.

Debbie

Debbie does not actually appear in the story, but she is mentioned by Tracy—and later Lisa—as a rival for Eddie's affections.

Eddie

Eddie is a boy from Susan's school. He is very popular and all the girls like him. This includes Susan's friend Tracy, but she has a rival in a girl named Debbie. Eddie arrives late for the carol singing. It turns out that he is dating Debbie, and this leaves Tracy disappointed.

Saleh Hamadi

Saleh Hamadi immigrated to the United States from Lebanon when he was eighteen. He is now elderly, although his exact age is unknown. He has never married. To Susan, he is a grandfatherly figure. Hamadi is an old friend of Susan's father, although his fellow Arab immigrant cannot recall how they met. A dignified and rather old-fashioned man, Saleh lives a simple life in a cheap downtown hotel in a run-down area. He says he has little need for material possessions. He never seems to travel anywhere, although he does claim that when he was younger, he met the famous Lebanese poet Kahlil Gibran in a big city, probably New York. However, it is never clear whether he knew Gibran in person or just through his books. Saleh has a philosophical, reflective nature that Susan finds very interesting, and he in turn is fond of her.

Susan's father, though, is rather exasperated by Hamadi, saying that he talks in riddles. Susan also regards Hamadi as a rather melancholy person.

Lisa

Lisa is a friend of Susan's who is one of the carol singers. She has a soprano voice. It is Lisa who lets everyone know that Eddie is dating Debbie by speaking about it to him in a loud voice. Lisa is a chatty, outgoing girl who is already planning for the Sweetheart Dance in February and the dinner that will follow it.

Susan

Susan, who is a freshman in high school, is the main character in the story. She is a studious girl who works as a proofreader on the school literary magazine. She likes to read Gibran's *The Prophet* with her friend Tracy, and she tries to absorb and invoke some of Gibran's wisdom, as when she tells Tracy what love really is—a way of connecting deeply to all of life, not just trying to own one person. Susan has an inquisitive nature and is at an age when she has many questions about life and the way things are. Unlike her friends, she is not interested in acquiring a boyfriend, since everyone she knows who has either a boyfriend or a girlfriend has problems with the relationship. Susan lived for three years in Jerusalem with her family before she was ten, and she is eager to learn more about the Arab culture that her father comes from, often trying to get him to tell stories about his childhood. She seems to find American culture uninteresting by comparison. She is particularly drawn to Saleh Hamadi, whom she has known since she was very young. She likes his unconventionality, and his pithy sayings make her think.

Susan's Father

Susan's father immigrated to the United States from Palestine. He has brothers in the United States, but he also goes back to Jerusalem once every year to visit his family. He appears to have adjusted well to living in the United States, although Susan believes that he thinks a lot about Palestine and lives very much in two cultures. He goes caroling with the group, but he does not know the words of the carols and does not bother to sing.

Susan's Mother

Susan's mother is American. She likes to go carol singing, and Susan thinks she has an excellent voice. She knows the carols without even looking down at the words or music. She also knows more songs than anyone else.

Tracy

Tracy is a junior in high school and a friend of Susan's. Like Susan, she has literary interests, working for the school literary magazine and reading Gibran's *The Prophet* aloud with Susan during lunch. Tracy is romantically interested in Eddie and is jealous of Debbie, who also likes Eddie. When they all go caroling together, Tracy learns that Eddie is in fact dating Debbie, and this reduces her to tears. Hamadi comforts her.

THEMES

Wisdom

The two main characters, Susan and Hamadi, are both seekers of wisdom. They are interested in the deep truths of life. Susan is only fourteen, so there is much to for her to learn, but she is an eager student, as is her friend Tracy. They both respond to the wisdom contained in Kahlil Gibran's *The Prophet* and try to apply it to a real-life situation. Tracy says she feels hatred for Debbie because Debbie is a rival for Eddie's affection, but she is fighting against her emotion because she has read the following passage in Gibran's work: "Hate is a dead thing. Who of you would be a tomb?" Susan, although she is not interested in relationships with boys, understands what Gibran says about love and tries to educate her friend about its real nature: "Gibran says that loving teaches us the secrets of our hearts and that's the way we connect to all of Life's heart." She points out that this is quite different from the sort of love that Tracy seems to have in mind, where one person simply wants to take ownership of another while calling it love.

The fact that Susan is drawn to the kind of universal wisdom expressed by Gibran also explains her affection for the eccentric Hamadi, because it is exactly this wisdom that he seems to embody. He takes a rather mystical approach to life, in which everything is connected to everything else, and a wise person senses that connection. Hamadi feels connected to Gibran, for example, and says, "I meet him every day in my heart." When the subject is why he never married, he says that he "married the wide horizon," which suggests an intimate communion with all of life. When Susan's father suggests that Hamadi should take a trip back to his village in Lebanon so that he can find out what happened to everyone since he was a boy there, Hamadi replies, "I already know. It is there and it is not there." He does not explain this enigmatic and paradoxical remark (which may be why Susan's father complains that he talks in riddles), but perhaps the sense is that Hamadi feels spiritually connected to his family and his former country in some way that does not require actual physical presence. In addition to this kind of mysticism, Hamadi also has a practical wisdom. Right at the end of the story, when he sees that Tracy is upset, he says, "We go on. On and on. We don't stop where it hurts. We turn a corner. It is the reason why we are living. To turn a corner. Come, let's move." An eccentric and a mystic Hamadi may be, but it would be hard to think of better advice than this, in the context in which he gives it.

Immigrant Life

In the background of the story, and giving it something of its flavor, is a picture of what it means to be an immigrant. Immigrants live in two worlds: the culture from which they came and the new culture in which they must learn to live. Susan's family has its roots in both Arab Palestinian culture and American culture. Her father travels to Jerusalem, where he is originally from, to visit his family every year. Susan lived for three years in Jerusalem and is very aware of her dual cultural heritage. She likes to hear from her father about what life was like in Palestine when he was a boy. She also has some awareness that immigrants can be caught between two different worlds. As she watches her father gazing off into the distance during the carol singing, she imagines him thinking "about all the refugees in camps in Palestine.... Maybe he thought about the horizon beyond Jerusalem when he was a boy, how it seemed to be inviting him, 'Come over, come over.'" Her father had left his home to live thousands of miles away, and now, Susan thinks, he is "doomed to live in two places at once." Life for immigrants is therefore not entirely comfortable, because so much has been left behind. It is as if they live in

TOPICS FOR FURTHER STUDY

- Research the recent history and current status of Jerusalem. What government currently presides over it? Why do both Israel and the Palestinians claim Jerusalem as their capital city? How might the conflict be resolved? For background, read Nye's poem "Jerusalem" (available at the Poetry Foundation website) and selections from *Teen Voices from the Holy Land: Who Am I to You?* (2007), by Mahmoud Watad and Leonard Grob, which presents the views of Israeli and Palestinian teenagers on the conflict between their two countries. Write an essay on the issue in which you propose a resolution, titled "A Plan for Jerusalem."

- What kind of obstacles do immigrants face when they first come to the United States? Are the difficulties greater for some immigrant groups than for others? Should immigrants seek to maintain their own cultures or should they assimilate into mainstream American culture? With the aid of Internet research, give a class presentation on the issue. You might like to read Nye's poem "My Uncle's Favorite Coffee Shop"

(available at the Poetry Foundation website). Consider what that poem conveys about the life of an immigrant and weave it into your presentation.

- Go to the Poetry Foundation website and read some of the twenty-three poems by Nye that are reproduced there. Pick two or three poems you like, memorize them, and recite them aloud to your class. Explain why you picked those poems and what you like about them.

- In a *PBS NewsHour* interview, available at http://www.poetryfoundation.org/features/video/319, Nye encourages young people to write their own stories and poems and by doing so discover how much material they have to write about. Following her encouragement, write your own poem or short story in which you draw directly from events in your own life. Post it to your blog with an author's note in which you discuss the autobiographical nature of the piece, why you were inspired to write it, and what techniques you used to express yourself.

---

between two cultures. Susan finds immigrants always "slightly melancholy" for that reason. Immigrants are often unable to participate in key aspects of their new culture, even if they have been living in it for a long time. Susan's father, for example, though willing to go caroling with the group, does not know the words of any of the carols. He points out to Susan that Saleh Hamadi, another immigrant, will not know the words either. Susan is incredulous at first. She says, "How could you live in America for years and now know 'Joy to the World' or 'Away in a Manger'?" Her father makes a wry but also amusing remark in reply: "I grew up right down the road from 'Oh Little Town of Bethlehem' and I still don't know a single verse."

Little things like this can mark off even longtime immigrants as strangers in their new country. The lack of knowledge of Christmas carols on the part of Susan's father and Hamadi is contrasted sharply with the easy mastery of them that Susan's American mother shows.

Hamadi also reveals the immigrant experience in some of his remarks. Sometimes, when he is with Susan's father or her uncles, Hamadi will speak Arabic, his native tongue, but he does not do so often. He says it makes him sad, "as if his mother might step into the room at any minute, her arms laden with fresh mint leaves." He also recalls the experience familiar to any immigrant of culture shock on first arrival in the United States. When he was young, he says, he was

Susan and Tracy always eat their vegetarian lunches outdoors instead of eating in the cafeteria. (© *Beth Swanson / Shutterstock.com*)

"shocked by all the visions of the new world—the tall buildings—the wild traffic—the young people without shame—the proud mailboxes in their blue uniforms." Hamadi continues to live as something of an oddity or an outsider in American life. He seems to live in his own world of philosophical wisdom gathered from his reading of Gibran and other writers, and he does not participate directly in American culture.

Another, rather different picture of life for immigrants in the United States is fleetingly suggested in Susan's comments about her uncles. These are uncles on her father's side of the family, since they speak Arabic with their brother and Hamadi. Susan finds them boring, though, because they like to shop at the mall and watch television. This suggests that they have found a way of integrating themselves into American life, since consumerism and a love of popular entertainment are embedded in American culture. It seems that not all immigrants feel the need to maintain close ties with the culture they left behind.

STYLE

Limited Third-Person Narrator

Nye's story is told from a limited third-person narrator's point of view. *Third-person* means that Susan, the main character, is referred to as "she"; she is not telling the story herself using "I." The narrator of "Hamadi" has insight only into the thoughts and feelings of Susan. For example, the first page and a half is devoted to her thoughts about her life and descriptions of it. Every other character, including Hamadi himself, is seen only through Susan's eyes. These characters reveal themselves entirely through what they say, what they do, how they look, and what others say about them. The narrator does not penetrate their minds directly, as an omniscient (all-knowing) narrator would be able to do.

Hamadi yet emerges as a fully realized character because he is given more direct, quoted speech than any of the others, and his actions and gestures are described in telling detail. For example, before he gives advice, Hamadi "would raise his hands high," which gives an image of him as a kind of prophet dispensing wisdom and knowledge. Other people react to him, too, which also helps to characterize him. After he goes around the group of carolers introducing himself, "a few people laughed silently when his back was turned." This tells the reader a lot about how Hamadi is perceived by others.

Epigraph

An epigraph is a short quotation that appears at the beginning of a literary work in order to suggest a theme. The epigraph in "Hamadi" is a quotation from one of the works of Kahlil Gibran. It is appropriate not only because Gibran and his work are mentioned several times in the story but also because it has implications for how a reader might interpret the story. The quotation suggests that truth has two aspects before it can be complete. It is not enough for one person to express a truth; there must also be another person who can understand it. When applied to the story, perhaps this implies that Hamadi is a lonely figure because people do not always understand his pithy sayings. Or it could mean the opposite. There are two main characters in the story, Hamadi and Susan, and perhaps the truths Hamadi likes to speak are complete because Susan finds him interesting and either does or will soon learn to understand his way of seeing the world.

COMPARE
&
CONTRAST

- **1990s:** There is a boom in Arab American literature in a variety of genres. In addition to the work of Nye, Suheir Hammad publishes her poetry collection *Born Palestinian, Born Black* in 1996. Joseph Geha, who was born in Lebanon, publishes a collection of eight short stories, *Through and Through: Toledo Stories* (1990). Elmaz Abinader publishes a memoir, *Children of the Roojme: A Family's Journey from Lebanon* (1991). Diana Abu-Jaber and Rabih Alameddine publish their first novels, *Arabian Jazz* (1993) and *Koolaids: The Art of War* (1998), respectively.

  Today: Arab American poetry flourishes, thanks to poets such as Fady Joudah, Deema Shehabi (both of whom, like Nye, are Palestinian Americans), Lawrence Joseph, Samuel Hazo, Khaled Mattawa, and Hayan Charara. Notable novels include Rabih Alameddine's *I, the Divine: A Novel in First Chapters* (2002) and *The Hakawati* (2009); Randa Jarrar's *A Map of Home* (2008); *Birds of Paradise* (2011), by Diana Abu-Jaber; *The Bullet Connection* (2003), by Patricia Sarrafian Ward; *Once in a Promised Land* (2008), by Laila Halaby; and *The Moor's Account* (2014), by Laila Lalami.

- **1990s:** In 1990, there are 850,000 people in the United States who report Arab ancestry, according to the US Census Bureau.

  Today: According to the US Census Bureau, in 2010 there are an estimated 1.5 million people of Arab ancestry living in the United States, representing a 76 percent increase since 1990. Of this group, 83,241 people claim Palestinian ancestry. The largest group in terms of Arab ancestry are Lebanese Americans, with 485,917 people claiming Lebanese ancestry.

- **1990s:** The Oslo Accord of 1993 raises hopes for a peaceful settlement of the Israeli-Palestinian conflict. In 1994, Israel withdraws its forces from the Gaza Strip, which becomes self-governing under the Palestinian National Authority. Negotiations over the future of the West Bank continue, but the entire peace process is dealt a blow in 1995 when Israeli prime minister Yitzhak Rabin is assassinated by a Jewish extremist.

  Today: The UN General Assembly regards the State of Palestine as a nonmember observer state within the United Nations. The State of Palestine is recognized by 134 members of the United Nations, but this does not include Israel or the United States. Conflict between Israel and the Palestinians continues. In 2014, an Israeli military action against Hamas, the organization that governs the Gaza Strip, leaves about 1,800 dead in Gaza, a large number of them civilians. Israel states that it launched the attacks in response to rocket attacks by Hamas on Israel.

HISTORICAL CONTEXT

Kahlil Gibran

Born in 1883, Kahlil Gibran was a Lebanese poet and artist who immigrated with his family to the United States in 1895, where they lived in a poor immigrant area in Boston. Over the next decade he returned to Beirut and traveled in Europe, studying art in Paris in 1908 and also publishing short stories in Arabic. In 1911, Gibran moved to New York, where he became known as an up-and-coming writer and met many leading figures of the day, including psychologist Carl Jung and poet William Butler Yeats. His first book written in English was *The Madman: His Parables and Poems*, published in 1918.

Mr. Hamadi is out of place with the other Christmas carolers, but he seems to enjoy himself.
(© Mandy Godbehear / Shutterstock.com)

Gibran's most famous book, *The Prophet*, about a spiritual teacher who counsels his people, was published in 1923. First written in Arabic and then translated by Gibran into English, it consists of twenty-six short sections written in highly poetic prose. *The Prophet* was published during the period known as modernism, which was characterized by the more intellectual poetry of T. S. Eliot and Ezra Pound, and the mystical romanticism of Gibran found little favor among critics and scholars. However, the general public responded to his work enthusiastically, and *The Prophet* grew steadily in popularity. In 1957, for example, it sold one million copies, and over the course of the twentieth century many millions of copies were sold.

In 1926, Gibran published the collection of aphorisms *Sound and Foam*, a quotation from which serves as the epigraph for "Hamadi." Two years later, he published *Jesus, the Son of Man: His Words and His Deeds as Told and Recorded by Those Who Knew Him*, a work that, like *The Prophet*, has remained popular throughout the twentieth century and into the twenty-first.

So phenomenal has Gibran's success been that he is the best-selling English-language poet of the twentieth century. Nonetheless, American literary critics have remained unimpressed by his work, and Gibran is not considered a significant poet in the American literary canon, although he remains one of the pioneers of Arab American literature. Gibran, who was an alcoholic, died of cirrhosis of the liver in New York City in April 1931, at the age of forty-eight.

Palestine

In "Hamadi," Susan's father comes originally from Palestine, and refugee camps in Palestine are mentioned. It is also stated that his family lives near Jerusalem. Jerusalem is a city which is under the rule of Israel but claimed by both Israel and the Palestinians. This situation must be understood in the context of the ongoing conflict between Israel and the Palestinians.

Beginning in 1920, the area known as Palestine was under British rule. The British had pledged to establish a home within Palestine for the Jewish people, and during the 1920s and

1930s, many Jews emigrated to Palestine with that hope in mind. In 1948, the nation of Israel was formed, but its creation was immediately followed by a war between Israel and surrounding Arab states, including Lebanon, Syria, Iraq, Jordan, and Egypt. The Arab armies were defeated, and hundreds of thousands of Palestinians (including Nye's father) became refugees. In the Six-Day War in 1967, Israel again defeated a coalition of Arab armies. It also took control of East Jerusalem and the area known as the West Bank, which were previously part of Jordan. Israel also captured the Gaza Strip and the Sinai Peninsula from Egypt. The United Nations Security Council called for the withdrawal of Israeli forces from the occupied territories. The Six-Day War created another five hundred thousand Palestinian refugees, who fled to Egypt, Syria, Lebanon, and Jordan. (In "Hamadi," Susan's father is a Palestinian, likely a refugee from 1948 or 1967 who at some point found his way to the United States.)

In the meantime, the Palestine Liberation Organization (PLO) had been formed with the goal of creating a Palestinian state. In 1987, an intifada, or uprising, began in the occupied territories of the West Bank and the Gaza Strip. More than one thousand people died in clashes with Israeli security forces over a period of several years. In 1988, the PLO declared the State of Palestine as an independent state, even though the territories concerned, the West Bank and Gaza Strip, were still occupied by Israel. The PLO also declared that Jerusalem was the capital of the State of Palestine, even though, following Israel's annexation of East Jerusalem, the city was entirely under Israeli control.

In the early 1990s, when "Hamadi" was written, the PLO had accepted Israel's right to exist and sought a two-state solution to the conflict: the recognition of a Palestinian state alongside Israel. In 1994, after an agreement was reached between Israel and the PLO in Oslo in 1993, the Palestine National Authority was set up to govern the West Bank and Gaza Strip.

CRITICAL OVERVIEW

Nye is known primarily as a poet, and as such she has won high praise from reviewers and literary critics. Bert Almon, in "Poetry of the American West," comments, "This poet is

always vigilant: the rhythms are sharp, the eye is keen. She excels at the unexpected and brilliant detail that underwrites the poetic vision." According to Samina Najmi in "Naomi Shihab Nye's Aesthetic of Smallness and the Military Sublime," "Nye's voice is among the most passionate, tender, and instructive for our times." In a comment that might well be applied to "Hamadi," Najmi notes that "Nye draws on varied cultural traditions that acknowledge her multifaceted identity; as Texan, Arab, and American, she is positioned to discern the connections among disparate groups of people." Other commentators have also noted this aspect of Nye's work. According to Jane L. Tanner in her entry on Nye in the *Dictionary of Literary Biography*, Nye

> observes the business of living and the continuity among all the world's inhabitants, whether separated by oceans or time. She lives in Texas but is regional only insofar as she has a strong sense of place wherever she happens to be; she is international in scope and internal in focus.

Similarly, in a review of Nye's 1995 poetry collection *The Red Suitcase* in the *Women's Review of Books*, Alison Townsend writes that Nye "can imagine herself into other people's lives with empathy and authenticity, and her work is distinguished by a generosity—of insight and spirit—that transcends geography."

Much of Nye's work is autobiographical or semiautobiographical, and Townsend comments on the poem "My Grandmother in the Stars," which concerns Nye's Palestinian grandmother (suggested in "Hamadi" by Susan's grandmother), anticipating with regret that they may not meet again. Townsend writes, "Ultimately, love is the emotion that animates this book, and in many ways the collection as a whole is a praise-song to what the poet loves—to what endures and to what is ephemeral."

CRITICISM

Bryan Aubrey

Aubrey holds a PhD in English. In the following essay, he discusses the presence in "Hamadi" of Kahlil Gibran's work and how that provides insight into the character of Hamadi.

The flavor of Naomi Shihab Nye's short story "Hamadi" is very much in keeping with

WHAT DO I READ NEXT?

- Nye's *There Is No Long Distance Now: Very Short Stories* (2011) contains forty short stories of no more than one thousand words each. These are all uplifting stories showing that the divisions between people are never as great as they might appear. The stories, which all feature teenage characters, are set in a variety of places, including the United States and abroad. Some take place against a background of current events, including wars in Iraq and Afghanistan and unrest in Jerusalem. Some show immigrants to the United States facing prejudice.

- *Habibi* is Nye's 1997 young-adult novel about Liyana, a fourteen-year-old girl who moves with her Arab father, American mother, and brother from St. Louis, Missouri, to the West Bank, which is under Palestinian rule and is where her father had grown up. Liyana feels like a stranger in a new land until she forms a friendship with an Israeli boy named Omer. But this raises problems, given the hostility between Israel and the Palestinians.

- *Looking for Palestine: Growing Up Confused in an Arab-American Family* (2013), by Najla Said, is a memoir by the daughter of the renowned Palestinian American scholar Edward Said. Najla was raised in Manhattan and as a child spent many summers in Beirut, Lebanon. As she grows up she struggles to come to terms with her dual cultural identity as an Arab and as an American.

- *A Treasury of Kahlil Gibran* (1951), translated by Anthony Rizcallah Ferris and edited by Martin L. Wolf, is a generous selection from the works of the famed Lebanese poet, including both poetry and prose.

- *Drinking Coffee Elsewhere* (2003) is a collection of eight short stories by American author ZZ Packer. The stories were highly praised by reviewers, who admired Packer's gift for characterization. Most of the stories feature African American teenage girls and deal with issues such as race and racial identity. Packer usually finds a way in these stories to present a moral lesson.

- *Dinarzad's Children: An Anthology of Contemporary Arab American Fiction* (2009), edited by Pauline Kaldas and Khaled Mattawa, contains thirty short stories by Arab Americans that explore the experience of being Arab American from many different angles.

- *Growing Up Ethnic in America: Contemporary Fiction about Learning to Be American* (1999), edited by Maria Mazziotti Gillan and Jennifer Gillan, is an anthology of short stories and memoirs about how immigrants and other racial minorities go about assimilating into American culture. Writing from a wide variety of perspectives, the authors discuss some of the difficulties they have encountered as immigrants and try to balance what they have left behind with what they gain from being in a new land. Writers represented include Sherman Alexie, Amy Tan, Toni Morrison, Sandra Cisneros, E. L. Doctorow, Gary Soto, Daryl Pinckney, Gish Jen, and others.

- In *Funny in Farsi: A Memoir of Growing Up Iranian in America* (2003), Firoozeh Dumas presents an amusing account of her family's life as Iranian immigrants in America. In 1972, at the age of seven, she moved with her family from Iran to Southern California. Her father was an engineer who loved his new country. In a series of sketches, Dumas describes how the family learned American culture and traditions.

> HAMADI IS AN OUTSIDER, AN ISOLATED FIGURE WHOM OTHERS REGARD AS ECCENTRIC. HAMADI IS LIKE HIS MENTOR GIBRAN IN THAT HE LIKES TO PONDER THE TRUTHS OF LIFE, BUT UNLIKE GIBRAN, HE DOES NOT OFTEN FIND A RECEPTIVE AUDIENCE."

that of her poetry: she shows a warm appreciation of life and a sympathetic approach to all her characters, and the setting, though in Texas, reaches out to the Middle East as well in a number of different ways. The main characters—Susan, her father, and Saleh Hamadi—are all Arab Americans, and the presiding spirit of the story is that of the Lebanese American poet Kahlil Gibran. Not only does his work supply the epigraph to the story, but the studious Susan regards him as one of her favorite writers, as does her friend Tracy. Also, Hamadi, who like Gibran was originally from Lebanon, claims to have met Gibran in person when he, Hamadi, first came to the United States at the age of eighteen. That meeting had a profound effect on him, and it appears that Hamadi became something of a disciple of the older man. "He has stayed with me every day of my life," he tells Susan; "I meet him in my heart every day." Like Gibran, Hamadi is a serious, reflective man with an abiding interest in truth. Also like his mentor, he enjoys offering up aphorisms (wise sayings) about life, as when he tells Susan, who is curious about whether he really met Gibran in person or just through his books, that she should not make such distinctions, "or your life will be a pod with only dried-up beans inside. Believe anything can happen." The image could have been lifted from almost any page of Gibran's works.

Gibran is a highly unusual, enigmatic figure. His books have sold millions of copies, and many people are moved by them. People who otherwise read no poetry or serious literature may well have Gibran's work on their bookshelves and regard him as a wise teacher. But literary critics tend to look askance at his work, often regarding it as sentimental, shallow, or pretentious. Where does the truth lie? A reading

of *The Prophet*, Gibran's most popular work (which is read by both Susan and Tracy in the story), provides material to support both views. The prophet of the title is a man named Almustafa, who is described as "the chosen and the beloved" who is about sail back from the city of Orphalese to the island of his birth after a long absence. Before he departs, the people of the city persuade him to impart the wisdom he has learned. Almustafa speaks to the people on a wide range of topics, each of which occupies a short chapter in the book. He speaks, for example, about marriage, love, children, joy and sorrow, crime and punishment, laws, freedom, self-knowledge, friendship, prayer, beauty, religion, death, and many other topics. He utters his pronouncements in poetic, image-laden prose that marks the book, according to the biography of Gibran on the Poetry Foundation website, as "a Middle Eastern work that stands closer to eastern didactic classics such as the Book of Job and the works of the twelfth- and thirteenth-century Persian poets Rumi and Sa'di than to anything in the modern American canon." The book has a distinctly spiritual and often mystical flavor, although it is not specific to any religion. Gibran himself was a Maronite Christian—the Maronite Church has its headquarters in Lebanon—but readers who profess other faiths will not find their beliefs undermined.

Gibran's style may appeal to some while repelling others. Take, for example, the prophet's pronouncements on work:

> You work that you may keep pace with the earth and the soul of the earth.
>
> For to be idle is to become a stranger unto the seasons, and to step out of life's procession, that marches in majesty and proud submission towards the infinite.
>
> When you work you are a flute through whose heart the whispering of the hours turns to music.

Some may find this profound, beautiful, evocative; others may regard it as tedious and rather empty—something that sounds profound, perhaps, but whose meaning evaporates on close inspection. Certainly, Gibran had set himself a hard task. Throughout the book, his prophet must keep up his persona of the enlightened teacher; if Gibran loses his inspiration at any point, the prophet may end up sounding more like a Hallmark greeting card than someone who knows reality.

Susan and Tracy, of course, are in the camp of Gibran's uncritical admirers. Although they are young, just teenagers, they feel the power of Gibran's work and like to quote him to each other. It seems that they try to use him as a guide to life and how to live it. When Tracy is upset because she has competition from Debbie regarding Eddie, the boy she has a romantic interest in, Susan immediately zeroes in on a passage from *The Prophet* in which he discusses love. Her statement that, according to Gibran, "loving teaches us the secrets of our hearts and that's the way we connect to all of Life's heart" is an excellent paraphrase of Gibran's words in *The Prophet*. Susan correctly interprets these words, too, when she tells Tracy that she is too concerned with owning Eddie, which is not love at all. As Gibran says, "Love possesses not nor would it be possessed."

Susan, the eager young girl lapping up the words of the seer Gibran, is a good illustration of the words of Gibran that appear as the epigraph to the story: "It takes two of us to discover truth: one to utter it and one to understand it." Susan shows that she can complete this twofold process.

Like Susan, Hamadi appears to have a deep understanding of Gibran, but the words of the epigraph also suggest a way of understanding Hamadi himself. Hamadi is an outsider, an isolated figure whom others regard as eccentric. Hamadi is like his mentor Gibran in that he likes to ponder the truths of life, but unlike Gibran, he does not often find a receptive audience. He may utter his truth but few are there to understand it. One suspects that when Hamadi makes one of his characteristic pronouncements about small matters of life, such as when he says, hands raised high (perhaps as he has always imagined Gibran's prophet might do), that "it is good to drink a tall glass of water every morning upon arising," he is greeted with indulgent smiles but not taken seriously. Even after many years in America, he remains quite outside American culture. When Susan asks him to go caroling with them, he thinks that means they are going out with a woman named Carol. Then he says he knows about the holiday spirit: "I was just reading about it in the newspaper." It sounds like he has not encountered it personally, but has just learned about it rather like one might learn a fact about a distant country.

Hamadi seems to study and contemplate in silence and alone, and unlike Gibran he does not appear to write much. Like Gibran, though, he thinks a lot about love. When Susan notices a lot of US postage stamps on his desk, all of which have the word "Love" on them, she thinks he must write a lot of letters, but Hamadi says, no, he just likes to focus on the word "love." "I particularly like the globe in the shape of a heart," he says. In fact, although he does not explain it, his remark about the heart-shaped globe—the letter *o* on the stamp, which resembles the earth and thus becomes an image of the universality of love—is his own version of Gibran's words about love that Susan later summarizes. Gibran's actual words in *The Prophet* are that love acts in a person so "that you may know the secrets of your heart, and in that knowledge become a fragment of Life's heart."

The caroling expedition also reveals a great deal about Hamadi. When Eddie joins the carol singers late, Hamadi, who is unfailingly courteous and has very formal manners, is the only one to greet him. "Welcome, welcome to our cheery group!" he says. The greeting is sufficiently unusual, and when coupled with the fact of Hamadi's odd appearance, as if he had "stepped out of a painting," it produces from Eddie the exclamatory question "Who is this guy?" Eddie is young and has no idea he is being rude to the kindly gentleman who greeted him. The reader may sense from this—although it is unstated—the pain that a sensitive man like Hamadi must have endured on many occasions due to his oddness, the fact that he stands out from the crowd and does not seem to fit anywhere.

The final incident in the story makes this a little more explicit and suggests both Hamadi's wisdom and his sadness. When Tracy is in tears because Eddie is going with another girl, Hamadi inquires as to why she is upset. Tracy turns to him and presses her face against his coat, continuing to weep. He does not touch her, which he would not think appropriate, but he does say the following words: "We go on. On and on. We don't stop where it hurts. We turn a corner. It is the reason why we are living. To turn a corner. Come, let's move." What is noticeable about this is how unlike Gibran it sounds. Gibran prefers a more high-flown and poetic mysticism, and indeed, Hamadi does not

No one seems to understand why Tracy begins to cry but Mr. Hamadi. (© DarkBird | Shutterstock.com)

normally speak like this either. But here he offers clear, practical, and simple wisdom, the very opposite of the "riddles" that were all Susan's father could see in his words. Hamadi speaks to help Tracy, but it is apparent that he is expressing his own experience of going "on and on," despite whatever hurts he has encountered in his long and unusual life. Although his response may go over young Tracy's head, and most of the carolers do not hear or take notice of his words, this for once is not an example of a truth left incomplete because it is not heard. Though she and Hamadi are far separated in years, Susan hears him and is struck by what he says, so much so that she remembers his words many years later. This particular nugget of truth therefore finds a willing receptacle and continues to resonate over the years. The final impression, then, of Hamadi is not of an eccentric and an outsider but of a long-suffering man made wise through difficulties and ready to pass his wisdom on to anyone who is ready and able to hear.

Source: Bryan Aubrey, Critical Essay on "Hamadi," in *Short Stories for Students*, Gale, Cengage Learning, 2015.

Dawn Talbott

In the following review, Talbott concedes that Nye has a beautiful writing style but finds the stories in her 2011 collection repetitive.

In this collection of thirty-nine short stories, award-winning poet Nye gives very brief snapshots of the lives of various characters. The selections provide glimpses inside the existences of protagonists of both genders, as well as many characters of different ages, locations, and backgrounds.

Because stories are limited to one thousand words, they are good for readers with limited time or short attention spans. A reader with more stamina can easily get through the book in a few hours. The stories, however, feel repetitive and a little unoriginal. They center on a character whose dad died, mom died, sibling died, dad left when they were young, or mom left when they were young. Although these are life-changing events, and reading about a character triumphing over this adversity makes a good tale, readers do not need thirty-plus entries with the same overall tone and plot in one collection, so readers who do choose to read the entire book may find themselves feeling like they are reading the same story again and again. Adding to the confusion, a few stories feature the same character but do not appear in the collection in chronological order, which makes it hard for readers to make the connections and follow the story. All in all, the stories are well written and do reflect a beautiful poetic style, but readers may feel a sense of deja vu if they choose to read the entire book.

Source: Dawn Talbott, Review of *There Is No Long Distance Now: Very Short Stories*, in *Voice of Youth Advocates*, Vol. 34, No. 4, October 2011, p. 390.

Kathleen T. Horning

In the following review, Horning calls Nye's very short stories "persistently hopeful."

The protagonists of each of these thirty-nine very short stories (one thousand words or fewer) are intelligent, articulate adolescents who crave meaningful connections with the wider world. We enter each story quickly, see something happening, get a flash of insight or two, and then exit, often wanting to know more about the characters and their lives. In one of the most moving stories, "Are We Friends?" a chatty cab driver complains about many things, including mosques ruining the whole coast of Texas, and his teenage fare blurts out, "Well, my dad is an Arab...from a Muslim family... and he's adorable. Not very religious in any way but super-sweet. I think you might like him." Her honest response elicits a heartfelt apology from the cabbie, and then the two search for and finally find one thing they can agree on—the bravery of Elizabeth Smart. Some of the characters recur, but the events don't necessarily occur in chronological order, so the stories do not need to be read in sequence. In "Johnnie," for example, we see the death of a girl named Annie's great-aunt Spitzy, who has mysteriously left a note for a man the family doesn't know. A few stories later, in "Where We Come From," Spitzy is alive and vibrant, telling Annie, "I've become one of the little old ladies I used to make fun of." The stories are persistently hopeful, and they will resonate most deeply with teens who, like the stories' protagonists, have that same craving for meaningful connection.

Source: Kathleen T. Horning, Review of *There Is No Long Distance Now: Very Short Stories*, in *Horn Book*, Vol. 87, No. 6, November–December 2011, pp. 106–107.

Ann Kelley

In the following review, Kelley praises Nye's prose, which "reads like poetry."

In 40 short stories, each 1,000 words or less, award-winning poet Nye introduces characters dealing with difficult life situations. There's Margo, whose parents' divorce feels as if it came out of the blue; Jane, whose father, reeling from the death of his wife, restlessly moves his daughter from one European city to the next; and Liyana, who learns over e-mail that her friend is in an Israeli jail. A few characters reappear intermittently, and careful readers will enjoy piecing together the connections. Nye sets her short stories in the U.S. and abroad, and her characters run the gamut from Texas natives to immigrants facing prejudice in this country. Current events are important to the narratives; news of the wars in Iraq and Afghanistan and protests in Jerusalem, for example, reach her characters via newspaper, e-mail, and TV. With prose that reads like poetry, Nye's powerful book can be savored story by story over time or devoured in one sitting. This offers a unique perspective on today's teenagers, who

TRUTH IS, I GUESS, WE ARE ALL STORYTELLERS IN DIFFERENT WAYS."

are growing up in an increasingly troubling, and increasingly small, world.

Source: Ann Kelley, Review of *There Is No Long Distance Now: Very Short Stories*, in *Booklist*, Vol. 108, No. 8, December 15, 2011, p. 56.

Rachel Barenblat and Naomi Shihab Nye

In the following interview, Nye talks about how she got her work published and her writing process.

Rachel Barenblat: When did you start writing? Were you writing poems from the start?

Naomi Shihab Nye: I started writing when I was 6, immediately after learning HOW to write. Yes, I was writing poems from the start. Somehow—from hearing my mother read to me? from looking at books? from watching Carl Sandburg on 1950's black and white TV?—I knew what a poem was. I liked the portable, comfortable shape of poems. I liked the space around them and the way you could hold your words at arm's length and look at them. And especially the way they took you to a deeper, quieter place, almost immediately.

RB: What did you write about, in the beginning? What provided your first inspiration?

NSN: I wrote about all the little stuff a kid would write about: amazement over things, cats, wounded squirrels found in the street, my friend who moved away, trees, teachers, my funny grandma. At that time I wrote about my German grandma—I wouldn't meet my Palestinian grandma till I was 14.

RB: How did you first get published? I'm curious about the "nuts and bolts" of becoming published for you.

NSN: "Nuts and bolts of becoming published"—well, I have this theory. You start anywhere you can, anyplace that seems inviting or possible to you. For me, it was magazines for kids, since I read them at the library and subscribed to a few. They often had pages that invited their readers to send work. So, I sent it. I had no delusion that everything I wrote would or should get published. This has served me well. There was never any great "mystique" about publishing to me, since I started when I was 7.

As a teenager I published in places like *Seventeen*. As a college student, I started reading literary journals, publishing in places like *Modern Poetry Studies* and *Ironwood*. One little thing always led to another. No way around that. All of my books since have been invited by various publishers or editors. I never have had an agent to this day. To publish, one needs to read widely, and find what's out there, then send one's own work to places you feel particular links with—that is my philosophy of publishing.

RB: Place plays an important role in your writing, especially the places you have lived and the places that hold your roots. Tell me about the places that have been important to you.

NSN: The 3 main places I have lived—St. Louis, Jerusalem, San Antonio—are each deeply precious to me indeed, and I often find them weaving in and out of my writing. Each place has such distinctive neighborhoods and flavors. Gravity interests me—where we feel it, how we feel it.

RB: What about travel? How is writing about travel different from writing about home?

NSN: Sometimes while traveling in Mexico or India or any elsewhere, I feel that luminous sense of being invisible as a traveler, having no long, historical ties, simply being a drifting eye . . . but after awhile, I grow tired of that feeling and want to be somewhere where the trees are my personal friends again.

RB: Where is your favorite place to travel?

NSN: My heart will probably always belong to the Middle East, travel-wise, but I have never been anywhere I disliked.

RB: If you were leaving here today and could only take one thing with you, what would it be?

NSN: If I could take only one thing with me? Our son!!!!!

RB: How do teaching and writing intersect for you? Are they separate activities, or are they connected?

NSN: Teaching and writing are separate, but serve/feed one another in so many ways. Writing travels the road inward, teaching, the road out—helping OTHERS move inward—it

is an honor to be with others in the spirit of writing and encouragement. I never wanted to be a full-time teacher for a minute, though, only an itinerant visitor. It's that nomad in my blood.

RB: Do you consider yourself a storyteller?

NSN: No, I don't consider myself a storyteller, per se. I think of storytellers as being those fabulous people sitting on bales of hay at folk festivals. Truth is, I guess, we are all storytellers in different ways.

RB: Do you think of yourself/your poetry as political?

NSN: Yes, I do think of myself as political, alas, because politics is about people, and I am interested in the personal ramifications of everything, for everybody. How can we get away from it?

RB: Who are your favorite poets to read? Are there books you return to again and again, and if so, what are they?

NSN: William Stafford will always be my favorite poet. I read LOTS of poets, constantly. Recently read & loved Hettie Jones & Koon Woon, always read W.S. Merwin, Molly Peacock, Jane Hirshfield, Jane Kenyon, Lucille Clifton, on and on and on. I never stop reading. I'm reading manuscripts for a contest now. Very exciting.

RB: Tell me a little bit about the anthologies for young readers that you have edited.

NSN: My anthologies have been acts of love and secretarial madness (I have no secretary, and each book involves ENORMOUS amounts of correspondence!) I think of them as being for teenagers and for adults, both. My editor, Virginia Duncan, of Greenwillow Books, is my brilliant guiding light. It seemed to me in the beginning there was room for more anthologies on the shelves of schools and in young people's bedrooms, for international voices, for intriguing, odder twists and true poetic journeying without that "cutesey" flair that has characterized the ways many people think of poetry. I was challenged to make my first anthology *This Same Sky* by teachers who said they wanted more international poetry for their students and did not have access to it. Each book has been warmly received beyond my dreams. I am so happy people like these anthologies. Personally, of course, I love them. I am their choreographer—that's what editing them feels like.

RB: Where do you usually write? Do you have a desk, an office, a favorite chair, a favorite tree?

NSN: I have a long wooden table where I write. Not a desk, really, as it doesn't have drawers. I wish it had drawers. I can write anywhere. Outside, of course, is always great. I am one of the few people I know who LOVES being in airports. Good thing. I can write and read well in them.

RB: What is your advice to writers, especially young writers who are just starting out?

NSN: Number one: Read, Read, and then Read some more. Always Read. Find the voices that speak most to YOU. This is your pleasure and blessing, as well as responsibility!

It is crucial to make one's own writing circle—friends, either close or far, with whom you trade work and discuss it—as a kind of support system, place-of-conversation and energy. Find those people, even a few, with whom you can share and discuss your works—then do it. Keep the papers flowing among you. Work does not get into the world by itself. We must help it. Share the names of books that have nourished you. I love *Writing Toward Home* by Georgia Heard, for example. William Stafford's three books of essays on the subject of writing—*Crossing Unmarked Snow* is the most recent—all from the Poets on Poetry series of the University of Michigan Press, Ann Arbor—are invaluable. I love so many of these new anthologies that keep popping up. Let that circle be sustenance.

There is so much goodness happening in the world of writing today. And there is plenty of ROOM and appetite for new writers. I think there always was. Don't let anybody tell you otherwise. Attend all the readings you can, and get involved in giving some, if you like to do that. Be part of your own writing community. Often the first step in doing this is simply to let yourself become identified as One Who Cares About Writing!

My motto early on was "Rest and be kind, you don't have to prove anything"—Jack Kerouac's advice about writing—I still think it's true. But working always felt like resting to me.

Source: Rachel Barenblat and Naomi Shihab Nye, "Interview with Naomi Shihab Nye," in *Pif Magazine*, August 1, 1999.

SOURCES

Almon, Bert, "Poetry of the American West," in *Western American Literature*, Vol. 31, No. 3, Fall 1996, pp. 265–66.

Asi, Maryam, and Daniel Beaulieu, "Arab Households in the United States: 2006–2010," US Department of Commerce, Bureau of the Census, http://www.census.gov/prod/2013pubs/acsbr10-20.pdf (accessed August 11, 2014).

Fadda-Conrey, Carol, *Contemporary Arab American Literature: Transnational Reconfigurations of Citizenship and Belonging*, New York University Press, 2014, pp. 20–21.

Gibran, Kahlil, *The Prophet*, Knopf, 1973, pp. 3, 12–13, 25.

"Israel and the Palestinians: A History of Conflict," BBC News website, http://news.bbc.co.uk/2/shared/spl/hi/middle_east/03/v3_ip_timeline/html/1929_36.stm (accessed August 8, 2014).

"Kahlil Gibran," Poetry Foundation website, http://www.poetryfoundation.org/bio/kahlil-gibran (accessed August 6, 2014).

Najmi, Samina, "Naomi Shihab Nye's Aesthetic of Smallness and the Military Sublime," in *MELUS*, Vol. 35, No. 2, Summer 2010, p. 151.

Nye, Naomi Shihab, "Hamadi," in *America Street: A Multicultural Anthology of Stories*, edited by Anne Mazer, Persea Books, 1993, pp. 134–46.

Shivani, Anis, "What Is Distinctive about Arab-American Writing Today?," in *Huffington Post*, September 29, 2010, http://www.huffingtonpost.com/anis-shivani/arab-american-writing_b_741205.html (accessed August 11, 2014).

Tanner, Jane L., "Naomi Shihab Nye," in *Dictionary of Literary Biography*, Vol. 120, *American Poets since World War II, Third Series*, edited by R. S. Gwynn, Gale Research, 1992, pp. 223–26.

Townsend, Alison, Review of *The Red Suitcase*, in *Women's Review of Books*, Vol. 13, No. 3, December 1995, p. 26.

FURTHER READING

Berrol, Selma Cantor, *Growing Up American: Immigrant Children*, Twayne's History of American Childhood Series, Twayne Publishers, 1995.

This is a nonfiction account of what immigrant children—whether from Central America, Europe, Asia, or elsewhere—go through as they become adults in a new country far from their original homes. Topics covered include discrimination, poverty, and the conflict between different cultural values.

Bunton, Martin, *The Palestinian-Israeli Conflict: A Very Short Introduction*, Oxford University Press, 2013.

Bunton traces the history of the conflict between the Israelis and the Palestinians from the decline of the Ottoman Empire to the present.

Orfalea, Gregory, *The Arab Americans: A History*, Olive Branch Press, 2005.

Orfalea tells the story of Arab Americans from the earliest immigrants in the mid-nineteenth century to the challenges faced by Arab Americans in the twenty-first century following the terrorist attacks against the United States on September 11, 2001.

Waterfield, Robin, *Prophet: The Life and Times of Kahlil Gibran*, St. Martin's Press, 1998.

This is a biography of Gibran. Waterfield gives some attention to Gibran's personal failings but also provides a positive assessment of his work, which has influenced so many people for almost a century.

SUGGESTED SEARCH TERMS

Naomi Shihab Nye

Hamadi AND Nye

Kahlil Gibran

The Prophet AND Gibran

Palestinian refugees

Arab American

Lebanese American

Palestinian American

The Isabel Fish

JULIE ORRINGER

2003

"The Isabel Fish" is a short story from Julie Orringer's 2003 collection *How to Breathe Underwater*. Originally published in the *Yale Review* in July of that year, the story chronicles the strained relationship between fourteen-year-old Maddy and her sixteen-year-old brother Sage after a devastating car accident. Maddy survived the accident, but Sage's girlfriend of six months, Isabel, was killed. When Maddy's parents suggest that the siblings take a class in scuba diving, they are forced to deal with issues surrounding the accident. Through Maddy's and Sage's struggles, Orringer explores themes of grief, guilt, isolation, and the trials of adolescence. Readers are cautioned that the story contains some profanity and innocent nudity. The story can also be found in *Poolside* (2007), edited by Duncan Bock.

AUTHOR BIOGRAPHY

Julie Orringer was born on June 12, 1973, in Miami, Florida. In her early years, her parents were both medical residents. In an interview for Oprah.com, she said that when she was about the age of two or three, her father asked her to tell him a story and then recorded her answer on index cards. Together they made the cards into a book. By the time she was five they had written ten or more of these books together. Orringer was a lover of books and reading throughout her childhood.

Orringer (right) with fellow author Maggie Shipstead at a book discussion in 2014
(© *Boston Globe via Getty Images*)

The family moved often as Orringer's parents continued their medical careers. When she was five, they moved to New Orleans, where they lived until Orringer was twelve. Her mother was diagnosed with breast cancer when Orringer was ten, the beginning of a ten-year battle; she succumbed to the disease when Orringer was twenty. The shared strain of her mother's illness brought her closer to her two siblings, a younger brother and sister.

Orringer attended Cornell University as an undergraduate and then attended the famed Iowa Writers' Workshop. After graduating in 1996, she held a two-year teaching fellowship there as well. She was awarded a Stegner Fellowship for Stanford University's creative writing program from 1999 to 2001, and she continued there as a lecturer from 2001 to 2003.

In 2003, Orringer's first short-story collection, *How to Breathe Underwater*, which includes "The Isabel Fish," was published. Many of the stories were first published in literary journals. Critical response was overwhelmingly positive; the collection was named a New York Times Notable Book and won several awards.

Orringer then began a novel, *The Invisible Bridge*, for which she received a grant from the National Endowment for the Arts. It was published in 2010 and selected as Amazon's Best Book of the Month for May. In June 2010, Orringer, who is married to fellow writer Ryan Harty, gave birth to her first child, a boy. She also began work on a second novel, this one based on the life of Varian Fry, a journalist who went to France during World War II to rescue artists and writers blacklisted by the Gestapo. Orringer received a Guggenheim Fellowship in 2013 for her work on the novel. As of 2014, Orringer was still at work on this book and living in Brooklyn, New York, with her husband and son.

PLOT SUMMARY

As "The Isabel Fish" begins, fourteen-year-old Maddy and her sixteen-year-old brother Sage are on their way to their first scuba-diving class at the YMCA. Maddy is the first-person narrator, and

MEDIA ADAPTATIONS

- Director and writer Lara Zizic presented *The Isabel Fish*, a short film adaptation of Orringer's story, at the Columbia University Film Festival in 2005, starring Addison Timlin as Maddy and Cal Robertson as Sage.

she tells the reader that Sage has been especially mean to her since "the accident." The reader will gradually learn that Maddy and Sage's girlfriend Isabel were in a car accident in which their vehicle plunged into a pond, and Isabel drowned.

Now, four months later, Maddy's parents are planning on taking the family to St. Maarten, in the Caribbean, for spring break, and have suggested that Maddy and Sage get their scuba certification so that they can dive while on the island. They hope that the prospect of diving among the tropical fish at St. Maarten will be enough to get Maddy past her fear of the water. Maddy is an avid ichthyophile, or lover of fish, and has several aquariums of pet fish. She is also conducting a science experiment on the blood pressure of fighting fish.

At the YMCA, Maddy befriends a Romanian girl in the class. For the first class, all they learn is how the equipment works and how to fall backward into the water, as they would fall out of a boat to begin a dive. Maddy is nervous, and Sage is no help—he ignores her and will not even stand near her during the class. When it is Maddy's turn to fall in the pool and swim, she falls in and just sinks, her limbs paralyzed with fear. She has to be pulled from the pool, coughing and shaking. On the drive home, Sage does not speak to her.

When they get home, Maddy tells her parents that she is not ready to learn scuba. They encourage her to at least consider it, maybe try one more class. She agrees to think about it a little more.

She goes to her room and checks on her fish. There are twenty-six experimental fish, and she has given them all names, one for each letter of the alphabet. There is an Isabel fish, and a Sage fish. The Sage fish is "mean and small with high blood pressure."

The next morning, Sage has a migraine and stays home from school. Maddy takes some medicine up to his room, but he is in the bathroom. She sees Isabel's bass guitar in Sage's room (Sage and Isabel were in a band together), and she picks it up. Sage returns from the bathroom and sees her with the guitar; he yells at her, shoves her out of his room, and slams the door.

That day at school on her lunch break, Maddy sits and relives the accident in her mind, and the reader learns the full story. Maddy was hanging out with Sage and Isabel and a few of their friends, when one of them said that he knew of a house under construction nearby with a newly installed hot tub. Isabel invited Maddy to come along to the hot tub, against Sage's protests.

At the hot tub, with everyone drinking beers, Sage tried to embarrass Maddy by telling a story about when Maddy was five years old and peed in the pool. When he would not stop teasing her, Isabel got angry with him. Then one girl tried to get into the house to use the bathroom and tripped the security alarm. The kids scrambled, running for their cars; Isabel took Maddy in her car, leaving Sage behind. They took off down the street, speeding. Isabel suggested they keep driving all the way to Chicago, three hundred miles away, where they could stay with her aunt and come back the next day. Still speeding, the car hit a curb and sailed into a pond. Isabel was unconscious and pinned by the steering wheel; Maddy's leg was cut open by the jagged metal of the car, but she managed to swim to the surface.

Since Isabel's death, Maddy feels that Sage blames her for not saving Isabel from the car. She blames herself, too.

When Maddy returns home from school, she finds eleven of her experimental fish dead, floating on the surface of the water. She is sure that Sage has deliberately killed them, but she says nothing about it to her parents or to Sage. She takes the dead fish to the pond—the same pond where Isabel drowned—and throws them into the water. Both the Sage fish and the Isabel fish are among them.

On the way to their second scuba lesson the next evening, Maddy finally brings up the subject of the dead fish. Sage tells her he will buy her some replacement fish. He apologizes for being so mean to Maddy, and confesses that he was a terrible boyfriend to Isabel, was not nice enough to her. Maddy reassures Sage that Isabel loved him very much.

At the scuba lesson, the students are diving with scuba equipment for the first time. Maddy is nervous, but this time Sage stands nearby and encourages her. Together they complete the dive successfully.

CHARACTERS

Dad

Maddy and Sage's father is a dentist. While the siblings' mom deals with their situation more directly, their dad tries to keep things light, "distracting us with jokes."

Isabel

Isabel was Sage's free-spirited, beautiful girlfriend, who died in the car accident that Maddy survived. She was outgoing and treated Maddy with kindness and acceptance. Isabel played the bass guitar in Sage's band, and now he keeps her guitar in his room. Although Sage treats Maddy as though Isabel's death was her fault, the accident was the result of Isabel's reckless driving; exhilarated by the prospect of getting away and driving all the way to Chicago, she was driving sixty miles an hour in the neighborhood when they hit a curb and flew into the pond.

Althea London

Althea is one of Sage's friends who was at the hot tub with them just before the accident. She was friendly to Maddy before the accident but now is cold toward her. Althea was the one who tripped the alarm at the unfinished house. Maddy feels that Althea, like Sage, blames her for Isabel's death.

Maddy

Maddy is an extremely bright fourteen-year-old girl, suffering the same sorts of anxieties that many fourteen-year-old girls do—insecurity about her body and her looks, concerns about not fitting in with her peers, and so on. Her only friends are the Padmanabhan sisters, and when they are out of school for a Hindu holiday, Maddy has no one to eat lunch with. The trauma from the recent car accident, in which Sage's girlfriend Isabel drowned and Maddy was injured, makes teen life even more of an ordeal. Maddy suffers from survivor's guilt, which is only intensified by her brother's cruel treatment of her since the accident. "I know Sage blames me, and in my heart I agree," Maddy tells the reader.

Maddy is an ichthyophile—a fish enthusiast—and loves her collection of tropical fish. She is in the process of performing a sophisticated science experiment, manipulating the blood pressure of twenty-six fish that she has raised from eggs. Her love of sea life leaves her conflicted about taking the scuba certification class; since the accident, the idea of being underwater terrifies her, but the prospect of diving amid the tropical fish in St. Maarten is very tempting.

Mom

Maddy and Sage's mother is a psychologist and attempts to counsel the siblings after their traumatic loss. She is positive and encouraging, but Maddy does not fully confide in her about Sage's cruelty. Despite her training as a psychologist, she is not the perfect parent; she smokes and tells stories about old boyfriends that Maddy finds embarrassing.

The Romanian Girl

Maddy befriends a girl with a Romanian accent in her scuba class. The girl is friendly to Maddy and sympathetic when she "bricks" during the first class and has to be pulled from the pool. Maddy shows her the scar from the accident, and the girl reveals her own scar, on her neck, from when her younger sister threw a broken glass.

Sage

Sage, Maddy's brother, is a sixteen-year-old boy filled with anger over his girlfriend's death. Though he knows, intellectually, that her death is not Maddy's fault, Maddy makes the most convenient target for his wrath. He is angry with life, and angry with himself; "I was a terrible boyfriend," he confesses to Maddy near the end of the story. When he deliberately kills eleven of Maddy's experimental fish, he realizes he has gone too far and tries to apologize.

Sage is cooler and more popular than Maddy; he plays drums in a band and has his own car and a larger group of friends. Before the accident, Sage and Maddy used to have a more typical brother-sister relationship; Sage teased her but was not as cruel as he is now. Sage suffers from severe migraine headaches, and in the story, he misses school one day as a result.

Ty Thibodeaux

Ty is another of Sage's friends. He works for a company that installs hot tubs; he was the one who told the group about the newly installed hot tub nearby.

THEMES

Adolescence

While Maddy's ordeal with the accident and Isabel's death is certainly not a common experience of adolescence, it magnifies many of the normal adolescent problems she experiences. For instance, Maddy, like many teen girls, is insecure about her body; now the scar she bears from the accident gives her one more reason to be self-conscious: "My chest is too flat, my legs too skinny, and there is a scar running the length of my left thigh." When the Romanian girl says, "I also have a scar," and shows Maddy the scar on her neck, Orringer may be suggesting that no one gets through adolescence without some lasting reminder of its difficulties.

Like Maddy, Sage was already going through a lot of changes before the accident, the normal changes of adolescence. Maddy notices how his body has changed when she sees him naked at the hot tub ("I hadn't seem him naked since we were kids"). But even though his body has changed, he still teeters on the line between boyhood and manhood; shortly after Maddy notes his more mature body, Sage begins teasing her about peeing in the pool when she was five years old, calling her "the Mad Pisser," and demonstrates that he still has a lot of maturing to do.

At her first scuba lesson, Maddy tells the reader, "Tonight, for the first time, I'll begin to know what my fish have known all their lives: how to breathe underwater." It is telling that the title of the collection in which "The Isabel Fish" appears is *How to Breathe Underwater*. Many of the stories feature adolescent girls enduring

TOPICS FOR FURTHER STUDY

- Because Maddy is the narrator of "The Isabel Fish," the reader never gets to hear Sage's thoughts or feelings about the tragedy. Write an inner monologue for Sage, or a story from his perspective, beginning with how he felt upon hearing the news of Isabel's death and detailing the progress of his emotional state in the four months since. Try to include as many of the stages of grief as you can—denial, anger, bargaining, depression, and acceptance.

- Do some Internet research on the subject of fighting fish, the type of fish Maddy is studying in her experiment. What similarities and differences do you see between fighting fish and characters in the story? Make lists for both Sage and Maddy, and then write an essay discussing how they are each like and unlike the fighting fish.

- Maddy and Sage are planning to go to St. Maarten with their parents for spring break. Find the island on a map, and research which areas are considered best for scuba diving. Using images you find online, create a travel brochure for St. Maarten, touting the best spots for scuba diving and encouraging divers to vacation there.

- Read Cynthia Kodohata's 2005 novel *Kira-Kira*, the story of two very close Japanese American sisters growing up in 1950s Georgia. When the older sister develops lymphoma, the younger must not only take care of her, but also figure out a way to continue life without her. Do you think it would be more difficult to lose a loved one suddenly, as Sage loses Isabel, or after a long debilitating illness, as in this story? Why? Write your opinion in a response. Use details from both stories to support your opinion.

isolation, peer pressure, bullying, and other experiences in which they are, figuratively speaking, just barely keeping their heads above water.

After the accident, Maddy tries to learn scuba diving. (© *Roy Pedersen / Shutterstock.com*)

Grief

Sage is mourning the loss of his girlfriend Isabel, and to some extent, the loss of the carefree days of childhood. In 1969, American psychiatrist Elisabeth Kübler-Ross first outlined the psychological stages of grief in her book *On Death and Dying*. The stages are said to be denial, anger, bargaining, depression, and acceptance. Clearly, Sage is in the anger stage. He torments Maddy throughout the story, cruelly describing how easy it would be for someone to tamper with her oxygen tank underwater while scuba diving, exploding in anger when he finds her in his room, and finally, deliberately killing eleven of her experimental fish. Because the story is told from Maddy's point of view, the reader has no access to Sage's real feelings about Isabel's death, but his confession that he was not a good boyfriend to Isabel implies that he is angry also with himself, not just Maddy. He may feel anger toward Isabel, as well, for driving recklessly, endangering both herself and his sister. Isabel has already been punished by death, however, and besides himself, Maddy is the most convenient target for his anger.

Isolation

Maddy is largely isolated, due to a collection of factors. She is exceptionally smart and interested in science (especially as it relates to fish and other aquatic life), neither of which are characteristics of the typical popular teenage girl. Her brother, who used to be more of an ally, now wants nothing to do with her and treats her harshly. Finally, the tragedy of the accident marks her even more distinctly as someone different or "weird." She feels that other kids, like Sage's friends, blame her for Isabel's death. Because the story is told from Maddy's first-person point of view, the reader cannot be sure if these other characters actually blame her or if Maddy's perceptions are colored by her own guilt over Isabel's death.

Maddy's only friends are two Hindu girls, Salma and Meena Padmanabhan, and the Romanian girl from her scuba class—all girls who are marked as different because of their ethnicity, their names, or their accents. On the day Maddy goes to school in the story, the Padmanabhan sisters are gone for a Hindu holiday, leaving Maddy even more isolated.

Sibling Relations

Before the accident, Maddy and Sage have a fairly typical brother-sister relationship: they have times where they get along and enjoy each other's company, and times when Sage teases and irritates Maddy, as big brothers everywhere do. For instance, Maddy recalls staying home sick from school with Sage when they both had mononucleosis: "We spent a week at home by ourselves, ordering videos our parents would never have let us watch and shooting Chloraseptic into each other's throats." The accident substantially alters their relationship. Even from before the accident, the reader can see that Sage is uncomfortable with Maddy being a part of his relationship with Isabel; he wants her to himself. When Isabel invites Maddy to come with them to the hot tub, Sage instantly nixes the idea, even though his other friends have no objection. "She's just a kid," he says; "she can't." Isabel overrides his suggestion. When Maddy and Isabel are in the accident together, Maddy has intruded even more profoundly into their relationship; Maddy has shared Isabel's last moments on earth. If Sage had not made Isabel angry by teasing Maddy at the hot tub, it is likely that he, too, would have been in the car. Guilt, jealousy, anger—Sage is experiencing a toxic mix of emotions. Maddy, too, is dealing with survivor's guilt, which is made even worse by Sage's harsh treatment of her. She tells Sage, "You make me wish I died instead of her."

STYLE

First-Person Point of View

Orringer's choice of Maddy as the first-person narrator has some important effects on the story. First of all, because only Maddy's thoughts and emotions are shared, the reader experiences the isolation Maddy feels, and even a bit of paranoia. When she sees Althea London at school, Maddy thinks, "I know she's thinking about Isabel when she looks at me, maybe wishing it had been me who died instead." Of course, Maddy cannot know what Althea is thinking; she assumes the worst. While Althea may be uncomfortable speaking to Maddy, it is unlikely that she wishes her dead. It is a common reaction for people to feel uncomfortable speaking to those who have recently endured a tragic experience or loss. However, the reader experiences only Maddy's reaction to Althea, not Althea's true motivation.

Likewise, the reader is not privy to the storm of emotions that is likely oppressing Sage at this difficult time, only his outward reactions, especially his cruelty to Maddy. Orringer offers some clues—Sage's migraines, for example—but experiencing Maddy's point of view, the reader understands her bewilderment, frustration, and despair at her brother's transformation.

Finally, Maddy's first-person narration makes her description of the car accident more harrowing and immediate:

> The windshield crunched and everything was dark and water poured in through the open windows, so cold it erased every part of me it touched, and suddenly it was in my mouth with its pond-scum taste and I couldn't breathe.

Setting

Orringer keeps the setting of the story somewhat vague and generic; the reader does not learn the name of the town they are living in, or even the state. There are a few clues to their location: Maddy says her mother drove her to Detroit to buy the fish eggs for her experiment, and bought her new swim fins at the Arbor Valley Sea and Ski. Orringer's family moved many times during her childhood, and one of the places she lived was Ann Arbor, Michigan, a college town about forty miles west of Detroit. The name of the nearby neighborhood where the accident occurred—Gettyswood Townhomes—with its man-made ornamental pond, indicates that the family probably lives in a suburban area.

Keeping the location generic and suburban helps emphasize the universality of the story's themes. Tragedy and adolescent turmoil happen everywhere, to everyone. This is not a story about the difficulty of adolescence in the city, or in the slums, or in an isolated rural community; it is a story about the difficulty of adolescence, period. Except for the accident, and Maddy's love of fish, the other details of the story are almost stereotypically suburban: a professional mom and dad, a mildly rebellious older brother who plays drums in a band, a class at the YMCA. The centerpiece of the story is the relationship between Maddy and Sage; the setting and other details fairly fade into the background.

Vocabulary

Maddy uses a more sophisticated vocabulary to describe her life than one would expect from a fourteen-year-old girl, which emphasizes how advanced she is intellectually. For instance, in describing how Sage continues to punish her for Isabel's death, she says, "A quiet private criminal justice system is what we've created, with Sage as judge, jury, jailer, and executioner. Our system has no checks and balances, and it allows multiple punishments for the same crime." Her experiment with the fish is titled "The Relationship between Aggression and Hypertension in *B. Splendens*." But Maddy's advanced intellect does not give her advanced emotional capabilities. She still struggles to process the trauma that she has been through and the pressures of growing up.

HISTORICAL CONTEXT

Terrorist Attacks of September 11, 2001

According to her writing notebooks, Orringer first made preliminary, conceptual notes for "The Isabel Fish" in December 1999. The actual writing of the story took place in both 2000 and 2001, while the story was not published until July 2003, in the *Yale Review*. With the creation of the story occurring over such a span of time, numerous historical influences could have affected it, or at the least the reception of it.

Y2K, as the transition from the twentieth to twenty-first centuries came to be known, was fraught with anxieties. There was a small contingent who believed the world would actually come to an end at 12:01 a.m., 2000. A much larger group was concerned about the effect that the change of date, from 1900s to 2000s, would have upon computer systems worldwide. With so many social, commercial, and governmental systems dependent upon computer systems, citizens braced themselves for total chaos, stocking up on basic necessities like water, canned goods, and generators for electricity. The irony for America was that while the Y2K transition turned out be fairly unproblematic, the event that would completely alter Americans' view of life was still to come, on September 11, 2001, when the terrorist attacks on the World Trade Center

shaped an entire generation. Four commercial planes were hijacked by nineteen terrorists; two planes were deliberately flown into the World Trade Center in New York City, resulting in 2,753 deaths. A third hijacked plane crashed into the Pentagon building, in Washington, DC, killing 184, and the fourth plane crashed in Pennyslvania when passengers and crew attempted to take the plane back from the terrorists; forty were killed.

The terrorist attacks of 9/11 significantly affected the psyche of the millennials, roughly the generation born between 1980 and 2000. The attacks and the war on terrorism are cited as a defining event for this generation. Many millennials, especially those who were old enough at the time of the attacks to understand and remember them, have a greater awareness of the brevity and fragility of life than young people of previous generations. They place a greater value on relationships and are less likely to postpone "bucket list" experiences to the future, as they are aware that this future is not guaranteed. In "The Isabel Fish," Isabel's death functions as a kind of microcosm of 9/11 for Maddy and Sage, a defining event that gives them an earlier experience of tragedy and a more heightened sense of the fragility of life than is known by most kids their age.

Impeachment of President Clinton, Edward Kennedy, and Chappaquiddick

On December 11, 1998, the House Judiciary Committee voted to recommend the impeachment of President Bill Clinton, on the grounds that he had committed perjury in a sexual harassment lawsuit brought against him earlier; the lawsuit was dismissed. It was revealed that Clinton had had an affair with a White House intern, Monica Lewinsky.

While this particular scandal may not be relevant to Maddy and Sage's story, it did cause some in the media to bring up an earlier scandal involving a prominent Democrat and a young worker in his employ. In 1969, Senator Edward Kennedy left a party he was attending to drive campaign worker Mary Jo Kopechne home. On the way home, he drove off a bridge on Chappaquiddick Island. While Kennedy swam free of the accident, Kopechne was unable to and drowned in the car. Kennedy was prosecuted for leaving the scene of an accident.

Sage seems to blame Maddy for Isabel's death.
(© Rynio Productions / Shutterstock.com)

CRITICAL OVERVIEW

Reviews of Orringer's first short-story collection, *How to Breathe Underwater*, were overwhelmingly positive. Emily Perkins, of the London *Guardian*, calls the collection "exquisite" and crowns Maddy "the true heroine of the book," for her patience and compassion for her brother Sage. Likewise, Michael Schaub of the *Austin Chronicle* writes that "it's impossible not to feel for the pained and alienated young women in Orringer's stories, and impossible not to be stunned and moved by their quests for redemption." Orringer was praised by more than one reviewer for her empathetic, realistic views of teen life. Lisa Dierbeck, writing for the *New York Times*, seems startled by the "harsh landscape" of Orringer's stories, but also praises her "assured voice, restraint and eye for detail."

In one discordant note, a writer for *Kirkus Reviews* calls the stories in the collection "mordant snapshots of lives under stress" and claims

regarding "The Isabel Fish" that "there's no movement in the story." Even this reviewer, however, concedes that "one could definitely do worse than this debut collection of nine stories." The general consensus of reviewers was that *How to Breathe Underwater* made for an impressive debut by Orringer, containing stories that show both understanding of and compassion for teens in the difficult transition from adolescence to adulthood.

CRITICISM

Laura B. Pryor

Pryor has a master's degree in English literature and almost thirty years of experience as a professional writer. In the following essay, she explores what Maddy does not tell the reader of "The Isabel Fish" about her struggle with Isabel's death, and how Sage's anger may not be the worst way to deal with grief.

In Julie Orringer's short story "The Isabel Fish," fourteen-year-old Maddy is a precociously bright girl going through many of the usual trials of adolescence, including insecurity about her body, a preoccupation with what others are thinking about her, and the development of her sexual identity. The tragic accident in which Isabel dies not only compounds these trials but also reveals Maddy's ambivalence about her sexual orientation.

One of Maddy's most unique characteristics is her passionate love of tropical fish. Through a carefully monitored experiment, Maddy alters the blood pressure and aggression of her fighting fish. Through her experiment with the fish, she is able to exert a level of control over their behavior that she cannot experience in her own life. She is able to "play God"; she raises the fish from eggs, alters their behavior with drugs, isolates them from the other fish. However, this is the only area of Maddy's life over which she has such control. She is meanwhile the subject of her parents' "experiment," their hoping that scuba diving will help Maddy "form positive associations with water," as her psychologist mother puts it. They do not force her to take the lessons, but Maddy says, "After all their planning, how could I say no thanks?" Out of obligation and the anticipation of guilt, then, Maddy agrees to the lessons. She already feels guilty for Isabel's

WHAT DO I READ NEXT?

- "Note to Sixth-Grade Self" is another story by Orringer in the same collection as "The Isabel Fish," *How to Breathe Underwater* (2003). In this story, a group of popular girls torment an awkward sixth grader, who does her best to avoid attracting their attention.

- In *Autobiography of My Dead Brother* (2005), written by Walter Dean Myers, the main character, Jesse, must deal with the loss of his close friend Rise, who was killed in a drive-by shooting after getting involved in dealing drugs. Fifteen-year-old Jesse is a talented artist and cartoonist, and the book includes his sketches of life in Harlem—sketches provided in reality by illustrator Christopher Myers, the author's son.

- In John Green's *Looking for Alaska* (2005), the main character, Miles, nicknamed Pudge, must cope with the loss of a dear friend who dies in a car accident. Sixteen-year-old Pudge, his roommate Chip, and Alaska Young, a beautiful, bright, but troubled girl, all live at a boarding school in Alabama.

- *On Grief and Grieving: Finding the Meaning of Grief through the Five Stages of Loss* (2005) was the last book written by renowned psychiatrist Elisabeth Kübler-Ross, who died in 2004; David Kessler is the book's coauthor. Kübler-Ross first delineated the five stages of loss—denial, anger, bargaining, depression, and acceptance—in her ground-breaking first book, *On Death and Dying* (1969). She was experiencing what she termed "anticipatory grief" herself while writing the book, because her own health was failing.

- *Scuba Diving* (2009), 4th ed., by Dennis Graver, is a comprehensive guide for those who want to learn the sport. It includes tips on how to select a good training course, what equipment is needed, and how to find the best equipment, among many other topics. The book is illustrated with color photographs of aquatic life.

- Orringer's first novel, *The Invisible Bridge* (2010), is a love story set against the backdrop of World War II and the Holocaust. The two lovers are Jewish and spend much of the war in Hungary, where they endure many trials. An epic tale rich with historical detail, the novel has been compared to Boris Pasternak's *Doctor Zhivago* (1957).

- Norman Maclean's classic novella *A River Runs through It* (1976) tells the story of two siblings, the narrator (also named Maclean) and his brother Paul, and of Paul's untimely fate. The two brothers, who live in Montana, bond through fly-fishing. The story is narrated by a much older Maclean, trying to makes sense of his brother's life many years later.

---

death, for not having saved her from the car after it crashed in the pond.

Maddy is an overachiever who hates to disappoint anyone, who tries to do the right thing regardless of her own feelings. She judges herself even for random thoughts; when it briefly occurs to her that the Romanian girl might recognize her from newspaper accounts of the accident, she instantly dismisses the notion as "an extremely egotistical thought, given how many unfortunate things there are on the news and in newspapers."

She judges her body as well, calling her physical shortcomings "the mistakes of my body," as though she is somehow responsible for them. Unlike Sage, whose grief is obvious, Maddy tries to function as always. She takes care of her fish, goes to school, does her homework, "just as if I were fully recovered. Which I'm not."

THE ANSWER MAY BE THAT MADDY, TOO, WAS IN LOVE WITH ISABEL."

While Maddy may appear to be functioning more normally and recovering faster than Sage, she may actually be doing worse. While Sage has moved on to the anger stage of grief—the second of the five stages, which are denial, anger, bargaining, depression, and acceptance—Maddy may still be in denial. She has named one of her experimental fish Isabel and gives it a calming drug daily. The fish she has chosen is a rare one with a unique blue marking on its fin. (In contrast, the fish she has named Sage is "mean and small with high blood pressure.") When Maddy goes to the first scuba class and sinks into the water, she says, "It feels like...if I go down farther still I will reach Isabel, her hair floating mermaidlike around her." Later, she says, "It's impossible to believe how gone she is, how untouchable." Maddy cannot accept Isabel's death. The question is, why should Maddy have more difficulty coming to terms with Isabel's death than Sage, who was in love with her and spent far more time with her than Maddy? The answer may be that Maddy, too, was in love with Isabel.

The typical media stereotype of a teenage girl is one who is boy crazy, fashion obsessed, highly emotional, and usually uninterested in math or science. Maddy fits none of these stereotypes. She is extraordinarily self-contained—as she describes herself in the final sentence of the story—is not subject to emotional outbursts, and observes life around her in great detail, like the scientist she is. She seems to have little interest in clothes, unless we count her new swim fins. And she never mentions even passing interest in a boy. When Maddy goes with Sage and his friends to the hot tub, there is no physical description of Sage's friend Ty Thibodeaux at all, though he is naked in the hot tub with them and treats Maddy nicely, refusing to join Sage in teasing her. On the other hand, Maddy describes Isabel in great detail:

> Isabel was naked, too.... She opened her arms and let the wind hit her and she laughed and shivered, her hair all loose and messed up, her skin going pink. She was so beautiful that for

a minute I forgot to be freaked out by what was happening. I started taking off my clothes like everyone else.

When Maddy gets into the hot tub next to Isabel, she says, "Our thighs pressed together under the water, her skin slick-smooth." Later, when they are speeding away from the hot tub in Isabel's car and Isabel suggests they drive to Chicago together, Maddy says, "I felt light-headed and frightened and almost in love with her." Even Maddy's interaction with Isabel's bass guitar has romantic overtones: "I pick it up and touch the smooth neck and the polished black body." She says she felt "almost" in love with Isabel—but given Maddy's strong desire to do what is expected of her, to not disappoint, would she ever go so far as to admit being in love with her brother's girlfriend? If saying no to scuba lessons is too much guilt for Maddy to stomach, could she ever confess to such a betrayal of Sage, even to herself? She is aware of how Sage would feel about the trip to Chicago: "Sage would be so jealous he would spontaneously combust."

Maddy, like most fourteen-year-old girls, is coming to terms with her body, her sexuality, and her insecurities about both. The story abounds with bodies—Sage and his friends at the hot tub, the locker room at the YMCA, Maddy's own inferior evaluation of herself in comparison to "the magazine look nowadays" (breasts but no hips). But of all the bodies Maddy is surrounded by throughout the story, the only one Maddy evaluates as "beautiful" is Isabel's.

On the surface, Sage's cruel behavior and Maddy's controlled, responsible demeanor give the impression that Maddy is coping more effectively with the loss of Isabel than Sage is. But while Sage allows his grief some release in the form of his angry outbursts, Maddy internalizes everything. Even Sage's name indicates that he may be taking the wiser course in venting his grief. Maddy's name, on the other hand, may be a foreshadowing of the eventual explosion that could occur if she continues to repress her emotions—she may become too "mad" to be self-contained any longer. Her experiments with her fighting fish, trying to make some sense of anger, "what makes it ebb and flow, how it can be controlled," may have more to do with keeping her own anger at bay than understanding Sage's.

Maddy sets exotic fish free in an ornamental pond, though she knows they will not likely survive.
(© Nastya Pirieva / Shutterstock.com)

Maddy makes some progress, however, after Sage deliberately kills her fish. She finally lashes out at Sage, in a small way, calling him some names and refusing his apologetic offer to buy her more fish. However, the guilt of her betrayal—her love for Isabel—prevents her from feeling fully justified in fighting back. Shortly after being angry with Sage, she ends up comforting him by telling him how much Isabel loved him.

In the end, the grieving process may be one scenario in which Maddy's intellect works against her. It is an emotional process, not a scientific, analytical one. And Maddy's tendency to put the emotions of others—her parents', Sage's—before her own hampers her ability to process her own grief. The process is further stunted by the forbidden nature of her feelings for Isabel. However, Maddy's progress with her scuba lessons, and the healing of her relationship with Sage, offer hope that she is moving forward, "self-contained and breathing underwater."

Source: Laura B. Pryor, Critical Essay on "The Isabel Fish," in *Short Stories for Students*, Gale, Cengage Learning, 2015.

Carmen Callil

In the following review, Callil admits that Orringer has talent but harshly criticizes her novel The Invisible Bridge.

This excessively long epic of war and love is almost impossible to review with charity, yet charitable criticism must be included in any assessment of it because the author is ambitious, has done prodigious research, and has certain remarkable talents. Julie Orringer is a young American whose first book, the much-praised collection of short stories *How to Breathe Underwater*, was noted for its ironic humour and verbal precision. Such attributes have been entirely discarded in this, her first novel, in which she takes a great story—in part based on the experiences of her grandparents—and flattens it beneath a mountain of incident and often embarrassing prose.

Andras Lévi is a poor young Hungarian who goes to Paris in 1937 to study architecture, while his elder brother Tibor goes to Modena to study medicine; in their native land, quotas for Jewish students prevent such education. Andras and Tibor have a younger brother, Mátyás, who aspires to the stage, as well as unassuming parents in the Hungarian village of Konyár; their story expands to include the fates of the Jewish fellow students Andras meets at the École Spéciale d'Architecture in Paris.

Andras is only 19. He meets an older, mysterious ballet teacher, Klara Morgenstern, and falls tumultuously in love. Their passionate relationship constitutes the first part of the saga and the destinies of Klara's family in both Paris and Budapest join that of Andras's in the complex narrative. Orringer is to be praised for her capacity to recreate the atmosphere of Paris in the febrile year which preceded the Munich pact, during which French antisemitism was on the rise. Her mastery of historical detail is admirable, as is her microscopic consideration of every visual feature of Andras's surroundings. The colour of every object—from "sandwiches so pale they looked like snow," through the varying shades of white, grey or silver in ice, beards or hay, to the "dusty yellow light" of a staircase—is painstakingly recorded.

But her lack of control over this descriptive torrent makes it impossible for her characters to come to life. Cardboard creatures, they drown in a sea of florid language, while their emotions and their dialogue—never for one moment containing any of the banter which is so much a part of most human life—are decorated with every available cliché. Clara looks up "from under the graceful arch of her brows." Always a dozen adjectives are used when one—or none—would do, as when Tibor and Andras visit the Louvre, "taking in the velvet-brown shadows of Rembrandt and the frivolous curlicues of Fragonard and the muscular curves of the classical marbles." As every sensation, every meal, doorway and incidental character receives similar attention, the narrative suffers and becomes infected: "That was what made her like a nymph, Andras thought; the way she seemed to embody both timelessness and the irrevocable passage of time."

And yet, a skeleton of brilliant storytelling can be spotted, and it almost comes to life in the second part of the book, which uses the experiences of these two Hungarian-Jewish families to tell the story of the Hungarian Holocaust. As war approaches, Andras's visa renewal is refused. Forced to return to Budapest, with the outbreak of war he is conscripted into the Munkaszolgalat, the state labour service which by 1938 consisted only of Jewish Hungarians. The horrific labour camps of the second world war, in which millions died, have always received less notice than the Nazi death camps. Death in these labour services was gradual, always wretched, and usually agonising. Here Orringer's grasp of fact and circumstance is used to best effect, as she observes the lingering disintegration of each starving and diseased human body and recreates the minute attention devoted to ensuring that so many died with as much suffering as possible.

Her formidable aptitude for research also triumphs in her account of the fate of Hungary's Jews. Protected from Nazi deportation orders by the Hungarian state until March 1944, in the few months that followed before the final defeat of Hitler more than half the Hungarian-Jewish population was deported to death. This will always be a heartbreaking story, and Orringer tells it well.

She can master anguish and history, but her style rarely matches her subject. Whenever her characters re-enter the story, purple prose accompanies them. "Andras had thought of Klara's womb, that sacred inward space they'd taken pains to keep empty." And, later: "Nest of my children, he thought, placing a hand on her womb." Nor is this helped by Orringer's insistent use of American idiom, as the text swells with "gottens," each sounding out of place on the desperate tongues of hounded European Jews in the 1930s and 40s.

Certainly Orringer has the talent to write. Has some sinister creative writing course twisted her obvious ability and deafened her ears? Only another cliché can truthfully describe her heroic failure in *The Invisible Bridge*: it is a perfect curate's egg of a book. That egg was famously good in parts. But of course an egg cannot manage this; such an egg cannot be eaten at all.

Source: Carmen Callil, Review of *The Invisible Bridge*, in *Guardian* (London, England), July 23, 2010.

Jessica Swaim

In the following review, Swaim calls Orringer's stories in How to Breathe Underwater *"spellbinding."*

Each of these nine stories, written with all the depth and complexity of a novel, probes the joy and anguish of coming of age. Girls trapped in the mystical universe of childhood grapple with religious conflict, sexual awakening, and the subtle tyranny of their elders as they negotiate the perilous passage to adulthood. Although the subject matter rings familiar, the language soars to poetry and the author's insights slice bone-deep. In "Stations of the Cross," mob mentality takes over when children reenact the crucifixion.

"I am the canker of my brother Sage's life," begins the story entitled "The Isabel Fish," in which 14-year-old Maddy is encouraged by her parents to take scuba diving lessons in order to overcome the trauma of a submerged car accident. In "Care," Tessa weighs responsibility to her young niece against her longing for the pills in her pocket. "Notes to My Sixth-Grade Self" documents the humiliating ritual of the school dance with the unattainable boy in the form of the narrator's notes to herself on how to dress and how to act to avoid being ostracized. Spellbinding stories to read for pleasure or to study as fine examples of the craft.

Source: Jessica Swaim, Review of *How to Breathe Underwater*, in *Kliatt*, Vol. 39, No. 4, July 2005, p. 34.

Steve Inskeep and Julie Orringer

In the following radio show transcript, Orringer explains the inspiration behind some of the stories in her collection How to Breathe Underwater.

STEVE INSKEEP, host: Many writers explore the agony of growing up, but not many examine childhood quite as brutally and unsentimentally as Julie Orringer. Her first book of short stories tells the tales of a girl whose mother died, a girl whose mother is dying, a girl who feels like nothing next to her cousin, a boy who kills his sister, entire classrooms full of children who ostracize one of their classmates. One of these stories is called "Note to Sixth-Grade Self." In it, a girl writes down some of the elaborate instructions that she tries to follow in an effort to get through a dance class without being tormented.

Ms. JULIE ORRINGER (Author): 'At 4:00, go inside with the others. Line up against

> WE'RE ALLOWED TO TURN AWAY FROM WHAT'S MOST DIFFICULT, OR WE'RE ALLOWED TO RENDER IT IN A FORM THAT'S DISTANT ENOUGH FROM OUR OWN EXPERIENCE THAT WE CAN LOOK AT IT HEAD ON."

the wall with the girls. Watch how the boys line up against their wall—popular ones in the middle, awkward ones at the sides. Watch how the girls jockey to stand across from the boys they like. Watch Brittney Wells fumble with the zipper of her nylon Le Sportsac. Don't let her get next to you with that thing. Try to stand across from someone good. Do not let yourself get pushed all the way out to the sides, across from Zachary Booth or Ben Dusseldorf. Watch how Patricia and Cara stand, their hips shot to one side, their arms crossed over their chests. Try shooting your hip a little to one side. Rest your weight on one foot. Draw a circle on a wooden floor with one toe. Do not bite your fingernails. Do not give a loud sniff. Think of the word nonchalant. Imagine the 11th-graders, the way they look when they smoke on the bus. Let your eyes close halfway.'

INSKEEP: The book is called "How to Breathe Underwater," and its excruciating but memorable stories have won wide praise. The author, Julie Orringer, is in the studios of KQED in San Francisco. Julie, thanks for the reading, and welcome.

Ms. ORRINGER: Thanks so much, Steve.

INSKEEP: I think that a lot of childhood angst is perhaps in the mind of the child, things that they don't understand, but you write about kids that have had very real tragedies. Repeatedly your main character will be someone whose mother has died.

Ms. ORRINGER: Mm-hmm. Mm-hmm. Yeah. And this is one of the ways, I think, that kids are sometimes subjected to the realities of the adult world long before they're ready to be. We do experience loss. We do experience pain that we don't have words for yet, and that's part of the difficulty of going through those years.

INSKEEP: You experienced some of that pain.

Ms. ORRINGER: Yeah, that's true. My mother died when I was 20 years old, after a 10-year battle with breast cancer.

INSKEEP: Did that affect things other than your relationship with your mother, even when you went away from the household to school, out to college, you were thinking about these things?

Ms. ORRINGER: Yeah. Absolutely. I think one of the deepest effects that it had in my life was to make me very, very close to my younger brother and sister. I have a brother who's five years younger and a sister who's eight years younger, and the sense that we were going through this thing together, this thing that was unimaginably horrible, made us have to communicate and be consistently close in a way that we might otherwise have not.

INSKEEP: Can I ask about a story in here called "Care"?

Ms. ORRINGER: Sure.

INSKEEP: And I just want to very briefly summarize this. It's about a young woman whose mother died when she was four. Her life is going nowhere. She's unemployed. She's hooked on pills. She's given her niece to look after for the day and she can't even do that. She gets stoned and the niece disappears.

Ms. ORRINGER: Right.

INSKEEP: She does find the girl before the end of the story again, but I wonder if you could read on page 141 for me?

Ms. ORRINGER: 'Now would be the time to take Olivia back to the hotel to get her cleaned up in Gayle's hotel room, to wait for her sister to be finished with her conference. Tessa and Olivia could both pretend everything was fine, and maybe Gayle would believe them, or maybe she wouldn't and everything would begin to change. The nightmare that has become Tessa's life might crack open and begin to fall away. Maybe that's what she's been hoping for all day. Maybe that's why she let herself lose Olivia, to make things so terrible they'd have to change. But Olivia is back now and Tessa feels almost as if she's been tricked. She feels as if she doesn't have the power to decide anything anymore, as if she's being pulled along slick tracks by a strong and twisted steel rope underground, like a cable car.'

INSKEEP: Julie Orringer reading from her book How to Breathe Underwater. *Julie, you have there a troubling story of a young woman, but the most interesting thing to me about that story was that that young woman has a sister. Obviously . . .*

MS. ORRINGER: Yeah.

INSKEEP: . . . her mother also died, but she seems to have pulled out of it.

Ms. ORRINGER: Yeah, it's interesting. I think that when I wrote this story, I was at a time in my life when the possibilities for a good outcome, a positive entry into adulthood seemed maybe just as likely or equally balanced against the possibilities of a really bad outcome. I wanted to explore both of those possibilities. What would it be like to have this happen at once in a single family? I was looking back on a time when I had recently moved to San Francisco, and I was trying to set up a life alone for the first time. I was in my very early 20s, and that was truly scary.

INSKEEP: Did you end up, you know, taking a lot of pills, sharing an apartment with a stoner, you know, like this girl does?

Ms. ORRINGER: Well, you know, my father just read this collection in its entirety pretty recently. There was a lot that I was kind of reluctant to have him read. He'd read quite a few of the stories, but not all of them, and this was one of them, and he said, 'You know, I've got to ask you. Did you—just confidentially, did you use drugs when you were in San Francisco?' And I thought, my God, of all the things he could've asked me about this collection, thank God you've asked me the one that I could say no to.

INSKEEP: You did worse things. You did other things.

Ms. ORRINGER: Yeah. Right. But we won't talk about that. No, I was lucky enough not to have an experience that was like this young woman's experience.

INSKEEP: Must be kind of a fine line between mining your difficult experiences of youth for these wonderful creative efforts that you've made here, and obsessing over the experiences of your youth and getting hung up on it.

Ms. ORRINGER: Well, you know, I think sometimes fiction acts as a kind of veil between the writer's experience and what's on the page in a way. We're allowed to turn away from what's most difficult, or we're allowed to render it in a form that's distant enough from our own experience that we can look at it head on.

INSKEEP: The book is called How to Breathe Underwater. *I know that refers to a specific event in one of the stories, but I wonder if it has a larger meaning for you.*

Ms. ORRINGER: Yeah. That's a great question. When I was looking back at the stories and I saw this line about breathing underwater from a story called "The Isabel Fish," in which a young girl who has survived a car accident and a near drowning is now taking scuba lessons with her brother, and I found this line, you know, 'Soon I will begin to learn what my fish have known all their lives, how to breathe underwater,' and I felt like this has something to do with the seeming impossibility of the transition between adolescence and adulthood, where we're being asked to take our young selves and move into a completely different social medium with different rules, and if we were allowed to do this gradually, adolescence might not be the incredibly fraught time it is. You know, the problems really arise when the adult world moves toward us before we're ready to experience it, either, you know, through sexuality or personal loss or tragedy or premature independence from our parents, and so I suppose I'm amazed that we're able to do it at all, and perhaps, you know, in the best-case scenario this book stands as a kind of appreciation to people who are doing that as we speak.

Source: Steve Inskeep and Julie Orringer, "Interview: Author Julie Orringer Discusses Her New Book *How to Breathe Underwater*," in *Weekend All Things Considered*, October 18, 2003.

Kirkus Reviews

In the following review, an anonymous writer faults "The Isabel Fish" for having "no movement."

As a career calling card, one could definitely do worse than this debut collection of nine stories. In the opening piece, "Pilgrims," a simple Thanksgiving Day visit by a family to the house of some friends takes a macabre turn when the game being played by the children in the backyard goes too far. This dark-tinged flavor is echoed in "Stations of the Cross," the volume's climactic story, which has deeper things on its mind—the travails of a Jewish girl trying to figure out where she stands in an almost entirely Catholic small Louisiana town—before going

off the rails with a children's reenactment of the Crucifixion that starts to mirror a lynching. If Orringer has a problem, it's one endemic to the modern short story: that these are for the most part still lives; they don't go anywhere. "The Isabel Fish" is an extremely competent and well-wrought tale about a teenaged girl who recently almost died in a car wreck that killed her older brother's girlfriend—something he now hates her for, a strange variant of survivor guilt. But as convincingly as Orringer is able to travel the strange by-ways of the adolescent mindset, there's no movement in the story, just the usual onionskin peeling away of memory until the details surrounding the primal crash are revealed. One piece that breaks the mold is "Stars of Motown Shining Bright," in which a young girl (another one) is made an accomplice by a friend who's planning to elope with a guy who doesn't exactly seem like husband material. While it's not the best entry here, it at least progresses from A to B and gives you a reason to persevere to the final lines; it's unlike most of these stories, which just peter out, albeit in a quiet and artful manner.

Still, Orringer stakes out some ground for herself with these compact little pieces about growing up in tough circumstances.

Source: Review of *How to Breathe Underwater*, in *Kirkus Reviews*, Vol. 71, No. 15, August 1, 2003, p. 986.

Publishers Weekly

In the following review, an anonymous writer commends Orringer's strong storytelling skills.

Trapped in awkward, painful situations, the young protagonists of Orringer's debut collection discover surprising reserves of wisdom in themselves. Their trials are familiar if harsh—the illness and death of parents and friends, social ostracism—but Orringer's swift, intricate evocation of individual worlds gives depth and integrity to her nine stories, set everywhere from Florence to New Orleans to Disney World. The collection's title comes from "The Isabel Fish," in which 14-year-old Maddy is learning how to scuba dive after surviving a car accident in which her older brother's girlfriend drowned. Maddy is sure her brother hates her, and when he kills the fish she is raising for a science fair project, she can hardly blame him. It is only when they go diving together that she realizes he feels as guilty as she does. In "Note to Sixth-Grade Self"— written in a telegraphic second person—the narrator details her torments at the hands of a popular girl who speaks with a stutter. The cruelty of children is also dissected in "Stations of the Cross," in which Jewish Lila Solomon attends her friend's first Communion in the Deep South, and finds herself reluctantly playing a part in an enactment of the Crucifixion. In "When She Is Old and I Am Famous," fat Mira must cope with the arrival of her supermodel cousin: "Aida. That is her terrible name. Ai-ee-duh: two cries of pain and one of stupidity." By the end of the story, Aida has won over Mira, who finally empathizes with her bids for attention. No matter how wronged they have been, Orringer's characters are open to reconciliation and even willing to save their tormentors. It is this promise of grace—and Orringer's smooth, assured storytelling—that distinguishes the collection.

Source: Review of *How to Breathe Underwater*, in *Publishers Weekly*, Vol. 250, No. 34, August 25, 2003, p. 38.

Donna Seaman

In the following review, Seaman praises Orringer's "fiercely beautiful" style.

How apt it is that water is Orringer's ruling element and reigning metaphor, because her short stories are exceptionally translucent, deep, and fluid. Her young characters—primarily girls whose mothers are gravely ill with cancer, depressed in the wake of divorce, missing, or dead—are drawn to ponds, pools, and hot tubs where immersion in water is cleansing, even holy, but also deadly. In Orringer's sensuous yet edgy fictional universe, disease, accidents, rivalry, and ostracism are rampant; therefore, smart and determined girls and young women must devise their own covert strategies for survival. In one eerie tale, the young daughters of a cancer sufferer spend Thanksgiving in a similarly stricken household where the parents practice healing meditation while the children turn violent. In the Salingeresque "The Isabel Fish," a sister and brother struggle to reconcile in the aftermath of a drowning. Elsewhere summer's heady eroticism seduces Hasidic teens. Radiant in their explicit sensory descriptions, penetrating in their eviscerating discernment of both the cruelty and the resiliency of children, and exquisitely attuned to the overwhelming tide of emerging sexuality, Orringer's unnerving and fiercely beautiful stories delve to the very core of life's mysteries.

Source: Donna Seaman, Review of *How to Breathe Underwater*, in *Booklist*, Vol. 100, No. 1, September 1, 2003, p. 61.

SOURCES

"About Julie Orringer," Julie Orringer website, http://www.julieorringer.com/about.html (accessed September 9, 2014).

Dierbeck, Lisa, Review of *How to Breathe Underwater*, in *New York Times*, October 19, 2013, http://www.nytimes.com/2003/10/19/books/survival-of-the-meanest.html (accessed September 7, 2014).

"How Did We Get Here?," in *Washington Post* online, http://www.washingtonpost.com/wp-srv/politics/special/clinton/how/how.htm (accessed September 10, 2014).

Inskeep, Steve, "'How to Breathe Underwater,'" Interview with Julie Orringer, *All Things Considered*, NPR website, October 18, 2003, http://www.npr.org/templates/story/story.php?storyId = 1471019 (accessed September 7, 2014).

Kübler-Ross, Elisabeth, *On Death and Dying*, Simon and Schuster, 1969, pp. 27–132.

Orringer, Julie, "The Isabel Fish," in *How to Breathe Underwater*, Vintage Contemporaries, 2005, pp. 47–75.

Perkins, Emily, Review of *How to Breathe Underwater*, in *Guardian* (London, England), April 2, 2004, http://www.theguardian.com/books/2004/apr/03/featuresreviews.guardianreview6 (accessed September 7, 2014).

Rainer, Thom S., and Jess W. Rainer, *The Millennials: Connecting to America's Largest Generation*, B&H Pub. Group, 2011, pp. 151–76.

Review of *How to Breathe Underwater*, in *Kirkus Reviews*, August 1, 2003, https://www.kirkusreviews.com/book-reviews/julie-orringer/how-to-breathe-underwater/ (accessed September 7, 2014).

Sabato, Larry J., "Ted Kennedy's Chappaquiddick—1969," in *Washington Post* online, http://www.washingtonpost.com/wp-srv/politics/special/clinton/frenzy/kennedy.htm (accessed September 10, 2014).

Schaub, Michael, Review of *How to Breathe Underwater*, in *Austin Chronicle*, October 10, 2003, http://www.austinchronicle.com/books/2003-10-10/180979/ (accessed September 7, 2014).

"September 11th Fast Facts," CNN website, September 8, 2014, http://www.cnn.com/2013/07/27/us/september-11-anniversary-fast-facts/ (accessed September 10, 2014).

"20 Questions with *The Invisible Bridge* Author Julie Orringer," Oprah.com, June 18, 2010, http://www.oprah.com/oprahsbookclub/20-Questions-with-The-Invisible-Bridge-Author-Julie-Orringer/ (accessed September 9, 2014).

FURTHER READING

Edward, Joyce, *The Sibling Relationship: A Force for Growth and Conflict*, Jason Aronson, 2012.

> In this book Joyce Edward, a clinical social worker for more than twenty-five years, examines the complexities and influences of the sibling bond. Edward explores a wide range of topics, including sibling rivalry, cultural differences in sibling relationships, the psychological effects of a sibling death, and many more. Edward uses case studies to illustrate each of her topics.

Felder, Leonard, *Fitting In Is Overrated: The Survival Guide for Anyone Who Has Ever Felt Like an Outsider*, Sterling, 2008.

> Author and psychologist Felder offers advice, encouragement, and coping strategies for anyone who feels "different," especially creative and intellectual types whose unique interests are often viewed as "weird" by peers and family. Felder includes tales of famous achievers such as Oprah Winfrey and psychologist Elisabeth Kübler-Ross, who were ridiculed and ostracized growing up. Questionnaires, exercises, and meditations are included to help readers pinpoint their personal strengths and ignore destructive criticism.

Fletcher, Nick, et al., *What Fish? A Buyer's Guide to Tropical Fish: Essential Advice from a Team of Experts*, Barron's Educational Series, 2006.

> For those inspired by Maddy to create their own collection of tropical fish, this helpful guide provides advice on choosing, feeding, and caring for them. Fletcher helps the reader select the right size aquarium and gives advice on water temperature, the compatibility of different species of fish, and much more. The volume features more than two hundred color illustrations.

Gootman, Marilyn E., *When a Friend Dies: A Book for Teens about Grieving & Healing*, rev. ed., edited by Pamela Espeland, Free Spirit Publishing, 2005.

> Gootman, who holds a doctorate of education, offers advice to teens who have lost a friend around their own age, an experience for which most are unprepared. The book features quotes from real teens who have lost a friend, a list of reference books that might help, and suggestions for finding a therapist or counselor if needed. Comforting quotes and small steps to take to relieve sadness are also included in an easy-to-read graphic style.

SUGGESTED SEARCH TERMS

Julie Orringer

The Isabel Fish

The Isabel Fish AND short story

Julie Orringer AND The Isabel Fish

Julie Orringer AND How to Breathe Underwater

The Isabel Fish AND Maddy

Julie Orringer AND coming-of-age

Julie Orringer AND grief

Julie Orringer AND adolescence

The Isabel Fish AND fighting fish

Man from the South

ROALD DAHL

1948

Appearing initially in *Collier's* magazine in 1948, Roald Dahl's "Man from the South" was originally called "The Menace" and then renamed "Collector's Item" before getting its final title via a conversation with a particularly demanding publisher. An intricately constructed story of a mysterious stranger with a liking for gruesome games and meat cleavers, the tale traces the manipulation of a young cadet whose confidence in his prized lighter will be put to the ultimate test. Part horror story and part social satire, "Man from the South" was published at a time when the capacity for human cruelty had been underscored by two world wars. Appearing the same year as Shirley Jackson's iconic story "The Lottery," Dahl's tale continues to resonate in a modern world in which the dark history of inhumanity seems determined to repeat itself.

A favorite of television and film writers since its original publication, "Man from the South" boasts a rich catalogue of adaptations by directors and actors such as Alfred Hitchcock, Steve McQueen, and Quentin Tarantino. The story can be found in the Dahl collection *The Umbrella Man and Other Stories* (1998) and his *Collected Stories* (2006).

AUTHOR BIOGRAPHY

Roald Dahl was born on September 13, 1916, in Cardiff, Wales, to parents of Norwegian descent: Harald Dahl, co-owner of a business

British author Roald Dahl
(© Horst Tappe | Hulton Archive | Getty Images)

that arranged for cargo to be carried by ships, and Sofie Magdalene Hesselberg. Named after the polar explorer Roald Amundsen, a national hero in Norway, he was the only son in a family of four children. As a young child, Dahl endured the death of an older sister from appendicitis, as well as the death of his father from pneumonia while on a fishing trip in the Antarctic.

Following his education at a number of English boarding schools, Dahl worked briefly with the Shell Petroleum Company before joining the Royal Air Force in 1939, where he was trained as a fighter pilot. Hospitalized following a crash landing in the fall of 1940, Dahl returned to action early in 1941 and saw aerial battle action until severe headaches caused him to be sent back to England. He was later appointed to a post at the British Embassy in Washington, DC.

After World War II, Dahl married American actress Patricia Neal in 1953. The couple remained together for thirty years and had five children: Olivia Twenty (1955; she died at seven from measles encephalitis), Chantal Tessa Sophia (1957), Theo Matthew (1960), Ophelia Magdalena (1964), and Lucy Neal (1965). The couple divorced in 1983, and Dahl married a much younger woman, Felicity Ann d'Abreau Crosland.

A prolific writer, Dahl published his first short story in 1942, one about his wartime adventures, for which he was paid relatively handsomely by the *Saturday Evening Post*. His first children's book, *The Gremlins*, was published in 1943 and launched a string of remarkable successes that included *James and the Giant Peach* (1961), *Charlie and the Chocolate Factory* (1964), and *Matilda* (1988). He also adapted two novels by his friend Ian Fleming into screenplays, both of which became popular films: the James Bond movie *You Only Live Twice* (1967) and *Chitty Chitty Bang Bang* (1968). Often overlooked is the fact that Dahl is also the author of a smaller but still very distinct body of fiction for adults, including "Man from the South" (1948). Book-length titles include *Over to You* (1946), *Someone like You* (1953), *Kiss Kiss* (1960), and *Switch Bitch* (1974).

Most critics agree that by the mid-1960s and throughout the 1970s, Dahl had reached financial stability from the spectacular success of his books for children, but his works for adults declined. Some would suggest, too, that his "misanthropic sneer" (in the words of Stephen Amidon in the *Nation*) was distinctly out of sync with the increasingly explicit and open sexuality of the 1960s.

Among the numerous awards and recognitions that Dahl received during his life are the World Fantasy Award for Life Achievement (1983) and the Children's Author of the Year (British Book Awards, 1990). He died from a blood disease, myelodysplastic syndrome, on November 23, 1990, in Oxfordshire, England. He was seventy-four years old.

PLOT SUMMARY

Dahl's "Man from the South" opens casually as a day winds to an end, which marks the opportunity for the narrator to buy a beer and catch the evening sun as he relaxes by the pool. The setting is tropical Jamaica, with a beautiful garden and an abundance of "white tables and huge brightly coloured umbrellas and sunburned men and women sitting around in bathing suits." The narrator observes that the people here are a mix of English and American;

MEDIA ADAPTATIONS

- "The Man from the South" was adapted as a thirty-minute television episode directed by Albert McCleery. It originally aired in August 1955 as part of the *Cameo Theatre* series.

- The story was also adapted as a thirty-minute television episode for the *Alfred Hitchcock Presents* series. It was directed by Norman Lloyd and aired in January of 1960.

- Another half-hour anthology series, *Tales of the Unexpected*, included an adaptation of "The Man from the South" that was directed by Michael Tuchner and originally aired in March 1979.

- A 1980s revival of the *Alfred Hitchcock Presents* series presented the story as another television episode in May 1985.

- The story appeared on film in 1995 as one of four vignettes that make up *Four Rooms*. The film was produced and distributed by Miramax Films, and this segment was directed by Quentin Tarantino.

- In December 2009, the story was adapted as a fifteen-minute radio drama on BBC Radio 4 in England.

the Americans are probably connected with a naval training vessel that had arrived earlier that day.

After the narrator settles into his deck chair, he notices a "small, oldish man . . . immaculately dressed in a white suit" and "creamy Panama hat" circling the deck in quick, bouncing strides. He joins the narrator at his table and, in heavily accented English, strikes up a conversation that focuses in part on the group of young people frolicking in the pool. As if on cue, one of the young American cadets and one of the English young women ask if they may join the two men at the table. As the cadet and narrator light cigarettes, the man in the suit begins the ritual of cutting and lighting a cigar.

The conversation turns to the lighter that the young sailor pulls out to use. When the man in the suit expresses doubt as to whether the lighter will work in the wind, the cadet notes, with some arrogance, that it always works. This statement triggers an intensity in the man in the suit, who lures the younger man toward gambling on the notion that his lighter will work flawlessly for ten consecutive attempts. The cadet is drawn in, open to the opportunity to bet a quarter or a dollar on this game. But the man in the suit has a different idea: he will bet his new Cadillac, and the cadet will bet the little finger on his left hand, which will be chopped off should the lighter fail to light.

Despite the deeply disturbing nature of the proposal, the young cadet is drawn toward the possibility of winning a luxurious car. The man in the suit continues to provoke the younger man, suggesting that he might be afraid or has been boasting about the lighter just to impress his female companion. At the same time, he adds details to the scenario, often in response to questions from the cadet. When asked how the finger would be removed, the man is very specific: "What I should do," he explains, "I should tie one of your hands to de table before we started and I should stand dere with a knife ready to go chop de momint your lighter missed." The young cadet agrees to the bet, despite the concerns voiced by both the English girl and the narrator. The latter is drawn into the event as the referee.

As the group moves through the garden to the man's room, a windless and private setting for the game, the man in the suit gets more excited and animated with each step. On their way, they pass a beautiful green Cadillac, which the man points out as the one being wagered. In the room, the man offers martinis before ringing a small bell and asking the maid for a somewhat shocking list of items, which will be used in the upcoming game: "I want some nails, I want a hammer, and I want a chopping knife, a butcher's chopping knife which you can borrow from de kitchen."

As preparations continue, the narrator continues to think through the logistics of the game, as well as the motivations, which he concludes are "silly." Voicing his opinion, the narrator must acknowledge that the cadet's resolve to go through with the bet is growing stronger as minutes pass and martinis are consumed.

The cadet is quick to rationalize his decision: "I can't remember ever in my life having had any use for the little finger on my left hand," he comments. The man in the suit commences preparations, hammering nails in a pattern that will allow the cadet's hand to be held securely and with a finger presented perfectly to the butcher's knife should he lose the bet. The narrator grows increasingly disturbed by what he sees, thinking to himself that this is not the first time the man in the suit has played this game. With preparations complete, the cadet's hand is tied in place, and the game begins.

Tension builds with each attempt, even as the lighter never falters in the first seven attempts. As the eighth successful lighting concludes, a "small, black-haired woman" comes into the room. Rushing forward, she calls out urgently to the man in the suit, calling him Carlos, and ends the game. Grabbing Carlos, she shakes him violently and chastises him fiercely "in some Spanish-sounding language." The narrator's earlier hunch is proven accurate, as the woman explains that Carlos has, in fact, done this often, collecting forty-seven fingers and losing eleven cars over the years. With nothing left to gamble with, Carlos has been forced to flee to Jamaica for his own safety, and he has taken to betting the Cadillac that is owned by the small woman. Her own ultimately successful participation in the game is also revealed, as the narrator notices her hand, which has only a finger and thumb remaining.

CHARACTERS

American Boy

The young American cadet remains nameless throughout the story. Nineteen or twenty years old and ashore on leave in Jamaica, he is described as having "a long freckled face and a rather sharp bird-like nose," and a sunburned chest with "a few wisps of pale-reddish hair." Apparently, he represents to Carlos a challenge: he is youthful (with an implication of virility, or sexual potency), confident to the point of arrogance, and lacking the strong moral center that would have told him to avoid the bet as something dangerous. Rather than walking away from Carlos's challenge, he buys in philosophically to the risk-versus-reward dilemma that the older man has tempted him with. He is

quick to rationalize the uselessness of a little finger when offered the chance for a new Cadillac, and he never steps back to reflect upon the game as a degradation of individual and social values.

In the film and television adaptations of Dahl's story, the cadet has been played by Steve McQueen (1960), Michael Ontkean (1979), Steven Bauer (1985), and Paul Calderon (1995).

Black-Haired Woman

The older, unnamed woman who ends the game with her arrival seems a moral counterpoint to the other characters in the story, all of whom are willing to go along with Carlos's sadistic game. As she reminds the observers (and by extension the reader), what might seem like a darkly intriguing gamble will have very real consequences for real people. Carlos has collected forty-seven fingers, including several from her, meaning that many people have given in to his temptation and are now carrying the physical and emotional scars of their decision. She is now caring for a man who is financially destitute (having lost eleven cars) and has been forced to flee his homeland due to his inability to control his urge to continue the game. As she is quick to point out, Carlos is a menace, and she feels obligated to protect the world from him even if it means her own freedom.

Carlos

Carlos is the "man from the South" of the title. He remains nameless for much of the story, defined almost wholly by his particular attire (white suit and Panama hat—a light-colored straw hat) and, more ominously, by the almost wild energy that builds in him as his sadistic game progresses. With his heavy Spanish-sounding accent, he is clearly a man who has come to Jamaica from elsewhere. He is also a man who has a deep understanding of human nature and, one may deduce, an intense hatred for much of what he sees as defining characteristics of the world around him, including youth, arrogance, greed, and weak moral fiber.

When confronted by the small, dark-haired woman who disrupts the game immediately after the eighth attempt with the lighter, the reader's perception of Carlos shifts: no longer a menacing sadist, he is revealed as a weak man, unable to control his gambling obsession. He has lost everything and must now be watched daily by a woman who effectively controls his life. His legacy is a dark one, indeed, but also pathetic and sad.

The character of Carlos has a rich tradition in the film and television adaptations of Dahl's story. He has been played by Peter Lorre (1960), Jose Ferrer (1979), John Huston (1985), and Quentin Tarantino (1995).

English Girl

Unnamed throughout the story, the cadet's companion is described as "a large-boned fair-haired girl wearing a pale blue bathing suit." On the border of the main action, she objects to the game but in the end is a passive, consenting observer. The question lingers: why does she go to the room to watch when she could just as easily have decided to return to her friends at the pool? On another level, her presence is part of the context that Carlos exploits as he offers the young cadet the chance to play the game. The young cadet might be trying to prove his masculinity to the young woman, whom he might see as a possible sexual conquest should he win the Cadillac through his perceived fearlessness.

The character of the young woman has been played by Neile Adams (1960), Pamela Stephenson (1979), Melanie Griffith (1985), and Jennifer Beals (1995).

Narrator

The first-person narrator, who remains unnamed throughout the story, functions as a kind of disengaged consciousness for the reader. Appalled by the game unfolding before his eyes, he is, at the same time, a participant in the action by his own free will. Despite his growing concern with the proceedings of the day, he does nothing to effectively stop the game. This passive involvement generates a second layer of discomfort in the story, as readers are forced to recognize that the narrator, at some level, is as intrigued with the potentially bloody game as Carlos and the young cadet.

THEMES

Capitalism

Capitalism, which is the most widely used economic system in the modern world, focuses on the freedoms and benefits associated with private ownership: that is, both the resources and

the means of producing goods and services are owned by individuals and not the government. In one form of capitalism, prices are set freely by the forces of supply and demand and are allowed to reach their natural point of exchange without the intervention of outside forces (most notably, government). In this sense, the cadet's decision to risk the loss of his little finger and possibly gain a new green Cadillac is a perfectly valid decision, based solely on his decision that a finger is of little value compared with the value that he places on the car. More broadly, the cadet's finger is his personal asset and can be used as he wishes.

At the same time, the cadet's decision underscores many of the key questions facing philosophers, economists, and politicians when confronted with the extremes of a capitalist or free-market system. While they might acknowledge that the cadet does, theoretically, have the freedom to use his personal assets as he wishes, they would also recognize that there might be a higher-order value at play. For instance, does respect for the human body take precedence over the right of an individual to sell or trade body parts? If the answer is no, the question remains as to who is to set the value for not only a little finger, but a more important organ such as an eye or kidney. Finally, it must be decided whether these resources should even be given a value, or whether they should be placed outside economic considerations. Dahl's story brings many of these questions to the front of the reader's mind.

Corruption

"Man from the South" is, on one level, a story of corruption, though not in the most commonly understood terms as referring to bribery, embezzlement, or other unethical business/government practices. The a story takes a broader philosophical or moral view of corruption as being a condition of moral or spiritual degradation, or a failing to hold to a principle of behavior. *Corrupt* literally means "utterly broken," and the term may apply to all characters in the story, from Carlos, the morally degraded perpetrator of the game, to the woman and cadet who have both succumbed to the temptation of the gamble. Indeed, even the narrator and English girl are guilty: given the free will to either engage with or disengage from the game (or even attempt to stop it), they willingly participate in an event that is very likely, given

TOPICS FOR FURTHER STUDY

- Dahl's "Man from the South" was originally called "The Menace" and then "Collector's Item" before it settled into a long history with its current title. Develop a well-designed and detailed poster in which you trace the various implications for each of the three titles in terms of the impact and presentation of the story. You might have three columns, for instance, with each one dedicated to a series of key points relating to each of the titles. Be creative, but remain focused on the details of the story itself.

- "Man from the South" echoes Shakespeare's *The Merchant of Venice* (written around the year 1596) in its focus on business contracts that reach out of the world of commerce and into the world of flesh and blood. Both works also put a woman in a position of authority, and both women eventually embarrass the men at the heart of the dealings. Write a detailed and well-researched essay in which you compare and contrast the roles of the women in each work.

- A number of television adaptations of Dahl's story have appeared over the years, but none as star laden as the 1960 version that appeared in season 5 (episode 15) of *Alfred Hitchcock Presents*. Narrated by Hitchcock himself, it starred Steve McQueen as the gambler and Peter Lorre as Carlos. Imagine that you have been asked to cast a new adaptation of "Man from the South." Prepare a thoughtful and well-structured multimedia "pitch" in which you argue for your choices of current actors for each of these two key roles. Who would you choose to play the cadet, and

why? Who would you choose to play Carlos, and why? Present your pitch to your class, showing video clips of your casting choices and of former interpretations of the roles.

- An interesting tendency in adaptations of the story for radio or television is the naming of all of the characters, despite the fact that only one character (Carlos) is actually named in Dahl's original story. Write a well-considered essay in which you discuss why Dahl chose to leave most of his characters nameless in the original story. Also consider why he chose to give a name to Carlos, when the other characters are nameless. You may want to further analyze the names that have been given to each of the characters.

- Read Richard Connell's "The Most Dangerous Game," a story first published in *Collier's* magazine (as was Dahl's story) in January 1924. Both stories focus on games taken to almost surreal extremes. Write an essay in which you compare and contrast how games are used in these two stories.

- Suzanne Collins's *The Hunger Games* (2008) is a young-adult novel that blends a combination of skill, luck, and potentially fatal danger (along with a good dose of money, power, and ego) into a game in an expanded future state. The spectacle of the game in Collins's world is more dramatic than that in Dahl's story, but the social commentary (notably around issues of complicity and collective morality) in both works is similar. In an oral report, discuss the similarities and differences of how games operate in these two works.

Carlos's record, going to end with a meat cleaver cutting through human bone and flesh. Read in this way, the story raises the question:

what has become of a world in which people will gamble fingers for cars while others watch, as though it is some form of entertainment?

The story begins in an idyllic setting: a hotel pool with deck chairs and umbrellas.
(© paul prescott / Shutterstock.com)

Sadism

The question of Carlos's motivation inevitably leads readers to a discussion of sadism, which is the derivation of pleasure from inflicting pain, degradation, or humiliation on others. Violence is not a necessary element of sadism. It can also be seen as a power relationship that expresses itself in control, manipulation, and humiliation, all of which can be seen to varying degrees in Carlos's tempting of the young cadet. Carlos watches closely for the perfect situation (a young man trying to impress a young woman) in combination with the ideal personality (the arrogance of youth) and opportunity (captured in the cadet's boastful statements "It always works" and "It never fails"); Carlos is clearly a predator in search of his next victim. Once he identifies the cadet as a potential gambler, he systematically tests the younger man's personality to expose any potential flaws in character. As the narrator comments, Carlos attempts to "embarrass the boy" and then moves quickly to challenging his bravery, appealing to his greed, and eventually locking him into a horrific game of skill and chance.

STYLE

Complex Characters

As David Propson notes,

> the true perversity of Dahl's tales lies not in their high-concept conceits, but in the characters. Dahl clearly enjoyed creating genuinely clever characters, particularly ones that prove too clever for their own good. These practical folk encounter a fantastical situation and see not the cruel caprice of an absurd universe, but an angle.

The complex layering of characters in "Man from the South" is a wonderful case in point, as Dahl creates an obviously manipulative character (Carlos) and embeds him within a community of characters that is itself seemingly without a sense of right and wrong or moral certainty. None of these characters follow clearly defined paths, as they seem to wander into the confusion of Carlos's world without a well-established compass to guide their behavior or judgment. These are not simple or one-dimensional characters; they are multidimensional and imperfect people who might voice a concern with the events as they unfold but will go along with them nonetheless.

Surprising Denouement

A French word meaning "the unknotting," *denouement* refers to the point of resolution of the conflict or plot complexities that have accumulated throughout the story. Like many of Dahl's stories, "Man from the South" leads readers to what Amidon calls "the twist, the sting in the tail, the comeuppance" when many of the complexities and ambiguities of the story are made clear. The arrival of the small, dark-haired woman shifts the story from horror to satire. Carlos is made powerless upon her arrival, which also signals the elimination of all threat of violence to be delivered to the young cadet as he sits tied to the table.

Her appearance also marks a clear shift of focus to the consequences of the actions not only of Carlos but of those who play along with his game in hopes of winning a new car. Without a willing (or greedy) audience, the woman suggests, Carlos would be merely irritating or eccentric, someone to be tolerated. But as she notes, there is a deep cost to having this willing audience available to Carlos, which is calculated in fingers, in lost cars, and in a forced dislocation from their homeland. With this deepening message of the denouement, "Man from the South" rebalances, moving off the extreme of the macabre toward the more balanced vision of a social satire.

First-Person Point of View

"Man from the South" is told from the point of view of a classic first-person narrator—that is, a storyteller who speaks as "I" and is a character in the story—who can give readers access to his own thoughts but not those of any other character. Serving to move the plot forward with a fine balance of psychological depth and anticipation, Dahl's use of this point of view effectively allows the narrator to stand in for the reader. Like the narrator, readers are at once repulsed by the story unfolding and, somewhat disturbingly, drawn to it. Will the lighter light? Will the cleaver come crashing down? Will the narrator's sense that Carlos has done this before prove to hold any truth as the events unfold? All these elements of the page turner are made more powerful by the insights shared and hesitations voiced internally by the narrator.

HISTORICAL CONTEXT

Initially published in 1948, "Man from the South" appeared shortly after the second of two devastating world wars that raised deep and disturbing questions about the human capacity for cruelty towards other humans. More than sixteen million troops and civilians were killed during World War I (1914–1918), in part because of a previously unheard-of commitment to the technology of mass destruction. From advances in such hand-deployed weaponry as grenades and flamethrowers through to more insidious applications of chlorine, mustard, and phosgene gases, this war set in motion a wave of military technologies that continues today.

With the results of World War I still shaping the cultural landscape two decades later, humanity was rocked again by the events of World War II: the devastation of Germany's advance across Europe; the shocking attack by Japan on the US military base in Pearl Harbor, which led the United States to enter the war; the horrors of the extermination camps of Nazi Germany, in which millions of people were systematically killed as undesirables; and the American use of nuclear weapons in Hiroshima and Nagasaki, Japan, in 1945. Combined with other shocking events—the assassination of Indian leader Mohandas Gandhi in January 1948, the intensification of the Arab-Israeli War, the murder of a three-year-old child in Blackburn, England—1948 seemed to be a year that offered plenty of reasons to energize a new questioning of the modern human condition.

Not surprisingly, a number of important cultural works from this time explored the willingness of people to participate in acts that, under ordinary circumstances, they would shy away from in repulsion. Dahl's "Man from the South" presented readers with the moral dilemma of Carlos's game, while Shirley Jackson's "The Lottery" (also published in 1948) pushes readers to reflect upon how far people will go in the name of ritual and tradition.

Economically, a brief recession in 1948 was a mild precursor to a more sustained downturn in 1949, all of which rekindled anxieties about national and personal finances as well as tensions between those with financial stability and those in search of it. All of this occurred at a time when the average cost of a new house in

COMPARE
&
CONTRAST

- **1948:** Dahl is very particular in establishing that the hotel pool in "Man from the South" is populated primarily by visitors from the United States (naval cadets) and Britain (the girls), thereby positioning Jamaica as a country with particular appeal to visitors from two of the great military powers in the Western world. Jamaica in 1948 is still a British colony (it will become independent in 1962) and is entering into a major out-migration of people to England, where a labor shortage (combined with falling sugar prices on the island) makes relocation a viable economic option.

  Today: Jamaica, the third-largest island in the Caribbean Sea, is an independent country and major tourist destination and cruise ship port of call. Over two million visitors annually are increasingly arriving more than ever from continental Europe (especially Germany, Russia, and Spain) as well as from various Latin American countries.

- **1948:** While smoking is a key element of Dahl's story, in 1948 the dangers associated with the habit are beginning to receive media attention worldwide. Despite the increasing body of knowledge, cigarette sales in the United States continue to show strong increases beyond World War II. This is often seen as a reflection of increases in domestic employment rates and postwar purchasing power. The average retail price for a pack of twenty cigarettes in 1948 is under twenty-five cents. Cigar smoking in the United States, however, experiences a slight decline in 1948.

  Today: Jamaica officially bans cigarette and cigar smoking in public places as of July 2013, so the entire poolside scene that triggers discussion around the reliability of the cadet's lighter would now be unlikely. Moreover, public knowledge of the dangers of smoking as well as of secondhand smoke, in combination with increases in taxation on tobacco products, has reduced the number of smokers globally. That said, the World Health Organization still recognizes tobacco use as one of the main health threats worldwide; it is one of the main risk factors for such chronic conditions as lung and cardiovascular diseases.

- **1948:** The Cadillac offered to Dahl's cadet as the prize for surviving the game is most likely a Series 62, which is a slightly modified version of the first Cadillac to enter production after World War II and remains by far the most popular model (over 60 percent of Cadillac sales in 1947 and 1948 are the Series 62). The car represents luxury, power, and fine taste to an entire generation of postwar buyers drawn to its brand name as well as its airplane-like design features.

  Today: The Series 62 is no longer a luxury item, having been replaced by a plethora of models bearing names like Audi, Lamborghini, and Ferrari (to name only a few). In terms of luxury, such brands as BMW, Mercedes-Benz, and Lexus push Cadillac down the list. In fact, the best-selling Cadillac is a crossover vehicle (the SRX) rather than a straight luxury car. That said, the Series 62 is still a sought-after collector's piece, with prices at auction often topping the twenty-thousand-dollar mark.

---

the United States was just over $10,000, a new car was $1,500, and the average annual salary edged just over $3,500. For a young cadet, the temptation to risk a finger in order to win a new Cadillac can be seen as a sign of a culture that was to become increasingly fixated on what is now known as disposable or discretionary income. As Carlos's impressive collection of

The boy is confident his lighter will always light, even in the wind. (© *Vladimir Arndt | Shutterstock.com*)

forty-seven fingers suggests, the gamble he offered was one that held particular appeal in an age of growing consumerism.

Appropriately, the 1947–1948 Cadillac was seen by many as an early example of postwar optimism and confidence in the United States. Inspired in part by airplane design, it was one of the cars credited with ushering in the age of tail fins—seen as flashy, confident, and powerful— in American automotive style. For a young American, this car, especially in the trademark Cadillac green, would have been seen as the peak of American automotive styling and luxury.

CRITICAL OVERVIEW

Erica Wagner, reviewing Dahl's *Collected Stories* for the *New York Times* in an article titled "Cruel World," observes that readers and critics most often "think of Roald Dahl as a writer for children, the magical creator of James, Charlie, Matilda and the BFG, who worked in a shed in his English garden with a silver ball of chocolate-wrappers by his side." Almost a classic example of a writer whose reputation has been pigeon-holed by success in one form or genre, Dahl remains unknown to many readers for the breadth of his work as a writer for screen and "of clever, often savage, stories for adults." As Joyce Carol Oates observes, Dahl's reputation as a story writer focuses primarily on his "macabre, blackly jocose tales that read, at their strongest, like artful variants of Grimm's fairy tales." It is in his finest stories that Dahl "exhibits the flair of a natural storyteller," she continues, "for whom no bizarre leap of the imagination is unlikely." His seemingly natural inclination, she suggests, is toward a fiction in which "intimacy is rejected for distance, [and] sympathy for an Olympian detachment."

Howard Lachtman is more specific, arguing that despite his great success as a contributor to a number of the most influential magazines of his time, Dahl's short fictions "are not great stories, but great plots—expertly contrived, told with charming ingenuity and perfect plausibility, and enlivened with a deliciously nasty wit that borders on wickedness." Wagner claims that Dahl's stories have a power that "derives, in large part, from the reader's simple desire to know what happens next." David Propson, in the article "Guys & Dahls" for *New Criterion*, states that Dahl's stories were most often noted for culminating in dramatic "and often shocking endings" at a time when more complex plots or political subjects were increasingly coming into favor with readers.

Regardless of the changing tastes of readers, the experience of reading one of Dahl's adult stories is "never completely comfortable," as Wagner admits. She goes on to say, "This is not simply because so many of these tales have endings that depend on cruelty or vengeance," but because of "the deep vein of misogyny that runs through them." It is a discomfort shared by other critics, such as Oates, who notes: "It must be that such misogynist female portraits are self-portraits of the misogynist's malformed soul, since they draw forth such quivering, barely containable loathing."

This loathing extends, Stephen Amidon suggests, to traditional values as well. "In Dahl's stories," he notes, "the core family values are not respect and love but torment and retribution. Intimacy doesn't just breed contempt; it breeds contempt in action." It is not surprising, given these well-founded concerns with Dahl's tone and sexual politics, that his adult fiction (both short and long) struggled to find an audience in the sixties and onward. For a few of his best stories, like "Man from the South," there remains an almost macabre fascination with the constructed worlds that Wagner describes best as "utterly heartless," but at the same time "strange, enchanting...and bloody tremendous, terrific, fantastic, too."

CRITICISM

Klay Dyer

Dyer is a freelance editor and writer specializing in topics relating to literature, popular culture, and emerging technologies. In the following

> LIKE THE YOUNG CADET, THE YOUNG WOMEN OF 'CINDERELLA' CONSIDER THE BLOODY LOSS OF A BODY PART A FAIR EXCHANGE FOR THE WEALTH, STATUS, AND POWER THAT ARE PROMISED SHOULD THEIR GAMBLES PAY OFF."

essay, he discusses the parallels between Dahl's "Man from the South" and the long-established traditions of the folktale.

The American story writer and critic Joyce Carol Oates points out a very important element of many of Dahl's so-called adult fictions with her observation that these stories are, in many ways, "like artful variants of Grimm's fairy tales," which were, in turn, equally artful variants of traditional folktales. Many of the elements of "Man from the South" do, in fact, align neatly with what David L. Russell, in the 2001 book *Literature for Children: A Short Introduction*, lists as the familiar conventions of the classic folktale. It is a story that moves readers to a place that is in some sense removed from the real world. As Dahl is quick to establish, the setting for his story, Jamaica, is an exotic land far removed from either the American homeland of the young cadets or the British one of the young women with whom they frolic in the pool. It is a place of fine gardens "with lawns and beds of azaleas and tall coconut palms," with a wind that blows "strongly through the tops of the palm trees, making the leaves hiss and crackle as though they were on fire." Although not necessarily a place of magic, it is a geography in which beauty and a sense of threat (the leaves crackling as though on fire) coexist. It is, in short, a perfect setting for a man like Carlos to offer the temptation of power and status but with a dark, violent undertow at play.

Although Dahl's characters tend to be somewhat more complicated than those found in folktales (which tend to be flat and relatively simple, Russell suggests), they are familiar in that the motivations of the two male players in the game—Carlos and the cadet—are singular in nature. As Russell explains, traditional folk characters "are motivated by one overriding

WHAT DO I READ NEXT?

- No list of recommended readings after this story would be complete without reference to the works for which Dahl is best remembered: *James and the Giant Peach* (1961), *Charlie and the Chocolate Factory* (1964), and *Matilda* (1988). When a reader revisits these after absorbing "Man from the South" (or "Skin"), these modern classics of children's literature reveal dark undertones that many readers overlook in early readings.

- Another of Dahl's adult stories, "Skin" (1952) is a disturbing satire on the world of art and art dealers in which a starving old man is literally forced to sell the skin off his back in order to survive in war-torn Paris of 1946.

- Dahl's nonfiction work *Going Solo* (1986) is an autobiographical recounting of his adventures working in Africa as well as his trials as an ace fighter pilot during World War II.

- O. Henry (a pseudonym for William Sydney Porter) was a strong influence on Dahl's story writing, as can be seen by reading any of the selections in *The Best Short Stories of O. Henry* (1994). Dahl was an open admirer of the subtle yet complex plot development, the detailed characterization, and the clever endings of his fellow story writer.

- Shirley Jackson's "The Lottery" (1948) is one of the most famous stories in American literature in its exploration of conformity pushed to the limits of madness. Covering the preparation for and follow-through of an annual stoning within a small, rural community, this story, like "Man from the South," interrogates the willingness of individuals and communities to participate in senseless yet deeply ritualized acts of almost unimaginable violence. Jackson's story has been taught in middle schools and high schools since its publication.

- British writer Angela Carter's *The Bloody Chamber* (1979) is a powerful, dark collection of modern rewritings of classic fairy tales and folktales. Written in a lush prose, these ten stories draw out many of the traditional elements of the classic tales into wholly engaging feminist challenges to the archetypes of violence and stereotypes of women that have long been a part of fairy tales.

- Given that Dahl was asked specifically to work on the film adaptations of two novels written by his friend Ian Fleming, a reading of Fleming's *Chitty-Chitty-Bang-Bang: The Magical Car* (1964) provides an interesting context for readings of both Dahl's adult stories and his children's books.

---

desire such as greed, love, fear, hatred, jealousy—unlike characters in novels where motivations are usually more complicated."

As the dark-haired woman explains late in the story, Carlos is a man possessed by a singular obsession (one might call it an addiction) to the game that he lures the cadet to play. He is, as she observes, unable to stop his gamesmanship despite the fact that it has cost him his homeland and everything he owns. As Amidon notes, Dahl's lessons in the addictive gambling side of human nature might have had their roots in his time as an assistant air attaché at the British Embassy in Washington, DC. In this position,

> Dahl found himself plunged into the sophisticated network of espionage, propaganda, blackmail and sexual intrigue the British used against their American allies to insure they stayed the course in the great struggle against fascism. The lesson was simple—even the best of friends were entitled to lie and cheat if the stakes were high enough.

For the young cadet, the motivation is equally focused: he wants to own the green Cadillac and is willing to risk his little finger to get it. Despite the fact that both the narrator and the English woman voice some concern over the game, the young gambler explains his thinking, which echoes through the story as a perfect example of rationalization: "Come to think of it," he reflects, "I can't remember ever in my life having had any use for the little finger on my left hand."

In terms of plot, "Man from the South" again exhibits some of the common characteristics of the folktale. There is a journey, though it is brief, from poolside to Carlos's room in the annex in which the game will take place, which can be seen to mark not self-discovery (as is often the case with folktale journeys) but almost a kind of collective degradation, as all parties (Carlos, the narrator, the cadet, and the English girl) give a kind of consent to the event by agreeing to participate or be witnesses to it. Repetitious patterns are also evident, both in the game itself (there will be ten attempts to light the lighter) but more ominously in the rituals that seem to bring so much pleasure to Carlos. Even the narrator is quick to note this aspect of the older man's detailed and careful preparations: "Anyone would think . . . [he] had done this before, I told myself. He never hesitates. Tables, nails, hammer, kitchen chopper. He knows exactly what he needs and how to arrange it." Finally, as Russell observes of folktales, "conflicts are quickly established and events move swiftly to their conclusion," which is also a necessary condition of a story as short as "Man from the South." Dahl wastes no words in establishing secondary plot lines. His stories are carefully constructed to lead readers to the ending.

Moreover, Dahl's careful plotting reflects a common folktale technique known as "stylized intensification." As Russell explains, this technique "occurs when with each repetition" of a central pattern, the repeated "element is further exaggerated or intensified." In this story, the intensity grows through the series of one-word paragraphs that count the cadet's successful attempts to light his lighter.

Interestingly, Dahl's take on the folktale tradition of conflict is where "Man from the South" both aligns most elegantly with and breaks most dramatically from the folk tradition. As Russell

notes, a thematic focus on violence permeates the long history of folktales. He explains, "Among the issues most often discussed regarding folk literature is the prevalence of violence. Foolish and irresponsible little pigs are devoured, wolves are cooked in boiling water, witches are pushed into hot ovens, characters are mutilated in any number of ways." Carlos's threat does, in many ways, echo the mutilation in the earliest versions of what would become the story of Cinderella, for instance, when the sisters willingly cut off parts of their feet in an attempt to fit into the much-desired glass slipper, which would guarantee them fortune as the wife of the prince. Like the young cadet, the young women of "Cinderella" consider the bloody loss of a body part a fair exchange for the wealth, status, and power that are promised should their gambles pay off.

But what is important to recognize, Russell continues, is that while "many folktales contain violent actions . . . few exploit that violence and most leave the details up to the reader's own imagination." In Dahl's story, the violence is deflected by the arrival of the black-haired woman, but the emotional impact is never fully undone. Readers have experienced through the eyes of the narrator a story obliging them to confront their own morality and put themselves in various positions in relation to the events of the evening. They are invited, in other words, to consider their own reactions to this or similar situations. While trading a finger for a Cadillac might not register as possible in their reality, similar moral dilemmas might. For example, a wallet discovered on the street, or the offer of a lottery ticket (with stupendous odds against winning), might tempt people to take a risk in search of massive financial gains. The story invites readers to ask how individuals act in times of moral ambiguity.

Similar questions arise around the decisions of the narrator and the young English woman, specifically their willingness to bear witness to the potential cruelty. A reader is invited to imagine himself or herself in this position. Would the reader follow the group to the room or return to the pool? Would the reader act more directly to stop the game, or stand by quietly to watch? And what guilt would belong to a participant should the lighter fail to ignite? Although the narrator

Carlos promises to give the boy a Cadillac if he wins the bet. (© *Kevin M. McCarthy | Shutterstock.com*)

does pause to reflect on this possibility, his thoughts never translate to action:

> But hell, what if the boy lost? Then we'd have to rush him to the hospital in the Cadillac that he hadn't won. That would be a fine thing. Now wouldn't that be a really fine thing? It would be a damn silly unnecessary thing so far as I could see.

Despite this focus on violence (albeit more implied than actual), "Man from the South" fails to either deliver the traditional happy ending or align with what Russell identifies as the kind of global theme of traditional folktales: "Wisdom comes through suffering." Readers would be hard pressed to argue that the arrival of the black-haired woman signals the turn to a happy conclusion to the events of the evening, or that anyone involved gained wisdom. The young cadet has escaped with his fingers intact, but the lingering taint of his rationalization has not been erased by either a final statement of remorse or a sigh of relief at the ending of the game. Although Carlos is defeated in his latest attempt to add to his collection (or lose yet another car), he shows little remorse or sign of understanding the error of his ways. His mumbled repetition of a single sentence ("We were only having a little bet") suggests, in fact, that he remains unchanged in his understanding of either his motivations or the implications that his actions have for himself and others.

Rather than offering a clear and strong moral, Dahl's folktale is generally an unproductive activity in terms of the positive lesson or moral value to be gained from reading it. Readers are left, in the end, with more questions than answers, and a lingering sense that Carlos has not played his last game.

Source: Klay Dyer, Critical Essay on "Man from the South," in *Short Stories for Students*, Gale, Cengage Learning, 2015.

Heather Worthington

In the following excerpt, Worthington discusses whether Dahl's writing is appropriate for children.

'VULGAR, VIOLENT, SEXIST, RACIST, CRIMINAL': CHILDREN'S LITERATURE?

In the oft-quoted words of Arthur Ransome, 'You write not for children but for yourself, and if, by good fortune, children enjoy what you enjoy, why then you are a writer of children's books.' These words could have been written with Roald Dahl in mind; he wrote about what he knew and enjoyed, and although in his writing for children he generally adopted a different narrative voice from that of his fiction for adults, the themes of and the humour in the two formats are uncannily similar. But, as Peter Hunt has noted, Dahl had a worldwide reputation as a writer of sinister short stories 'that dealt with the very dark corners of human nature before he became a writer for children.' Hunt goes on to query whether Dahl's 'zestful exploitation of childish instincts for hate and revenge, prejudice and violence, [can] be as innocent as it appears.' In the developed world, societies tend to define the child precisely as that which is not adult, endeavouring thus to set up clear demarcations between the two states of being, a position evident in children's literature. In this context, given the thematic similarities in his writing for children and for adults, particularly the pervasive presence of violence and the frequent representation of crime, can Dahl's juvenile fiction be considered to constitute a 'suitable' read for a child?

" "

THIS SLIPPAGE IN DAHL'S WRITING, BETWEEN
HIS ADULT AND CHILD REGISTERS, IS A MAJOR
CONTRIBUTOR TO ADULT ANXIETIES ABOUT THE
SUITABILITY OF HIS TEXTS FOR CHILD READERS, AS
ISSUES MORE OFTEN FOUND IN TEXTS FOR ADULTS
FIND THEIR WAY INTO HIS JUVENILE FICTION."

Of course, the very concept of 'suitability' is problematic; decisions as to what is 'suitable' or indeed 'unsuitable' for children are inescapably subjective and temporally and culturally contingent, as critical analyses of Dahl's fiction demonstrate. In 1991, Jonathon Culley offered a defence of Dahl's fiction, noting that while his texts had 'been heavily criticised for ... vulgarity, fascism, violence, sexism, racism, ... promotion of criminal behaviour,' because they are located in the folklore and fairy tale tradition they escape these charges. The child reader, Culley suggests, implicitly already familiar with the conservative patterns of such narratives (good triumphing over evil, virtuous characters rewarded and wicked ones punished, the triumph of the underdog), understands the imaginary status of the stories and so is unaffected by their content. In his 2010 biography of Dahl, Donald Sturrock devotes five pages to the adverse critical reception of Dahl's fiction for children. And yes, Dahl's juvenile texts wrap their violence and other potentially controversial aspects in a tissue of fantasy and they make the representation of crime acceptable either by moral justification or by ensuring its containment and punishment. Twenty years after Dahl's death and Culley's defence, in a world that in its reliance on television and electronic media would undoubtedly have horrified Dahl and which exposes children to actual violence and crime in unprecedented ways, his children's fiction seems less controversial and, I suggest, might now have more positive functions that outweigh the often negative adult perceptions of its suitability in moral terms of its content for their imagined child reader.

My contention here is that for the child of the twenty-first century and in the context of the contemporary emphasis on representing the 'real' in literature for children, Dahl's juvenile canon affords escapist reading par excellence. As in crime fiction, Dahl's writing for adults offers its readers a variety of potentially cathartic reading positions—protagonist, antagonist, victim—and this is equally true, I suggest, of his stories for children. These allow child readers a safe space in which to explore their personal and social anxieties and to vent, in their imagination and/or unconsciously, their own feelings of anger and resentment towards the adults who control their world. In many ways, modern children are given unprecedented and often unmediated access to the trappings of the adult world, particularly in terms of clothing and popular culture: they are less imitation adults than simulacra, having the appearance of—but without the substance or properties of—adulthood. More visibly perhaps than ever before, adult power is revealed to but denied the child. In Dahl's narratives, adult and juvenile, a constant theme is the reversal or circumvention of normative power relations and the revenge taken by the disempowered upon the empowered, but where in the adult stories the social and narrative status quo is, disturbingly, not necessarily restored, the children's fiction mostly adheres to the normative conservatism of happy, if quirky, endings.

The stories which Dahl produced specifically for children are, for the most part, clearly marked out as fantasy. They accord with Rosemary Jackson's concept of narratives, which 'assert that what they are telling is real—relying upon all the conventions of realist fiction to do so—and then they proceed to break the assumption of realism by introducing what—within those terms—is manifestly unreal.' Jackson is speaking of adult fiction, but Dahl's writing for a juvenile audience conforms to her description, presenting to the child reader a recognisable and often familiar world, peopled with everyday figures and events, and then introducing the patently unreal—animals and insects that can speak, children with magic fingers and kinetic powers, witches, giants. In Jackson's model, fantasy literature is precisely a literature of subversion, and the empowerment of the child and the (temporary) reversal of normative social structures in children's literature are subversive. In Dahl's texts the representation of adults is equally subversive; frequently they are depicted as at best thoughtless and at worst actively and intentionally cruel. Furthermore, this cruelty is always punished by a means that is directly or indirectly orchestrated by the child—or animal—victim. Once this has occurred, however, the subversion of the narrative is curtailed and conservative values and the proper status quo are restored, if in unconventional or reconfigured forms.

This containment of temporary subversion within conservatism, the veiling of violence in fantasy and the essentially restorative closures of the narratives are, in part, what make the majority of Dahl's fiction for children unthreatening and construct it as acceptable and morally appropriate, so making it 'suitable' reading for a child. They are also what make it escapist literature: for the space of their reading, child readers can live in their imagination and can possess the control over their lives and circumstances that reality does not afford. This is a space in which the child can be naughty, scatological, empowered and, perhaps most importantly, be metaphorically revenged on the adults who control children's lives. From the child's perspective, the methods of control are not always pleasant and the rationale behind them unclear; from the adult perspective this control is conventionally seen to be part of the process of civilising the child. For Dahl and perhaps for other adults, 'children...are only semi-civilised' and need training to become good (conformist) adult subjects. What Dahl's writing for children recognises is the child's perspective, particularly when adult behaviour is inconsistent or evidently unfair. Consequently, justice is often implicit in the revenge that is at the centre of much of Dahl's fiction. In *Matilda* the eponymous heroine decides to revenge herself on her parents every time they mistreat her: 'A small victory or two would help her tolerate their idiocies and stop her from going crazy.'

FANTASIES OF VENGEANCE, NATURAL JUSTICE AND EMPOWERMENT

Vengeance and a sense of natural justice are evident from the very beginning of Dahl's writing for children. *James and the Giant Peach* (1961), Dahl's first successful story for children, features orphaned James's distinctly unpleasant guardians, Aunts Sponge and Spiker. Their cruelty to their ward is punished when the giant peach, now containing James and his new friends the Centipede, the Grasshopper, the

Ladybird, the Earthworm, the Glow-worm and the Spider, accidentally rolls over the Aunts and crushes them to death. The world outside the peach is relatively realistically portrayed, as is the admittedly exaggerated treatment meted out to James by his aunts; the world of the peach is decidedly fantastic, with creatures the same size as James that initially—and understandably—terrify him. But it is in the 'real' world outside the peach that the Aunts are subjected to a process of 'natural' justice and punished, while James's fantasy life continues into a fairy tale 'happy ever after' with his friends, who in various ways also function as his (idealised) family. Revenge in *James and the Giant Peach* is not actively carried out by James; rather it is the narrative, and implicitly its author, that ensures the Aunts receive their just deserts, suggesting that in reality cruel adults should—and will—be punished.

Charlie and the Chocolate Factory (1964) is less overt in terms of violence and vengeance; the objectionable children there seem to bring their own punishments—which are clearly marked as fantastic—upon themselves, but it is their parents, and perhaps implicitly real-life parents, who are being castigated for their improper parenting skills. *The Magic Finger* (1966) allows its unnamed female child protagonist-narrator to ensure that the punishment fits the crime when her supernatural digit turns her gun-happy neighbours into human birds and their duck victims into quasi-humans. In *Fantastic Mr Fox* (1970) the fox of the title, in part representing the child, defeats the adult human farmers who seek to kill him; *The Twits* (1980) sees the unpleasant Mr and Mrs Twit's performing (child) monkeys literally turn the tables—and chairs—on their (adult) trainers. Crime and violence, accidental in *James and the Giant Peach* and implicit in *Fantastic Mr Fox*, where Mr Fox's theft from the farmers is excused both by the fantasy and by the natural eating habits of the fox, is rather more troubling in *George's Marvellous Medicine* (1981). George's purpose in creating the magic medicine is to make better his 'horrid old witchy' grandmother, famously described as having 'a small puckered-up mouth like a dog's bottom.' But his father's motive in giving his mother-in-law a later version of the medicine has definite criminal aspects. He knows that it will, at the very least, shrink the old lady down to a minute size; in the event, she disappears entirely in what might be read as an act of deliberate murder. The narrative is obviously fantastical, but the revenge here is not of the child upon the adult but of one adult upon another, aligning the text with much of Dahl's short fiction for adults.

This slippage in Dahl's writing, between his adult and child registers, is a major contributor to adult anxieties about the suitability of his texts for child readers, as issues more often found in texts for adults find their way into his juvenile fiction. While children will enjoy the humour of *George's Marvellous Medicine*, the potentially realistic depiction of family dynamics in which an elderly relative is seen as intrusive and unwanted—indeed, the entirely negative representation of old age—is relatively unusual in children's literature, which tends to support rather than criticise the ideology of family. *The Witches* (1983), by contrast, offers a positive depiction of the elderly in the figure of the grandmother. If the word 'marvellous' in the title of *George's Marvellous Medicine* suggests its fantastical status, *The Witches* is even more clearly labelled and the events of the narrative confirm it as fantasy; apparently-ordinary women are revealed to be witches intending to carry out by magical means the mass murder of children. While the criminal aspects of the text seem to have escaped criticism, *The Witches* has been castigated for its negative representation of the feminine. Dahl's witches are truly frightening creations made doubly unnatural through their deformed non-human appearance once unmasked and by their clear rejection of the nurturing child-centred traditional ideology of the feminine maternal. Violence is implicit in the desire to dispose of children by turning them into mice which will then be killed in mousetraps; the crime is self-evident. The very excess of the plot in part locates it as pure fantasy, as does the boy-turned-mouse protagonist and narrator. Thus far, thus fantastic, and so escapist and acceptable—the child reader can enjoy the frisson of fright safely contained in the fiction.

But the reality suggested by the frame narrative of the orphaned child protagonist is perhaps less enjoyable, despite the loving relationship between boy and grandmother. When she becomes ill, the unnamed boy faces the very real possibility of being orphaned for a second time by her death—she is after all, 80 years old (and a

smoker of cigars). His subsequent fate—being turned permanently into a mouse by the Witches, using a magic spell which would more usually in children's fiction later be reversed—has the effect of shortening his life dramatically, ensuring that he and his grandmother will have a better chance of dying at the same time and so removing the threat of his being abandoned. The avenging fantasy in the concluding pages of the narrative, where the boy/mouse and his grandmother plan to track down all the Witches, use their own potion to turn them into mice and then release cats to kill them, perhaps to some extent ameliorates the bleak message of finite life and the certainty of death implicit in the text. As in many of Dahl's texts intended for children, fantasy permits what might otherwise seem an inappropriate preoccupation with death. And for a child reader exposed to or anxious about family loss or abandonment, the promise of boy and grandmother being together until both their deaths provides a consolatory and comforting conclusion. Surprisingly, then, despite its gruesome and violent aspects, *The Witches* can perhaps be seen, certainly in bibliotherapeutic terms, to be an eminently 'suitable' read for some children.

This is perhaps because, as in much of his writing, Dahl's own life inflects the fiction; although set in England, *The Witches* begins and ends in Norway, the home of Dahl's parents and grandparents: in the fiction, the boy and his grandmother have to move to England in order for the boy to continue his English education, while in Dahl's own life his family move from Wales to England for the same reason. The idealised intergenerational relationship also has its origins in Dahl's own childhood holidays with his grandparents in Norway, related in the autobiographical *Boy* (1984). The self-referential frame narrative of *The Witches* is less a story for children than the story of a child directly drawn from the memory of the adult, both making it appropriate for the child reader but equally aligning it with Dahl's writing for adults and therefore making it problematic in terms of its suitability. *Matilda*, perhaps the last of Dahl's children's texts to engage closely with justice and revenge, adult-child power relations, violence and crime, was, in its original incarnation, also in adult rather than child mode. Dahl's original version features the compulsive gambler Miss Hayes, transformed in the published version into the adorable Miss Honey, while the delinquent

THE CONVENTIONAL WISDOM IS THAT
HIGHLY CULTURED PEOPLE ARE WISER AND
MORE COMPASSIONATE THAN THOSE WITH
LESS EDUCATION, BUT THIS GENERALIZATION
DOES NOT APPLY TO DAHL'S CHARACTERS. IF
ANYTHING, HIS AESTHETES AND ART COLLECTORS
ARE EVEN MORE DEVIOUS AND CRUEL THAN
HIS OTHER CHARACTERS."

Matilda's magical powers are used to fix the outcome of a race on which they have laid a large bet. The plot resonates with that of the adult 'Claud's Dog' story sequence, where in 'Mr Feasey' (1953) there is also an attempt to fix a race, although by rational rather than supernatural means....

Source: Heather Worthington, "An Unsuitable Read for a Child? Reconsidering Crime and Violence in Roald Dahl's Fiction for Children," in *Roald Dahl*, edited by Ann Alston and Catherine Butler, Palgrave Macmillan, 2012, pp. 123–29.

Mark I. West

In the following excerpt, West examines the macabre stories Dahl wrote in the 1940s, including "Man from the South."

In the late 1940s Dahl began writing macabre short stories. Although he always came up with new and unusual plot lines, these carefully constructed stories soon began to follow a discernible pattern: seemingly respectable characters are confronted with peculiar problems or opportunities and respond by committing, or at least contemplating, cruel or self-destructive acts. In most of these stories Dahl used sardonic humor, implied violence, and surprise endings. Often he incorporated material that related to his own recreational pursuits, such as collecting paintings and fine wines.

As he had done with his war stories, he submitted his macabre stories to American magazines, which quickly accepted them. The *New Yorker*, often seen as the most prestigious magazine in America, published eight of these stories between 1949 and 1959. This impressive

record helped establish Dahl as a major figure on the American literary scene. Building upon this reputation, Dahl brought out three important collections of his macabre stories: *Someone Like You* (1953), *Kiss Kiss* (1960), and *Switch Bitch* (1974). He published another anthology in 1977 under the title *The Wonderful Story of Henry Sugar and Six More*. Although not as well known as his three earlier collections, this anthology does include some macabre stories. He also wrote a novel entitled *My Uncle Oswald*, which came out in 1979. This novel directly relates to two of the stories in *Switch Bitch*, but it is somewhat less macabre than most of Dahl's short stories.

SOMEONE LIKE YOU

Almost all of the 18 stories in *Someone Like You* deal with characters whose daily routines are disturbed, resulting in various types of personal crises. When first introduced, these characters usually give every appearance of being upstanding members of society. They are generally wealthy, well educated, and highly regarded by their peers. Unlike most of the pilots in Dahl's war stories, however, these characters do not behave nobly under pressure. They often experience intense feelings of confusion, fear, anger, greed, or jealousy. These feelings cloud their judgment and cause them to lose their moral bearings.

Although most of the characters in these stories find themselves in situations that test their moral fiber, the central characters in "The Soldier" and "The Wish" confront a more basic problem: they lose touch with reality. "The Soldier," the only story in the collection that directly relates to Dahl's earlier war stories, deals with a character who floats in time, unable to distinguish between the present and the past. Although the story is set in peacetime, he still thinks he hears gunfire and still ducks when planes fly overhead. His paranoia also affects his relationship with his wife. He suspects her of playing tricks on him, such as tinkering with the taps in the bathroom so that hot water comes out of the cold-water tap. He eventually becomes so tangled up in his delusions that he mistakes another woman for his wife. "The Wish" is about a boy with a very active imagination. He pretends that a multicolored carpet in his home is a dangerous obstacle course. He imagines that the red patches are hot coals and the black patches are poisonous snakes. Pretending that the yellow parts are the only ones upon which he can safely step, he sets out to cross the carpet. In his mind this game soon becomes a life-threatening experience. His emotional reactions to the imagined dangers are the same as they would be if the coals and snakes were real. In both of these stories the characters' behavior is governed much more by their fantasies and emotions than by reality and reason.

Disturbing memories and imagined foes also haunt the central character in "Galloping Foxley." At first glance this man appears to be completely rational and businesslike. Over the 36 years that he has been working, he has developed a rigid routine, part of which involves riding the train to and from his job. He loves the predictability of his routine and is annoyed when anything varies from the norm. One day a stranger shows up at the station where he catches the train each morning, and this disturbs him a great deal. After listening to the stranger's voice, he becomes convinced that this man is Galloping Foxley, the bully who beat him when he was a schoolboy almost 50 years earlier. The memories of these beatings come flooding back, tormenting him to the point that he becomes obsessed with the stranger. He finally decides to confront his old foe, only to discover that he is completely mistaken about the man's identity. This story exemplifies a major theme that runs through many of Dahl's stories: that adherence to daily routines can give one the false appearance of psychological stability.

Mary Maloney, the main character in "Lamb to Slaughter," is a prime example of a person who at first glance seems perfectly normal. She is the wife of a police officer, and she goes to great lengths to please him. When he comes home from work she always takes his coat and fixes him a drink. The couple then sit quietly together for a little while before she prepares their dinner. On the day in which the story takes place, this routine is disturbed when the husband confesses that he is having an affair and wants a divorce. Mary responds by bashing in his head with the frozen leg of lamb that she had planned to cook for dinner. For the rest of the story she calmly and cleverly goes about averting suspicion and disposing of the murder weapon. What is so unsettling about this character is not the anger that she feels

but the way in which she expresses it. She so easily makes the transition from housewife to murderer that one wonders about her mental state prior to the day she killed her husband. Perhaps she had always been a killer but had carefully hidden this aspect of her personality. The more chilling interpretation is that she is normal and that normal people, in certain circumstances, can turn into murderers.

Another Dahl character who becomes hostile under pressure is Harry Pope, the protagonist in "Poison." He is an Englishman who lives in India. His housemate, who serves as the story's narrator, comes home late one night to find Pope lying motionless in bed and looking terrified. The narrator asks what is wrong, and Pope whispers that under the covers a poisonous snake is lying asleep on his stomach. Not knowing what to do, the narrator calls the town's native doctor. The doctor hurries over and painstakingly pours chloroform through a tube, one end of which he has placed under the bedcovers, in order to make the snake unconscious. When the doctor finally turns back the covers, however, there is no snake to be seen. The doctor asks Pope if he is sure that he had actually seen a snake, and Pope responds by calling the doctor a "dirty little Hindu sewer rat." The doctor shrugs off the insult and suggests that Pope simply needs a vacation, but the reader is not so ready to forgive Pope's hostility, ingratitude, and racism. It seems quite possible that the crisis with the snake brought out Pope's true personality.

In several of these stories the characters' undoings are caused not by anger or fear but by greed and competition. Two such stories are "Man from the South" and "Dip in the Pool." Both involve gambling, but the forms that the gambling takes are out of the ordinary. In "Man from the South" a young American sailor boasts that his cigarette lighter never fails to work. An elderly gentleman from South America overhears this boast and asks if the sailor is willing to "have a good bet on dis ting" (*Someone*, 42). The South American offers to give the sailor his Cadillac if the lighter works 10 times in a row; if the lighter fails this test, the South American proposes, he will chop off one of the sailor's little fingers. Although it is obvious that the South American is mentally unbalanced, the sailor's competitive spirit and desire for the fancy car cause him to ignore his better judgment, and he accepts the bet.

The self-destructive behavior exhibited by the sailor, though certainly dramatic, pales in comparison to the actions taken by the central character in "Dip in the Pool." While crossing the Atlantic on an oceanliner, this character decides to participate in a contest sponsored by the ship's crew. The contest involves guessing the number of miles the ship travels each day, and the winner will collect a considerable sum of money. The protagonist guesses a low figure, assuming that an unexpected storm they have encountered will delay the ship. The storm blows over, however, and the ship resumes its normal speed. Determined to win the contest, he concocts a daring plan to slow down the ship. His idea is to jump overboard and then call for help, forcing the ship to stop so that he can be rescued. He makes sure that a woman passenger sees him as he deliberately falls overboard, but it never occurs to him that she might not sound the alarm. His downfall, like the downfalls of many other Dahl characters, comes about because he allows his emotions and egotism to overwhelm his ability to think clearly.

Most of the remaining stories in the collection deal with characters who belong to society's artistic and intellectual elite. The conventional wisdom is that highly cultured people are wiser and more compassionate than those with less education, but this generalization does not apply to Dahl's characters. If anything, his aesthetes and art collectors are even more devious and cruel than his other characters. Although they give the appearance of being considerate, they are fully capable of committing evil and sometimes violent deeds. . . .

Source: Mark I. West, "Mastering the Macabre," in *Roald Dahl*, Twayne Publishers, 1992, pp. 36–40.

SOURCES

Amidon, Stephen, "Getting Even," in *Nation*, Vol. 283, No. 20, December 11, 2006, pp. 21–22.

Dahl, Roald, "Man from the South," in *The Umbrella Man and Other Stories*, Viking, 1998, pp. 54–68.

Lachtman, Howard, "Roald Dahl's *Tales of the Unexpected*," in *Studies in Short Fiction*, Vol. 17, No. 2, Spring 1980, pp. 189–90.

Oates, Joyce Carol, "The Art of Vengeance," in *New York Review of Books*, April 26, 2007, http://www.nybooks.com/articles/archives/2007/apr/26/the-art-of-vengeance/ (accessed August 19, 2014).

Propson, David, "Guys & Dahls," in *New Criterion*, Vol. 25. No. 6, February 2007, pp. 75–77.

Russell, David L., *Literature for Children: A Short Introduction*, Longman, 2001, pp. 158–64.

Wagner, Erica, "Cruel World," in *New York Times*, December 3, 2006, http://www.nytimes.com/2006/12/03/books/review/Wagner.t.html?_r=0 (accessed August 19, 2014).

FURTHER READING

Bingham, Jane, *Roald Dahl*, Raintree, 2010.
    Part of the Culture in Action series, this book provides young readers with interesting facts, imaginative activities, and fascinating photographs that explain both the life and creative force of Roald Dahl.

Craats, Rennay, *Roald Dahl*, Weigl, 2003.
    The books in the My Favorite Writer collection, a biography series for young readers, follow an accessible and easy-to-follow format. This work guides readers through discussions of Dahl's early childhood and his time spent learning the craft of writing. Other sections include "Creative Writing Tips," "Fan Information," and "Quiz."

Kelley, True, *Who Was Roald Dahl?*, Grosset & Dunlap, 2012.
    Part of the popular Who Was series, this illustrated biography is accessible to young readers.

Sturrock, Donald, *Storyteller: The Authorized Biography of Roald Dahl*, McClelland & Stewart, 2010.
    Despite his already astonishing life as a Norwegian growing up in Wales whose father died when he was just a child, as an ace fighter pilot, as a British intelligence agent, and as a husband for a while to one of Hollywood's top stars, Dahl nonetheless persistently embroidered the truth about himself. Facts bored him, as this biography reveals, so he openly rewrote history, ignored reality, and reshaped his vulnerabilities with great skill. This is a carefully researched and gently nuanced book that draws on a wealth of sources and resources to construct a rich and compassionate biography of one of the most beloved storytellers of the twentieth century.

Treglown, Jeremy, *Roald Dahl: A Biography*, Faber and Faber, 1994.
    The first full biography of Dahl, Treglown's volume is in turns an intimate psychological study of the man behind the stories and a book that illuminates some of the more subtle intricacies of the publishing industry that affected Dahl throughout his career.

SUGGESTED SEARCH TERMS

Man from the South AND Dahl

Roald Dahl

gambling AND short fiction

macabre AND short fiction

cruelty AND short fiction

vengeance AND short fiction

greed AND short fiction

satire AND short fiction

The Nightingale and the Rose

OSCAR WILDE

1888

Oscar Wilde was a well-known public figure in Victorian England during the fin de siècle—the end of the nineteenth century, a period sometimes known as the Decadence because of dandies like Wilde who professed to have no morals and to live only for pleasure and sensation. His scandalous wit was enjoyed by the upper classes in his popular comedic plays, such as *The Importance of Being Earnest* (1895). A darker side came out in his novel, *The Picture of Dorian Gray* (1890), which thumbed its nose at Victorian prudery by exposing the life of a debauched man. Wilde himself became a symbol of the folly of flirting with immorality in the public arena when he was sentenced to two years in prison for homosexuality.

There is another side to Wilde found in his two volumes of fairy tales, which present allegories of kindness and unselfish behavior. The first volume, *The Happy Prince and Other Tales* (1888), contains five tales: "The Happy Prince," "The Nightingale and the Rose," "The Selfish Giant," "The Devoted Friend," and "The Remarkable Rocket." They were well received in his time and have had enduring interest for both children and adults. "The Nightingale and the Rose" was made into an opera by Elena Frisova in 1994 and into a ballet in 2007 by Christopher Wheeldon.

Wilde's fairy tales are a pleasure to read because they are lush in sensuous language

Irish writer and poet Oscar Wilde (Library of Congress)

AUTHOR BIOGRAPHY

Oscar Fingal O'Flahertie Wills Wilde was born on October 16, 1854, in Dublin, Ireland, the son of Sir William Wilde and Jane Francesca Wilde. His parents were Dublin intellectuals, and he grew up with famous literary guests in the house. His mother wrote revolutionary poetry and was an Irish nationalist. Lady Wilde gave Oscar his love of the arts. His father was a surgeon knighted for his service to the government. He wrote books on archaeology and folklore and treated the poor at his dispensary.

Wilde was educated at home until he was nine, learning French and German fluently from servants. He attended Portora Royal School in Enniskillen, County Fermanagh. He read classics at Trinity College, Dublin, from 1871 to 1874. He was at Magdalen College, of Oxford University, from 1874 to 1878 on a scholarship in Greek studies. At Oxford, he became known for his involvement in the aesthetic movement under the influence of art critics John Ruskin and Walter Pater.

In the early 1880s, Wilde lived in London and traveled as a lecturer. He published poems in magazines, bringing out a *Collected Poems* in 1881. In 1883, he produced his first play, *Vera*, in New York. He married Constance Lloyd in 1884, and they had two sons, Cyril and Vyvyan. In 1886, however, he became lovers with Robert Ross, rebelling against the Victorian prohibition against homosexuality. After editing *The Woman's World* in 1887, a journal of fashion and the arts, he published a book of fairy tales, *The Happy Prince and Other Tales*, including "The Nightingale and the Rose." Wilde's only novel, *The Picture of Dorian Gray* (1890), was criticized for its decadent philosophy. In 1891, a second volume of fairy tales was published, *A House of Pomegranates*. His tragedy in French, *Salomé*, published in 1893, was censored in London.

Wilde became a public hit with his drawing-room comedies. *Lady Windermere's Fan* (1892), *A Woman of No Importance* (1893), *An Ideal Husband* (1895), and *The Importance of Being Earnest* (1895) were wildly popular plays, but his career came to a halt with his arrest and conviction for a homosexual relationship with Lord Alfred Douglas. Wilde was sentenced to hard labor for two years, which broke his health. He published "The Ballad of Reading

and beautiful imagery. They often imitate a biblical cadence. He seems quite at home writing symbolic fantasies that contain subtle messages about his theory of art, his criticism of society, and above all his moral vision. Wilde's anarchism and rebellion have so long been emphasized that it is only recently that critics have turned to the fairy tales to find his sympathy with the poor and those who dare to follow their own hearts instead of social authority. It is surprising to find Christian values in Wilde's work and even the figure of Christ himself in the fairy tales as an example of human charity. "The Nightingale and the Rose" ends with a tragic but noble sacrifice that characterizes and foretells Wilde's own fall and his view of it. Though his philosophy can be extracted from the tales, one should bear in mind that they are indeed children's stories, and he enjoyed reading them to his own sons.

Gaol" (1898) after his release from prison, and his memoir, *De Profundis*, was published after his death in 1905. He spent his last three years in exile in France, converting to Catholicism on his deathbed. Wilde died of cerebral meningitis on November 30, 1900, at the Hôtel d'Alsace in Paris. Although he died in poverty and social disgrace, he retained his fame as an important Victorian author of plays, tales, poetry, essays, and a novel.

PLOT SUMMARY

Wilde published two volumes of fairy tales. The "Nightingale and the Rose" appears in the first volume, *The Happy Prince and Other Tales* (1888). A second volume, *A House of Pomegranates*, came out in 1891. The stories are reminiscent of the style of Hans Christian Andersen and tell of the spiritual power of sacrificial love.

In "The Nightingale and the Rose," a young Student cries out that the girl he is in love with will only dance with him if he brings her a red rose, but there are no red roses in his garden. He is overheard by the Nightingale in her nest in the Oak-tree. The Student continues to lament that though he has studied the wisdom of philosophy, his life is failing because he does not have a red rose to achieve his desire. The Nightingale is impressed, saying that she has finally found a true lover. Every night, she sings of love to the world, and now she knows what a lover looks like. She describes his dark hair, red lips, and pale face.

The Nightingale comments to herself that love is the most beautiful thing in the world, and it brings her joy to sing of it, yet it brings the Student pain; therefore, he must be a true lover. The Student throws himself on the grass in mourning, explaining how his love will dance to the music but not with him because he cannot give her what she asks.

The creatures in the garden are disturbed by his grief. A Green Lizard asks why the Student weeps, as do a Butterfly and a Daisy. The Nightingale explains that he weeps for a red rose. They do not understand, but the Nightingale feels she understands the mystery of love. She flies through the garden and, seeing a beautiful Rose-tree, sits on it. She asks it to give her a red rose, and she will sing it the sweetest song. The tree says its roses are white and tells the

MEDIA ADAPTATIONS

- *Fairy Tales of Oscar Wilde: In Aid of the Royal Theatrical Fund* is an audiobook available at Audible.com featuring Jeremy Irons, Joanna Lumley, Derek Jacobi, Sinead Cusack, Robert Harris, Geoffrey Palmer, and others as readers of the unabridged tales. The recording, which has a running time of almost four hours, was released in 2010. "The Nightingale and the Rose" is read by Dame Judi Dench.
- *Stephen Fry Presents: A Selection of Oscar Wilde's Short Stories* is an audiobook of *The Happy Prince and Other Tales*, including "The Nightingale and the Rose," read by the noted English comedian, actor, and author. It was recorded in 2008 and is available from Audible.com and iTunes.
- "The Selfish Giant" is a British film loosely inspired by the fairy tale of that name from *The Happy Prince and Other Tales*, starring Connor Chapman and directed by Clio Barnard for IFC Films in 2013. The award-winning film is set in contemporary northern England and concerns the story of two poor boys and their employer, who first exploits the boys and then performs an unselfish act.

Nightingale to go to its brother by the sundial. The Nightingale visits the tree growing by the sundial, but it says its roses are yellow and encourages her to go to the Rose-tree beneath the Student's window. The Nightingale visits this Rose-tree, who admits it has red roses but explains that it will not produce roses this year because of last winter's frost affecting its buds and branches.

The Nightingale pleads for only one red rose. The Rose-tree says there is only one way, but it is a terrible way. The Nightingale says she is not afraid, so the Rose-tree tells her she must build the rose out of music and stain it with her own heart's blood. If she sings all night to the

Rose-tree with a thorn piercing her heart, giving her life blood to the tree, then the red rose will appear.

The Nightingale says that death is a great price for a red rose. She speaks of the sweetness of life in the garden with the Sun and Moon and the scent of the flowers. She decides, however, that love is even more precious than life. The heart of a bird is nothing compared to the heart of a man. She flies over the garden and sees the Student still weeping on the grass.

She tells him she will give him the red rose, sacrificing her life, but he must promise to be a true lover. Love is wiser than philosophy and better than power. The Student hears but does not understand what the Nightingale tells him. The Student only understands things in books. The Oak-tree, however, understands what the Nightingale is saying and feels sad. The Oak-tree asks the Nightingale to sing one last song, and she grants the request.

The Student listens but criticizes, seeing the Nightingale as having style but no feeling. He thinks she is shallow like most artists; the arts are selfish. He believes that the arts are beautiful but have no meaning and are not practical.

That night when the Student is asleep, the Nightingale flies to the Rose-tree and sets her breast against a thorn, singing all night as the thorn goes deeper and deeper into her heart. The Moon listens as the bird's life ebbs away. She sings of how love is born in the hearts of boys and girls. While she sings, a rose begins to bloom on top of the Rose-tree. At first it is pale, but the tree tells the Nightingale to press the thorn more closely so it will redden before dawn with her blood. She sings of passion and is pierced by the thorn. The rose begins to turn pink, but the thorn has not yet reached the Nightingale's heart. Finally, the thorn reaches her heart as she sings, and the pain is bitter. She sings of love that does not die with death. The rose becomes crimson as the day dawns. The Nightingale's voice is fainter, and as the rose is finished she dies and falls to the ground with a thorn in her heart.

At noon the Student wakes up and looks out his window to see the wonderful red rose. He picks the rose and goes to the Professor's house, where the Professor's Daughter is sitting in the doorway. The Student presents her with the reddest rose in the world and reminds her of her promise to dance with him. When she wears the rose, he says, it will announce to the world how much he loves her.

The girl replies that the red rose will not go with her dress. Besides, the Chamberlain's nephew sent her some jewels that are more costly than flowers. The Student is angry and throws the flower in the street, where a cart runs over it. The girl belittles the Student for his poverty, and the Student comments that love is a silly thing, not as important as logic. Love is impractical. He wants to go back to his study of philosophy and metaphysics. He returns to his room to read.

CHARACTERS

The Butterfly
The Butterfly fluttering after a sunbeam is only vaguely curious about the intruder, the Student, weeping in the garden.

The Daisy
The Daisy is a common garden flower, unlike the more royal rose. It whispers in something like gossip to its neighbor, wondering at the Student's emotions. The Daisy is given a male personality.

Echo
Echo amplifies and carries the song of the Nightingale to wake the hills and the sea and the shepherds. The Nightingale's song is powerful enough to move all of nature.

The Green Lizard
The Green Lizard runs with his tail in the air and seems stuck up. He is called a cynic and laughs at the Student's distress. Wilde contrasts the responses of various members of the garden to the plight of the Student's grief. The Lizard has no sympathy.

The Moon
The Moon is necessary for the Nightingale's song, especially while she makes the special rose. The moon is cold and crystal and has a chariot of pearl, but her beauty inspires the bird's song. When the Moon hears the last burst of the Nightingale's song, she forgets about dawn and lingers in the sky. This implies that nature answers to the Nightingale's song. She has power over the elements and creatures.

The Nightingale

The Nightingale is the main character of the tale. She is an artist with extraordinary talent and love of beauty. She has complete sympathy with the Student's distress, imagining that he is a true lover of the kind of ethereal love she sings about. The Nightingale is shown to be a naïve idealist but one with great sensitivity to everything around her. The Student is her foil, for he cares only for his own feelings. The great virtue of the Nightingale is not only her willingness to sacrifice for the happiness of another but her willingness to live her art in life. She not only sings of beauty but also creates it through her song and life, living out her ideal of love. The fact that she misjudges the sincerity of the Student's situation leads to her tragedy, but she is triumphant in her art. She is able to create a supernatural rose that does not exist in nature, even more beautiful than a real rose.

This is Wilde's philosophy, that art is superior to nature and can repair the deficiencies of nature. The Red Rose-tree was damaged by frostbite and could not produce any roses of its own, but with the Nightingale's help, it can. It is interesting though, that the Nightingale can only produce this exotic rose through the pain of a thorn at her breast that finally kills her. This is part of Wilde's idea that sympathy and moral beauty arrive with pain. It is pain that moves one beyond egotism to sympathy with others. This song was not the bird's usual song that she sang in the garden but something special, and it is hinted that it is sacred, for it is a song about the love that transcends death and is perfected by death. It is perfected by death because the Nightingale gives up everything, even her life, for another's love. This suggests a Christlike act of love. The Nightingale is thus both victim and hero.

The Oak-tree

The Oak-tree is the Nightingale's friend and admirer. He has given shelter to the Nightingale, who built a nest in its branches. The Oak-tree appreciates the song of the Nightingale, while the Student does not. When the Oak-tree understands that the Nightingale means to give up her life, he is sad and asks for one last song, which the Nightingale obligingly gives him. He will miss her in the garden.

The Professor's Daughter

The Professor's Daughter is the most cruel and thoughtless character in the story. She never enters the garden but is only associated with the town. She first causes the Student suffering by demanding the red rose for a dance with her, and when he produces it against all odds, she humiliates him by turning it down for the jewels of the other suitor, the Chamberlain's nephew. She only weighs gifts in terms of material cost. Her fickleness is the reason the Student turns against love and returns to his intellectual studies, unable to trust the heart.

The Red Rose-tree

The Red Rose-tree has been damaged by the winter's frost and cannot produce the rose the Student needs. It grows under his window, suggesting that it is actually his coldness that blights the tree, for he is not the true lover the Nightingale assumes from his tears. Because the Rose-tree has weathered terrible storms, she seems to know what it will take for the Nightingale to make her bloom. The Nightingale will have to go to the brink of death to find enough force in her to sing the song of blooming. This paradox of blooming on the brink of death illuminates one facet of the aesthetic philosophy of Wilde and the students of Walter Pater, who were exhorted to burn always with a hard gem-like flame to extract every bit of intensity out of life. The Rose-tree coaches the Nightingale as she sings to keep up her passion to finish the rose before daylight. Red is the color of blood and passion and of sacrifice, as the Nightingale has to produce the red color with her heart's blood.

The Rose

The rose created by the Nightingale is a miracle beyond nature. The Nightingale manages to make a barren tree grow a single red rose overnight with her song and heart's blood. The emphasis is on the fact that the rose is "built" out of a song sung in moonlight and stained with the blood produced by a thorn at the heart. This image evokes W. B. Yeats's poem "Sailing to Byzantium," which celebrates the artifice of eternity of the artist, who can go beyond flesh and death to create something lasting. This supernatural rose created by the Nightingale is red like the flame-colored body of love itself and represents love's passion. The last note of the Nightingale's song wakens the rose to life as it shivers with ecstasy and opens its petals. Wilde's sense of humor surfaces in the Student's remark that this unusual rose must have a Latin name. He can only classify it rather than perceive it innocently. The fact that the rose is trampled in the street is a reference to the beauty of true art and love sometimes being ignored or even ruined in the world. The garden is the paradisal place of the magic birth of the rose. The rose only becomes crimson as the Nightingale sings of the degrees of love: first, the love of a boy and girl; then the love of the man and maid; finally, the (Christlike) love that survives the tomb.

The Student
The Student first appears as a disconsolate romantic lover weeping in the garden for his love. This is a conventional image for lovers, and Shakespeare used it in his plays for adolescent love or false love. In many ways, the Student is an intruder, out of sympathy with the rhythms and beauty of the garden. The animals and trees have mixed reactions towards him. The Rose-tree beneath his window does not bloom. When the Nightingale tries to sing to him to cheer him up and tell her she can produce the rose for him, he does not understand her and scorns her song as useless. He is a philosopher who studies about life from books. When life does not conform to his ideas, he retreats to his room. The Student treats art in a utilitarian fashion. He only cares if the rose serves as the currency for his girl's attention. When it does not work, he throws it in the street as having no value. The Student gives an extended criticism of art when he thinks that the Nightingale has style but no meaning to her song. He thinks artists are selfish, just pleasing themselves. In reality, he is evaluating himself, not the Nightingale who gives her all. The Student stands for logic and the coldness of critics.

The Sun
The Sun has a chariot of gold, and the Nightingale enjoys the beauty of day, though it is the beauty of night that makes her sing. She has to finish her song before the sun rises. Daylight often implies the everyday world to romantic artists, while moonlight provides the magic for art.

The White Rose-tree
The White Rose-tree is in the center of the garden with its pure white roses. The white suggests purity and virginity. It cannot grant what the Nightingale needs for the Student to complete his love quest.

The Yellow Rose-tree
The Yellow Rose-tree suggests an association with the sun. It is near the sundial. Wilde frequently uses color symbolism, and here, he makes yellow part of the daytime world of the daffodil before the mower comes. The yellow roses are associated with the noontime of life before the mower Death comes to cut them down. A yellow rose does not contain the passion needed for the heart.

THEMES

Art and Society
Wilde includes his philosophy of art in symbolic form in this tale. The Nightingale is the passionate artist who cannot help singing about the beauty she sees around her. The artist is thus represented as the supreme lover, a lover of life and beauty. The Nightingale assumes that because the Student speaks passionately of love, he must love as she idealizes. She takes pity on him and wants to help him because he represents true love for her. He has thrown himself on the ground and weeps, which she sees as evidence of his sincerity.

When she finds she must give up her own life to further his suit with the young woman he adores, by producing a red rose for her, she is willing to give it. She sings and bleeds her own life into the rose as an offering that will please the young woman enough to respond to the Student. The other beings in the garden, such as the Oak-tree and Rose-tree, understand the value of the Nightingale's song and her sacrifice; but the Student and the girl he loves do not value the rose or know what it cost the Nightingale to produce it. It is thrown away and trampled as being of lesser value than the jewels from the Chamberlain's nephew. Wilde felt this was true of the taste of the public in general, which was unable to appreciate the refinement of art.

The Student himself criticizes the Nightingale's song when he hears her singing to console him. He compares her to artists who have style but no substance. As a student of philosophy, he feels he can judge the arts as without value;

TOPICS FOR FURTHER STUDY

- In class, discuss the characteristics of fairy tales. What kinds of characters and plots do they tend to have? Do they take place in the present as well as the past? Do they teach lessons or are they just good stories? Considering such facets, write your own fairy tale, and post it on a class blog. After receiving feedback and revising, publish a collection of class fairy tales in book form, in e-book form, or as a website.

- Do an oral report, followed by discussion, of Michael Jackson as a figure like Oscar Wilde who held a larger-than-life symbolic relationship to his art and to his age. Document his career and the controversies surrounding his life and death using various media, such as slides, video clips, music clips, photos, magazine articles, books, and interviews. Why did people admire him or condemn him? In your presentation, try to go to a deeper view of the issues of being such a public figure.

- Read one of the following biographies of teens who did whatever it took to develop as an individual in an environment where that was not encouraged: Ishmael Beah's *A Long Way Gone: Memoirs of a Boy Soldier*

(2007) is about a boy in Sierra Leone who was forced to become a soldier but later became a civil rights activist. Irene Gut Opdyke's *In My Hands: Memories of a Holocaust Rescuer* (1999) tells the story of a young Polish girl who hid Jews during World War II. Lori Gottlieb's *Stick Figure: A Diary of My Former Self* (2000) describes the struggles of an anorexic girl. Divide into groups responsible for each book, and present these stories to the larger class. Everyone faces challenges trying to be who they are, overcoming conventional expectations of parents, society, and friends. Then write a personal essay comparing the journey these teens took to self-discovery and the one you are engaged in or would like to be engaged in.

- Read some other fairy tales by Oscar Wilde. Then write a critical paper comparing "The Nightingale and the Rose" to another story, finding common themes, characters, and subject matter. Do these tales teach the values people need today? Justify your argument and conclusion with quotes and examples.

---

the arts are selfish, he says. They do not give anything practical; they are a waste of time.

The fairy tale also explains symbolically how art is produced. The Nightingale is sensitive, moved by the beauty of the Moon and the garden and the love of a man for a woman. She spontaneously sings out the beauty she sees without premeditation or purpose, except to express herself and add to the happiness of others. Her innocence and naïveté about the motives of human society prevent her from seeing the young woman's demand for a red rose as a selfish move to control the Student. The girl humiliates the boy and his gift when he does what she asks of him.

As an artist who believed in the value of art for its own sake, Wilde shows the Nightingale as the primordial artist singing because she is full of life and love. He also shows that the process of producing the art is not always visible to the society that passes judgment on artists. The Student has never seen a rose as beautiful as the one the Nightingale sings into existence as a product of the imagination. This is Wilde's idea that the artist improves upon nature. The fact that the artist suffers, killed by a thorn to get to the deepest part of experience, is also seen as a prophetic statement about Wilde's own death in the pursuit of art and pleasure. He, like the Nightingale, became a victim of the shallowness of society.

The nightingale hears the student's words and believes that he feels a pure and rare kind of love.
(© Markus Plank / Shutterstock.com)

Love

Love motivates the Nightingale to sing. It motivates the Student's tears over the girl he wants to dance with. The fairy tale, however, distinguishes between shallow and deep love. The Nightingale assumes that the Student feels what she imagines because of his actions. In love poetry, the nightingale is often invoked as the bird of love, singing its melancholy, sweet air by moonlight. The Student, supposedly in love, is unable to make anything of the Nightingale's song. It is a pretty song to him, but without feeling or meaning, yet it is he who lacks feeling. When thwarted by the young woman, the Student becomes disillusioned about love and immediately gives it up as silly.

The Nightingale's idea of love is far grander, nobler, and more mystical than that of the shallow people around her. Her love and song come from the beauty of nature and connect the listener to that universal love exhibited in the garden. To her, love is so exalted that she does not see death as too great a price to pay for it. In fact, even though in pain, she creates a song about love that is perfected by death, that goes beyond mortality. Though she dies, and the rose is trampled, the song remains as her triumph. This is love that approaches the divine, suggesting the sacrifice of Christ, a theme that Wilde uses frequently in his work.

The nightingale and the rose are well-known symbols from Eastern art. Eastern visual arts and poetry were popular with aesthetic writers like Wilde. The nightingale and rose, for instance, were used in Persian verse, in Divan poetry. The nightingale was the lover, either the suffering lover in a human relationship or else the seeker of God in Sufi mysticism. The rose was therefore either erotic love or divine love. The garden was the garden of the world, or the garden of heaven. Wilde's rich symbolic imagery, ornate style, and blending of mystical love with worldly love in this tale suggest Oriental literature.

Sacrifice

The Nightingale's sacrifice for love and art constitute the primary act in the plot. In Wilde's fairy tales, sacrifice is a common theme, for it distinguishes those who are loving from those who are selfish. In "The Selfish Giant" and "The Happy Prince," for instance, sacrifice is praised as ennobling to the soul, even if not rewarded on earth. The Happy Prince is a statue that gives up his own beauty and value to provide for the poor in the city. The little swallow that helps him do this by taking the statue's jewels and giving them away is, like the Nightingale, sacrificed to the greater good. The people, however, do not appreciate this unselfishness and pull down the ugly statue, once the swallow distributes its jewels. God finally sends for the statue and the swallow to adorn his own garden. Similarly, the Selfish Giant creates a wasteland when he chases children away from his garden, but eventually, beauty returns when he is kind to one child and helps him climb a tree. That child is shown to be the Christ Child and rewards the now Unselfish Giant by taking him to his garden in heaven after he dies. The Nightingale's sacrifice, however, goes unrecorded and unappreciated except by the reader and the trees in the garden.

STYLE

Literary Fairy Tale

Fairy tales and folktales are part of the oral tradition in ancient cultures. They are stories of magic told by tribes or by the common folk all over the world that include witches, fairies, princes and princesses, secrets, prophecies, transformations, wish fulfillment, talking animals and plants, the origins of things, and how the cleverness of poor folk triumphs over the rich. Often full of the monstrous as well as the marvelous, they are tales passed along by the uneducated or illiterate, as opposed to the literary fairy tale, created by authors and written down. A literary fairy tale may take bits of folktales or retell an oral tradition, but generally, the literary fairy tale is written by an individual and given a new or specific purpose.

The Victorian fairy tale, for instance, was very popular as a genre and saw works written by well-known authors such as Charles Dickens ("A Christmas Carol"), George MacDonald ("The Light Princess"), William Makepeace Thackeray ("The Rose and the Ring"), John Ruskin ("The King of the Golden River"),

and Oscar Wilde ("The Happy Prince" and "The Nightingale and the Rose"). One of the most famous makers of literary fairy tales in the nineteenth century was Danish writer Hans Christian Andersen, an important influence on Dickens and Wilde. Andersen added to his created tales an emotional and psychological depth and often a spiritual or moral dimension, as in "The Little Mermaid," the heroine of which is trying to get a human soul. Literary fairy tales are included as part of children's literature but are usually meant for adults, too, and contain wisdom that prefigures the interest in modern fantasy.

Aestheticism

Wilde was one of the most famous proponents of the aesthetic movement in art in England (1868–1900). Aestheticism, meaning the love of beauty and art for its own sake, was part of a larger European movement in style in the late nineteenth century influencing literature, music, interior design, painting, and architecture. It emphasized beauty of design over function or morality. It was also called Pre-Raphaelitism in England in the 1860s and 1870s, *symbolisme* in France, and the Decadence during the 1890s, when Wilde was writing his drawing-room comedies. The arts were thought to provide pleasure rather than preaching morality. It was the enjoyment of "art for art's sake" and nothing more.

Wilde's poetry and prose are ornate with beautiful symbols and colors that suggest a Pre-Raphaelite painting or Persian miniature, as in "The Nightingale and the Rose." The garden is a place of beauty, presided over by the Nightingale, whose song concentrates all the colors, scents, and feelings into a heightened passion. The Student classifies her as the kind of aesthetic artist who is all style and no heart, not understanding Wilde's view of aestheticism as spiritual rather than moral art. Spiritual art feeds the spirit, which can ascend to divine realms through beauty. The Nightingale can only sing because she is sensitive and sings by giving her very lifeblood. The Student wants to know things through the intellect, and thus aestheticism seems selfish to him for worshipping beauty over morality.

Allegory and Symbol

Although Wilde subscribed to the notion of art for art's sake and having nothing to do with morality, he often contradicts himself by providing morals to his stories in symbolic form. Wilde's fairy tales are highly allegorical, teaching lessons for life. Allegory is a way of telling a story through a parable, making one thing stand for another thing, such as the Christian parable of the prodigal son returning home to his forgiving father, standing for the sinner returning to God. There is a hidden or second meaning behind the literal images. For instance, John Bunyan's *The Pilgrim's Progress* (1678), with a main character named Christian and others named Mr. Worldly Wiseman and Obstinate, is an obvious Christian allegory for the journey of the soul to salvation. The characters stand for certain types or certain principles.

In "The Nightingale and the Rose," the Nightingale stands for the aesthetic artist who creates out of intensified sensitivity to life. She is thought impractical by the Student, who studies philosophy. The Student and the Nightingale stand for different philosophies of life. Thus, the tale becomes a symbolic dialogue in which Wilde means to show the superiority of feeling over thinking, even if extreme sensitivity leads to death. Though in an allegory a moral can be stated, it is often shown through the symbolism, as in this tale. The love of the Nightingale is symbolized in her sacrifice as she sings with a thorn to her breast to turn the rose red. The selfishness of the girl is shown in her dismissing the precious rose (true love) after receiving jewels from the Chamberlain's nephew (social standing). Wilde also liked to use color and imagery symbolically, much like music, to create a mood. Each color of rose evokes a different feeling, as do the Green Lizard and the homely Daisy.

HISTORICAL CONTEXT

The Victorian Age

Wilde wrote during the reign of Queen Victoria (1837–1901), when Britain changed from an agrarian economy controlled by landowners to an industrial power run by entrepreneurial financiers. The Reform Bill of 1832 was a watershed in English history that shifted power towards working- and middle-class interests. Britain was the superpower of the nineteenth century, with its vast world empire that included colonial domination of countries from South Africa to India to Australia. The British believed themselves at the pinnacle of civilization with a superior navy, technological and industrial advances, and great wealth.

English culture also led the world with its stable political and legal systems, popular writers like Charles Dickens and Rudyard Kipling, and engineering discoveries. Queen Victoria's promotion of middle-class morality and family values led, however, to a repressive atmosphere for women, minorities, and artists. An explosion in scientific knowledge, marked by Darwin's ideas of evolution in *The Origin of Species* (1859), challenged the notion of a divinely set hierarchy in nature. Other questions about religion came up with David Friedrich Strauss's *The Life of Jesus* (1835) and Ludwig Feuerbach's *The Essence of Christianity* (1841), which debated the traditional interpretation of Christ's life and the literal truth of the Bible.

Belief in technological and philosophical progress replaced the old received truths. Wilde grew up in an era that still embraced the status quo but also thrived on the influx of new ideas. He played both these trends for his own purposes, posing as a stylish society dandy and an iconoclast at the same time.

Victorian Rebels

Though the growing wealth of the middle classes created new possibilities for successful writers of novels, the ugliness of industrialism and materialism was severely criticized by the rebellious aesthetes, those artists who believed true art had nothing to do with morality or middle-class values. Wilde was influenced by the aesthetic philosophy while at Oxford through the art critic Walter Pater (1839–1894). In essays published in 1867 and 1868, Pater announced his belief that life should be lived intensely in the pursuit of beauty, in every moment. His *Studies in the History of the Renaissance* (1873) was a key text in Wilde's life for its descriptions of the beauties of Renaissance art that needed no didactic purpose. A number of young men, both artists and social dandies, subscribed to the cult of beauty, as Wilde did. They were rebels who declared that life should imitate art, dressing and behaving outrageously, as does Algernon Moncrieff in Wilde's play *The Importance of Being Earnest*.

COMPARE
&
CONTRAST

- **1888:** Homosexuality is a punishable offense in England. Wilde spends two years at hard labor in prison after his conviction for an affair with Lord Alfred Douglas.

  Today: The Civil Partnership Act of 2004 and the Marriage (Same Sex Couples) Act of 2013 give legal rights to gay couples and make gay marriage legal in England.

- **1888:** The literary fairy tale is a popular genre, with many major authors trying to write one. Victorian fairy tales are enjoyed by children and adults.

  Today: The literary fairy tale is only one type of speculative fiction, which includes the whole fantasy and science-fiction industry.

The audience for speculative fiction is vast and includes children and adults.

- **1888:** High art and commercialism are opposed, with the rising middle classes wanting morality in their fiction and artists like Wilde reserving the right to experiment with controversial themes and style.

  Today: The boundaries between high art and popular art are blurred, with themes and styles transferring from traditional art to popular media and vice versa. There is little left to shock the public in books, films, or theater, though rating systems and reviews are employed to warn the consumer.

The predominant realism of Victorian novels was associated with middle-class utilitarianism, examining how useful a thing is, as the Student does in the fairy tale. Aesthetic artists preferred to celebrate beauty for its own sake with sensuous color and imagery and myth and fantasy. Famous aesthetic writers in England were Wilde, Dante Gabriel Rossetti, and Algernon Charles Swinburne. They were influenced by French symbolists like Charles Baudelaire, Arthur Rimbaud, and Paul Verlaine. Rossetti was also a visual artist, along with other Pre-Raphaelite painters such as William Morris, John Everett Millais, and Edward Burne-Jones, as well as the later impressionist painters. Aesthetic art often displays amoral or rebellious ideas, as in Wilde's comedies. The 1890s, the decade of Wilde's greatest social triumph and his disgrace, was called the *fin de siècle* (end of the century) or the Decadence. The last half of the nineteenth century saw the rise of adult fantasy and literary fairy tales by writers like Wilde and George MacDonald. These imaginative works tried to be a corrective to the materialism of the age with alternate worlds of beauty.

Socialism

In his novel *Sybil; or, The Two Nations* (1845), Benjamin Disraeli proclaimed a division in England between the rich and the poor. Disraeli described the miseries of the lower classes of Manchester, who were fodder for the factories, but he could offer no solution to this industrial nightmare. Karl Marx (1818–1883), the German economist, wrote much of his work on capitalism and communism as an answer to these conditions while living in London. Many nineteenth-century reformers espoused socialism of some kind. Socialism is a general philosophy of social ownership instead of private ownership, with the economy planned and regulated for the use of all, instead of goods being accumulated for the profit of the few. George Bernard Shaw and his wife, Charlotte Payne-Townshend, were founding members of the Fabian Society, a British socialist movement (still existing) that believes in social democracy through gradual change rather than revolution. It advocates principles of the welfare state to bring about social justice and equal opportunity, with capitalism controlled through

The nightingale gives his heart's blood to stain the white rose red. (© *Brzostowska | Shutterstock.com*)

regulation. The movement attracted such artists as the Shaws, Leonard and Virginia Woolf, H. G. Wells, and Sidney and Beatrice Webb. Wilde supported many of its initiatives.

Aesthetic artists, such as John Ruskin and the designer William Morris, also embraced socialist ideas as part of their artistic theory, denouncing mechanization and advocating handcrafts produced by and for the working class. Oscar Wilde's essay "The Soul of Man under Socialism" attempts to reconcile art, socialism, and individualism. His fairy tales have implied socialist themes couched in Christian ethics, as when the Happy Prince distributes the jewels on his statue to the poor and when the Selfish Giant opens his garden to the children instead of keeping it for himself. In "The Nightingale and the Rose," the Professor's daughter represents a thoughtless and soulless middle class unaware of beauty and kindness, figuratively trampling the artistic rose created by the Nightingale from its lifeblood.

CRITICAL OVERVIEW

By the time *The Happy Prince and Other Tales*, which includes "The Nightingale and the Rose," was published in 1888, Wilde was happily married and the father of two boys whom he adored and to whom he read his tales. He was already famous in Britain and America for his poetry, journalism, and lectures on aestheticism. His darkest works, *The Picture of Dorian Gray* and *Salomé*, had not yet appeared, nor had his popular comedies. The fairy tales were generally well received, especially the first volume, *The Happy Prince*.

Donald H. Ericksen summarizes contemporary criticism of the tales in his book *Oscar Wilde*. The *Athenaeum* compares Wilde's fairy tales to those of Hans Christian Andersen, considering this high praise. Alexander Ross in the *Saturday Review* feels the stories go beyond Andersen's in their degree of satire, making them suitable for thinking adults. Walter Pater,

Wilde's famous tutor in aesthetic philosophy at Oxford, wrote to him that he especially liked "The Remarkable Rocket" and "The Selfish Giant," tales that are "gems" with "delicate touches and pure English."

Although Wilde's literary reputation declined immediately after his trial and prison sentence, and his life and aesthetic philosophy came to be seen as a cautionary tale against excess and arrogance, the fairy tales remain popular with readers and stand on their own outside controversy, though they gained little critical attention until recently. With the publication of Wilde's letters in 1962, there was greater scholarly interest in both the man and the author. The tales are now seen as prefiguring major themes in his poetry and drama and as foretelling his own sexual orientation and perceived moral fall. As Jerusha McCormack remarks in the 1997 article "Wilde's Fiction(s)": "The love of women, as the fairy tales explicitly show, is shallow and cruel."

Wilde's fairy tales are still republished with various illustrations highlighting aspects of his ornate aesthetic sensibility. Ruth MacDonald, for instance, reviewed a 1982 edition of *The Nightingale and the Rose* for *School Library Journal*, praising illustrations by Freire Wright and Michael Foreman that bring out "the surreal aspects of the story and its delicacy in their color washes and swirling patterns." She questions, however, bringing out a new edition of a negative story about love. Karen T. Bilton commented for *School Library Journal* on a 2004 edition of *The Fairy Tales of Oscar Wilde*, illustrated by P. Craig Russell, which is presented in a format like a graphic novel that opens "Wilde's tragic stories to a new audience while remaining true to his thoughtful, moral prose." Wilde's tales, like Andersen's, have entered the popular imagination and have become part of the reading public's moral vocabulary.

CRITICISM

Susan K. Andersen

Andersen is a writer and teacher with a PhD in English literature. In the following essay, she considers "The Nightingale and the Rose" as a fable of Wilde's own philosophy of art in which the artist becomes a sacrificial, Christlike figure in society as he strives to realize his individuality and art.

CHRISTIAN THEMES SUCH AS SUFFERING, REBELLION AGAINST WORLDLY AUTHORITY, SELF-SACRIFICE, AND UNSELFISHNESS INFORM THE FAIRY TALES, WITH WILDE'S UNIQUE TWIST TOWARD DEFENDING THE ARTISTIC TEMPERAMENT."

Oscar Wilde's fairy tales, such as "The Nightingale and the Rose," seem to be a far cry from the fashionable cynicism he is known for in the social comedies that celebrate the aesthetic philosophy of the Victorian Decadence. Algernon Moncrieff, for instance, the idle spoiled dandy in *The Importance of Being Earnest*, complains, "It is awfully hard work doing nothing." The only thing required of Algy is that he be rich and live for pleasure as long as he can be fashionably witty. The fairy tales, on the other hand, concern the injustice of the rich toward the poor. The stories praise moral acts of kindness and unselfishness. The noblest characters are those who sacrifice for love or the common good, like the Nightingale, the Happy Prince, and the Giant.

This paradox, of Wilde's artistic stance of living for pleasure on the one hand and showing the moral consequences of doing so on the other, seen in the tragic outcomes of his play *Salomé* and his novel, *The Picture of Dorian Gray*, is explained by Wilde in his memoir, *De Profundis*. Wilde says he always had the goal of complete self-development, to taste all experience both good and bad, as his mentor, Walter Pater, had recommended for the artistic sensibility. He feels he achieved his goal of becoming a true individual but at a great cost, as did his model, Jesus Christ, the example he proposes for the artist and total individual in *De Profundis*. Christian themes such as suffering, rebellion against worldly authority, self-sacrifice, and unselfishness inform the fairy tales, with Wilde's unique twist toward defending the artistic temperament. From this angle, Wilde perhaps saw the Nightingale's story as his own symbolic drama.

"The Nightingale and the Rose" is a fable of Wilde's philosophy of art. To begin with, the Nightingale is an artist. She sings of all the beauty she sees in the garden. At first the

WHAT DO I READ NEXT?

- Maya Angelou's first autobiography, called *I Know Why the Caged Bird Sings* (1969), is titled from a line in African American poet Paul Laurence Dunbar's poem "Sympathy," about a caged bird singing in pain but singing because it must, recalling Wilde's metaphor. Angelou was a dancer, singer, writer, and civil rights activist. This autobiography is on young-adult lists because it describes the first seventeen years of her long and remarkable life.

- Boy George (George Alan O'Dowd), English singer from the 1980s to the present, is a nonconformist who has spent time in jail, not for his gay affairs but for his drug abuse. While accepted as a gay artist, he, like Wilde, places himself in the margins of acceptability. He has written two autobiographical books, *Take It like a Man* (1995) and *Straight* (2005), both best sellers in the United Kingdom.

- F. Scott Fitzgerald's novel *The Great Gatsby* (1925) recalls the decadence of the Jazz Age and living for pleasure in high society. Jay Gatsby tries to please and win the socialite Daisy Buchanan, who is unworthy of his sacrifices. Fitzgerald's lush poetic prose reminds the reader of Wilde's aesthetic sensibility.

- "The Artist of the Beautiful" is a short story by Nathaniel Hawthorne in his collection *Mosses from an Old Manse* (1846). The protagonist is an artist who is ridiculed for creating something beautiful and intangible rather than something practical. The woman he loves does not understand and prefers to marry a practical man.

- Merlin Holland's *The Real Trial of Oscar Wilde* (2004) is an account of the trial in 1895 that led to Wilde's downfall and imprisonment. Holland is the grandson of Wilde and has included transcripts of the trial and legal analysis. He concludes that Wilde was convicted because of bad advice

and his flippancy in court, treating the trial as a bit of theater.

- *One Thousand and One Nights* (1548), also known as *The Arabian Nights*, is a traditional collection of fairy tales written in Arabic, first translated into French by Antoine Galland in 1706. The scenes are set in Baghdad and Cairo, with Scheherazade telling stories to the sultan each night to save her life. This was one of the most popular books in Victorian England, coming out in many editions since 1840. It is found in a 2008 edition.

- Doreen Rappaport's retelling of a Malagasy fable for young readers, *The New King* (1995), illustrated by E. B. Lewis, tells of Prince Rakoto of Madagascar, who cannot accept his father's death and orders him to be brought back to life. A wise woman tells him a tale to comfort him about the truth of life and death.

- *The Victorian Fairy Tale Book* (1988), edited by Michael Patrick Hearn, includes Robert Browning's "Pied Piper of Hamelin," J. M. Barrie's *Peter Pan*, and other classic tales of the period, with illustrations by famous Victorian artists such as Dante Gabriel Rossetti, Maxfield Parrish, and Arthur Rackham.

- Oscar Wilde's novel, *The Picture of Dorian Gray* (1890), scandalized the public with its story of a spoiled aristocratic dandy living for pleasure at the expense of others. Dorian's sins, however, are mysteriously exhibited on the portrait of himself he keeps hidden in the attic, and eventually he must pay for his crimes.

- William Butler Yeats's *Fairy and Folk Tales of the Irish Peasantry* (1888) came out the same year as *The Happy Prince and Other Tales*. Rather than literary fairy tales, the volume includes retellings of traditional Celtic myths of fairies, witches, leprechauns, druids, kings, and queens. A recent edition was published in 1993.

garden is unspoiled like Eden. The trees, the talking animals, and flowers are friends of the Nightingale and appreciate her song. Then, suddenly, there is a Student in the garden weeping about his unrequited love. If he does not produce a red rose, his girl will not dance with him. The garden has no red roses. The Nightingale is enchanted by the situation, assuming she is witnessing the true love of which she always sings: "What I sing of he suffers: what is joy to me, to him is pain. Surely love is a wonderful thing. It is more precious than emeralds." She believes the Student is sacrificing for his love, so the Nightingale tries to fulfill the Student's wish. Because the one Rose-tree is frostbitten and cannot produce red roses, it tells the Nightingale how to create a red rose with her song: "You must build it out of music by moonlight, and stain it with your own heart's-blood. You must sing to me with your breast against a thorn."

Wilde shows the artist infusing her creation with her own life, thus making it manifest to the world through imagination, but this involves sacrifice. The Nightingale is fully aware that the price for this artistic rose that does not exist in nature is her own death from using her life force with such intensity. In *De Profundis*, Wilde claims the artist is a type of Christ, a sacrificial victim for others who attack or consume the artist in an irrational ritual: "I was a man who stood in symbolic relations to the art and culture of my age." The artist is often a scapegoat, living out dreams and desires symbolically on a public stage. Surely Wilde would have understood the tragedies of Marilyn Monroe and John Lennon, torn to pieces by their artistic success. Similarly, the Nightingale participates in a public sacrifice to what she thinks is romantic love and is crucified.

The Nightingale explains that she will perform the creation of a red rose for the Student and die doing it: "All I ask of you in return is that you will be a true lover, for Love is wiser than Philosophy." She wants to know that her act means something and that the result is felt in the world. The reader knows immediately that the Student is not worthy of this sacrifice, for he cannot hear the meaning of her song. He criticizes her as the critics did Wilde and the aesthetic artists, calling their art selfish and not useful to society because it was dedicated to pleasure and beauty.

The Nightingale is passionate. As she sings of love, the rose begins to blossom on the tree. By dawn, the rose is finished, and so is the Nightingale as she drops down dead. The fickle girl does not accept the rose created at great cost, however, because "it will not go with my dress." She prefers the more worldly courting of the Chamberlain's nephew, who can give her jewels. The Student is disillusioned about love and goes back to his books. The Nightingale's song is not appreciated, and her wish, that the artistic act might actualize the love she sings of, does not happen. The rose, symbol of the work of art, remains in the ideal world, not available to the people for whom she sang.

This fairy tale ends negatively and is given many interpretations by critics, such as that it represents Wilde's disgust with heterosexual love. It also seems to prefigure his own disappointment about his art and his life. His works *De Profundis* and "The Soul of Man under Socialism," in which he compares the artist to Christ, seem to some to be a melodramatic justification of his suffering and punishment by society. The two essays, however, establish a deeper view of the meaning of art to Wilde and what he feels it takes to produce something worthy.

"The Soul of Man under Socialism" (1891) calls attention to the need for social justice and lauds the socialism of Christ, who cared for the beggar as well as the rich man. This is the kind of socialism found in the fairy tales when the Happy Prince gives away all his riches to the poor and when the Young King, though a lover of beauty, gives away his rich robes and crown when he learns they are made by slaves, preferring an ascetic coronation under the statue of Christ. The fairy tales caution against accumulation of wealth for selfish purposes, when the many are needy. Regenia Gagnier in her introduction to *Critical Essays on Oscar Wilde* points out that Wilde's socialism, however mainstream in thought, is different because Wilde tried to integrate socialism and individuality. He did not want the authoritarianism of any state to interfere with self-development. The example of Christ, he thought, leads to freedom for everyone to have the basic needs in life taken care of so they can fulfill their inner potential. The essay mostly stresses his compassion rather than his politics. "The state is to make what is useful. The individual is to make what is beautiful," he says.

In "The Soul of Man under Socialism," Wilde invokes Christ as the great individualist who calls for perfecting the personality rather than accumulating things: "And so he who would lead a Christ-like life is he who is perfectly and absolutely himself." The Nightingale is that artistic individual who is herself and can thus sing beauty most successfully by creating out of her imagination. An artist who has developed individuality has the widest sympathy with others, as the Nightingale exhibits. The boy and girl, by contrast, are narrow-minded, only knowing what books or society tell them. They cannot understand the secret of true love. They have not perfected themselves. In his essay, written before his prison sentence, Wilde claims pain is not necessary for developing sympathy and individuality. The pursuits of beauty and pleasure are enough. Wilde later argues in *De Profundis*, however, that the artist only realizes himself fully through sorrow and pain. The artist becomes a Christlike sacrifice in order to realize himself and his art, as Wilde claims he did, and as the Nightingale did.

De Profundis was written in 1897 in Wilde's cell in Reading Gaol. It was a long letter to Lord Alfred Douglas, the man for whose sake he ruined his life. It was not published until 1905, after Wilde's death, with the personal confessional parts left out. Often, the philosophical parts are printed without the personal accusations to Douglas, and this part of *De Profundis* is most moving, for Wilde sums up a justification of his life, showing how he actually lived his philosophy of art. In spite of his great fall, he perfected his individuality through sorrow. He began as an artist in search of pleasure and beauty, but, "tired of being on the heights, I deliberately went to the depths in the search for new sensation." What he found in the depths was not depravity, as the public judged, but pain and humility and sympathy with others. He had to lose everything, he admits, in order to be who he is, to become an individual. The Nightingale is a symbol of the journey he details in *De Profundis*, a journey like Christ's toward the artist's complete surrender to art and love. Wilde understands that external things are not of any importance, nor is what society says, for it is all an inner journey to perfect one's self. He believes that only through sorrow can the soul of man reach perfection:

"Pleasure for the beautiful body, but pain for the beautiful soul."

Art, he claims, is a manifestation of the soul, "the soul made incarnate." Instead of avoiding forbidden fruit, "I wanted to eat of the fruit of all the trees in the garden." He asserts that he had to experiment with his life without regret in order to perfect himself: "Humility in the artist is his frank acceptance of all experiences." He finds Christ to be the prototype of this ultimate artist who takes all on himself and transmutes it into beauty.

Critics try to understand the place of Christ and the Christian ethics in the fairy tales. Wilde did convert to Catholicism on his deathbed, so there are those like Brother John Albert, a solemnly professed Trappist monk, who in "The Christ of Oscar Wilde" sees "an Oscar Wilde of intense religious feeling" in his works. Stephen Arata, on the other hand, in "Oscar Wilde and Jesus Christ" finds the Christ of Wilde an artistic strategy to confer meaning on the pattern of his life, especially its ending. Wilde frequently compares himself to Christ and the poet Lord Byron, public martyred figures of their times.

The contemporary trend is to see Wilde as ahead of his time. Though originally a son of privilege, Wilde put himself in the margins of society and wrote fairy tales supporting those who have been left out—the poor, the ugly, the unloved, children, the weak, the humble, artists, social rebels, and those who desire beauty and social justice. The German critic Norbert Kohl, in *Oscar Wilde: The Writings of a Conformist Rebel*, sums up the paradox of Wilde as being that of a Janus-like artist who looks backward to sum up the Victorian age and forward to embody the seeds of modernism. Regenia Gagnier in "Wilde and the Victorians" details the ways in which Wilde was a Victorian as well as a precursor of modernism and postmodernism. He was modern in his fables of socialism and individuality. He was postmodern in understanding that the self could be constructed in language. The triumph must therefore belong to the artist Nightingale (and Wilde), who had the power to realize herself through art, in spite of the response.

Source: Susan K. Andersen, Critical Essay on "The Nightingale and the Rose," in *Short Stories for Students*, Gale, Cengage Learning, 2015.

After his beloved scorns the rose, the student returns to his studies, concluding that love is silly.
(© Stokkete / Shutterstock.com)

Nicholas Ruddick

In the following excerpt, Ruddick points out that it is helpful to compare Wilde's story to Hans Christian Andersen's tale "The Nightingale."

It is not difficult to get students to read and enjoy Oscar Wilde's works, and it is all too easy to get them to debate the significance of his life. But how does an instructor convey to a class Wilde's importance as the late nineteenth century's foremost theorist and advocate of aestheticism? Wildean aestheticism was far more than a rehearsal of the slogan "art for art's sake." It offered both a radical critique of the crudely utilitarian materialism of the late Victorian era and a decadent (or precociously protomodernist) insight into the superannuated state of nineteenth-century Romanticism. Students can certainly come to evaluate Wilde's role in intellectual history through an examination of his major essays in tandem with his novel *The Picture of Dorian Gray* (1891). However, I have found that the study of a pair of shorter and more accessible works can quickly lead classes to a clear and by no means superficial understanding of the significance of Wildean aestheticism. Students of late-nineteenth-century literary and cultural history will greatly benefit from instructors who can lead them through a careful analysis of "The Happy Prince." Instructors who can reveal something of the complex engagement of "The Nightingale and the Rose" with the Romanticism of Hans Christian Andersen will illuminate for fairy-tale classes a key moment in the development of the literary fairy tale in English.

Oscar Wilde's first important book was a slim volume, *"The Happy Prince" and Other Tales* (1888), containing five short fairy tales. The proposition that short fantastic fictions apparently intended for children can be used to introduce undergraduates to weighty matters of intellectual history might seem excessively paradoxical to instructors unfamiliar with the fairy tale as a genre. Yet although the fairy tale, through the famous collections of the Grimms and Andersen, had by the mid-nineteenth century come to be associated with young readers, there is no essential connection between the genre and children (see, e.g., Zipes, Introd. xi). There is evidence that adults were the primary intended readership of Wilde's fairy tales. Wilde sent copies of *The Happy Prince* collection to such childless luminaries as John Ruskin and Walter Pater, and in a letter of 1888 he noted that the tales "are studies in prose, put for Romance's sake into a fanciful form: meant partly for children, and partly for those who have kept the childlike faculties of wonder and joy, and who find in simplicity a subtle strangeness" (*Complete Letters* 352). In 1891, in response to criticism that his later volume of tales might not please children, he wrote, "Now in building this *House of Pomegranates* I had about as much intention of pleasing the British child as I had of pleasing the British public."

"The Happy Prince" is unlikely to be much enjoyed by children today. Its plot is too static, its vocabulary too complex, and its style, influenced by the fin de siècle prose poem, too stilted. Undergraduates, by contrast, may dismiss the tale at first reading as too slight or childish to merit much attention. Instructors might begin by asking the class for their thoughts on the Councillor's description of the statue of the late Happy Prince: "He is as beautiful as a weathercock . . . only not quite so useful." Depending on the level of the course, it may be necessary to provide a little Victorian intellectual context to get the discussion rolling. The Councillor, who articulates the values of the dominant class in the city, is a utilitarian of the crudest kind. That is to say, he believes that if something is useful to oneself, then it is likely to make one happy, therefore it must be morally good, and therefore it may be called beautiful. As money can be very useful, and someone who has a lot of it is likely to be happier than someone who has none, then—so the utilitarian argument went—wealth must be morally good, and the more expensive an object is, the more beautiful it must be. (Such logic could also be used to explain why the poor lived in ugly squalor and were predisposed to crime.)

To Wilde, this utilitarian philosophy was nothing more than a specious justification of selfish acquisitiveness, and it may be necessary to remind students at this point that utilitarianism, the ethical theory formulated by Jeremy Bentham (1748–1832), was supposed to conduce to the greater good of the majority, not of the already privileged individual. The Happy Prince's statue is "useful" and "beautiful" to the city's ruling class because it demonstrates the equation between happiness and high monetary value. Put another way, in life the Prince was happy because he was rich; now that he is dead, his gilded and bejeweled statue usefully advertises the city's dominant ideology—namely, that wealth equals happiness. More sophisticated students, when asked why the Councillor adjudges the statue to be not as useful as a weathercock, will be able to deduce that his failure to understand how an ideological tool might be as valuable as a literal one marks him as a truly crude utilitarian.

. . . When discussing Andersen's influence on Wilde, fairy-tale critics have tended to emphasize the differences between the writers, often at Andersen's expense. It can be a useful heuristic strategy to ask students who have read first Andersen's, then Wilde's tales to evaluate some critical extracts comparing the two writers. For example, Isobel Murray feels that Wilde "avoids Andersen's cloying moments, and generally transcends him." Responding to Murray, Jack Zipes claims that "Wilde's underlying purpose in writing his tales would be 'subversion' rather than 'transcension.' He clearly wanted to subvert the messages conveyed by Andersen's tales" (*Fairy Tales* 114). Maria Tatar, who believes that Andersen's female protagonists tend to promote the virtues of subservience and "cheerful self-effacement," notes that "despite the superficial resemblance to Andersen's tales, Wilde's stories sound very different ideological chords" (216, 249), for Wilde was a shrewder and more radical social critic than Andersen.

Students are likely to find some truth in such observations, but many will probably also come to feel that the critics insufficiently acknowledge Wilde's considerable positive debt to Andersen. They will have noted that Wilde took from Andersen not only characters and motifs (e.g., the Little Match Girl's cameo in "The Happy Prince" and the many borrowings from "The Little Mermaid" in "The Fisherman and His Soul" [1891]) but also the technique of using the fairy tale as an allegorical vehicle "to express his own inner development in a form free from social scrutiny" (Martin, "Oscar Wilde" 74). Student essays comparing Andersen and Wilde often begin by noting, for example, that without the precedent set by Andersen, Wilde's most powerful fairy tale, "The Nightingale and the Rose," could not have been written.

In courses on the fairy tale, I find that "The Nightingale and the Rose" is best approached after students have familiarized themselves with two tales by Andersen. "The Swineherd" (1842) and "The Nightingale" (1844). In "The Swineherd," an impoverished young prince disguised as a swineherd seeks the hand of an emperor's daughter, to which end he gives her a nightingale that sings "as though all the melodies ever composed lived in its throat" (Hallett and Karasek 238) and a rose from a tree on his father's grave that blooms only once every five years. But she, unable to see the value in a real nightingale and rose (as opposed to costly artificial ones), rejects him. By making her a musical rattle, he eventually purchases from her the kisses she did not give him before, but when her father catches her in the act of embracing a swineherd, he has them both thrown out of his castle. The reader expects the lovers now to rejoice in their union as a compensation for their reduced circumstances, but the quasi-Romantic plot takes a harshly realistic turn. The swineherd-prince rounds on the princess: "I have come to despise you.... You did not appreciate the rose or the nightingale, but you could kiss a swineherd for the sake of a toy. Farewell!" Students need not be familiar with "The Happy Prince" to see that there can be no happy ending for the swineherd-prince and the former object of his affection, because the couple's value systems are incompatible. She, a materialist, shares the dominant values of her society; he, a true Romantic, recognizes that the emotional, aesthetic, and spiritual values represented by the nightingale and the rose are far more precious than the kind of gifts that she covets.

From Andersen's tale, Wilde borrowed not only the motifs of the nightingale and rose but also the theme of irreconcilable value systems. Careful readers may conclude that Wilde in "The Nightingale and the Rose" neither transcends nor subverts "The Swineherd." Rather, he intensifies the social critique already strongly evident in Andersen's tale, as if to track, by maintaining a close intertextual relation between his tale and Andersen's, the development of a sociohistorical process. During Andersen's time, Wilde implies, true love was still possible—the swineherd might have found a simple girl of the people who shared his uncorrupted values. By Wilde's time, however, the rampant and pervasive materialism of society has made romantic love impossible.

For Andersen, the emperor's court represents the corrupt values of the wealthy, the swineherd the unspoiled values of the poor. To ask a class why Wilde sets the tale not in the feudal class structure of the traditional fairy tale, as Andersen did, but among the bourgeoisie, the dominant class of the nineteenth century (and today), often provokes an interesting discussion. Many students will have discovered the direct relevance of Wilde's sociological critique to their own lives. The girl is the daughter of a professor, not an emperor; the Student is poor only temporarily. Having given up the impractical nonsense of romantic love and returned to his dusty books, the Student will undoubtedly earn his degree (his study of philosophy was only a utilitarian means to an end), join the professional middle class, and eagerly subscribe to their philistine values. As one of my class once observed with an uneasy smile, once the Student is earning a handsome salary, he will be sure to attract plenty of eligible young philistine women.

In "The Nightingale and the Rose," Wilde made a further significant change from "The Swineherd" by using a bird as protagonist rather than a human lover. But even here he was beholden to Andersen, who often made effective use of a nonhuman protagonist—for example, in such tales as "The Ugly Duckling," "The Daisy" (1838), and "The Butterfly" (1861). But the tale that most clearly influenced Wilde's elevation of the bird to protagonist is Andersen's "The Nightingale."

Set in a fairy-tale China, this story concerns an emperor's court of fabulous wealth and beauty that is nevertheless culturally moribund, totally constrained by its own absurd rituals.

The emperor has learned that visitors to China always praise the song of a nightingale who haunts the margins of his palatial gardens. Never having heard of this creature, he orders that it be brought before him. Despite its drab appearance the bird sings so beautifully that the emperor, weeping for joy, has it caged and allowed out only for walks with its legs bound with silk ribbons. But then the emperor is presented with an artificial nightingale, which sings as well as the real one and is studded with costly jewels. This he prefers to the real bird, which, now ignored, leaves the palace. Soon the artificial nightingale breaks down, and the emperor himself falls mortally ill. But just as Death is about to claim the emperor, the real nightingale returns from the gardens and charms Death away by its song. The grateful emperor offers the bird any reward it might choose, but the nightingale refuses a material recompense, wanting only its freedom to roam China so that it can sing to the emperor of both the good and evil it finds there. To the emperor, it confides that it has already been amply rewarded by "the tears from your eyes; and to a poet's heart, those are jewels" (Hallett and Karasek 216).

Instructors will find that a comparison between Andersen's "The Nightingale" and Wilde's "The Nightingale and the Rose" will help classes understand the extent to which Wilde broke with the belated Romanticism dominating his own age. It has been noted that Andersen's tale is "a virtual primer in Romantic imagery and values, with the nightingale itself representing the artist in defiance of the complacent narrow-mindedness of society" (Hallett and Karasek 184). For Andersen, the nightingale as Romantic poet is able to rejuvenate society on certain conditions: that the powers that be are responsive to his song (this is the redemptive significance of the emperor's tears), that they are able to understand that there can be no replacement for an authentic poet, that they learn to value the poet's art more highly than material things, and that they allow the poet complete freedom of expression....

Source: Nicholas Ruddick, "Teaching Wilde's Fairy Tales: Aestheticism as Social and Culture Critique in 'The Happy Prince' and 'The Nightingale and the Rose,'" in *Approaches to Teaching the Works of Oscar Wilde*, edited by Philip E. Smith II, Modern Language Association of America, 2008, pp. 93–94, 96–98.

Patrick M. Horan

In the following excerpt, Horan explores how fairy tales, including Wilde's stories, are used to illuminate truths about human nature.

Speranza and Sir William were active in the Irish literary revival; naturally, the telling of ancient stories and Irish legends was a favorite pastime in their household. Two years before Wilde was born, Sir William even published a collection of Irish fairy stories entitled *Irish Popular Superstitions*. He never finished his second manuscript on Irish fairy lore, but some of this information was taken over by Speranza who included it in her most famous work, *Ancient Legends, Mystic Charms, and Superstitions of Ireland* published in 1888. This was the same year that Wilde published his first collection of fairy tales entitled *The Happy Prince, and Other Tales*. Three years later, he published his second collection, which he entitled *A House of Pomegranates*. These works, along with his *Poems in Prose* and his 1891 short story collection, are said to be written versions of some of the numerous tales that he frequently and spontaneously told.

Serious analyses of Wilde's tales have been scarce. For example, Hesketh Pearson theorizes that Wilde wrote fairy tales because he was emotionally undeveloped. Arthur Ransome argues that the tales are merely Wilde's experiment to show that he could have been Hans Christian Andersen and, at the same time, to please his wife with a charming book. To dismiss Wilde's tales as whimsical literary exercises, however, is an injustice.

Studies in child psychology, such as Bruno Bettelheim's influential study, *The Uses of Enchantment*, indicate that fairy stories teach us much about the inner problems of humans. Bettelheim maintains that fairy tales "describe inner states of the mind by means of images and actions." This is certainly true of Wilde's tales. Nowhere in his oeuvre is he so pessimistic. His cynical tone is appropriate, however, because his tales invariably illustrate two paradoxes of life: humanity is often inhumane and lovers frequently refuse to reciprocate love.

Sir William's infidelity and his inhumane treatment of Speranza most likely helped Wilde to conclude that humanity can be inhumane.

Wilde's observations of Speranza, who continually idealized and sacrificed for her husband, enabled him to understand that love can be unreciprocated. Sir William loved Speranza; nevertheless, he did not sacrifice for her or reciprocate her idealization of him. Tragically, Wilde's future lover Lord Alfred Douglas would follow suit: the young man refused to sacrifice for Wilde or reciprocate the Irish writer's idealization of him. Wilde's tales, therefore, approach autobiography; they often revolve around an altruistic protagonist who sacrifices inordinately for his or her partner.

Wilde borrowed from many sources for his fairy stories. Hans Christian Andersen is the most obvious, but Speranza's presence, however subtle, is also there. David Upchurch theorizes that Speranza's work with legends even influenced Wilde's famous novel, *The Picture of Dorian Gray*, especially in its Celtic folklore attributes. Sometimes Wilde borrowed heavily from his mother's legends as in "The Fisherman and His Soul." Most of his stories, however, differed from Speranza's legends because her characters were usually one-dimensional and her concerns were primarily moralistic.

Wilde's stories also differ from his sources because they are cynical in tone. Wilde was a humanitarian; yet he understood that humanity can be selfish. The death of innocents, social injustice, and unhappy marriages frequently occur in his stories. Consequently, John Updike identifies the author's dark tone and, in his edited version of Wilde's tales, he wisely warns his young readers that "Oscar Wilde wrote in a time when grown men wrote very seriously for young readers."

Wilde's tone, however, helps to make his stories unique. He often reworked the writings of previous authors, as evidenced by his early poetry and drama (especially his famous *Salomé*). Yet, he was a master at making his retold stories seem original. Thus, Speranza's friend, the Comtesse de Bremont, asserted that Wilde was addicted to plagiarism, but stated that he "had the power to make old sayings and situations appear fresh and sparkling"; this is clearly the case with his fairy tales.

When Wilde was editor of *The Woman's World*, he acknowledged that he adored fairy tales for their imaginative quality (*WW*, 2, 221–24). For instance, he praised W. B. Yeats for gathering fairy and folk tales that were "a collection of purely imaginative work." Nevertheless, Wilde's own tales (as well as his novel *The Picture of Dorian Gray*) hover somewhere between fantasy and "reality" or, as Harold Bloom so eloquently states, they wander "in the regions of Lewis Carroll."

Wilde told the American novelist Amelie Chanler that his stories were not written for children (*L*, 237); later, he informed the editor of the *Pall Mall Gazette* that he did not write *A House of Pomegranates* "for the purpose of giving pleasure to the British child" (*L*, 301). Wilde concluded that in writing these stories he had about as much intention of pleasing the British child as he had of pleasing the British public (*L*, 302). In Wilde's words, his tales were an attempt to "mirror modern life in a form remote from reality—to deal with modern problems in a mode that is ideal" (*L*, 237). This is exactly what he did by identifying the topical issue that inhumane and unreciprocated relationships are destructive.

. . . To summarize, Wilde wrote fiction, in part, to show that love is frequently unreciprocated because idealized lovers are often inhumane. Certainly this was the case with his parents' marriage as well as his relationship with Lord Alfred Douglas. The scenarios of Wilde's tales question why people idealize their lovers and unduly sacrifice for them. Ultimately, Wilde's stories ennoble the idealizer and therefore enabled him to validate Speranza's inordinately altruistic treatment of Sir William.

Wilde always wanted to be popular, even though his readership included the sexually repressed thinkers of nineteenth-century England. Thus, the fairy-tale genre enabled him to affirm the naturalness of homosexual relationships because it was a "safe" medium in which to proclaim such a liberal idea.

Wilde shared Speranza's notion that fairy tales help to explain "reality," and he recognized that children are frequently more perceptive than adults. Certainly they are often less narrow-minded because they believe rather than judge. In the conclusion of "The Priest's Soul," Speranza asks,

> What is the use of going so far to learn when the wisest man in all Ireland did not know if he had a soul till he was near losing it; and was only saved at last through the simple belief of a little child?

Wilde echoes his mother because his tales acknowledge the profundity of childlike beliefs. His "simple" belief that both homosexual and heterosexual relationships should be partnerships is profound. Nevertheless, partnership was lacking in his parents' union as well as his own marriage to Constance and his relationship with Lord Alfred Douglas.

In his plays, Wilde continued the theme that heterosexual marriages are often unreciprocated. Moreover, Speranza's presence is evident in Wilde's dramas because the plots frequently involve the actions of a self-sacrificing mother who is perceived to be a wayward Bohemian.

Source: Patrick M. Horan, "1888–1891: Wilde's Stories, Fairy Tales, and Novel: The Nature of Love," in *The Importance of Being Paradoxical: Maternal Presence in the Works of Oscar Wilde*, Fairleigh Dickinson University Press, 1997, pp. 75–92.

SOURCES

Albert, John, O. C. S. O., "The Christ of Oscar Wilde," in *Critical Essays on Oscar Wilde*, edited by Regenia Gagnier, G. K. Hall, 1991, p. 241.

Arata, Stephen, "Oscar Wilde and Jesus Christ," in *Wilde Writings: Contextual Conditions*, edited by Joseph Bristow, University of Toronto Press, 2003, pp. 255–57, 262–64.

Bilton, Karen T., Review of *Fairy Tales of Oscar Wilde*, illustrated by P. Craig Russell, in *School Library Journal*, Vol. 50, No. 11, November 2004, p. 153.

Bristow, Joseph, Introduction to *Wilde Writings: Contextual Conditions*, edited by Joseph Bristow, University of Toronto Press, 2003, p. 338.

Calloway, Stephen, "Wilde and the Dandyism of the Senses," in *The Cambridge Companion to Oscar Wilde*, edited by Peter Raby, Cambridge University Press, 1997, pp. 34–54.

Ericksen, Donald H., *Oscar Wilde*, Twayne's English Authors Series No. 211, Twayne Publishers, 1977, p. 60.

Gagnier, Regenia, ed., Introduction to *Critical Essays on Oscar Wilde*, G. K. Hall, 1991, pp. 6–7.

———, "Wilde and the Victorians," in *The Cambridge Companion to Oscar Wilde*, edited by Peter Raby, Cambridge University Press, 1997, pp. 18, 20, 27–28.

Holland, Merlin, "Biography and the Art of Lying," in *The Cambridge Companion to Oscar Wilde*, edited by Peter Raby, Cambridge University Press, 1997, pp. 3–17.

Kohl, Norbert, *Oscar Wilde: The Works of a Conformist Rebel*, translated by David Henry Wilson, Cambridge University Press, 1989, pp. 49–67.

MacDonald, Ruth, Review of *The Nightingale and the Rose*, illustrated by Freire Wright and Michael Foreman, in *School Library Journal*, Vol. 28, No. 10, August 1982, p. 109.

McCormack, Jerusha, "Wilde's Fiction(s)," in *The Cambridge Companion to Oscar Wilde*, edited by Peter Raby, Cambridge University Press, 1997, p. 107.

Wilde, Oscar, *De Profundis*, Project Gutenberg, 2007, http://www.gutenberg.org/files/921/921-h/921-h.htm (accessed August 15, 2014).

———, *The Importance of Being Earnest*, in *The Complete Illustrated Stories, Plays and Poems of Oscar Wilde*, Chancellor Press, 1991, p. 503.

———, "The Nightingale and the Rose," in *The Complete Illustrated Stories, Plays and Poems of Oscar Wilde*, Chancellor Press, 1991, pp. 163–67.

———, "The Soul of Man under Socialism," Project Gutenberg, 2003, http://www.gutenberg.org/cache/epub/1017/pg1017.txt (accessed August 16, 2014).

FURTHER READING

Andersen, Hans Christian, *The Annotated Hans Christian Andersen*, edited by Maria Tatar, W. W. Norton, 2007.
> This collection of Andersen's beloved tales and Tatar's fascinating notes on Andersen and the Victorian and European authors he knew, as well as comments by contemporary writers like Ursula Le Guin, enhance understanding of a major influence on Wilde's fairy tales.

Ellman, Richard, *Oscar Wilde*, Knopf, 1988.
> Considered the definitive biography of Wilde, this book won the Pulitzer Prize and was the basis of the 1997 film *Wilde*.

Mikhail, E. H., ed., *Oscar Wilde: Interviews and Recollections*, 2 vols., Macmillan, 1979.
> All known interviews are included, as well as recollections by various friends and authors. The volume establishes Wilde's balanced wit and humor.

Quintus, John Allen, "The Moral Prerogative in Oscar Wilde: A Look at the Fairy Tales," in *Virginia Quarterly Review*, Vol. 53, No. 4, Fall 1977, pp. 708–17.
> Quintus shows the moral side of Wilde, to correct the image of the unrepentant rebel, through his interpretation of the fairy tales.

SUGGESTED SEARCH TERMS

Oscar Wilde

The Nightingale and the Rose

The Happy Prince and Other Tales

fairy tale

literary AND fairy tale

aestheticism

Decadence

fin de siècle

Victorian England

De Profundis AND Wilde

Parker's Back

FLANNERY O'CONNOR

1965

"Parker's Back" is one of Flannery O'Connor's best and best-known stories. It is typical of the southern gothic style and illustrates O'Connor's theory of the grotesque. It tells the story of an ordinary man who is seized out of his everyday life by a mystical experience that impels him on a journey to redemption. He has an eye-catching tattoo etched on his skin and endures a dramatic transformation with strong religious echoes. The story was published in O'Connor's posthumous collection *Everything That Rises Must Converge* (1965) and can be found in *The Complete Stories* (1971) and the Library of America's edition of her *Collected Works* (1988).

AUTHOR BIOGRAPHY

Mary Flannery O'Connor was born on March 25, 1925, in Savannah, Georgia, to Edward F. O'Connor, a real-estate broker, and his wife Regina (née Cline), both members of socially prominent families. O'Connor first gained national recognition when she was six years old, as a pet chicken she had trained to walk backward was featured in a Pathé newsreel (the equivalent of a network evening news broadcast today). Her father died of lupus, a genetic disease, when she was fifteen. O'Connor attended the Peabody Laboratory School, a progressive

American writer and essayist Flannery O'Connor (© *Mondadori via Getty Images*)

high school that largely allowed students to design their own curricula, with hers centering on literature. She also drew cartoons for the school paper. She considered becoming a professional cartoonist, but she was discouraged from this by the fact that her teachers did not consider such a career a serious endeavor and by rejections from the *New Yorker* and similar national publications. She took a degree in social science from the Georgia State College for Women and an MFA from the prestigious Iowa Writers' Workshop. She had success publishing short stories in academic journals like the *Sewanee Review* but needed to gain acceptance from mainstream publications to support herself as a writer. While living with Robert Fitzgerald—one of the twentieth century's greatest translators of Greek and Latin literature—and his wife in Redding, Connecticut, between 1949 and 1951, O'Connor wrote her first novel, *Wise Blood*, which was published successfully in 1952.

Already in 1951, however, O'Connor herself was diagnosed with lupus. She returned to her family's farm, Andalusia, in Midgeville, Georgia, outside of Savannah, where she lived for the next fourteen years, far longer than her doctors expected her to survive. O'Connor took up the hobby of raising exotic fowl, including peacocks, emus, and ostriches. Especially after the publication of her short-story collection *A*

Good Man Is Hard to Find (1955), whose title story is her best-known work, O'Connor was recognized as a leading southern writer and an exponent of the style known as southern gothic. Given her fame, she was frequently invited to give public speeches, which she usually devoted to theoretical analysis of the southern gothic and of Catholic literature. These talks and other writings would be collected in the posthumous volume *Mystery and Manners: Occasional Prose* (1969). She published her second novel, *The Violent Bear It Away*, in 1960.

O'Connor died of lupus on August 3, 1964, at the county hospital near her farm. She was racing against death to finish her second short-story collection, *Everything That Rises Must Converge*, which was published in 1965 and many of whose stories deal with racial and other issues in southern culture. "Parker's Back," included in that volume, was her last story, which she worked on until her final hospitalization. Other posthumous works collected her letters, in *The Habit of Being* (1969); her book reviews, in *The Presence of Grace* (1983); and the contents of *A Prayer Journal* (2013), from her time as a student in Iowa. *The Complete Stories* (1971), an anthology of all her short stories, won the National Book Award.

PLOT SUMMARY

"Parker's Back" begins as Parker and his wife, Sarah Ruth, are sitting on their porch in the evening. As she snaps beans, Parker glumly looks on and recalls the events of his life.

Theirs is an unlikely marriage since Sarah Ruth is a Low Church fundamentalist Christian—that is, she forsakes the trappings of organized religion—while Parker has no faith and no interest in religion. He works as a farmhand for an elderly widow, but he leads his wife to believe that his employer is a voluptuous beauty half in love with him, in an (unsuccessful) effort to torment Sarah Ruth with jealousy.

Parker was a womanizer who had never intended to marry, but one day his truck breaks down in front of a house, and to attract the attention of the woman he senses watching him (Sarah Ruth), he pretends to hurt his hand while working on the engine and begins cursing loudly and outrageously. Her religious sensibilities offended, the woman suddenly attacks him with a broom. The one thing that distinguishes Parker is the fact that nearly his whole body is covered with tattoos. Sarah Ruth is disgusted when she sees the ones on his arms. He has cultivated tattoos because he was deeply impressed when he was fourteen years old and saw a tattooed man in a carnival sideshow. He soon started getting his own tattoos and found that the kind of woman he liked was attracted to them.

A few years after seeing the tattooed man, Parker's mother took him to a revival meeting, but he ran away rather than go into the church, and he kept on running to join the navy. Parker got a new tattoo in each port. Over the years, he switched from inanimate objects to flowers and animals. After five years in the navy, he went AWOL and was discharged after spending some nine months in jail. He worked odd jobs, mainly to pay for tattoos, until meeting Sarah Ruth.

Parker begins courting her by stopping by her family's house to give them gifts of the fruit he has purchased in order to resell. He feels the need to seduce her in order to prove he is superior to her. Sarah Ruth's father is a preacher traveling the revival circuit and so is rarely at home. Sarah Ruth considers ordinary church service to be idolatrous. Parker thinks he is losing his mind, but he feels more and more strongly attracted to her. He has always gone by his initials, O.E., but she worms out of him his full name, Obadiah Elihue. When he attempts to seduce her, she makes clear that nothing will happen until they are married.

Parker swears never to see her again, but they are nevertheless soon married, in a civil rather than a religious ceremony. Even then, unfulfilled, each morning he affirms that he will leave and never come back, but each night he returns to her. Sarah Ruth remains disgusted by his tattoos. The only part of Parker's body lacking tattoos is his back, since he would not himself be able to see them there, except by standing awkwardly between two mirrors. Parker takes a steadier job to support his family after Sarah Ruth becomes pregnant. He begins to try to torment her with the idea of having an affair with his employer, but she remains unfazed. Parker thinks that if he gets the right tattoo, he will at last be able to make an impression on his wife.

A few days later, Parker is driving a tractor through his employer's field, considering the problem of his next tattoo. Distracted, he runs the tractor into a tree. The tractor explodes into flames, but Parker is thrown clear, losing his shoes in the process. While flying through the air, he hears his own voice call out unbidden, "GOD ABOVE!" Without any conscious thought or intention, Parker runs to his truck and drives away, past his own house, to the nearest city, fifty miles away. He finally arrives at his regular tattoo artist. Parker asks to look through the sample book with religious images, since he wants a tattoo of God. He eventually sees a Byzantine-style mosaic image of Christ and flips past it, but the ensuing silence tells him to go back to the image. Although it is late in the day, Parker insists that the artist begin right away, and indeed he starts tattooing the image on Parker's back. He estimates that the whole job will take two days. The session ends at midnight, and Parker spends the night in a Christian mission shelter, where he is given a pair of shoes. All night Parker tells himself that once the tattoo is finished, he will never look at it and will dismiss the whole affair as an episode of insanity and go back to his usual way of life.

The next day the artist, while working, asks Parker if he wants the tattoo because he underwent a religious conversion. Parker maintains he has no use for being saved and merely wants it to impress his religious wife. The artist finishes at the end of the day. He makes Parker look at the tattoo against his will. Taken aback, Parker buys a bottle of whiskey and drinks himself to intoxication in a few minutes. He then goes to a nearby pool hall where some of his friends hang out. One greets him by slapping him on the back. He tells the man not to since he just got a fresh tattoo there, and the friends want to see it. He refuses, but they grab him and pull his shirt up. They are all shocked into a long silence when they see the new image. They too suspect he has found religion, but Parker denies it. They disagree about it so strenuously that Parker fights with them, and they throw him out of the pool hall. Parker lingers in the alley through the night.

Before dawn, Parker drives back to his own house to find the door locked. His wife, apparently infuriated by his absence, refuses to recognize him and disingenuously asks who is there. At first he says he is O.E., but then he says his full name, and upon turning and seeing light branching up from the rising sun, he is seized by a sort of mystical ecstasy. At that moment, Sarah Ruth opens the door. She says that she had a long talk with the woman Parker works for, discovering that she is not the seductress Parker made her out to be, and besides reporting that, she demands payment for the cost of replacing the tractor. Parker at once shows her the new tattoo, but Sarah Ruth does not recognize what the image represents. When Parker tells her it is God, she denies that God could have a human appearance—his face cannot be seen, since he is a spirit. When he explains it is only a picture of God, Sarah Ruth loudly denounces him as an idolator and attacks him (again) with her broom, striking him across the back and raising welts on the face of the image of Jesus. Parker makes his way to the shelter of the pecan tree, where Sarah Ruth spies him weeping like a baby.

CHARACTERS

Mr. Cates

Sarah Ruth's father is a fundamentalist preacher. He is constantly away from home traveling on the revival circuit. He does not seem to derive much income from his work, leaving his family to welcome the slight charity that Parker provides them.

Mrs. Cates

Sarah Ruth's mother is not a profoundly developed character. She has a large number of children to provide for from very limited means and welcomes Parker's attentions to her eldest daughter as a financial boon to the family.

Large Man

The unnamed large man in the red and black checkered shirt is the friend of Parker's who first greets him in the pool hall. He appears little different from Parker, or at least Parker's old self, seeming to hold religion in contempt as something unmanly, or at least something not to be taken seriously. Allegorically, he and Parker's other friends in the pool hall take on the role of the soldiers who torture Jesus in his prison cell the night before his crucifixion.

Old Woman

The old woman whom Parker works for owns a large and relatively prosperous farm, but must hire men like Parker to work it for her. She is probably a widow. She is constantly critical of Parker's work, meanwhile underpaying him. Parker represents her as a beautiful young romantic rival in an effort to torment Sarah Ruth with jealousy, although Parker's wife learns the truth when the old woman finally visits Parker's house to demand payment for the destroyed tractor.

Ordinary

The Ordinary is the title of the county clerk who marries Parker and Sarah Ruth. They have a civil rather than a religious wedding since Sarah Ruth considers organized religion to be corrupt, while Parker claims he has no use for it.

Betty Jean Parker

Parker's mother is present in the story only briefly, when she tries to take him to a revival meeting to be saved. She seems to play no very important role in Parker's affections. His father is never mentioned in the story, nor does the reader receive any information about how Parker's parents came to choose his rather flamboyant biblical names.

Obadiah Elihue "O.E." Parker

Parker, generally known by his initials O.E., is the protagonist of "Parker's Back." Of Parker's biblical names, *Obadiah* means "servant of Yahweh," while *Elihue*, more commonly spelled *Elihu* in English, means "he is God's." Both names are used of several characters in the Bible. Perhaps the Obadiah alluded to by O'Connor is the steward of King Ahab who protects a group of righteous prophets at the cost of his own fortune (1 Kings 18:3–4), who has been identified (quite improbably) with the author of the book of Obadiah in Jewish and Christian tradition. O'Connor's Elihue may be the friend of Job who argues that God is capable of making even the righteous suffer to protect them from the human propensity to sin (Job 32–37).

Aside from his tattoos, Parker is an ordinary man, with no particular education, status, or importance and no particular religion. He is neither good nor bad: capable of acts of charity (the gifts of food to the Cates family) but also capable of using them for his own ends (courting Sarah Ruth). It is precisely for this reason, perhaps, that O'Connor has chosen him to become a type of Christ in "Parker's Back." Once he is marked as Christ by having the deity's image tattooed on his back, he symbolically relives the last hours of Jesus's life as he is tortured and crucified, until he is finally born again, left crying in the darkness like a baby.

For O'Connor, salvation is not something that automatically happens to the Christian, not a matter of saying a certain formula and accepting Jesus, but rather is a matter of becoming Christlike. God became human through the incarnation, and the human must become divine by re-creating that point of contact. Just as Christ is both fully man and fully God according to the Nicene Creed, the Christian does not lose his humanity in his salvation, but rather his physical, human identity becomes seamlessly joined to a larger divine identity. The Christian is an arabesque of humanity and divinity. Parker's whole life has been aimless and meaningless because he has been only human. But he has had his vision of the divine-human arabesque, received upon viewing the tattooed man, to guide him. That vision grew like a seed within him until he finally flourishes in his new Christlike identity. It comes upon him like a thief in the night without his ever understanding it, until the moment of transformation.

Sarah Ruth Parker (née Cates)

Sarah Ruth is Parker's wife. She is a thin, remarkably plain-looking woman. She is essentially the antagonist of "Parker's Back." If Parker's theophoric biblical names help to define his identity, Sarah Ruth's names seem to have been assigned to her by O'Connor in mockery. Sarah and Ruth figure in the Old Testament as the ancestors of Isaac and David and in their beauty and true faithfulness seem to be the opposite of O'Connor's Sarah Ruth.

The authoritarian figure of Sarah Ruth seems at first to represent Parker's religious goal, at least insofar as his conscious efforts are concerned. But her religion is degraded, as O'Connor confirmed in calling her a "heretic" in one of her letters from 1964, and Sarah Ruth rejects the salvific validity of Parker's conversion. She is not able to understand true Christianity. She rejects the church and imagines that

she can in some sense re-create primitive Christianity based entirely on the Bible. This is a genuine and important tendency in much southern religion, and is generally referred to as Low Church, but is highly antithetical to O'Connor's Catholicism. Remarkably, Sarah Ruth thinks of God as being a spirit who cannot even be represented in anthropomorphic form, such that human representations of God are equivalent to idolatry. This view, however, would entail a rejection of the incarnation and the Trinity, and is heretical by any modern Christian standard; the implication of Sarah Ruth's statement that a traditional depiction of Christ is not an image of God is that Jesus must not have been God in any true sense. This is the Arian heresy (named for Arius, its third-century proponent) and transports her back to a world of anti-Trinitarian doctrine that flourished in late antiquity but has been rejected as false for over fifteen hundred years.

O'Connor would have required a whole novel to unpack her theology in full detail. She had no interest in providing such an explanation, but she clearly felt that the rejection of Jesus's humanity—the rejection of Christians' use of the incarnation of God in a visceral, physical, all-too-human body as a bridge to finding salvation in God—was a fault of modern American spirituality. She revealed as much in her 1964 letter about "Parker's Back." Sarah Ruth, appropriately then, takes on the role of the soldiers who scourge Jesus as he carries the cross through the streets of Jerusalem. Her false beliefs do far more damage to Christianity than physical blows ever could.

Tattoo Artist

The unnamed tattoo artist inscribes the Byzantine Christ on Parker's back and was also responsible for several others of Parker's tattoos. His attitude to his work is that of a serious craftsman. He has taken advantage of his baldness to tattoo his own scalp (using a series of mirrors to see the work area) as an advertisement of his skill. Although it is not a main theme of the story, he witnesses the misogyny of American southern culture in the 1950s, easily accepting Parker's explanation of having gotten married as accounting for his disheveled and diminished appearance (he at first thought Parker must have served a jail sentence but sees marriage as a comparable hardship) and for his desire for the Christ tattoo as a means of winning over his wife.

Tattooed Man

Parker saw the tattooed man in a circus sideshow when he was fourteen. Although the reader learns nothing of his character, the lush, organic arabesque of his tattoos represents for Parker a theological vision tantamount to Eden and salvation. Parker comes to grips with the overwhelming impression this made on his young sensibilities only over the course of the entire story.

THEMES

Grotesque

O'Connor explains something of her theory of the grotesque in her lecture "Some Aspects of the Grotesque in Southern Fiction." Somewhat paradoxically, she suggests that it is a kind of realism, but a realism focused on the forgotten and the excluded:

> We find that connections which we would expect in the customary kind of realism have been ignored, that there are strange skips and gaps which anyone trying to describe manners and customs would certainly not have left. Yet the characters in these novels are alive in spite of these things. They have an inner coherence, if not always a coherence to their social framework.

The grotesque character is, in O'Connor's terms, a freak, someone who cannot be explained within the ordinary framework of society because he is not part of that framework. She is quick to supply an alternative framework which makes sense of the grotesque:

> Whenever I'm asked why Southern writers particularly have a penchant for writing about freaks, I say it is because we are still able to recognize one. To be able to recognize a freak, you have to have some conception of the whole man, and in the South the general conception of man is still, in the main, theological.

In other words, the grotesque is that which can only be explained in a religious framework, which in the 1950s was already becoming peculiar to southern culture. Parker, with his mismatched tattoos, is certainly a freak in what O'Connor calls the comic-grotesque tradition,

TOPICS FOR FURTHER STUDY

- Search the Internet for religious tattoos and make a multimedia presentation with interpretative commentary for your class. What do the various symbols mean?

- Write an essay comparing the grotesque and other southern gothic themes in "Parker's Back" and William Faulkner's story "A Rose for Emily."

- Tattooing is an ancient and popular art form in Japan. Its history and culture have been the subject of scholarly investigation such as *Irezumi: The Pattern of Dermatography in Japan* (1982), by W. R. van Gulik, and *A History of Japanese Body Suit Tattooing* (2006), by Mark Poysden and Marco Bratt. Using these or similar sources, write an essay comparing tattooing in Japan and its presentation in "Parker's Back."

- The carnival sideshow is a popular setting for literature. Read a book from the *Cirque du Freak* series, by Darren Shan. Drawing on this background, write a story imaginatively constructing the life of the tattooed man who is such an influence on Parker in "Parker's Back."

but his actions, which are senseless to those around him and only meaningful in light of his new mystical inner direction, are what make him into an outcast. Parker becomes a Christlike figure, and his friends and his wife reject him by scourging him as Jesus was scourged. It is not hard to perceive that just as Parker becomes a type of Jesus, Jesus is the type of O'Connor's freak, a social outcast whose actions make no sense in the world and is therefore rejected by the world.

Christianity

O'Connor was, by her admission, even more a Catholic than a southern writer. It is hardly surprising, then, that she was deeply influenced by the leading Catholic intellectual of her day, the Jesuit priest Pierre Teilhard de Chardin. The title of her last short-story collection, *Everything That Rises Must Converge*, in which "Parker's Back" was first published, is a quotation from his work expressing his central idea.

Historians and physical scientists generally think of history as an unfolding process whose future course, while dependent on the past, is neither predetermined nor moving in any particular direction. Christianity, however, has a doctrine of eschatology which teaches that history is moving in a very definite direction, toward the end of the physical world and the return of Christ at the end of time, an event which is always believed to be in the immediate future.

Teilhard de Chardin's main effort in his own philosophical writings was to selectively use the results of scientific research to argue that history was in fact moving toward a definite end. This was not necessarily the literal mythological last day described in the book of Revelation, but something he called, in *The Future of Man*, the *Omega point*, which he described as "a divine center of convergence." He thought that human consciousness was evolving (an idea popular in science fiction of the 1950s and 1960s, such as Arthur C. Clarke's novel *Childhood's End* and the film *Children of the Damned*) and would finally become part of the godhead, a sort of scientifical equivalent of the final redemption of humankind. Teilhard de Chardin found evidence for this conception in the idea that mystical experience was on the increase in the 1950s, although without offering any demonstration of this assertion.

"Parker's Back" certainly can be read merely in light of traditional Christianity. When Parker first meets Sarah Ruth, he has a vision of her as an angel even while she beats him with a broom. This recalls the expulsion from the Garden of Eden and the fall from grace of humankind. Later he achieves redemption, when he whispers his first name and the arabesque of the life in the Garden animates his soul, leading to her again beating him with a broom, scourging him as the Roman soldiers did Jesus. In this way Parker's experience encapsulates in itself the entire drama of salvation, from the Fall to Christ's

Parker is fascinated by a tattooed man he sees at a fair. (© GOLFX | Shutterstock.com)

redemptive sacrifice. In turn, the sudden irruption of mystical revelation into Parker's consciousness, at the time of the tractor crash and again later in his selection of the Byzantine Christ tattoo, certainly has a Teilhardian flavor. One can see the weeping Parker at the end of the story as an infant of the new Teilhardian mystical race.

STYLE

Southern Gothic
The gothic tradition in literature goes back to eighteenth-century Europe, rising with the novel. Hallmarks of this tradition include, among other things, explorations of taboo themes and unsettling motifs: the supernatural, mystery, darkness, haunted mansions with hidden passages, family secrets, madness, incest—in other words, the gothic explores the darker

side of human nature, the parts of themselves people keep hidden from others. The style has a number of commonplace tropes, such as ruined castles, ancient blood feuds, and young women in peril of their chastity. The gothic is the romantic vision of the Middle Ages and takes its name from the common appellation of that era, as in Gothic cathedrals. It concentrates on the freakish and the horrible—dwarves, scenes of torture, frightful animals such as rats, and so forth.

With the establishment of America, many of the older European gothic traditions were continued with a few new components; this came to be called American gothic. The three most famous American gothic writers were Nathaniel Hawthorne, Edgar Allan Poe, and Herman Melville. One of the distinctions Hawthorne established was a reaction to the romantic idealization of nature; he established a tension between civilization and nature with nature representative of the unknown and of mystery. When a character in a Hawthorne tale leaves the city or town and goes into the woods or the garden, the reader pretty quickly perceives that the character is going to encounter something horrible rather than find solace and understanding in nature.

After defeat in the Civil War, the South suffered a crisis of identity from which it never fully recovered, giving rise to a distinctly southern gothic tradition that includes and expands the themes of the gothic in general along with American gothic themes as well, but with a uniquely southern character. Much Reconstruction and post-Reconstruction literature concerns itself with southern identity, and one often sees the southern literary persona as fragmented, mirroring the southern sense of identity crisis. A longing for the past is also a hallmark of southern gothic literature, a desired return to the glory days of the South, when every person knew and understood his or her place in the social order turned upside down by the Civil War. One can see this in real life as well, in the membership of the Ku Klux Klan organization, with their outlandish titles such as Grand Wizard or Cyclops, their referring to themselves as knights, and their adopting Catholic penitential garb as their uniform. They are figures directly out of gothic romances fighting against modernity. In the

stories in *Everything That Rises Must Converge*, O'Connor address the South's past in the midst of the final breakdown of segregation that was underway during the 1960s. While this is not a main theme of "Parker's Back," Sarah Ruth represents the freakish and heretical character type that would fight against equality for southern blacks in the name of Christian virtue. The grotesque is the hallmark of the southern gothic, above all for O'Connor, and can be seen in the landscape of tattoos covering Parker's body as much as in the violence he suffers from his wife.

Narrative Voice

The narrative voice and its relationship to the characters is always an important element of O'Connor's fiction. Usually it offers a critique of the characters' actions and beliefs. But in "Parker's Back" Sarah Ruth plays this role, while the narrator is much nearer expressing Parker's thoughts and feelings.

In Medias Res

In medias res means "in the middle of things," or, in a story, in the middle of the plot. "Parker's Back" begins in the middle of the story, some months after Parker and Sarah Ruth's marriage. The story then proceeds with flashbacks of various temporal depth, describing Parker's life from the time he was fourteen years old and saw the tattooed man up to the present marked by the story's beginning. The remainder of the story is then a temporally continuous narrative proceeding from the tractor crash, a few days after the beginning, through Parker's last tattoo and his confrontation with Sarah Ruth.

HISTORICAL CONTEXT

Tattooing

In the ancient Near East, tattoos were used for various cultic and magical purposes. For this reason the Israelites were forbidden to bear any tattoos by biblical law: "Ye shall not... print any marks upon you" (Leviticus 19:28, King James Version). This is why Sarah Ruth considers Parker's tattoos to be idolatrous, and why, indeed, they seem to be an unlikely instrument of divine grace. But it is precisely

COMPARE & CONTRAST

- **1960s:** An initial review of "Parker's Back" notes that Parker's tattoos are part of the grotesque atmosphere of the story because tattooing is not in fashion.

  Today: More Americans have tattoos than at any time in history, and in many subcultures they are an important part of personal fashion.

- **1960s:** Church and big-tent meeting revivals are an important feature of American, especially southern, religious culture.

  Today: Evangelical Christianity is dominated by televangelism and megachurches, but traveling revivals still exist.

- **1960s:** Pool halls are an important part of lower- and middle-class life.

  Today: Pool halls still exist but have declined in number and social importance, replaced in part by video gaming.

---

their idolatrous quality that makes them grotesque from a Christian perspective and which attracts O'Connor's attention to them.

There are several ambiguous texts in the New Testament that may refer to tattoos. The best known of these is condemnatory. In the world described in the vision in the book of Revelation, the beast "causeth all, both small and great, rich and poor, free and bond, to receive a mark in their right hand, or in their foreheads: And that no man might buy or sell, save he that had the mark, or the name of the beast, or the number of his name" (Revelation 13:16–17, KJV). A tattoo would seem to be the only way that an individual could bear such a mark in his body. The number in question is 666, which is the numerological value of *Neron Kaisar*, the Greek title of the emperor Nero. But no such requirement was put in place in the Roman Empire, nor was there any use of tattoos in Roman religion, such as in the imperial cult. The biblical passage seems to mix themes from the real world in a weird conspiracy theory, perhaps combining the role of Nero as the first persecutor of Christians with the fact that worshippers of the Syrian goddess Atargatis would receive a tattoo on their hands as a sort of souvenir after a pilgrimage to her temple at Hierapolis.

A parallel with Atargatis worship is also sometimes suggested to explain another very unclear statement of the apostle Paul, when he claims, "From henceforth let no man trouble me: for I bear in my body the marks of the Lord Jesus" (Galatians 6:17, KJV). The New American Standard version is even more suggestive, with the wording "I bear on my body the brand-marks of Jesus," while other versions refer to "scars." However the wording may be, this passage at least comes much closer to being a possible model for Parker's Christ tattoo. Magicians would also validate their power by tattooing divine names and signs on themselves, and this practice may also be reflected in Revelation when Christ is described during his return: "And he hath on *his* vesture and on his thigh a name written, KING OF KINGS, AND LORD OF LORDS" (Revelation 19:16, KJV). In any case, Parker's salvation is certainly accomplished by the image of Jesus he has tattooed on his back and by his speaking his own theophoric names, so O'Connor is operating in the same thought world as the New Testament authors. For O'Connor, the tattoo of Christ is a symbol that flesh and spirit are inseparably joined, and that neither nature can be ignored, though Sarah Ruth heretically ignores the physical. Similarly, worshippers of the god Dionysus believed that they would be saved in the next life by bearing an amulet on which was written a formula expressing their participation in the divine.

While working, Parker becomes distracting by thinking about his next tattoo and crashes a tractor into a tree. (© Ollyy / Shutterstock.com)

CRITICAL OVERVIEW

O'Connor's exceptional literary talent was recognized in her lifetime, so serious analysis of "Parker's Back," published in her last short-story collection, *Everything That Rises Must Converge* (1965), began with the initial reviews. (Those cited here are reprinted in *Flannery O'Connor: The Contemporary Reviews*). Stanley Edgar Hyman, writing in the *New Leader* on May 10, 1965, already isolated the main themes in the story:

> Parker has a Byzantine mosaic of a staring Christ reproduced on his back. He is then literally *christophoric*, Christ-bearing, "witnessing for Jesus" on his hide. Under this coloration Parker is transformed and reborn, resuming the Old Testament names he has always concealed behind his initials, and suffering a Punch and Judy martyrdom as he passively allows his wife to punish his "idolatry" by beating him with a broom.

Hyman finds the story "simultaneously uproarious and deeply moving, and the metaphor of tattooing—bloody, painful, indelible; garish, out of fashion, ludicrous—for the burden of Redemption is uncanny and perfect, a true metaphysical conceit." While Hyman considers "Parker's Back" antithetical to the main body of O'Connor's work, the anonymous review in the *Savannah News* of May 23, 1965, relates its themes to O'Connor's larger purpose:

> There seems to be a common conviction that she was concerned with the power of grace. The very violence involves compassion, and in the horrendous portrayal of the intractability of man, it is frequently the tragic plight of the non-violent which stays with us to haunt.

Later, more considered analyses of O'Connor, like Marshall Bruce Gentry's *Flannery O'Connor's Religion of the Grotesque*, can only refine these insights. Gentry notes, "The comic elements and religious message of 'Parker's

Back' have led many critics to name this story O'Connor's best." He agrees that it is unique among O'Connor's writing, not because the protagonist's unconscious uses the grotesque as his means of redemption, but because it is the narrator who communicates the personal sense of this redemption, rather than adopting a more neutral tone, as if the narrator were Parker's unconscious. Gentry makes explicit what Hyman implies, that Parker becomes a type of Christ.

Irwin Howard Streight's important article in the *Flannery O'Connor Bulletin* for 1993–1994 sees Parker's tattoos, in distinction to Parker's wife's view of them as idolatry, as a signification of the incarnation of the logos that is the theological basis of the Gospel of John. Joanne Halleran McMullen, in her O'Connor study *Writing against God*, reads against O'Connor's assertion that Sarah Ruth is heretical in relating the commonly expressed opinion that Sarah Ruth is the instrument of Parker's salvation, since it is her violence that martyrs him like Christ.

Among third-generation critics of O'Connor, Sue Brannan Walker, in her "Flannery O'Connor's 'The Temple of the Holy Ghost' and 'Parker's Back' as Dermatology/Theology," interrogates O'Connor's work for subjects of postmodern interest. She finds in O'Connor's use of the grotesque a mask for the expression of her concerns about her lupus, in the same way that Parker's tattoos both conceal and reveal his unconscious desire for redemption, a view which never occurred to earlier scholars.

CRITICISM

Rita M. Brown

Brown is an English professor. In the following essay, she examines the psychological and theological dimensions of "Parker's Back."

Although not the protagonist of "Parker's Back," Sarah Ruth, presenting an image of Christianity by which Parker is both attracted and repelled, plays a driving role in the plot. Sarah Ruth's personality is an easily recognizable type, but one for which there is no generally used English term.

This personality type is described in its political dimension in Richard Hofstadter's

WHAT DO I READ NEXT?

- "A View of the Woods" (1957) is another southern gothic story of O'Connor's which views the modern world as at odds with salvation. It is also contained in *Everything That Rises Must Converge* (1965) and later collections.

- *Wise Blood* (1952) is O'Connor's first novel and perhaps her greatest work. As with most of her writing, it deals with alienation and redemption. John Huston made an outstanding film adaptation of it in 1979.

- O'Connor's *The Violent Bear It Away* (1960) is her second novel. Perhaps her most Catholic work, it concerns a teenaged boy trying to escape his destiny as a prophet.

- *Flannery O'Connor* (1986), edited by Harold Bloom, is a collection of older criticism of O'Connor especially intended for students.

- The essays in *Inside the Church of Flannery O'Connor: Sacrament, Sacramental, and the Sacred in Her Fiction* (2007), edited by Joanne Halleran McMullen and Jon Parrish Peede, concentrate on the Catholic aspects of O'Connor's work.

- Japanese manga, like the series *Yu Yu Hakusho* (1990–1994; English translation, 2003–2010), often use supernatural elements from Japanese folklore, mixing them with the modern world in a way analogous to the gothic.

- *Beautiful Creatures* (2009), by Kami Garcia and Margaret Stohl, is a young-adult novel that uses elements of the southern gothic.

"The Paranoid Style in American Politics" and in its psychological dimension in Erich Fromm's *The Anatomy of Human Destructiveness*, where Fromm points out that there is a conventional German term for it, *Schnüffler*, which means "sniffer." Fromm and Hofstadter agree that this personality type is important because of its role in popular support for

> PARKER, HOWEVER, BECAUSE HE SEES
> THAT A WHOLE HUMAN BEING IS COMPOSED
> OF FLESH AS WELL AS SPIRIT, IS OPEN TO
> REDEMPTION AND THE COMPLETION OF
> SALVATION HISTORY IN THE FUTURE."

fascism and other right-wing political movements. Fromm finds the basis of the *Schnüffler* in what Freud called the death instinct. Every animal, including every human being, has a life instinct, to expend energy on procreation and to risk its own life in that cause, but also a death instinct, to conserve energy and preserve its own stasis above all. In the *Schnüffler*, which Fromm more clinically calls the necrophilous personality type, the death instinct is predominant. The *Schnüffler* has perhaps felt the exuberant impulse toward sexual freedom and all of life's pleasures, but has repressed such desires in favor of the longing for stasis and the denial of pleasure. The repressed desires are thus expressed in the form of condemnation of anything that might give rise to pleasure. The personality type can be seen in certain common traits expressed in everyday life, such as cold deadness in conversation, a preference for dark colors, especially black, and an obsession with bad odors (i.e., the odor of decay), for example in complaining about them when they do not exist. According to Fromm,

> their fascination with bad odors frequently gives such persons the appearance of being "sniffers."...Not infrequently this sniffing tendency even shows in their facial expression. Many necophilous individuals give the impression of constantly smelling a bad odor. Anybody who studies the many pictures of Hitler, for instance, can easily discover this sniffing expression in his face.

More importantly for the *Schnüffler*, the bygone past is surrounded by a holy aura, and anything exciting and new is deemed an offense against the natural order. Destruction is preferred over creation, force and violence over reason and cooperation, and the nonliving over the living.

The narrative voice of "Parker's Back" clearly marks out Sarah Ruth as a *Schnüffler*:

> In addition to her other bad qualities, she was forever sniffing up sin. She did not smoke or dip, drink whiskey, use bad language or paint her face...Her being against color, it was the more remarkable that she had married him.... At other times he had a suspicion that she actually liked everything she said she didn't.

Sarah Ruth also opposes everything new, because it is new. Even in the story's setting in the 1960s, she considers the automobile to be a modern device she has no use for. She believes in the most conservative possible type of religion, even rejecting the idea of a church with a congregation meeting on Sundays because it does not reflect the usages of the most primitive form of Christianity. For Sarah Ruth, all art is idolatry, something to be rejected on religious grounds. Predictably, then, her response to Parker confronting her with an image of Christ, after she gets over her denial that it even is a depiction of Christ, is to make a violent attack against him. Her perverted version of Christianity leads her to the most un-Christian response, reenacting the scourging of Jesus by Roman soldiers.

In a letter of July 25, 1964, addressed to "A.," O'Connor says flatly that "Sarah Ruth was the heretic." Because she is a *Schnüffler*, she can only privilege the past. She hates the sin that was imposed on humankind by the fall from Eden, but she cannot embrace the redemption that looks to the future. Parker, however, because he sees that a whole human being is composed of flesh as well as spirit, is open to redemption and the completion of salvation history in the future.

Viewed in the same terms as Sarah Ruth's necrophilia, Parker's redemption is a journey from death to life. He begins his obsessive tattooing with inanimate objects, particularly instruments of violence like rifles and cannons, but shifts over time to animals, symbols of life, and finally ends with an image of Christ. His original inspiration is seeing a tattooed man in a circus, whose tattoos are notably alive: "the arabesque of men and beasts and flowers on his skin appeared to have a subtle motion of its own." This becomes Parker's ideal, which he tries to emulate on his own body. But he fails miserably. Parker adds tattoos piecemeal, getting a new one whenever the novelty of the last one wears off, with no overarching scheme or meaning: "The effect was not of one intricate arabesque of colors but of something haphazard and botched." The repeated word *arabesque* is important. It means an intricate, interwoven design, something that the tattooed man achieved but which Parker cannot.

Yet Parker does create an arabesque, though in a quite different way, after he receives the Christ tattoo. When he comes home to show the Christ image to Sarah Ruth, she refuses to admit him to the house. She pretends not to recognize him, calling out to him to identify himself, as if she thought her husband were a stranger. He repeatedly identifies himself by his initials, O.E., the name he usually goes by, but finally calls himself by his proper name: "'Obadiah,' he whispered and all at once he felt the light pouring through him, turning his spider web soul into a perfect arabesque of colors, a garden of trees and birds and beasts." When he calls himself Obadiah, which in Hebrew means a servant of Yahweh, Parker accepts his new, or perhaps his true, identity. That is the moment at which he is saved in religious terms. His salvation is expressed through the internal arabesque. His soul had been a spider web, a brutal and animalistic means of acquisition, a grotesque expression of monstrous life feeding on death, but it is transformed into the whole pattern of life, the Garden of Eden as it had been intended before the Fall.

Parker's salvation is marked by his becoming a type of Christ. Since his salvation is presented as a journey, it begins with small signs. The earliest event narrated in "Parker's Back" is his encounter with the tattooed man in the circus. The arabesque printed on the man's body alerts Parker to the possibility of salvation, but he denies that it is necessary and runs away from any conventional path to redemption in the church. His fallen condition is confirmed when Sarah Ruth beats him with a broom to punish him for blaspheming. She seems to him something like the angel driving Adam and Eve from Eden with a flaming sword: "Parker's vision was so blurred that for an instant he thought he had been attacked by some creature from above, a giant hawk-eyed angel wielding a hoary weapon. As his sight cleared, he saw before him a tall raw-boned girl with a broom." His redemption begins when he crashes a tractor into a tree. During the accident he does not take the lord's name in vain, as

he did when he pretended to hurt his hand, but invokes God legitimately, shouting out "GOD ABOVE!" He does not consciously choose to do so, but rather the narrator says that Parker heard his own voice utter the cry, as if he were inspired by some external, or internal, force. When he is thrown off the tractor, his shoes fly off and catch fire, and he spends the rest of the day barefoot, only getting new shoes when he spends the night in a Christian mission ministering to the homeless. In the Middle Ages, regular clergy often went barefoot as a mortification, but also in imitation of the poverty of Christ. Parker's reaction to the irruption of grace into his life is to get another tattoo, but this time a religious one. His choice is a portrait of Christ in the Byzantine style (often said to be Christ Pantocrator by commentators, although O'Connor does not mention that particular iconographic type).

After Parker gets the tattoo, his life begins to parallel the last day of Jesus's life. He goes to the local pool hall, where his friends pull up his shirt and mock him for getting a Christian icon tattooed on him. He becomes involved in a brawl with them and is thrown out into the street. This recalls the scene from the synoptic Gospels in which the soldiers who beat Jesus the night before his crucifixion make it into a game. They blindfold him, pull off his clothes, and begin to beat him and mock him by commanding, "Prophesy, who is it that smote thee?" (Luke 22:64, KJV; cf. Mark 14:65, Matthew 27:27–31). After Parker is in the street, "a calm descended on the pool hall as nerve shattering as if the long barn-like room were the ship from which Jonah had been cast into the sea." In Christian theology, the great fish spitting Jonah up onto the land is seen as a type of the resurrection, with Jonah's being cast into the sea corresponding to the Crucifixion. When Sarah Ruth sees the tattoo, her rejection of it as idolatry is, in effect, a rejection of Jesus's divinity. She insists that God is spirit only, which denies the Christian doctrine of the incarnation, by which God is both fully man and fully God. The idea of mixing the two elements, however, is antithetical to Sarah Ruth's whole personality. She again beats Parker with a broom, this time recalling the scourging of Jesus as he carries his cross through Jerusalem. O'Connor drives the point home when she notes that "large welts had formed on the face of the tattooed Christ." In the last sentence of the story Parker is finally born again: "There he

For his final tattoo, Parker decides on the image of a Byzantine Christ. (© *Antony McAulay | Shutterstock.com*)

was—who called himself Obadiah Elihue—leaning against the tree, crying like a baby.''

The theological dimension of ''Parker's Back'' invokes the ambiguity of the title. Upon first reading it, one might imagine that it means *Parker is back*. But the narrative of the story will convince the reader that the apostrophe-*s* is possessive, referring to the character's back, where the tattoo of Christ is inscribed. But it is finally possible to read it as signifying the cycle of fall and redemption, such that indeed Parker has returned to the state of grace. Most likely O'Connor intended the play on words implicit in the title's ambiguity.

Source: Rita M. Brown, Critical Essay on ''Parker's Back,'' in *Short Stories for Students*, Gale, Cengage Learning, 2015.

Miles Orvell
In the following excerpt, Orvell discusses the ironic ending of ''Parker's Back.''

…The history of Parker's conversion, if we may call it that, is extravagant, whimsical, and ludicrous. What first awakens the spiritual passion that will lead him, all unknowingly, to Christ is the sight of a tattooed man at a fair. ''The man's skin was patterned in what seemed from Parker's distance…a single intricate design of brilliant color.'' As the tattooed man flexes his muscles, ''the arabesque of men and beasts and flowers on his skin appeared to have a subtle motion of its own. Parker was filled with emotion, lifted up as some people are when the flag passes.'' Although that last sentence suggests a cool amusement at Parker's emotion, it would be a mistake to underestimate the importance of this initial sense of wonder. It is akin to the earlier association of the aesthetic and the spiritual in ''The Displaced Person'' when the priest exclaims rapturously over the beauty of Mrs. McIntyre's passing peacock. In both cases, a grotesque blend of the familiar and the exotic seems to be at the root of ''wonder,'' and, in Parker's case, it leads him to marvel at the strangeness of life itself. ''Until he saw the man at the fair, it did not enter his head that there was anything out of the ordinary about the fact that he existed.'' O'Connor's first principle is thus rooted in the perception of the world and not in some disembodied cogito: rather, video ergo sum.

Thus begins Parker's spiritual career: in emulation of the tattooed man at the fair, he offers the tabula rasa of his body to a series of artists for their lines and colors, figures and words. And, what is more, the operations hurt him ''just enough to make it appear to Parker to be worth doing. This was peculiar too for before he had thought that only what did not hurt was worth doing.'' Parker thus receives O'Connor's characteristic initiation into suffering, and we know that, spiritually, he is henceforward a marked man.

Yet the mass of creation on his skin is, in a manner, without a Creator, and, with a subliminal urgency, Parker seeks some means of ordering his world. Thus he marries Sarah Ruth—for no apparent reason—and stays with her too—also for no apparent reason (she was ''both ugly and pregnant and no cook'')—although the reader may well perceive in his attachment to the Bible zealot an as yet unrealized attraction to the Word. Still, Sarah Ruth is not enough, and, with his vague dissatisfaction

> **" AND IT IS SIMPLY THE FINAL IRONY OF THE STORY THAT OUR LAST PICTURE OF PARKER, AFTER WE HAVE CAREFULLY OBSERVED HIS SECOND BIRTH INTO GRACE, SHOULD BE—THROUGH HIS WIFE'S EYES—AS A PATHETIC CRYING BABY."**

growing, Parker takes himself to a tattoo parlor, where at last he fixes upon an image that will contain his malaise. Or, rather, the image chooses him, for staring out from the artist's catalog of possible pictures is "the haloed head of a flat stern Byzantine Christ with all-demanding eyes."

What is so impressive in this story of course is how convincingly O'Connor manages to render the almost magical powers of this image of Christ; in a way that is more like Hawthorne than anything else she wrote (compare "The Birthmark" and "Egotism; or the Bosom Serpent"), O'Connor enforces a peculiar amalgam of literal physical detail and symbolic meaning. Thus, as the tattoo sinks into Parker's skin, the transformation—or second birth—begins: his heart beats slowly, "as if it were being brought to life by a subtle power." When the image is fully complete, Parker is shocked into silence by the powerful eyes of the Christ—"eyes to be obeyed." He drives back home to Sarah Ruth and, on the way, he experiences that alienation from self and surroundings that one recognizes, in O'Connor, as the sign of an impending revelation. Outside his own house at last, the image of the sun denotes a transformation in nature that is the mirror of Parker's own metamorphosis. "Then as he stood there, a tree of light burst over the skyline. Parker fell back against the door as if he had been pinned there by a lance." The foreshadowing crucifixion imagery is unmistakable, and not without a humorous self-consciousness.

But the metamorphosis is not yet complete. Sarah won't let him into the house until he utters his full name ("'I don't know no O.E.'" that literalist says); but when he does utter the name—Obadiah (lit.: worshiper of Jehovah)

Elihue (lit.: whose God is He)—he at last fully creates for himself his new identity: and a gracious light pours through him, turning the unimportant "spider web of facts and lies" that had earlier been his soul "into a perfect arabesque of colors, a garden of trees and birds and beasts." The deliberate echo of Parker's initial perception of the carnival tattooed man implies the fulfillment at last of Parker's "notion of wonder."

The fulfillment of his suffering soon follows. For although Parker had sought, in having tattooed on his back "just God" (that is, only God), an image that would finally satisfy his wife's obsession with the Bible, Parker painfully discovers that Sarah Ruth does not recognize "God" when he is pictured right before her eyes. The word, for his wife, is disembodied. It is not "with God."

> "Another picture," Sarah Ruth growled. "I might have known you was off after putting some more trash on yourself." . . .
>
> "Don't you know who it is?" he cried in anguish.
>
> "No, who is it?" Sarah Ruth said. "It ain't anybody I know."
>
> "It's him," Parker said.
>
> "Him who?"
>
> "God!" Parker cried.
>
> "God? God don't look like that!"
>
> "What do you know how he looks?" Parker moaned. "You ain't seen him."
>
> "He don't *look*," Sarah Ruth said. "He's a spirit. No man shall see his face."
>
> "Aw listen," Parker groaned, "this is just a picture of him."
>
> "Idolatry!" Sarah Ruth screamed. "Idolatry!"

And the woman whose broomstick is mightier than her word proceeds to beat still another tattoo on the poor man's flesh.

> Parker was too stunned to resist. He sat there and let her beat him until she had nearly knocked him senseless and large welts had formed on the face of the tattooed Christ. Then he staggered up and made for the door.
>
> She stamped the broom two or three times on the floor and went to the window and shook it out to get the taint of him off it. Still gripping it, she looked toward the pecan tree and her eyes hardened still more. There he was—who called himself Obadiah Elihue—leaning against the tree, crying like a baby.

The ritual scourge Parker endures in this, the last scene of the story, is the perfection of his "suffering" and exaltation. In some respects, its effect might be compared with the scaffold scene in Hawthorne's *Scarlet Letter* and too with the conclusion of Kafka's "Hunger Artist," in both of which, as Edwin Honig has written perceptively, the ironic reenactment of Christ's ordeal "becomes terrifying and credible because it is revealed as an actuality of daily life which repeats the original archetypal situation of Christ's lonely death on the Cross. Passing into fiction in this way, the scriptural event is given a new and different, one might say more starkly religious, value from the one now rigidified in the dogma."

And yet it would be false to the overall effect of "Parker's Back" to push the analogy with Hawthorne and Kafka too far. For Christ's "terrifying" and "lonely death on the Cross," in Honig's words, seems after all to be somewhat distant from the tone of O'Connor's story. The narration of the tale is quite clearly designed to place Parker's "crucifixion" in a comic context, so that we may well associate Parker, at the end, with blind, ascetic, suffering Hazel Motes who is also the hero of a Christian comic plot (the Resurrection is implied paradoxically in the Crucifixion). In addition, the structure of the tale seems analogous to the traditional motif of the henpecked husband who can do nothing to please his shrewish wife. Our recollection of Parker's first meeting with Sarah Ruth (she smacks his face for cursing) casts a comic light on the repeat performance that closes the tale.

Moreover, the narrative style of "Parker's Back" suggests that O'Connor took her usual rare delight in adopting the ironic, humorous voice of the storyteller.

> Sarah Ruth's father was a Straight Gospel preacher but he was away, spreading it in Florida.
> When he could, [Parker] broke in with tales of the hefty girl he worked for. "'Mr. Parker,'" he said she said, "'I hired you for your brains.'" (She had added, "So why don't you use them?")
> "And you should have seen her face the first time she saw me without my shirt," he said. "'Mr. Parker,' she said, 'you're a walking panner-rammer!'" This had, in fact, been her remark but it had been delivered out of one side of her mouth.

And it is simply the final irony of the story that our last picture of Parker, after we have carefully observed his second birth into grace, should be—through his wife's eyes—as a pathetic crying baby. So outrageous, indeed, is the story, so humorous the telling of it, so overt the symbolism, that one hesitates to decide whether it is not as much a parody of the Christ figure in fiction as a seriously ironic achievement of that figure; or whether, through parody, O'Connor has not ironically reinvigorated the source.

While it is lacking in the deadly violence that characterizes many of her best tales, early and late, "Parker's Back" evinces a confidence in handling that is indicative of the writer who is sure of himself and his materials. In this respect, it bears comparison with earlier tales like "The River" (also an overtly "theological" tale) and "A Temple of the Holy Ghost" (where the symbol of the grotesque body also carries a theological meaning)—in both of which that maturity seems lacking. And if we take O'Connor's attitude toward Parker as at once playfully comic and seriously ironic, one cannot but marvel at the rightness of her symbolism. For the tattooed body of O. E. Parker becomes at once a splendid and beautiful microcosm of the world, an embodiment of his "spider web soul," and a literal emblem of his Christlike suffering—besides being the perfect naturalistic medium for Parker's aesthetic emotions.

And too, as Theodore Gaster has written, the tattoo has a long history in religious faiths as a sign confirming a belief in, and covenant with, God.

> The custom of tattooing passed even into Christianity. In early centuries, baptism was known as "sealing," and this was also the ancient name for the rite of Confirmation, which originally followed immediately. Nor did the custom survive only in a figurative sense. To this day the Catholics of Central Bosnia tattoo themselves with religious symbols; while in the neighborhood of Loreto (Italy) it is common to do likewise in honor of the celebrated local Madonna.... and it is recorded of the German mystic, Heinrich Seuse, that he impressed the name of Jesus over his heart.

Caroline Gordon has written, in an article on O'Connor, of a visit she paid to the writer in May, 1964, when the latter was hospitalized in Atlanta. This was of course a few months before O'Connor's death, and she was working at the time on "Parker's Back," hoping that she would be able to finish it for her forthcoming volume of stories, *Everything That Rises Must Converge*. Miss Gordon writes: "After the nurse had left the room Flannery pulled a notebook out from under her pillow. 'The doctor says I mustn't do any work. But he says it's all right for me to write a little fiction.'"

Source: Miles Orvell, "The Short Stories: 'Parker's Back,'" in *Flannery O'Connor: An Introduction*, University Press of Mississippi, 1991, pp. 167–72.

Streight, Irwin Howard, "Is There a Text in This Man? A Semiotic Reading of 'Parker's Back,'" in *Flannery O'Connor Bulletin*, Vol. 22, 1993–1994, pp. 1–11.

Teilhard de Chardin, Pierre, *The Future of Man*, translated by Norman Denny, Image Books/Doubleday, 2004, pp. 115–16.

Walker, Sue Brannan, "Flannery O'Connor's 'The Temple of the Holy Ghost' and 'Parker's Back' as Dermatology/Theology," in *Scribbling Women & the Short Story Form: Approaches by American & British Women Writers*, edited by Ellen Burton Harrington, Peter Lang, 2008, pp. 142–53.

SOURCES

Fromm, Erich, *The Anatomy of Human Destructiveness*, Holt, Rinehart and Winston, 1973, pp. 325–68.

Gentry, Marshall Bruce, *Flannery O'Connor's Religion of the Grotesque*, University Press of Mississippi, 1985, pp. 77–81.

Gooch, Brad, *Flannery: A Life of Flannery O'Connor*, Little, Brown, 2009, pp. 363–73.

Hofstadter, Richard, "The Paranoid Style in American Politics," in *The Paranoid Style in American Politics, and Other Essays*, Vintage Books, 2008, pp. 3–40.

Hyman, Stanley Edgar, "Flannery O'Connor's Tattooed Christ," in *Flannery O'Connor: The Contemporary Reviews*, edited by R. Neil Scott and Irwin H. Streight, Cambridge University Press, 2009, pp. 207–11; originally published in *New Leader*, May 10, 1965, pp. 9–10.

Jones, C. P., "*Stigma*: Tattooing and Branding in Graeco-Roman Antiquity," in *Journal of Roman Studies*, Vol. 77, 1987, pp. 139–55.

McMullen, Joanne Halleran, *Writing against God: Language as Message in the Literature of Flannery O'Connor*, Mercer University Press, 1996, pp. 91–93.

O'Connor, Flannery, "The Catholic Novelist in the Protestant South," in *Collected Works*, Library of America, 1988, pp. 853–64.

———, "Parker's Back," in *Collected Works*, Library of America, 1988, pp. 655–75.

———, "Some Aspects of the Grotesque in Southern Fiction," in *Collected Works*, Library of America, 1988, pp. 813–21.

———, "To A.," July 25, 1964, in *Collected Works*, Library of America, 1988, p. 1218.

"O'Connor's Tales of Gothic Horror Left Deep Impact on Modern Letters," in *Flannery O'Connor: The Contemporary Reviews*, edited by R. Neil Scott and Irwin H. Streight, Cambridge University Press, 2009, pp. 214–15; originally published in *Savannah News*, May 23, 1965, p. 8.

FURTHER READING

Hewitt, Avis, and Robert Donahoo, eds., *Flannery O'Connor in the Age of Terrorism: Essays on Violence and Grace*, University of Tennessee Press, 2010.
>   This collection of essays is among the most important recent O'Connor criticism.

Lake, Christina Bieber, *The Incarnational Art of Flannery O'Connor*, Mercer University Press, 2005.
>   Lake is principally concerned with O'Connor's use of the body in her fiction.

O'Connor, Flannery, *A Good Man Is Hard to Find, and Other Stories*, Harcourt, Brace, 1955.
>   This is O'Connor's first short-story collection. The title story, O'Connor's best known, has many points of contact with "Parker's Back," especially concerning the main character's unlikely redemption.

———, *A Prayer Journal*, edited by W. A. Sessions, Farrar, Straus, and Giroux, 2013.
>   O'Connor kept this prayer journal, recently discovered among her papers, while taking her MFA degree at the Iowa Writers' Workshop. It gives unique insight into her private life.

SUGGESTED SEARCH TERMS

Flannery O'Connor

Parker's Back AND O'Connor

Everything That Rises Must Converge

southern gothic

grotesque

Teilhard de Chardin

Byzantine art

Christ Pantocrator

tattooing

The Problem of Cell 13

In 1905, the editors of the *Boston American* wanted to boost sales, so they asked one of the staff writers, Jacques Futrelle, to come up with a fiction story they could publish serially. Futrelle had an idea for a brilliant, modern, logical detective, Professor Augustus S. F. X. Van Dusen, who could think his way out of anything, including a high-security prison cell. Futrelle divided his story into six installments, the first of which appeared in the *American* on Monday, October 5, 1905, along with the announcement of a contest for readers: whoever could figure out how the professor might manage to escape from his cell in Chisholm Prison could send the solution to the newspaper and win one hundred dollars. What began as a sales stunt launched a career in detective fiction—a career that tragedy cut short less than a decade later. Nonetheless, Futrelle's first story, "The Problem of Cell 13," remains a classic example of early detective fiction. It can be found in Futrelle's *Best "Thinking Machine" Detective Stories* (1973); *The Classic Tales of Jacques Futrelle*, Volume 1, *The Thinking Machine* (2004); and other Futrelle volumes, as well as such anthologies as *Detective Fiction: Crime and Compromise* (1974) and *The Best American Mystery Stories of the Century* (2001).

JACQUES FUTRELLE

1905

AUTHOR BIOGRAPHY

Jacques Heath Futrelle was born on April 9, 1875, in Pike County, Georgia, to Wiley Harmon Heath Futrelle and Linnie Bevill Futrelle.

The prison cell contains nothing other than an iron bed. (© Mmroz | Shutterstock.com)

His father was of French Huguenot ancestry and taught at Atlanta College. In addition to his studies in public school, Futrelle was tutored by his father at home in French and other subjects.

When Futrelle finished high school, he found newspaper work, first with the *Atlanta Journal* and then with the *Boston Post*. Living in Boston, however, turned out to be difficult for a young man in love: in 1895, Futrelle moved back to Atlanta to marry his sweetheart, Lily May Peel. He went back to work for the *Atlanta Journal*, where he founded the newspaper's sports department.

The couple then moved to New York, where Futrelle took a job with the *New York Herald*. They had a lively social life there, moving in literary circles that included writers O. Henry and Edith Wharton. In 1902, the couple settled in Richmond, Virginia, where Futrelle had secured a position as the manager of a small theater. While employed there, Futrelle

tried his hand at writing plays and even acted in a few. His wife also found some success as a writer, publishing several magazine articles and novels.

It was when Futrelle's stint in the theater ended and he went back to his roots in journalism that he got the idea for his most memorable character: Augustus S. F. X. Van Dusen, the "Thinking Machine." "The Problem of Cell 13," the first story to feature Professor Van Dusen, was published in the *Boston American* in installments, with the first part appearing on October 5, 1905. The story and its main character were immediately popular with readers, and the next year, Futrelle published the first full-length Thinking Machine novel: *The Chase of the Golden Plate*.

Many other novels in the mystery and detective genre followed. His books sold well in the United States, so in 1912, Futrelle and his wife traveled to Europe to make a deal to publish his work there as well. After conducting his business successfully, Futrelle booked passage home on the maiden voyage of the *Titanic*. He died in the *Titanic* disaster on April 15, 1912, after persuading his wife to take a place in a lifeboat, though she resisted leaving him. She returned home to their two teenaged children and oversaw the publication of two more of Futrelle's novels: *My Lady's Garter* (1912) and *Blind Man's Bluff* (1914).

PLOT SUMMARY

I

The protagonist of "The Problem of Cell 13," Professor Augustus S. F. X. Van Dusen, is introduced. He has a long list of degrees after his name, showing that he is highly educated as well as highly intelligent. Van Dusen is "above all . . . a logician": he believes that rational, logical thought can accomplish just about anything.

While discussing a scientific theory with a couple of colleagues, Dr. Charles Ransome and Mr. Alfred Fielding, Van Dusen insists that logical thought can even effectively dissolve prison walls, by finding a way through them to escape. Dr. Ransome expresses his disbelief, annoying Van Dusen, and Mr. Fielding suggests putting Van Dusen's claim to the test.

Van Dusen takes up the challenge. He agrees to enter Chisholm Prison with nothing other than what any prisoner might be allowed to take into his cell and asserts that he will escape within the week. He is so confident of his success that he orders his housekeeper, Martha, to prepare a celebratory dinner one week hence.

The three men drive to the prison. Van Dusen is searched. He asks for a few items: tooth powder and twenty-five dollars in cash. He also asks if he might have his shoes polished. The warden grants these requests. Prisoners are not usually allowed money, but the warden is confident that his guards cannot be bribed at all, much less for so small a sum. Van Dusen is led into his cell, which is filled with the scurrying of rats.

II

Van Dusen looks out his barred window at the prison grounds. There are high, smooth walls around the prison yard, which is brightly lit at night. The wire leading to the light on that side

MEDIA ADAPTATIONS

- Jimcin Recordings released an Audible audio edition of "The Problem of Cell 13" in 2007, read by Walter Covell. Running time is thirty-one minutes.

of the prison passes near the window. Van Dusen recalls the guard's booth and the seven locked doors he passed through to get to Cell 13. There are no furnishings in his cell to help him.

A rat runs across his foot. He watches the movement of the rats, realizes that none of them run out through the small gap under the door, and looks for another exit. After a brief search, he finds the opening of a drainage pipe.

A guard brings a simple lunch. Van Dusen asks a few questions and learns from the guard that the prison has a new plumbing system and that there is a playground between the prison and the river nearby. Van Dusen says he is thirsty and is allowed to keep a small bowl of water in his cell.

The guard sees Van Dusen catching rats. Another guard later finds a note written on a small piece of linen that Van Dusen threw out his window with a five-dollar bill. The guard takes the message and the money to the warden. The note is written in code and addressed to Dr. Ransome. The warden and the guard wonder where Van Dusen acquired ink and an implement to write the note with.

III

The warden searches Van Dusen's cell for his writing supplies. He has Van Dusen change his own white shirt for a striped inmate's shirt and sees that part of the white linen was used for the note. Van Dusen refuses to explain what he used for pen and ink.

The following day, Van Dusen offers a guard a bribe to help him escape. The guard refuses and points out that even if he agreed, he does not have all of the necessary keys. He can only unlock two of the seven doors that stand between Van Dusen and freedom.

That evening the guard catches Van Dusen sawing at the bars on his window. The guard fetches the warden, and they find that Van Dusen was using pieces of metal from his shoes to rub at the bars. The jailers take the small metal bits, search his cell thoroughly, and urge him to give up.

At four o'clock the next morning, a scream echoes through the prison. The warden and several guards rush to Van Dusen's cell. The section ends on this exciting note, reminding the modern reader that the story was originally published serially. Leaving a cliffhanger at the end of the installment made readers eager to see the next section.

IV

When the warden and guards arrive at Van Dusen's cell, he is snoring on his bed. Another scream comes from above. The warden goes to the prisoner in Cell 43, two floors directly above Van Dusen's cell. The inmate of Cell 43 is Joseph Ballard, who is accused of causing a woman's death by throwing acid on her face. Ballard is babbling in fear, begging to be moved to another cell. He claims to have heard a ghostly voice.

Van Dusen throws another note out his window. The warden cannot understand where Van Dusen might have gotten the linen for this note, because the warden accounted for both of the missing pieces of the prisoner's shirt during his last search.

Van Dusen asks one of the guards about the lights outside each of the prison walls and who maintains them. Van Dusen returns to his perch at his window, looking out.

Later in the day, Van Dusen tosses a five-dollar bill to one of the guards, calling it a tip. The guard dutifully takes it to the warden, who realizes that the money originally given to Van Dusen contained two ten-dollar bills and only one five-dollar bill, which had already been found with the last note. The warden cannot imagine where Van Dusen acquired the other five-dollar bill.

The warden surprises Van Dusen at three o'clock in the morning with a thorough inspection of his cell and discovers the old drainage pipe. He reaches in and finds a dead rat. When the warden finds five one-dollar bills in the prisoner's trousers, he questions Van Dusen, who denies that any of the guards gave him change for his ten-dollar bill. Van Dusen refuses to explain where he did get the change, which aggravates the warden.

Before the warden can get to sleep, he hears screaming. It is Ballard again. He confesses to the crime of throwing acid on the woman, swearing he heard a voice saying, "Acid—acid—acid." When he also claims to have heard the phrase "No. 8 hat," the warden concludes that he has gone mad.

V

It is the fifth day of Van Dusen's week in prison, and the warden is worn down from fretting over the situation. Van Dusen tosses another note out the window, this time with a half dollar. The coin, fresh evidence of Van Dusen's cleverness, frustrates the warden, as does the memory of the mysterious voice Ballard claims to have heard.

The next day, the warden receives a note in the mail indicating that Dr. Ransome and Mr. Fielding will come to the prison the following evening—the deadline for Van Dusen's escape. Van Dusen throws several more notes out the window. On the afternoon of the seventh day, the warden checks on Cell 13, but Van Dusen seems to be sleeping on his bed.

When Ransome and Fielding arrive, the warden receives them in his office. A guard interrupts to report that a light in the prison yard will not light, so the warden calls an electrician to come repair it. A special delivery letter arrives, and Dr. Ransome takes note of the return address, but the reader does not yet learn where the letter is from.

The electricians come to repair the broken light. The warden confirms that four electricians entered the prison: "three workmen in jumpers and overalls" and the manager in a "coat and silk hat." After instructing the guard at the gate to be sure that only four men leave the prison when the work is finished, the warden turns his attention back to his guests as he opens the special delivery letter. It is a dinner invitation sent from Cell 13.

Two reporters arrive, asking to speak to the warden. He tells a guard to allow them to come in but asks that no one mention the situation. A guard checks on Van Dusen and says that he is still lying on his bed. The reporters enter the office. One of them is Hutchinson Hatch, whom the warden knows, and the other is—Van Dusen.

Van Dusen leads everyone to Cell 13 and shows them the blond wig and the pile of rope, wire, and other supplies that he covered with his blanket to make it appear he was still asleep on the bed. He also demonstrates that some of the bars in the cell door and window have been dislodged.

VI

At Van Dusen's supper party, everyone is eager to hear how he accomplished his escape. Because he observed that the rats were field rats and knew they had come in through the drain pipe, he surmised that the pipe exited near the playground he knew to be between the prison wall and the river. By unraveling the tops of his socks, he had a long thread, which he tied to one of the rats. He then sent a frightened rat scurrying through the drainpipe with a note to be delivered to Hatch. Van Dusen was sure Hatch's reporter's instincts would not let him give up the chance for a good story.

Hatch did indeed begin helping. He was able to make contact with Van Dusen and bring supplies that he needed, including a stronger cord and wire for passing things through the pipe and acid to eat through the prison bars. The pipe also served as a speaking tube, though the unfortunate Ballard overheard their exchanges, understanding only Van Dusen's instructions for acid and for a No. 8 hat for the disguise he would need later in the plan.

The notes on linen scraps—which had been taken from an extra layer in Van Dusen's shirt, while the ink was made from shoe polish and water—and the sawing at the window bars were meant to be false trails to distract the warden from the real escape plan. The secret code used in the first note only entailed spelling the message backwards. Van Dusen's hope was to frustrate the warden so much with the false trail and changing money that he would stop searching the cell, which he indeed finally did.

On the final evening, Van Dusen broke the yard light by severing its wire using his own wire tipped with acid. Then he slipped out the window, replaced the bars so that they looked undisturbed, and climbed down to hide in the shadows until he could meet Hatch, who came in with the electricians—his father being the

company's manager. Hatch gave Van Dusen overalls and a size 8 cap so that he would appear to be one of the workmen, and the two simply walked out of the prison gate.

CHARACTERS

Joseph Ballard

Ballard is the prisoner in Cell 43, which is above Van Dusen's cell. Ballard is accused of throwing acid on the face of a woman who later died from her injuries. Ballard is terrified when he hears a ghostly voice in his cell. Although the voice is actually Van Dusen instructing Hatch to bring acid to eat through the prison bars, Ballard fears he is hearing a ghost, which finally drives him to confess.

Mr. Fielding

Fielding's first name is given as both Alfred and Albert in some versions, likely because of carelessness in editing. At the beginning of the story, Fielding is arguing some obscure theory with Van Dusen. Along with Dr. Ransome, Fielding challenges the Thinking Machine to think his way out of a cell on death row in Chisholm Prison.

Guards

Throughout the story, the guards bring Van Dusen his meals. By answering seemingly harmless questions, the guards give Van Dusen some of the information he needs to escape. The guards also report to the warden about anything unusual, such as the notes that Van Dusen throws out the window.

Hutchinson Hatch

Hatch is a reporter for the *Daily American* newspaper. Van Dusen sends a letter to him from inside Cell 13, guessing that he would help simply to have the inside scoop on an interesting story for his paper. The two men set up communication through the drainage pipe: they quietly voice messages, and Hatch sends materials in to Van Dusen. Hatch also helps Van Dusen escape by coming in with the electricians from the company his father manages and by providing a disguise for Van Dusen to wear so that he can simply walk out of the prison.

Martha

Martha is Van Dusen's housekeeper. He instructs her to prepare a meal to celebrate his escape before he even enters the prison.

Dr. Charles Ransome

Dr. Ransome argues with Mr. Fielding and Van Dusen about a scientific or philosophical theory at the start of the story. Then Ransome and Fielding challenge Van Dusen to escape from Chisholm Prison without any special treatment beyond what is always given to prisoners. When Van Dusen is laying false trails for the warden to follow, he addresses one of his notes to Dr. Ransome. Of the several people present in the warden's office at the close of the story, Dr. Ransome seems the most impressed and amused by Van Dusen's escape: "'Wonderful!' he exclaimed. 'Perfectly amazing.'"

Professor Augustus S. F. X. Van Dusen

Professor Van Dusen is the protagonist of a series of stories and novels by Futrelle that feature the solution of crimes or puzzles through logic and deduction. Van Dusen has earned the nickname of the "Thinking Machine" because of his brilliant mind. He has an unusual appearance, with bushy blond hair, stooped shoulders, thick glasses, and squinting blue eyes.

Van Dusen enters into the challenge from Dr. Ransome and Mr. Fielding to escape from a high-security prison cell, certain that he can escape using only the powers of his mind, even if given no special treatment. He becomes annoyed at the suggestion from Dr. Ransome that he could not escape from a cell unless he "entered it with tools prepared to get out."

Professor Van Dusen leaves false trails to throw off the warden, writing notes and throwing them out the window and pretending he intends to saw through the window bars with bits of metal from his shoe. He cleverly uses his meager resources to engineer his escape. He unravels his socks and ties the string, ten dollars, and a message to a rat, which creeps through a drain pipe. The note gets delivered to Hutchinson Hatch, a reporter, who then communicates with Van Dusen by using the pipe like a speaking tube and delivers materials to help with the escape, such as wire and acid.

Once Van Dusen escapes, he cheerfully discloses all of the details of his plan to the men gathered in the warden's office. Van Dusen is confident to the point of seeming arrogance. However, he follows through on his claim that he can escape from the prison and even suggests that he came up with two alternate plans that would have worked equally well.

The Warden

The warden agrees to have Van Dusen in the prison, certain that he will not be able to escape. The warden is sure that his security is tight and that his guards cannot be bribed to help a prisoner escape or even deliver a message. Although he is determined not to let Van Dusen escape and searches the cell frequently, he allows what he considers fair treatment of his guest, including allowing him to keep a bowl of water. The warden is continually puzzled and frustrated by Van Dusen's actions, both the ones left as false trails and the ones actually leading to his escape. At the end of the story, when all of the characters meet in his office, the warden is amazed that the escape was successful and is curious to hear exactly how it was accomplished.

THEMES

Escape

The entire plot of "The Problem of Cell 13" revolves around the idea of escape. Van Dusen is challenged by his fellow intellectuals to escape from Chisholm Prison using only what any prisoner might be allowed to take into his cell with him. Throughout the story, the reader is given clues as to how Van Dusen might accomplish this, as well as details about false trails that he plants to throw off the warden, who is doing his best to thwart the escape attempt, as is his duty for any prisoner.

The story does not focus on a desperate, serious kind of flight. Instead, it centers on a staged escape—the actors are essentially pretending to be concerned about the prisoner's predicament. Futrelle's light touch on this theme is appropriate when one considers that detective fiction reflects, in part, a desire on the part of the reader to escape from day-to-day cares. Some people do not take mystery and detective fiction seriously as a genre; it sometimes is not considered "significant literature" the way more realistic fiction is. Whether this

TOPICS FOR FURTHER STUDY

- Many detective stories are appropriate for young adults. Popular author Philip Pullman selected the fiction presented in *Detective Stories* (1998) specifically for a young-adult audience. Tales by Ellery Queen, Agatha Christie, Dorothy L. Sayers, and E. C. Bentley are included. After reading several of the selections, choose your favorite. Reread the story again carefully, considering how the story would be different if Professor Van Dusen were the detective in the story. Then write a play, substituting Van Dusen for the original detective character. With some friends, perform your play for the class. Alternatively, record and post the performance so that your classmates can view it online.

- Professor Van Dusen is often compared with fellow literary sleuth Sherlock Holmes. Read a few of Arthur Conan Doyle's stories featuring this character. Think about how his methods compare with Van Dusen's, and write a paper in which you conclude, based on what you see in the stories, which character would likely solve a mystery first.

- Create a "locked room" situation like that of Cell 13 in Chisholm Prison, where one must either escape from a seemingly inescapable place or retrieve an item from a seemingly impenetrable room. Plan out your puzzle in detail, including both diagrams and descriptions of your setting. Make sure there are at least two paths by which someone could beat your safeguards. Post your locked room brainteaser online, and invite your classmates to try to solve the puzzle.

- Using online and traditional resources, research past prison breaks, such as the possibly successful 1962 escape attempt from Alcatraz. Select one in which you feel the escapee(s) used the most ingenuity and resourcefulness. Make a PowerPoint presentation to explain the path to escape, and share it with your class.

opinion is justifiable or not, it is true that many people read mysteries in their leisure time to relax. Most readers of the genre are not usually interested in learning about crime; rather, they enjoy seeing crime solved and order restored. The solution of the crime is a big part of the fun, allowing readers to fix their thoughts on an intellectual puzzle that has no bearing on the real world—much like Van Dusen's challenge.

Futrelle's theme of escape also represents the social trends of his time, which were moving away from the rigid structures of Victorian times. It was a new era with more social equality and new technology. Dr. Ransome and Mr. Fielding, with their doubt and their questions, can be seen to represent the old ways, while Van Dusen and his confident, logical approach represent a newer, more progressive way of looking at the world.

Intellectualism

Intellectualism characteristically entails the belief that true knowledge comes from pure reason, or a process of logic. This concept is related to rationalism, which is the theory that one's actions should be based on logic, reason, and experience rather than emotions or unverifiable beliefs. The theme of intellectualism or rationalism is represented in "The Problem of Cell 13" by Professor Van Dusen.

Van Dusen's nickname, the Thinking Machine, reflects his belief that logic and rational thought can accomplish anything. Dr. Ransome insists that "there are some things that can't be *thought* out of existence, or rather which would not yield to any amount of thinking." He gives the example of a prison's walls. "No man can *think* himself out of a cell," Ransome says. Van Dusen, however, believes he can indeed think himself out of a cell and agrees to do exactly that.

Van Dusen's certainty that "a man can so apply his brain and ingenuity that he can leave a cell," which he asserts amounts to "the same thing" as thinking the walls out of existence, illustrates the theme of intellectualism. Van Dusen's ultimate success in escaping from Cell 13 hints that Futrelle likely feels much the same way as his character.

Cell 13 is plagued by rats. (© Heiko Kiera / Shutterstock.com)

STYLE

Detective Story

Detective and mystery stories have long been popular, and to some extent the terms are interchangeable. Both genres involve secrets and typically recount the solution of a crime that has been committed. John Cawelti, an expert on the academic study of popular culture, has examined the detective story and determined four classes of characters common to a vast majority of them: the victim of the crime, the perpetrator of the crime, those threatened by the crime but unable to solve it, and the detective.

Detective fiction became very popular at the end of the nineteenth century and the beginning of the twentieth. This may be because of the huge changes that were happening in society, industry, and science. Reading about fictional heroes who used scientific methods to fight crime was reassuring as well as entertaining to a populace unsettled by what was going on around them.

The balance between good and evil or right and wrong is a common theme in mystery and detective fiction, but perhaps the most important element is the puzzle at the heart of the plot. Many devoted readers of detective stories enjoy the challenge of getting to the bottom of the crime before the author reveals the solution. Because so many readers attempt to solve the mystery, authors in this genre have a difficult task. They must present the facts of the case so that solving the crime is theoretically possible for careful readers, but they must make it difficult enough to maintain suspense and to impress and amaze most readers with the skills of the fictional detective. "The Problem of Cell 13" is different from typical detective fiction in that no crime is committed—rather, a staged escape is anticipated—but the story contains many of the elements of the typical detective story.

Locked-Room Story

A locked-room story is a particular type of detective fiction. In locked-room stories, the crime happens under seemingly impossible circumstances. For example, there could be a theft of an object from a room where it is apparently

COMPARE
&
CONTRAST

- **c. 1905:** Futrelle enjoys a great amount of popular success with his readers. His detective stories, along with those of popular fellow mystery writers like Arthur Conan Doyle, E. W. Hornung, and G. K. Chesterton, set up the conventions of the genre, many of which are still used in stories today.

  Today: Futrelle's reputation has declined, perhaps because of his early death, although "The Problem of Cell 13" is anthologized fairly frequently. Detective fiction and mysteries continue to be hugely popular with readers, as well as with fans of mystery television shows and films. Popular writers today include Gillian Flynn, Michael Connelly, Lee Child, and J. D. Robb, to list just a few.

- **c. 1905:** "The Problem of Cell 13" appears in installments in the *Boston American* newspaper. Many popular authors, including Charles Dickens, Herman Melville, Henry James, and Doyle, achieve great popularity by publishing their novels serially.

  Today: The growing use of tablets and other portable devices spurs the publication of more short fiction that readers can complete in a single sitting. Many kinds of literature—from historical novels to science fiction to serial web comics—now appear in installments, attracting loyal readers.

- **c. 1905:** In theory, prisons are intended to rehabilitate inmates, but conditions are harsh, with very few opportunities for education or psychological help. Many prisoners are very isolated and are forced to remain silent, wear striped clothes, and perform physical labor for no payment.

  Today: The United States has the highest incarceration rate in the world. The rate in 1999 is at least five times the rate in western Europe—although the crime rate there is comparable—and seventeen times that in Japan. The vast majority of federal prisoners are incarcerated for nonviolent crimes. It is estimated that 16 percent of the nation's approximately two million inmates are mentally ill. Some inmates are forced to work for wages as low as a quarter per hour in private, for-profit prisons.

---

impossible for someone to have entered, taken the object, and then escaped. One common variation on the locked room is sometimes called the "English" or "country house" story, in which the isolation of the setting limits what happens in the story to a small community of possible suspects.

"The Problem of Cell 13" is a variation on the classic locked-room story. No crime is committed, but as with other locked-room tales, the reader is presented with the puzzle—here, a seemingly inescapable cell—and all of the clues—from the rats to the bowl of water to the questions about the exterior lighting—and can try to figure out the solution before the dramatic revelation at the close of the story.

HISTORICAL CONTEXT

Detective Fiction

Edgar Allan Poe is often credited with the creation of the first modern detective story, but there were several other works that can be considered detection fiction that were published before Poe's "The Murders in the Rue Morgue" in 1841. In the United States, the story "The Rifle," by William Leggett, appeared in the 1827 special Christmas edition of the *Atlantic Souvenir*. Danish author Steen Steensen Blicher published the novella *The Rector of Veilbye* in 1829. In 1839, Philip Meadows Taylor released *Confessions of a Thug* in Britain, and Maurits Christopher Hansen published *Mordet på maskinbygger Roolfsen* (*The

Dr. Van Dusen realizes that the rats enter his cell through a drainpipe and begins to formulate a plan of escape. (© Erni / Shutterstock.com)

Murder of Engine Maker Rolfsen) in Norway. In France, Émile Gaboriau is sometimes called the father of the *roman policier* (detective novel). The first of his twenty-one mystery novels was *L'affaire Lerouge* (*The Widow Lerouge*), which came out in 1866.

For American and British audiences, however, it was Poe's detective, C. Auguste Dupin, who captured their imaginations. Dupin was an intelligent man with an upper-class background, and his methods were logical, relying on close observation and detailed clues. In addition to the original 1841 story, Poe published only two other stories featuring Dupin, "The Mystery of Marie Rogêt" (1842) and "The Purloined Letter" (1844), but this popular character set the standard for later heroes.

Detective fiction was also influenced by true-to-life stories. Allan Pinkerton penned stories inspired by actual cases solved by his detective agency, a national company that was founded in 1850. Pinkerton National Detective Agency was famous for its methods: compiling information about and photographs of suspects and perfecting

surveillance work to catch those doing wrong in the act. The procedures used by Pinkerton's detectives and the style of his writing influenced many authors who came after him.

The new genre of detective stories was so popular that even successful mainstream authors like Charles Dickens were influenced by it. His novel *Bleak House* (originally published serially between March 1852 and September 1853), along with the novels of his friend and fellow writer Wilkie Collins, established some of the iconic conventions of detective stories, such as the bumbling efforts of the regular police officers investigating the case, the idea of the "inside job," and the final twist to the plot to surprise the reader.

Perhaps the most popular and well-known detective is Arthur Conan Doyle's Sherlock Holmes. From 1887 to 1923, Doyle published four novels and fifty-six stories featuring Holmes and his associate, Dr. Watson. These tales have fascinated fans from the original newspaper serials to the modern film and television adaptations. As Mark Lawson explains in the London *Guardian*,

So long and so strong is the shadow of Holmes that anyone subsequently creating a detective in any culture has had to make a deliberate gesture of homage or avoidance to the resident of 221B Baker Street.

The influence of Holmes can be seen in many subsequent literary detectives, including Agatha Christie's Hercule Poirot and Georges Simenon's Commissaire Jules Maigret. Lawson theorizes that Christie, though British, made Poirot Belgian in an effort to avoid comparisons to Holmes.

In the United States in the 1930s, "hard-boiled" detective stories were popular in pulp magazines—inexpensive publications meant for wide circulation. They were called hard-boiled because of their rough urban settings, the rapid, slang-infected dialogue, and the no-nonsense, streetwise attitudes of the protagonists. Dashiell Hammett, who worked for the Pinkerton National Detective Agency, invented the style when his 1929 story *The Maltese Falcon* was serially published in *Black Mask* magazine. This genre of detective fiction was new and distinctly different from the English style of mystery story made so popular by Doyle and followed eagerly by American writers until that point.

During World War II, American readers turned to policemen rather than private eyes. Police investigators had been mocked by authors from Poe through Doyle, but, perhaps motivated by the patriotism of the war effort, authors began to show public officers a new level of respect in crime fiction. As crime solving became more intricate, with legal complications and new procedures requiring scientific expertise, the idea of working alone to catch criminals became less feasible. Modern detective fiction is more likely to feature a team than a lone detective. The continued popularity of the older stories, however, proves that the classic formula and detectives like Holmes and Van Dusen have an appeal that does not fade.

CRITICAL OVERVIEW

In spite of the popularity that Futrelle enjoyed during his few years writing fiction, his reputation has dwindled to almost nothing in the years since his death aboard the ill-fated *Titanic*. Indeed, there is not much critical attention to Futrelle—his dramatic end is discussed much more than his work. Mary Anne Hutchinson, writing in the *Cyclopedia of World Authors II*, asserts that had Futrelle "not died so tragically and suddenly only five years after beginning his career as a mystery writer, he would now be remembered as one of its most celebrated practitioners."

Hutchinson praises "the lightness of Futrelle's touch, the ingenuity of his plots, and the modernity of his settings." She believes that Futrelle is "one of the first mystery writers to give that genre scientific and intellectual respectability," and she points out that "critics generally regard the novel *The Diamond Master*...as Futrelle's best novel." Roger Johnson, reviewing a biography of Futrelle, calls his stories "witty, challenging and stimulating" and marvels at his "astonishing ingenuity and logical creativity" as he matches his "professor against all manner of extraordinary problems." Just as Futrelle was influenced by fellow mystery writers such as Doyle, scholars Luis Velez, Eric-Jan Noomen, George Behe, and Phillip Gowan note of Futrelle in the *Encyclopedia Titanica* that "it has been suggested that his detective was an inspiration for Agatha Christie" in the creation of her beloved Hercule Poirot.

CRITICISM

Kristen Sarlin Greenberg

Greenberg is a freelance writer and editor with a background in literature and philosophy. In the following essay, she compares Futrelle's "The Problem of Cell 13" with Arthur Conan Doyle's Sherlock Holmes stories.

"You really are an automaton—a calculating machine." This sounds like a comment that might be directed at Professor Van Dusen—the "Thinking Machine" whom Jacques Futrelle introduces in the story "The Problem of Cell 13." This sentence, however, is actually uttered by Dr. Watson to Sherlock Holmes, who was clearly an inspiration for Futrelle, in *The Sign of Four* (1890). Detective fiction was hugely popular in 1905, when Futrelle first published "The Problem of Cell 13" in the *Boston American* in installments, and the stories about Holmes by Arthur Conan Doyle accounted for much of the popularity of the genre.

WHAT DO I READ NEXT?

- After "The Problem of Cell 13" was published, Futrelle continued the story of the Thinking Machine in his novel *The Chase of the Golden Plate* (1906).

- Futrelle's Professor Van Dusen is often compared with Arthur Conan Doyle's famed Sherlock Holmes. There are fifty-six short stories and four novels featuring Doyle's genius detective, all of which are widely available. Readers who are interested in variations of the locked-room story like "The Problem of Cell 13" might try "The Adventure of the Speckled Band" (1892), which appears in the collection *The Adventures of Sherlock Holmes*, and "The Adventure of the Norwood Builder" (1903), which appears in *The Return of Sherlock Holmes*.

- Popular and critically acclaimed mystery writer P. D. James analyzes her own genre in *Talking about Detective Fiction* (2009). James provides a personal but comprehensive look at British and American authors and characters from the nineteenth century through the modern day.

- Mark Haddon's *The Curious Incident of the Dog in the Night-Time* (2003) is an unconventional mystery novel featuring fifteen-year-old Christopher John Francis Boone, who investigates the death of his neighbor's pet dog, Wellington. Christopher, much like the classic detectives Holmes and Van Dusen, looks at the world through logic and patterns, but he falters when faced with human emotion.

- *The Final Bet*, by Abdelilah Hamdouchi, was published in 2001 in its original Arabic and then released in English in 2008, as translated by Jonathan Smolin. The publishers claim that it is the first Arabic detective novel to be translated into English. The Moroccan setting and unstable political situation add interest to Hamdouchi's light mystery.

- Many name Edgar Allan Poe's "The Murders in the Rue Morgue" (1841) as the first true detective story. Poe's tale recounts the puzzling murder of a mother and daughter in a Paris apartment, with Detective C. Auguste Dupin stepping in to solve the case. The tale is available in most Poe collections.

- Dandi Daley Mackall won the 2012 Edgar Award in the young-adult category for *The Silence of Murder*, in which Hope Long tries to clear her brother's name after he is accused of murder. The book's title reflects its central problem: Hope's brother has not spoken in years, so he is unable to explain why the evidence points in his direction as the culprit.

There are a lot of similarities among most detective stories. They feature clever puzzles solved by logic and attention to detail. The authors tease out the solutions, giving readers tantalizing hints but holding some things back to create tension for the narrative. Perhaps the reader can sometimes figure out the solution, though often the details are too obscure and defy the most dedicated attempts. Many read detective stories less to become armchair investigators and more for the pleasure of watching the hero solve the puzzle. Like Dr. Ransome watching Van Dusen, we can sit back and say, "Perfectly amazing."

In addition to the factors common to most stories in the genre, Futrelle and Doyle had analogous protagonists: both are brilliant, eccentric men who solve seemingly impossible mysteries. For anyone reading "The Problem of Cell 13," comparisons between Van Dusen and Holmes are inevitable. Given the characters' similarities, it is curious that Van Dusen has

" "

FUTRELLE MAKES CLEAR THROUGH HIS
IMPERSONAL NARRATOR THAT VAN DUSEN'S
ACCOMPLISHMENTS 'DEEPLY STIRRED THE
WORLD AT LARGE,' BUT DOYLE MAKES MORE OF
AN IMPACT ON THE READER BY SHOWING FROM
DR. WATSON'S POINT OF VIEW HOW INCREDIBLE
HOLMES'S SKILLS ARE."

been largely forgotten, whereas Holmes has remained a huge part of our modern culture. There have been countless adaptations of Doyle's work over the years: films, television series, plays, and pastiches, as well as scholarly works. Even those who have never read a Holmes story find called to mind the fog of Victorian London and the dark, thin, pipe-smoking genius of Baker Street when they hear his name. Why is Sherlock Holmes a central figure in popular culture, while Futrelle's character has been relegated to a mere footnote?

Mary Anne Hutchinson, writing in the *Cyclopedia of World Authors II*, proposes that Futrelle's early death on the *Titanic* is to blame for his lack of reputation today. "Had he not died so tragically and suddenly only five years after beginning his career as a mystery writer," Hutchinson believes, "he would now be remembered as one of its most celebrated practitioners." Perhaps that is so. Doyle certainly was more prolific, but Doyle's tales also have something, right from the beginning, that Futrelle's stories lack. It is Doyle's use of Watson as his narrator that brings Holmes himself to life.

The tradition of the brilliant detective having a sidekick of sorts was already established before either Futrelle or Doyle set pen to paper. Edgar Allan Poe, in "The Murders in the Rue Morgue" (1841), which is widely credited as the first modern detective story, gave his C. Auguste Dupin a friend, though unnamed, who narrates the story. In "The Problem of Cell 13," we meet Van Dusen and his circumstantial friend and partner, Hutchinson Hatch. Hatch, however, is little more than a pair of legs for

Van Dusen to send out into the world where he cannot go given the parameters of the escape challenge. The two men have little contact throughout the story, and Futrelle does not make any effort to establish the nature of their friendship. The reader has little sense of who Hatch is, other than the bare facts that Futrelle includes: he is a reporter, always keen for a sensational story. Futrelle's third-person narrator competently presents the puzzle and describes for us Van Dusen's "peculiar, almost grotesque, personality," but we have no idea what Hatch might think about him.

Doyle, on the other hand, perfected the sidekick trope, creating in Watson a character far easier to love than his famous friend. In the opening pages of *A Study in Scarlet*, the first published Sherlock Holmes novel, we learn that Watson is a doctor who has been wounded in military service in Afghanistan. He has returned to England and, having neither family nor friends, must find a place to live that he can afford. Watson is a three-dimensional character from the very start, and because we see Holmes through Watson's eyes, he becomes real to us as well.

Consider how Van Dusen got his moniker, the "Thinking Machine": it is "a newspaper catch-phrase applied to him at the time of a remarkable exhibition at chess." This is a rather impersonal way to get a nickname and gives the impression of an unfeeling man. Contrast this to the scene in which Watson calls Holmes a "calculating machine." Watson levels this accusation at Holmes in *The Sign of Four* because he does not seem to notice the attractiveness of their client, a Miss Mary Morstan, who later becomes Watson's wife. Therefore this comment from Watson is less about Holmes lacking feeling or personality and more about a man starting to fall in love and unable to understand how his friend could fail to notice the virtues of the woman he admires.

In "The Problem of Cell 13," Futrelle tells us that Van Dusen's mental faculties are amazing: "He spent week after week, month after month, in the seclusion of his small laboratory from which had gone forth thoughts that staggered scientific associates and deeply stirred the world at large." Doyle, on the other hand, portrays Holmes's cleverness through Watson's bafflement, amusement, and amazement. Watson meets his old medical-school chum Stamford,

At first, the warden is puzzled and frustrated that he cannot figure out how Van Dusen is sending notes and acquiring materials, but in the end he is smiling in amazement at Van Dusen's cleverness.
(© Lipowski Milan / Shutterstock.com)

who mentions Holmes as a possible flatmate. Holmes is "sure to be at the laboratory," Stamford explains, then continuing: "He either avoids the place for weeks, or else he works there from morning till night." The reader, with Watson, wonders about this obsessive behavior, but Doyle does not yet reveal the reasons for it. Then, rather than simply being told that our hero comes up with "thoughts that staggered scientific associates," we walk into the lab with Watson and find Holmes in the very midst of one his experiments—he has just perfected a new test for detecting blood stains that will revolutionize the collection of incriminating evidence.

Futrelle makes clear through his impersonal narrator that Van Dusen's accomplishments "deeply stirred the world at large," but Doyle makes more of an impact on the reader by showing from Dr. Watson's point of view how incredible Holmes's skills are. When Holmes explains his work as a consulting detective, Watson is all amazement: "Do you mean to say . . . that without leaving your room you can

unravel some knot which other men can make nothing of, although they have seen every detail for themselves?" Throughout "The Problem of Cell 13," the warden is frustrated because he does not understand Van Dusen's plan. He is "sadly puzzled" when he cannot figure out how Van Dusen is getting his materials into the cell, and, after Van Dusen escapes, he is desperate to know how. When Van Dusen explains everything at the close of the story, Dr. Ransome is thrilled and impressed, exclaiming, "Wonderful! . . . Perfectly amazing." However, because neither the warden nor Dr. Ransome is a fully fleshed character like Watson, their reactions remain one step removed. We are not as interested in what they think and feel—we cannot be certain we can trust their reactions the way we can rely on dear old Watson.

It may be that the nature of "The Problem of Cell 13" as a "locked-room" story is the problem. Because Van Dusen spends most of the story isolated and locked in a cell, he and Hatch have no face-to-face interaction. However, in Doyle's story "The 'Gloria Scott'" (originally published as "The Adventure of the 'Gloria Scott'"), Holmes relates to Watson his very first case, which happened long before the two friends met. In this tale, we see a clear illustration of how the use of Watson as a first-person narrator increases the reader's interest in Holmes's adventures, even when Watson himself is not present during the action. On a quiet winter's night by the fire, Holmes gives Watson "a little tarnished cylinder" that contains an "enigmatical message," and immediately the reader, like Watson, wants to know the story behind the note. The rest of the story is told by Holmes, and Watson is not involved in the mystery, but the structure of the framing story allows the reader to be infected by Watson's curiosity as the story begins.

Detective fiction is by nature largely driven by the plot. The author must reveal the clues artfully to move the story along to a dramatic revelation of the solution. But good detective fiction gives the reader a little something more along the way: characters who are as intriguing as their cases. Having Watson tell Holmes's stories gives insight into both characters and makes readers more interested in the plot. Watson's reactions to Holmes humanize him, whether the detective is being condescending or witty. In contrast, readers might find it challenging to think of Futrelle's Van Dusen as anything other than a machine. We do not see glimpses into his personality or his relationships, and therefore the clever plot is left as the only draw to a story like "The Problem of Cell 13."

Source: Kristen Sarlin Greenberg, Critical Essay on "The Problem of Cell 13," in *Short Stories for Students*, Gale, Cengage Learning, 2015.

Eddie McIlwaine

In the following essay, McIlwaine describes Futrelle as an author whose work has been "unjustly neglected."

The re-appearance on the book shelves today of a mystery novel called *The Chase of the Golden Plate* is a reminder of how the author Jacques Futrelle, (37), perished in the *Titanic* tragedy nearly 101 years ago.

He was returning home to Massachusetts after a holiday visit to the British Isles and Europe, including a few days in Belfast during which it is thought he was researching his next detective story on this side of the ocean.

As the liner was sinking Futrelle (right) refused the offer of an empty seat on a lifeboat next to his wife Lily May Peel, another writer, even though he had to force her to be among the rescued.

Later Lily had her husband's final book *My Lady's Garter*, published posthumously, dedicated "to the heroes of the Atlantic."

The Chase of the Golden Plate, Futrelle's first book, is re-issued today by Hesperus Press whose mission is to revive works written by special authors which they feel have been unjustly neglected. It's the story of a cheeky robbery at a high society fancy dress party by a thief dressed as a robber and accompanied by a beautiful girl accomplice.

Futrelle was a journalist, born in Georgia who wrote for the *Atlanta Journal*, the *Boston Post* and the *New York Herald* before he became a full time author and produced scores of bestsellers with titles like *The Problem of Cell 13*, *Jackdaw*, *The Man Who Was Lost* and *A Piece of String*.

Most of his yarns featured Professor S.F.X. Augustus Van Dusen—nicknamed by his police friends as The Thinking Machine—because, like Sherlock Holmes, he always applied logic to every crime he encountered, including the one involving the theft of the golden plate.

In the end of course it is The Thinking Machine and a journalist called Hatch who solve the mystery.

Source: Eddie McIlwaine, "He Died on *Titanic*, Now Author Gets Print Return," in *Belfast Telegraph*, December 29, 2012, p. 26.

R. A. Whay

In the following review, Whay praises the ingenuity of Futrelle's stories.

For sheer ingenuity, the stories which Mr. Futrelle has built up about Professor Augustus Van Dusen, the Thinking Machine, are equalled by little, and surpassed by nothing in contemporary fiction. The soundest criticism that is to be brought against this second series of tales is that, as was the case with the first series, the invention is at times almost too clever. The deductions of the Thinking Machine are so swift and astonishing that the reader is often puzzled in following them. Mr. Sherlock Holmes had an uneven disposition and occasionally made mistakes. Professor Van Dusen is also more or less irritable, but his invariable infallibility proves in the end a strain on the credulity. Yet his exploits taken in homeopathic doses must appeal to the most jaded appetite.

Throughout the tales of *The Thinking Machine on the Case* the varied results of man's mechanical cunning play a prominent part. In the first story it is a motor boat carrying a dead man wearing a uniform that leads the authorities to think him a captain in the French navy, which crashes into a wharf in Boston Harbour. Another tale deals with the mysterious murder at his key board of the operator of the wireless of an ocean steamship. Of particular grimness is the story of "The Crystal Gazer," which introduces an elaborate device by which the victim, peering into a crystal, sees what he takes to be a vision of his own murder. Again there is "The Phantom Motor," which, night after night, enters one end of a short road lined on both sides by ten-foot walls, never comes out the other end, and cannot be found between. But what, above all, marks Mr. Futrelle's work in this as well as the earlier book, is not the cleverness of any particular tale, but rather the consistent excellence and fertility of invention of them all.

Source: R. A. Whay, "Jacques Futrelle's *The Thinking Machine on the Case*," in *Bookman*, Vol. 27, June 1908, pp. 496–97.

Rafford Pyke

In the following review, Pyke compares Van Dusen with Sherlock Holmes.

In sheer inventiveness and ingenuity [the stories in *The Thinking Machine*] at times surpass the now classical problems which interested the mind of Sherlock Holmes. "The Thinking Machine" is a name given to a certain Professor van Dusen, who is the incarnation of unemotional science. His logic is without a flaw; his mental processes are infallible. Sherlock Holmes was partly a man of action; but Professor van Dusen is wholly a man of thought. In this respect he resembles Mycroft Holmes, but without the amiable eccentricities of that cogitator. The problems that are given to him to solve are often, on the face of them, so impossible as to make the reader absolutely certain that they cannot in any way be mastered.

Take, for example the problem of Cell 13. Professor van Dusen consents to be placed in a certain cell of Chisholm Prison. The prison is

built of granite. It is surrounded by a wall of solid masonry eighteen feet high and topped by a five-foot fence of steel rods. Armed guards are stationed in the yard both night and day, and electric lights dispel darkness as soon as the sun sets. Cell 13 is usually occupied by some person under sentence of death. Its walls are of solid masonry; its door is of chilled steel. Its window is a narrow slit. Outside the door are heavily barred gates, at which a sentinel is always watching.

Into this cell The Thinking Machine is thrust, after being thoroughly searched, and the doors are locked and barred upon him. The warden is especially warned to keep him in confinement, for The Thinking Machine has declared that within a week's time he will pass out of this dungeon unhindered and without the knowledge of his keepers. Here, surely, is a problem that seems insoluble, and the reader is quite as incredulous as are the friends of The Thinking Machine who arrange the test.

This story is perhaps the most absorbingly interesting and puzzling in the book; but the others are all extremely clever. If, after the reading is over, one still ranks them below the adventures of Sherlock Holmes, it is because the latter have greater realism and accord more closely with the conditions of actual life. Holmes sometimes makes mistakes, and this fact renders him more real as a human being. The incidents which befall him are also far more usual, and for that very reason are the more convincing. But *The Thinking Machine* is a book that will be read with avidity for its great cleverness; and other stories by the same author are certain to receive an appreciative welcome.

Source: Rafford Pyke, "Mr. Futrelle's *The Thinking Machine*," in *Bookman*, Vol. 25, June 1907, p. 433.

Nation

In the following review, an anonymous writer looks at Futrelle's work (along with Arthur Morrison's) as part of the genre of the detective story.

The short detective story has become so thoroughly conventionalized within the last few years that it would be as unfair to accuse an author of imitating Sir Conan Doyle by describing the exploits of an unofficial detective of marked personal peculiarities, rapid and incisive deductive powers, as to accuse him of imitating Pinero by writing a play in three acts.

Mr. Futrelle has been bold enough to christen his elucidator in so many words the "Thinking Machine," mentioning only now and then his real name, Prof. Augustus S. F. X. Van Dusen, the scientific man who is consulted on occasions of great stress by Hutchinson Hatch, reporter, a journalistic counterpart of Dr. Watson. "Nothing is impossible," is Professor Van Dusen's dictum. "The mind is master of all things." Martin Hewitt, Mr. Morrison's detective on the other hand, always maintains, more modestly, that he has "no system beyond a judicious use of ordinary faculties."

The criminals with whom Prof. Van Dusen has to deal in the seven tales [of *The Thinking Machine*] are, perhaps, as modern a lot as fiction affords. They turn scientific knowledge to their own purposes in ways that are dark indeed; in fact, rather beyond the scope even of legitimate science. Mr. Morrison's criminals, equally ingenious, employ more familiar agencies for their nefarious business. Mr. Futrelle, it might be said in generalization, is the more fertile devising enigmas, Mr. Morrison in answering them without straining.

On this point, the detective story must be judged by canons of its own. It is the first duty of the writer to carry out his implied contract to provide for every problem a solution that shall be complete and adequate, with the minimum of evidence left in the detective's sole possession till the last moment. From this point of view, it is hard to justify the use of an actually false clue under any circumstances. The reader should have the chance to match his wits on even terms against the writer, who must give as much information as possible, without disclosing the final solution. Now Mr. Futrelle is guilty of keeping up suspense by false evidence. The whole mystery in one of these stories is sustained through twenty-six pages, on the supposition that a revolver shot fired in a certain direction struck nothing. It is only explained at the very end of the story that the constable merely missed his mark. The mistake might easily happen in an actual criminal case, but it does not properly belong in a detective story. For a narrative that complies with the same condition, giving substantially all the necessary clues before the final revelation comes, the first of the Martin Hewitt stories, "The Lenten Croft Robberies" may be cited.

Source: Review of *The Thinking Machine* and *Martin Hewitt, Investigator*, in *Nation*, Vol. 84, No. 2185, May 16, 1907, p. 457.

SOURCES

Alter, Alexandra, "The Return of the Serial Novel," in *Wall Street Journal*, April 11, 2013, http://online.wsj.com/news/articles/SB10001424127887324020504578396742330033344 (accessed September 7, 2014).

Behling, Laura L., "Mystery and Detective Fiction," in *American History through Literature, 1870–1920*, edited by Tom Quirk and Gary Scharnhorst, Vol. 2, Charles Scribner's Sons/Thomson Gale, 2006, pp. 737–42.

Doyle, Arthur Conan, "The 'Gloria Scott,'" in *Sherlock Holmes: The Complete Novels and Stories*, Vol. 1, Bantam Classics, 2003, p. 584.

———, *The Sign of Four*, in *Sherlock Holmes: The Complete Novels and Stories*, Vol. 1, Bantam Classics, 2003, p. 135.

———, *A Study in Scarlet*, in *Sherlock Holmes: The Complete Novels and Stories*, Vol. 1, Bantam Classics, 2003, pp. 6, 17.

"Émile Gaboriau," in *Encyclopædia Britannica*, July 6, 2006, http://www.britannica.com/EBchecked/topic/223197/Emile-Gaboriau (accessed September 7, 2014).

Futrelle, Jacques, "The Problem of Cell 13," in *Detective Fiction: Crime and Compromise*, edited by Dick Allen and David Chacko, Harcourt Brace Jovanovich, 1974, pp. 122–50.

"Hard-Boiled Fiction," in *Encyclopædia Britannica*, October 10, 2013, http://www.britannica.com/EBchecked/topic/254914/hard-boiled-fiction (accessed September 7, 2014).

Hutchinson, Mary Anne, "Jacques Futrelle," in *Cyclopedia of World Authors II*, edited by Frank N. Magill, Vol. 2, *Day–Kel*, Salem Press, 1989, pp. 560–61.

"Jacques Futrelle," *Biography.com*, http://www.biography.com/people/jacques-futrelle-283814 (accessed September 6, 2014).

Johnson, Roger, Review of *The Thinking Machine: Jacques Futrelle*, http://www.lagergaard.dk/books/rev/thinking.html (accessed September 6, 2014); originally published in *District Messenger*, No. 177, 1998.

Lawson, Mark, "Crime's Grand Tour: European Detective Fiction," in *Guardian* (London, England), October 26, 2012, http://www.theguardian.com/books/2012/oct/26/crimes-grand-tour-european-detective-fiction (accessed September 7, 2014).

Pelaez, Vicky, "The Prison Industry in the United States: Big Business or a New Form of Slavery?," Global Research, March 31, 2014, http://www.globalresearch.ca/the-prison-industry-in-the-united-states-big-business-or-a-new-form-of-slavery/8289 (accessed September 7, 2014).

"Prisons and Executions—the U.S. Model: A Historical Introduction," in *Monthly Review*, Vol. 53, No. 3, July–August 2001, http://monthlyreview.org/2001/07/01/prisons-and-executions-the-u-s-model/ (accessed September 7, 2014).

Routledge, Chris, "Detective Fiction," in *Bowling, Beatniks, and Bell-Bottoms: Pop Culture of 20th-Century America*, edited by Sara Pendergast and Tom Pendergast, Vol. 2, *1920s–1930s*, UXL, 2002, pp. 441–43.

Siegel, Mark R., "The New Serial Revolution," in *Huffington Post*, October 8, 2012, http://www.huffington post.com/mark-r-siegel/the-new-serial-revolution_b_1936625.html (accessed September 7, 2014).

Sjavik, Jan, "Hansen, Maurits Christopher," in *Historical Dictionary of Scandinavian Literature and Theater*, 2006, http://scandinavian_literature.enacademic.com/114/Hansen,_Maurits_Christopher (accessed September 7, 2014).

Sundstrom, Alison, "From Sherlock to SVU: The History of Detective Fiction," in *Breaking Character*, November 19, 2012, http://www.breaking-character.com/post/2012/11/19/From-Sherlock-to-SVU-The-History-of-Detective-Fiction.aspx (accessed September 6, 2014).

Velez, Luis, Eric-Jan Noomen, George Behe, and Phillip Gowan, "Jacques Heath Futrelle," in *Encyclopedia Titanica*, http://www.encyclopedia-titanica.org/titanic-victim/jacques-futrelle.html (accessed September 6, 2014).

FURTHER READING

Brickhill, Paul, *The Great Escape*, Buccaneer Books, 1993.

> This nonfiction book, originally published in 1950, recounts the experiences of a group of British and Commonwealth soldiers in prison camp in Germany during World War II. The men worked for over a year on their plan, forging uniforms and paperwork and digging tunnels to freedom. The story was adapted into a 1963 film that has become a classic.

Chesterton, G. K., *The Complete Father Brown Stories*, Wordsworth Editions, 1989.

> Chesterton is perhaps best known for his short stories featuring Father Brown, a priest and detective. Chesterton began publishing the Father Brown stories only a few years after "The Problem of Cell 13" appeared.

Futrelle, Jacques, *The Diamond Master*, Kessinger Publishing, 2007.

> This volume is a reprint edition of the novel some consider Futrelle's best work. Four mysterious packages containing flawless diamonds are the beginning of an intriguing mystery.

Mansfield-Kelley, Deane, and Lois A. Marchino, eds., *The Longman Anthology of Detective Fiction*, Pearson/Longman, 2005.

> In addition to award-winning stories, editors Mansfield-Kelley and Marchino include a history of the detective genre and information and criticism on the included authors.

SUGGESTED SEARCH TERMS

Jacques Futrelle AND The Problem of Cell 13

Jacques Futrelle AND Thinking Machine

Jacques Futrelle AND detective fiction

Thinking Machine AND Sherlock Holmes

golden age of detective fiction

Titanic victims and survivors

locked room mystery

detective fiction

A Turn with the Sun

John Knowles is best known for his young-adult novel *A Separate Peace*. His 1968 short story "A Turn with the Sun" shares the novel's setting at the fictional Devon Academy, an elite prep school, as well as its main theme of ambiguity of intention in the death of a boy at the school. In "A Turn with the Sun," Knowles signals to the reader that he is going to follow the redemption of a socially ambitious but awkward boy, only to chronicle instead his moral decline. The tale can be found in Knowles's *Phineas: Six Stories* (1968).

JOHN KNOWLES

1968

AUTHOR BIOGRAPHY

John A. Knowles was born on September 16, 1926, in Fairmont, West Virginia. His parents came from Lowell, Massachusetts, but moved to West Virginia for his father, James Knowles, to become an executive of a coal company. Knowles attended the public high school in Oyster Bay, New York, but in 1942, he transferred to the boarding school Phillips Exeter Academy, in New Hampshire. He graduated in 1945 and served briefly in the US Army Air Corps. He attended Yale University, where he worked on the *Yale Daily News*, becoming the editorial secretary in his senior year (1948–1949). Knowles worked for several years as the European correspondent for the *Hartford*

American writer John Knowles
(© Everett Collection Inc. | Alamy)

several of whose stories, including "A Turn with the Sun," are also set at Devon. In an article published in the *Exeter Bulletin*, Knowles acknowledges that he fell in love with the school during the summer he spent there largely alone for remedial study. He describes himself and most of his fellow students as leaving each other alone, except for a few close friends, including a member of the school diving team. None of Knowles's later writing, however, ever enjoyed the same kind of reception as his first novel. As reported by Honan in his obituary,

> Mr. Knowles once told an interviewer that he did not mind having his reputation rest on a single book. "It's paid the bills for 30 years," he said. "It has made my career possible. Unlike most writers, I don't have to do anything else to make a living."

Knowles retired to Florida in the 1990s. He died in a convalescent home in Fort Lauderdale after a short illness on November 29, 2001.

Courant newspaper. He became an associate editor at the travel magazine *Holiday* in 1957.

Encouraged by the prominent playwright Thornton Wilder, who took an interest in his writing, Knowles began work on his first novel, *A Separate Peace*, which was published in 1960. It was a phenomenally successful book, in terms of both critical reception and sales. It was awarded the William Faulkner Foundation Award (for best new writer) and the Rosenthal Award of the National Institute of Arts and Letters. It was quickly included in the new young-adult curriculum that was then becoming fashionable in public schools. The novel was adapted as a film in 1982. It concerns a boy at a fictional elite boarding school, Devon Academy (based on Exeter), who causes an accident that maims a fellow student and eventually results in his death. The tension of the novel is created by Knowles's never revealing whether the fatal action was intentional or accidental. The book's mystery was perpetuated even at the time of Knowles's death when his brother-in-law, Bob Maxwell, told *New York Times* reporter William H. Honan, "John used to say he would never answer that question. . . . He took that one with him."

Knowles wrote half a dozen books, including the short-story collection *Phineas* (1968),

PLOT SUMMARY

"A Turn with the Sun" begins very near the end of its chronological sequence. It is dusk on an early spring day, in the middle of the athletic fields of what the reader will learn is Devon Academy, a prep school (short for "preparatory school," a secondary school aimed at preparing students for college). One of the fields is bounded by a stream that is crossed by a bridge. The school buildings can be seen in the distance. An intramural lacrosse game has just ended, and the boys, walking back to the school, drop one of the balls into the stream. One of the boys is Lawrence Stewart, who tells the others about his exploits in the lacrosse match, scoring the winning goal. Another boy, Bead, invites him to go to the movies. Bead had already arranged to go with an older boy, Bruce, so Lawrence would go along with them. Lawrence is terribly conscious of social rank among his schoolmates and knows that Bruce holds a relatively lofty position. He finds it amazing that Bead, a new student like himself, would be socializing with Bruce. Still, Lawrence realizes that his recent performance will, ever so slightly, raise his own social standing. Lawrence observes to himself that while he has no close friends at school, he has never been bullied either, but simply ignored: "He merely inhabited the nether world of the unregarded, where no one bothered him or bothered about him. Why, after all, should they?"

As Lawrence crosses the bridge, he recalls an incident that turns out to be crucial to the story, though its description by the narrator is surprisingly minimal. Last September, he first came to the attention of the socially dominant boys on his fourth day at the school when he made a spectacular double-somersaulting dive off the same bridge. One of the senior boys, Ging Powers, who came from his own hometown, invited him to dinner with some of the others. Later that afternoon, after his dive, Lawrence visited the trophy room in the gymnasium, examining the "James Harvey Fullerton Cup, Awarded Each Year to That Member of the Sixth Form Who, in the Opinion of his Fellows and Masters, Most Closely Exemplifies the Highest Traditions of Devon." It went without saying that the boy's achievements had to be mainly athletic and that the trophy room was a shrine at the heart of the school because athletic achievement was the currency of social capital at Devon. Lawrence hurried back to his room to get dressed for dinner and wrote a letter to someone named Janine, saying he thought he was making a social success at school.

On the day that he made the dive, Lawrence is having dinner with the other boys at the Devon Inn. This is a restaurant, perhaps with a small hotel attached, within walking distance of Devon Academy. The older, more mature boys prefer to have dinner there because it gets them out from under the control of their teachers (called "masters" at this school), at least to a degree. The other boys, besides Lawrence and Ging, are also upperclassmen: Vinnie James, an official of the senior class, and Charles Morrell (known as Captain Marvel), the leading athlete at the school. When Lawrence joins them, they are discussing "punching" as a way to get into social clubs at Harvard, called "final clubs." Although the members of clubs represent the highest society at any of the elite Ivy League schools, Vinnie dismisses them as "crashing bores." Vinnie explains that at these colleges, younger students are invited to a party at which punch is served; when the invitations stop arriving, a student knows he is no longer being considered for membership. Vinnie also comments that while

it is possible to join a final club coming from Devon, it is more certain for graduates of Groton, perhaps the most exclusive prep school in the United States. Ging immediately declares that he would never attend Groton, but Lawrence knows this is an outrageous lie: Ging's mother had tried everything in her power to get him into Groton, only accepting Devon as a poor substitute when that proved impossible. Lawrence mentally compares Ging to Morrell and finds him lacking in every way.

Lawrence decides that he wants to be like Morrell, but instead he proceeds to act like Ging, making up his own lie, that he has two cousins who are in a club at Harvard. Relieved that Ging seems to accept his tale, Lawrence proceeds to babble out a comparison between Devon and Harvard, finally wandering back to his impressive dive, which Morrell says he witnessed. Lawrence goes incoherently on, launching an attack against the dean of Devon, Eleazer Markham Bings-Smith, "the one who looks like Hoover with an Oxford accent.... Why does he talk that way and look that way? Like my beagle, that's the way he looks, like the beagle I've got at home, my beagle looks just like that right after he's had a bath." This does not go down well with the senior boys, and just at that moment, an elderly couple get up from their dinner at a nearby table. Lawrence, in horror, asks whether that is the dean, and if he overheard what Lawrence said. Not waiting for an answer, Lawrence childishly sinks out of his chair to sit beneath the table and bang his head against it in embarrassment. The older man was not the dean but rather the registrar, and Lawrence's comments had not been overheard. Still, the other boys are aghast at Lawrence's behavior, and they also get up and leave.

In the weeks following this social disaster, Lawrence has to deal with and try to understand his failure. He is generally ignored by his own socially marginal housemates and he gives in to terrible fits of anger. In one case, he throws a steamer trunk down the staircase, sending it crashing into the proctor's door. Judging himself entirely by his fellow student's opinions of him, Lawrence concludes: "This was the final, the unbearable affront; they thought him strange, undisciplined, an inferior little boy given to pettish tantrums." As fall is ending, Lawrence decides that his only hope is to make something out of himself through his single talent: self-discipline. From then on, he would work for internal improvement and turn his back on the social world of Devon.

The narration moves its focus outward, describing the passing of the seasons. Lawrence, meanwhile, works on his self-discipline. He follows school athletics; deciding that football is too chaotic for his performance to be under his control, he takes up swimming and makes the junior-varsity swimming team. He views his life at Devon as a contest and feels he has won. He therefore adopts a superior attitude toward his housemates. He implies to others that he will be going to Bermuda for spring break, but one of his housemates, Billy Baldwin, gets him to admit that he is not. Instead of mocking him, Baldwin invites Lawrence to come and visit him over the break. Lawrence lashes out at him in anger, however, as though the possibility of going to Connecticut were too ridiculous to consider. Baldwin retaliates with an accusation that Lawrence's family is unable to keep up with the tuition payments. This wounds Lawrence because it is close to the truth (though the story never reveals the details). Lawrence returns to his family in Virginia for spring break, where his air of superiority alienates Janine.

Lawrence has been excelling academically, but this begins to slip after spring break as he neglects to prepare for classes. He continues to follow school athletics closely. He is persuaded to participate in an intramural lacrosse match that he intended only to watch, and he scores the winning goal. After he showers and dresses, he revisits the trophy room, reliving his frequent daydream of seeing his own name inscribed on the Fullerton Cup. However, looking at it now, he realizes that there is very little room left for new names. Captain Marvel, who will surely win the honor this year, will be the last; there would be no room for his own name in 1954.

Lawrence walks back to school over the bridge where he made the dive last September. The narrative now reaches the point where it began. He and some other boys, Bead and Bruce, decide to go diving again, and in a very understated description, it is revealed that Lawrence drowns.

Two days later, the school masters, led by Dean Kuzak, conduct a sort of inquest, interrogating Bead and Bruce about the incident. The boys are very anxious to shape their testimony to preclude any possibility of negligence on their part, while the masters are keen to establish that he was *happy*—that is, he had not been suicidally depressed. They seem alarmed to learn that Lawrence had no close friends. They conclude that it was an accident, probably caused by a leg cramp. They memorialize Lawrence by placing a portrait of him in the gymnasium trophy room.

CHARACTERS

Billy Baldwin
Baldwin is a housemate of Lawrence's who tries to befriend him by inviting him to visit his family over spring break. Lawrence, however, makes the situation impossible and responds with hostility, engaging in lengthy, scheming calculations about Baldwin's social worth.

Bead
Bead is a housemate of Lawrence's and in the same class year as him. He is one of the boys who goes diving with Lawrence and witnesses his death. Lawrence is amazed at and jealous of Bead's ability to get on friendly terms with prominent upperclassmen like Bruce.

Dean Eleazer Markham Bings-Smith
Bings-Smith, a dean of the school, evidently gave the welcoming speech to the boys on the first day of school. During Lawrence's dinner with Morrell, he goes on a long rant depicting the man as ridiculous, beginning with his name and ending by likening his appearance to that of a wet dog.

Bruce
Bruce is one of the boys who goes diving with Lawrence and witnesses his death. He seems to be somewhat older than Lawrence and a more prominent athletic figure at the school.

Vinnie James
James is a senior and a friend to Morrell, who is a member of the group Lawrence is invited to dine with after his first dive. He provides information about the social life at Harvard during the dinner.

Janine

Janine is the girl to whom Lawrence writes when he seems on the verge of social success after his dive. When he sees her over spring break, the change in his character distresses her. Their exact relationship is not specified; she may be a girlfriend (his letter to her is described as "ardent," meaning forceful or passionate), or she may be his sister.

Dean Kuzak

Dean Kuzak leads the investigation undertaken by the school into Lawrence's death. He is skilled at his rhetorical task of proving that the death was not a suicide, as opposed to discovering what actually happened.

Captain Marvel

See Charles Taylor Morrell

The Masters

The masters, or teachers, at Devon are conspicuous by their absence from the narrative. They are scarcely mentioned at all, and only two of the deans are named, one because Lawrence finds the name ridiculous and the other because he leads the investigation into Lawrence's death. Only Lawrence's French master is even mentioned by his title. This contributes to Lawrence's characterization: he evidently has no interest in his teachers. This is unexpected, since many aspects of Lawrence's character would lead the reader to think he would be naturally subservient to authority, but Lawrence reserves this attitude for socially prominent boys, and is in contrast to the close relationships that Knowles himself had with his teachers at Exeter. Although the point is not emphasized in "A Turn with the Sun," one of the main subjects of study at an elite school like Devon at the time would have been Latin, and the teachers were traditionally called masters as a closer translation of the Latin word *magister*, which means both master and teacher (it is also the root of the English term *magistrate*).

Charles Taylor Morrell

Morrell is the leading athlete at Devon and, in Lawrence's opinion, the ideal image of a mature, promising boy. He is nicknamed Captain Marvel by the other students. To Lawrence he appears "cool, unconcerned, [someone] who would easily rise to the top of every group he entered." He is the leader of the group that invites Lawrence to dinner after his impressive dive, which Morrell witnessed. He seems certain to be the winner of the Fullerton Cup for his year. Like his companions, he is appalled by Lawrence's childish behavior.

Ging Powers

Ging is in Captain Marvel's social circle and comes from Lawrence's hometown in Virginia, so he is the one who extends the dinner invitation to Lawrence after his first dive. Like the other boys, Ging is seen through Lawrence's eyes. Lawrence immediately identifies him as a hypocrite and sycophant (someone who flatters those in authority), trying to do nothing but impress the other boys to increase his own prestige. Since he knows Ging's family, Lawrence realizes that his attack against rival school Groton is a case of sour grapes: "The climber! What a lying climber! He had never realized before what a fool Ging was." This evaluation really reveals more about Lawrence's character than Ging's, since he seems oblivious to the fact he is doing just the same. The reader sees all of the other characters in "A Turn with the Sun" through Lawrence's eyes, so nothing learned about them can be accepted as impartial.

"Fruitcake" Putsby

Putsby is the boy who lives in the room next to Lawrence's. He is bullied and stigmatized as homosexual, as indicated by his derisive nickname. Bullying of this kind does not necessarily seek out boys who are gay, but can attach the stigma of being a victim to any boy, and it may have fallen on Putsby simply because of his name (*putz* being the Yiddish word for the male organ).

Lawrence Bates Stewart

Lawrence is the main character of "A Turn with the Sun," and although there is an impersonal narrator, the story is essentially told from his perspective and mostly concerns the development of his inner life during his year at Devon Academy. He is most likely fourteen years old at the time the story begins. The narrator summarizes Lawrence's position for the reader:

> He had entered in the fourth-form year, when the class was already clearly stratified, he arrived knowing only one person in the school, he came from a small Virginia town which no one had ever heard of, he was unremarkable athletically, his clothes were wrong, his vocabulary was wrong, and when he talked at all it was about the wrong things.

As this reveals, Lawrence is deeply conscious of his perceived inferiority to the other boys at the school.

One of the main functions of a school like Devon is to establish social connections between boys from elite families, fostering networks that will support them in later life. Lawrence is dimly aware of this and takes as his own purpose the goal of worming his way into the most elite circles at Devon. He rightly senses that the easiest way to do this is by showing himself to be athletically gifted. This is the purpose behind the spectacular dive he makes on his fourth day at the school. His efforts are noticed and result in a dinner invitation from the inner circle of Charles Morrell—Captain Marvel—the star athlete and social leader of Devon. But Lawrence ultimately fails because he is too immature and unsophisticated, as yet, to play the role he covets.

Lawrence's response to failure is to turn inward, to build up his inner worth through self-discipline, but he still lacks the ability to turn anything he gains in this way into social capital. In fact, his self-absorption causes him to reject integration into the social life of the school. He imagines that he is superior to those he is in fact inferior to, and he thinks that things should be given to him when in fact he has to earn them. He builds up detailed fantasies of his success, seeing himself as a natural winner of the cherished Fullerton Cup, but does nothing to effectively work toward success. He spends a tremendous amount of effort on self-criticism, such as mentally rewriting, in a better style, every line he speaks during his dinner with Morrell and his friends as soon as it leaves his mouth, but he refuses to critique and thereby change his core identity. His vanity prevents him from understanding his own shortcomings:

> His failure to strike out in some, in any, direction puzzled him in October, when he had been at Devon six weeks, angered him in December, made him contemptuous in February, and on this burgeoning April day when everything else stirred with life, took on the coloration of tragedy.

He does work to change himself, but he becomes more thoroughly what he already was, rather than becoming something new. When he finally realizes that his position is hopeless, not because real change is impossible but because he is unwilling to do what is necessary to change, he has no desire to continue playing a game he has lost and exits.

TOPICS FOR FURTHER STUDY

- *Little Men* (1871) is Louisa May Alcott's sequel to her better-known work *Little Women*. It follows several characters form the first novel as they go off to a boarding school. It was adapted as an animated television program in Japan, *Little Women II: Jo's Boys* (1993). Give a talk to your class, including clips from the show, comparing the view of boarding-school life it presents with that given in "A Turn with the Sun."

- "A Turn with the Sun" shares not only the setting at Devon but also many thematic similarities with Knowles's *A Separate Peace*. Read that novel and write a paper comparing the treatment of shared themes in the two works.

- The websites of elite boarding schools such as Phillips Exeter Academy (http://www.exeter.edu) or Rugby School (http://www.rugbyschool.net) include sections on student life. Give a talk to your class comparing these statements with the view of boarding school life given in "A Turn with the Sun."

- One of the most successful series of historical novels ever written is the Flashman Papers series by George MacDonald Fraser. These stories chronicle the fictional history of a minor character from the 1857 novel *Tom Brown's School Days*. Write your own short story about the experience of one of the minor characters in "A Turn with the Sun" during the Korean War (1950–1953). The plot should turn on life lessons he learned at Devon, particularly through his having known Lawrence.

THEMES

Ambiguity

The climax of "A Turn with the Sun" is the death of its main character, Lawrence Stewart. In warm weather, according to the story, it is a

For a long while, Lawrence feels out of place at Devon. (© *Cynthia Farmer | Shutterstock.com*)

common practice for the boys at Devon to dive from a bridge into a small river that runs through the campus. On one April evening at the end of the story, Lawrence and two of his fellow students do so, and Lawrence drowns. The story leaves ambiguous (uncertain) whether his death is an accident or a suicide. On the surface, everything points to it being an accident. The masters at the school conduct an investigation and find that the death was accidental; presumably, any formal investigation by the police or coroner would have had the same result, although this is never mentioned in the text. However, the masters are keenly aware that suicide is a possibility, and they work not to find the truth but to make a plausible case that the death was an accident. It would reflect poorly on them and on the reputation of the school if one of the boys in their charge intentionally killed himself. During their questioning they shamelessly lead the other two boys who witnessed the incident, to get them to say that

Lawrence was *happy*, in other words that he was not in a suicidal depression. The boys are relieved to be led in this direction since it will relieve them of any guilt they might feel over failing to identify and prevent a suicide. The interests of the parties in reaching the verdict of accident betray its potential falsity. The judgment is made not because it is true but because it is easier for everyone.

The facts, even as they are revealed in the "investigation," suggest a different conclusion. In the first case, Lawrence was a very strong swimmer, and even if he had had a leg cramp (as everyone decides must have been the case), he could surely have managed to make some effort to surface even with only three limbs working. One could believe that he might have succumbed after a struggle, but the fact is, he went under the water and never came up, making no effort to save himself. Since it is never mentioned as a possibility, it is apparent that there was no bruise on Lawrence's head from being knocked unconscious. The masters are rightly alarmed to discover that Lawrence had no close friends after a year at the school, evidence of a disturbed psychology. During the investigation, one of the boys blurts out, "I don't think he cared." This gets to the heart of the matter, as the masters recognize, but they quickly guide the boy to make his statement mean that he was merely confident in his diving ability. It is clearly a possibility that Lawrence, incapable of feeling any pleasure in life, did not care whether he lived or died. However, the story never provides a definitive answer.

Natural Cycles

The title of "A Turn with the Sun" is a poetic description of the passage of a year. At many points, the narrator swoops far away from the story to give an overview of the passing of the seasons:

> [Lawrence] returned in the middle of April to find Devon transformed. He had forgotten that the bleak lanes and roads, winding between gaunt, skeletal trees, were beautiful when the earth turned once again toward the sun. Tiny leaves of callow green sprouted from the gray branches, and the living scents of the earth hung softly in the air.

In fact, the narrative does not occupy the space of a year, but only part of an academic year—not quite seven months. The annual cycle is emphasized so that the attentive reader will realize that it is incomplete. The cycle cannot be finished because Lawrence's death intervenes. This interruption calls attention to Lawrence's incompleteness of another kind, his thwarted, misshapen personality, the exploration of which is the true purpose of the story.

STYLE

In Medias Res

"A Turn with the Sun" takes place during Lawrence's fourth-form year (equivalent to tenth grade) at Devon. The title refers to the passage of that year. The story begins very near the end, in April, when Lawrence is about to make a second dive off of the bridge over the stream that runs through the campus. The bulk of the narrative consists of Lawrence's introspectively recalling the academic year. This is a common pattern in fiction, for the story to begin near its climax and fill in the details necessary to understand its significance through flashback. It is

described by the Latin phrase *in medias res*, meaning "in the middle of the story." The classic example is Homer's long poem the *Odyssey*, which begins a few weeks before its conclusion and fills in the events of the preceding twenty years through a series of nested recollections by various characters. Knowles's handling of the approach is somewhat unusual, however. When Knowles reaches the point where his narrative catches up with the first scene, he gives the reader no clue, but merely presses on with the narrative as though he has simply been telling it in chronological order.

MacGuffin

The two key events in "A Turn with the Sun" are Lawrence's two dives from the bridge on the Devon campus, first in September and again the following April. The first dive brings Lawrence some hope of swift acceptance into the social hierarchy of the school (a chance he throws away though his own foolish behavior), while the second one is the climax of the story and results in Lawrence's death. The odd thing about these events is that Knowles does nothing to play them up. They are not described in detail but rather are mentioned so casually that the reader can easily miss their significance. This is particularly true of the second case: the brief description, "he drowned that night," is buried in the middle of a sentence. The dives are what movie director Alfred Hitchcock called a MacGuffin: something that is of intense interest to the characters in the story but otherwise irrelevant to the audience. A classic example, from one of Hitchcock's films, is the microfilm that a Soviet spy is attempting to smuggle out of the United States in *North by Northwest*. The MacGuffin allows the storyteller to organize a narrative around a conventional plot while creating space for a second narrative, usually psychological in nature, to emerge and engage the audience's attention. Knowles, on behalf of the reader, has no interest in the dives themselves, but wishes to explore how Lawrence's character is shaped by the first one, and how the consequences of the first one lead to his probable suicide in the second.

HISTORICAL CONTEXT

Boarding Schools

The fictional Devon Academy is an aristocratic boarding school. Schools where the sons of elite families would live away from their families had

COMPARE
&
CONTRAST

- **1950s:** Boarding schools like the fictional Devon or its real-life inspiration Exeter are generally limited to male students.

  Today: Most elite boarding schools, including Exeter, are coeducational (accepting both male and female students).

- **1950s:** Student social clubs (called "final" clubs) at Harvard University are overseen by the school administration.

  Today: Although membership is still limited to Harvard students, the final clubs disassociated themselves from the school and became private entities in 1984 in order to avoid Title IX regulation, which helps equalize the educational resources available to boys and girls. Although a few final clubs have recently been founded for women, the traditional clubs remain to a remarkable degree segregated by sex.

- **1950s:** Devon, likes its inspiration, Exeter, caters to the sons of socially and economically elite families.

  Today: Exeter, with an endowment of more than a billion dollars (the largest of any secondary school in the world), is refocusing its admission policy toward academic promise rather than social connections.

---

their origin in medieval Europe, especially England (where these institutions, generally associated with the Church of England, are paradoxically called public schools). At the time, there were only a few universities; they were essentially religious centers where young men could gain the education and social polish necessary to function at court, the center of power, and to prepare to practice a profession such as law, which was necessary for any meaningful role in political governance. The opportunity to gain connections with other young men who would soon play leading roles in government was just as important as the education at public schools, even more than at university. Especially after the Industrial Revolution, the isolation from home and the strict discipline of the schools were seen as necessary training for an aristocratic class that might be called upon to suppress class revolt and govern a colonial empire. This is why violent sports like rugby and later American football were favored by the schools, as was a culture of class and national superiority. Lawrence clearly undergoes this kind of aristocratic hardening at Devon. It becomes obvious to him that the only way he can succeed is by cultivating an arrogant manner and becoming dead to ordinary human feeling.

Of course, the historical role of such schools in grooming the aristocracy is much less prominent in a twentieth-century American institution like Devon. Nevertheless, these schools are still looked upon as an entrance to an elite world based on both superior education and social networking. At Devon, the students are well aware that the main purpose of their boarding-school education is to prepare them to attend even more elite centers of higher learning, such as Harvard University, and to enter the elite social network of its final clubs. The sudden separation of a boy from his family is now seen as more traumatic than was long supposed, and it contributes to the common characterization of the schools as a kind of prison. The English novelist Evelyn Waugh observes in his novel *Decline and Fall* that "anyone who has been to an English public school will always feel comparatively at home in prison." Lawrence is alive to this aspect of the boarding school when he observes, "Devon is like some kind of country club–penitentiary, where the inmates don't take walks around the courtyard, they go to the private penitentiary golf course for eighteen holes."

An infamous aspect of boarding-school life is bullying, where weaker boys are the object of

Lawrence hopes to gain status and acceptance by excelling in lacrosse, but he comes to realize that he cannot base his identity on the regard of others. *(© kml | Shutterstock.com)*

aggression generated largely in reaction to the general circumstances of school life. Lawrence comments on this when he muses that "he had never found a mixture of sour cream and Rice Krispies in his bed at night, no one had ever poured ink into the tub while he was bathing." Lawrence was spared this treatment because of his insignificance. He did not seem important enough to the other boys even to bully. As one would expect in an atmosphere in which teenage boys are crammed together without female companionship, homosexual acts are a common part of boarding-school life, often abusively in the context of bullying. One boy at Devon is given the humiliating nickname of "Fruitcake" Putsby (*fruit* being a slur used for gay men). This does not necessarily mean that

he was a homosexual or engaged in homosexual acts, but the insulting of fellow students as homosexuals remained a common means of attack among teenagers.

CRITICAL OVERVIEW

Knowles's first major publication was his 1960 novel *A Separate Peace*, which, like "A Turn with the Sun," is set at a fictional private boys' school called Devon Academy. It won the William Faulkner Foundation Award for the best novel by a new author but did not attract much critical attention or popular success. This changed in the late 1960s when the fashion for using a curriculum of young-adult literature in American high schools began. Many novels whose principal characters are adolescents, such as William Golding's *Lord of the Flies* (1954) and J. D. Salinger's *A Catcher in the Rye* (1951), originally written for a general audience, were retrofitted into this category. *A Separate Peace* benefited from the same treatment.

Although Knowles's books and stories are now frequently assigned in American high schools, they still do not attract much scholarship. The only analytical treatment of "A Turn with the Sun" was undertaken by Zia Hasan in the entry on Knowles in the 1981 *Critical Survey of Short Fiction*. In Hasan's view, the story, like Knowles's fiction generally, possesses "a universality which leaves the reader with an insight about the condition of man." Regarding the stories in the collection *Phineas*, which includes "A Turn with the Sun," the "final effect is aimed at more than one level, a symbolic timelessness coming from the context of each story. The plot is only half of each story; the other half is the matrix of the earth from which the author, the story, and the phenomenon of life emerge." Hasan explains, "Structurally, 'A Turn with the Sun' is a modern short story following in the mode of such writers as Katherine Mansfield, James Joyce, and Sherwood Anderson and sharply distinct from the contemporary mode of stories with a surreal surface structure." Hasan finds that "A Turn with the Sun," as suggested by the story's title, contrasts the serenity of the natural world with the violent and chaotic events in the characters' lives, even at the smallest level: "The positioning of words in the first sentence,... together with the punctuation and the soft vowel sounds grouped together, suggests the softness of dusk and is in direct contrast to Lawrence's experience." Hasan expands, "Everything that Lawrence does or experiences is set against a backdrop of changing seasons, of a beautiful nature indifferent to the upheavals around it." At the same time, the combination of the natural and the human builds up the totality of the story: "The important images and recurring motifs—the steamy heat, the bridge and the stream, the quest for athletic glory—come together at the end of the story to symbolize Lawrence's intense efforts to be 'regarded.'" The school takes on "microcosmic proportions not through the story line, but by repetitive patterns.... Lawrence's accidental death assumes universal meaning."

> NO MATTER HOW STRONG SOMETHING IS, IF IT DOES NOT BEND, IT WILL EVENTUALLY BREAK."

CRITICISM

Bradley A. Skeen

Skeen is a classicist. In the following essay, he explores "A Turn with the Sun" as a postwar meditation on fascism.

Redemption is a common theme in literature. Countless stories show their characters changed for the better by their experiences in the narrative. After a few pages of John Knowles's "A Turn with the Sun," the reader may well expect that this will turn out to be an account of redemption. The main character, Lawrence, is given a chance to become what he wants and at first fails miserably. A predictable way to develop that beginning would be to show how Lawrence is changed by his failure, becoming able to succeed when he is given a second chance, providing a satisfying conclusion to the narrative. One might expect such a development from the story's obvious and early emphasis (including the title) on the cyclical nature of time: when the opportunity comes around again, Lawrence will seize it. Knowles prepares the reader for such a story: he describes Lawrence's first dive as a sort of baptism. "Everything within him was released; it was as though his dive into the river had washed away his boyhood, and he now stood, clean and happy, wondering dreamily what he would be like now." Initiated in this way, Lawrence ought to be prepared for a brighter future.

However, all of this is misdirection on Knowles's part. He has it in mind to tell a very different kind of story. To start with, the baptismal initiation comes too soon. So far from his boyhood being washed away, Lawrence fails precisely because he persists in acting in a childish manner. He reacts to embarrassment by sinking beneath the table at dinner, like an ostrich burying its head in the sand or like a scolded toddler. In the remainder of the story, Lawrence is given many chances for redemption; he is not unable but rather unwilling to

WHAT DO I READ NEXT?

- John Green's *Looking for Alaska* (2005) is a young-adult novel set at a boarding school. The plot revolves around the death by uncertain causes (accident or suicide) of one of the characters.

- *Spring Snow* (1969), by Yukio Mishima, is a novel whose main characters are prep-school students. The story is set in Japan in the early twentieth century. The novel ends with the protagonist's suicide, under circumstances that make his intentions unclear to the other characters.

- *The Rector of Justin* (1964) is a novel by Louis Auchincloss set at Groton School. The main character is a fictional headmaster of the school whose character must be deciphered from accounts given by six different narrators over a period of sixty years.

- *A Separate Peace* (1960) is Knowles's first novel and his principal work. It also takes place at Devon and is remarkably similar in its themes to "A Turn with the Sun." In the novel, a younger boy, Phineas, shakes a branch from which several boys are diving, causing the star athlete of the school to fall and injure himself, resulting eventually in his death. The tension of the novel derives from the unresolved issue of whether the shaking was accidental or intentional.

- Axel Bundgaard's 2005 title *Muscle and Manliness: The Rise of Sport in American Boarding Schools* is a historical investigation of the role of athletics in the boarding-school experience. Playing sports became accepted as a way of building character and cultivating leadership skills.

- *Goodbye, Mr. Chips* (1934), by James Hilton, is a sentimental exploration of life at English public schools in the late nineteenth and early twentieth centuries, celebrating them as a little world cut off from the larger concerns of political and social change.

take them. He never changes for the better. Instead of a climactic redemption, the story ends in self-destruction. Since Knowles directs the reader in this way, with a false expectation that gradually falls away, leaving only the terrible truth of Lawrence's insufficiency, it will be worth examining just how Knowles develops Lawrence's character.

Lawrence clearly has in mind what his redemption would consist of: becoming someone like Captain Marvel:

> The answer was athletics; not just winning a major D, not health or muscles or some other by-product, but the personality of the athlete itself, the unconscious authority which his strength, his skill, his acclaim gave him.

Lawrence sees Captain Marvel as a mature, powerful figure and wants to be like him, but his opinion of the older boy is tinged by envy, which from the first works against any proper use of him as a model.

Lawrence's first response to his childish failure to enter Captain Marvel's circle is still essentially childish. He throws a tantrum, tossing his luggage dangerously down the steps. But he soon turns to an analytical response to his failure:

> After the first storms had subsided, Lawrence tried again and again to analyze his failure. Whom had he offended, how, why? Why was everything he had ever wanted sparkling like a trophy in his hands one minute and smashed to bits at his feet the next?

Although he evidently fails to answer these questions, he develops a plan for future success:

> There remained this one quality on which he could rely: his capacity for self-discipline. He would turn his back upon the school and the way things went there; he would no longer be embroiled in Devon's cheap competition for importance.... And by God, if only he could, he would be the greatest athlete ever to electrify a crowd on the playing fields of Devon. The greatest, and the most inaccessible.

The inadequacy of this response can be seen in its hypocrisy and inconsistency. His original ideal of the athlete lay precisely in the way that the athlete interacts with those around him, becoming a natural leader. If he cuts himself off from interaction with the school, how can Lawrence hope to achieve that? Even more curiously, Lawrence simultaneously maintains his desire for athletic triumph, while devaluing athletic competition. He will electrify Devon with his success, but he now considers Devon to be *cheap*. He is now struggling not to become a natural leader at Devon, but against Devon. If he fails, as one would reasonably expect, it will be because Devon had become something beneath him. Going to such lengths to insulate himself against failure, he must be expecting it. But Lawrence is also building himself into something greater than Devon, greater than the need for the human relationships it represents. This is a kind of dark narcissism, like the melodramatic villain cackling, *You laughed at me, but I'll show you all!*

Lawrence's attempt to build himself up through self-discipline seems, in fact, to have some effect. Lawrence

> felt his own inner strength grow as it waned in those about him. He had in fact a stronger character now, although it was the strength of the season of Steam Heat, of pale faces and insistent wills.

Knowles makes it clear, though, that this newfound strength is a kind of desperation, more useful for combat than friendship. Lawrence's strength is not only unnaturally aggressive, but also excessively rigid, as reflected in his choice of sports: "there was too much freedom on a football field"; instead, "he turned to the pool where the lanes were rigidly predetermined and he had only to swim up and down, up and down. Into this he poured all the intensity he possessed." No matter how strong something is, if it does not bend, it will eventually break. Lawrence's personality becomes authoritarian, privileging control over freedom.

As Lawrence succeeds in making something of himself, both academically and athletically, on the junior-varsity swim team, the other students' attitude toward him changes. He is treated with more respect, and even with some overtures of friendship. The reader might imagine that this is what Lawrence wanted at the beginning. But the new Lawrence has no use for it:

> Lawrence sensed this at once and became more thoroughly disturbed than at any time since the dinner at the Inn. He loathed them all, of course, and he felt cheated; now that his defenses were invulnerable they were calling off the assault, inviting him to talk terms, asking for a conference out in the open.

Lawrence no longer wants for the other boys to be his friends (if he ever did), or to lead them; he wants them to surrender to him. But even when he imagines that they are doing so (probably no such idea ever occurred to his classmates), that is not enough for him. He seems to want them to go on fighting him and being defeated by him. Lawrence's character has become not only narcissistic (self-involved), but decidedly fascistic, finding fulfillment only in conflict. Politically, *fascism* means government by a dictator representing industrial interests, but as a philosophy it looks toward the violence of warfare as its ideal. Lawrence in the same way now sees perpetual conflict as the only way he has of relating to his fellow students. The only thing that Lawrence remains interested in is power. Human relationships are now meaningless to him. He believes that "he had proved the strongest of all, for what was strength if not the capacity for self-denial? He had divorced from them so successfully that now he didn't care." Lawrence does not see the other students as part of the fascist mob he could merge into, but as the enemy, leaving him to seek virtue in struggle against the whole world. No individual can be as strong as a community. By cutting himself off, Lawrence has actually made himself the weakest of all. His abusive rejection of Billy Baldwin's overture of friendship shows that Lawrence's failure has done nothing to positively transform or redeem him, but rather he has become incapable of wanting the acceptance that had once been his goal.

Lawrence blows up his narcissistic self-regard into an ideology, or belief system: "Life was conquered by the strong-willed, success was demonstrated by austerity; it was the bleak who would inherit the earth." It is not hard to see that this is a description of fascism, that ideology in whose defeat Knowles's generation found its meaning and purpose. Knowles is teaching in miniature the same lesson that William Golding teaches in *Lord of the Flies*: community is the essential basis of human civilization, but power is destructive. The fascist states created a sort of substitute for civilization in which power was the only objective. Knowles is interested in showing how that could have happened on an individual level, through Lawrence's descent into isolation, narcissism, and obsession as substitutes for friendship and accomplishment.

What Lawrence has triumphed over is human feeling. After he has done that, what point can there be for him to go on living? He can expect no further happiness or fulfillment. Fascism aims at death as its objective, whether the death of a vanquished foe or one's own death through self-sacrifice. What death could matter to Lawrence other than his own? This is the truth

Lawrence's realization is closely followed by his accidental drowning.

(© Balazs Kovacs Images / Shutterstock.com)

that the masters of Devon decidedly did not want to discover about Lawrence's drowning.

Source: Bradley Skeen, Critical Essay on "A Turn with the Sun," in *Short Stories for Students*, Gale, Cengage Learning, 2015.

Jay L. Halio

In the following essay, Halio praises Knowles's craftsmanship.

[It is] heartening to see a few like John Knowles who, taking his cue from [Ernest Hemingway's] *The Sun Also Rises* rather than from [Hemingway's] *For Whom the Bell Tolls*, has brought back to recent fiction some of the clear craftsmanship and careful handling of form that characterizes our earlier and best fiction in this century....

[Before] man can be redeemed back into social life, he must first come to terms with himself, he must first—as has been said so often of American writers—discover who and what he is. That we must look inward and learn to face honestly what we see there and then move onwards or anyway outwards is necessary if in the long run we are to salvage any part of our humanity—if, indeed, humanity is in the future to have any meaning or value. This is the enterprise carried forward in contemporary literature by such novelists as Angus Wilson in England and Saul Bellow at home; and alongside their novels John Knowles has now placed two brilliant pieces of fiction, *A Separate Peace* (1960) and *Morning in Antibes* (1962...). His gift is different from theirs as theirs is different from each other, for he speaks with a voice that is at once personal and lyrical in a mode that, with the possible exception of Bellow's *The Victim*, neither of the others has as yet attempted. In his first novel, moreover, Knowles achieves a remarkable success in writing about adolescent life at a large boys' school without falling into any of the smart-wise idiom made fashionable by *The Catcher in the Rye* and ludicrously overworked by its many imitators.

A Separate Peace is the story of a small group of boys growing up at an old New England prep school called Devon during the early years of World War II. The principal characters are the narrator, Gene Forrester, and his roommate, Phineas, or "Finny," who has no surname. As yet but remotely aware of the war in Europe or the Pacific, the boys give themselves up during Devon's first summer session to sports and breaking school rules under the instigations of the indefatigable Finny. It is the last brief experience of carefree life they will know, for most of them will graduate the following June. But within this experience, another kind of war subtly emerges, a struggle between Gene, who is a good student and an able competitor in sports, and Finny, who is the school's champion athlete but poor at studying. Believing Finny's instigations aim at ruining his chances to become valedictorian of their class—and so upset the delicate balance of their respective achievements—Gene awakens to a mistaken sense of deadly enmity between them. (Anyone who has attended such schools will immediately recognize this conflict between intellectual and athletic glory.) Impulsively, Gene causes his roommate to fall from a tree during one of their more spectacular games, and cripples him. This is the central episode of the novel, and the fear which lies behind such destructive hatred is its major theme.

How Gene eventually loses this fear, and so is able to enter that other war without hatred, without the need to kill, is the business of the succeeding episodes. Confession by Gene of deliberate viciousness is alone insufficient release; indeed, far from bringing release, it causes deeper injury to Finny and to himself because of its basic half-truth. Freedom comes only after an honest confrontation of both his own nature and that extension of it represented by Finny, whose loss at the end of the novel he must somehow accept and endure. For if, as the book shows, Finny is unfit for war, and hence unfit for a world engaged in a chronic condition of war, it is because of his fundamental innocence or idealism—his regard for the world not as it is, but as it should be—that renders him unfit. Under Finny's influence, most of the summer of 1942 was, for Gene, just such a world; and it is briefly restored during the following winter when, after convalescing, Phineas returns to Devon. But the existence of this world, and the separate peace this world provides, is doomed. In Finny's fall from the tree Gene has violated, or rather surrendered, his innocence, and he learns that any attempt to regain it, to "become a part of Phineas,"... is at best a transient experience, at worst a gesture of despair. Nor will either of the twin expedients, escape or evasion, serve him. Escape, as it presents itself to Gene after Finny's second fall, the final crisis in the novel, is rejected as "not so much criminal as meaningless, a lapse into nothing, an escape into nowhere."... And evasion—any recourse into the various dodges of sentimentality, such as aggressive arrogance, insensitive factionalism, or self-protective vagueness as variously portrayed by other boys at Devon—such evasion, Gene comes to realize, is only a mask behind which one does not so much seek reality, as hide from it, for it is a mask to cover fear. "Only Phineas never was afraid, only Phineas never hated anyone," the book concludes. The essential harmony of his nature could not allow such emotions, and his "choreography of peace" in a world he alone could create and sustain, as for example during Devon's first, only, and illegal "Winter Carnival," is not the dance of this world. His death,

coming as it does on the eve of graduation, is, then, for Gene a kind of necessary sacrifice before he can take the next step. And his forgiveness is Gene's way of forgiving himself for what he at last recognizes is "something ignorant in the human heart,"... the impersonal, blind impulse that caused Finny's fall and that causes war. It is an acceptance, too, the acceptance (as [T. S.] Eliot shows in *Four Quartets*) of a reality which includes ignorance and prepares for humility, without which the next step remains frozen in mid-air.

In *Morning in Antibes*, Knowles prepares to take the next step—or to complete the first—the step that leads to the possibility of human encounter, of real and fruitful meetings with others. But before actually taking this step, he repeats much of what he has already presented in *A Separate Peace*. Perhaps this repetition is necessary for the shape of the novel, which ostensibly is not a continuation of the first (as part of a trilogy, for example) and must tell its own story. But to readers of Knowles's first book, *Morning in Antibes* unavoidably appears as a retelling, in part, of what he has already demonstrated; and so it drags a bit, if only just slightly. The novel opens with the separation of a young couple, Nicholas and Liliane Bodine, after a brief and unhappy marriage. Nick has left Liliane in Paris for the pleasures and transparent lures of the Riviera and for the love he mistakenly hopes to find there: but his unfaithful wife, now deeply troubled and wanting to reconcile, follows him to Juan-les-Pins. It is the summer of 1958, and reflected against this portrait of impending marital dissolution is the mounting struggle of Algeria to free itself from France during the last days of the Fourth Republic: as in *A Separate Peace*, the private and the public war are clearly related. Before reconciliation is possible, however, or even desirable, both Nick and Lili must suffer an agonizing inward look, recognize their self-limitations with neither exaggeration nor minimizing, and with this knowledge of both good and evil in the human heart, discover the means and the will to forgive, and to love....

[Significantly, a character] enters Nick's life, a young man called Jeannot, whom Nick at first distrusts implicitly: he is an Algerian and all Algerians in France are naturally suspect. But Nick's distrust gradually gives way before Jeannot's gentleness and his profound need to be treated as a human being, even though he is an unemployed Algerian in France during her most stressful period since the War. Nicholas learns a great deal from Jeannot during Liliane's absence, much of it having to do with Jeannot's love for the country which has misprised and misused him....

For it is through Jeannot as much as by his wife's absence—to go on a prolonged cruise with a cynical, degenerate French nobleman—that Nicholas begins to understand what love means and what it demands. Through Jeannot, Nick learns that love begins by valuing (or loving) ourselves justly; only then can we take others at their own just evaluation. Love prevents either party from imposing false valuations upon themselves. In this way Nick's relationship with Jeannot grows and flourishes....

As a second novel, *Morning in Antibes* stands up well against *A Separate Peace*, although readers will doubtless recognize the superior achievement of Knowles's first book. Finny's fall from the tree, while it makes use of old and familiar symbolism, loses none of its power but gains instead by its complete integration within a realistic design. By contrast, Nick's skin-diving episode just before Liliane returns to Juan-les-Pins, though it draws upon equally ancient symbols, parallels too closely Jake Barnes' deep dives off San Sebastian in *The Sun Also Rises*. Here, as in other places, such as a few clipped passages of dialogue, or some detailed descriptions of French cuisine, a purely literary recollection intervenes, detracting from the reader's experience of the presentation and robbing it of some of its felt reality. Nevertheless, in his second novel Knowles retains much of the individual voice mentioned earlier; despite the occasional ventriloquism, it is still there. Moreover, he demonstrates an important development of his theme, and we may well wait for what he has to say next with aroused expectations....

Source: Jay L. Halio, "John Knowles's Short Stories," in *Studies in Short Fiction*, Vol. 1, No. 2, Winter 1964, pp. 107–12.

SOURCES

Hasan, Zia, "John Knowles," in *Critical Survey of Short Fiction*, Vol. 5, edited by Frank N. Magill, Salem, 1981, pp. 1764–69.

Honan, William H., "John Knowles, 75, Novelist Who Wrote *A Separate Peace*," in *New York Times*, December 1, 2001, http://www.nytimes.com/2001/12/01/arts/john-knowles-75-novelist-who-wrote-a-separate-peace.html (accessed September 2, 2014).

Knowles, John, "A Turn with the Sun," in *Phineas: Six Stories*, Random House, 1968, pp. 3–27.

———, "A Special Time, a Special School," in *Exeter Bulletin*, 1995, http://www.exeter.edu/libraries/553_4390.aspx (accessed September 1, 2014).

Waugh, Evelyn, *A Handful of Dust, and Decline and Fall*, Dell, 1959, p. 392.

FURTHER READING

Delderfield, R. F., *To Serve Them All My Days*, Hodder & Stoughton, 1972.
    This is a classic of boarding-school literature. It concerns a badly shell-shocked officer who comes to work as a history teacher at the fictional Bamfylde school after World War I. Its plot mirrors the political trends of the 1920s and 1930s that would lead to World War II. In one respect it is an answer to the apolitical novel *Goodbye, Mr. Chips*.

Gaztambide-Fernandez, Ruben A., *The Best of the Best: Becoming Elite at an American Boarding School*, Harvard University Press, 2009.
    The Best of the Best is a case study of how boarding schools act in networking in American elite culture.

Hughes, Thomas, *Tom Brown's School Days*, Macmillan, 1857.
    Tom Brown's School Days created the genre of boarding-school literature. Unlike most of its successors, it is set at a real school, Rugby, and is intended in part as a tribute to its headmaster during the 1830s, Thomas Arnold, father of the poet Matthew Arnold, who revolutionized public-school education.

Knowles, John, *Peace Breaks Out*, Bantam, 1981.
    Peace Breaks Out is a sequel to Knowles's novel *A Separate Peace*. It concerns a boy who returns to Devon after service in World War II to become a history teacher.

SUGGESTED SEARCH TERMS

John Knowles

A Turn with the Sun AND Knowles

modernism

American AND boarding school

athletics

fascism

New England

MacGuffin

Glossary of Literary Terms

A

Aestheticism: A literary and artistic movement of the nineteenth century. Followers of the movement believed that art should not be mixed with social, political, or moral teaching. The statement "art for art's sake" is a good summary of aestheticism. The movement had its roots in France, but it gained widespread importance in England in the last half of the nineteenth century, where it helped change the Victorian practice of including moral lessons in literature. Oscar Wilde and Edgar Allan Poe are two of the best-known "aesthetes" of the late nineteenth century.

Allegory: A narrative technique in which characters representing things or abstract ideas are used to convey a message or teach a lesson. Allegory is typically used to teach moral, ethical, or religious lessons but is sometimes used for satiric or political purposes. Many fairy tales are allegories.

Allusion: A reference to a familiar literary or historical person or event, used to make an idea more easily understood. Joyce Carol Oates's story "Where Are You Going, Where Have You Been?" exhibits several allusions to popular music.

Analogy: A comparison of two things made to explain something unfamiliar through its similarities to something familiar, or to prove one point based on the acceptance of another. Similes and metaphors are types of analogies.

Antagonist: The major character in a narrative or drama who works against the hero or protagonist. The Misfit in Flannery O'Connor's story "A Good Man Is Hard to Find" serves as the antagonist for the Grandmother.

Anthology: A collection of similar works of literature, art, or music. Zora Neale Hurston's "The Eatonville Anthology" is a collection of stories that take place in the same town.

Anthropomorphism: The presentation of animals or objects in human shape or with human characteristics. The term is derived from the Greek word for "human form." The fur necklet in Katherine Mansfield's story "Miss Brill" has anthropomorphic characteristics.

Anti-hero: A central character in a work of literature who lacks traditional heroic qualities such as courage, physical prowess, and fortitude. Anti-heroes typically distrust conventional values and are unable to commit themselves to any ideals. They generally feel helpless in a world over which they have no control. Anti-heroes usually accept, and often celebrate, their positions as social outcasts. A well-known anti-hero is Walter Mitty in James Thurber's story "The Secret Life of Walter Mitty."

Archetype: The word archetype is commonly used to describe an original pattern or model from which all other things of the same kind are made. Archetypes are the literary images that grow out of the "collective unconscious," a theory proposed by psychologist Carl Jung. They appear in literature as incidents and plots that repeat basic patterns of life. They may also appear as stereotyped characters. The "schlemiel" of Yiddish literature is an archetype.

Autobiography: A narrative in which an individual tells his or her life story. Examples include Benjamin Franklin's *Autobiography* and Amy Hempel's story "In the Cemetery Where Al Jolson Is Buried," which has autobiographical characteristics even though it is a work of fiction.

Avant-garde: A literary term that describes new writing that rejects traditional approaches to literature in favor of innovations in style or content. Twentieth-century examples of the literary avant-garde include the modernists and the minimalists.

B

Belles-lettres: A French term meaning "fine letters" or "beautiful writing." It is often used as a synonym for literature, typically referring to imaginative and artistic rather than scientific or expository writing. Current usage sometimes restricts the meaning to light or humorous writing and appreciative essays about literature. Lewis Carroll's *Alice in Wonderland* epitomizes the realm of belles-lettres.

Bildungsroman: A German word meaning "novel of development." The *bildungsroman* is a study of the maturation of a youthful character, typically brought about through a series of social or sexual encounters that lead to self-awareness. J. D. Salinger's *Catcher in the Rye* is a *bildungsroman*, and Doris Lessing's story "Through the Tunnel" exhibits characteristics of a *bildungsroman* as well.

Black Aesthetic Movement: A period of artistic and literary development among African Americans in the 1960s and early 1970s. This was the first major African-American artistic movement since the Harlem Renaissance and was closely paralleled by the civil rights and black power movements. The black aesthetic writers attempted to produce works of art that would be meaningful to the black masses. Key figures in black aesthetics included one of its founders, poet and playwright Amiri Baraka, formerly known as Le Roi Jones; poet and essayist Haki R. Madhubuti, formerly Don L. Lee; poet and playwright Sonia Sanchez; and dramatist Ed Bullins. Works representative of the Black Aesthetic Movement include Amiri Baraka's play *Dutchman,* a 1964 Obie award-winner.

Black Humor: Writing that places grotesque elements side by side with humorous ones in an attempt to shock the reader, forcing him or her to laugh at the horrifying reality of a disordered world. "Lamb to the Slaughter," by Roald Dahl, in which a placid housewife murders her husband and serves the murder weapon to the investigating policemen, is an example of black humor.

C

Catharsis: The release or purging of unwanted emotions—specifically fear and pity—brought about by exposure to art. The term was first used by the Greek philosopher Aristotle in his *Poetics* to refer to the desired effect of tragedy on spectators.

Character: Broadly speaking, a person in a literary work. The actions of characters are what constitute the plot of a story, novel, or poem. There are numerous types of characters, ranging from simple, stereotypical figures to intricate, multifaceted ones. "Characterization" is the process by which an author creates vivid, believable characters in a work of art. This may be done in a variety of ways, including (1) direct description of the character by the narrator; (2) the direct presentation of the speech, thoughts, or actions of the character; and (3) the responses of other characters to the character. The term "character" also refers to a form originated by the ancient Greek writer Theophrastus that later became popular in the seventeenth and eighteenth centuries. It is a short essay or sketch of a person who prominently displays a specific attribute or quality, such as miserliness or ambition. "Miss Brill," a story by Katherine Mansfield, is an example of a character sketch.

Classical: In its strictest definition in literary criticism, classicism refers to works of ancient Greek or Roman literature. The term may also be used to describe a literary work of recognized importance (a "classic") from any time period or literature that exhibits the traits of classicism. Examples of later works and authors now described as classical include French literature of the seventeenth century, Western novels of the nineteenth century, and American fiction of the mid-nineteenth century such as that written by James Fenimore Cooper and Mark Twain.

Climax: The turning point in a narrative, the moment when the conflict is at its most intense. Typically, the structure of stories, novels, and plays is one of rising action, in which tension builds to the climax, followed by falling action, in which tension lessens as the story moves to its conclusion.

Comedy: One of two major types of drama, the other being tragedy. Its aim is to amuse, and it typically ends happily. Comedy assumes many forms, such as farce and burlesque, and uses a variety of techniques, from parody to satire. In a restricted sense the term comedy refers only to dramatic presentations, but in general usage it is commonly applied to nondramatic works as well.

Comic Relief: The use of humor to lighten the mood of a serious or tragic story, especially in plays. The technique is very common in Elizabethan works, and can be an integral part of the plot or simply a brief event designed to break the tension of the scene.

Conflict: The conflict in a work of fiction is the issue to be resolved in the story. It usually occurs between two characters, the protagonist and the antagonist, or between the protagonist and society or the protagonist and himself or herself. The conflict in Washington Irving's story "The Devil and Tom Walker" is that the Devil wants Tom Walker's soul but Tom does not want to go to hell.

Criticism: The systematic study and evaluation of literary works, usually based on a specific method or set of principles. An important part of literary studies since ancient times, the practice of criticism has given rise to numerous theories, methods, and "schools," sometimes producing conflicting, even contradictory, interpretations of literature in general as well as of individual works. Even such basic issues as what constitutes a poem or a novel have been the subject of much criticism over the centuries. Seminal texts of literary criticism include Plato's *Republic,* Aristotle's *Poetics*, Sir Philip Sidney's *The Defence of Poesie,* and John Dryden's *Of Dramatic Poesie.* Contemporary schools of criticism include deconstruction, feminist, psychoanalytic, poststructuralist, new historicist, postcolonialist, and reader-response.

D

Deconstruction: A method of literary criticism characterized by multiple conflicting interpretations of a given work. Deconstructionists consider the impact of the language of a work and suggest that the true meaning of the work is not necessarily the meaning that the author intended.

Deduction: The process of reaching a conclusion through reasoning from general premises to a specific premise. Arthur Conan Doyle's character Sherlock Holmes often used deductive reasoning to solve mysteries.

Denotation: The definition of a word, apart from the impressions or feelings it creates in the reader. The word "apartheid" denotes a political and economic policy of segregation by race, but its connotations—oppression, slavery, inequality—are numerous.

Denouement: A French word meaning "the unknotting." In literature, it denotes the resolution of conflict in fiction or drama. The *denouement* follows the climax and provides an outcome to the primary plot situation as well as an explanation of secondary plot complications. A well-known example of *denouement* is the last scene of the play *As You Like It* by William Shakespeare, in which couples are married, an evildoer repents, the identities of two disguised characters are revealed, and a ruler is restored to power. Also known as "falling action."

Detective Story: A narrative about the solution of a mystery or the identification of a criminal. The conventions of the detective story include the detective's scrupulous use of logic in solving the mystery; incompetent or ineffectual police; a suspect who appears guilty at first but is later proved innocent; and the detective's friend or confidant—often the narrator—whose slowness in interpreting clues emphasizes by contrast the detective's brilliance. Edgar Allan Poe's "Murders in the Rue Morgue" is commonly regarded as the earliest example of this type of story. Other practitioners are Arthur Conan Doyle, Dashiell Hammett, and Agatha Christie.

Dialogue: Dialogue is conversation between people in a literary work. In its most restricted sense, it refers specifically to the speech of characters in a drama. As a specific literary genre, a "dialogue" is a composition in which characters debate an issue or idea.

Didactic: A term used to describe works of literature that aim to teach a moral, religious, political, or practical lesson. Although didactic elements are often found inartistically pleasing works, the term "didactic" usually refers to literature in which the message is more important than the form. The term may also be used to criticize a work that the critic finds "overly didactic," that is, heavy-handed in its delivery of a lesson. An example of didactic literature is John Bunyan's *Pilgrim's Progress.*

Dramatic Irony: Occurs when the reader of a work of literature knows something that a character in the work itself does not know. The irony is in the contrast between the intended meaning of the statements or actions of a character and the additional information understood by the audience.

Dystopia: An imaginary place in a work of fiction where the characters lead dehumanized, fearful lives. George Orwell's *Nineteen Eighty-four,* and Margaret Atwood's *Handmaid's Tale* portray versions of dystopia.

E

Edwardian: Describes cultural conventions identified with the period of the reign of Edward VII of England (1901–1910). Writers of the Edwardian Age typically displayed a strong reaction against the propriety and conservatism of the Victorian Age. Their work often exhibits distrust of authority in religion, politics, and art and expresses strong doubts about the soundness of conventional values. Writers of this era include E. M. Forster, H. G. Wells, and Joseph Conrad.

Empathy: A sense of shared experience, including emotional and physical feelings, with someone or something other than oneself. Empathy is often used to describe the response of a reader to a literary character.

Epilogue: A concluding statement or section of a literary work. In dramas, particularly those of the seventeenth and eighteenth centuries, the epilogue is a closing speech, often in verse, delivered by an actor at the end of a play and spoken directly to the audience.

Epiphany: A sudden revelation of truth inspired by a seemingly trivial incident. The term was widely used by James Joyce in his critical writings, and the stories in Joyce's *Dubliners* are commonly called "epiphanies."

Epistolary Novel: A novel in the form of letters. The form was particularly popular in the eighteenth century. The form can also be applied to short stories, as in Edwidge Danticat's "Children of the Sea."

Epithet: A word or phrase, often disparaging or abusive, that expresses a character trait of someone or something. "The Napoleon of crime" is an epithet applied to Professor Moriarty, arch-rival of Sherlock Holmes in Arthur Conan Doyle's series of detective stories.

Existentialism: A predominantly twentieth-century philosophy concerned with the nature and perception of human existence. There are two major strains of existentialist thought: atheistic and Christian. Followers of atheistic existentialism believe that the individual is alone in a godless universe and that the basic human condition is one of suffering and loneliness. Nevertheless, because there are no fixed values, individuals can create their own characters—indeed, they can shape themselves—through the exercise of free will. The atheistic strain culminates in and is popularly associated with the works of Jean-Paul Sartre. The Christian existentialists, on the other hand, believe that only in God may people find freedom from life's anguish. The two strains hold certain beliefs in common: that existence cannot be fully understood or described through empirical effort; that anguish is a universal element of life; that individuals must bear responsibility for their actions; and that there is no common standard of behavior or perception for religious and ethical matters. Existentialist thought figures prominently in the works of such authors as Franz Kafka, Fyodor Dostoyevsky, and Albert Camus.

Expatriatism: The practice of leaving one's country to live for an extended period in another country. Literary expatriates include Irish author James Joyce who moved to Italy and France, American writers James Baldwin, Ernest Hemingway, Gertrude Stein, and F. Scott Fitzgerald who lived and wrote in Paris, and Polish novelist Joseph Conrad in England.

Exposition: Writing intended to explain the nature of an idea, thing, or theme. Expository writing is often combined with description, narration, or argument.

Expressionism: An indistinct literary term, originally used to describe an early twentieth-century school of German painting. The term applies to almost any mode of unconventional, highly subjective writing that distorts reality in some way. Advocates of Expressionism include Federico Garcia Lorca, Eugene O'Neill, Franz Kafka, and James Joyce.

F

Fable: A prose or verse narrative intended to convey amoral. Animals or inanimate objects with human characteristics often serve as characters in fables. A famous fable is Aesop's "The Tortoise and the Hare."

Fantasy: A literary form related to mythology and folklore. Fantasy literature is typically set in non-existent realms and features supernatural beings. Notable examples of literature with elements of fantasy are Gabriel Gárcia Márquez's story "The Handsomest Drowned Man in the World" and Ursula K. Le Guin's "The Ones Who Walk Away from Omelas."

Farce: A type of comedy characterized by broad humor, outlandish incidents, and often vulgar subject matter. Much of the comedy in film and television could more accurately be described as farce.

Fiction: Any story that is the product of imagination rather than a documentation of fact. Characters and events in such narratives may be based in real life but their ultimate form and configuration is a creation of the author.

Figurative Language: A technique in which an author uses figures of speech such as hyperbole, irony, metaphor, or simile for a particular effect. Figurative language is the opposite of literal language, in which every word is truthful, accurate, and free of exaggeration or embellishment.

Flashback: A device used in literature to present action that occurred before the beginning of the story. Flashbacks are often introduced as the dreams or recollections of one or more characters.

Foil: A character in a work of literature whose physical or psychological qualities contrast strongly with, and therefore highlight, the corresponding qualities of another character. In his Sherlock Holmes stories, Arthur Conan Doyle portrayed Dr. Watson as a man of normal habits and intelligence, making him a foil for the eccentric and unusually perceptive Sherlock Holmes.

Folklore: Traditions and myths preserved in a culture or group of people. Typically, these are passed on by word of mouth in various forms—such as legends, songs, and proverbs—or preserved in customs and ceremonies. Washington Irving, in "The Devil and Tom Walker" and many of his other stories, incorporates many elements of the folklore of New England and Germany.

Folktale: A story originating in oral tradition. Folk tales fall into a variety of categories, including legends, ghost stories, fairy tales, fables, and anecdotes based on historical figures and events.

Foreshadowing: A device used in literature to create expectation or to set up an explanation of later developments. Edgar Allan Poe uses foreshadowing to create suspense in "The Fall of the House of Usher" when the narrator comments on the crumbling state of disrepair in which he finds the house.

G

Genre: A category of literary work. Genre may refer to both the content of a given work—tragedy, comedy, horror, science fiction—and to its form, such as poetry, novel, or drama.

Gilded Age: A period in American history during the 1870s and after characterized by political corruption and materialism. A number of important novels of social and political criticism were written during this time. Henry James and Kate Chopin are two writers who were prominent during the Gilded Age.

Gothicism: In literature, works characterized by a taste for medieval or morbid characters and situations. A gothic novel prominently features elements of horror, the supernatural, gloom, and violence: clanking chains, terror, ghosts, medieval castles, and unexplained phenomena. The term "gothic novel" is also applied to novels that lack elements of the traditional Gothic setting but that create a similar atmosphere of terror or dread. The term can also be applied to stories, plays, and poems. Mary Shelley's *Frankenstein* and Joyce Carol Oates's *Bellefleur* are both gothic novels.

Grotesque: In literature, a work that is characterized by exaggeration, deformity, freakishness, and disorder. The grotesque often includes an element of comic absurdity. Examples of the grotesque can be found in the works of Edgar Allan Poe, Flannery O'Connor, Joseph Heller, and Shirley Jackson.

H

Harlem Renaissance: The Harlem Renaissance of the 1920s is generally considered the first significant movement of black writers and artists in the United States. During this period, new and established black writers, many of whom lived in the region of New York City known as Harlem, published more fiction and poetry than ever before, the first influential black literary journals were established, and black authors and artists received their first widespread recognition and serious critical appraisal. Among the major writers associated with this period are Countee Cullen, Langston Hughes, Arna Bontemps, and Zora Neale Hurston.

Hero/Heroine: The principal sympathetic character in a literary work. Heroes and heroines typically exhibit admirable traits: idealism, courage, and integrity, for example. Famous heroes and heroines of literature include Charles Dickens's Oliver Twist, Margaret Mitchell's Scarlett O'Hara, and the anonymous narrator in Ralph Ellison's *Invisible Man*.

Hyperbole: Deliberate exaggeration used to achieve an effect. In William Shakespeare's *Macbeth,* Lady Macbeth hyperbolizes when she says, "All the perfumes of Arabia could not sweeten this little hand."

I

Image: A concrete representation of an object or sensory experience. Typically, such a representation helps evoke the feelings associated with the object or experience itself. Images are either "literal" or "figurative." Literal images are especially concrete and involve little or no extension of the obvious meaning of the words used to express them. Figurative images do not follow the literal meaning of the words exactly. Images in literature are usually visual, but the term "image" can also refer to the representation of any sensory experience.

Imagery: The array of images in a literary work. Also used to convey the author's overall use of figurative language in a work.

In medias res: A Latin term meaning "in the middle of things." It refers to the technique of beginning a story at its midpoint and then using various flashback devices to reveal previous action. This technique originated in such epics as Virgil's *Aeneid.*

Interior Monologue: A narrative technique in which characters' thoughts are revealed in a way that appears to be uncontrolled by the author. The interior monologue typically aims to reveal the inner self of a character. It portrays emotional experiences as they occur at both a conscious and unconscious level. One of the best-known interior monologues in English is the Molly Bloom section at the close of James Joyce's *Ulysses*. Katherine Anne Porter's "The Jilting of Granny Weatherall" is also told in the form of an interior monologue.

Irony: In literary criticism, the effect of language in which the intended meaning is the opposite of what is stated. The title of Jonathan Swift's "A Modest Proposal" is ironic because what Swift proposes in this essay is cannibalism—hardly "modest."

J

Jargon: Language that is used or understood only by a select group of people. Jargon may refer to terminology used in a certain profession, such as computer jargon, or it may refer to any nonsensical language that is not understood by most people. Anthony Burgess's *A Clockwork Orange* and James Thurber's "The Secret Life of Walter Mitty" both use jargon.

K

Knickerbocker Group: An indistinct group of New York writers of the first half of the nineteenth century. Members of the group were linked only by location and a common theme: New York life. Two famous members of the Knickerbocker Group were Washington Irving and William Cullen Bryant. The group's name derives from Irving's *Knickerbocker's History of New York*.

L

Literal Language: An author uses literal language when he or she writes without exaggerating or embellishing the subject matter and without any tools of figurative language. To say "He ran very quickly down the street" is to use literal language, whereas to say "He ran like a hare down the street" would be using figurative language.

Literature: Literature is broadly defined as any written or spoken material, but the term most often refers to creative works. Literature includes poetry, drama, fiction, and many kinds of nonfiction writing, as well as oral, dramatic, and broadcast compositions not necessarily preserved in a written format, such as films and television programs.

Lost Generation: A term first used by Gertrude Stein to describe the post-World War I generation of American writers: men and women haunted by a sense of betrayal and emptiness brought about by the destructiveness of the war. The term is commonly applied to Hart Crane, Ernest Hemingway, F. Scott Fitzgerald, and others.

M

Magic Realism: A form of literature that incorporates fantasy elements or supernatural occurrences into the narrative and accepts them as truth. Gabriel García Márquez and Laura Esquivel are two writers known for their works of magic realism.

Metaphor: A figure of speech that expresses an idea through the image of another object. Metaphors suggest the essence of the first object by identifying it with certain qualities of the second object. An example is "But soft, what light through yonder window breaks? / It is the east, and Juliet is the sun" in William Shakespeare's *Romeo and Juliet*. Here, Juliet, the first object, is identified with qualities of the second object, the sun.

Minimalism: A literary style characterized by spare, simple prose with few elaborations. In minimalism, the main theme of the work is often never discussed directly. Amy Hempel and Ernest Hemingway are two writers known for their works of minimalism.

Modernism: Modern literary practices. Also, the principles of a literary school that lasted from roughly the beginning of the twentieth century until the end of World War II. Modernism is defined by its rejection of the literary conventions of the nineteenth century and by its opposition to conventional morality, taste, traditions, and economic values. Many writers are associated with the concepts of modernism, including Albert Camus, D. H. Lawrence, Ernest Hemingway, William Faulkner, Eugene O'Neill, and James Joyce.

Monologue: A composition, written or oral, by a single individual. More specifically, a speech given by a single individual in a drama or other public entertainment. It has no set length, although it is usually several or more lines long. "I Stand Here Ironing" by Tillie Olsen is an example of a story written in the form of a monologue.

Mood: The prevailing emotions of a work or of the author in his or her creation of the work. The mood of a work is not always what might be expected based on its subject matter.

Motif: A theme, character type, image, metaphor, or other verbal element that recurs throughout a single work of literature or occurs in a number of different works over a period of time. For example, the color white in Herman Melville's *Moby Dick* is a "specific" motif, while the trials of star-crossed lovers is a "conventional" motif from the literature of all periods.

N

Narration: The telling of a series of events, real or invented. A narration may be either a simple narrative, in which the events are recounted chronologically, or a narrative with a plot, in which the account is given in a style reflecting the author's artistic concept of the story. Narration is sometimes used as a synonym for "storyline."

Narrative: A verse or prose accounting of an event or sequence of events, real or invented. The term is also used as an adjective in the sense "method of narration." For example, in literary criticism, the expression "narrative technique" usually refers to the way the author structures and presents his or her story. Different narrative forms include diaries, travelogues, novels, ballads, epics, short stories, and other fictional forms.

Narrator: The teller of a story. The narrator may be the author or a character in the story through whom the author speaks. Huckleberry Finn is the narrator of Mark Twain's *The Adventures of Huckleberry Finn.*

Novella: An Italian term meaning "story." This term has been especially used to describe fourteenth-century Italian tales, but it also refers to modern short novels. Modern novellas include Leo Tolstoy's *The Death of Ivan Ilich,* Fyodor Dostoyevsky's *Notes from the Underground,* and Joseph Conrad's *Heart of Darkness.*

O

Oedipus Complex: A son's romantic obsession with his mother. The phrase is derived from the story of the ancient Theban hero Oedipus, who unknowingly killed his father and married his mother, and was popularized by Sigmund Freud's theory of psychoanalysis. Literary occurrences of the Oedipus complex include Sophocles' *Oedipus Rex* and D. H. Lawrence's "The Rocking-Horse Winner."

Onomatopoeia: The use of words whose sounds express or suggest their meaning. In its simplest sense, onomatopoeia may be represented by words that mimic the sounds they denote such as "hiss" or "meow." At a more subtle level, the pattern and rhythm of sounds and rhymes of a line or poem may be onomatopoeic.

Oral Tradition: A process by which songs, ballads, folklore, and other material are transmitted by word of mouth. The tradition of oral transmission predates the written record systems of literate society. Oral transmission preserves material sometimes over generations, although often with variations. Memory plays a large part in the recitation and preservation of orally transmitted material. Native American myths and legends, and African folktales told by plantation slaves are examples of orally transmitted literature.

P

Parable: A story intended to teach a moral lesson or answer an ethical question. Examples of parables are the stories told by Jesus Christ in the New Testament, notably "The Prodigal Son," but parables also are used in Sufism, rabbinic literature, Hasidism, and Zen Buddhism. Isaac Bashevis Singer's story "Gimpel the Fool" exhibits characteristics of a parable.

Paradox: A statement that appears illogical or contradictory at first, but may actually point to an underlying truth. A literary example of a paradox is George Orwell's statement "All animals are equal, but some animals are more equal than others" in *Animal Farm.*

Parody: In literature, this term refers to an imitation of a serious literary work or the signature style of a particular author in a ridiculous manner. Atypical parody adopts the style of the original and applies it to an inappropriate subject for humorous effect. Parody is a form of satire and could be considered the literary equivalent of a caricature or cartoon. Henry Fielding's *Shamela* is a parody of Samuel Richardson's *Pamela.*

Persona: A Latin term meaning "mask." Personae are the characters in a fictional work of literature. The persona generally functions as a mask through which the author tells a story in a voice other than his or her own. A persona is usually either a character in a story who acts as a narrator or an "implied author," a voice created by the author to act as the narrator for himself or herself. The persona in Charlotte Perkins Gilman's story "The Yellow Wallpaper" is the unnamed young mother experiencing a mental breakdown.

Personification: A figure of speech that gives human qualities to abstract ideas, animals, and inanimate objects. To say that "the sun is smiling" is to personify the sun.

Plot: The pattern of events in a narrative or drama. In its simplest sense, the plot guides the author in composing the work and helps the reader follow the work. Typically, plots exhibit causality and unity and have a beginning, a middle, and an end. Sometimes, however, a plot may consist of a series of disconnected events, in which case it is known as an "episodic plot."

Poetic Justice: An outcome in a literary work, not necessarily a poem, in which the good are rewarded and the evil are punished, especially in ways that particularly fit their virtues or crimes. For example, a murderer may himself be murdered, or a thief will find himself penniless.

Poetic License: Distortions of fact and literary convention made by a writer—not always a poet—for the sake of the effect gained. Poetic license is closely related to the concept of "artistic freedom." An author exercises poetic license by saying that a pile of money "reaches as high as a mountain" when the pile is actually only a foot or two high.

Point of View: The narrative perspective from which a literary work is presented to the reader. There are four traditional points of view. The "third person omniscient" gives the reader a "godlike" perspective, unrestricted by time or place, from which to see actions and look into the minds of characters. This allows the author to comment openly on characters and events in the work. The "third person" point of view presents the events of the story from outside of any single character's perception, much like the omniscient point of view, but the reader must understand the action as it takes place and without any special insight into characters' minds or motivations. The "first person" or "personal" point of view relates events as they are perceived by a single character. The main character "tells" the story and may offer opinions about the action and characters which differ from those of the author. Much less common than omniscient, third person, and first person is the "second person" point of view, wherein the author tells the story as if it is happening to the reader. James Thurber employs the omniscient point of view in his short story "The Secret Life of Walter Mitty." Ernest Hemingway's "A Clean, Well-Lighted Place" is a short story told from the third person point of view. Mark Twain's novel *Huckleberry Finn* is presented from the first person viewpoint. Jay McInerney's *Bright*

Lights, Big City is an example of a novel which uses the second person point of view.

Pornography: Writing intended to provoke feelings of lust in the reader. Such works are often condemned by critics and teachers, but those which can be shown to have literary value are viewed less harshly. Literary works that have been described as pornographic include D. H. Lawrence's *Lady Chatterley's Lover* and James Joyce's *Ulysses*.

Post-Aesthetic Movement: An artistic response made by African Americans to the black aesthetic movement of the 1960s and early 1970s. Writers since that time have adopted a somewhat different tone in their work, with less emphasis placed on the disparity between black and white in the United States. In the words of post-aesthetic authors such as Toni Morrison, John Edgar Wideman, and Kristin Hunter, African Americans are portrayed as looking inward for answers to their own questions, rather than always looking to the outside world. Two well-known examples of works produced as part of the post-aesthetic movement are the Pulitzer Prize–winning novels *The Color Purple* by Alice Walker and *Beloved* by Toni Morrison.

Postmodernism: Writing from the 1960s forward characterized by experimentation and application of modernist elements, which include existentialism and alienation. Postmodernists have gone a step further in the rejection of tradition begun with the modernists by also rejecting traditional forms, preferring the anti-novel over the novel and the anti-hero over the hero. Postmodern writers include Thomas Pynchon, Margaret Drabble, and Gabriel Gárcia Márquez.

Prologue: An introductory section of a literary work. It often contains information establishing the situation of the characters or presents information about the setting, time period, or action. In drama, the prologue is spoken by a chorus or by one of the principal characters.

Prose: A literary medium that attempts to mirror the language of everyday speech. It is distinguished from poetry by its use of unmetered, unrhymed language consisting of logically related sentences. Prose is usually grouped into paragraphs that form a cohesive whole such as an essay or a novel. The term is sometimes used to mean an author's general writing.

Protagonist: The central character of a story who serves as a focus for its themes and incidents and as the principal rationale for its development. The protagonist is sometimes referred to in discussions of modern literature as the hero or anti-hero. Well-known protagonists are Hamlet in William Shakespeare's *Hamlet* and Jay Gatsby in F. Scott Fitzgerald's *The Great Gatsby*.

R

Realism: A nineteenth-century European literary movement that sought to portray familiar characters, situations, and settings in a realistic manner. This was done primarily by using an objective narrative point of view and through the buildup of accurate detail. The standard for success of any realistic work depends on how faithfully it transfers common experience into fictional forms. The realistic method may be altered or extended, as in stream of consciousness writing, to record highly subjective experience. Contemporary authors who often write in a realistic way include Nadine Gordimer and Grace Paley.

Resolution: The portion of a story following the climax, in which the conflict is resolved. The resolution of Jane Austen's *Northanger Abbey* is neatly summed up in the following sentence: "Henry and Catherine were married, the bells rang and every body smiled."

Rising Action: The part of a drama where the plot becomes increasingly complicated. Rising action leads up to the climax, or turning point, of a drama. The final "chase scene" of an action film is generally the rising action which culminates in the film's climax.

Roman a clef: A French phrase meaning "novel with a key." It refers to a narrative in which real persons are portrayed under fictitious names. Jack Kerouac, for example, portrayed various friends under fictitious names in the novel *On the Road*. D. H. Lawrence based "The Rocking-Horse Winner" on a family he knew.

Romanticism: This term has two widely accepted meanings. In historical criticism, it refers to a European intellectual and artistic movement of the late eighteenth and early nineteenth centuries that sought greater freedom of personal expression than that allowed by the strict rules of literary form and logic of the eighteenth-century neoclassicists. The Romantics preferred emotional and imaginative expression to rational analysis. They considered the individual to be at the center of all experience and so placed him or her at the center of their art. The Romantics believed that the creative imagination reveals nobler truths—unique feelings and attitudes—than those that could be discovered by logic or by scientific examination. "Romanticism" is also used as a general term to refer to a type of sensibility found in all periods of literary history and usually considered to be in opposition to the principles of classicism. In this sense, Romanticism signifies any work or philosophy in which the exotic or dreamlike figure strongly, or that is devoted to individualistic expression, self-analysis, or a pursuit of a higher realm of knowledge than can be discovered by human reason. Prominent Romantics include Jean-Jacques Rousseau, William Wordsworth, John Keats, Lord Byron, and Johann Wolfgang von Goethe.

S

Satire: A work that uses ridicule, humor, and wit to criticize and provoke change in human nature and institutions. Voltaire's novella *Candide* and Jonathan Swift's essay "A Modest Proposal" are both satires. Flannery O'Connor's portrayal of the family in "A Good Man Is Hard to Find" is a satire of a modern, Southern, American family.

Science Fiction: A type of narrative based upon real or imagined scientific theories and technology. Science fiction is often peopled with alien creatures and set on other planets or in different dimensions. Popular writers of science fiction are Isaac Asimov, Karel Capek, Ray Bradbury, and Ursula K. Le Guin.

Setting: The time, place, and culture in which the action of a narrative takes place. The elements of setting may include geographic location, characters's physical and mental environments, prevailing cultural attitudes, or the historical time in which the action takes place.

Short Story: A fictional prose narrative shorter and more focused than a novella. The short story usually deals with a single episode and often a single character. The "tone," the author's attitude toward his or her subject and audience, is uniform throughout. The short story frequently also lacks *denouement*, ending instead at its climax.

Signifying Monkey: A popular trickster figure in black folklore, with hundreds of tales about this character documented since the 19th century. Henry Louis Gates Jr. examines the history of the signifying monkey in *The Signifying Monkey: Towards a Theory of Afro-American Literary Criticism,* published in 1988.

Simile: A comparison, usually using "like" or "as," of two essentially dissimilar things, as in "coffee as cold as ice" or "He sounded like a broken record." The title of Ernest Hemingway's "Hills Like White Elephants" contains a simile.

Socialist Realism: The Socialist Realism school of literary theory was proposed by Maxim Gorky and established as a dogma by the first Soviet Congress of Writers. It demanded adherence to a communist worldview in works of literature. Its doctrines required an objective viewpoint comprehensible to the working classes and themes of social struggle featuring strong proletarian heroes. Gabriel García Márquez's stories exhibit some characteristics of Socialist Realism.

Stereotype: A stereotype was originally the name for a duplication made during the printing process; this led to its modern definition as a person or thing that is (or is assumed to be) the same as all others of its type. Common stereotypical characters include the absent-minded professor, the nagging wife, the troublemaking teenager, and the kindhearted grandmother.

Stream of Consciousness: A narrative technique for rendering the inward experience of a character. This technique is designed to give the impression of an ever-changing series of thoughts, emotions, images, and memories in the spontaneous and seemingly illogical order that they occur in life. The textbook example of stream of consciousness is the last section of James Joyce's *Ulysses.*

Structure: The form taken by a piece of literature. The structure may be made obvious for ease of understanding, as in nonfiction works, or may obscured for artistic purposes, as in some poetry or seemingly "unstructured" prose.

Style: A writer's distinctive manner of arranging words to suit his or her ideas and purpose in writing. The unique imprint of the author's personality upon his or her writing, style is the product of an author's way of arranging ideas and his or her use of diction, different sentence structures, rhythm, figures of speech, rhetorical principles, and other elements of composition.

Suspense: A literary device in which the author maintains the audience's attention through the buildup of events, the outcome of which will soon be revealed. Suspense in William Shakespeare's *Hamlet* is sustained throughout by the question of whether or not the Prince will achieve what he has been instructed to do and of what he intends to do.

Symbol: Something that suggests or stands for something else without losing its original identity. In literature, symbols combine their literal meaning with the suggestion of an abstract concept. Literary symbols are of two types: those that carry complex associations of meaning no matter what their contexts, and those that derive their suggestive meaning from their functions in specific literary works. Examples of symbols are sunshine suggesting happiness, rain suggesting sorrow, and storm clouds suggesting despair.

T

Tale: A story told by a narrator with a simple plot and little character development. Tales are usually relatively short and often carry a simple message. Examples of tales can be found in the works of Saki, Anton Chekhov, Guy de Maupassant, and O. Henry.

Tall Tale: A humorous tale told in a straightforward, credible tone but relating absolutely impossible events or feats of the characters. Such tales were commonly told of frontier adventures during the settlement of the west in the United States. Literary use of tall tales can be found in Washington Irving's *History of New York,* Mark Twain's *Life on the Mississippi,* and in the German R. F. Raspe's

Baron Munchausen's Narratives of His Marvellous Travels and Campaigns in Russia.

Theme: The main point of a work of literature. The term is used interchangeably with thesis. Many works have multiple themes. One of the themes of Nathaniel Hawthorne's "Young Goodman Brown" is loss of faith.

Tone: The author's attitude toward his or her audience maybe deduced from the tone of the work. A formal tone may create distance or convey politeness, while an informal tone may encourage a friendly, intimate, or intrusive feeling in the reader. The author's attitude toward his or her subject matter may also be deduced from the tone of the words he or she uses in discussing it. The tone of John F. Kennedy's speech which included the appeal to "ask not what your country can do for you" was intended to instill feelings of camaraderie and national pride in listeners.

Tragedy: A drama in prose or poetry about a noble, courageous hero of excellent character who, because of some tragic character flaw, brings ruin upon him- or herself. Tragedy treats its subjects in a dignified and serious manner, using poetic language to help evoke pity and fear and bring about catharsis, a purging of these emotions. The tragic form was practiced extensively by the ancient Greeks. The classical form of tragedy was revived in the sixteenth century; it flourished especially on the Elizabethan stage. In modern times, dramatists have attempted to adapt the form to the needs of modern society by drawing their heroes from the ranks of ordinary men and women and defining the nobility of these heroes in terms of spirit rather than exalted social standing. Some contemporary works that are thought of as tragedies include *The Great Gatsby* by F. Scott Fitzgerald, and *The Sound and the Fury* by William Faulkner.

Tragic Flaw: In a tragedy, the quality within the hero or heroine which leads to his or her downfall. Examples of the tragic flaw include Othello's jealousy and Hamlet's indecisiveness, although most great tragedies defy such simple interpretation.

U

Utopia: A fictional perfect place, such as "paradise" or "heaven." An early literary utopia was described in Plato's *Republic,* and in modern literature, Ursula K. Le Guin depicts a utopia in "The Ones Who Walk Away from Omelas."

V

Victorian: Refers broadly to the reign of Queen Victoria of England (1837-1901) and to anything with qualities typical of that era. For example, the qualities of smug narrow-mindedness, bourgeois materialism, faith in social progress, and priggish morality are often considered Victorian. In literature, the Victorian Period was the great age of the English novel, and the latter part of the era saw the rise of movements such as decadence and symbolism.

Cumulative Author/Title Index

Cumulative
Nationality/Ethnicity Index

Subject/Theme Index

Prejudice
Man from the South: 195
Prophecy
The Nightingale and the Rose: 209
Psychoanalysis
Afterward: 12
Punishment
Man from the South: 197
Puzzles
The Problem of Cell 13: 254, 255

R

Race relations
Bang-Bang You're Dead: 63
Rationalization
Bang-Bang You're Dead: 58
Man from the South: 185, 195
Realism
Back Windows: 25, 31
Bang-Bang You're Dead: 52–53
Haircut: 137
The Nightingale and the Rose: 213
Parker's Back: 231
Realization
Afterward: 9, 12–15
Reason
The Problem of Cell 13: 254
Reconciliation
Brothers Are the Same: 95–96
The Isabel Fish: 180
Redemption
The Isabel Fish: 172
Parker's Back: 232, 235, 236, 239
A Turn with the Sun: 271–272
Reflection
The Facts behind the Helsinki Roccamatios: 120
Rejection
Bang-Bang You're Dead: 47
Haircut: 132, 133
Religion
Bang-Bang You're Dead: 44, 63
The Facts behind the Helsinki Roccamatios: 111
The Isabel Fish: 177
Parker's Back: 226–228, 231, 235–237, 241
Remorse
The Isabel Fish: 167
Repression (Psychology)
Afterward: 17–19
The Facts behind the Helsinki Roccamatios: 121
The Isabel Fish: 174
Resentment
Man from the South: 196
Resistance
The Beautiful People: 67, 83

Respect
A Turn with the Sun: 273
Responsibility
Back Windows: 30
Restraint
Back Windows: 34–36
The Facts behind the Helsinki Roccamatios: 118–122
Retribution. *See* Revenge
Revelation
Parker's Back: 240
Revenge
Afterward: 5, 6, 16
Haircut: 129, 131, 132, 141–142
Man from the South: 195–198
Rituals
Brothers Are the Same: 88
Rivalry
Brothers Are the Same: 90
Romantic love
The Nightingale and the Rose: 217, 221
Romanticism
Brothers Are the Same: 95–96

S

Sacrifice
Back Windows: 37
The Nightingale and the Rose: 204–206, 208, 210–212, 215, 217, 223, 224
Parker's Back: 232
A Turn with the Sun: 275
Sadism
Man from the South: 185, 188
Sadness
Back Windows: 25
The Facts behind the Helsinki Roccamatios: 121
Salvation
Parker's Back: 232, 236
Satire
Bang-Bang You're Dead: 64
Science
The Problem of Cell 13: 250
Science fiction
The Beautiful People: 67
Secrecy
Afterward: 1, 9, 14
Self destruction
Back Windows: 35
Man from the South: 199, 200–201
A Turn with the Sun: 272
Self determination
A Turn with the Sun: 264, 266, 273
Self judgment
The Isabel Fish: 173
Self reliance
Back Windows: 3, 25, 30–31, 34
Self respect
Bang-Bang You're Dead: 65

Self worth
Brothers Are the Same: 93
Selfishness
Back Windows: 36
The Nightingale and the Rose: 207–209, 212, 217, 220
Sensitivity
The Nightingale and the Rose: 207, 209
Serenity. *See* Tranquility
Setting (Literature)
Afterward: 8, 9
Haircut: 131
The Isabel Fish: 170
Man from the South: 192
Sex roles
Afterward: 1, 5, 6–7, 11, 18, 20–21
Back Windows: 32, 41
Bang-Bang You're Dead: 49–51
Brothers Are the Same: 92
Haircut: 139–142
Sexual orientation
The Isabel Fish: 172
Sexual politics
Man from the South: 192
Sexuality
The Beautiful People: 85
The Isabel Fish: 174, 177
Sibling relations
The Isabel Fish: 170, 178, 180
Silence
Afterward: 23
Simplicity
Hamadi: 149
Skepticism
The Beautiful People: 76
Small town life
Haircut: 129, 133
Social change
Afterward: 9–11
Back Windows: 32
Social class
Afterward: 1
Bang-Bang You're Dead: 56, 63
Haircut: 141, 142
A Turn with the Sun: 262, 266, 269
Social conventions
Back Windows: 35
Bang-Bang You're Dead: 51
The Beautiful People: 71
Social criticism
The Nightingale and the Rose: 204, 220, 221
Social identity
The Beautiful People: 75
Social order
Afterward: 11
Social roles
Afterward: 1
Haircut: 141